W9-BUD-745

Fundamentals of Sport Marketing

— FOURTH EDITION —

Brenda G. Pitts, EdD
Georgia State University

David K. Stotlar, EdD
University of Northern Colorado

FiT

Fitness Information Technology

A Division of the International Center
for Performance Excellence
West Virginia University
262 Coliseum, WVU-CPASS
PO Box 6116
Morgantown, WV 26506-6116

Copyright © 2013 by West Virginia University

All rights reserved.

Reproduction or use of any portion of this publication by any mechanical, electronic, or other means is prohibited without written permission of the publisher.

Library of Congress Card Catalog Number: 2012954215

ISBN: 978-1-935412-40-3

Cover Design: Bellerophon Productions

Cover Photos: Front cover photo courtesy of iStockphoto.com. Back cover photos, from left to right: Courtesy of BigStockPhoto.com; © Jianbing lee | Dreamstime.com; Courtesy of Photos8.com; © Adam gregor | Dreamstime.com; © Ratmandude | Dreamstime.com

Typesetting: Bellerophon Productions

Production Editor: Rachel Tibbs

Copyeditor: Rachel Tibbs

Proofreader: Maria denBoer

Indexer: David denBoer

10 9 8 7 6 5 4 3 2 1

Fitness Information Technology
A Division of the International Center for Performance Excellence
West Virginia University
262 Coliseum, WVU-CPASS
PO Box 6116
Morgantown, WV 26506-6116
800.477.4348 (toll free)
304.293.6888 (phone)
304.293.6658 (fax)
Email: fitcustomerservice@mail.wvu.edu
Website: www.fitinfotech.com

Contents

Acknowledgments

Writing or updating a textbook is a major undertaking. Although the authors spend significant amounts of time researching to stay current and to bring the best knowledge to the book, it is done with the patience, support, work and help of several individuals. We wish to acknowledge and thank the following.

Dr. Pitts wishes to acknowledge her coauthor, Dave Stotlar, who has been a wonderful partner in writing and accomplishing this great task since its inception and first edition many years ago.

Dr. Stotlar is also appreciative of Dr. Pitts' contributions and their 30-year friendship. Working as colleagues on this and many projects has been an immense pleasure. Dr. Stotlar also acknowledges the support of his wife Sylvia and the many students with whom he has worked over his career.

Several students were instrumental in research efforts to help discover the newest information out there while working for Dr. Pitts. They include: Jenny Arnold, Dusty Bennett, John Carter, Pasquale DeMatteo, and Chandrika Smith. These students were either graduate assistants to Dr. Pitts or completed some of this work as a directed study assignment.

Last, but not least, Dr. Pitts wishes to acknowledge her partner of over 28 years, Melita Reeves, for being patient and helping get through all of those late night writing sessions. Additionally, Dr. Pitts recognizes the "furry kids" in her life—the Corgi, Jazz; the mutt, Tucker; and the cat, Buster. They provide the unconditional love and never-ending comic relief needed in life. Live—laugh—love.

Thank you and enjoy the book.

Introduction

*F*undamentals of Sport Marketing, Fourth Edition* is a textbook on the theories, fundamentals, and practical application of marketing to sport business. Our approach has been to apply sound principles of marketing to the sport industry, modify and refine, define and develop, and eventually present theories and fundamentals of sport marketing that we know work in the sport business industry.

In this book, we use the definition of sport management and sport industry as it has been defined in the field of sport management by leading scholars who have extensive experience working in both academia and industry. According to these definitions, the sport industry is broad and varied, includes the many segments of businesses that toil behind the scenes, and is not limited to the selling of sports events. Two schools of thought regarding sport management and sport industry have emerged through the development of sport management as a field of study over the last three decades. One supports the notion that sport management is limited to the study of mainstream sports events and how to market and sell those to spectators. The other supports the position that sport management is the study of all businesses that exist in the sport industry, and the sport industry is defined as all businesses and enterprises whose products are sport or recreation-business related.

Like no other book in the field, *Fundamentals of Sport Marketing, Fourth Edition* covers the diversity of sport business, not merely professional and collegiate sport. This would include, for example, sport marketing research companies, sport sponsorship management companies, sporting goods manufacturers and retailers, sports broadcast companies, web sport enterprise, and sport tourism companies. All of these different types of companies are places where sport management and sport marketing students will be working. It is therefore incumbent upon sport management educators to prepare students with foundational knowledge that can be carried into any one of these types of companies. Therefore, our fourth edition is once again designed to meet these needs: sound foundational sport marketing knowledge that students can apply in any sport business.

This book is designed to introduce students to the business and practice of sport marketing. It provides an overview of the sport business industry, sport management, and sport marketing. It further provides detailed theories, fundamentals, and practical applications about how to conduct sport marketing.

SCOPE AND ORGANIZATION OF THE BOOK

This book is based on the belief that current and future sport industry professionals should be able to apply the fundamentals of sport marketing to any sport business. Therefore, different types of sport businesses are included as examples throughout the book.

Chapter 1 presents an updated overview of contemporary sport management definitions and concepts for sport, sport industry, sport business, sport management, and sport marketing.

Chapter 2 introduces the student to the global characteristics of sport business and how sport and global markets merge.

Chapter 3 orients the student to the foundations of sport marketing and introduces the Sport Marketing Management Model, which provides an illustration of the elements and tasks of the practice of sport marketing.

Chapter 4 introduces sport marketing research and its importance, as well as new examples of actual survey instruments that can be used for sport marketing research.

Chapter 5 presents the important sport marketing element of segmentation. Used to categorize and focus marketing efforts for consumer and business-to-business marketing, the importance of both consumer and industry segmentation are presented and thoroughly explained.

Chapter 6 provides the necessary tools for information management.

Chapter 7 lays the groundwork for the four Ps of marketing, which serve as the foci of Chapters 8 (product), 9 (price), 10 (place), and 11 (promotion). Each chapter has been updated with new information from the sport business industry that arms the student with contemporary knowledge in relation to product, price, place, and promotion.

Chapter 12 explains how to effectively utilize various forms of traditional media for marketing purposes.

Chapter 13 describes the ways in which marketing efforts can be enhanced with the use of athlete endorsements and sponsorship deals.

Chapter 14 explores trademark licensing and distinctive logos as methods of distinguishing and protecting a sport organization's products.

Chapter 15, new to this edition, focuses on the multitude of ways that the Internet and social media in particular are aiding sport marketers in reaching a wider audience.

The appendices are very important and are continued in this edition. Appendix A provides a brief directory to sport businesses. Appendix B contains a directory of sport business trade organizations. Appendix C provides a directory of sport business trade publications. For nearly every specific area of sport business, there is a trade publication to which you may subscribe. Appendix D provides a directory of sport management, sport marketing, and sport law journals and their information; it also contains directories of related sport business journals, sport management associations, sport management conferences, and information about the sport management curriculum standards. Appendix E contains several examples of sport marketing academic research. These will be helpful in finding research and locating where it is published. Finally, Appendix F contains seven different examples of research instruments commonly used in sport marketing that can be modified and used for actual research. This book is the only textbook that offers sport marketing instructors, students, and practitioners actual research instruments at their fingertips. Further, each instrument is provided with a description of the topic of study, its purpose, type of instrument, methodology, and some practical uses of the data gathered by this instrument. Actual studies may be conducted using these instruments with appropriate guidance from the sport marketing course instructor.

UNDERLYING PHILOSOPHIES OF THIS BOOK

Readers will welcome that fact that this book, like no other, is inclusive of diverse populations, such as people of various ages, genders, races, abilities, classes, sexual orientations, and cultures. The sport business industry contains these diverse populations, therefore, our philosophy of sport marketing reflects this position. For example, there are examples and information offered throughout the text concerning the many different populations and sport businesses. Further, the unbiased language used throughout the text is reflective of our recognition and embraces the diversity in sport business.

The sport business industry is vast and varied. We believe that today's sport business management and sport marketing students will attain jobs and careers in any one of the many different types of sport businesses in the industry. Therefore, we believe the student should be educated about fundamental sport marketing theories and practices that can be used and applied in any sport business. As such, we present a variety of sport businesses in discussions and as examples throughout the text.

Further, although this book is grounded in marketing theory as its conceptual framework and "parent discipline," we have intentionally presented the material in such a way that it can be used as a practical guide to sport marketing. In addition, the sport marketing theories and models developed and presented in this book may serve researchers in sport marketing well as their conceptual frameworks for important academic sport marketing scholarship.

BENEFITS TO THE READER

Fundamentals of Sport Marketing, Fourth Edition is a book written by authors with unparalleled academic and sport business industry experiences, knowledge, consulting, research, and practical experience in sport marketing, both in the U.S. and in countries around the world. Some of their international experiences include speaking, working, teaching, or consulting in South Africa, the Netherlands, Spain, England, France, Singapore, Malaysia, Hong Kong, Mauritius, Australia, Zimbabwe, Japan, Cyprus, Scotland, China, Saudi Arabia, Hungary, Greece, Italy, Germany, Korea, and Taiwan. Both authors have received the top awards in the field: the North American Society for Sport Management Research Fellow Award and the Dr. Earle F. Zeigler Scholar Award, both of which recognize top scholars each year in sport management. Therefore, readers can be assured that the book is developed by years of scholarship and practical experience in sport marketing.

It is a book that can be used on the job as a handbook, guide, and reference. Since the first edition was published, students working in the industry report that they continue to use it and follow it as a handbook. The fourth edition builds on the foundation laid in the first, second, and third editions.

We also believe that this textbook can be used in practically any country. Even though the examples and businesses cited are primarily North American, the theories, fundamentals, and the Pitts & Stotlar Sport Marketing Management Model (found in Chapter 3) can be applied to any sport business in any country.

1

The Sport Business Industry

"Sport has the power to change the world. It has the power to inspire. It has the power to unite people in a way that little else can. Sport can awaken hope where there was previously only despair."

—Nelson Mandela, Laureus World Sports Awards Ceremony 2000

INTRODUCTION

Welcome to one of the world's largest and most popular industries! The sport business industry is certainly among the top largest industries in the United States. In many other countries, regions and territories around the world, sports (and thus the sport business industry) is also one of the largest industries. This also means that the profession of sport management (also called sport business management) is one of the largest professions in the world. This is because wherever sports are being played, there are numerous people working to organize, manage, service, broadcast, officiate, build, facilitate, promote, finance, and produce them.

The underlying reason is the popularity of sports for people. People everywhere engage in or with sports in a number of different ways. In fact, in the U.S., we are literally surrounded by sports. Many of us are touched daily in some way by sports, whether we realize it or not. Sports events and news about sports are mentioned in nearly every newscast on TV and radio, and are blasted to our computers and cell phones. Moreover, there are countless television and radio channels and companies, newspapers, magazines, websites, and varying forms of social media whose business is covering sports and sending sport-related information around the world.

Secondly, many of us participate in sports or engage in fitness and/or recreational activities of all kinds. Some do this daily, while others engage either weekly or at least monthly. Table 1.1 shows 2010 participation rates as researched and reported by the National Sporting Goods Association (NSGA; www.nsga.org). Figure 1.1 shows information from the United States Department of Labor revealing that in an average 24-hour work day, employed individuals aged 25–54 with children engage in sports and leisure activities 2.6 hours per day.

Participant sport is comprised of all sports activities in which amateurs participate. That is, if an individual is not paid as a professional to participate in a sports activity, then that individual is part of the participant sport industry segment. As you can imagine, this is the segment comprised of all of those millions, probably like you the reader, who participate in sports activities. Millions of individuals are walking; hiking; camping; boating; playing soccer, softball, and basketball; climbing; fishing; kayaking; biking; working out; hang gliding; swimming; playing tennis, volleyball, and golf; and participating in yoga, aerobics, weight training, and scuba diving. And those are only a few of the multitudes of sports, recreation, leisure, and fitness activities around the world. Thus, it is easy to see that the largest segment of the sport business industry is participant sports.

For example, consider the following information about a few participant sports. The Outdoor Industry Association (OIA) is one of many sports-related organizations that conduct research and track sports activities. This particular organization, however, tracks just eight outdoor activities. Their research can be accessed for free online at www.outdoorindustry.org. The eight sports activities are bicycle-based, camp-based,

Table 1.1. 2010 Sports Participation— Ranked by Total Participation

Sport	Total (in millions)	Percent Change *	Sport	Total (in millions)	Percent Change *
Exercise Walking	95.8	2.6%	Backpack/Wilderness Camp	11.1	−9.3%
Exercising with Equipment	55.3	−3.4%	Softball	10.8	−8.4%
Swimming	51.9	3.4%	Volleyball	10.6	−1.0%
Camping (vacation/overnight)	44.7	−12.0%	Dart Throwing	10.5	−14.1%
Bicycle Riding	39.8	4.3%	Football (tackle)	9.3	4.8%
Bowling	39.0	−13.3%	Skateboarding	7.7	−8.5%
Aerobic Exercising	38.5	16.3%	In-Line Roller Skating	7.5	−5.4%
Hiking	37.7	10.9%	Scooter Riding	7.4	−9.4%
Workout at Club	36.3	−5.3%	Skiing (alpine)	7.4	5.6%
Running/Jogging	35.5	10.3%	Mountain Biking (off road)	7.2	−13.5%
Fishing	33.8	2.8%	Archery (target)	6.5	−8.3%
Weight Lifting	31.5	−8.8%	Paintball Games	6.1	−2.7%
Basketball	26.9	10.1%	Snowboarding	6.1	−1.2%
Billiards/Pool	24.0	14.8%	Kayaking	5.6	14.8%
Golf	21.9	−2.0%	Target Shooting—Air gun	5.3	2.4%
Yoga	20.2	28.1%	Hunting w/Bow and Arrow	5.2	−16.7%
Boating, Motor/Power	20.0	−16.2%	Water Skiing	5.2	0.6%
Target Shooting (net)	19.8	0.3%	Gymnastics	4.8	23.5%
Hunting with Firearms	16.3	−13.5%	Hockey (ice)	3.3	7.9%
Soccer	13.5	−0.3%	Muzzle Loading	3.1	−19.6%
Table Tennis	12.8	−3.7%	Wrestling	2.9	−0.9%
Baseball	12.5	8.9%	Skiing (cross country)	2.0	19.5%
Tennis	12.3	13.2%			

Note: Participated more than once; Seven (7) years of age or older; *Percent change from 2009.
Source: National Sporting Goods Association, www.nsga.org

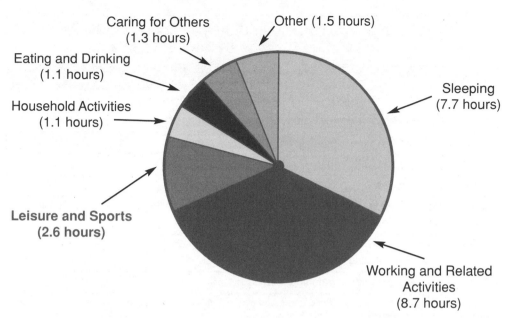

Caring for Others
(1.3 hours)

Other (1.5 hours)

Eating and Drinking
(1.1 hours)

Household Activities
(1.1 hours)

Sleeping
(7.7 hours)

Leisure and Sports
(2.6 hours)

Working and Related
Activities
(8.7 hours)

Figure 1.1. Time use on an average workday for employed persons ages 25 to 54 with children: Sports and Leisure activities is 3rd largest reported.

NOTE: Data include employed persons on days they worked, ages 25 to 54, who lived in households with children under 18. Data include non-holiday weekdays and are annual averages for 2009.

SOURCE: United States Department of Labor; Bureau of Labor Statistics. 2009. http://www.bls.gov/tus/charts/

paddle-based, fishing, hunting, snow-based, trail-based, and wildlife viewing (Outdoor Industry Association, 2011). As part of their research, the OIA reports that "Nearly half of Americans ages 6 and older, or 137.9 million individuals, participated in at least one outdoor activity in 2010, making 10.1 billion outdoor outings," according to the *2011 Outdoor Recreation Participation Topline Report* (see Table 1.2). The research shows significant increases in adventure sports such as kayaking, backcountry camping and climbing, as well as slight increases in youth participation among those individuals ages 13–24.

Moreover, it's not just the large number of individuals that make the "participant sport" segment the largest segment of the industry, it's also the amount of money involved. The OIA has reported that these eight outdoor activities account for a contri-

A Few Segments of the Sport Business Industry

- Participant sport
- Sporting goods manufacturing and retail: Equipment, apparel, footwear
- Sports facilities: Design, construction, management
- Athlete management companies
- Professional sports
- High school and college sports
- Outdoor sports
- Sports governing bodies
- Sport management education
- Sport business advertising
- Sport sponsorship
- Sports tourism and travel
- Sports law
- Sports betting/gambling
- Sports media: TV, Internet, radio, mobile devices
- Sport marketing
- Water and marine sports
- Sports media and broadcasting

Table 1.2. The Outdoor Industry Association Study: Participation Rates of 8 Outdoor Sports	
Outdoor Sport	**Participation**
1. Bicycle-based Recreation—on paved roads or off-road	60 million
2. Camp-based Recreation—RV, tent, or lodge at a campsite	45 million
3. Paddle-based Recreation—kayaking, rafting, canoeing	33 million
4. Fishing—all types	13 million
5. Hunting—all types	24 million
6. Snow-based Recreation—cross country or Nordic, downhill, telemark, snowboarding, and snowshoeing	16 million
7. Trail-based Recreation—trail running or day hiking on an unpaved trail, backpacking, climbing ice or natural rock	56 million
8. Wildlife Viewing—wildlife watching, birding	66 million
Note: Nearly half of Americans ages 6 and older, or 137.9 million, participated in at least one outdoor activity in 2010, making 10,1 billion outdoor outing.	
Note: There are significant increases in adventure sports such as kayaking, camping and climbing as well as slight increases in youth participation ages 13–24.	
* Source: Outdoor Industry Association (2011). www.outdoorindustry.org	

bution of $730 billion USD annually to the U.S. economy! The outdoor recreation industry of these eight activities, according to the research, provides nearly 6.5 million jobs in the U.S., generates $88 billion in annual state and national tax revenue, and generates $289 billion annually in retail sales and services (Outdoor Industry Association, 2011). Further, as was previously mentioned, sports are part of our everyday lives, whether we realize it or not, and the OIA report shows that this industry segment ". . . touches over 8 percent of America's personal consumption expenditures—more than 1 in every 12 dollars circulating in the economy"(p. 3).

The second largest industry segment is the "sporting goods" industry. The many people engaging in different sporting, recreation, and fitness activities all need equipment, clothing, uniforms, socks, and shoes. These three product categories—equipment, apparel, and footwear—comprise the sporting goods industry. According to current research, this industry has an economic value of $114.2 billion USD in the United States alone (Plunkett Research Ltd., 2011; see Table 1.11).

And let us not forget about our beloved spectator sports, which in this country are primarily comprised of professional, college, and high school sports. Millions of Americans are fans of these sports and can be categorized on a continuum from what we call the "hardcore fanatical fan" to the "I'm just here for the party fan." Even though some professional and college sports enjoy massive media coverage while other spectator sports receive only minor coverage, spectator attendance drives the existence and popularity of spectator sports. That is to say, if it were not for spectators, professional and college sports might not exist. It can easily be argued that sports' very purpose is to pro-

Without the dedication of fans, sport businesses would be unable to thrive. Courtesy of stockphotography.com

vide a form of entertainment. Hence, many scholars argue that professional and college sports are nothing more than an entertainment pastime. Regardless of their spectator attendance, media coverage, or economic impact, professional, college, and high school sports are also big business.

The sport business industry consists of numerous other segments, some of which are sports tourism, semi-professional sports, recreation, high school and college sports, outdoor sports, and sports service businesses such as sport marketing firms, sport sponsorship management companies, and sport governing bodies. In addition, each of the segments is comprised of a plethora of sub-segments. Throughout this chapter, as well as the rest of the book, we will present a multitude of these segments to illustrate how large and varied this industry is. This is important for many reasons. First, anyone who will be working in this industry should understand its scale and complexity. Second, by introducing as many segments as possible, you might be introduced to one that will interest you and which could become your future career area.

JOBS AND CAREERS IN THE SPORT BUSINESS INDUSTRY

Jobs and careers in the industry are seemingly endless and are as varied as the segments and businesses that comprise the overall industry. For every sports activity, such as a college basketball game, the number of sport management professionals required to produce it can range from as few as five or six to as many as thousands. For instance, consider how many workers are needed for a simple basketball game, from a local recreation game to a university Division I level game. The local city recreation women's basketball league requires a facility, which in turn requires workers who designed it, workers who built it, and workers who maintain and manage it, as well as the workers who are coaches, officials, and staff for the game. For the college basketball game, the same types of workers are needed, but professionals are also needed for sport marketing, sports information, sports medicine, sport finance and budget, sports law, sponsorship, supporters, sports ticket businesses, game-day operations staff, fan gear merchandising, fan gear licensing, traffic control, parking facilities, food and drink workers for concessions and restaurants, luxury suite workers, and security. Additionally, because this game might be televised or transmitted in other media—radio, web, social media—professionals are needed in sports media, journalism, photography, production team, electricians, lighting, sound, on-camera announcers, and Web producers. Further, several industries are critical to the game as well. They are the stakeholders—those who have a "stake," or vested interest, in the success of the production of the game. This includes whole industries such as the transportation industry for airline flights and local transportation such as buses, subways, or taxis; the hotel industry for places for spectators, teams, media, and workers to live during the event; the restaurant industry for food and drink for everyone; and sponsors for provision of much-needed items such as funding, promotional items, advertising dollars, and a variety of gifted equipment or materials. Therefore, the number of jobs needed for a simple basketball game can be in the hundreds!

At yet another level are sports events that are called "sports mega events." These include such events as the Winter and Summer Olympic Games, the Men's and Women's World Cup championship tournament, the World University Games, or the World Equestrian Games. These are called "sports mega events" because they are of an enormous size in relation to all other sports events in terms of years of preparation, facilities needed, marketing efforts, organizations involved, volunteers needed, sponsors and sponsorship dollars needed, governments involved, and the number of paid sport management professionals needed. Consider how much is involved in organizing one of these events.

Moreover, this is an industry in which a person can often find success by linking an interest in sports with an interest in something else. It is a unique industry in which you can have two loves—one being sports and the other being something else—and there is most likely a job that incorporates both of them. For example, an individual loves sports, but also loves photography. That individual does not have to choose between the two because there are plenty of jobs for sports photographers. As another example, an individual loves to write computer programs, but also loves sports. Again, that individual does not have to choose one or the other—there are plenty of jobs in the sport industry for individuals to write computer programs for sports equipment, such as the fitness workouts on screens on treadmills or rowing machines; for keeping up with one's fitness workouts at a fitness center; for programming a Jumbotron for digital displays at a large sports arena; or for gauging the air drag of race cars, speed-skating suits, or bobsleds. Essentially, in the sport business industry, there are numerous jobs that combine two interests into one job. There are not many other industries in which that is true.

SPORT MANAGEMENT IS A POPULAR
COLLEGE DEGREE PROGRAM TODAY

With the widespread love of sports and the sport business industry's size, variety, and flexibility, it is no wonder that sport management is a fast-growing and popular college degree program today. Because so many students want a career in the sport business industry, many colleges and universities are adding degree programs in sport management. Although sport management programs are more typically found in a department including other sports-related degree programs, such as sports medicine, physical education, and exercise science, there has been a recent increase in the number of programs being offered in departments or colleges of business. But despite the constant increase in the number of programs, there are still too few programs and too few students in sport management to fill all of the jobs in the sport business industry. Additionally, there are still many jobs in the industry for which a degree in sport management is not yet required. It will be perhaps several years, probably decades, before there are enough students trained in sport management programs to fill all of the available jobs.

EVOLUTION OF SPORT MANAGEMENT

There is plenty of evidence that humans have created and played sports and recreational activities throughout their history. The proof can be found in a number of historical records and artifacts, such as sculptures, monuments, carvings, paintings, depictions, artifacts, equipment, clothing, and facilities.

In fact, the word "sport" is derived from the Old French word "desport," which means "leisure" (Desport, 2011). The oldest use of the word "sport" found in English is from the 15th century, and at that time the word meant anything humans find amusing or entertaining (Harper, 2011). Labeled as the oldest "sport" is *Pitz*, the Mayan ball game played by everyone—women, men, and children—dating from around 2500 B.C. (Authentic Maya, 2011). Hundreds of the ancient ball courts, called Halaw, have been discovered in Central America (around 500 in Guatemala alone) where the game was played.

One can easily draw the conclusion that sport management is among the oldest professions. First, where there are sports activities, there are people who are working to organize and govern the events, plan and build the facilities, invent and manufacture the equipment, and design and produce the clothing. Second, if sports and recreational activities were being played, there must have been people who were also teaching others how to organize, build, design, produce, and manage sports activities, equipment, clothing, and events. Thus, sport management was being practiced at the very beginning of human sports. Therefore, humans have been participating in sport management ever since sports have been played. It can readily be concluded that this makes sport management among the oldest professions on Earth (Pitts, 2008, 2011).

In the United States, the evolution of sport management as an academic field can be partially attributed to a course in physical education titled "Administration and Organization of Physical Education and Athletics" in the early 1950s. It was the only course a

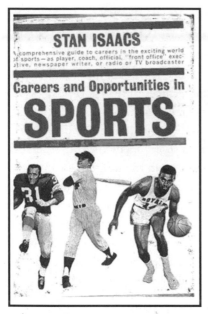

The 1964 Sports Careers Book by Stan Isaacs

college student could take with any content about the management of sports. Eventually, students demanded more and the "college athletics administration" course was created. Soon after, more courses were developed. For several years, and unfortunately still today, some programs were ". . . primarily physical education curricula with a sport management title" (Pitts, 2001, p. 6).

In response to greater and increased varied interests in all of the different segments of the sports industry beyond college sports, other courses were added with a much broader focus. Many courses, years, curriculum standards, and sport management associations later, that first course has evolved into the academic field of study that exists today. Most programs are housed in physical education, health, and exercise science departments, some programs comprise their own departments, and more recently some programs are housed in a school of business or a department or school of hospitality, entertainment, and tourism (Mahony, 2008; Schwarz, 2010).

It is intriguing, then, that even though humans have been practicing sport management ever since humans have played sports, sport management as an organized and named academic area of study is rather new. In fact, it has perhaps only existed for a few decades! There has been no organized study to determine the historical development of sport management as a degree program. Some sport management scholars credit Ohio University having the first sport management program in the U.S. in 1966 and with perhaps coining the term "sports administration." In fact, a recent discovery reveals that perhaps the first known use of the term is found in a book published in 1964 (Isaacs, 1964; Pitts, 2008). In this book, titled *Careers and Opportunities in Sports*, Stan Isaacs has a chapter titled "Careers in Sports Administration." Further, Isaacs describes a sport management degree program titled "Baseball Administration School" that was offered from 1949 to 1959 at Florida Southern University. That curriculum had courses very similar to sport management programs today with courses such as "Legal Responsibility and Insurance," "Daily Game Operations," "Park Maintenance," "Tickets and Tax Laws," "Finances, Accounting, and Payroll Systems," and "Player Contracts and Related Paperwork" (see Isaacs, 1964, p. 183 [Appendix IV]). Table 1.3 presents those courses and their course descriptions. As you can see in the course descriptions, they are very similar to courses offered today in sport management programs. Additionally, the chapter in Isaacs' book lists and discusses various sport management jobs such as general manager, public relations manager, lawyer, commissioner, scouting, traveling secretary, statistician, ticket director, groundskeeper, and even batboy.

Table 1.3. The Florida Southern University Courses in 1949

Appendix IV

The curriculum of the Baseball Administration School operated at Florida Southern University from 1949 to 1959 is of interest in its reflection of the details involved in sports administration.

DETAILS OF CURRICULUM

    1. THE NATIONAL AGREEMENT—Since all functions of club management are based upon the rules and regulations of the National Association Agreement, a comprehensive and analytical study of this governing instrument {is undertaken}. In conjunction with this study, there will be an analysis of the general structure of organized baseball and the relationship of the minor leagues to the major leagues.

    2. PLAYER CONTRACTS AND RELATED PAPERWORK—All player contracts and related paperwork must be written and processed according to the precise rules established in the National Association Agreement. So that class members may familiarize themselves with these forms and processes . . . extensive emphasis {is} placed upon the subject, with active drills being conducted on forms supplies by the National Association of Professional Baseball Leagues.

    3. TICKETS AND TAX LAWS—A study of the correct pricing of tickets and the taxes thereon; kinds of tickets; ticket sales and promotions. Sample tickets and problems are used in the classrooms.

    4. LEGAL RESPONSIBILITY AND INSURANCE—Students thoroughly discuss workman's compensation, hospitalization, robbery and liability insurance; responsibility to employees and spectators; dual responsibility in city-owned and -leased parks; and responsibility of sub-contractors.

    5. FINANCES, ACCOUNTING, AND PAYROLL SYSTEMS—Sample budgets, social security and withholding tax regulations, proper handling of tax funds and tax reports.

    6. PARK MAINTENANCE—Importance of neatness and cleanliness. Clubhouse and restroom facilities. Suggestions for proper layout and upkeep of the playing field and lighting system.

    7. DAILY GAME OPERATIONS—Stadium personnel; reserved- and box-seat sales and reservations; game reports; public address and scoreboard operations; ball boys; barking and traffic problems; police protection; checking tellers in and out.

    8. CONCESSIONS—Program advertising and layout; sale of concession items; commissions to vendors; inventory and records; sales personnel.

    9. PROMOTION AND PUBLIC RELATIONS—Press and radio, T.V. relations; use of passes; year-round promotional programs; special nights and group ticket sales; the value of off-seasons promotions—hot-stove meetings and home-plate clubs; use of baseball films; importance of working with youth and women's organizations." (page 183)

The program at Florida Southern was focused on the business of baseball. The catalog described it this way: "Florida Southern College, recognizing that baseball business management was a profession in which no training at the college academic level had heretofore been offered, instituted at the Baseball Administration School to provide students an opportunity to study and learn at first hand the major problems of the baseball business executive" (Isaacs, 1964, p. 136).

It is important for all students in sport business management to know and understand as much as possible about their chosen career and industry. For example, it is vital that every sport management student have an understanding of sport marketing. The student must understand sport marketing fundamentals and how they can be used in every segment of the sport industry. This knowledge will positively affect the student's success in a chosen career in any sport industry segment.

The application of sport marketing fundamentals to the sport business industry is best accomplished when the student has full knowledge and understanding of the sport business industry and its segments. It is important to understand what this industry is, how it develops, how it grows, what feeds its growth, who its consumers are, and the nature of its linkages with society and culture.

Throughout this chapter, the student will learn about the sport business industry. Toward this goal, it is first essential to understand the "sport business industry" as it is being defined in sport business management today. To do this, it is important to understand the terms *sport* and *industry* individually and also as they are defined in sport management today.

WHAT IS AN INDUSTRY?

An "industry" is a market in which similar or closely related products are sold to buyers. Some industries may contain only one product. It is more typical that an industry comprises a variety of product items sold to many existing or potential consumers who vary demographically and psychographically, and whose needs, wants, desires, or demands may change over time. The tennis racket industry is an example of a single-product industry. Within this industry, there are different variations of tennis rackets ranging in size, color, material, and price to meet the demands of the many different consumer markets. Additionally, the tennis racket industry is part of a multi-product industry, the sporting goods industry.

The sporting goods industry is an example of an industry that is composed of many different but related products. It includes all products sold as goods, equipment and apparel for use in sports, recreation, and fitness activities. This industry can be subdivided into several segments using different ways to define those segments. To see the many segments of the sporting goods industry, look inside a sporting goods store. There are departments (representative segments of the industry) for a variety of sports and activities, categorized according to their similarities such as aquatic sports, camping activities, and soccer apparel. Keep in mind, however, that local sporting goods stores do not carry goods for every sport that exists. For example, to find equestrian or rodeo equipment, one would have to go to a specialty store.

Within a department, the products can be further subdivided into groups of individual sports or closely related sports. In the aquatic sports department, for example, you will find equipment, goods, accessories, and apparel for several different sports such as scuba diving, fishing, water skiing, snorkeling, and swimming. In the tennis department, you will find tennis rackets from the single-product tennis racket industry, but you will also find many other tennis products—tennis balls, shoes, socks, bags, towels, tennis ball holders, water bottles, caps, shirts, and many more. You will also find products not needed to play tennis. These are products that promote the sport of tennis such as tennis bumper stickers, key rings, jewelry, posters, and T-shirts. As you can see in the examples, an industry can be composed of one product or many products. Those products can be very closely related and similar in nature or very loosely related and dissimilar. Moreover, it is important to recognize that products can be goods, services, people, places, or ideas. An industry can be composed of one of these or a combination of them. Either way, the products are usually related in some way as defined by those involved in the industry.

> **Product Examples in the Sport Industry Include:**
>
> - Participation
> - Entertainment
> - Equipment and apparel
> - Promotional items
> - Sports facilities
> - Sport marketing research
> - Management services
>
> It is important to recognize that products can be goods, services, people, places, or ideas.

SPORT AND SPORT BUSINESS MANAGEMENT

"Sport" is defined in different ways depending on the context in which it is used. In fields such as sport sociology, physical education, and recreation, sport is used to denote sporting activities such as basketball, hiking, snowboarding, and running. The term *sport*, as used in the field of sport business management and in relation to the sport business industry, is a broad, conceptual term used to denote all people, activities, businesses, and organizations involved in producing, facilitating, promoting, or organizing any activity, experience, or business enterprise focused on fitness, recreation, sports, sports tourism, or leisure. Sport management is also called sports administration, sport business, and sport business management.

To classify an enterprise as a sport business, then, doesn't necessarily mean it is a business that sells sports. It might be a company in the business of sport marketing research, a sports tourism business that sells snow ski packages, a Web-based sport company that sells Women's World Cup souvenirs via the Internet, a sponsorship management business specializing in handling sports sponsorship packages, or a sporting goods company that manufactures mountain-climbing gear.

Notice that the title of this book uses the contemporary term *sport marketing* and not *sports marketing*. Also note the use of the term *sport management* or *sport business management* throughout the book instead of *sports management*. The term *sport* has a very different meaning than *sports*. According to the North American Society for Sport Management (NASSM), "sports implies a collection of separate activities such as golf, soccer, hockey, volleyball, softball, and gymnastics—items in a series that can be counted" (Parks & Zanger, 1990, p. 6). This is the way most people define sports—as sports activities. This reflects primarily two things: first, exposure to sports in our schools and colleges; second, exposure to sports every day through the media. That is, what the average person sees and hears through television coverage of sports events, the sports section in the newspaper, and the sports report on TV news broadcasts covers sports activities as they take place or a report of the outcome—the final score and who won. Therefore, *sports management* implies only managing sports activities. "Sport," however, is a collective noun and a more all-encompassing concept. Therefore, NASSM (the professional association composed of university academicians, students, and scholars in

Sport Management Defined

Sport management is the study and practice of all people, activities, businesses, or organizations involved in producing, facilitating, promoting, or organizing any sport-related business or product.

sport business management) chose the word *sport* as a term that more correctly identifies and defines the sport management field of study.

Sport business management implies a much broader concept. Therefore, the contemporary definition of sport business management is as follows: *Sport business management* is the study and practice in relation to all people, activities, businesses, and organizations involved in producing, facilitating, promoting, or organizing any sport-related product. Sport products can be goods, services, people, places, or ideas. This includes, for example, a company that manufactures sports equipment, clothing, or shoes; a person or company who offers promotion services for a sports organization; an organization charged with governing a sport; a person who represents a professional athlete as an agent; people who own and manage a sports facility; people who design and construct those sports facilities; a person who teaches golf; a company that manages the promotional merchandise and licenses for a sports event; the local recreation business that offers basketball, tennis, and swimming leagues; and television companies that are involved in broadcasting sports events.

This is what *sport* means when used in the context of sport management, sport marketing, and the sport industry. It is an all-inclusive term representing every person and business involved in producing, facilitating, promoting, or organizing sports, fitness, play, leisure, or recreation activity and all related products.

THE SPORT BUSINESS INDUSTRY

A variety of research in sport management provides descriptions of the many different products and businesses that make up the sport industry. The products and businesses focus on sports, fitness, recreation, or leisure products. There are many different groups of consumers for these products, and they can be broadly categorized as either end consumers or business consumers.

Based on this research and the definitions of *sport* and *industry* presented earlier, the definition of *sport business industry* follows: The *sport business industry* is the market in which the products offered to buyers are related to sport, fitness, recreation, or leisure and may be activities, goods, services, people, places, or ideas.

Here are some examples of the types of products offered in the sport business industry:

- participation products such as participation in a women's recreational basketball league;
- entertainment products, primarily for spectating, such as the offer to watch a field hockey game, a snow-boarding competition, or the X-Games;
- equipment and apparel such as softball uniforms, ice-hockey pads, bodybuilding apparel, in-line skates, and bicycle helmets;

- promotional merchandise used to promote a sport business, sports league, sports event, or fitness activity such as logo caps and shirts, fitness club shirts or towels, stadium cushions and blankets with the company logo;
- sports facilities such as the construction of a new sport stadium or the remodeling of racquetball courts to accommodate wallyball (the design and the construction company for the facility are also products);

> ## Sport Business Industry Defined
>
> The *sport business industry* is the market in which the products offered to its buyers are related to sport, fitness, recreation, or leisure and may be activities, goods, services, people, places, or ideas.

- sport products offered by service businesses, such as sport marketing research, tennis racket stringing, or golf course care;
- recreational activities sold as participation products, such as mountain bicycling, hiking, camping, horseback riding, boating, cross-country skiing, sailing, and mountain climbing;
- complete management and marketing professional services offered for a variety of markets, such as the management of a large marathon, the promotion and management of a sports tourism package, or the management and marketing for an athlete; and
- products offered by sport media businesses, like magazines about specific sports such as *Runner's World* magazine and trade magazines targeted to industry business such as *The Boat Dealer* (there also are these products and companies: sports television companies, sports radio shows, and Internet sports companies).

ORGANIZING THE INDUSTRY TOWARD BETTER UNDERSTANDING AND COMPETITIVE ADVANTAGE

The sport business industry is one of the largest industries in the U.S. and in the world. In the U.S., it might be the largest, or at least in the top five largest. It is very diverse and is composed of numerous different segments filled with many types of businesses. In fact, it is so large that it is easier to study a segment or a small part of the industry than it is to study the entire industry. However, it is important for anyone working in this industry to truly understand the depth and breadth of the industry in order to better understand how it operates and for competitive advantage. This knowledge will help in making decisions and developing marketing strategies.

There have been attempts to study the entire industry, and some of those studies will be presented in the next section. There have also been attempts to study the industry in an attempt to organize it so that it can be understood for business purposes. Several models have been created to organize the many segments of the sport business industry. This kind of research can help sport management and sport marketing professionals better understand their products and their consumers, and therefore enhance their decisions regarding their particular sport business. Three of these models are presented here.

Product Market Model

Figure 1.2 presents the industry segmentation model developed by Pitts, Fielding, and Miller (1994). Their research utilized "functions" of products to formulate categories or segments, also called product markets. This model indicates that products in the industry fall into three segments: sport performance, sport production, and sport promotion. For example, if a business manufactures tennis rackets, this product falls into the sport production segment in this model because a tennis racket is a product needed or desired for the production of, or to influence the quality of, sport performance. To play tennis, one must have a tennis racket. There are, however, a great variety of tennis rackets, and they vary by color, material, grip size, weight, head size and configuration, and string. As a player increases in skill level, the player might desire a custom-made racket in order

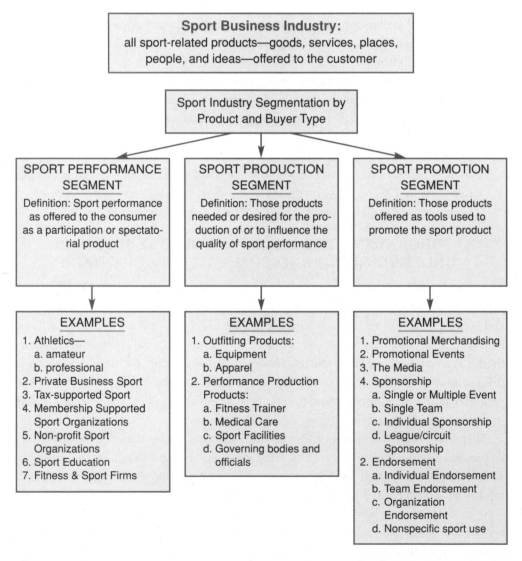

Figure 1.2. The Sport Business Industry Segment Model: Product Market Model.

to try to enhance performance. Your tennis racket company, then, might consider manufacturing a line of rackets that range from the inexpensive one-size-for-all racket to an expensive custom racket. Your knowledge of the function of this product, purposes of the racket, the product market segment, and your consumer greatly enhances decision-making. You will learn more about segmentation in later chapters.

Economic Activity Model

This approach was developed by Meek (1997) and is presented in Figure 1.3. Meek categorized the industry into segments based on its economic activity. This model depicts three segments: (1) sport entertainment, comprised of professional sports; (2) sport products, comprised of sporting goods; and (3) sport support organizations, comprised of management and organizational businesses that manage the other segments. Meek's model presents the idea of understanding the industry based on how its different segments are linked economically, as well as how similar the types of businesses are.

Sports Activity Model

This model, developed by Li, Hofacre, and Mahony (2007) and presented in Figure 1.4, depicts segments of the industry as divided by sports activities. This model places sports activity production companies and organizations at the "core" of the industry and suggests that all other businesses exist to support, build, facilitate, produce, manage, or promote the "core" product.

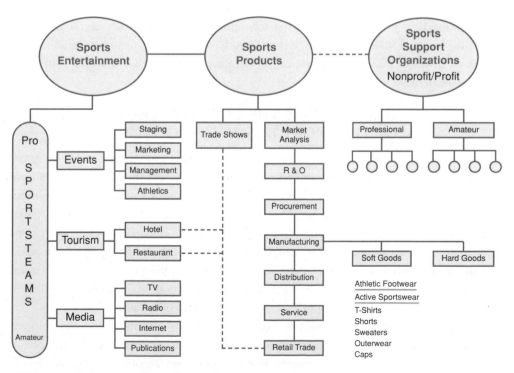

Figure 1.3. The Meek Economic Activity Model.

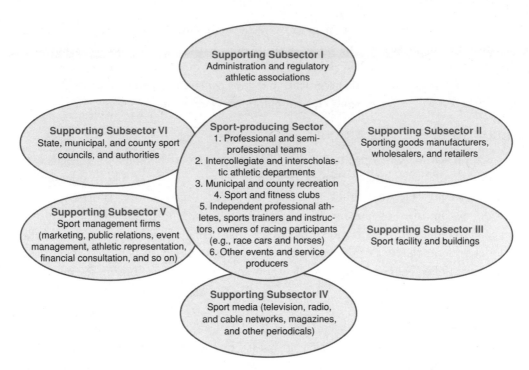

Figure 1.4. Sport Industry Segmentation: The Sport Activity Model.

All of the models have some similarities, and all give us ways to categorize the entire industry. Each one helps with making sense of where a particular business fits into the industry and how it is related to all other segments. Knowing as much as you can about your business and how it is related, either directly or indirectly, to other types of businesses is critical to making decisions and developing strategies that will give your company a competitive advantage.

DETERMINING THE ECONOMIC SIZE OF THE SPORT BUSINESS INDUSTRY

The sport business industry has experienced phenomenal growth in a relatively short period of time. Although sports and recreational activities, events, and businesses have been around for about as long as humans, there has never been a period of explosive growth like that of the last 40 years. There are many reasons for this growth; those reasons are presented in the next section of this chapter. These changes represent both horizontal and vertical expansion. Horizontal growth involves the addition of new markets and products, such as new sport businesses like sport marketing research firms. Vertical growth involves the growth of existing markets and products, such as the explosion of girls and women in traditional sports like basketball and volleyball.

Researchers and some organizations have attempted to determine the dollar value or economic impact of the sport business industry. There are many reasons to do this, one of which is to gain a sense of size in relation to other industries. Another is to know the extent of an industry. This important information is helpful in determining jobs needed and

Table 1.4. Studies of the Economic Size of the Sport Business Industry Over 35 Years

This table shows 8 different studies of which several claim to be a study on the overall size of the sport business industry. However, none of the studies included all of the segments of the industry. Nonetheless, they provide a estimate of the size of some segments of the industry.

Study	Year	Size of Industry by This Study	Rank in Top 50 Industries	Segments Included
The Lineberry Analysis[1]	1973	$132 billion	not given	several
The 1st Sports Inc. Study[2]	1986	$47.3 billion	not given	several
The 2nd Sports Inc. Study[3]	1987	$50.2 billion	23rd	several
The 3rd Sports Inc. Study[4]	1988	$63.1 billion	22nd	several
The Meek Study[5]	1995	$152 billion	11th	several
The SBJ Study[6]	1999	$213 billion	6th	four men's professional sports leagues
The Outdoor Industry Association Study[7]	2010	$730 billion	not given	8 outdoor sports categories
The Plunkett Study[8]	2011	$422 billion	not given	12 segments

Sources: (1) Lineberry, 1973; (2, 3, 4) Sport Inc. and Sporting News with WEFA; (5) Meek, 1997; (6) Broughton, Lee, and Nethery, 1999; (7) outdoorindustry.com; (8) Plunkett Research Ltd., 2011

jobs growth as well as the type of education needed for workers and professionals in the industry. Although the studies were not conducted the same way and did not look at the same factors or parts of the industry, they at least provide an estimate of the size of the industry and the various segments that have constituted the industry since the first known analyses in 1973. You may be surprised to learn that the men's professional sports segment is not the largest segment of the industry, even though it certainly seems that way because of the media coverage those sports receive. As you will see in the figures presented in this section, the largest segments of the industry are participant sport and sporting goods. When you learn what constitutes these segments, then you see that it makes sense.

To date, eight studies on the size of the sport business industry offer an illustration of its size, segments and growth over nearly 35 years (see Tables 1.4–1.16). These studies will be presented first; then we present a different method for attempting to determine the size and scope of the industry. We believe that the reader will get a sense of how large the sport business industry is, how varied it is, and how extensive its reach is. Something else to keep in mind when studying all of this information is the number and different types of jobs in the different segments of the industry. As a student, you might have come into sport management thinking that your goal is to get a job in the college or professional sports settings. Perhaps this is because you have not really considered the different segments or the multitude of other areas of the industry. Perhaps after reading the following information, you will be introduced to a part of the industry that is very interesting to you.

Table 1.5. The Lineberry Analysis— Some of the Industry Segments Included	
Industry	**Value**
Nondurable toys and sports supplies	$5.6 billion
Camping equipment	$5.0 billion
Swimming pools/accessories	$1.0 billion
Spectator sports admissions	$400 million
Commercial recreation	$1.6 billion
Hunting and fishing licenses and equipment	$4.0 billion
Boating	$3.4 billion
Federal expenditure outdoor recreation	$450 million
State park and recreation	$295 million
Local recreation and parks	$2.0 billion
Tennis	$420 million
Snow skiing	$1.0 billion
Source: Lineberry, 1973	

The Lineberry Analysis: 1973

The Lineberry analysis of the industry attempted to gather several different reports and studies on economic values of different segments of the industry (Lineberry, 1973). Refer to Table 1.5. As Lineberry reports: "In the mid-1960s, the financial communist, Sylvia Porter, wrote of recreation as 'a big booming professional business—dazzling even the most optimistic projections of a few years ago . . .'" (p. 204).

Further, Lineberry reported the following about an article in the *New York Times*: "At the dawning of the seventies, leisure has become an essential part of American life, with a pattern of growth significantly greater than that of the economy. The varied groups in the highly diversified leisure 'industry' expect therefore continued expansion of their revenues . . . as the market for their products and services broadens" (p. 204).

Lineberry reported and outlined several statistical economic studies and reports about sports and recreation accounting for the 1960s and early 1970s. The analysis and all of the economic data presented in Lineberry's book show that the sports industry was at the beginning of its boom times.

The Sports Inc. Studies: 1986, 1987, 1988

These were a series of three studies about the industry in 1986, 1987, and 1988 (Comte & Stogel, 1990)—see Tables 1.6 and 1.7. What is significant here is that the sport industry is shown to be the 23rd largest industry in the country in 1987. It is revealing to note which industries are larger than the sport business industry, and which ones are smaller. We all know that the sport industry is big, but it is not until we see numbers

Table 1.6. Top 50 Industry Rankings of 1987—From the Sports Inc Study			
Industry	Value	Industry	Value
1. Real estate	$519.3*	26. Paper and allied products	$39.5
2. Manufacturing	479.9	27. Auto repair garages	38.9
3. Retail Trade	427.4	28. Security/commodity brokers	36.7
4. Regulated Industry	408.2	29. Primary metals	36.4
5. Manufacturing (non-durable goods)	373.6	30. Lodging	35.7
6. Wholesale trade	313.0	31. Personal services	34.4
7. Health services	223.7	32. Air transportation	34.2
8. Business services	179.3	33. Petroleum and related products	33.6
9. Communications	120.9	34. Rubber and plastics	29.9
10. Radio and television	108.3	35. Educational services	29.6
11. Insurance	101.3	36. Insurance agents and brokers	28.6
12. Miscellaneous professional organizations	86.4	37. Lumber	27.7
13. Electrical machinery	85.0	38. Stone, clay, and glass	27.5
14. Banking	84.8	39. Instrument manufacturing	26.9
15. Chemicals and allied products	77.1	40. Amusement and recreation services	24.0
16. Food and kindred products	74.0	41. Apparel	22.5
17. Insurance carriers	72.7	42. Textile mills	19.9
18. Trucking and warehousing	64.2	43. Credit agencies	17.0
19. Legal services	62.3	44. Holdings and other investment firms	16.2
20. Fabricated metals	60.3	45. Tobacco	15.5
21. Printing and publishing	58.2	46. Furniture and fixtures	14.9
22. Non-auto transportation equipment	56.0	47. Miscellaneous repairs	13.9
23. SPORTS	50.2	48. Miscellaneous manufacturing	13.9
24. Motor vehicles and parts	49.9	49. Telephone and telegraph	12.7
25. Social and membership organizations	45.3	50. Transportation services	12.0

* In billions; Source: The Comte & Stogel study of 1986, 1987, 1989.

from studies like these that we begin to understand the true size of the sport business industry in relation to the size of other industries. For instance, the sport business industry was larger than the air transportation industry in 1987.

Table 1.7. From the Sports Inc Study—Sport Industry Segment Rankings			
Segment	**1987** (millions)	**1988** (millions)	**Percent Change**
Leisure and participant sports	$21,599.5	$22, 789.3	+ 5.5
Sporting goods	18,069.3	19,012.8	+ 5.2
Advertising	4,058.6	4,388.5	+ 8.1
Net take from legal gambling	3,504.8	3,618.3	+ 3.2
Spectator sports receipts	3,050.0	3,240.0	+ 6.2
Concessions, souvenirs, novelties	2,100.0	2,348.1	+ 11.8
TV and radio rights fees	1,209.2	1,415.8	+ 17.1
Corporate sponsorships	1,012.0	1,140.0	+ 12.6
Golf course, ski area construction	542.3	946.9	+ 74.6
Sports insurance	722.0	830.0	+ 15.0
Magazine circulation revenues	658.6	773.0	+ 17.4
Royalties from licensed properties	584.0	735.0	+ 25.9
Athlete endorsements	520.0	585.8	+ 12.7
Trading cards and accessories	350.0	408.3	+ 16.7
Sports book purchases	241.0	330.7	+ 37.2
Stadium and arena construction	250.0	319.3	+ 27.7
U.S. Olympic Committee, NGB budgets	98.2	114.2	+ 16.3
Youth team fees	95.3	97.0	+ 1.8
Halls of fame	5.4	6.0	+ 11.1
TOTAL	**$58,670.2**	**$63,099.0**	**+ 7.5**

Source: The Comte & Stogel study of 1986, 1987, 1989; 1990.

A key piece of data from this set of studies is the size and rankings of the different industry segments that were included in this study. Note that the largest two segments are participant sport and sporting goods. This might surprise you as well, since most people tend to think that professional sports is the largest segment of the industry. This is a common misperception; professional sports receives a massive amount of television and other media coverage, giving the impression that it is the largest part of the industry.

The Meek Study: 1997

Tables 1.8 and 1.9 present key information from the next study about the economic size of the sport business industry. Note that this study was done ten years after the Sports Inc. study and that the sport business industry is ranked much higher at number 11. So, in just a decade, the sport business industry had grown so much that its ranking had practically doubled. It is important to keep in mind that these studies were done using

Table 1.8. Top 25 Industry Rankings of 1997—From the Meek Study—The Sports Industry has moved up from 23rd to 11th Rank in Ten Years			
Industry	**Value**	**Industry**	**Value**
1. Real Estate	$850.0	14. Industrial machinery and equipment	123.3
2. Retail Trade	639.9	15. Insurance carriers	115.4
3. Wholesale Trade	491.0	16. Food and kindred products	113.3
4. Health Services	443.4	17. Trucking and warehousing	100.6
5. Construction	277.6	18. Legal services	100.5
6. Business Services	275.3	19. Printing and publishing	89.7
7. Depository Institutions	225.9	20. Motor vehicles and equipment	88.7
8. Utilities	205.3	21. Fabricated metal products	86.0
9. Other Services	195.0	22. Farms	85.0
10. Telecommunications	156.0	23. Security and commodity brokers	75.6
11. SPORTS	**152.0**	24. Oil and gas extraction	62.7
Source: The Meek Study; 1997.			

different methodology. Still, these studies give us vital information about our industry.

The Meek study also looked at different segments of the industry. Note that again, participant sport and sporting goods ranked as the largest two segments of the industry. This is important to note because as you will see in the next studies, a similar pattern will emerge.

Table 1.9. From the Meek Study— Sport Industry Segment Rankings	
Segment	**Value**
1. Sporting goods, footwear, apparel	$71.0 billion
2. Participant sports	$32.0 billion
3. Sports medicine	$18.5 billion
4. Construction	$11.8 billion
5. Sponsorship, endorsements, radio, TV, newspapers	$ 7.5 billion
6. Admissions (spectators)	$ 5.3 billion
7. Trading cards, video games, tapes, books, magazines	$ 3.5 billion
8. Concessions and souvenirs	$ 3.4 billion
9. Betting	$ 3.3 billion
Source: The Meek Study; 1995.	

The *SportsBusiness Journal* Study: 1999

In 1999, a fifth study was conducted. This one was done by the *SportsBusiness Journal* (*SBJ*). This study estimated the size of the industry to be $213 billion ("The Answer," 1999). This study was widely cited during that period of time and unfortunately became the label of the size of the industry. This label was wrong because the *SportsBusiness Journal* study did not include the whole of the sport business industry—it was highly exclusive and included only four men's professional sports leagues and some of the businesses associated with operating those spectator sports. Additionally, at that time it was determined that this study showed the value reported was "twice the size of the auto industry, and seven times the size of the movie industry" (Adams, 2004). While it would be fair to state that the four pieces of the industry could be determined to be larger than the auto industry and the movie industry at that time, it was not accurate to claim that the study was about the size of the whole industry.

Tables 1.10 and 1.11 show the information from the *SBJ* study. Table 1.10 illustrates the rankings of industries, with the sport business industry appearing as the 6th largest industry. Table 1.11 shows the segments of the industry that were included in the *SBJ* study. It is important to point out that although this study was limited to a very small part of the industry—four men's professional sports leagues—the economic size reported placed it in 6th place among the largest industries in the U.S.

When you compare this study to the previous studies, you can see that the *SBJ* study included the fewest segments of the industry. Their study was limited to organized sports that they defined as "spectator sports" and their related industries.

Table 1.10. The *SportsBusiness Journal* Study—Rank of Industry	
Industry	**Value**
1. Real Estate	$935 billion
2. Retail Trade	$713 billion
3. Health Care	$460 billion
4. Banking	$266 billion
5. Transportation	$256 billion
6. SPORTS BUSINESS	**$213 billion**
7. Communications	$212 billion
8. Public Utilities	$210 billion
9. Agriculture	$132 billion
10. Mining	$121 billion
11. Motor Vehicles and Equipment	$85 billion
12. Motion Pictures	$31 billion
Source: The SBJ study: *SportsBusiness Journal*, December 20–26, 1999.	

Table 1.11. The *SportsBusiness Journal* Study of 1999		
Four Men's Professional Sports—Spectator Sports Segment	**Estimated Value**	**% of Total**
1. **Travel** (transportation, accommodations, meals of spectators, colleges, the "big four" leagues, other)	$44.47 billion	20.92
2. **Advertising** (telecasts, cable, regional, print, signage, radio)	$28.25 billion	13.29
3. **Equipment, Apparel, Footwear** (sportswear in competition)	$24.94 billion	11.73
4. **Gate Receipts** (admission, concessions, merchandise, parking)	$22.56 billion	10.61
5. **Team Operating Expenses** ("big four" player salaries and operating expenses, colleges)	$19.23 billion	9.05
6. **Legal Gambling** (wagers, horses, dogs, jai alai, internet)	$18.55 billion	8.73
7. **Licensed Goods** (apparel, footwear, housewares, media, miscellaneous)	$15.10 billion	7.10
8. **Professional Services** (agents, sport marketing firms, facility management, financial, legal, and insurance services)	$14.03 billion	6.60
9. **Media Broadcast Rights** ("big four", college, other radio telecasts)	$10.57 billion	5.00
10. **Sponsorships** (events, teams, leagues, broadcasts)	$5.09 billion	2.40
11. **Medical Treatments** (baseball, football, basketball, soccer, softball, other)	$4.10 billion	1.93
12. **Facility Construction** (stadium, track, arena construction)	$2.49 billion	1.17
13. **Publications/videos** (magazines, videos, video games, books)	$2.12 billion	1.00
14. **Endorsements** (value of top 80 athletes and coaches)	$730 million	0.34
15. **Internet** (revenue from advertising and access fees)	$300 million	0.14

*The SBJ study included only these segments of four men's professional sports. *SportsBusiness Journal*, December 20–26, 1999.

The Outdoor Industry Association Study: 2010

The Outdoor Industry Association is one of many sports-related organizations that conduct research and track sports activities. This particular organization, however, tracks just eight outdoor activities. They are bicycle-based, camp-based, paddle-based, fishing, hunting, snow-based, trail-based, and wildlife viewing activities (Outdoor Industry Association, 2011). The Outdoor Industry study shows the size of the industry to be $730 billion (see Table 1.12). This study did not show an industry ranking. It would be interesting to learn where these segments place among the top largest industries in the U.S.

Table 1.12. The Outdoor Industry Association Study	

Total Economic Contribution: ....$730 billion

Categories Within:
  Jobs Generated: ....6.4 million
  Gear Retail Sales: ....$46 billion
  Trip-related Sales: ....$243 billion
  Taxes (federal, state): ....$87 billion

The 8 Sports Activities Included in the Study

Bicycle-based recreation—on paved roads or off-road
Camp-based recreation—Camping in an RV, tent, or lodge at a campsite
Paddle-based recreation—kayaking, rafting and canoeing
Fishing—all types
Hunting—all types
Snow-based recreation—all types of snow-skiing, snowboarding and snowshoeing
Trail-based recreation—running or hiking on an unpaved trail, backpacking, and
   climbing ice or natural rock
Wildlife viewing—wildlife watching and birding

Source: Outdoor Industry Association (2011). www.outdoorindustry.org

The Plunkett Study: 2011

Table 1.13 shows the most recent study on the sport business industry. This company included 11 segments of the industry, as shown in the table, and the total economic value of the 11 segments as $422 billion. Note that the largest segment in this study is the sporting goods segment at a total of $114.2 billion—consistent with the earlier studies.

Table 1.13. The Plunkett Study of 2011	
Segment	**EstimatedValue**
1. Annual Company Spending for Sports Advertising	$27.8 billion
2. MLB League Revenue	$7.2 billion
3. NFL League Revenue	$9.0 billion
4. NBA League Revenue	$4.1 billion
5. NHL League Revenue	$3.0 billion
6. Sporting Equipment Sales . . . Wholesale Revenues > . . . Retail Sporting Equipment Sales >	$74.2 billion $40 billion
7. NCAA Sports Revenue (Div. I, II, III)	$757 million
8. Spectator Sports (racetracks, sports teams, and other sports)	$31.4 billion
9. U.S. Health Club Revenue	$20.1 billion
10. European Health Club Revenue	$31.4 billion
11. NASCAR Revenue	$645.4 million

*The Plunkett Study of 2011 included the above segments of the industry. Source: Plunkett Sports, 2011.

WHAT IS THE CORRECT ECONOMIC VALUE SUM OF THE SPORT BUSINESS INDUSTRY?: USING INDUSTRY SEGMENT STUDIES TO DETERMINE INDUSTRY SIZE

Determining "one number" for the sport business industry is next to impossible. The industry is so massive and diverse that it would take a gargantuan effort to attempt to reach a magic "one number." As was just presented, each of the eight studies on the industry helps us to see the whole picture of the size of the industry. However, none of the studies includes *all* of the segments of the sport business industry. Therefore, perhaps a better way to gain a more comprehensive understanding of the size of the industry is to collect numerous completed studies and other data on the many different parts of the industry. This method will also just provide an estimate because data about every part of the industry simply doesn't exist, and there are other limitations, such as double-counting and overlap. However, it will give us a more complete picture of the industry and a better understanding of its economic value.

To begin, Table 1.14 presents data from just one industry—the boating industry. You can see that this type of information is valuable to those working in that industry. Tables 1.15 and 1.16 present lists of several different sport business segments, sports events, and facilities in the U.S. and their economic impacts or values. Table 1.15 presents data on 30 parts of the industry that could be found, and Table 1.16 shows 31 single sports events and 5 sports facilities. You can see that the sum of just a few of these segments of the sport industry exceeds any of the studies just presented in the previous section on the overall size of the industry. Table 1.15 shows 30 different segments in the industry and their economic values. These 30 pieces of the industry total $2.142 trillion dollars. That number is far beyond any of the totals given in the previous studies. Table 1.16 shows 31 sports events and 5 sports facilities and their economic impact or value. These 36 sport industry events and facilities values total $24.438 billion.

These tables present only a small fraction of what is in the sport business industry. What if we could possibly find data about every segment, activity, business, event, facility, organization or other type of entity that comprises the industry—what do you think the number would be? Right now, write down as many different sports events that you know about that took place last week, or that will take place during the coming week. Try to calculate the economic value of each event. Add that to the two tables and their figures. Second, try to determine how many sports organizations are in your city and calculate their value. All together, you will have quite a large number. As you

Table 1.14. Economic Value of Recreational Boating in America	
Total Contribution:	$51.8 billion
Boating Sales and Service	$30.8 billion
Boating Trip Expenditures	$21 billion
Source: Haas, 2010.	

Chapter One

can see, determining the economic impact or value of every part of the industry would be a very large and time-consuming task. However, this method will give us a more complete picture of the industry.

Using studies and reports about numerous different industry segments is perhaps a better way to study the economic impact or value of the sport business industry. Each sport management student will work in one or more of these industry segments and so must continuously monitor the research about that segment as well as the entire sport industry. This information can be found in a variety of resources such as the following:

(page 28)

Table 1.15. Some Sport Industry Segments and their Economic Values: Total Value of these 30 segments is $2.142 trillion

Industry Segment	Value	Industry Segment	Value
1. Eight Outdoor Sports Activities 2011	$730 billion	16. Golf Equipment, Apparel, and Footwear 2010	$6.8 billion
2. USA Sports Tourism, 2011	$600 billion	17. Golf Charitable Giving Impact Estimate 2010	$5.8 billion
3. Outdoor Recreation 2010	$394 billion	18. The Tennis Industry, USA, 2011	$5.6 billion
4. Angling (fishing and products)	$125 billion	19. NASCAR Licensed Products 2010	$3.63 billion
5. Sporting Goods Industry	$114.2 billion	20. Snow Sports 2010–2011 season	$3.3 billion
6. Recreational Boating 2010	$44 billion	21. Indianapolis, Indiana Sporting Goods Industry 2010	$3 billion
7. Gym, Health and Fitness Clubs 2010	$24.2 billion	22. The New York Yankees 2011	$1.6 billion
8. Golf Courses 2009	$19.5 billion	23. The Boston Red Sox 2011	$1.5 billion
9. Sports Gambling 2010	$18.9 billion	24. Bicycling Industry in Wisconsin 2010	$1.5 billion
10. Sports Sponsorship 2010	$18.2 billion	25. Golf Facilities 2010	$1.2 billion
11. Sports Licensed Products 2010	$15 billion	26. Nike Apparel Sponsorship Price to NFL 2010	$1.1 billion
12. Online Sports Advertising 2010	$12.1 billion	27. Sports Endorsements 2010	$897 million
13. The 30 NBA Team Franchises 2011	$10.9 billion	28. Sponsorship by Anheuser-Busch for the NFL 2010	$700 million
14. Spectator Sports Expenditures 2010	$10 billion	29. NCAA Sports Division I, II, and III 2010	$757 million
15. Corps of Engineer Lakes and Area 2010	$7.1 billion	30. NASCAR 2010	$645.4 million
Total Economic Value of these 30 entities = $2.142 trillion			

(1) outdoorindustry.com; (2) wikipedia.org/wiki/Sports_tourism; (3) USCGboating.org; (4) American Sportsfishing Association; (5) SGMA.com and Plunkettsports.com; (6) uscgboating.org; (7) Forbes.com; (8) scribd.com; (9) sports businesssims.com (projected); (10) sportsbusinesssims.com (projected); (11) teamfanshop.com; (12) mediacom.com; (13) SportsPro Magazine, March 2011; (14) includes pro, amateur and racetracks; teamfanshop.com; (15) USCG boating.org; (16) cybergolf.com; (17) cybergolf.com; (18) tennisindustry.org; (19) sportsbusinesssims.com; (20) SnowSports.org; (21) Forbes.com; (22) Forbes.com/Yankees; (23) Forbes.com/RedSox; (24) www.bikingbix.com; (25) cybergolf.com; (26) Sports Illustrated, March 14, 2011; (27) sportsbusinesssims.com; (28) Sports Illustrated, March 14, 2011; (29) Sports Illustrated, March 14, 2011; (30) Sports Illustrated, March 14, 2011.

Table 1.16. Economic Impacts or Values of 36 Single Sport Event and Facilities: Total $24.438 billion

Industry Segment	Value	Industry Segment	Value
1. Super Bowl XLV[1]	$10.1 billion	19. XIX World Masters Athletics Championship, 2011[14]	$24 million
2. Itinerant sports events market[2]	$6.65 billion	20. USA Volleyball Big South National Qualifier, 2010[15]	$19.4 million
3. Indianapolis 500, 2010[3]	$336 million	21. USA Volleyball Association 2011 Girls Championship[15]	$19.3 million
4. Daytona 500, 2010[3]	$230 million	22. NCAA SEC Men's Basketball Tournament, 2010[16]	$18.4 million
5. Alltech FEI World Equestrian Games, 2010[4]	$201.5 million	23. Navistar LPGA Classic, 2010[17]	$13 million
6. Kentucky Derby, 2010[3]	$167 million	24. USA Junior Olympic Boys' Volleyball Championship, 2010[18]	$11 million
7. U. S. Open Championship (PGA) 2010[5]	$150 million	25. Annual Suncoast Super Boat Grand Prix and Festival 2011[19]	$9.6 million
8. IAAF World Junior Championships, 2010[6]	$127.5 billion	26. Snohomish Bigfoot Soccer Tournament, Washington, 2010[19]	$4.2 million
9. Tour de France (21 days), 2010[3]	$63 million	27. Amateur Softball Association National Finals Under 12 2011[20]	$3 million
10. Alamo Bowl, 2010[7]	$56.7 million	28. Ironman 70.3 Lake Stevens Washington, 2010[19]	$1.4 million
11. British Open (a PGA event) 2010[5]	$56 million	29. U.S. Rowing Masters Regional Championships, 2010[21]	$694,000
12. Houston Marathon, Houston, Texas, 2010[8]	$51.1 million	30. FLW EverStart Bass Fishing Tournament, 2010[22]	$535,000
13. NCAA Men's Final Four tournament, 2010[3]	$50 million	31. Washington Junior Golf Assoc. State Championship 2010[21]	$475,000
14. Central Intercollegiate Athletic Association Women's and Men's Basketball Tournament 2011[9]	$44 million	32. FACILITY: New Jersey Nets Proposed Arena[22]	$4.9 billion
15. U.S. Bowling Women's Championship, 2011[10]	$40 million	33. FACILITY: Red Bull Arena in Harrison, New Jersey, 2010[23]	$200 million
16. Chick-Fil-A Bowl event annual average[11]	$35 billion	34. FACILITY: PPL Park arena in Philadelphia, 2010[23]	$120 million
17. AT&T U.S. Figure Skating Championships, 2011[12]	$27.4 million	35. FACILITY: Allen Texas High School Football Stadium[24]	59.6 million
18. Big Sur Marathon, 2011, Carmel, California[13]	$27 million	36. FACILITY: Girls Softball Complex, Chattanooga, Tennessee[25]	$11.8 million

Total Economic Value of these 36 entities: $23.738 billion

Sources: (1) SportsPro, April, 2011; (2) www.sportseventsmagazine.com (itinerant sports events are those that move around to different destinations; includes youth, college, professional, and senior sports; limited study data); (3) www.fastasticnetwork.com; (4) www.kentucky.com/2011; (5) www.businessweek.com/aug2010; (6) www.canadian sporttourism.com (IAAF = International Association of Athletics Federation; this is a track and field event); (7) www.valeroalamobowl.com; (8) time-to-run.us; (9) www.hbcudigest.com; (10) www.faqs.org/periodicals (estimate); (11) cms.metroatlantachamber.com; (12) www.myfox8.com/news; (13) www.runnersweb.com; (14) www.27x7 .com/2011; (15) www.gwinnettcenter.com; (16) www.nashvillesports.com; (17) navistarlpgaclassic.com; (18) www.usa volleyball.org; (19) www.bizjournals.com/tampabay/news2011 (estimate); (20) 222.waka.com/news (estimate); (21) www.sportscommissions.org/documents/2011; (22) www.paysonroundup.com/news/2011; (22) en.wikipedia.org; (23) www.goal.com; (24) highschool.rivals.com; (25) www.n-n-a.com/recreational/about429280.html

- *Industry publications*—These include trade or business magazines, journals, newsletters, and websites.
- *Sport business conventions and exhibitions*—These include such annual conventions and trade shows as the Snow Sports Industries of America and the National Sporting Goods Association's Super Show.
- *Sport management or marketing research businesses*—There are numerous companies that specialize in conducting research. Some of these include Joyce Julius & Associates and Simmons Market Research Bureau.
- *Local or national news publications*—Much can be learned about sport industries from published articles in newspapers and magazines. Local papers carry information about local sports

> **You can keep up with the latest in your industry by**
>
> - Reading trade or business magazines, journals, newsletters, and websites
> - Attending sport business conventions or exhibitions
> - Obtaining research from sport marketing firms
> - Reading local or national news publications and websites

businesses, and national papers provide articles with a more national focus about individual sport-related businesses and whole industries.

This method of collecting research offers a new way to estimate the economic size of the industry. It is obvious with the few studies presented here that the sport business industry is among the largest industries in the U.S. Moreover, with numbers this large, perhaps the sport business industry is the number one largest industry. There is no tried-and-true method for studying its depth and breadth and determining its economic value, so the method suggested here is at least one way to provide a viable estimate.

WHY THE SPORT BUSINESS INDUSTRY IS SO LARGE AND DIVERSE: FACTORS INFLUENCING ITS GROWTH AND DEVELOPMENT

The sport business industry is a massive industry comprised of many segments and many different types of sports, products, and sport businesses. But why? Why is this industry so large and diverse? There are many factors that influence the growth and development of the sport business industry—those that have impacted it in the past, those that affect it currently, and those that will have an influence in the future. Table 1.17 presents eight broad categories of factors along with some of their many different individual factors. This section presents these factors and describes each one.

One's career in the sport business industry will be greatly enhanced by an understanding of why the industry is so large and diverse and what drives its growth. The sport business professional must constantly analyze what is affecting the industry because such influences may affect the success or failure of a product or business. If the sport businessperson studies and understands these factors and how they affect the product or business, then that individual can develop decisions and strategies that will greatly enhance success.

Table 1.17. The Eight Factors that Influence Growth in the Sport Business Industry*	
Factor Categories	**Individual Factors**
I. People	1. Human interest in sports and recreation is constant 2. Increase in sports and sport business among diverse market segments
II. Sports Activities and Events	1. Constant increase in the number of new and different sports, recreational and fitness activities and events 2. Constant growth in the offering of traditional sports 3. Constant increase in the number and type of professional level sport, fitness, and recreational activities 4. Increase in sports tourism and adventure travel products
III. Sporting Goods: Equipment, Apparel, and Footwear	1. Increase in distribution and availability of sports equipment, apparel, and footwear 2. Increase in sports equipment, apparel, and footwear designed for the diversity of markets and their demands 3. Influence of technology on sports equipment, apparel, and footwear
IV. Sports Facilities, Sports Medicine, and Fitness Training	1. Increase in number and type of sports facilities 2. Movements of facilities from single-purpose to multi-purpose and full-service facilities 3. Growth in the amount and type of sports medicine and fitness training services
V. Commercialization and Marketing of Sports and Sport Business	1. Development of packaging sport as an entertainment product 2. Increased marketing and marketing orientation of the sport industry 3. Increased understanding and knowledge of conusumers in the sport business industry from marketing efforts 4. Growth in sports sponsorship, endorsements, and licensing and merchandising
VI. Professional Service Businesses	1. Growth of sport business-specialized professional service businesses in areas such as facility, event, legal, financial, marketing, tourism, research, management, governance, human resources
VII. Media and Electronic Technology	1. Increase in television, radio and print media exposure and distribution of sports and sport business 2. Increase in electronic media—the Internet—exposure and distribution of sports and sport business 3. Exposure and distribution of sport and sport business by mobile device media: data phones, wifi-enabled mobile devices 4. Growth of social media types and marketing use for exposure and distribution of sports and sport business 5. Growth of electronic games such as video and fantasy sports games
VIII. Sport Management Education	1. Increase in sports and sport business management education 2. Increase in competency of sport management professionals 3. Growth of sport management as an academic discipline and career

*Source: Developed by Dr. Brenda Pitts; original source: Pitts & Stotlar (2007).

In addition, studying these factors can help identify the number and types of jobs and careers in the industry. When reading about the factors presented and explained in this section, think about the number and types of jobs needed in that area. You just might discover your future career.

Factor Category I: People

Humans are the reason sports and the sport business industry exists. If it were not for our interest in and demand for sports, recreation, fitness, adventure travel, and sports tourism, the industry would not exist. We humans have played sports nearly as long as we have been on this earth. There is plenty of evidence from the earliest of human record-keeping in the most ancient of types, such as paintings on pottery, carvings, and drawings in caves, that depict humans engaging in sports and recreational activities such as stone and stick games, hunting and fishing, archery, running, and wrestling.

Sports are a major area of human interest and activity. Sports command so much attention from humans that they account for a large portion of media content of all kinds. It is perhaps the only industry that enjoys newspaper, television, radio, and Internet coverage in most outlets around the world on a daily basis. People are fascinated with sports and recreational activities of all kinds, and participate in and/or watch sports several times a week. As you learned earlier in the chapter, "participant sports" is the largest segment of the industry. Here are some factors relating to people and the sport business industry.

Constant Human Interest in Sports and Recreation

A look at the studies presented earlier in this chapter on the size of the sport business industry shows that *participant sports* constitute the largest segment of the industry. People participating in sports, recreation, and fitness activities are the primary reason the sport industry exists. It is people who drive the growth of the sport industry because they are the consumers of sports, recreation, fitness, tourism, and leisure products.

In the U.S., millions of individuals participate in such activities. They play, run, climb, scoot, ride, and perform numerous other skills for a variety of reasons, including to have fun, to compete, to improve, to lose weight, to socialize, to have a good workout, and to learn a new sport.

As an example of research that shows the popularity of playing and engaging in sports, Table 1.18 presents some of the analyses from the Physical Activity Council's 2011 study. The council measured participation in 119 different sports and grouped them into these categories: Individual Sports, Racquet Sports, Outdoor Sports, Winter Sports, Water Sports, and Fitness Sports (Physical Activity Council Topline Report,

---

Studying the factors that influence the sport industry can reveal what types of jobs are available and help you decide on a future career.

Table 1.18. Physical Activity Council Study Findings
• There is increased participation in a number of sports and recreational activities
• There is an expressed desire to increase the amount of travel specifically to participate in sports and activities
• Sports labeled as "Aspirational Activities"—those activities that survey responders say they aspire to participate in—show demand to participate in the future
• There is a desire to participate in favorite sports and recreational activities even though the recession may cause some spending changes
• Niche sports continue to see new participants and growth in participation is expected
• There is growth in participation rates in sports of the Generation Y group
Source: Physical Activity Council, 2011.

2011). Due to the recession that began in 2008, participation rates showed signs of being negatively affected, with participation rates lower in 2008 and 2009. However, the research also showed signs of rebounding with an increase in participation rates beginning to appear in 2010. The research reveals many points of information about participation in sports, some of which include the points listed here in Table 1.18. The Physical Activity Council stated that its members feel optimistic about the future of continued and increasing participation in sports and recreational activities.

Table 1.19 presents information on one sports activity that is a major industry—boating. These are numbers about recreational boating; keep in mind that there are also segments of boat racing as amateur, Olympic, and professional sports; such as sailing, kayaking, motor-boat racing, rowing, and jet skiing. Further, boats are used for a number of activities including fishing, shrimping, scuba diving and snorkeling, search and rescue, research, and racing.

Table 1.20 presents information about participation numbers for some outdoor sports activities. This information is from the Outdoor Industry Association and presents a study involving eight categories of outdoor sports. As you can see, the participation numbers are significant.

A large portion of the dollars spent on sports is the millions spent for items needed or desired in order to participate, such as equipment and apparel. For example, to play softball, the player needs a softball glove and a bat. This player might also want to use other products that are produced for a variety of reasons. These might be bat-

Table 1.19. Participation in Recreational Boating in America
Boating Businesses — 18,940
Boaters — 82 million
Registered Boats — 12.7 million
Fishing while Boating — 25.8 million
Jobs Generated — 154,300
Projections of Boating Participants for 2020
Motor Boaters — 60.4 million
Canoers — 23.3 million
Jet Ski Users — 21.1 million
Rafters — 20.9 million
Water-Skiers — 19.1 million
Kayakers — 13.5 million
Sailors — 11.4 million
Rowers — 9.7 million
Source: Haas, 2010

Table 1.20. The Active Outdoor Recreation Economy of 8 Sports Activities	
The 8 Sports Activities and Participation Rates	
Bicycle-based recreation (on paved roads or off-road)	60 million
Camp-based recreation (Camping in an RV, tent, or lodge at a campsite)	45 million
Paddle-based recreation (kayaking, rafting and canoeing)	33 million
Fishing (all types)	13 million
Hunting (all types)	24 million
Snow-based recreation (cross-country/nordic, downhill, telemark skiing, snowboarding and snowshoeing)	16 million
Trail-based recreation (trail running or day hiking on an unpaved trail, backpacking, and climbing ice or natural rock)	56 million
Wildlife viewing (wildlife watching and birding)	66 million
The Participation Numbers from the research	
• Nearly half of Americans ages 6 and older, or 137.9 million individuals, participated in at least one outdoor activity in 2010, making 10.1 billion outdoor outings. • The research shows significant increases in adventure sports such as kayaking, back-country camping and climbing as well as slight increases in youth participation among those individuals ages 13–24.	
Source: Outdoor Industry Association (2011). www.outdoorindustry.org	

ting gloves, cap, helmet, specialized softball shoes, specialized socks, sunglasses, customized uniform shirts, undershirts, pants or shorts, and a customized softball bag in which to carry it all. Finally, many players will want merchandise that speaks to their identity as a softball player, such as funny softball T-shirts, a softball-glove key ring, and a tiny softball glove and bat to hang on their car's rearview mirror.

Moreover, this continuous interest in sports and recreation activities influences many other segments of the sport industry. Consider this: For every coed basketball league, there must be many people and products in order for that league to exist—a basketball facility, basketball officials, scorekeepers, score sheets, facility managers, facility maintenance people, facility groundskeepers, a league director, a league on-site supervisor, staff for such jobs as paperwork, record keeping, registration and other forms, a certain number of teams registered, coaches, team managers, uniforms, shoes, socks, water bottles, towels, a coach's note pad, officials' evaluation forms, rulebooks, pens and pencils, and basketballs.

There are many different companies needed to supply all of these people and to create and produce all the necessary products. Further, if the basketball league is the WNBA or the NBA, many more businesses are needed to provide additional items and services needed or desired to produce just one game. Some of these are special officials, statisticians and other specialists, reporters, radio, television, facility security, concessions and concession stand staff, office staff, hospitality staff, promotions and promotions staff, parking facilities and parking lot staff, and trophies and awards.

It is easy to see that because so many people participate in sports, fitness, and recreation activities, the sport industry is especially affected. People who participate are the primary reason the industry exists and is so large and diverse. Additionally, they are the reason that the industry has so many other segments.

Increase in Sports and Sport Business Among the Diverse Market Segments

The sport business industry is a vast multi-business and multicultural industry. It always has been and always will be. There has been significant growth, development, and commercialization of the multitudes of sports activities, events, businesses, and organizations that are created and managed for and by the many different populations of people who live in the U.S. Table 1.21 illustrates some of the different diverse market segments. As diverse market segments—such as people who are African-American, Asian-American, Jewish, Hispanic, lesbian and gay, young and old, female and male, and disabled—grow and emerge as viable markets, two things are happening. First, existing sports companies are targeting them and courting them as potential consumers either for existing products or potential products. Second, many of these groups are creating their own sports companies and industries. Here are some examples:

Race. The National Brotherhood of Skiers (NBS) is an organization for African-American snow skiers; it has 60 clubs in 43 cities, and 3,000 members. The NBS hosts over 800 events each year. One annual event can reach an estimated economic impact of $10 million. The primary mission of the NBS is to identify and financially support athletes of color to train and compete in Olympic and other international competitions. See www.nbs.org for more information.

Gender. Growth and development of girls and women's sports, and the increase in participation numbers of girls and women, has been phenomenal over several decades. In one example, the FIFA Women's World Cup was created by FIFA to meet the demands of women's soccer worldwide. Since the first championship in 1991, the tournament has been held every four years and is growing in both the number of teams entering and the number of spectators world-wide. The media and fan attention has grown at an extraordinary rate, with record-breaking numbers of spectators at the games and watching on television or following on other media at nearly every event. The final championship match in 2011 brought about another record: the highest rate of tweets (on Twitter) at 7,196 tweets per second.

Sexual Orientation. There is a gay and lesbian sports organization, business, league, or team in almost every city in the U.S. These organizations offer tens of thousands of sports and recreation events each year for the lesbian and gay sports market. The events range from archery to equestrian events to rodeo to snow sports to volleyball.

Table 1.21. Examples of Diverse Market Sports Events and Organizations

Market	Sports Activities, Events, Organizations
1. Geographic Region	African Games
	Australian Games
	National Games of France
	National Games of India
	Pan American Games
	Russian Games
2. USA States	Alabama State Sports Festival
	Empire State Games (New York)
	Georgia State Games
	Northwest Adventure Sports Festival (Washington)
	Rocky Mountain State Games (Colorado)
	Southeastern Sports Festival
3. Disability	Disabled Swimming
	Paralympic Games
	Special Olympics
	O & P Extremity Games
	World Games for the Deaf—Deaflympics
	Georgia Blind Sports Association
4. Religious Affiliation	Maccabi Games (Jewish Olympics)
	Athletes in Action (Christian)
	Women's Islamic Games (Muslim Sports)
5. Career or Profession	Australian Corporate Games
	U.S. Corporate Games
	West African Corporate Games
	World Police and Firefighter Games
	World Student Games
6. Sexual Orientation	European Gay and Lesbian Sports
	Federation of Gay Games
	Gay and Lesbian Rowing Federation
	International Gay and Lesbian Aquatics
	International Gay and Lesbian Ice Hockey Association
	World OutGames

Continued on next page

Table 1.21 (cont.). Examples of Diverse Market Sports Events and Organizations	
Market	**Sports Activities, Events, Organizations**
7. Race or National Origin	Cherokee National Youth Fitness Camp
	Colorado Indigenous Games
	First Nation Golf Association
	National Association of Black Scuba Divers
	National Brotherhood of Skiers (Afrian American)
	North American Indigenous Games
	Northwest Hispanic Soccer League
	Seattle Asian Sports Club
8. Age	International Senior Softball Association
	National Senior Games
	National Youth Soccer Champinoships
	National Youth Bowling Championships
	Pan Pacific Masters Games
	U.S. Masters Swimming
	World Masters Weightlifting
9. Nation or Country	Olympic Games
	Commonwealth Games
	FIFA World Cup

The top event, the Gay Games, held every four years, is a major sports event and festival. Table 1.22 presents facts about the Gay Games since the first one, held in 1982. See www.GayGames.com for more information.

Age. Master's swimming organizations offer swimming opportunities, events, and competitions for a variety of age groups from 20 to 90 years of age. People of different ages compete in groups of their ages only. See www.usms.org for more information.

The ESPN X Games were invented specifically for an age group—18 to 34—labeled Generation X, or GenX. There are now Summer and Winter X Games with sports such as skateboarding, downhill and aggressive in-line skating, bicycle stunt racing, street luge, snowboarding, snow mountain biking, and skysurfing. Started in 1995, the 1998 X Games boasted over 400 athletes, $450,000 in prize money, 225,000 spectators, and a proclaimed economic impact of $20 million. Having grown in popularity since then, today the X Games boasts EXPN.com, EXPN radio, official X Games sporting goods and X Games merchandise, EXPN Podcasts and more. See expn.go.com for more information.

Table 1.22. Facts About The Gay Games Since 1982				
Gay Games Event	**Athletes**	**Countries**	**Sports**	**Economic Impact**
Gay Games I—1982 San Francisco, California, USA	1,300	12	16	unknown
Gay Games II—1986 San Francisco, California, USA	3,482	22	17	unknown
Gay Games III—1990 Vancouver, BC, Canada	7,300	28	31	$30 million
Gay Games IV—1994 New York City, New York, USA	10,864	40	31	$112 million
Gay Games V—1998 Amsterdam, Netherlands	14,864	78	31	$300 million
Gay Games VI—2002 Sydney, Australia	15,000	70	31	$116 million
Gay Games VII—2006 Chicago, Illinois, USA	12,000	50	30	$60 million
Gay Games VIII—2010 Cologne, Germany	10,000	70	35	$80 million
Gay Games IX—2014 Cleveland, Ohio USA	estimate[1] 10,000	estimate[1] 70	35	estimate[1] $60 million
Gay Games X—2018[2] To Be Decided	TBA	TBA	35	TBA

Notes: 1. As of the writing of this book, the 2014 event had not taken place. The numbers here reflect the estimated numbers from sources; 2. As of the completed writing of this text, the site for the 2018 Gay Games had not been decided.

Disability. There is a growing number of sports organizations that focus specifically on the many different categories of disabilities. The Paralympic Games are the Olympic Games for people with physical disabilities. Disabled Sports USA, established in 1967, offers nationwide sports programs, activities, and events to anyone with a permanent disability. Table 1.23 shows a few of the many events offered by Disabled Sports USA. Go to www.dsusa.org to find out more about this organization. Additionally, disability sports organizations are found at the local and state level. An example of a new one is the Georgia Blind Sports Association.

One of the reasons so many groups of people create their own sports businesses and organizations is to socialize and participate in sports with individuals who have similar backgrounds and interests. A second reason is that as populations fight for and gain civil rights, new legislation brings about increased opportunities in sport, fitness, and recreational activity. For some populations, the increase in sports opportunities has almost paralleled the fight for civil rights. The involvement of the African-American population in sport, fitness, and recreation activity increased as their struggle for civil and equal rights progressed. Women and girls gained more opportunities in organized high

Table 1.23. Some Events Offered by Disabled Sports USA	
BlazeSports Ability Games	BlazeSports Quad Rugby
First Swing Golf Clinic	STRIDE Swimming
Desert Challenge Games	Adaptive Adventures Adaptive Cycling
Women's Wheelchair Basketball	DS/USA Far West Water-Skiing
STRIDED Wounded Warriors Weekend	Ability First Camp
Northern California/Nevada Ride Series	WAVE Camp
Adaptive Adventures Rafting Experience	The NorCal-Nevada Handcycling Series

school and collegiate athletics because of legislation aimed at stopping discrimination based on gender in educational institutions. The number of women and girls participating in sports and athletics has increased significantly since the early 1970s.

A third reason for the creation of these businesses and organizations is that people like to enjoy sports activities with their friends. Typically, a person wants to spend time with and participate in activities with people they like, who have similar characteristics, who enjoy the same things, who share the same culture, and with whom they are most comfortable. It is no surprise that most groups of people with common interests organize their own sports activities and businesses. For example, the number of sport businesses, organizations, and events for the lesbian and gay population has grown at a very fast rate (Pitts, 1997, 1999a, 1999b). In the Gay Games' early years, the number of participants increased 1200% from the first Gay Games in 1982 to the fifth Gay Games in 1998. That success and popularity continues today. Over 10,000 athletes from over 70 countries compete at every event (refer to Table 1.22).

Laws and other legislation have been passed to stop discrimination against the handicapped population. The passage of the Americans with Disabilities Act of 1990 has helped facilitate increased opportunities in sports and fitness activity for the handicapped and has had a significant impact on forcing the accessibility of sports facilities for the disabled. The Paralympics receives major sponsorship today. In addition, there are now numerous sports organizations and equipment designers for people with disabilities.

Factor II: Sports Activities and Events: Sports, Recreation, Fitness, Leisure, Sports Tourism

The creation, management, marketing, and production of sports, recreation, fitness, leisure, and sports-tourism activities and events offer a world of opportunities to people. Many sports activities are created specifically for a particular group. For example, the popularity of these sports has led to the creation of state games such as the Bluegrass Games (Kentucky), the Sunshine State Games (Florida), and the Big Apple Games (New York). These events are multisport festivals designed for recreational athletes who live in a particular region.

Earlier in the chapter, Table 1.1 showed some of the many different sports and recreational activities today and the changes in participation rates over a period of time as compiled by the National Sporting Goods Association (NSGA). Indeed, the SGMA believes that participation figures are the most important information in defining the size of a market. According to the SGMA, "sports participation defines the size, composition, and ultimately the trend of the product market and is, in effect, the 'gold standard' to which all markets eventually return" (Sporting Goods Manufacturer's Association, 2010, p. 4).

Increase in New and Different Sports, Recreational, and Fitness Activities and Events

Since the mid-1970s, the United States has experienced a consistent and fast growth in the number and type of new sport, fitness, or recreation-related activities and events offered to a variety of sport market consumers. Consider the following examples. In the late 1970s, a seemingly new way to get fit was offered. This was called aerobics—exercising to music. Today, there are hundreds of different kinds of aerobics offered to a wide variety of consumers. Some of these programs are soft aerobics, hard aerobics, jazzerobics, elderobics, and baby-robics.

During the past two decades, in-line skating made its way across the continent. Boogie-boarding and snow-boarding were invented. Here are a few more recently invented sports: snow kayaking, wingsuit flying, ice surfing, mountain boarding, dirt surfing, beach volleyball, extreme golf, Parkour (free running), snow kiting, skydive dancing, street luge, ice climbing, and the X Games. With this fast and diverse innovation in sport and fitness activities comes increased participation by a wider spectrum of consumers. Whereas the traditional sport of outdoor 11-on-11 soccer played for two 45-minute halves might not interest someone, that person might be interested in trying a modified game of indoor soccer, 5-on-5, and consisting of four 12-minute quarters. These innovations have increased the number and types of sport-activity products offered to the consumer and have reached an increased number and type of consumer market segments. This kind of new product development is one key to success in competitive strategy.

Consistent Growth in the Offering of Traditional Sports

Even though there is a multitude of new sports activities, traditional sports have not been set aside. Instead, there has been growth in the offerings of traditional sports and activities. In other words, if you wanted to play volleyball a few decades ago, you most likely would have had to join a YWCA, YMCA, or a local city parks and recreation league. Today, volleyball is offered by many different businesses and organizations such as multisport centers, clubs, independent organizations, individual tournament organizers, and even by local pubs or bars. Along the same line, soccer was a sport almost unknown in the U.S. just a few decades ago. Today, soccer may be found at many parks and recreation facilities, privately owned facilities, state facilities, and on the campuses of schools and colleges. It is offered to consumers of all ages. There are leagues for children who are 4 years old as well as the fast-growing leagues for the 30-something, 40-something, and 50-something year-old player.

In addition, fueling this growth are the increasing numbers of sports and recreation organizations among the many diverse populations. For example, the number and variety of sports and recreational activities and events for people with disabilities have exploded. Limited only by imagination, people with a vision or hearing impairment, for example, can participate in a multitude of sports, recreation, and fitness activities.

Constant Increase in the Number and Type of Professional-Level Sport, Fitness, and Recreational Activities

When a new sport activity is invented, sometimes that sport will become a professional sport activity. A professional sport is one in which the participant is paid to perform or in which the participant is making a career. Consider the number and range of sport and fitness activities that are professional today: racing cars, trucks, boats, horses, dogs, and other items; Frisbee throwing; aquatic sports such as water skiing, knee boarding, trick skiing, jet skiing, surfing, boogie-boarding, windsurfing, sailing, yachting, fishing, and other water activities; snow sports such as downhill and cross-country racing, trick skiing, ice sailing, the Iditarod, ice fishing, and others; bowling; billiards; hang gliding; aerobics competition; and body building. These have increased the number of professional sports participants as well as the number of opportunities available for the sport management and sport marketing professional in producing, facilitating, promoting, or organizing the events. In addition, such a growth in activity increases the need for sports equipment and apparel designed for the sport and participant.

Growth in Sports Tourism and Adventure Travel

Although combining travel and sports is not new, what is new is the specific development of sports-related tour and travel companies. Every time a person travels to another city to participate in a marathon or to go hiking in the Himalayas, this is sports tourism. Every time a group of baseball fans travels to another city to watch the World Series, this is sports tourism. When people travel to Fort Lauderdale to see the Swimming Hall of Fame or travel to tour a sports facility to pay homage to it, this too is sports tourism. Hence, sports tourism and adventure travel can be defined as an activity in which people travel to a particular location as a sport event participant or spectator, or to attend sport attractions or business meetings.

Additionally, both large and small sports events can be big business for countries, cities, and/or communities. Cities and countries that host sports events, such as the Olympic Games, the Rugby World Cup, or the FIFA World Cup, receive benefits that significantly outweigh the time and money invested across the life cycle of the event from pre-bid through post-event legacy. Hence, most cities and states have sports commissions or organizations whose specific duty is to attract sports events to be staged in their city. Destination marketing has been growing significantly as these sports commissions use the city's (destination's) attractiveness as one of the primary purposes for staging an event in that particular city.

There is now a national organization for sports commissions—the National Association of Sports Commissions (NASC). Other organizations that are related to sports

events and travel include the Association of Chief Executives of Sport, Sports Destination Management, and Sports Events Magazine (an online source).

Some sports businesses such as snow ski resorts rely heavily on people's willingness to
travel to their place of business in order to participate in a sports activity. Others, such
as golf, promote their resort as a golf-vacation destination even though local consumers
support the resort. Some companies are in the business of developing sports travel packages by developing a trip specifically for the purpose of participating in an activity. For
example, numerous companies now specialize in organizing trips for hiking, camping,
climbing, running, kayaking, scuba diving, and many other activities.

There are now many companies that specialize in putting together travel packages for
the purpose of attending sports events. A few of the many sports events designed for
spectatorial and entertainment purposes include the Super Bowl (a national football
championship game), the Women's or Men's World Cup (the international soccer championship held every four years and requiring more than a month of time for several
matches), or local college women's or men's basketball play-off games. In addition, people also engage in sports-related travel not to participate in a sports activity or to watch
a sports event, but to see sports-related places such as sports museums, halls of fame,
arenas, stadiums, facilities, memorabilia, or monuments.

Factor Category III: Sporting Goods—
Equipment, Apparel, and Footwear

It should be no surprise that sporting goods are a significant reason the sport business
industry is large and diverse. As you just learned about Factor Category I: People, and
in the earlier sections of this chapter, participation in sports is a massive industry. Participating and engaging in sports, fitness, leisure, and recreational activities requires
sports equipment, apparel, and footwear. Therefore, people's participation in sports creates the demand for and thus the development and growth in the sporting goods industry. The opposite is true as well. There are many sporting goods entrepreneurs who invent and create sports equipment, apparel, and footwear that actually encourages people
to engage in sports. That is, when you browse through a sporting goods store, you may
see equipment for sports that are new to you. This can sometimes catch your interest
and you will purchase that equipment and learn how to play that sport. Additionally,
sporting goods companies use popular professional athletes to endorse their products,
creating demand for those products. As an example, the Michael Jordan Air Jordan shoe
has been one of the all-time best selling shoes in sports.

Following are some of the many factors about sporting goods that have affected the
growth and development of the sport business industry.

What is new about sports tourism is the increasing number of businesses, types of
products offered, and focus on sports tourism as a developing identifiable industry.

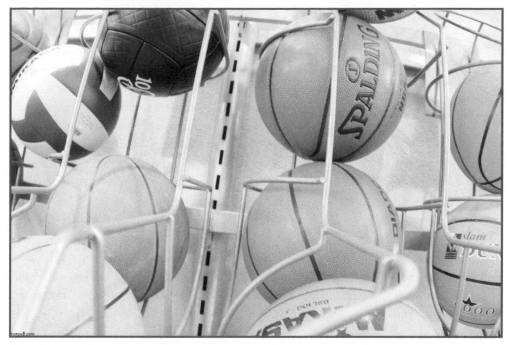

Sporting goods stores provide a wide range of sports equipment. Courtesy of Photos8.com

Increase in Distribution and Availability
of Sports Equipment, Apparel, and Footwear

Long ago, nearly all products and goods could be found in the local "general store." Today, department stores are the "general stores." However, slowly, speciality stores were developed and today sporting goods stores can be found in nearly every city and town around the world. With this development, the ability to distribute sports equipment, apparel, and footwear to nearly every corner of the world has been achieved. Additionally, today the Internet is now the 'general store' and provides access to sporting goods to anyone with a computer and Internet access. The growth in sporting goods as well as distribution possibilities has influenced the growth and development of the sport business industry.

Increase in Sporting Goods and Apparel Designed
for the Diversity of Markets and Their Demands

It wasn't so long ago that all sporting goods, equipment, and services were designed and made only for the male participant. Today, sporting goods manufacturers are designing goods and equipment for a variety of market segments. Further, the number of companies, retail or manufacturer, owned and managed by people who are not white males is increasing. These companies are set up to specifically design sports equipment, apparel, and services for other markets. A woman, for example, may look for running shoes made for a woman's foot instead of having to purchase a shoe made for a male. A child who wants to play soccer can buy soccer shoes made specifically for children. A person

> The sporting goods industry is increasingly focused on developing products for non-traditional markets such as women, disabled athletes, and children.

with only one leg can purchase specially designed snow-ski equipment. A Jewish person can participate in an Olympic-style event created just for Jewish people. At the same time, technology and design have influenced sports equipment and apparel. Tennis rackets are available in a variety of sizes: The grip is offered in several sizes, shapes, and materials; the racket head is offered in several sizes and materials; the string is offered in a variety of types; and the weight of the racket varies. Uniforms also come in a variety of styles, sizes, and materials. Most sports have clothing or equipment custom designed for enhancing performance. Consider the one-piece rubberized suits worn in the sport of luge. The style and material are aerodynamically designed for speed.

Today, sporting goods and sport activity are much more available, more affordable, and more accessible to more consumer segments. Historically, tennis was enjoyed exclusively by the wealthy. Today, tennis is affordable to and enjoyed by people of many income levels. Services surrounding sport and fitness activities have also expanded. Services offered in some fitness clubs include laundry service, racket stringing, golf-club cleaning, childcare, concessions, restaurants, lounges, tanning beds, valet parking, and massage.

The variety of goods and services is expanding to accommodate the many diverse populations participating in sport. The demographics and psychographics of the people in the U.S. change almost constantly. At one time a marketer could safely assume that the greatest majority of people living in the U.S.

> The sporting goods industry is one of the largest segments of the sport business industry because people must have equipment and apparel in order to participate in most sports activities.

were white, Christian, and heterosexual, and that a household consisted of a traditional family consisting of a woman, man, and children. The general make-up of the current "household" is very different today. Knowledge of and sensitivity to current household structure is important in decisions concerning all marketing strategies.

Sports equipment designed for the disabled is being developed more frequently today. There are softballs that emit a beeping sound. These are used in softball games for people with vision impairments. There are wheelchairs designed for speed. Materials are very lightweight, and the chairs are aerodynamically designed and constructed. This type of wheelchair is used in basketball, running, and tennis participation, for example.

Influence of Technology on Sport-Related Goods, Services and Training

Imagine playing tennis with a racket made of wood! Well, if you played tennis before the late 1960s, you played with a laminated wood racket. The invention of a variety of metals and other composite materials has led to some amazing advances in technology for sports equipment, apparel, and footwear in nearly every sport.

The sport industry has benefited greatly from advances in technology. Technology has influenced sports equipment, facilities, clothing, and shoes and has affected athlete performance through sophisticated training programs. Some specific examples include computer-assisted programs in nutrition, training, skill analysis, and equipment design; and materials used in equipment, uniforms, shoes, and other gear.

A few other examples include the following. Instant replay is now commonplace for some sports. It is used by officials to be very specific with calls, and is also used for spectators and can be either exciting or excruciating for the fans. Sports surfaces have been enhanced by technology often called "Turf Technology." The surfaces on which we play have never been so technologically innovative. Today, even dirt can be artificially produced!

Technology is not only used for improving performance, but also for keeping the athlete safe. In NASCAR, the technology for a neck and head brace saves lives. And in the sport of football, helmets are specially constructed to decrease head injuries.

Factor Category IV: Sports Facilities, Sports Medicine, and Fitness Training

Is it the facilities or an athlete's natural skill that enhances performance? If an athlete believes that a facility makes him or her perform better, is it true? Perhaps we will never know the answer to such questions. We do, however, know that what people believe can be a powerful influence on their mental or physical state. Sports facilities today are state-of-the-art and place the athlete in an ultimate surrounding for enhanced performance. In addition, many modern sports facilities are designed with the spectator in mind. At no other time in history have so many multimillion-dollar facilities been built than in the 1990s. The diversity of the people who will watch the spectacle, as well as their needs, are being taken into consideration. Facilities influence and are a major segment of the sport industry.

Increase in the Number and Types of Sports Facilities and Events

The increased interest in sport, fitness, and recreation activity over the last few decades has influenced the number and type of facilities and events offered. Sports and fitness facilities are constantly being built to meet the demand for sports, fitness, and recreation activities; new sports; and sports entertainment purposes. For example, a record number of football stadiums for professional teams were built in the late 1990s. These facilities incorporate full-service communities including restaurants, shopping malls, hotels, and fitness centers.

Another factor influencing this growth in building sport facilities and offering events is money. Call any city's visitors and convention office, and they can tell you how many sports events were hosted in the city during the prior year. They can also give you an estimate of the economic impact of each of those events. Economic impact includes the money brought in to the city because of the event—money spent by the event attendees on lodging, eating, shopping, and transportation. Realizing the money involved, many cities build sports facilities and have committees whose primary responsibility is to attract sporting events. The sporting events might include small events such as a 10k run, a car race, a three-on-three basketball tournament, a beach volleyball tournament, or a rodeo. The committees may also try to attract events as large as the Olympics.

Movement of Facilities From Single-Purpose to Multi-Sport and Full-Service Facilities

Early sport, fitness, and recreation facilities were typically single sport or single purpose. Today, sport facilities are built with the capability to serve many purposes and to accommodate many sport events as well as nonsports events. Consider today's fitness centers. Most will have the usual weight-lifting room, sauna, and tanning beds. Further inspection will reveal large multipurpose rooms for aerobics and other activities, an indoor and outdoor pool, steam rooms, whirlpool baths, plush locker rooms and full-service dressing rooms, childcare services, restaurants, lounges, volleyball courts, racquetball courts, basketball courts, tennis courts, massage services, a pro shop, and many auxiliary services such as racket stringing, laundry services, hair dryers, shampoo, and even toothbrushes and toothpaste.

The multipurpose, multisport facility serves the modern fitness and health-minded consumer as a home away from home. Such facilities are more accessible, more convenient, and more efficient; they can accommodate the consumer's desires for something different when he or she becomes bored with one sport.

There are still some single-sport facilities built today whose primary purpose is to accommodate one sport. As examples, consider the Toronto Sky Dome, the Joe Robbie Stadium in Miami, and the Super Dome in New Orleans. However, even though they were built to primarily service one or two sports, other events are staged in the facilities.

Constant Increase in the Amount and Types of Sports Medicine and Fitness Training Services

Regardless of status, skill, or fitness level, if an individual wants or needs medical treatment for a sports injury or professional training, it is available today as in no other period of time in history. During the late 1970s and throughout the 1990s, the importance of keeping college, professional, and Olympic athletes healthy, in top physical condition, and in the game produced a need for professionals who specialized in taking care of sports injuries with an emphasis on speedy and accurate recovery and professionals who specialized in perfecting the physical. Hence, the athletic training, sports medicine, and fitness training fields of study proliferated. Today, every city has sports medicine, sports-injury rehabilitation, and fitness training clinics. It is a growing industry segment of the sport business industry. For the professional, there are degrees, certification clinics, workshops, seminars, exhibitions, conferences, magazines, newsletters, professional journals, websites, and even consultants—all designed to support and make money from this growing industry.

The effects of this increase in sports medicine and related services on sport businesses have been many, but the individuals reaping the benefits are people who

> Taking care of the athlete, regardless of level, has become big business.

participate in sports. Getting professional attention to injuries and professional training enhances an athlete's performance. Therefore, fewer sports participants have to give up participating due to an injury. Furthermore, the growth of such services is one reason for the growing numbers of people participating throughout their lifetimes, regardless of age. It is no secret that one of the fastest growing age segments in the sport industry are people 45 years of age and older. The industry is scrambling to meet the demand, offering increasing numbers of age-group categories in most sports for those who are 50, 60, 70, 80, and even 90-plus. Readers of this textbook who want to play sports forever should know that this is increasingly becoming possible.

Factor Category V: Commercialization and Marketing of Sports and Sport Business

The word *commercialization* is derived from the word *commercial*. A check of any thesaurus will give you these words: ad, advertisement, business, marketable, mercantile, salable, plug, promo, promotion, sponsorship, sport, trade, trading, vendible, and wanted. Most sports and recreational activities are all these things today. The increasing commercialization and marketing of more and different sports, recreation, fitness, tourism, and leisure activities and events, as well as sport-related products such as sports magazines, are having a tremendous impact on the growth and development of the sport industry.

Development of Sport Packaging as an Entertainment Product

Companies with sports events for sale have done an increasingly better job of packaging sports to attract a wide variety of consumers. Fitness centers and sports clubs have enhanced their offerings to attract and keep consumers. As you learned earlier, fitness centers have become almost a "home away from home." Every convenience and service is offered to catch and to keep the consumer's attention.

Sports for sale as a spectatorial or entertainment product are being packaged to attract more and a greater variety of consumers. For example, consider a minor league men's professional baseball game. The consumer is lured to the park with accommodations for tailgating (partying in the parking lot before and after a game) and offered a chance to be one of the first 2,000 people through the gate to receive a huggie (a plastic can cooler); he or she might win a brand-new truck during the seventh-inning stretch (as the result of a ticket-stub number drawing); and, for one hour after the game, a local country music band will play their hearts out while consumers two-step on the infield. What a bargain!

In another example, the Kentucky Derby offers over 70 events leading up to and surrounding the Kentucky Derby horse race. The actual race lasts only about two minutes,

Table 1.24. Official Kentucky Derby Festival Events in One Year	
An Evening with Vincenzo Benefitting KDFF	Da'Ville Classic Drum Line Showcase College Fair
Kentucky Derby Festival Yard Sale	TheSlice: Spice, Style & Soul
Pegasus Pin Sponsorship Grand Prize Drawings	Sonic Saturday Featuring Soul Asylum
Derby Eve Jam featuring Justin Moore	U.S. Bank Derby Festival Great Balloon Rush Hour Race
Illumination Derby Ball Presented by The Steward's Staff	U.S. Bank Derby Festival Great Balloon Glow
Republic Bank Pegasus Parade	Running Wild Pasta Dinner & Expo
100 Black Men of Louisville Derby Gala	Movie Night on the Great Lawn Featuring "Twilight"
Tune It Up Thursday Concert featuring Cage the Elephant	Chow Wagon at Waterfront Park
Battle of the Bounce	Running Wild Expo
Wednesday Evening Concert Featuring Todd Snider	U.S. Bank Derby Festival Great Balloon Tour
Big Brother Open Casting Call	BlueMile Lounge
Fifth Third Bank Derby Festival $1 Million Hole In One Finals	U.S. Bank Derby Festival Great Balloon Glimmer
Republic Bank Parade Preview Party	U.S. Bank Derby Festival Great BalloonFest
Run for the Rose	Kroger's Fest-a-Ville on the Waterfront
Kentucky Proud Derby Festival WineFest	Kentucky Bourbon Bar
Ramble for the Roses	Pajama Party
Anthem Blue Cross and Blue Shield Healthy Lifestyle Showcase	Fifth Third Bank Derby Festival $1 Million Hole In One Ladies Day
RhythmFest by State Farm featuring The S.O.S. Band and The Dazz Band	Bed Making Competition
Stock Yards Bank Great Bed Races	NPC Fitness and Physique Championship
AT&T Derby Festival Morning Line	Derby Festival Basketball Classic presented by papajohns.com
Don Fightmaster Golf Outing for Exceptional Children	Fifth Third Bank Derby Festival $1 Million Hole In One Golf Contest
Discovery Day	Night of the Future Stars
HappyTail Hour at Kroger's Fest-a-Ville	Taste of Derby Festival
Knights of Columbus Charity Dinner	King Southern Bank Derby Festival Foundation Pro-Am Golf Tournament
Fifth Third Bank Derby Festival $1 Million Hole In One Semi Finals	The Fillies Children's Tea with the Derby Festival Princesses presented by Goldberg Simpson
Louisville Youth Orchestra Concert	Volleyball Classic
Celebration Sunday with 88.5 WJIE	Thunder Over Louisville
Marathon/miniMarathon presented by Walmart	Boomtown Presented by Tumbleweed
U.S. Bank Derby Festival Great Balloon Race	Thunder Over Louisville Waterfront Chow Wagon
DerbyHole Tournament	

but the events surrounding the race now last about four weeks! The primary reason for offering the consumer more than just the sports event is to make the sports event the centerpiece of a larger event. Of course, another reason is money. Many people and businesses profit from the Kentucky Derby. Therefore, everyone cooperates in order to bring in more consumers. Table 1.24 illustrates a sample of the events. Notice how many are sports events!

Increased Marketing and Marketing Orientation of the Sport Business Industry

As more sport management professionals learn and then apply the fundamentals of sport marketing to the sport industry, the industry is treated more as a business than as a recreational interest, and sport products are designed with consumer needs in mind. Maybe you have heard the expression "give consumers what they want!" This certainly applies to the sport industry. Take, for example, basketball rules changes specifically for entertainment value: The dunk was legalized because the fans loved it, and there are TV time-outs because television's advertisers need the time for their commercials. Why is soccer not televised in the U.S. on a regular basis? Because there are no time-outs in order to assure advertiser's commercials? Television officials are pressuring soccer officials to change the rules in order to make it "TV-friendly." In other words, rules in sports are changed to make the sports more marketable.

Many in the sport business industry have perfected the art of promotion, partially out of a desire to truly promote a product and partially out of the increasingly competitive nature of the industry. For example, there are more home fitness equipment products on the market than ever before. In order to entice the consumer to purchase one company's product instead of the other company's product, sport marketing professionals go to great lengths to create the optimal promotional plan.

In another example, it might seem that sport marketing professionals have taken the art of promotion perhaps too far. Modern spectators of sporting events expect more than just the event. They expect to be entertained before, during, and after an event. They expect to be bombarded by advertising messages, and they expect promotional activities such as giveaway merchandise, souvenir stands, food and drink, instant replay on gigantic screens, and much, much more. At any rate, sport marketing professionals have perfected this craft.

Increased Understanding and Knowledge of Sport Business Industry Consumers

As you will learn in this book, there are a multitude of different consumer groups. Gone are the days when a sport business such as college men's basketball could simply offer the game and expect large crowds. Gone, too, are the days when an athlete-management consulting company was the only one in existence. Because of the increased competitive structure of the industry, there are many more products from which to choose. For a sport company to thrive, therefore, it must constantly analyze its consumers. Sport management professionals are increasingly doing a better job of studying consumer groups and meeting their demands for products. Additionally, literature in sport management and sport marketing has begun to recognize that there is much more to the industry and many more types of consumers than sports participants and spectators. Therefore, sport management education professors and educational materials are better preparing students for careers throughout the industry.

Growth in Sport Sponsorship, Endorsement, and Licensing and Merchandising

Sponsorship is a multibillion-dollar industry and growing. There are a multitude of opportunities for sponsorship companies because there are hundreds of thousands of sports events, organizations, governing bodies, and athletes, many of which are looking for sponsorship. Sponsorship is such a large industry segment that there are conferences, trade shows, magazines, companies, and directories serving the industry. Sponsorship is the exchange of something for something. In its simplest form, sponsorship occurs when a company or person gives money to financially support an event, organization, or person. The return is an advertising benefit.

> Decisions in the sport industry are increasingly based on consumers' desires.

Some exchanges can be quite complex and involve goods and services as well as funds. In exchange, the company might receive such benefits as advertising, having the event or facility named for the company, product tie-ins, on-site sales or giveaways, goods, and tickets.

Companies are heavily involved in sponsorship in the sport industry today. Because it is such a large and popular industry, companies use sponsorship primarily as an advertising tactic. Other reasons are to reach specific market segments, to increase grassroots marketing, to be associated with sports, and to participate in cause marketing. Watch any racecar driver step out of her or his car. Look at the uniform, and what do you see? The uniform is covered with patches of the many companies that provided money to the racing team organization. It is almost impossible to see the car because it is covered with sponsors' logos. Why do companies get involved in sponsorship? The most common reasons include the company's desires to have the public think of it as a caring company, to

> **Company sponsorship:**
>
> • promotes a caring image
> • familiarizes the public with the company name
> • provides relatively inexpensive advertising

have the public see and remember its name, and to use its resources wisely (in many cases, sponsorship is less expensive than other forms of advertising).

Endorsement. Over the last couple of decades, the use of endorsement as an advertising and promotional tool has increased. The product may or may not be a sport product. The agreement may involve a fee, goods, and/or services traded for the individual's or company's time. Use of the endorser brings attention to the product by capitalizing on the popularity of the endorser.

Licensing and Merchandising. Licensed merchandise in the U.S. is a multi-billion-dollar industry. NASCAR, for example, reports an estimated $2 billion in licensed merchandise sales. A way to promote and to add extra income for many sports companies is to use licensing and merchandising. In the last decade, licensing and merchandising have become big business. They involve copyright protection for a company's name, logo, mark, or events and using those to create lines of souvenir merchandise. This has become so much a part of sports events that spectators expect to be able to purchase souvenir merchandise. Licensing and merchandising have had a tremendous impact on the sport business industry, primarily as income boosters, but also as ways to develop brand-loyal consumers.

Factor Category VI: Sport Industry Professional Service Businesses

There are a number and variety of businesses that offer such professional services as legal, sport marketing, sport finance, sport management, and consulting to the sport business industry. These have become an integral part of the industry.

Extraordinary Growth in Service Businesses for the Sport Industry

Those service businesses provide legal representation, consulting, and research, marketing, and financial services. For almost every area of the industry, there are now businesses that want to provide services to help (and profit from) that part of the industry. For example, for professional athletes, there are several service businesses and consultants to help them with their legal, financial, licensing, sports equipment, clothing, and endorsement possibilities. These offers of help now start when athletes are very young, even sometimes when they are still preteens. For other areas of the industry, there are service businesses. For example, if your company is a laundry detergent company and you want to know exactly how effective your $15-million racing boat sponsorship is, you can hire a sport marketing company to do the research for you. Moreover, although these service businesses have sprung up to offer help in the sport industry, and, of course, to profit from it as well, they have created new professions, which translates into new jobs and careers for people.

Factor Category VII: Media and Electronic Technology

The sport industry and the media have a relatively long history. Sports have been broadcast or reported through such media forms as television, radio, newspaper, and magazines. There are more forms of media today, and the sport business industry has benefited greatly from most of them. Additionally, a new sport business industry segment, sports media, has emerged as a result of the popularity and growth of both media and sports as well as media technology. For instance, sports events were first televised by existing broadcasting companies. During the 1960s, a couple of hours per week might be programmed for broadcasting sports coverage. The growth in popularity of sports, fitness, and recreation gave rise to new sport media businesses such as ESPN and FOX Sports, whose exclusive programming focus was sports events and news. The continued popularity of such businesses has spawned specialization. There are individual channels for individual sports. Other forms of sport media include print media, the Internet, film, radio, social media, video and fantasy games, and mobile devices. Following are some of the many factors related to media and electronic technology that have affected the growth and development of the sport business industry.

Increase in Television, Radio, and Print Media Exposure; and Distribution of Sports and Sport Business

Coverage of sport activities and events on television and radio is big business. Most major and minor broadcasting companies compete for the rights to broadcast events, large and small, traditional and contemporary. In addition, there are several sports broadcasting companies whose full-time coverage is sports activities and events. This constant and growing coverage of sports, recreation, and fitness events has helped increase the popularity of sports.

The advent of television and certainly the broadcasting of sports on television have had a tremendous impact on the growth of the sport industry. Through television, people are exposed to a variety of sports and sport events. The demand for sport on television gave way to advertising dollars for the networks and for the sport enterprise as well. The exposure has influenced the awareness of sport, popularity of sport, and participation in sport. Television has also created new sport business opportunities and a new sport industry segment has taken off—TV sports. Gone are the days when people were limited to watching a few select sports events on national broadcasting channels sandwiched between other programming. Today, numerous sports channels offer the consumer the chance to watch sports and recreational events 24 hours a day, 7 days a week.

Fueling this increase is target marketing. Sports channels are being created to meet the desires of target markets. Some of those targeted channels include the Golf channel, the Tennis channel, the Speed channel, NBA channels, soccer channels, and the outdoor life channel.

These sports channels are having profound effects on the sport business industry. Not only are they an enormous industry segment that is creating millions of jobs, but they also introduce, educate, and entertain millions of consumers each day. They have launched two more industry segments: non-sports companies that use televised sports events for advertising their products, and sports created for TV. In the first instance, which is sometimes called "marketing through sports," many companies pay millions of dollars to advertise during televised sports events, or to sponsor the event, in order to reach certain markets. In the second instance, sports, fitness, and other recreational activities and events are invented specifically for television. For example, ESPN2 created the X Games as a television sports event commodity.

> Exposure to TV, the radio, and the Internet has increased popular interest in sports and the sport industry.

Another mass media outlet includes print media such as newspapers and magazines (see Table 1.25). No other industry enjoys its own separate section in nearly every newspaper worldwide. Reading about sports and recreation increases the awareness of sport and the desire to participate in sports and recreation. Walk into any local bookstore and go to the magazine section. How many magazines can you count that are sports, fitness, health, leisure, travel, and recreation magazines? If the activity exists, there is or soon

Table 1.25. Examples of Sports Magazines		
Aikido Today	Hoop	Southern Sports Journal
Auto Racing Digest	Horse Illustrated	Sporting News
Backpacker	Inside Kung Fu	Stock Car Racing
Baseball Digest	Inside Pool Magazine	Surfer's Journal
Basketball Times	Inside Wrestling	Swimming World
Billiard Times	International Figure Skating	Tae Kwon Do Journal
Black Belt	Junior Baseball	Tennis
Blue Water Sailing	Kite Boarding	Thoroughbred Times
Bowling Digest	Motorcycle World	Track & Field News
Buffalo Sports Report	National Masters News	Transworld Skateboarding
Camping Life	Personal Watercraft Illustrated	USA Gymnastics
Canoe & Kayak	Pro Bull Rider	Velo News
Climbing	Racer	Volleyball
Dick Berggren's Speedway Illustrated	Road & Track	Volleyball Canada
Diehard	Rugby	Wahine (women's surfing)
Dirt Rag (bicycle racing)	Runner's World	Wake Boarding
ESPN Deportes	Scuba Diving	Wind Surfing
Fantasy Sports	Senior Golfer	Women's Basketball
Footbag World	Ski	Women's Soccer World
Golf	Skydiving	Yachting
Golf for Women	Snowboarder	
Hockey Business News	Soccer Digest	

will be a magazine for it. The variety includes boating, sailing, in-line skating, fishing, flying, running, walking, adventure travel, camping, hiking, mountain biking, four-wheeling, canoeing, aquatic sports, and snow sports.

What are the purposes of these magazines? What do they offer the consumer? They expose the consumer to a sport. They educate the consumer about the sport, and encourage and support participating in the sport or becoming a spectator of the sport. They also serve as a source of information, as a resource for networking, and as a catalog of sport equipment and apparel, thereby offering manufacturers a source of advertising directly to a target market.

Consumer magazines serve to address a sport consumer's interest in a sports activity. Trade magazines serve industry individuals who want industry news, ideas on marketing, and business information. Academic journals serve teachers, professors, and students studying sport business.

Table 1.26. Examples of Trade Publications from the NSGA	
NSGA Retail Focus Magazine	**NSGA Huddle Newsletter**
NSGA Research Newsletter	**HAD Hockey Voice Newsletter** (Hockey Dealers Association)
Sporting Goods Intelligence newsletter—SGI delivers the news and analysis that matters, focused on the sporting goods marketplace and the emerging retail landscape. NSGA Retailer/Dealer Members: Take $200 off the subscription rate of $495 . . . making an annual e-mail subscription only $295!	
Sporting Goods Business—Monthly issues cover the entire sporting goods industry, from how to better run a retail store and sell more merchandise to product information including, footwear, apparel, equipment and accessories. NSGA Retailer/Dealer Members: Free and and unlimited subscriptions.	
Sporting Goods Dealer—Bimonthly issues cover industry insiders, new products and merchandising trends affecting team dealers and retailers who serve schools, colleges, consumers, pro and local team and organizations. NSGA Retailer/Dealer Members: Free and unlimited subscriptions.	
Sports Executive Weekly—Offers more in-depth analysis and insight on the news of the week and also provides additional feature stories and commentary covering the broader issues of the sporting goods, athletic footwear, and athletic apparel markets. The subscription for Sports Executive Weekly is normally offered at $429 per year. NSGA Retailer/Dealer Members: Take 20% off annual subscription rate and pay just $343!	
Source: NSGA	

Trade magazines are primarily for people in the various careers and trades in the sport business industry. For example, there are magazines that provide boating industry information, market data, and business strategies for the owners and managers of boat dealerships. For the sports tourism company, there are sports travel magazines, and for snow sports businesses, there are snow sports business magazines such as *WinterSport Business* and *Snowboarding Business*. Table 1.26 shows examples of trade publications.

Additionally, there are annual conventions and trade shows for many businesses such as the annual sporting goods manufacturers' trade show held annually in Atlanta and the snow sports industries trade show held annually in Las Vegas. Table 1.27 shows examples of trade organizations and publications for the golf industry.

This proliferation of information has influenced both the popularity and growth of participation in sport-, fitness-, and recreation-oriented activities and the effectiveness of the sport business. As people read about, hear about, or see sports, they are more inclined to become involved. As sport businesses study and learn more about their business and industry segment, they more effectively manage and market their business. Both groups reap great benefits.

Table 1.27. Trade Associations, Organizations, Exhibitions, Conferences, and Publications Examples for the Golf Business Industry
American Society of Golf Course Architects (ASGCA)—www.asgca.org
Club & Resort Business—www.clubandresortbusiness.com
Club Managers Association of America (CMAA)—www.cmaa.org
CMAA Club Careers—www.clubcareers.org
Environmental Institute for Golf (EIFG)—www.eifg.org
GCSAA Education Conference—held annually
Golf Builder's Association of America (GCBAA)—www.gcbaa.org
Golf Business Advisors—www.golfbusinesadvisors.com
Golf Business Magazine—www.golfbusiness.com
Golf Business Development Magazine (GBD)—www.golfbusinessdevelopment.com
Golf Course Industry Magazine—www.golfcourseindustry.com
Golf Course Superintendents Association of America—www.gcsanc.com
Golf Industry Show—held annually
International Golf Course Equipment Managers Association (IGCEMA)
National Golf Course Owners Association (NGCOA)—ww.ngcoa.org
National Golf Foundation (NGF)
Society of Golf Appraisers—www.golfappraisers.org
PGA Magazine—www.pgamagazine.com
Professional Golfers Association of America (PGA)—www.pga.com
United States Golf Association (USGA)
Women in the Golf Industry—www.wigi.info
World Conference and Club Business Expo—held annually

Increase in Electronic Media and Its Exposure and Distribution of Sports

The Internet, which continues to revolutionize business and the way people shop, interact, and communicate, has also had an enormous impact on the sport industry. There are already numerous sport businesses and other opportunities on the Web. To find some of them, simply go to any search engine and type in "sports" or "sport business" as the subject. In one example, www.CBSsportsline.com is a company created specifically to be a Web-based company. It offers information and is a sports shopping mall. Figure 1.5 shows the top ten sports websites.

Additionally, the Internet has become a significant way for sports companies to gain exposure for and to distribute their sports and other sport business. With the advances

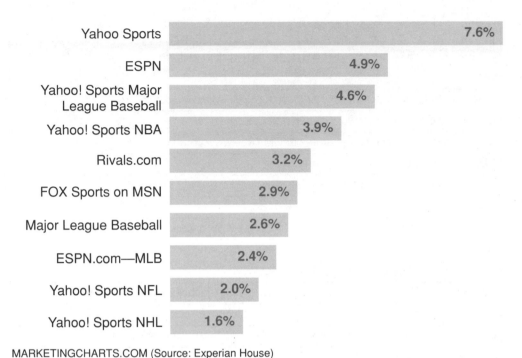

MARKETINGCHARTS.COM (Source: Experian House)

Figure 1.5. Top Ten Sports Websites ("Top 10 Sports Websites," 2011).

in streaming video and live events on the Internet, sports businesses have vigorously sought to put their events and other products on the Internet. This exposure increases the popularity of sports, and thus affects participation and spectator rates.

Exposure and Distribution of Sports and Sport Business by Mobile Device Media

The explosion of mobile and Wi-Fi enabled devices and their technologies have allowed sport businesses to expand their distribution and exposure. With a data phone or other mobile device, such as an iPad or other similar tablet, one can now watch sports events on a phone or tablet device. Further, as these products proliferate, the willingness of consumers to shop via these devices increases. Many sport businesses are taking advantage of the popularity of these devices.

Cell phone descriptions are starting to read like computer descriptions: A phone introduced in 2011 described it as ruggedized, water-resistant, dust-proof, scratch-resistant, equipped with a 10 megapixel camera with LED flash and VGA camera for video chatting, powered by a 600 MHz processor and 512MB of RAM with support for microSD cards up to 64GB storage, with a 1,650mAh battery with 10 hours of talk time or 21 days of standby time.

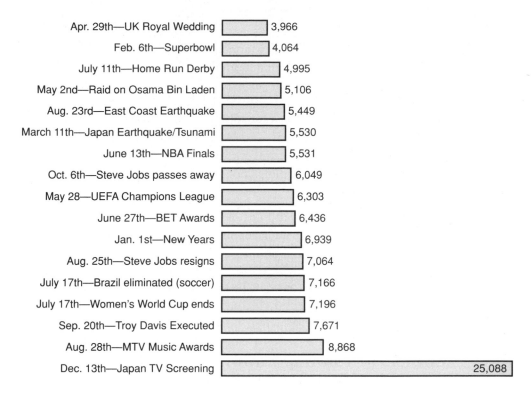

Figure 1.6. Of the Top 17 "Tweets Per Second" Records in 2011, 6 (35%) Are Sports Events. Source: (http://yearinreview.twitter.com/en/tps.html)

Growth of Social Media Types and Marketing Use for Greater Exposure and Distribution

"Like" us on Facebook! Social media websites have recently caught on and are exponentially popular and being used in an ever-growing number of ways. One of these ways is that sport businesses are creating their own connections with consumers by developing their own social media accounts. Sports fans can go to their favorite team's Facebook page and interact in a number of ways. This increases the popularity of sports and thus is having a significant effect on the growth of the industry. Figure 1.6 shows data about Twitter and "tweets per second" records in 2011. This data shows that a little over a third of the records set were sports events.

Growth of Sport-Related Electronic Games

Games about sports have exploded in popularity. The newest research shows the growth and development of the sports video game industry in a number of ways (Cianfrone,

The plethora of magazines devoted to particular sports not only promotes awareness of specific sports, but also provides education, encouragement, and support for the sport's participants.

Zhang, & Ko, 2011). Sports fans are most likely to consume sports video games such as Madden NFL. Sports video games and fantasy league sports games have the positive potential to influence participation and interest in sports.

Factor Category VIII: Sport Management Education

Where there is an industry, there is a need for appropriately educated individuals. The vastness and diversity of segments, jobs, and careers in the sport business industry have led to a constant increase in the number and type of educational opportunities. From certifications to doctoral degrees, educational opportunities for sport industry professionals cannot grow fast enough.

Increase in Sport-Related Education for Executives, Administrators, Athletes, and Other Personnel

There are several categories of people who are interested in sport education. There are people who want to learn how to play sports, games, and other activities. Some want to learn how to officiate, coach, or train athletes. Some want to learn how to organize and manage sporting enterprises. Others want to learn how to produce or promote sports events. When people desire something, it is usually (eventually) offered for sale. Today's consumer is offered an abundance of sports and/or sport business educational opportunities that range from rock-climbing lessons and biking instruction to sport business CEO workshops and coaching clinics. In addition, there are meetings and clinics to educate officials.

Many books, videos, and magazines offer lessons, suggestions, hints, and tips for improving performance. All of these products have positively affected the sport industry. The opportunities help educate people who are already working in the industry and people who want to work in the industry.

Increase in Competency of Sport Business Management Professionals

Although sport business management is still a new field of study when compared to most other disciplines, it is having a positive influence on the competency level of those working in the sport business industry. The number of undergraduate, graduate, and doctoral programs of study in sport management continues to increase in the United States, Canada, and around the world. In 1993, the members of the North American Society approved curriculum standards for sport management, and in 1994, an approval process began, headed by a joint committee called the Sport Management Program Review Council of NASPE-NASSM (Fielding, Pitts, & Miller, 1991; Parks & Zanger, 1990). In 2009, a new accreditation commission replaced the original one: the Commission on Sport Management Accreditation (COSMA). As students complete degrees in sport management, they will fill the jobs in the sport industry. Eventually, there will be more employees and executives in the sport industry who have a sport management degree than those who do not. As appropriately educated sport administrators begin to manage in the sport industry, they will have a positive effect on the industry.

Growth of Sport Management as an Academic Discipline and Career

Sport management continues to grow in demand as an academic discipline and career. In the U.S. alone, there are approximately 350 undergraduate programs, 200 master's degree programs, and 12 doctoral programs. The growth of sport management academic programs is creating jobs for those interested in education, research, and the sport business industry. Today, there are more sport management faculty than ever before. With the growth in the number of programs comes growth in sport management as an academic discipline, and an academic discipline must have a scholarly body of knowledge. Today, the body of knowledge in sport management is larger than ever before. For example, there are now over a dozen sport management academic journals; some of these journals are the *Journal of Sport Management*, the *International Journal of Sport Management*, *European Sport Management Quarterly*, the *Sport Management Review* (Australia), *Sport Marketing Quarterly*, the *International Journal of Sports Marketing and Sponsorship*, the *International Journal of Sport Management and Marketing*, the *International Journal of Sport Finance*, *Choregia: The International Sport Management Journal*, and the *Journal of Sports Economics*. Additionally, there are closely related journals such as the *Journal of Vacation Marketing*, the *Journal of Sport and Social Issues*, and the *Journal of Sports Tourism*. For a more complete list, see Appendix D.

There is a scholarly society in North America (the North American Society for Sport Management), and these types of societies are increasing in number around the globe. Here are a few examples: the Sport Management Association of Australia and New Zealand (SMAANZ), the European Association for Sport Management (EASM), the Taiwan Association for Sport Management (TASM), the Asian Association for Sport Management (AASM), the Latin Association of Sport Management (ALGEDE), and the Mongolian Association for Sport Management. Each of these groups holds annual conferences during which numerous academic papers are presented, and hundreds of professors, industry professionals, and students attend.

The newest organization formed during 2011 is the cornerstone of all organizations everywhere: the World Association for Sport Management (WASM) (Pitts, 2011).

It is certainly a sign that sport management is an academic field in great demand with growth that will continue for as long as people play sports.

CHAPTER SUMMARY

The student in sport business management and in sport marketing must develop an understanding of the sport business industry, sport management, and sport marketing. An industry is a market containing similar products. Some industries contain only one product. The sport industry contains many. The sport industry is a market in which the products offered to its buyers are related to sport, fitness, recreation or leisure; these products may be activities, goods, services, people, places, or ideas. The sport industry is a large, broad, and very diverse industry. Its products serve a large and diverse base of consumers. Studies have created categories or industry segments as a way of organizing the sport industry in order to better define and understand it.

Many factors have affected and will continue to affect the sport industry. Some impact the growth and development of the industry. Some will continue to have an effect on the industry. The sport management professional and sport marketer should constantly monitor these factors and others in order to develop educated decisions and strategies.

DISCUSSION QUESTIONS

1. What is the sport business industry? Give some examples.
2. What is sport business management?
3. What is the North American Society for Sport Management, and what is the Sport Marketing Association?
4. What are the many factors that influence the growth and development of the sport industry? Give examples and explain how each factor influences the industry. Why is it important to know this?
5. How do you use media to consume sports and sport business?

SUGGESTED EXERCISES

1. Discover the sport business industry in your city by doing the following: (a) Create a list of sport industry businesses, organizations, clubs, and other enterprises in your city or community; (b) Categorize everything according to the three sport industry segments created by the Pitts, Fielding and Miller (1994) model: sport performance, sport production, and sport promotion; (c) For each item on your list, list the jobs within each; (d) For each item on your list, list the sport products offered to the consumer; (e) For each category, list consumer markets.
2. Access the Internet and do searches for sports entities' economic impacts or values. Try to find 5 different ones. Give a brief presentation of what you found to the class. Email your results to the authors of this book—they might be chosen to be included in the next edition and you will be given credit in the book.
3. Subscribe to sport management-related journals such as the *Journal of Sport Management, Sport Marketing Quarterly*, and the *Seton Hall Journal of Sport Law*. Read and summarize the studies you find in the journals. Describe how sport management and sport marketing professionals can use the information.
4. Use the chapter's case study for a group discussion in class. Then, with a group, create your own case study based on the topics covered in this chapter.

2

The Global Market for the Sport Industry

INTRODUCTION

Globalization hit its stride with the 2008 Summer Olympic Games in Beijing. The battle for world domination between Nike, adidas and Li Ning was front and center during the Games. Nike secured the podium apparel rights for the USOC and outfitting rights for 22 of 28 Chinese national teams. Li Ning sponsored the Chinese gymnastics, table tennis and diving teams (high-profile and eventual medal winning teams). Li Ning also signed an agreement to outfit all Chinese television broadcasters (CCTV) during the Games. Adidas was an official Beijing Olympic Organizing Committee supplier with outfitting rights for all personnel and volunteers working the Games. Adidas also secured a selection of national team podium rights, including host country China. Stage set, battle on!

The value of the global sports equipment market is estimated to be near $100 billion, rebounding after the 2009 recession. The cumulative world market for all sport spending is just over $1 trillion. A reasonable estimate of the total U.S.

> "Many people believe that nowhere is the triumph of globalization more clear than in the world of sport" (Bairner, 2003, p. 34). The NBA, NFL, UFC, and nearly every major sport enterprise in the United States are doing business in a global environment. Sport management professionals clearly must develop an understanding of the issues associated with globalization and craft appropriate strategies.

sports market would be $400 to $425 billion yearly, with U.S. sporting equipment sales at retail sporting goods stores totaling roughly $39 billion annually (Miller, 2011).

As a multinational corporation, Nike has cornered 32% of the worldwide market in athletic footwear, bringing in over $19 billion in annual sales. Adidas was second in the market with the 2005 merger with Reebok. According to their annual report, adidas plans to grow 45–50% to €17 billion (about $22.4 billion) by 2015 (Parker, 2010). In total, the United States exported more than $1.5 billion in sporting goods in 2010 and imported over $10 billion (Hamilton, 2011). Not only sports products companies are going global; sports services are involved as well. World-renowned sports agency International Management Group (IMG) has 3,000 employees and offices in 30 different countries ("IMG Connects," n.d.). As you can see, the sport industry is a global marketplace.

The purpose of this chapter is to enable sport marketers to think in international and global terms. The chapter is not intended to provide a complete overview of the billion-dollar multinational market. Although many lessons and examples can be learned from such companies, one does not have to play in their league to learn from their experiences. To illustrate the complexities of international sport marketing, IMG founder Mark McCormack once commented that "I worry that the people in our Stockholm office don't talk to the people in our Sydney office. I worry that they don't know our people in the Sydney office. Worse yet, I worry that they don't know we have a Sydney office!" (McCormack, 2000, p. 248). This chapter has been written with the following objectives in mind: a) to provide information about the global marketplace for the sport marketer, b) to identify information and knowledge necessary for entry into a global market, and c) to present a context for thinking about marketing internationally.

According to Pride and Ferrell (2010), fewer than 15% of small to midsize companies participate in global marketing and trade, but 70% express an interest in international sales. Thus, it seems only natural that many businesses have limited knowledge of international trade. This information void may contribute to a reluctance to begin examining global aspects of the sport industry.

Traditional concepts of import and export arise when international markets are mentioned, yet these are not the only factors in a global approach. It will become increasingly necessary to view all corporate resources, finances, manufacturing, distribution, retailing, and human resource management from a global perspective. As Americans have experienced, much of our sports equipment is manufactured abroad, but have we truly examined foreign markets for the sale of our products and services? Are there markets in which our products or services could dominate? Could mergers and cooperative agreements provide increased revenue and markets for U.S. and foreign companies?

With these questions in mind, it becomes necessary to investigate the global market in more detail. Although the global marketplace is ever changing, the areas presented below may provide some knowledge and insight for international market exploration.

THE GLOBAL BUSINESS STRUCTURE

The structure of the international business environment is complex. Business schools offer complete courses in international business, and some graduate programs are designed with international commerce as their focus of study. Following is an overview for the sport marketing professional of the key topics in the area.

Several avenues are available for entering international markets. The Internet certainly provides opportunities for engaging in international commerce. However, because individual consumers are burdened with clearing items through customs and paying duty on goods (over $400 for goods imported into the United States), this option is not prevalent in the sport industry.

The easiest and least complicated avenue available for entering international markets is exporting. This practice depends on either corporate or agency interest in domestic products. For example, a sporting goods company in Argentina may contact Firm A about the possibility of purchasing in-line skates for export. Firm A would simply supply them with the product; the Argentinean company would deal with the issues of duties and tariffs to import the items into Argentina. The benefits are easy to see: Firm A's outlay of capital is negligible, and it is not overburdened with customs procedures. Perhaps the only modifications that Firm A would need to make would be in package labeling or modifications in color to satisfy local appeal. On the other hand, exporting in this manner depends on the emergence of demand, as opposed to activating demand (Pride & Ferrell, 2010).

In some instances, trading companies can more actively identify markets and move products more effectively into international channels. Trading companies typically purchase goods in one country and then resell them in various international markets. Again, the advantage is that the business's risks and capital outlay are minimal. If the products don't sell, the trading company absorbs the loss.

The formation of *joint ventures* and *strategic alliances* are two additional, prevalent ways to penetrate international markets in the sport industry. These marketing techniques involve a greater level of risk and the commitment of more corporate resources.

Joint ventures are characterized by partnering with a corporation residing in the target nation. This practice has been successfully implemented in the athletic footwear industry. Major U.S. shoe companies have formed partnerships with Asian factories to dedicate portions of their factory space or a percentage of their production-line time to the production of shoes. Pride and Ferrell (2010) noted significant growth in the implementation of strategic alliances in the late 1990s continuing into the 2000s.

What differentiates strategic alliances from joint ventures is that in the formation of a strategic alliance, partners "often retain their distinct identities, and each brings a distinctive competence to the union" (Pride & Ferrell, 2010, p. 128). Thus, a Korean golf equipment manufacturing group could receive much-needed capital for expansion and engineering innovation from a U.S. sporting goods company. The U.S. firm would obtain high-quality products manufactured at labor and material costs far lower than could have been secured domestically.

Direct ownership is the final alternative to entering a foreign market. In this instance, the domestic company commits significant resources in order to build a factory and corporate office and hire a local work force to manufacture goods and distribute them within the market. Because of the level of capital required and the tremendous risk involved, few sport firms are willing to select this strategy. Regardless of the structure selected for international marketing, a thorough understanding of the business environment is required. Additional topics presented below provide information that should prove useful.

INTERNATIONAL ECONOMICS AND FINANCE

A working understanding of world banking and finance is essential for sport marketers. Most Americans are accustomed to dealing with commercial banks through such services as deposits, loans, and checking accounts. In the United States, commercial banks are widespread and need only a license to operate. However, most industrialized nations have a system controlled by a central national bank. For the sport entrepreneur, two choices exist: Deal with the central bank of the host country, or deal with a foreign branch of an American bank.

American banks may have familiar-sounding names and executives who understand the American way, but overall, foreign banks have fewer restrictions and less regulations than do American banks. For that reason, many foreign banks are often easier to deal with, have lower fees and are less inclined to hassle the customer than their American counterparts.

In selecting a bank for foreign business activities, the size of the bank is not as important as are the services it can provide. Managers should look specifically for banking institutions that can:

1. Move money from banks in one country to banks in another through wire transfer.
2. Handle export financing through personnel in their internal department.
3. Arrange for collections and payments in various currencies.
4. Process foreign currency through exchange conversion at the lowest possible rate.
5. Issue and process letters of credit to guarantee payments and collections from clients.

A common nightmare for sport marketers is foreign currency. If the only experience you have in dealing with foreign currency is exchanging your dollars for pesos on your Mexican vacation, you are in for an education. Not all international monetary units are the same with regard to exchange and convertibility. The term *hard currency* has generally been defined as a unit of monetary value readily convertible to other units. In international business transactions, the U.S. dollar, Euro, the Japanese yen, and the British pound are all convertible with one another at established rates of exchange. However, because of fluctuating exchange rates, variance in financial backing, and government stability, not all world currencies are equally acceptable.

Problems can easily arise in situations where the standard payment method has not been well conceived. Suppose you close a deal to provide 100,000 baseball bats at 264 Chinese Yuan each ($1.00 U.S. = 6.58 Chinese Yuan). Once the shipment arrives, payment is required within 30 days. However, because of currency fluctuations within the international monetary system, the value of the payment may be less than expected at the time of delivery to your account in Shanghai. Until 2005, the Yuan was pegged (tied) to the U.S. dollar, but with the strength of the Chinese economy, it was allowed to float freely in the international system ("How China runs the world," 2005). The international monetary system may have devalued the dollar against the Yuan. In 2011, the U.S. government was pressuring China to allow for greater fluctuation such that U.S. exports to China might be cheaper. Without a clear understanding of the market, the result could be that you would actually lose money on your deal.

For the 2008 Olympics this change in monetary policy meant that the Beijing Olympic Organizing Committee received less money from the IOC's television contract, but paid a lower amount in rights fees to the IOC. In another example, the Golf Channel began negotiating with Taiwanese television officials to supply 24-hour programming. However, when the Taiwanese dollar plunged, the deal fell apart.

This same situation can also wreak havoc with international employees. If agreements for salary were negotiated in local currency, employees might find that their standard of living deteriorates considerably with inflation or devaluation. On the other hand, if they contracted to be paid in U.S. dollars and the local currency decreased in its value against the dollar, they could have expanded their buying power immensely. Precisely this situation occurred with the Asian Games in Bangkok. In an 8-month period, the Thai *baht* dropped in value against the U.S. dollar by more than 54%. However, because most of the expenses incurred by the organizers were in *baht* and their income from sponsors was in U.S. dollars, the event and revenues were protected. Most international corporations have contractual language that addresses this issue. When possible, avoid taking foreign currency in payment for an account. In dealing with the problems of international currency, many companies use countertrade agreements.

These agreements are similar to barter, in which products and services are exchanged for other products or services that can be resold to another party for hard currency. According to Tuller (1991), "countertrade is probably the best guarded secret in international trade" (p. 263).

One multinational sport corporation, ProServ, encountered a similar situation in negotiating with Eastern European backers for a professional tennis tournament. Although the promoters wanted television production and coverage of the event, they did not have any hard currency with which to pay. However, a German firm was located that needed to make a series of payments for their employees in the local currency, and ProServ agreed to make the payment for the German firm, which paid ProServ in deutsche Marks (Briner, 1992).

Finally, Tuller (1991) recommends the following guidelines for using the global banking system:

1. The education process—Get up to speed in internal finance as soon as possible. Take a college course in international finance. Spend some time with the head of the international department of a regional bank.
2. Read, read, read—The fastest way to learn about global banking and develop a global financial mentality is to read everything available on the subject.
3. Choosing a commercial bank—Determine which local bank has an international department. Interview the department manager.
4. Experiment—Open a foreign bank account. Transfer small amounts back and forth. Incorporate exchange rate variances in forecasts, even if you have to use fictitious entries.
5. Conquer the "big boy" syndrome—The more a person investigates global banking the more one realizes it is not just for the "big boys." (p. 221)

TRADE REGULATIONS

Since the industrialization after World War II, the General Agreement on Tariffs and Trade (GATT) has governed much of international trade. Through this accord, member nations agree to certain practices involving international commerce. Although it may be beneficial for sport marketers to review this agreement, relatively few of the member countries meticulously follow its bylaws. Many countries in the world continue to establish and enforce trade agreements and tariffs that protect their products and restrict competition. However, the success of GATT agreements between the 124 participating nations has reduced the average tariff on manufactured items from 45% to 5% (Pride & Ferrell, 2010). In 2004, the U.S. Congress passed legislation (Foreign Sales Corporation/Extraterritorial Income bill) that lowered tariffs for 1,600 products, including many sporting goods manufactured in the U.S.

Examples of trade regulation affecting sport organizations are numerous. In 1994, the United States, Mexico, and Canada entered into the North American Free Trade Agreement (NAFTA) and, in 2005, the Central American Free Trade Agreement (CAFTA), which reduced and eliminated many previously imposed tariffs across North and Central America. By 2009, almost all tariffs between these nations disappeared. Lifting of these trade regulations has provided greater access to Canada's more affluent population and has increased trade from the United States by 50% since NAFTA's inception. Although many consumers in Mexico and Central America are less affluent than those in either the United States or Canada, trade between the United States and Mexico was enhanced because of a strong desire for products made in the United States. U.S. firms were also able to redirect manufacturing to Mexico and Central America, where the costs of labor have traditionally been much lower. In the manufacture of sporting goods, this labor market may prove attractive in business relocation and product sourcing. As will be discussed later, the practice of using cheap labor to produce U.S. consumer goods has created considerable controversy in some segments of the sport industry. NAFTA and CAFTA could also have an impact on the export of products where previous tariffs may have priced U.S. goods too high for some consumers—

Free-trade agreements allow for the global distribution of sporting goods and equipment. © Jianbinglee | Dreamstime.com

additional markets for U.S. sporting goods and equipment companies could be more accessible ("A weighty matter," 2004; Pride & Ferrell, 2010)

Free-trade agreements could also affect sport-related corporations in terms of liability costs. In the last 20 years, many sporting goods corporations relocated to foreign countries because of the growing cost of equipment-related liability in the United States. If import tariffs were eliminated between the United States and the manufacturer's host country, some corporations might be able to realize greater profit margins by relocating to a foreign manufacturing site.

Specifically in Europe, the formation of the European Union (EU), as well as the multinational changes within it in 1992, also brought many challenges and opportunities in sport and had dramatic effects on the sport industry. For example, in Formula One (auto racing), officials in charge of regulating antitrust situations across the European Union have challenged F1 authorities' restrictive television contracts. One of the main issues pertains to whether or not sport is a business and subject to regulation.

Prior to the unification of the EU, sport marketers who desired to do business in Europe had to follow a multitude of rules and regulations specific to each country. However, with consolidation in many key business areas, the bureaucracy of transacting business in Europe has been standardized, if not reduced. The introduction of a standard currency, the Euro, in 1999 also helped with international transactions. Although not all member countries adopted the Euro as domestic currency, inter-European and international trade was calculated in euros.

In sport marketing, we must be careful not to become too restricted in our perceptions. Although EU regulations may allow for more standardized products to be sold, the sport marketer should not automatically conclude that European consumers have similarly homogeneous needs and desires. Specific demographic and psychographic research will continue to be required. As an example, the variation of income across the richest EU member nations to the poorest has been as high as 138%. Another area of concern has been in sports equipment. Manufacturers in England had previously been required to follow one set of product safety codes whereas those in France have followed another. These and other issues related to sport and commerce are continually being clarified.

The general strategy predicted for companies in the EU is that as new markets open, price-cutting is likely to be a popular move toward the increasing of initial market share. New products will also be used, as development will have been made less costly through standardization. New products will help attract consumers who may have been previously unfamiliar with a company's product line. Experts have also postulated that distribution of goods will be facilitated because regulations covering truck transport (used to move 80% of EU goods) will be reduced and border clearances will be considerably faster. These are some examples of serious issues brought to light by the EU unification.

Other areas of the world also offer opportunities for sport-related businesses. The United States Sports Academy, an American college located in Alabama, has conducted business affairs in Saudi Arabia since the mid-1970s, at one point having over 500 employees in the region. However, by modifying regulations in the 1980s, the Saudi government changed the rules for calculating taxes and income for foreign corporations. Excellent planning by the CEO provided for the formation of a locally held corporation to take over the sport and recreation services once provided by the United States Sports Academy. By seeking local executives and changing the business structure of the venture, the United States Sports Academy was able to continue to do business with the country.

Free-trade zones also provide interesting opportunities for sport marketers. These zones are regulated by government agencies in host countries. In the United States, such zones allow for the manufacture and/or assembly of goods that are not intended for national consumption. Thus, you could import parts for gymnastics equipment from Asia, assemble them in a Colorado free-trade zone, and ship them to Europe without paying customs duties. Similar situations have also been developed in foreign nations. On a recent trip to Taiwan, a sport executive planned to purchase a high-quality set of golf clubs that he had discovered were manufactured in Taiwan. Figuring that he could find a great bargain, he began to search for his prized clubs. Much to his surprise, he learned that they were manufactured in Taiwan, but they were produced for "export only." Yes, they could be purchased in Taiwan, but only when re-imported from the United States. With twice the shipping expense, the clubs were cheaper in the United States.

INTERNATIONAL MARKETING STRUCTURE

The structure of international marketing in contrast to that of domestic sport enterprises contains more similarities than differences. Tuller (1991) reported that many of the main concepts of selling directly to consumers or selling through agents are indeed the same. Other traditional marketing activities contained in this book are also required in global marketing efforts. The process is similar, but the information and sources will be significantly different.

Differences come in the format that facilitates transactions. Terms such as *foreign trading corporations* and *export management companies* are unique to international business. Sport marketers who choose to compete in the global market will invariably learn to deal with these terms and to work effectively with foreign distributors.

Probably the most difficult aspect of foreign trade is customs. If you are dealing in sports goods and products, successfully negotiating the customs system is key to your success. If you are importing goods into the United States that have been manufactured overseas, you will be required to clear the goods through customs at their port of entry.

Several other factors differentiate international marketing from domestic. There appears to be greater government regulation in foreign markets and consequently a greater need for feedback and control. In addition, more data is needed for marketing decisions because of the cultural differences that exist. Many marketing decisions are made in U.S. sport organizations because of a knowledge of sport in our societal context. This knowledge simply does not exist for U.S. sport managers making decisions in foreign countries. To offset this problem, most organizations will enlist the assistance of national experts from the target nation.

These experts can also be helpful in communicating value differences between cultures. For example, American and German executives typically value punctuality and promptness, whereas in other cultures a 10:00 a.m. meeting simply means sometime in the morning. It is not that executives in other cultures are being rude; punctuality is just not important in their value system. International managers must learn to respect the value systems of others, not merely tolerate them.

Another difference in international marketing is that in many countries, government-owned business can compete with privately held companies. For instance, one may own a sport concession management business similar to ARAMARK Corporation in the United States. ARAMARK Corporation has a variety of contracts with professional and collegiate stadiums around the country to supply concession and facility management services. However, in some foreign countries, government-owned corporations may be granted exclusive rights to public stadiums. Another complication could be government subsidies to local corporations. Either of these practices would severely restrict the ability of a successful U.S. company to compete in that market.

THE GLOBAL SPORTS STRUCTURE

A precursor to involvement in international sport management is a thorough understanding of the global sport environment.

The framework for comprehension begins in the United States with the recognition that the United States Olympic Committee (USOC) is chartered by Congress to oversee amateur sport in the country. This encompasses all sports that are in the Olympic and Pan-American Games. Sports that fall outside those parameters may hold membership with the USOC, but are not governed by them. Professional and collegiate sports in the United States are self-governing through private voluntary associations such as the major league offices and the National Collegiate Athletic Association.

In the international sports environment, the International Olympic Committee (IOC) maintains authority over the Olympic Games and regional Olympic-style competitions (Pan-American Games, Asian Games, etc.). The IOC retains control of these multi-sport competitions and manages and markets these events internationally. Furthermore, The Olympic Partners (TOP) sponsorship program includes multinational corporations such as Visa and Coca-Cola (USA), Panasonic (Japan), and Samsung (Korea).

Each specific sport is governed by an international federation for that sport. Track-and-field is a member of the International Amateur Athletic Federation, basketball has its International Amateur Basketball Federation, and each sport maintains an affiliation with its International Federation (IF). These federations work very closely with the IOC in staging the Olympics, but their main purpose is to set rules and regulations for their sports and conduct the world championships in their sport on a yearly basis.

The organizations are also linked through national governing bodies (NGBs). Each IF designates an NGB in each country to organize and govern a specific sport within national borders. This NGB must be recognized by its national Olympic committee (i.e., USOC). As such, the NGBs work with the IFs to develop rules and regulations within a one-sport setting, yet for Olympic competition, each NGB works with its national Olympic committee to ensure participation in the Olympic Games. Several corporations have secured official supplier contracts through positive relationships developed with Olympic-governing bodies. This official supplier status was effective in boosting product sales. As a sport marketer, it is imperative to become well versed in the relationships between each of these groups and tune into the political dynamics of the world sport community.

GLOBAL MARKET SELECTION AND IDENTIFICATION

Global markets can seem overwhelming if viewed as a whole. Only when they are dissected and analyzed individually can the sport marketer make wise marketing decisions. Market conditions vary considerably in different countries, and thus, the sport industry exhibits varying growth rates. For instance, the global growth rate for the industry was projected to be 12% for the athletic footwear market, yet the U.S. rate was 5% whereas the projected growth of the Asian market was 36%. These data indicated that average yearly per capita spending on athletic footwear in the United States was $30.88 at wholesale; Japanese consumers spent $10.36, whereas the Chinese market figures indicated spending of only $0.02 (but remember, the Chinese market is 1.3 billion people). Overall, 65% of the global sporting goods market is comprised of products made in China (Yang, 2005). China dominates among exporters of athletic footwear to the United States with a market share of 76% of the total import dollar value. Indonesia's share is about 9% and Vietnam's share is near 8%. Vietnam has been a significant producer of sporting goods for many years, with company-owned and licensed factories around the country. In 2005, a Taiwanese sportswear producer (Pou Yuen) under contract with Nike, adidas, Reebok, Puma, and Lacoste invested $480 million to build a new plant in Vietnam. For any single company like Nike, the percentage of company profit derived from international sales can run as high as 37%. Fortunately for the sport marketer, there are a variety of ways to investigate foreign markets, and the U.S. government is one of the best sources for this information.

As an example, the U.S. Information Agency (www.usia.gov) manages U.S. pavilions at the world trade expos around the globe. The expos create excellent opportunities for American firms to demonstrate their products and services to worldwide consumers. One example was the Volvo Sports Design Forum in Munich where snowboard manufacturer Burton utilized the opportunity to discuss and showcase their new snowboard products designed specifically for women (Walzer, 2005). Information and contacts obtained through the United States Information Agency offices and their numerous publications can be invaluable in developing a network of sport professionals.

Other government offices in the Department of State also have reams of information about foreign economies that is available at little or no cost. Consideration also should be given to contacting the U.S. Agency for International Development, which has as its main purpose improving trade with developing countries.

Interestingly, most foreign governments are also attempting to attract U.S. business and have personnel at their embassy to accommodate the needs of marketers. Brief meetings or telephone conversations with their staff are often beneficial during the early stages of project development. Other sources for international marketing contacts include international trade associations, economic development councils at the state or local level, and international trade shows. With a little digging, even small sport companies can obtain quality information for entering the global marketplace.

According to Tuller (1991), key issues include: whether a market economy exists or one that is government controlled, the existing market demand, growth, and competitive forces, U.S. government trade policies, and the local government policies toward trade with the United States. Each factor should be evaluated, and as Pride and Ferrell (2010) noted, a company must thoroughly analyze the environment before entering a foreign market. As when marketing to domestic customers, marketers must evaluate cultural, social, technological, political, and economic forces in target regions. Considerable attention over the past 15 years has been focused in varying degrees on Japan, the Pacific Rim, Europe, South America, and developing nations throughout the world. In no particular order, a discussion of several of these markets follows.

Japan, China and Asia

Why, you might ask, has this section been called Japan, China and Asia? Aren't Japan and China part of Asia? Yes, from a geographical perspective, but not from a marketing point of view. For many years Japan and China have presented obstacles to American sport marketers. The climate has appeared positive for marketers, with a stable hard currency and an attractive market size. However, as a result of the endless debate over Japan's high tariffs, its complex system of distribution and sales, and governmental reluctance to encourage foreign business activity, sport marketers have not generally been successful. Regardless, many sports companies have taken the approach of trying to sell the Japanese on American products.

China, with a population in excess of 1.3 billion people (22% of the world population), has commanded considerable attention from sport marketers. Trade with China has been hobbled by bureaucracy and political interference with business for many

Asia has proven to be a challenging market for many international brands. © Jianbing lee | Dreamstime.com

years. Yet the prospects for the future of the sport industry in China are based on a new policy of decreased government intervention and increases in private ownership (Yang, 2005). The increasing international focus on trade with China (2008 Olympics) and its participation in the World Trade Organization (WTO) has improved the situation (Yang, 2005). The official policy for the development of the sport industry in China is to create and market their own brands (as evidenced by the emergence of Li Ning). The government believes that too much of the productivity of China has gone to furthering international brands such as Nike and adidas and that the shift must now be to home-grown Chinese brands. Estimates reveal that China imported $1.2 trillion in products for 2008 from the international market, making it the world's largest consumer market. The staging of the 2008 Olympic Games in Beijing accelerated the pace of growth for Chinese brands as well as for the Chinese market.

Asia, as a geographic and social region, is extremely diverse. It ranges from Turkey to Saudi Arabia to the Pacific Islands. Social and political conditions affecting sport vary considerably from predominantly Muslim nations such as Malaysia to the socialist ideology in the People's Republic of China.

Some regions and other industrialized nations (Singapore, South Korea, Taiwan) can provide active, growing markets for both consumption and production of sports products, whereas other nations are still in the stages of economic development. As noted previously for other regions, the U.S. government has also worked to make entry into Asian markets easier. The Asia-Pacific Economic Cooperation alliance, in place since 1989, enabled its 21 member nations to work through many trade barriers to enhance both import and export business (Pride & Ferrell, 2010). Entry into the sports markets of Japan, China and Asia will demand considerable study and analysis, but the rewards can be immense.

Eastern and Western Europe

Considerable attention has already been given to Western Europe. The dynamic changes with the formation of the European Union have in some ways helped sport marketers and in other ways hindered their success. A unified Western European market has allowed much freer access to markets than was previously available, yet the increased competitiveness of EU companies has also increased competition. The generally held view is that in most sport industry segments, the opportunities are still limited and extremely competitive.

Eastern Europe, on the other hand, may provide more opportunities. With pent-up consumer demand and a reduction of government controls, sport purchasing and sponsorship avenues may greatly increase. However, some of the problems that sport marketers will encounter include the lack of hard currency and unstable governments (for example the EU's financial issues with Greece in 2010). It is also important to realize that sport expenditures are often considered luxuries and are made with discretionary funds. However, several marquee events are headed to Russia. Sochi will host the 2014 winter Olympics and Moscow will stage the World Cup in 2018. Other Eastern European communities may well expand their sport economies into the next decade.

The Caribbean and Central and South America

In 1983, the U.S. government passed a law that made trade with the Caribbean nations both more accessible and more lucrative. The Caribbean Basin Initiative (CBI) was designed to increase trade and assist in the economic development of this region. The 1989 report indicated that recreational items and sporting goods were some of the products that had benefited the most from this legislation (Tuller, 1991).

The business climate in the area has been enhanced through this Act. Sport marketers should examine the possibility of taking advantage of the benefits extended through the CBI Act. These include tax breaks and the elimination or reduction of import duties. In addition, special financing programs are available for start-up companies. Of special note is the fact that many of these nations also have special agreements with European nations for importing and exporting goods and services. Therefore, it may behoove the sport marketer to investigate the range of possibilities of operating out of the Caribbean.

Central America presents several points of interest. With the previously discussed free trade possibilities, manufacturing potential exists in the sports goods industry. Depending on the economic and political fortunes of the area, additional consumer demand for both goods and services may also exist. The rapid growth of the surfing industry in countries like Costa Rica may open the doors to increased U.S. exports.

South America has been under the shadow of its severe debt crisis for the past two decades. As mentioned in the section on international economics and finance, triple-digit inflation and hard-currency issues will hamper sports entrepreneurs in South America. The sport marketer should realize that the public interest in sport is especially high. Brazil has secured the 2014 World Cup and the 2016 Summer Olympic Games, so considerable potential exists in numerous market segments.

Conducting business in the Caribbean and Central and South America has positive attributes, but only if the sport marketer is able to cope effectively with the business and political idiosyncrasies of the region. The 2005 CAFTA agreement should accelerate business in the region.

Africa

As diverse and difficult to grasp as the Central and South American markets are, the African market is understood by fewer American companies (Tuller, 1991). Generally, the continent consists of Muslim North Africa, Central, East and West Africa, with South Africa presenting a special case of its own. Sports activities in North Africa are, in line with traditional Muslim view, predominantly male and rooted in tradition. For American sport managers to conduct business here demands an understanding of the culture and the emphasis on sport. Within that context, the markets are available to U.S. representatives.

West Africa has, for the most part, put political upheaval behind itself and is entering an era in which sport market development is possible. Of specific importance will be sports equipment and supplies as well as sport services in coaching and sport management. However, many of these markets offer limited growth potential. As recently as

1990, the product advertised in the window of a sporting goods store was a pair of adidas Rome running shoes, popular in the United States in the early 1970s. Central Africa has yet to achieve the stability conducive to market entry. This will be an area to watch for future growth and development in sport.

In South Africa, enough wealth exists for any multinational corporation to flourish. After the very successful 2010 World Cup, South Africa has played host to many international sport events. However, because of past economic and political practices, a two-tiered economic market exists—a large lower class and a growing upper class. For the sport marketer, both segments offer possibilities. With the political changes in the country in the early 1990s, the lower class was provided greater access to sport and recreational facilities. This created immense demand for sports equipment. Corporate sponsorship and financing for sport activities also created an atmosphere conducive to a growth market. Another factor in favor of expansion into South Africa is the abundance of well-educated and effective sport management personnel. These have been most apparent in South Africa's hosting major international sports events such as the aforementioned 2010 World Cup as well as rugby and auto racing.

As with other regions in the world, the problems of soft currency and political instability (i.e. 2011 unrest in Egypt and Tunisia) will restrict many African sport-marketing opportunities. Yet, with attention to these factors and a careful study of the market, sports marketers can successfully meet the demands of African consumers.

INTERNATIONAL SPORT MARKETING PERSONNEL

The selection of well-trained and experienced personnel is essential. Trying to enter global markets without the expertise of someone experienced in international trade is a common error made by American executives. To arrange financing, market products, or negotiate contracts with foreign customers without assistance from internationally experienced management personnel will always lead to disaster.

A study by *Sports Edge* magazine found that European companies preferred to have U.S. personnel manage U.S. offices and European executives staff their European operations. The issue seems to be that the U.S. market is relatively homogeneous, whereas success in the European market demands a multitude of language skills and cultural sensitivity lacking in many U.S. executives ("Going Global," 2004). One of the main difficulties experienced by foreign market managers was adapting to cultural diversity. The selection of personnel for managing foreign markets or for heading up foreign units is affected by several criteria. Among those found to be most important were: proven domestic marketing ability, foreign national status, prior international training, and a strong desire for global involvement. Personnel training can be performed through a variety of different methods. Some corporations conduct in-house training sessions using the expertise and experience of their existing staff. Some corporations handle the training through their foreign offices. Both of these methods have proven to be successful in the sports environment. Outside resources have also been retained for the training process. This method is often expensive, but without internal expertise, it is essential.

Adaptation to Cultural Diversity

Research has indicated that adaptability to foreign cultures is equal in importance to marketing skills developed in a domestic position. Sport business personnel have a common bond with sport executives in other nations through their athletic experiences; however, culture variations on appropriate business and sport etiquette can sabotage chances for success. The successful sport marketer needs to have a clear understanding of the dos and don'ts of foreign culture. What follows are some national and international customs in business relations.

Before traveling and dealing with international executives, be sure to review the special characteristics of the host nation.

Touching

In much of North America, touching is acceptable between friends, but overt touching of casual acquaintances in a business setting is not tolerated. The local custom in many Latin countries allows for hugs following an introduction. In the Middle East, on the other hand, you may find two men walking down the street holding hands to signify their friendship.

Relationships Between Males and Females

Women have for many years played increasing roles in the conduct of sport business in the United States. Many women serve as CEOs of major sport corporations, sport marketing firms, and professional team franchises. Yet, in other parts of the world, women may not be accepted in business meetings. We believe in equality of the sexes, but this does not mean that everyone in the world does. Your firm must decide whether to do business with countries that have different beliefs about the role of women in business relations and follow a strategy that will produce the best business results.

Drinking

The easiest rule for drinking is to follow the lead of the host. If the host orders a drink, you are welcome to imbibe. Be cautious about bringing alcoholic gifts for your host. Even though you are from the South, possession of a fifth of Southern Comfort will land you in prison in almost any Islamic nation. On the opposite end of the spectrum, refusing a glass of wine in France or a cup of sake in Japan is considered rude. One experience at the International Olympic Academy in Greece found that the Russian delegation's vodka was one of the most cherished barter items between participants—worth at least five Olympic pins.

Gifts

Exchanging gifts is a custom that is more prevalent in other countries than it is in the United States. In fact, in the 1970s the U.S. government passed the Foreign Corrupt Practices Act to curtail bribes and kickbacks. The line is very vague as to what constitutes a payoff and what is a generous gift. Most sport marketers will face difficulty in this area. Try to learn ahead of time from a confidante or fellow sportsperson the tradition and local custom. A good practice is to carry small company pins or souvenirs and to graciously accept similar offerings from your host.

Time and Schedules

In many parts of the world, time is a relative concept. This is especially true in many Latin countries and in the Middle East. Both of the authors of this text have conducted sport-marketing seminars around the globe and can attest to this phenomenon. In Malaysia, an 8:00 a.m. meeting means sometime in the morning, yet just across the bridge in Singapore, you had better be there at 7:30 a.m. to get a seat. One style is not right or wrong; it is just different. It is also important that everyone be clear on how dates are written. The U.S. military writes dates with the day first, then the month and year (i.e., 7 June 2011). This does not create confusion until it appears as 7/6/11. Much of the world uses the same style as does the U.S. military, so when placing the order for the delivery of sport equipment, be specific.

Business Etiquette

Every country will have its unique protocol for conducting business. In England, it is appropriate to wear a jacket and tie for the initial business meeting; however, in Manila, the heat calls for lighter clothing. Whether to wear business attire or casual sports clothing is something that should be explored carefully; it never hurts to ask. When and where to talk business should also be carefully decided. In England, work is work and play is play. Don't confuse the two. However, in many other countries, the best deals are put together on the golf course. You should also be perceptive about special interrelationships. In England, you seat the most important person to your right, according to British military custom. In South Africa, you rise to greet your Afrikaner guest, but don't when meeting a Zulu guest; according to tribal custom, such a movement is confrontational. In South Africa and other parts of southern Africa, sport marketers and event organizers have experienced problems from a simple question: "Do you understand this proposal?" When the answer was "yes," all matters seemed settled. Only later was it determined that all was not well. The polite answer to the question was "yes." To answer "no" would imply that you had not explained it well and be considered insulting. Better initial questions would have been "What is your understanding?" or "Do we have an agreement on these points?" Similarly, in negotiating with Asian executives, "we'll consider it" means "no."

The integration of international marketing into the domestic corporate culture is also of great importance. Depending on the size and nature of the international versus the domestic market, jealousies and conflicts can arise if executives are not adamant in clarifying the priority of both global and national marketing activities. The selection and training of international sport executives encompass many different considerations. They often involve difficult and awkward adaptations to normal business practices. However, if one invests the time, the results can be rewarding.

SPECIFICS OF INTERNATIONAL SPORT MARKETING

The expansion of professional and amateur sports internationally has been well recognized in the sport-marketing arena. Given the trend toward globalization, many U.S. professional leagues are looking to overseas markets. One of the first professional sport organizations to recognize the global demand for its product was the National Basketball Association (NBA). From a historical standpoint, professional boxing has conducted worldwide events for many years, but these have been primarily single events. Professional baseball had early opportunities to restructure and include demand in Asia and Latin America, but decided that such a move was not in its best interests. The NBA, on the other hand, has viewed international markets from an entirely different perspective.

In recognition of the over 200 million people around the world who participate in basketball, the NBA embarked on a global marketing campaign in the 1990s. Sixty-nine percent of international youth (age 12–17) play basketball ("NBA Global," n.d.). The NBA opened the 2010 season with 84 international players on team rosters. Games played in Europe and Asia spawned a growth in NBA television rights of 30% per year with the sales of licensed goods growing at twice that rate ("NBA Global," n.d.). They currently have marketing offices in London and Shanghai. The NBA also held development clinics in Africa and its first game in China (Shanghai) in 2004. The NBA hosts more than 40 international events, including its very successful Basketball Without Borders program for international youth development.

The NBA sells licensed products in more than 200 countries, with international sales accounting for 25% of product sold ("NBA Global," n.d.). Since the success of the 1992 U.S. Olympic (a.k.a. NBA "Dream Team") basketball team, the NBA commissioner recognized the global nature of basketball and positioned the league to capitalize on the phenomenon (Ober, 1992). In 2011, as part of the league's celebration of Martin Luther King, Jr. Day, the NBA gave international fans the chance to watch more live games and programming than ever on Slam Dunk Monday. Fans in 100 countries could watch up to 13 live games in 11 languages across Europe, Africa, Latin America, and Asia. The NBA typically schedules over 20,000 hours of international television programming in 43 languages to over 214 countries ("NBA Global," n.d.; NBA and Russell, 2005). International broadcasting produces 15% of the NBA's TV revenues and 20% of its merchandising dollars. In addition, 40% of the NBA's web traffic originates from outside the U.S. Major League Baseball (MLB) has also pushed the international spectrum, signing a $46 million per year television deal with Japanese agency Dentsu, which resold rights to the major broadcaster in Japan. The estimated per-game audience was pegged at 12.5 million with a total of 630 games aired in 2004. Still moving into international markets is the National Football League (NFL), where the popularity and understanding of the game lags. NFL Games are currently available to 500 million homes outside of the U.S. All of the major U.S. sports leagues (MLB, NHL and NFL) play regular season games in international markets (Rosner & Shropshire, 2011).

As the NBA has stressed global marketing, basketball equipment manufactures have followed suit. Nike, Reebok, adidas, and Spalding all saw tremendous growth in global sales of basketballs and basketball shoes in conjunction with NBA positioning. Spalding sells their NBA licensed basketballs through 18,000 retail outlets in 74 countries, which together with their backboards (Huffy division) totaled $3 billion in sales ("NBA and Russell," 2005).

The Ultimate Fighting Championships (UFC) has hosted 26 events internationally. Notable cities in which the UFC has held events are: London, Abu Dhabi, Sydney, Manchester, Cologne, Dublin, and Tokyo. Future events are expected to be held in Renfrewshire, Scotland and Rio de Janeiro, Brazil. In 2010, the UFC hired former NBA executive Mark Fischer to expand the league's presence in Asia. Fischer was the former director of NBA Asia, and speaks fluent Mandarin Chinese. The UFC bases its success on the notion that combat sports are truly more international in appeal than sports like American football and cricket.

World tournaments and international events are at the center of many international marketing activities. Because the recognition and value of international events grew considerably in the 1980s and 1990s, most television agreements, sponsorship contracts, and licensing programs have necessarily become international. Without attention

Group A	Group E
South Africa—adidas France—adidas Uruguay—Puma Mexico—adidas	Cameroon—Puma Japan—adidas Netherlands—Nike Denmark—adidas
Group B	Group F
Argentina—adidas Nigeria—adidas Greece—adidas South Korea—Nike	Italy—Puma Paraguay—adidas Slovakia—adidas New Zealand—Nike
Group C	Group G
England—Umbro Algeria—Puma Slovenia—Nike USA—Nike	Brazil—Nike North Korea—Legea Ivory Coast—Puma Portugal—Nike
Group D	Group H
Germany—adidas Australia—Nike Ghana—Puma Serbia—Nike	Spain—adidas Switzerland—Puma Honduras—Joma Chile—Brooks

Figure 2.1. World Cup Sponsors by Group.

to these details, sport marketers could find themselves in the same situation as Nike during the 1992 Olympic Games, when another company in Spain had registered the word *Nike*, thereby complicating the U.S. firm's marketing efforts.

The international reach of the fitness business is also noteworthy. Overseas clubs call on U.S. fitness experts to fashion American-style clubs that meet the demands of style-conscious clientele. The depth of the market is such that the IDEA Health & Fitness Association has representatives in 70 foreign countries. The sport of soccer (football, in the international community) is the most popular sport on television across the globe. The projected worldwide cumulative audience for the 2010 World Cup was over 40 billion. This popularity has affected the sport industry in many ways. Many of the world's top teams have been able to secure sponsorship from multinational corporations. Adidas outfitted the referees and supplied all World Cup licensed gear. In addition, they sponsored 12 national teams (including the champion Spain) and sold about $1.8 billion in licensed product. Nike sponsored 9 of the World Cup teams, including the runner-up Netherlands. After the Cup, Nike shelled out $64 million a year, four times what adidas had been paying, to grab sponsorship of the French national team from 2011 to 2018. A list of national teams and their sponsors can be found in Figure 2.1.

It should also be noted that global demographics are significantly different from those in the United States. An amazing 70% of the world's consumers reside in developing countries. The United States has an aging population, yet in much of the developing world, the population is considerably more young and becoming even younger. Children tend to buy shoes more frequently than adults do, which contributes to many of the marketing decisions for sporting goods manufactures.

TRENDS FOR THE FUTURE

As the United States and many leading economic powers evolve into information societies and reduce their strength in manufacturing, the licensing of sport manufacturing technology and professional services will be a major growth area in the sport industry. Sporting goods companies and sport consultants will protect products through extensive licensing and manufacturing agreements and will issue "covenants not to compete" to ensure the protection of their intellectual properties. The result will be a greater emphasis on strategic alliances, mergers, and joint ventures than has existed in the past.

Sport marketers will begin to think more of international demographics in the development of products and services in the sport industry. Pan-European consumers will begin to develop more similarities than differences as EU markets mature. Around the world, the newly industrialized nations will begin to demand more sport-related products and services, and new markets will emerge. However, friction between the countries that supply the cheap labor for sporting goods production and those that consume the goods will continue.

Cause-related sport marketing will also make favorable impressions on consumers. These humanistic trends must be incorporated into the operation of all sport organizations in the global environment. Further, the line between sport and entertainment events will continue to blur as the two industries collide.

As shown by the developments outlined in this chapter and evidence in the professional literature, there will undoubtedly be a greater need for internationally trained and educated sport managers. Professionals in the area and aspiring sport managers should become well versed in international sports affairs. This training will open a vast new job market and should provide an array of exciting experiences.

CHAPTER SUMMARY

The purpose of this chapter was to provide information about the global marketplace for the sport marketer. It is clear that sport is a major component in the global economy and that sport marketers must be prepared to work in this environment. Specific skills and knowledge regarding the international banking system, world sport structure, and the application of marketing principles in specific cultural contexts are necessary to succeed in international markets, and sport marketers must obtain the requisite training. Furthermore, Pride and Ferrell (2010) noted that marketers must "customize marketing mixes according to cultural, regional and national differences" (p. 115). The global sport marketplace provides a wealth of opportunities for corporations and organizations that commit to spending the time required for market research and flexibility in market perception.

DISCUSSION QUESTIONS

1. Diagram the relationship of the International Olympic Committee to a specific international federation. Include a discussion of how each functions with the United States Olympic Committee and a national governing body in the United States.
2. What are the keys to successful banking in international sport marketing?
3. How does marketing a sports product internationally differ from marketing the same product in the United States?

SUGGESTED EXERCISES

1. Investigate opening a Swiss bank account.
2. How would you handle the following situation? You have just completed a consulting project negotiating sponsorship deals for the Lithuanian National Basketball team and were due to be paid $10,000 in U.S. dollars. At the last minute, you are informed that they can pay you only in the local currency. What is that currency? How much of it would you get? Would you accept payment in that form, and if not, what would be an alternative?

PROFESSIONAL ASSOCIATIONS AND ORGANIZATIONS

World Federation of the Sporting Goods Industry

La Maison du Sport
CH-1936 Verbier Switzerland
www.wfsgi.org

United States Information Agency

301 4th Street SW
Washington, DC 20547

International Events Group

640 N. LaSalle, Suite 6000
Chicago, IL 60610-37777
www.sponsorship.com
1-800-834-4850

SUGGESTED READINGS

Axtell, R. E. (1991). Gestures: *The do's and taboos of body language around the world*. New York, NY: John Wiley & Sons.

Chalip, L., & Thoma, J. (1993). *Sport governance in the global community*. Morgantown, WV: Fitness Information Technology.

Morrison, T., Conaway, W., & Borden, G. (1994). *Kiss, bow, or shake hands*. Holbrook, MA: Bob Adams, Inc.

3

The Sport Marketing Process

INTRODUCTION

Chapters 1 and 2 described the sport business industry and its global nature. This chapter covers the process, tasks, and activities of sport marketing—in other words, *how to do sport marketing*.

As presented in Chapter 1, we know that sport business management is a field of study focused on and specializing in one industry—that of sport business. Sport marketing is a component of sport management. Thus, sport marketing also focuses on the sport business industry. In this chapter, we present the process of sport marketing with an overview of all of its activities and tasks. Chapters with in-depth details about each of the activities follow throughout the book.

Sport marketing is, simply, the process of offering products that the consumer wants. Of course, it's a little more complicated and involved than that! This chapter will provide an overview of the Sport Marketing Management Model, which is an illustration of the process, activities, and tasks related to sport marketing.

WHAT IS SPORT MARKETING?

What is different about sport marketing when compared to general marketing? In marketing, one studies basic marketing principles and fundamentals as generalized to numerous industries. What makes sport marketing different is that it is specialized to one industry. This allows the focusing of principles and fundamentals to one area of expertise, thus allowing for a more specialized area of study. In a sport marketing class, students study their industry of choice for a career; in a marketing class, however, students see examples of all kinds of vastly different industries, from toothpaste to cars and from apples to tires. This lack of specialization means that students will have to wait until they enter a particular industry in order to learn that industry, then apply and modify marketing principles while on the job. Students in a sport marketing class are able to study their singular choice of industry, learning exactly how the principles and fundamentals have been applied and already modified to that one industry, and will be able to "hit the ground running" upon beginning their jobs in the sport business industry.

Simply stated, sport marketing is the process to give the consumer what they want. It is the process that is the heart of the business. If the sport marketing process is successful, the business will be successful. The formal definition of sport marketing follows:

Sport marketing is the process of designing and implementing activities for the production, pricing, promotion, and distribution of a sport product to satisfy the needs or desires of consumers and to achieve the company's objectives.

Sport marketing is a complex and dynamic part of every sport business. In fact, most business decisions are based on the activities of marketing. All sport marketing activities are developed with specific and strategic decisions based on research and information. These activities are typically based on a strategic process, or model. This chapter will present the Sport Marketing Management Model, which illustrates the activities and process

> Simply stated, sport marketing is the process to give the consumer what they want. It is the process that is the heart of the business. If the sport marketing process is successful, the business will be successful.

> Sport marketing is the process of designing and implementing activities for the production, pricing, promotion, and distribution of a sport product to satisfy the needs or desires of consumers and to achieve the company's objectives.

of sport marketing (see Figure 3.2 on p. 93). Each activity is presented in an individual chapter after this one.

WHEN DID SPORT MARKETING ORIGINATE?

To understand sport marketing, it is first important to understand its components and how its definition was developed. The definition is derived primarily from sport marketing theory, which is built from various fields of study, marketing theory, sport business industry knowledge, and the sport marketing and sport management bodies of knowledge. Although sport marketing textbooks and courses are relatively new when compared to other fields of study, such as law or teaching, sport marketing is as old as ancient sports and sport events. Sport businesses have been practicing sport marketing for as long as sport events, activities, and other sport businesses have existed—and that is many thousands of years. As was mentioned in Chapter 1, it is ironic that although we have been practicing sport management forever, it is only within the past 50 to 60 years that we have created studies and degrees in sport management.

Historically, sport marketing evolved as sports managers invented ways to promote sports events and products, and borrowed marketing tactics used in other business ar-

> Sport marketing has been practiced for as long as sport events and activities have existed; however, it is a new academic field of study.

eas. The development of sport marketing fundamentals is therefore based on practitioner invention, basic marketing principles, and from bodies of knowledge in a variety of related fields. The practice and activities of sport marketing are primarily based on its primary and foundational discipline—marketing. However, as previously stated, it is not enough that students who will work in the sport business industry take only marketing classes in a business school. It is imperative that a sport management student's college education be primarily comprised of sport management courses.

Sport marketing is one of the most important functions of a sport business. This is because the sport marketing activities will define the business. The growth of the sport industry, especially over the past few decades, is phenomenal and shows no signs of slowing. By some accounts, it has grown from the 23rd largest industry in the early 1980s to perhaps the largest industry in the United States (see arguments in Chapter 1).

Growth partially means that there are increasing numbers of sport companies and products; each sport product or company is competition. The concept of competition in business is the idea that a sport business is competing against another business to win the consumer's dollar. Winning in business means staying in business at a successful level. Success is defined by the sport company and is usually measured by achieving the company's objectives.

Companies in the sport business industry have plenty of competitors, including those that are directly as well as indirectly related. A sport company today must employ sport marketing as a significant business function to the extent that every facet of the company is guided by sport marketing concepts. It is the function that

- guides the sport business toward identifying the products that consumers need or desire;
- identifies and analyzes competitors;
- develops pricing strategies;
- develops the promotional strategies to get the consumer to the product; and
- identifies how to get the product to the consumer.

DEFINING MARKETING

Marketing is a business process that developed and evolved along with the development and growth of business. Bartels (1988) wrote that marketing is the element that "revolutionized the economy of the country and gradually affected the whole world" (p. 1). The word *marketing* comes from the word *market*, which means a group of buyers and sellers (consumers and producers) negotiating the terms of exchange for something. Buyers are consumers, and there are many different categories of consumers. Sellers can be manufacturers, producers, retailers, promoters, and wholesalers. Negotiation takes many forms, such as deciding to buy or not to buy simply based on a nonnegotiable price; making offers and counteroffers until agreement is reached; and determining a fair or satisfactory exchange. Terms can involve negotiating over delivery and acceptance, warranty, after-sales service, payment methods, and promises of quality. The exchange can involve many factors, such as delivery, terms of payment or trade, and transaction. Finally, the word *something* in the definition usually involves the trade of something for something else; "something" could be goods, services, ideas, benefits, perks, deeds, and, of course, money. One example of the market at work is a flea market. It is an area, or a marketplace, where sellers bring their wares and buyers come to shop. At a flea market, it is expected that buyers and sellers will haggle in the exchange process to trade something for something else.

Usually, in this setting, the buyer and seller negotiate over the worth, or value (price), of a good. The seller has established a price based on factors of worth. It is highly likely that the buyer has an idea of price based on factors of worth. Sometimes the two align, but sometimes the buyer has is a different price in mind. Buyer and seller negotiate until some exchange agreement is reached.

In another example, the value of goods in a sporting goods store is set using pricing strategies, one of the activities of sport marketing. Pricing strategies are developed from information about the 4 Cs of sport marketing (refer to Table 3.5 on p. 96; Pitts & Stotlar, 2007). The buyer typically enters the store and decides whether or not to purchase the good at its "sticker" price. Usually there is no negotiating between buyer and seller like the kind of bargaining found, and expected, in a flea market setting. However, the buyer can send a message to the seller about price by making the decision to buy or not to buy. If a product is not selling, the company must determine why. If the company discovers the product does not sell because too many consumers think the price is too high, the company can relay this important information to the producer. The producer then has to analyze the situation and make a decision about whether to change the price. It is not a simple decision of lowering the price because perhaps the price is high due to the high cost of manufacturing the item.

Marketing as a business activity developed and evolved primarily from the study of people and what they buy, how much they will pay, where they want to purchase a product, and how they are affected by promotional tactics and messages. This is called "marketing orientation." Additionally, the elements, functions, principles, and theories of marketing were also developed through the study of many other factors such as industrial production expansion, the invention of new products, the study of human behavior (sociology and psychology), population studies, education and income studies, and studies of new and diverse markets. As a response to these and other factors, a market-driven economy developed. This meant that businesses paid increasing amounts of attention to consumers and studied what the consumers needed or wanted (Bartels, 1988).

Another historical model of marketing that developed was the "production orientation." Manufacturers utilized developments in machines, factory assembly, manufacturing, and transportation to simply make products without much thought to studying consumers first. Many of these manufacturers made products just because they could make them. To sell them, companies employed sales forces to go out and push the products for sales. One tactic was the use of door-to-door salesmen, whose job was to travel throughout neighborhoods, gain entrance, and once inside use pressure sales tactics to coax consumers into purchasing the product, whether or not the consumers wanted or needed the product. This and similar tactics are still used today and can be seen primarily through the use of television "infomercials."

Today's marketing concepts evolved from a simple concept to one that is complex and broad. The concepts are drawn from the social sciences and are more than merely a business activity. Although marketing is a business function that should be a significant part of every company, the functions of marketing should be a critical part of every department within the business. Companies faced with the challenge of achieving profitable growth in an environment of intense competition, product proliferation, and escalating costs must make marketing a priority function throughout the company. Marketing must be a total company effort, and every company should develop a marketing orientation—that is, every task and decision of a company should be made based on its marketing plan.

Today, the marketing orientation concept is more critical than ever, and so is widely used. In a country like the United States, the population has become complex and very diverse. This makes it absolutely necessary to study the consumer thoroughly and modify the company's strategies and products to be successful.

The marketing orientation, or concept, is a philosophy concerning the way a company should be managed. It consists of three requirements (Cravens & Woodruff, 1983):

1. Examine people's needs and wants as the basis of deciding what the business (or economy) will do.
2. Select the best way to meet the consumer's needs that are targeted by the firm.
3. Achieve the organization's performance objectives by meeting the consumer's needs satisfactorily.

In short, the company must study what the consumer wants and provide it. Although this seems like an easy rule to follow, there are many functions that must be performed, and must receive critical analysis and proper management in order for successful marketing decisions to be developed. It is not an easy task to identify what someone wants or needs and then to provide it. The human being is a complex organism affected by a remarkable variety of influencing factors. Although the marketer might discover what the consumer wants today, that desire may be different tomorrow. Therefore, studying consumers must be a constant activity.

Complicating the task of producing what the consumer wants is the company's capacity to manufacture it, distribute it, and offer it. In addition, the company must consider its values and objectives and decide if it can ethically offer the products. Therefore, careful management of the marketing functions and critical analysis before decision making can increase the company's chances for success. The incorporation of a marketing management strategy is critical.

SPORT MARKETING FUNDAMENTALS AND THEORY

Sport marketing is a relatively new academic field of study. It does not yet contain a substantial body of knowledge when compared to many other fields of study. However, the body of knowledge is growing. Sport marketing is very new when compared to fields of study like law, education, management, medicine, or marketing. For example, this textbook is one of only a few textbooks about the fundamentals of sport marketing. In addition, there are three academic journals that are specifically focused on sport marketing: *Sport Marketing Quarterly*, the *International Journal of Sport Management and Marketing*, and the *International Journal of Sports Marketing and Sponsorship*. There are other journals that focus on sport marketing elements, such as the new *Journal of Sport Communication*.

Table 3.1. The Sport Marketing Association
Mission:
SMA endeavors to develop beneficial relationships between sport marketing professionals and academicians through expansion of the field's body of knowledge and multiple forums for professional interaction.
Vision Statement:
The Sport Marketing Association (SMA) is established to develop a mutually beneficial relationship between professional practitioners and academicians engaged in the business of marketing sport. The Association's fundamental focus will be to develop and expand the body of knowledge in the sport marketing field, disseminating the resulting research findings and market-oriented solutions via mass as well as targeted media sources, internal and external to the Association. Secondarily, the Association will provide a forum for professional interaction among practicing sport marketers, sport marketing academicians, and students dedicated to this sport industry segment. The Association strives to include all members of the professional sport marketing community that seek to impact future developments within the academic discipline and the field of sport marketing.
History:
SMA was founded in 2002 by a team of sport marketing professors that included such individuals as Dr. Larry McCarthy, Dr. Greg Bennett, Dr. Richard Irwin, Dr. Brenda Pitts, Dr. David Stotlar, Mr. Jim Kahler, Dr. Jacquelyn Cuneen, Dr. Andy Ostrow, Dr. William Sutton, among others.   The Sport Marketing Association (SMA), a new professional association for sport marketing practitioners and academics, was founded recently at the International Conference on Sport & Entertainment Business in Columbia, South Carolina. The mission of the SMA, which will house business operations at the University of Memphis Bureau of Sport & Leisure Commerce, is to develop beneficial relationships between sport marketing professionals and academicians through expansion of the field's body of knowledge and multiple forums for professional interaction.   At its inaugural meeting, SMA's Founding Board appointed Dr. Richard L. Irwin of The University of Memphis as President. Mr. Jim Kahler, Executive Director of Arizona State University's MBA Sport Business Program, and former Senior Vice President of Sales and Marketing with the Cleveland Cavaliers/Gund Arena Corporation, to serve as Vice President for Industry Affairs. Dr. Brenda Pitts, Director of the Sport Management Program and the Sport Business Research Center at Georgia State University to serve as the Association's Vice President for Academic Affairs. Dr. Larry McCarthy, from the Center for Sport Management in the Stillman School of Business at Seton Hall University, to serve as the Association's Treasurer.
Source: www.sportmarketingassociation.com

Finally, sport marketing is growing as a singular academic discipline. There is an academic organization, the Sport Marketing Association (SMA), which was established in 2002 (see Table 3.1). Its primary mission is to serve professors and students who have a special interest in sport marketing. It offers a website, an associated journal, *Sport Marketing Quarterly*, and an annual academic conference. The conference program is filled with scholarly research presentations, keynote speakers, industry professional speakers, social activities, special sessions and activities for students, and industry and academic exhibitions. It produces an annual book of papers and a book of conference proceedings (found on the SMA website).

As a course of study, sport marketing has typically been offered as an individual course among several other sport management courses. Today, a few institutions offer two or more sport marketing courses, with the additional ones being focused on specific sport marketing activities such as sport and the media, sport communication, sport sponsorship marketing, sport consumer behavior, and sport marketing research. Additionally, a few institutions offer sport marketing as a concentration area of study. Although sport marketing is being established as an academic discipline, academicians have created two different sport marketing areas of focus (see Figure 3.1).

First, one group of academicians teaches that sport marketing involves just the selling of sports events to two groups of consumers: sports participants and sports specta-

Figure 3.1. Two Concepts of Sport Marketing.

tors. This group tends to use the terminology of "sports" marketing, or, the marketing of sports. One example is those few programs that have a focus on intercollegiate athletics. In these programs, courses and coursework have a focus on the management and marketing aspects of one industry segment, college sports. Students in these programs have an interest in specializing in college sports. This type of specialization is a sign of the positive growth of sport management as a field, showing that some programs now have enough faculty members to cover the basics of sport management and to offer additional courses for specialization in segments of the industry or content areas.

Second, other academicians believe that sport marketing is closely related to the contemporary definition of sport management and the sport industry. That is, sport management is the study and practice of management and business principles in the sport industry. The *sport industry* includes all businesses offering any sport, recreation, fitness, tourism, and leisure-related product (see Table 3.2). As you learned in Chapter 1, there are many different types of sport businesses that offer many different types of products to many different consumers. Therefore, sport marketing should be broad enough so that students will learn how to apply the fundamentals of sport marketing to any sport business, in any industry segment, and to all of its consumers.

In this book, we use the contemporary definitions of sport marketing and the broad concept of the sport business industry to define sport marketing and the Sport Marketing Management Model. Students in sport marketing and sport management might end up in jobs and careers in any one of the numerous different segments of the industry.

Although sport marketing is a developing field of study, this does not mean that marketing has never been used in the sport industry. As pointed out earlier, marketing practices and principles have been used in the sport industry throughout history and are still used today. Sport marketing professionals have drawn from and continue to draw from marketing and other fields of study, as well as consulting with each other, and borrowing ideas from competitors. In addition, academicians and practitioners are hard at work conducting research in sport mar-

Table 3.2. Some Segments of the Sport Business Industry

Participant Sport
College Sports
Sporting Goods
Sports Apparel and Footwear
Sports Television Media
Sports Social Media
Sports Marketing
Sports Facility Management
Sports Event Management
Sponsorship Management
Sports Athlete Management
Sports Medicine
Sports Governing Organizations
Sport Law Firms
Licensing and Merchandising
Sports Facility Architectural Design
Sports Tourism
Outdoor Recreation Sports
Auto Racing
Boat Racing
Extreme Sports
Adventure Sports
Snow Sports Industry
High School Sports
Sports Educational Books
Sport Management Education
Sports Magazine Media
Olympic Sports
Youth Sports
Masters and Senior Sports
Rodeo Sports
Fishing

keting, as is evidenced by the studies published in a variety of research journals and trade magazines. Further, this book adds to the young but growing body of knowledge in sport marketing. As marketing principles are applied to the sport industry, they are modified as necessary. As marketing strategies and models in the sport industry are studied and research is published, the body of knowledge will be developed. As higher education responds to the needs of the sport industry, textbooks, courses, and curriculum in sport marketing will be developed. Each will add to the development of the body of knowledge and to sport marketing as a field of study, and will serve as the foundation of a theory of sport marketing.

The theory of sport marketing as it is being produced in academia is still developmental and thus constantly evolving. These theories and fundamentals may be used as conceptual frameworks for research. To study the developing theory of sport marketing, we must study the foundation from which it is being built. Foundation includes research, fundamentals, principles, theories, and practices. The foundation of sport marketing knowledge is built primarily from five broad fields of study, and from studying and consulting with sport marketing professionals in the industry. The fields of study include sport studies, business administration studies, social science studies, technology, and communications (see Table 3.3).

Theory can be defined as "a system of assumptions, accepted principles, and rules of procedure devised to analyze, predict, or explain a set of phenomena" (Webster's, 1978). Theory is built from a foundation of research and knowledge and may be tested

Table 3.3. Contemporary sport marketing theory. These fields of study are serving as the foundation and framework to build the fundamentals of sport marketing.

Contemporary Sport Marketing Theory		
Sport Studies	Sport Management Psychology of Sport Recreation Management Sports Tourism	Sociology of Sport Leisure Management Legal Aspects of Sport Sports Information
Business Administration	Marketing Economics Consumer Behavior Entrepreneurialship	Finance Business Law International Business
Communications	Media Studies Broadcasting Journalism	Advertising Public Relations
Social Sciences	Cultural Studies Labor Market Studies Personnel Management	Population Studies Human Relations
Technology	E-commerce Internet marketing	Web business Web platform

through research and application. Research can be defined as a systematic and organized investigation. When the research is complete, the results may be used in a variety of ways, some of which are to add to one's knowledge, to add to a body of solutions for problems, and to discover answers to specific questions.

Table 3.4. Areas of Study in Sport Business Management
Sport Sponsorship Analysis
Sport Consumer Behavior
Consumer Market Identification
Legal Issues of Sport Marketing
Economic Impact of Sports Events
Sports Tourism
Sporting Goods Consumption Patterns
Sport and Destination Marketing
Cultural Factors and Sport Consumption
International Issues of Sport Marketing
Sport Facility Management Research
Social Media and Sport Research
College Sports Management
Olympic Sports Management
Youth Sports Administration
Masters and Senior Sports Consumer Patterns
Rodeo Sports Management
Fishing Consumer Behavior
Extreme Sports Trends
Licensing and Merchandising in Sport Business
Economic Impact in Sport
E-commerce and Sport

Within each broad field of study are specific or specialized areas of study from which sport marketing is developing its body of knowledge. Within sport studies, these specializations include sport management, sport sociology, sport psychology, leisure management, recreation administration, legal aspects of sport, sport tourism, and sport information. Within business, the specializations include marketing, economics, finance, business law, and consumer behavior. In communications, the areas include journalism, public relations, media studies, advertising, and broadcasting. The areas in the social sciences include human relations, cultural studies, population studies, and labor market studies. Technology includes e-commerce, Internet business, and web-based marketing.

Table 3.4 presents a list of some areas of study in sport marketing today. As an example of how academicians and practitioners in sport marketing are using other fields of study to develop the theories in sport marketing, let us consider how the social sciences may be used. Yiannakis (1989) suggested that sport marketing could be strengthened through the study and application of sport sociology. This is still true today. Sociology is the study of human behavior. Sport sociology is the study of human behavior and sport. In sport marketing, an understanding of people and sports will help a sport business be successful.

In a study of sport sociology literature, Yiannakis suggested that sport sociology could make significant contributions to sport marketing and management in the following ways:

1. conceptualization, design, and implementation of good market research;
2. instrument development;
3. interpretation of the findings by grounding both a priori and post hoc explanations in existing knowledge bases;

4. advertising effectiveness by providing essential information bases, especially in the area of lifestyle characteristics;

5. development of a general marketing information base (target market characteristics);

6. exploration and identification of new markets; and

7. introduction of social science orientation to the enterprise.

Yiannakis stated that this involves

> an appreciation of the interactive nature of system forces in the marketing environment and their impact on consumer preferences, underlying patterns and trends and their potential impact on consumer buying readiness, cultural differences and their influence on purchasing decisions, and the role that sport plays in society in terms of influencing values and attitudes, shaping tastes, providing role models, creating new fashions and the like. (p. 105)

Another author, Kates (1998), agrees that research and theory in sport marketing literature can be greatly enhanced by using each other's theory, methods, and insights. Kates writes that "some scholarly work within consumer research has focused upon the study of subcultures" in sport, and that this work is providing "theoretical frameworks and substantive findings regarding the enculturation of people into a new set of norms and values while interacting with others. . . . By linking these discourses, new marketing tactics can be formulated. . . . [By] bringing the discourses of consumer behavior, sport sociology, and sport marketing together, new research agendas and new marketing insights will result" (p. 29).

Sport Marketing knowledge is developed from the following fields of study:
• Sport Studies
• Business
• Marketing
• Communications
• Social Sciences
• Technology
• Social Media

Research "will significantly decrease the uncertainty in making marketing decisions" (Schwarz & Hunter, 2008, p. 43). It is important to note that the underlying purpose of research is "to generate information" (Li, Pitts, & Quarterman, 2008). As Chapter 4 will emphasize, information is critical for making decisions and developing strategies for the company, and research is the vehicle that provides the information needed.

One of the critical areas in which research is essential is the consumer. Throughout the evolution of sport marketing, critical analysis and research of the many different groups of such consumers in the sport industry as the African-American sport market (Armstrong, 1998), the Hispanic sport market (McCarthy, 1998), the gay and lesbian sport market (Pitts, 1998, 1999), and the Generation X sport market (Shoham, Rose, Kropp, & Kahle, 1997) can provide a sport business with the knowledge and understanding needed in today's increasingly diverse industry. Today's emphasis on studying consumers is just as critical. In fact, there are vast numbers of sport businesses developed and owned by these markets that offer sport products specifically for these markets, as we learned in Chapter 1. This new knowledge and understanding can then be used to formulate successful marketing strategies. Therefore, the theories existing in those fields must be used in sport marketing and in studying the sport industry; these theories should continue to be used in the development of a sport marketing theory.

Studying and Consulting with Sport Marketing Professionals

It is also important to study and consult with sport marketing professionals in the industry. These are the individuals who practice sport marketing. As such, they have key ideas about what works and what does not work for their business, or perhaps for their industry segment. Therefore, when working toward developing the fundamentals of sport marketing, it is important to study and gather the knowledge of practicing sport marketing professionals.

This can be done in a number of ways. Both authors of this textbook, for example, have worked in the industry and have studied and consulted with numerous sport marketing professionals. The following examples offer some ideas of working with, studying, or consulting with sport marketing professionals. One way to work with professionals is to develop a relationship with locals. In Atlanta, Georgia, the Georgia Dome is a world-class sports facility. Meet with the sport marketing professionals who work there and take time to talk with them about their jobs and responsibilities. Ask them about everything they do. Talk to them about what works and does not work at the facility. Use that knowledge and information to add to or make adjustments to what you already know about sport marketing.

As another example, conduct survey or interview research about sport marketing methods used at the local college in the athletics department. The purpose of the study might be to examine specific promotional methods, such as the use of sponsorship signage, to determine its effectiveness. Use the results to inform what you already know and to modify it if needed.

Lastly, share your information with the professional and ask him/her to critique it. As an example, the authors of this book share the book with local sport marketing professionals and ask them to evaluate what is correct and what is probably not correct about sport marketing fundamentals in the book. With this knowledge coming directly from professionals in the field, the content of the book can be adjusted. That means that students using the book receive information about sport marketing that is exactly what is being used in the field.

The Sport Marketing Management Model

Sport marketing is a process of activities designed to optimize the sport business. A process is a continuous cycle; therefore, marketing is a function that never ends. The Sport Marketing Management Model is an illustration of the sport marketing process, and shows its main components and activities (see Figure 3.2). This model should be the guide, or road map, for managing the company's marketing functions. The model illustrates the elements of marketing, the succession of elements and functions, the process of managing, and the interdependency of the elements.

Figure 3.2. The Sport Marketing Management Model.

An overview of the model, sport marketing management, each element, and the process as a whole is presented in the remainder of this chapter. Subsequent chapters present each sport marketing element with its activities in detail.

THE SPORT COMPANY'S MISSION AND GOALS

Every business exists for a purpose; each company strives to stay consistent with its purpose in order to enhance its chances for success. The company's purpose may be found in its stated mission. For example, an intercollegiate athletics program's mission may be "to provide sports participation opportunities for the college student." In another example, a city parks and recreation department's mission might be "to provide the means for leisure pursuit for the city's population." The company will offer products with the intention of meeting the company's mission; the mission is the reason the company exists. All marketing activities must begin with a clear understanding of the company's mission and the company's current situation. The stated mission must be accompanied by the company's objectives. The objectives provide specific and concrete direction, whereas the mission statement often may be broad and ambiguous. The objectives should state the exact direction that management wants for the company. For example, whereas the

A clear picture of a company's purpose can be found in its mission statement. © Adam gregor | Dreamstime.com

mission of the college athletics department is to provide athletic participation opportunities for the college student, its objectives will be detailed concerning what the athletic department wants to achieve within a given period of time.

An example of such an objective might be to win a national championship in track-and-field within five years. The direction is established in the objective, and the college will implement programs and strategies that will most likely achieve the stated objective.

In another example, a professional women's basketball league may have an objective to increase consumer awareness of its existence and to increase attendance by 20% by the end of the regular season. The marketer must make decisions and implement strategies that will take the league toward attaining the stated objective.

SPORT MARKETING RESEARCH AND INFORMATION COLLECTION

Information is critical to the sport business. Information is necessary in making every decision and for formulating strategies. Information is gained via collection and discovery through research. As you can see in the Model (Figure 3.2), research is the base upon which all decisions are made.

We exist in a world that seems small and interconnected because electronics, communication systems, and transportation are efficient, fast, and relatively affordable. The amount of information produced and disseminated through electronics and communication systems is massive. In fact, the last several years have been labeled the Information Era. Moreover, we are currently living and working in an era in which electronics, media, and communications are literally changing the face of business, and in some ways changing how business is conducted. A factor largely responsible for this is the Internet. Business on the Internet has acquired several names, including e-commerce (the e stands for electronic), e-business, web-based business, and emailing. The Internet has created a new mode of delivery for business. We can, if we wish, do nearly everything, from working to shopping for necessities, and never leave the chair in front of the computer. The marketer must be able to conduct research, obtain information, analyze the results of research and the data gathered, envision uses for the information, and formulate strategic decisions based on the research and information. In addition, the marketer must have or create a system to manage the information and research.

Sport marketing research is the collection and analysis of information. What types of information and how data are gathered is specifically organized and determined by what question is in need of answering. For example, if the company's product isn't selling, the question becomes, "Why isn't this product selling?" Research is then designed to gather and analyze data to try to answer this question.

The sport marketer will need the information gained through research to formulate decisions and strategies concerning every aspect of the company and its marketing plan. Marketing research usually focuses on one problem. At the same time, broad databases may be established and maintained concerning specific aspects of the company or the company's consumer markets and competitors.

The massive amount of information requires a sophisticated information management system. This is usually called a *marketing information system*, or MIS. The purpose of an MIS is to collect, store, and retrieve specific information. An MIS can be as simple as a few index cards or as complex as a state-of-the-art computer system. Some of the determining factors include the company's capability for funding a system, the amount and type of information to be managed, and the ways in which the marketer will need to use the information.

The research and information collected are needed to make decisions about all elements of the business. These elements are called the marketing mix, and also called the "4 Ps of marketing"—product, price, place, and promotion. Information is needed to make decisions about the company's product(s), about setting prices and formulating pricing strategies, about distribution (place) and strategies, and about promotion plans and strategies. The information needed falls into four categories called the "4 Cs of marketing"—consumer, company, competitor, and climate (Pitts & Stotlar, 2007). Information about any one or more of the 4 Cs is needed in making decisions about the marketing mix elements.

THE FOUR Cs: CONSUMER, COMPANY, COMPETITOR, AND CLIMATE

Everyone in a sport business must possess knowledge about many different things. These factors have direct and indirect influence on the company that must be used or referred to when making decisions and developing strategies. The sport business should develop a way to constantly study and analyze them. Most all of this information falls into four categories called "The 4 Cs of Sport Marketing"—consumer, company, competitor, and climate (refer to Figure 3.3; as developed and coined by Pitts & Stotlar, 2007). The following sections contain brief descriptions of each. Thorough details of each are presented throughout later chapters.

Figure 3.3. The 4 Cs.

Consumer

The sport marketer needs to know and understand the people (consumers) who need or want the company's products—see Table 3.5 and Figure 3.4. This is called *consumer analysis*. With this knowledge, the marketer may make educated strategic decisions for the company that will position the company for success.

The various factors of the *consumer* are demographics, psychographics, geographics, behavioralistic characteristics, and product functions and benefits (see Figure 3.4). *Demographics* include descriptive information about people such as age, gender, education, and income. *Psychographics* are psychological characteristics that relate to an individual's

Table 3.5. The 4 Cs of Sport Marketing: Consumer, Company, Competitor, and Climate		
Consumer:	Demographics Geographics Product Functions and Benefits	Psychographics Behavioralistic
Company:	Mission and Goals Financial Strength Brand Identity and Strength	Human Resources Market Share Competitive Advantage
Competitor:	Industry Data Market Share Strengths and Weaknesses Competitive Advantage	Competitors Data Brand Strength Trends
Climate:	Economic Climate Cultural Issues Technological Trends Community Industry Trends	Political Legal Issues Education Trends Ethical Issues Media Trends
Source: Pitts & Stotlar, 2007		

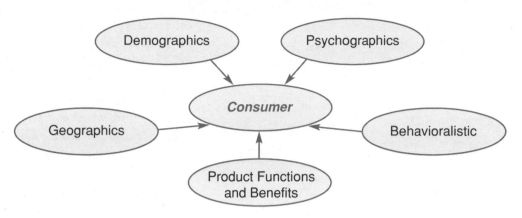

Figure 3.4. The 4 Cs—Consumer.

personal life and lifestyle, such as attitudes, opinions, values, interests, activities, and relationship status. *Geographics* are variables that relate to geographical information that are descriptive about location, area, region, or country. *Behavioralistic characteristics* are those that include behavior-related variables or attributes such as consumer behavior, purchase behavior, brand loyalty, product usage rate, benefits sought, and user status. *Product functions and benefits* are those variables that are related to the function(s) of the product for the consumer, and the benefits that the consumer derives from a product, such as function sought, quality, reliability, predictability, and trialability.

It is also important to identify potential consumers. These are consumers the company might want to attract. For example, you are the owner of a soccer club. You currently offer soccer leagues for two age divisions: 29 and under, and 30 and over. You should consider offering other age divisions as well because you are in the unique position to create a product for a new consumer. That is, you could create a 40-and-over division. All of your 30-and-over players will turn 40 one day. They will probably want to continue to play soccer, but they might not want to continue to play against younger players.

The sport marketer must constantly study and analyze existing consumers and the potential for new consumers. This will afford the sport marketer the knowledge needed to develop new products, change existing products, set new goals, and make other strategic decisions for the company.

Company

The study of one's own company is vital to success. One example of a method of company study is a SWOT analysis. SWOT is an acronym for Strengths, Weaknesses, Opportunities, and Threats. Other variables that should be studied include mission and goals, financial strength, production, market share, brand identity and strength, competitive advantage, and product management (see Figure 3.5).

The information is useful in informing most decisions concerning almost every move the company considers. For example, you wouldn't plan to buy another company unless you had a strong financial position, could absorb the other company under current company structure, and could take over the operation of the other company. In an-

Figure 3.5. The company and its factors that affect sport marketing strategies.

other example, your company might be considering entering a market with a product new to the company. A complete analysis of the barriers to entry, competitors, and whether or not your company can afford such a move is vital to this decision.

Market share, another critical factor to consider, is how well the company is positioned in the marketplace in relation to how much of the market the company commands. It is the percentage of a total market, either in sales volume or value, accounted for by a brand, product, or company.

Brand identity and strength are important factors. A company's brand is its distinctive name or product line that identifies the company or a product. Brand strength is a measure of consumer recognition and loyalty to a brand. The benefits of a company having a strong brand include such factors as increased purchase speed, increased product acceptance, increase in brand insistence and loyalty, and decrease in price erosion. Competitive advantage is a relative advantage in variables or attributes that one company has that allows it to outperform and hold an advantage over its competitors, and should also be carefully considered.

Competitor

Studying the competitor involves studying both the whole industry, industry segments, and closely related competitors (see Figure 3.6). For example, let's say that your company is a sport marketing research business. It is important for you to study sport marketing research companies that sell the same products. At the same time, it is important for you to study what is happening in the sport marketing research industry to help you make informed decisions.

The sport marketer must continuously study and analyze the competition to gain an understanding of what competitors are doing, what they are capable of doing, and how these activities might impact upon his/her business. With this information, the marketer will be able to change existing strategies, if needed, and formulate new strategies.

Competitor analysis involves collecting information about such important characteristics as market share, brand identity and strength, trends, and competitive advantage.

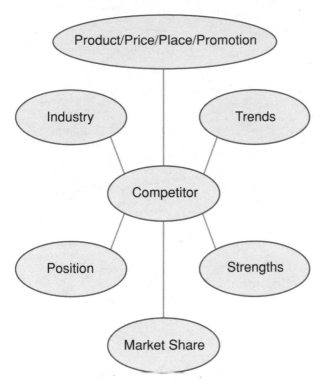

Figure 3.6. The competitor and its factors that affect sport marketing strategies.

Climate

An important responsibility of the sport business management team is to analyze the climate (see Figure 3.7). *Climate*, also referred to as environment or atmosphere, refers to the current situational factors in a society that can affect the sport business. These include the following aspects of society: economic, social and cultural, political, ethical, trends, technological, community, education, industry, media, and legal. With an analysis of each of these in specific relation to its effects on the sport business, the sport marketer must determine how each can influence the company (Gauws, 1997). For example, today there is heightened sensitivity toward civil rights and humanity and thus not offending groups of people. Therefore, titles, names, and logos of some sport businesses have been challenged in relation to their offensiveness to groups. For instance, some sports team's logos that were considered to be offensive and degrading to particular groups of people have been changed.

Economic Climate

The state of the economy could impact the sport company. The sport marketer must analyze the current economic situation and determine its effect on the company. There may be opportunities for success and, on the other hand, the possibility for financial disaster for the company. For example, how did the Great Flood of 1993 affect tourism in St. Louis and specifically spectatorship and gate receipt revenue at Major League Baseball games? How much of a financial impact did the flood have on the parks and recreation industry, and how would a specific recreation area be affected?

Social and Cultural Climate

Cultural and social traditions and attitudes may affect your company. The sport marketer must grasp the social and cultural structures within which the company exists as well as those that exist within the company and analyze the effects on the company and the effects of the company on society. Some examples include (a) public pressure on private golf clubs that have only white members to allow others, and (b) sport organiza-

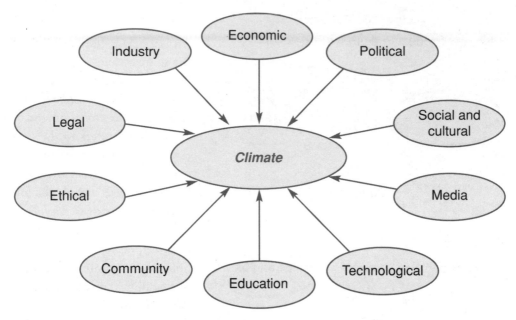

Figure 3.7. The 4 Cs—Climate.

tions such as professional fishing groups that do not allow women. Present and future social issues may affect your company.

Political Climate

This consists of individuals and organizations that strive to establish tolerance or intolerance within the public sphere for specific business practices. For example, those private golf clubs that do not allow women to reserve tee times on Saturday mornings are under pressure to change that practice. In another example, collegiate athletic programs are under pressure to change many aspects concerning women in athletics such as the number of opportunities to participate, which directly affects the number of sports offered, the number of scholarships offered, and the number of coaching and other staff positions directly involved with the women's athletic program.

Legal Climate

"When all else fails, sue." This seems to be the most popular way of handling issues today. However, it has resulted in a great variety of local, state, and federal legislation to protect the consumer. It is important that the sport business knows and understands laws, how those laws apply to specific products or segments of the sport industry, and how legislation may be used to reveal opportunities and threats for the sport business.

Ethical Climate

Society, culture, and business develop certain ethical mores that influence life and business. The ethical climate in the United States was studied intensely during President Clinton's impeachment investigation. People and businesses questioned and discussed their ethical philosophies. The current ethical guidelines will influence the sport business. The marketer needs to know how this is occurring in order to develop strategies.

Trends

Trends can affect the sport business in many ways. We cannot determine if a trend is simply a trend and will be short-lived, or if a trend will become the next commonplace and institutionalized phenomenon. For an example of the influence a trend can have on an industry, remember that aerobics was once considered a passing trend.

Technological Climate

Technology has tremendous effects on the sport business world in many ways. The rise of electronic commerce has reshaped business and marketing. Advances in materials for facility construction, equipment design, and even sports clothing have significant influences on the sport business industry. The sport marketing professional must study these advances, determine how best to utilize them to maximize success, and capitalize on the competitive advantages they can offer.

Educational Climate

The education of sport marketing professionals influences the business world. Imagine a world in which higher education, or any education for that matter, does not exist. It would be stagnant. Education is vital to the sport business industry. Because every segment of the industry constantly grows more complex, education is necessary to prepare individuals for those challenges. The sport business industry should work with sport management education to ensure professors are teaching future industry workers exactly what they need to know to be successful on the job.

Educators in sport management have curriculum standards that were designed based on the minimum knowledge every sport management student should have to go into any career in the industry. The sport management educator should make every effort to design a curriculum modeled on the standards and attempt to achieve program approval.

Every year there is an increase in the number of colleges and universities starting programs in sport management. Unfortunately, most programs have only one or two faculty members, and many times, these faculty members are expected to teach outside of sport management while managing the sport management program. There is a critical need for sport management faculty in general, candidates from doctoral programs designed to appropriately prepare them exclusively for sport management education, and those who are working exclusively in sport management. Moreover, there is a critical need for sport businesses to get involved with sport management education and support the efforts of the faculty. Indeed, it will be the sport business that benefits. One day, there just might be colleges or schools of sport business, just as there are colleges of education or business. There will be full departments based on the curriculum content areas such as sport marketing, sport finance, and sport law. The halls will be lined with nicely framed plaques showing sport businesses that have endowed faculty positions, research centers, and department chairs.

Community Climate

The local community within which the sport company resides will influence the company. Each area has different climates in relation to economic, legal, environmental, and cultural issues, for example. The sport business in that community must understand the community climate and how it will influence the business. All of these can have influences on the sport business. With that knowledge, the company can make educated decisions regarding its business in the community. For example, one person wanted to start a company with a driving range and lights for nighttime practice. However, people in the residential area that surrounded the new driving range complained that the huge lights would detract from their property values and quality of life. The future driving-range owner ignored the residents and installed the range and the lights. This led the residents to file a formal complaint with the city. The city investigated and sided with the residents. The driving-range owner was only allowed to use the lights one night a week, every other week. The owner learned a hard and expensive lesson. The lights cost several hundred thousand dollars to purchase and install, and it will be many years before the owner will recoup the costs. In addition, the local newspaper ran several stories about the disagreement, and the owner appeared to be insensitive to the needs and desires of the residents, resulting in negative publicity for the company.

Corporate (Industry) Climate

Each company develops what is called its "corporate climate" and is influenced by a regional or national corporate climate. This involves both trendy corporate factors and those that take on a long-time personality. Typically, top administration establishes both the spoken and unspoken rules or limitations and philosophy that govern the way a company conducts business and how it treats its employees. This makes employees believe they must follow the rules in order to stay with the company. Moreover, it creates an atmosphere for business in which an entire industry will operate. For example, it has become corporate practice for large companies to set up manufacturing plants in countries outside the United States because wages are extremely low compared to those in the U.S. This practice has backfired in that Americans have criticized those companies for exporting American jobs and for supporting poor working conditions in poverty-stricken countries. In certain situations, the consequences of this can be boycotting of the company's products, negative press, and a tarnished reputation. These consequences can sometimes be devastating to the company.

In another example, sexual harassment is no longer tolerated as a part of a corporate climate, at least by law. This is not to say that sexual harassment does not continue to take place—it does. However, the issue has been so well addressed that many corporations have stiff penalties for any employee who is found to be sexually harassing another employee.

A sport business must become aware of corporate climates, how they affect the company, and how the company can make corrections or utilize them to company advantage.

Media

The media include television, radio, print and electronic forms. All media have had significant influences on the sport business industry. Many are individual industries, such as broadcast television, and some are media forms that sport businesses use for a number of purposes for the benefit of the company. One of these examples is broadcast television. While sports broadcasting companies are individual media companies, they rely on the sports industries to provide programming. They have contracts with sports teams, leagues, and organizations for the right to broadcast their events. At the same time, these sports teams, leagues, and organizations are using television as a promotional tool.

In another example, the newest form of media, social media, is growing fast and reaching amazing proportions. While social media, such as Facebook and Twitter, use sports events for growth, these sports teams, leagues, and organizations use social media as a promotional tool.

In summary, the sport marketer needs to study and understand the many climates in which the company works and how each affects the company. This knowledge will guide the sport marketer in developing marketing decisions and strategies.

SEGMENTATION, TARGET MARKET DECISIONS, AND POSITIONING

The primary purpose of conducting research and analysis of the 4 Cs is to have information necessary for making decisions and formulating strategies. The next steps in the Sport Marketing Management Model (Figure 3.2, p. 93) are segmentation, target marketing, and positioning.

Segmentation, target marketing, and positioning are essential for every sport business. Without these, the sport business puts itself in serious jeopardy of failing. Segmentation, target marketing and positioning enable the sport business to develop strategies appropriate to different sets of consumers. *Segmentation* is dividing a whole into homogeneous groups. *Target marketing* is the selection of consumer segments (also called target markets) for which selective marketing mix strategies are developed. *Positioning* is telling the consumer what the business wants the consumer to think about the product, or the company. The company uses its marketing mix to influence the consumer's perception of a product. Such moves may influence what the consumer thinks about the product's quality, value, status, convenience, and many other factors.

Segmentation

For the consumer population, *consumer segmentation* involves differentiating groups of consumers based on unique characteristics. Through segmentation, the company identifies and understands the common characteristics of the consumers in that segment and can determine how to address their unique demands. There is also *industry segmentation*, which involves differentiating the whole sport business industry into homogeneous groups, or groups for business purposes. For instance, the entire industry may be segmented based on different types of sports, such as everything that is basketball may be the basketball industry. Even that can be further segmented—there may be the basketball shoe industry segment, the college basketball industry segment, the professional basketball industry segment, and the basketball facility design and construction industry segment.

The process of segmentation varies. Segmenting strategies can include the division of consumers by, for example, buyer identification, salespeople, purchase location, time of purchase, purchase quantity, product design, product bundling, product tie-ins, and pricing. Other strategies include those that identify consumer segments by sets of demographics, psychographics, and lifestyle. Typically, consumer segments are labeled for identification and definition. Some examples of labeled segments with which you might be familiar include the baby boomers, the senior market, the Generation X market, and the women's market. Some parts of the sport industry identify consumer segments according to loyalty. A few examples of these are the hard-core fan, soccer hooligans, and the occasional fan. Some labeled consumer segments in the participant sports segment of the industry include, for example, the thrill-seeker, the adventurer, the competitor, the weekend warrior, the elite athlete, and the recreational participant.

Segmentation is used in segmenting an industry in order to identify and understand the different segments in the sport industry. These are called *industry segments*. *Industry segmentation* is used to better identify, define, and understand the common characteristics of those businesses within that industry segment and to help with competitor analysis and competitive advantage strategies. The sport industry can be segmented in several different ways. One example is segmenting the industry by type of business. One industry segmentation study shows the industry segmented into three segments: sport performance, sport production, and sport promotion (Pitts, Fielding, & Miller, 1994). See Figure 1.2 on page 14 in Chapter 1. In this model, all sport businesses that are in the business of marketing, promotions, merchandising, and the media are categorized into the sport promotion industry segment. Sport businesses study this segment, analyzing its strengths and weaknesses, then develop competitive strategies. A sport business must identify its industry segment in order to formulate marketing objectives and long-term company goals. This knowledge allows it to make better decisions about product, price, place, and promotion and to determine positioning strategies.

Target Marketing

The marketer must direct the company in deciding which consumer segments the company is capable of serving. The segments chosen become the company's target markets. A target market is a segment of consumers who are homogeneous and who have purchasing power and the willingness to buy. Target markets should be the basis for all marketing strategies. It is the target market for which a product is produced and offered, a specific price is determined, locations at which to offer the product are selected, and promotion strategies are formulated. Here are a few examples of target marketing:

1. The Women's Basketball Hall of Fame opened in the spring of 1999 ("The Her-story of Basketball," 1999). The target market is the large and growing women's basketball consumer market. The Hall of Fame is based in Knoxville, Tennessee, the home of the fantastically successful and popular University of Tennessee women's basketball team, the Lady Vols, and Coach Pat Summitt. Speaking to the market, the advertisement for the hall of fame uses the slogan "Honor the Past. Celebrate the Present. Promote the Future."

2. Targeting Native American people, Snow-Riders.org is a website originally created to encourage the development of a Native American Olympic Ski & Snowboard Team for the 2010 Vancouver Winter Olympic and Paralympic Games. The sup-port has grown into a group called the Snow-Riders of the American Indian Na-tions. The group encourages Native American sports participation, with a goal of supporting Native American athletes striving for the Olympics. They have also added the Native American Olympic Team Foundation as a partnership between U.S. Tribal Leaders, Elders and Olympians to encourage future athletes (Snow Riders, 2011).

3. In 1998, the *SportsBusiness Journal* launched its first issue. Its target market is sport business industry management people and sport management educators. As such, the *SportsBusiness Journal* provides information for sport business manage-ment professionals with an emphasis on trade and business.

4. Combining the growing NASCAR fan popularity, and the popularity of sports fantasy leagues, NASCAR created NASCAR Fantasy Live (NASCAR, 2011). A fan can join league competition managing a roster of 5 Sprint Cup drivers through a season. The fans earn points in five categories toward winning prizes.

5. The Federation of Gay Games' primary target market is the lesbian and gay sports market around the world (Federation of Gay Games, 2011). The Gay Games was created to offer an "Olympic" experience for LGBT people. The event is held every four years and is modeled after the Olympic Games with one significant ex-ception: a Gay Games participant does not have to qualify in that individual's sport. Typically, the number of participants is around 12,000, making the Gay Games one of the largest sports events in the world.

6. Targeting the Hispanic population, several professional sports leagues, such as the NFL, WNBA, and MLB, have created specific marketing initiatives. In addition, sports television programmers have channels in Spanish, such as FOX Sports en Español.

In these examples, the products were planned and produced specifically for a particular group of consumers—a target market. It is the target market that informs decisions concerning the marketing process, especially the marketing mix.

Marketing Mix and Positioning

After information has been collected about the 4 Cs, and segmentation and target mar-kets have been developed, the next step is making decisions and formulating strategies about the marketing mix—the 4 Ps.

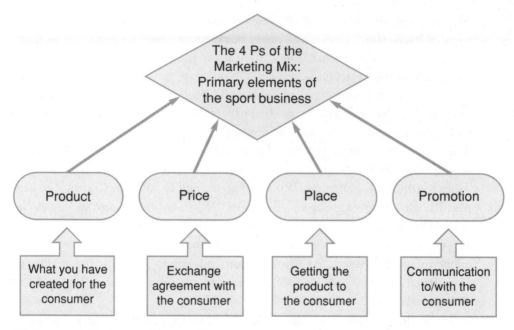

Figure 3.8. Marketing Mix Elements—The 4 Ps.

The *marketing mix* is the strategic combination of the product, price, place, and promotion elements (see Figures 3.8 and 3.9). These elements are typically called the *4 Ps of marketing*—a term coined by the American Marketing Association in the 1960s. These components are what the sport marketing professional can control. Therefore, it is critical that decisions and strategies for each component are thoughtfully and strategically determined. Information for making educated decisions involving the 4 Ps comes from marketing research involving primarily the 4 Cs—consumer, competitor, company, and climate (Pitts & Stotlar, 2007). A critical decision and one of the greatest challenges for the sport business is how to strategically combine the four Ps to best satisfy the consumer, meet company objectives, enhance market position, and enhance competitive advantages.

Market position, also called *positioning*, refers to the way a company uses its marketing mix to influence the consumer's perception of a product. Such moves may influence what the consumer thinks about the product's quality and what the consumer is getting for the money, features not found on another similar product, status, convenience, and many other factors.

PRODUCT

The centerpiece of a sport business, and thus the marketing mix, is the product. The product is what the consumer seeks. It should be understood as a concept and not simply as a singular item. A sport product is any good, service, person, place, or idea with tangible or intangible attributes that satisfy consumer sport, fitness, or recreation related needs or desires. The consumer is looking for functions and benefits. The product is the

Product	Price	Place	Promotion
Functions	Objectives	Objectives	Objectives
Features	Flexibility	Channel Types	Promotion Mix
Accessories	Product Life Cycle	Market Exposure	Sales People
Utility	Terms	Distribution Goals	Advertising Methods
Use	Warranty	Transportation	Market Demand
Instructions	Sales	Location	Publicity
Installation	Special Order	Service	Public Relations
Service	Exclusivity	Intensity	Media Relations
Warranty	Psychology	Efficient	E-commerce
Product Lines	Perceived Value	Effective	M-commerce
Packaging	Discounts	Inventory Mgmt	Social Media Mix
Branding	Allowances	Warehousing	

Figure 3.9. The 4 Ps of the Marketing Mix.

satisfaction agent for those. The product satisfies something that the consumer needs or wants. Price, place, and promotion strategies are designed specifically for the product in order to increase the probability that it will sell.

The sport company must constantly study the consumer in order to discover what the consumer wants or needs. The result could mean developing a new product or changing an existing product in some way. The sport business must use information concerning the competition when making these decisions. For example, if the mechanic for a sailing club discovers that the sailing club members are not buying sailboat hardware at the club's shop because they cannot get what they need, the prices are higher than at other stores, and the quality is not as good, the mechanic should tell the marketer.

The marketer may decide to survey the members to get more information. If the research supports what the mechanic reported, the marketer must determine if action is needed. In this case, the marketer should consider further research to determine what hardware the members need, prices other stores are offering, and if higher-quality products are available and can be sold at a specific price level.

A sport marketer will make many critical decisions concerning the sport company's products. One such decision involves the number and types of products to offer. This is called *product mix*, the complete set of all products that the sport company offers.

A sport company will determine what is, or will be, the right combination of products for the company. Product management involves tracking the sales of each product to determine if sales are increasing, maintaining, or decreasing. An analysis will provide the sport marketer with knowledge to make adjustments to specific products or to terminate a product.

The product is the company, and any changes, additions, or deletions to the product will have specific effects on the company. It is the sport marketer's job to try to forecast the effects and initiate only those changes that could have positive results for the company and the consumer.

Price

Price involves the exchange of something for something else—that is, one item of value is exchanged for another item of value. The price of something can have a tremendous effect on a consumer. The consumer's decision to buy something can be affected by many factors. Some of those factors include what the consumer can afford to pay, if what the consumer gets for the money is of value, if the consumer thinks he/she is getting "a good deal," friends' attitudes, family influences, how the product compares to another similar product in terms of features and other factors, and the product's warranty and extended services.

Setting the price for a product is a very important decision for the sport marketer because price affects the product's success, status quo for the product, and the consumer's perception of the product. The decision should be based on many factors such as knowledge of the consumer and what the consumer will pay, cost to the company to produce and offer the product, profit-making strategies of the company, the competition's prices, and supply and demand within the product market. Although Chapter 9 offers details regarding price and pricing strategies, here is one example of how setting prices works.

In Center City, USA, there exists one indoor soccer complex: Soccer City, Inc. The city's population is 600,000, and soccer leagues, both recreational and in schools, are full and growing. Soccer City opened five years ago, and its facility includes one indoor soccer court enclosed by a giant net, a concession bar, and a tiny soccer equipment and apparel store (rented space to a local soccer store). Soccer City enjoys a monopoly on indoor soccer. As the popularity of soccer has grown and proliferated in the city, so has indoor soccer. It offers a place to play soccer during the winter months, which are the off-season in all outdoor soccer venues. The demand is high. All leagues offered fill quickly even though the price has been increased. The adult league fees are $400 for an 8-week session of one game per week. The high school and youth fees are even higher. The fees for these teams are per person. The high school players will pay $75 per person for an eight-week session of one game a week. Although most of the players complain of the high fees, the leagues are always full.

However, a new indoor soccer facility will soon open, Pele's Palace. The CEO of Pele's Palace has a choice to make concerning prices. Pele's Palace could charge lower fees compared to Soccer City and probably win quite a few of Soccer City's customers. A second choice is this: Pele's Palace could charge the same fees as Soccer City because it has been established that those prices are what consumers will pay for indoor soccer.

Which would you do? Which is better for the company? Which is best for the consumer? Are there any other pricing strategies you could consider? How much does the product (indoor soccer) cost the company to produce and how will this affect your pricing decisions?

As you can see from the example above, pricing a product is not a simple matter. It involves many factors and critical analysis of those factors before determining marketing mix strategies.

Place

Place is how a company gets a product from its production or origination point to a place where the targeted consumer can have access to it. Remember that sport industry products include people, places, goods, services, and ideas. Goods that are typically manufactured in a factory must be transported from the factory to the market. Some products, such as services, must be delivered to the marketplace and the consumer in a different way. Sports activities are very different because a sports event does not exist until a person manufactures it—that is, basketball is intangible and doesn't exist until someone plays basketball. It is a product like a play in a theater or a live concert by a current famous musician that is manufactured and consumed simultaneously.

In a sports event, the consumer is the participant. The consumer has paid for the product—softball, for example—but does not take possession of it until the consumer actually creates it, or plays softball. In this example, the consumer will probably have to go to a softball field on a given day at a given time to get what he/she purchased. Getting this type of product to the consumer is different from transporting a good from a factory to the marketplace and requires the sport marketer to make specific decisions.

Place, or distribution as it is also called, requires knowledge of the type of product; how best to get that product to the consumer, or how to get the consumer to the product; efficient and effective distribution channels; packaging; and other factors. Analysis will lead to better decisions. Chapter 6 details the marketing mix variable place.

Advertising is a highly visible category of promotion. © Cthomas41 | Dreamstime.com

Promotion

Promotion is what the general public often thinks is marketing. That is because the promotions are what the public sees. More specifically, promotions are especially designed to get a person's attention. Advertising, one category of promotion, includes TV commercials, radio commercials and announcements; advertisements in magazines, in books, in movie theaters, in video movie rentals, on social media, on billboards on every highway, and on the sides of buses, trucks and cars; signs on tops and sides of buildings; and signs on athletic fields, stadia, arenas, and uniforms. In other words, it is everywhere. People are surrounded by advertising.

Sport businesses lure people to sporting events by incorporating special promotional events, sometimes called promos. Consider these examples: a Leanne Rimes concert the day before a NASCAR race event; a gift such as a coffee mug for the first 2,000 people through the gates; a prize such as a 45-inch television given away at the halftime break during the local college women's basketball game; and the appearance of a sport superstar who will sign autographs after the game. These are just a few of the many promotional methods that sport marketers use to get the attention of the consumer.

It is no wonder, then, that the general public thinks that marketing is promotion and promotion is advertising. Promotion, however, involves more than creating advertisements and inventing special events. As you will see in the chapters on promotion and promotional methods and strategies, promotion is multifaceted.

Promotion is the process of raising awareness. This process may involve a variety of methods for gaining the attention of potential consumers in order to tell them something and/or to educate them about something. In addition, once the marketer has the consumer's attention, the marketer must keep it long enough to get a message across. Usually, the message contains information about a product or a business. The marketer's purpose for promotion is to encourage the person to purchase the product. Therefore, the message must be developed in such a way that it serves three functions: First, it gets the attention of people; second, it gets across a message or educates people; and third, it tempts people to purchase the product. The promotion may be any one or more of a variety of promotional methods and strategies. The sport marketer may choose any one or a combination of promotional methods and strategies. The promotional message and strategies are put together to speak to a specific kind of person—a market segment. The sport marketer uses research data about the consumer and the competition to create strategies and the promotional message.

MARKETING MANAGEMENT STRATEGIES

A critical part of the marketing process is management strategies that involve implementation, management, evaluation, and adjustment (see Figure 3.2 on p. 93).

The sport business must have a system for managing the process of sport marketing. This system includes the implementation, management, evaluation, and adjustment of all of the sport marketing components. Management is a multidimensional step that involves setting objectives for the sport marketing strategy, developing the sport marketing plan, selecting and managing sport marketing personnel, establishing a financial plan, establishing and managing an organizational structure, establishing and overseeing deadlines and scheduling, acting as the liaison between sport marketing personnel and top management, and coordinating all sport marketing functions.

The development of the sport marketing plan is an important task. Strategic planning strengthens relationships between sport marketing and other management functional areas in the company. The sport marketing plan is the written, established plan of action for the company or for one of its elements (or products). It drives the company.

The plan contains the marketing objectives, identified target markets, financial strategies, and details of the marketing mix strategies. The marketing plan can be written for a single sport product, a group of products, a new promotional strategy, or the entire sport company.

The sport marketing plan should not be taken lightly. It requires time, research, and critical analysis. Every possible task, angle, financial analysis, and every function of the company and the product should be thoroughly studied and analyzed. The final plan should reflect informed decision making and strategy formulation.

Implementation involves establishing a system for planning and managing the implementation of the sport company's marketing strategies. Evaluation involves creating a system for analyzing marketing strategies to determine if the strategies are accomplishing the established objectives.

In developing evaluation strategies, every activity, process, and strategy put in place should have an evaluation plan. The evaluation plan will critically analyze each activity toward findings and conclusions. The findings will provide key information about whether or not the activity is performing the way the business wanted it to perform. For example, if a promotion activity was developed with the goal of selling more tickets to an event, there should be a plan for testing the activity to determine if it was successful.

CHAPTER SUMMARY

In this chapter, we presented the history of the development of sport marketing and the concept of sport marketing theory, defined sport marketing, presented the Sport Marketing Management Model, and briefly discussed the components of the model. Subsequent chapters will provide specific details, methods, and strategies of each component.

Theory is built from a foundation of research and knowledge. Sport marketing theory is in the process of being developed, as it is a new field of study when compared to many other fields of study. To study the developing theory of sport marketing, one must study the foundation from which it is being built. The foundation of sport marketing comes from several fields of study.

Sport marketing is the process of designing and implementing activities for producing, pricing, promoting, and distributing a sport product to satisfy the needs or desires of consumers and to achieve the company's objectives. Sport marketing is one of many management functions. It has become, however, one of the most important functions because the sport industry continues to grow at a phenomenal rate. The growth means competition and the sport industry is a highly competitive industry.

The Sport Marketing Management Model illustrates the process and elements of sport marketing, the succession of elements and functions, the process of managing, and the interdependency of the elements. The model should be used as a guide for the sport management or sport marketing professional. We encourage sport marketers to refer to the Sport Marketing Management Model (Figure 3.2) throughout their study and practice of sport marketing. It will serve as a reminder of the total marketing picture and where each component fits.

DISCUSSION QUESTIONS

1. What is sport marketing theory? What fields of study serve as the foundation of sport marketing fundamentals and theory? What are some of the areas of research in sport marketing?
2. Should sport marketing professionals be consulted when studying the methods of sport marketing? Explain why and how.
3. What is the Sport Marketing Management Model? What are the components of the model? Define and describe each one.
4. What are the 4 Cs of marketing? Describe each one.
5. What are the different climates within which a sport business exists? Describe each one and how it affects the business.

SUGGESTED EXERCISES

1. (a) Create a list of people who work in the sport industry in different types of sport businesses across the United States. Interview them about sport marketing at their company. Ask them what their theory of sport marketing is. (b) Now do the same with college professors of sport marketing. Interview them about teaching sport marketing. Ask them what their theory of sport marketing is. (c) Compare and analyze your results. Give a presentation in class.
2. Go to the university library and check out textbooks in marketing. Look for the definitions, fundamentals, and theory of marketing. Compare these to the definition, fundamentals, and theory of sport marketing in this book. Analyze your results. Give a presentation in class.
3. Take this book to some people who work in the industry. Ask them to look at the Sport Marketing Management Model and to tell you if it matches the marketing activities they perform (or someone performs) in the company. Compile their answers. Give a presentation in class.

4

Sport Marketing Research

"Knowledge is the foundation of all sport marketing and sport business activity."

—(Pitts & Stotlar, 2007)

INTRODUCTION

As you learned in the previous chapter, knowledge is the foundation of all sport marketing and sport business activity. All decisions in a company should be based on the information and knowledge gained from research. Good information that is timely, accurate, interactive, flexible, and accessible is the lifeblood of the sport company. Among many other reasons, good research can help maximize a company's sales, identify future product and market opportunities, identify potential threats to the company, provide information for understanding consumers, help in the advertising development process, provide consumer feedback on product improvements, and assist in determining prices.

Marketing research is a vital element of marketing. Marketers attempt to know what the consumer wants and what that consumer will exchange for it. The primary method for determining what the consumer wants is to communicate with the consumer or study the consumer's needs, wants, and desires in other ways. With this information, a sport business professional can make decisions that will greatly boost the success of that business.

Is it necessary to constantly conduct research just to collect information? Yes. However, you can conduct the research yourself, or you can find information from research that others have conducted, or you can hire a sport marketing research company to conduct specific research. Some information is free, and some must be purchased. For instance, there is a massive amount of information on the Internet. However, while the Internet has revolutionized how we acquire information, one must be careful about the characteristics of the source of the information. The important thing to remember is that making smart decisions comes from having information to guide you to a decision or strategy that significantly increases your odds to be successful.

Additionally, more successful businesses subscribe to the philosophy of the *marketing concept*—that companies should analyze the needs of their consumers and then attempt to satisfy those needs better than their competition. This is helpful in understanding the typical terms of "customer oriented" and "market driven." The key point is that a successful sport business marketer takes the time to find out what the customer wants and then provides it. Additionally, the sport marketing professional can use the information to determine the right price, the right place (distribution points), and the right promotional strategies. This provides the sport business with the right *marketing mix strategy*. "Right" means that each of the 4 Ps are what the consumer wants.

Acquiring good information requires good research (Li, Pitts, & Quarterman, 2008). That is, the research and its methods must be as accurate as possible. As illustrated in the Sport Marketing Management Model, the company needs information in four categories called The 4 Cs of marketing: consumer, company, competitor, and climate (see Figure 3.2 in Chapter 3). The decision-makers in the company must know as much as possible about their consumers, current and potential, about their competitors, about their own company, and about the many elements of climate (see Table 4.4).

Here are some typical questions that the marketing and management team of a sport business might need to answer in the course of doing business:

- Who are our competitors? Where are they? What is their market share? How do their products and prices compare to ours?
- Who are our consumers? Are they changing? How are they changing?
- What are the emerging consumer markets that our company could begin to target?
- Can our company get into M-commerce (mobile commerce), create a store targeted to mobile devices, and sell our logo merchandise through it?
- What new product can our company produce for a new consumer market?
- What do consumers like and dislike about our new sports facility?
- How can we upgrade our manufacturing process without having to add too much to the price of our product?
- Which sport businesses could benefit from our sport marketing research services?
- Do spectators at a major sporting event recognize that our company spent over $12 million to be a major sponsor for this event? Will they be more likely to buy our product because of our sponsorship?
- How does our company compare to others regarding employee benefits?
- Why are some consumers protesting our new advertising campaign? What do we need to do now?
- What is the hottest, newest sport? Can our company be involved in some way?
- How can we decrease our distribution costs and find a more effective and efficient way to move our products from the manufacturing plant to our distributors?
- If the national weather offices are predicting a warm winter, how can our snow ski resort lessen the potential financial damages and make up potentially low profits?
- What are the largest markets today, and how will they change in 10 years? How can our company plan for the change?
- What is the true economic impact of our marathon and 10K?
- How do our consumers perceive our new promotional gimmicks?
- What are the current laws concerning licensing?
- How is the current economy affecting our company?

At first glance, the questions seem like common, simple questions. But, try this: start with the first question and develop a thorough answer. How would you answer this question? What kind of information do you need? Does this information already exist? If so, where can you get this information? Will the information be accurate? Will it be current? Is it specific to your company, your product, and your part of the industry?

If it doesn't already exist, how can you collect the information you need? Do you need to conduct a study? What kind of study? What kind of measurement instrument do you need? Does an instrument already exist, or do you need to develop one? Will the instrument collect the right kind of information? Will it be accurate? Will the information be useful when it is collected, or will you need to manipulate it somehow? How do you analyze the information you collected? Will your analysis be accurate for your needs?

How will you be able to use the information for the company? Will you need to now study the company with the new information and determine how it will work within the company?

After doing this little exercise, you can see how what appears to be a simple question must be treated with a professional, organized, and calculated approach. That professional approach is research.

In this chapter, you will learn what sport marketing research is, how sport marketing research is conducted, and how it is used in the analysis and development of marketing decisions and strategies in the sport industry. In Chapter 5, you will learn how sport marketing research is the basis for segmentation, target marketing, and positioning; in Chapter 6, you will learn how to manage all of this information gathered through research.

SPORT MARKETING RESEARCH

Simply, sport marketing research is an activity conducted to collect information. Of course, there is more detail to it than a simple definition. A more descriptive and formal definition is as follows:

> Sport marketing research is the process of planning, collecting, and analyzing relevant information needed to make a decision or solve a problem in the sport business exchange process. In the academic world, sport marketing research is conducted to provide theoretical or practical knowledge and to further the body of knowledge in sport marketing as a field of study.

In both areas—the sport business and the academic world—research is critical in order to gain information or solve a problem. The use of the new information is essential; it

---

Sport marketing research is the process of planning, collecting, and analyzing relevant information needed to make a decision or solve a problem in the sport business exchange process. In the academic world, sport marketing research is conducted to discover and provide theoretical or practical knowledge and to enhance and progress the body of knowledge in sport marketing as a field of study.

is necessary for formulating decisions concerning the sport company's financial aspects, product development, pricing strategies, distribution strategies, promotional strategies, and all other functions and operations within the company.

In the academic world, research is conducted primarily to enhance the body of knowledge in sport marketing. Academics—sport marketing professors at universities—conduct research in many different areas of sport marketing. Often, the research is conducted on or within a sport business. The professor then shares the new knowledge primarily with other professors and with students so that their knowledge of the sport business is enhanced. Further, the professor attempts to publish the research in scholarly journals so that anyone can have access to the information. All of these journals, as well as textbooks, involving sport marketing are what comprises the sport marketing body of knowledge. A "body of knowledge" is a collection of all of the information known about a topic. The body of knowledge is studied and used by other professors, students, and industry professionals.

Research adds to the body of knowledge that tests theories and forwards the body of knowledge. Theories lead to the development or improvement of practice; research can be applied. Both theoretical and applied research can help answer questions, solve problems, test theories, or lead to new ideas for theories or practices.

Sport marketing research can range from simple to complex. Figure 4.1 illustrates the sport marketing research continuum. The type of research conducted is based on what information is needed, what problem needs solving, or what question is asked. For instance, if the sport marketer of an indoor soccer club needs to know the email addresses of current consumers in order to send direct-email promotional material, the information may be gathered easily from membership application forms that have included members' email addresses. If the publisher of a wakeboarding sports magazine wants to know what's happening in the sport, the company can read and study information published in industry trade publications. At the other end of the continuum, if the management of the LPGA (Ladies Professional Golf Association) needs to know how many

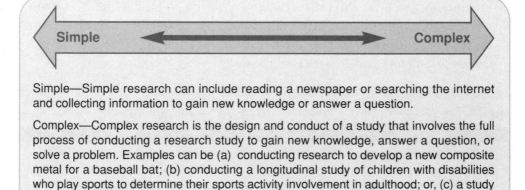

Simple—Simple research can include reading a newspaper or searching the internet and collecting information to gain new knowledge or answer a question.

Complex—Complex research is the design and conduct of a study that involves the full process of conducting a research study to gain new knowledge, answer a question, or solve a problem. Examples can be (a) conducting research to develop a new composite metal for a baseball bat; (b) conducting a longitudinal study of children with disabilities who play sports to determine their sports activity involvement in adulthood; or, (c) a study of arena advertising to determine if spectators can recall sponsors and advertisers.

Figure 4.1. The Sport Marketing Research Continuum.

people are attending each event, who they are, and why they attend, a study will be designed and then conducted in order to collect the appropriate data.

Research conducted by sport management academicians and scholars can also range from rather simple methods to more formal and complex methods. Appendix E contains examples of research conducted by academicians that adds to the body of knowledge in sport marketing and can be used by the sport business executive. For instance, many sport management professors have worked as consultants to sport businesses and conducted research for them. For example, each author of this textbook has served as marketing and marketing research consultants to businesses in the sport industry for over 20 years (see Table 4.1). This research is used by the sport business for their purposes. For instance, Carl Atkins, the general manager of the Georgia Dome in Atlanta, Georgia, uses the market

Table 4.1. Examples of Sport Market Research for the Georgia Dome in Atlanta, GA*
• Visitor spending and economic impact of the AMA SupercrossFactors that influence attendance of fans attending the 2011 NCAA men's SEC regional championship.
• Cultural tradition: amalysis of fans' attending the Atlanta Football Classic 2011.
• Consumer satisfaction: analysis of fans' satisfaction with Georgia Dome as a venue for sports events 2011.
• The Georgia Dome and Atlanta as destination: analysis of fans' satisfaction with the Georgia Dome and the city of Atlanta as a destination for sport events 2011.
*Research conducted by Dr. Brenda Pitts and Sport Management students at Georgia State University in Atlanta for the management team at the Georgia Dome.

research to inform decisions about sports events at the Dome. Some decisions have included changing seating charts, changing pricing structures, enhancing customer service, improving the fan experience, and enhancing client services.

Some research is published in journals such as those presented in Table 4.5 and in Appendix D. Some research is presented at academic conferences such as the annual conference of the Sport Marketing Association (SMA), the Sport Management Association of Australia and New Zealand (SMAANZ), and the European Association for Sport Management (EASM). Often, summaries (abstracts) of these research presentations are published in the conference proceedings of the association.

PURPOSES OF SPORT MARKETING RESEARCH

Why does a sport business need to do research? What are the purposes of research? Research is used to gather information, attempt to identify a problem, or to attempt to solve a problem. Without research and analysis, the sport business wouldn't have vital information: without information, decisions and strategies would be risky. When a decision is not based on real and accurate information gained from research, the sport company risks making a wrong decision. Decisions based on no information, or on inaccurate information, can have seriously negative consequences for the company. Therefore, decisions should be based on information and knowledge gained from research.

Some of the purposes of sport marketing research can be found in definitions of marketing from the American Marketing Association (AMA). One definition states that "marketing research links the consumer, customer, and public to the marketer through information—information used to identify and define marketing opportunities and problems; generate, refine, and evaluate marketing actions; monitor marketing performance; and improve understanding of marketing as a process. Marketing research specifies the information required to address these issues; designs the methods for collecting information; manages and implements the data collection process; analyzes the results; and communicates the findings and their implications" ("New Marketing," 1987, p. 1). In another definition offered by the MASB Common Language Project, marketing research is "the systematic gathering, recording, and analysis of data about issues relating to marketing products and services" (MASB Common Language Project, 2012).

Based on these definitions and the definition of sport marketing research, the following sections detail the purposes of sport marketing research.

To Gather, Analyze, Understand, and Use Information about the 4 Cs

The sport business must have information about the 4 Cs of marketing—consumer, company, competitor, and climate—in order to make sound decisions and develop good strategies about the 4 Ps—product, price, place, and promotion. As illustrated in Figure 4.2, information about the 4 Cs feeds decisions about the 4 Ps.

Consumer: The company must gain an understanding of the consumer's needs, wants, and desires, as well as study how the consumer makes consumption decisions (purchase behavior). The company must also understand the consumer's need for the function of the product, views on pricing, and perceptions and reactions to promotions. Table 4.2 presents a sample of a range of questions and information needed on the consumer. Further, Chapter 5 presents in-depth information on consumer research.

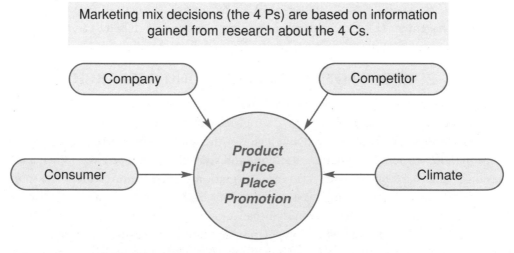

Figure 4.2. The 4 Cs and the 4 Ps.

Table 4.2. Information Needed About the 4 Cs				
	Consumer	**Company**	**Competitor**	**Climate**
Who ...	... are our consumers? ... consumes the competitor's products? ... could become our next 1,000 consumers?	... works for us? ... is making key decisions?	... is our competitor? ... does our competitor serve?	... can influence the economy, law, etc?
What ...	... do our consumers like/ dislike? ... are they willing to pay?	... does our company do? ... can our company do? ... is our financial status?	... does our competitor do? ... is their advertising like? ... is their financial status? ... are their prices?	... is the future of our economy? ... are the laws that affect my company?
When ...	... does the consumer want this product? ... can the consumer pay? ... should we advertise?	... can our company offer a product? ... does the company need to be paid? ... should the company advertise?	... does the competitor offer its products? ... does the competitor use attack marketing? ... does the competitor use sales promotions?	... do the new laws go into effect? ... will the economy get better? ... will the Hispanic market respond to cultural-based marketing
Where ...	... are our existing consumers? ... are our potential consumers?	... is our company located?	... is the competitor located? ... do the competitors put their products?	... will the economic setbacks hit hardest?
Why ...	... does the consumer want a product? ... does the consumer want to pay a particular price?	... does our company offer this service? ... doesn't our company offer this service?	... does the competitor offer a particular service?	... is the economy hit hardest in this area?
How ...	... can the consumer use this product? ... can the consumer pay for the product?	... can our company offer a product? ... does our company track sales of its products?	... do we compare with our competitor? ... are we different? ... does our competitor offer the product?	... will the economy be in three years? ... will the new law affect my company?

Company: The sport company must know itself deeply and critically. Research conducted on the company and its many elements, such as processes, financial strengths/ weaknesses, positioning, distribution strategies, and consumer perceptions, will help the management team make strategic decisions based on company strengths.

Competitor: The sport business should know its competitors as well as, if not better than, its own company. Knowing the competitor will help the management team make better decisions.

Climate: Understanding many climate elements, such as the economic situation, legal issues, and environmental concerns, will help the sport business make much better decisions and strategies.

The typical journalist's questions should be asked: who, what, when, where, why, and how. The sport marketer should seek to understand the answers to these questions concerning the sport company, its consumers, its competitors, and the climate. Examples of the many questions the sport marketing professional should constantly ask and monitor are shown in Table 4.2. Marketing decisions and strategies should be formulated based on real information and an accurate understanding of the 4 Cs. Again, making uneducated and uninformed decisions is risky.

Consider the information presented in Table 4.3. This chart shows the most popular sports activities participation by people in different countries. If you were in the sporting goods business and looking to get into international markets, how would you analyze this information? Try to answer the following questions by analyzing the information from the various positions:

- If you were a sporting goods retailer, how would you view this information in relation to your specific business?
- If you were a sport shoe manufacturer's sales representative, how do you think this information would affect your product and company?
- If you worked for a computer company and you were head of a team to seek sports activities events for sponsorship possibilities, how would you use this information?

Table 4.3. Top 10 Participation Sports by Country

	Japan	USA	Australia	Taiwan
1st	Bowling	Exercise Walking	Walking	Walking
2nd	Gymnastics (no equipment)	Exercising with Equipment	Aerobics/Fitness	Jogging
3rd	Jogging, Marathons	Swimming	Swimming	Basketball
4th	Swimming (pool)	Camping	Cycling	Hiking
5th	Catch ball, Baseball	Bicycle Riding	Golf	Excursion
6th	Training	Bowling	Tennis	Mountain Climbing
7th	Cycling, Cycle sports	Aerobic Exercising	Running	Bicycle Riding
8th	Fishing	Hiking	Bushwalking	Swimming
9th	Table Tennis	Workout at Club	Netball	
10th	Badminton	Running/Jogging	Soccer	

Table 4.4. Sports and Athletic Footwear Shoes Average Prices and Changes					
Shoe Type	2010	Changed	2009	Changed	2008	Changed
Aerobic shoes	49.22	6.9%	46.06	6.5%	43.23	−0.2%
Baseball/softball	43.72	0.6%	43.44	−0.5%	43.67	2.9%
Basketball shoes	62.13	3.0%	60.30	6.0%	56.91	0.7%
Boat deck	44.59	9.7%	40.63	17.2%	34.66	−2.2%
Bowling shoes	44.55	n/a	n/a	n/a	41.40	n/a
Cheerleading	n/a	n/a	42.53	n/a	n/a	n/a
Cross Training/Fitness	53.59	n/a	n/a	n/a	n/a	n/a
Cycling	n/a	n/a	56.94	n/a	n/a	n/a
Football shoes	51.88	7.5%	48.27	0.5%	48.05	9.4%
Golf shoes	63.34	4.5%	60.64	−5.9%	64.47	1.5%
Gym shoes/Sneakers	36.44	15.1%	31.65	1.0%	31.35	4.1%
Hiking shoes/Boots	64.30	8.9%	59.06	3.2%	57.25	7.7%
Jogging/running	62.33	4.9%	59.43	3.3%	57.53	2.8%
Skateboard shoes	40.75	2.2%	39.87	−1.3%	40.38	−4.9%
Soccer shoes	38.07	0.8%	37.78	2.5%	36.87	−1.4%
Tennis shoes	36.71	4.3%	35.18	7.0%	37.83	1.3%
Volleyball shoes	54.83	n/a	n/a	n/a	56.87	n/a
Walking shoes	48.01	4.9%	45.76	2.0%	44.85	1.6%
Source: NSGA.com						

In another example of research from the National Sporting Goods Association (NGSA), Table 4.4 shows data concerning prices and price changes in sports footwear. If you had the perception that sports shoe prices have been increasing, would this information change your mind? With this information, consider the following question: How can you use the data presented in Table 4.4 if your company manufactures tennis, soccer, softball, basketball, and running shoes?

Right away, you can see that even a simple survey can reveal interesting and sometimes surprising information, and that the information will be viewed and analyzed differently depending on the type of company that is studying the research. Each one of the different companies can use the information provided, but each needs it for different reasons.

To Form a Link between the Consumer and the Sport Company

The sport company can use the gathered information to get to know existing and potential consumers and what they want. The consumer receives a message from the sport company that it is trying to meet the consumer's needs. The following are examples of how this works:

1. Puma North America created sports shoes with the extreme generation in mind. For that, Puma received "the cool factor" rating from teens. The shoes are "cool" and "hip" according to alternative kids. Sales of the shoes have boosted profit an amazing 20-fold in a few years—to just over a billion dollars. By comparison, Nike sales grew less than 10 percent and adidas increased by only 5 percent. To continue their "coolness," Puma teamed with Fader Magazine, a music and culture magazine targeting the "Gen F" market, to support a live music tour. Puma used research on youth and teens to develop a product and promotional strategies to reach the market. The tour, called Gen F Live, involves several cities in the U.S. Both companies hope to cash in on the cool factor, attracting new fans—and consumers—of their products.

2. In 1970, the National Sports Center for the Disabled (NSCD) was started. It was a one-time ski lesson for children with amputations for the Children's Hospital of Denver. The NSCD has developed into one of the largest outdoor therapeutic recreation agencies in the world. From the NSCD website: "Each year, thousands of children and adults with disabilities take to the ski slopes, mountain trails and golf courses to learn more about sports—and themselves. With specially trained staff and its own adaptive equipment lab, the NSCD teaches a variety of winter and summer sports and activities to individuals with almost any physical, cognitive, emotional, or behavioral diagnosis. "The mission of the National Sports Center for the Disabled (NSCD) is to provide quality outdoor sports and therapeutic recreation programs that positively impact the lives of people with physical, cognitive, emotional, or behavioral challenges" (National Sports Center for the Disabled, 2012). Targeting individuals of all ages with nearly any disability, the NSCD reaches a market that is growing in both numbers and in the attention it is getting from more and more industry. Numerous companies and organizations offer sporting goods as well as sports activities. Using research conducted by several organizations now about individuals with disabilities, this organization and others develop their products and strategies.

To know the consumer requires research and constant monitoring. To conduct this research, the company must have contact with the consumer. This contact is done through formal research methods such as surveys and interviews, and through informal methods such as conversations and spending time together. In these ways, the company can learn about the consumer and can then make better decisions in relation to the 4 Ps.

New electronic media, such as Facebook and Twitter, are giving the sport business new ways to link directly with the consumer and nearly communicate on a one-to-one basis. For instance, the company will set up a Facebook account, develop the site in such a way as to attract consumers to the site, ask the consumer to "like" the company (or a product), and even ask the consumer to place the company's information, website, or Facebook page on the consumer's own Facebook page—essentially, asking the consumer to directly advertise for the company! Not a day goes by today without hearing the words "Follow us on Facebook and Twitter!"

To Identify and Define Marketing Opportunities, Problems, and Threats

A *marketing opportunity* is a chance for a sport company to capitalize on a new idea or new product, move to a new location, gain a specific consumer market, take advantage of a financial management technique, or engage in other activities that will most likely prove positive for the company. A *marketing problem* occurs when something is not quite right in the company. A *marketing threat* is usually more serious for the company. It means that something could have a serious adverse affect on the company. Only through research can the sport marketer discover opportunities, problems, or threats to the company. Let us consider some examples.

Fitness foe. Research can reveal threats. Let us consider fitness centers as an example. Today there are fitness centers everywhere. During the 1970s and 1980s, when the number of fitness centers was growing rapidly, the increase was a problem and a threat to the few existing fitness centers. For example, if the Downtown Fitness Center (DFC) is the only fitness center within a 20-mile radius, the DFC feels safe, knowing that competition is at least 20 miles away. When the owner of the DFC discovers through research that three other companies are making plans to open within the 20-mile radius, the owner becomes aware of a threat to the DFC. With this information, the owner is in a position to do something so that the new fitness centers will have either no effect or minimal effect on the DFC's business. Without the research effort, however, the owner of the DFC never would have known that competition was about to increase substantially.

Baseball bargains. Stacy Cavanaugh is a sales representative for a large baseball bat manufacturing company. The professional baseball leagues, which currently allow only wood bats, are considering allowing bats made of other materials. Spectator attendance has been slowly declining in the last four years, and leaders in the baseball leagues believe that bats made of other materials will result in more hits, and thus more excitement for fans, which will in turn lead to increased attendance. There are currently 12 professional baseball leagues in this particular country—4 men's leagues, 4 women's leagues, and 4 minor leagues. Changing the bat-material rule could have a significant impact on the bat manufacturing companies, especially those companies whose sole product is wood bats and who sell only to the professional leagues.

Stacy's company, the Acme Baseball Bat Company, manufactures bats made from two materials: wood and aluminum. The wood bats are all produced on machines that individually produce bats one at a time according to the specifications of each player who orders bats. The aluminum bats are mass produced in a factory in another country and shipped. The aluminum bats, however, are children's bats and much smaller than an adult's bat. The Acme Company started producing these bats as promotional items— autograph models of some of the professional players. Children using these bats choose according to the name. For example, a child whose favorite professional players include

Kelly Powers, Mike Star, and Jay Jay Homer can use the aluminum bats named for the players and dream of becoming that player one day.

Stacy figures that it ought to be easy for the company to make the transition and stay in business if the leagues decide to allow bats of materials other than wood because the company already makes bats out of other materials. Stacy proposes this idea to the company's top administration, and she is assigned to research the idea.

Stacy makes a trip to the aluminum bat factory to talk to the director and discovers that their aluminum-bat-making machines will not make bats large enough for an adult. The company would have to purchase all new machines. Stacy's research into this leads to the discovery that each new machine, along with reconfiguring the existing factory, will cost $1.2 million. There would also be additional expenses including personnel, extra space, and numerous overhead costs. Further research reveals that the company would have to have a factory with 30 of these machines in order to produce enough bats to sell to be efficient and cost effective.

After presenting the research to the company's top administration, it is determined that the cost of start-up and production is a problem that will require major, long-term commitment from the company in order to effectively produce these new bats. The administration also decides that the problem warrants further research, especially because they are the only wood bat company that already produces bats of other materials. However, more research is needed regarding how many companies currently produce adult-size bats of other materials that could more quickly meet the professional players' demands and perhaps corner the market.

In this situation, start-up costs to enter a product market present a problem for this company. Unless further research is conducted, it is not known whether a cost-effective solution might be found.

To Monitor Marketing Activities and Performance

Marketing activities include determining the company's products and all of their characteristics, determining pricing strategies, developing promotional methods, and deciding on distribution. Research is needed in order to first generate and design those actions. Decisions about what product to offer and how to offer it can only be made after the research is conducted. Once those decisions and actions are in place, they should be monitored constantly in order to evaluate effectiveness and performance.

Every sport business must determine if its marketing efforts are performing according to the established goals. That is, if one goal of a particular marketing effort was to increase brand awareness, how can the sport business determine if that goal was met? Of course, the answer is research. The sport marketing professional can use brand-awareness research tools to determine if consumers are aware of and recognize the company's brand.

As you will learn throughout this textbook, there are many different marketing efforts. For instance, there are numerous promotional methods. Some are newspaper advertisements, television commercials, promotional giveaways, licensed promotional merchandise, and sponsorship promotions. All of these efforts should be monitored in

Corporate sponsors may target other companies by advertising at corporate golf tournaments. © Ratmandude | Dreamstime.com

order to determine if they are working and if they are meeting the objectives set for them. The following are examples of this monitoring.

Example A: New Era in Sponsorship Marketing

It is no secret that the average spectator of many professional sports is being squeezed out of the prime seating areas of the sports venue. But who would have predicted that spectators would cease to be the prime target of sponsorship advertising? A growing trend in some professional sports, where sponsorship is a form of advertising, is business-to-business sponsors (Owens, 1999). That is, corporate sponsors whose products are only manufactured for and sold to other companies are targeting businesses with their advertising rather than spectators. The trend is not hard to spot. For example, which fans recognize the consumer products being touted by a chemical company such as Dupont? Only those who either work for or do business with DuPont. DuPont doesn't need the fans to recognize their product—their target is corporate. Constant research involving trends of consumers of many professional sports reveals the changing nature: there is an ongoing increase in the number of corporations that purchase box seats and tickets and also purchase (rent) the pricey spaces around the sports venue for a corporate party tent.

The tent space is, of course, an extra cost and can range from a small amount to hundreds of thousands of dollars. The increasing number of corporate consumers is causing sponsors to take notice. Companies who had never been sponsors for sports events are taking advantage of the opportunity to market to a target audience. Although most sponsors are still producers of consumer products, a growing number of companies whose consumers are businesses are getting involved. For instance, in NASCAR, many sponsors are not companies whose consumers are end consumers—they are retailers. That is, businesses who do business with other businesses. A sponsor in NASCAR can spend $8 million annually to support a race car and team. That sponsor will most likely spend another $8 million for promoting the sponsorship and using it to entertain and enhance business with clients and potential clients.

Many events now have enormous areas in which to create hospitality villages for sponsors. Although the average fan at the event may wander through the village and benefit from promotional giveaways or drawings, the village exists for the corporate sponsor executives and their business partners. The sponsor's focus is on the businesses that buy their products in huge quantities. In other words, a train shipment of sales is worth much more than an individual sale to one consumer. The retailers and whole-salers are being courted for their attention and their wallets.

Constant research and monitoring of existing and potential consumers and their needs and desires are the only ways the sport marketing professional can discover these needs and desires and then plan to meet them. In this instance, sports event executives should study the changing needs of current sponsors in order to best serve them. This will require changes in the product offered—the sponsorship deal, sponsor's needs, and sponsor's areas—in order to meet the desires of the new market: the business-to-business sponsorship.

Example B: It's My Turn

In a study of the WNBA's marketing tagline "We Got Next!" researchers found that only a small number of fans know what the phrase actually means (Shoenfelt, Maue, & Hatcher, 1999). The researchers studied basketball spectators and a generic group of undergraduate students and found that more basketball spectators than students had watched a WNBA game and could link the tagline to the WNBA.

However, very few of both groups knew the meaning of the phrase. The phrase is one used in basketball pick-up situations where players or groups line up for their time in the game or on the court. The phrase essentially means that the speaker is the next in line. The WNBA wanted to convey to the basketball world to move over, it's time for the women to shine. The slogan also refers to the season scheduling. The NBA season is played "first," and the WNBA season is "next."

If the WNBA now knows that its consumers don't really know what the phrase means, they can make some decisions to effect a change. For instance, they could mount a campaign to attempt to educate consumers as to the meaning of the phrase, or the WNBA could decide to develop a new phrase.

To Improve Understanding of Sport Marketing as a Process to Enhance the Sport Marketing Research Body of Knowledge

A process can be the routine execution of a method. To understand marketing as a process, research can provide answers to questions concerning why and how the process works. For instance, the sport marketing academic journals *Sport Marketing Quarterly*, *International Journal of Sports Marketing and Sponsorship*, and *International Journal of Sport Management and Marketing* provide outlets for the publication of sport marketing research conducted by people in both the academic and practitioner worlds of sport management. All of the studies and other materials published improve our understanding of sport marketing and its process. Table 4.5 provides a representative list of sport marketing, sport management, sport law, sport studies, and business administration journals in which sport marketing research can be found. Examples of this type of research are presented in Appendix E. These are brief summaries of the research. You

Table 4.5. Sport Business Journals	
Asian Sport Management Review (since 2009)	Journal of Intercollegiate Sport (since 2008)
Case Studies in Sport Management (since 2012)	Journal of Issues in Intercollegiate Sports (since 2008)
Choregia: Sport Management International Journal (since 2005)	Journal of Japan Society of Sports Industry (since 2009)
Cyber-Journal of Sport Marketing (deceased)	Journal of Korean Society of Sport Management (since 2009)
Entertainment and Sports Law Journal (since 2002)	Journal of Legal Aspects of Sport and Physical Activity (since 1985)
European Sport Management Quarterly (since 2001)	Journal of Leisure Research (since 1968)
International Journal of Leisure and Tourism Marketing (since 2009)	Journal of Sport Administration and Supervision (since 2009)
International Journal of Sport Finance (since 2006)	Journal of Sport & Tourism (since 1995)
	Journal of Sports Economics (since 2000)
International Journal of Sport Management (since 2000)	Journal of Sport Management (since 1987)
	Journal of Sports Media (since 2005)
International Journal of Sport Management, Recreation & Tourism (since 2008)	Journal of Vacation Marketing (since 1994)
International Journal of Sports Marketing and Sponsorship (since 1999)	Journal of Venue and Event Management (since 2009)
International Journal of Sport Management and Marketing (since 2005)	Korean Journal of Sport Management (since 2009)
International Journal of Sport Policy and Politics (since 2009)	Marquette Sport Law Review (since 1990)
International Sports Journal (since 1997)	SMART (Sport Management and Related Topics) Online Journal (ceased)
International Sports Law Review (since 1992)	Sport, Business and Management: An International Journal (since 2011)
Japanese Journal of Sport Management (since 2009)	Sport Management Education Journal (since 2007)
Journal for the Study of Sports and Athletes in Education (since 2007)	Sport Management Review (since 1998)
	Sport Marketing Quarterly (since 1992)
Journal of Hospitality, Leisure, Sport & Tourism Education (since 2002)	Women in Sport and Physical Activity Journal (since 1992)
	World Leisure Journal (since 1958)

should find the source and read the full study to gain a complete understanding of the research. In addition, all of the information presented in the "Sport Business Fact Book: Did You Know . . ." boxes throughout this book are examples of bits of information discovered through research.

The new knowledge and understanding gained through research leads to theory. Theory is the basis of sport marketing practice. The material in the field of sport marketing has changed and been enhanced over the last twenty years because of the research both in the academic field and in the industry. As new and more research is conducted, it adds to the body of knowledge, helping it grow and mature. As this happens, it is the student and the practitioner in the industry who will benefit from the information. For instance, Table 4.6 presents research from nine studies on sport sponsorship. The table

Table 4.6. Sport Marketing Research: Consumer and Sport Sponsorship Measured in Research

Consumer classification data and sponsorship effect that were measured in the nine papers.

1. Sponsored property consumer profile

- demographics
- buying habits
- image of sponsored property
- attitude toward sponsorship
- attitude toward sponsors
- perception of sponsored property symbols
- size
- frequency of sponsored property consumption
- perception of fit between sponsor and the sponsored property

2. Exposure

amount of exposure
- number of people who were exposed to the sponsor's message
- number of seconds signage was on TV
- number of mm of print (newspapers, magazines)

3. Effects on consumer

on awareness
- unaided awareness (compared with competitors)
- aided awareness (compared with competitors)
- share of voice/mind—% of total mentions compared with other sponsors/non-sponsors
- recall by viewing weight—i.e., by frequency of exposure
- signage recall
- high- versus low-profile brands share of voice analysis
- awareness of current and past sponsor
- association of sponsor with the sport generally (i.e. soccer, rugby)
- association of sponsor with the sponsored property (i.e., World Cup)
- change in share of voice/mind (compared with competitors)
- change in recall (compared with non-sponsors)

on image/attitude toward the company
- degree of image change (compared with non-sponsors)
- effect on company image (compared with non-sponsors)
- effect on product image (compared with non-sponsors)
- general image of sponsors (compared with non-sponsors)
- on attitudes among business decision makers (compared with non-sponsors)
- on employee satisfaction

on behavior
- effect on brand preference (compared with non-sponsors)
- rate of growth of brand preference (compared with non-sponsors)
- on buying intentions

4. Multimedia effects

- synergy with other communication mediums
- relative value return of sponsorship versus advertising
- awareness by means of message—advertising, sponsorship, product placement, spot advertising
- relative ability of sponsorship isolated from other communication efforts

Source: Brooks, 1998.

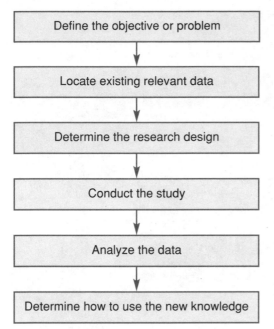

Figure 4.3. A basic process for designing sport marketing research.

summarizes the type of consumer information studied and the sponsorship effects that were measured in the research. Students, practitioners, and educators can benefit from this information, which can be used, for example, in designing sponsorship studies.

A BASIC PROCESS FOR DESIGNING RESEARCH

There are some specific models and methods for research design and activity. Figure 4.3 illustrates a basic process for designing sport marketing research. This illustration outlines the process and a series of questions to guide the sport marketer through it. Each step in the process should be carefully and thoughtfully developed and planned so that the research produces truthful and useful results.

Typically, information is available in two types of sources: primary and secondary. *Primary sources* include those sources from which information is gathered directly. Gathering information about consumers directly from those consumers is using the primary source—the consumer. Therefore, one's own marketing research is a *primary source of information*.

Secondary sources are those that contain information that is already compiled or published—in other words, someone else conducted the research and you are simply using it as information. A marketing report purchased from a sport marketing firm is a secondary source. Information on the Internet is *secondary source information*. The information comes to you secondhand. There are several secondary sources available to the sport marketer.

Step 1: Define the Objective or Problem

The first step is to define the objective of the project or specify the problem. What does the company need to know? What is the problem? Refer to the list of questions at the beginning of the chapter (Table 4.2). Defining the objective or problem can be as simple as knowing the question. Once the objective or problem has been identified, the development of the research will be guided by what is needed.

Step 2: Locate Existing Relevant Data

The second step is to locate existing information that might answer your question or solve your problem. If this can be done, there might be no need to conduct further research. That is, if you can find information that is accurate, specific, and timely enough

Collection of demographics and other consumer information can help companies target the most relevant audiences. Courtesy of BigStockPhoto.com

to address the objective or solve the problem, then this might be as far as you will need to go. If not, then further research is needed.

Determine the Kind of Information Needed

Typically, most information needs fall into the 4 Cs categories as previously discussed in Chapter 3: the consumer, competitor, company, and climate. For each one of these areas, there are numerous elements that must be studied. The following are descriptions of some of the kinds of information needed concerning each of the 4 Cs and the most common types of research methods used to study them.

Consumer. The sport business must know and understand its consumers and potential consumers. Chapter 3 presented specific information needed concerning the consumer and how that information is analyzed and used. Kinds of information studied include:

- demographics such as age, gender, disabilities, sexual orientation, income, ethnicity, and education;
- psychographics such as lifestyle preferences, favorite color, household, employment, purchase behavior, brand preferences, class, culture, reference groups, personality characteristics;

- consumer behavior such as consumer values, lifestyles, perceptions, purchase decisions, purchase decision process, problem recognition, perceived value, post-purchase behavior, and factors affecting purchase involvement level; and
- business consumer segments such as producers, retailers, service providers, resellers, governments, vendors, and business-to-business buying behavior.

Competitor. Studying the competition and the industry is necessary in order to ascertain what competitors are doing and how those actions will possibly affect one's own company. Additionally, thorough knowledge of the competition can reveal much information that might be helpful. That is, one company can learn from another company's successes. Sometimes, those successes have to do with hitting on a promotional idea that becomes popular. For example, the use of animals in advertising has been rising in popularity. Would you agree that the GEICO Insurance Company's gecko is one of the most highly recognized animals in advertising? Sometimes these popular advertising themes take on a life of their own. The popularity of the gecko spawned a full complement of licensed merchandise.

Study of the competition includes study of an industry segment and the industry as a whole. In an industry as enormous as the sport industry, it is essential to remember that oftentimes, one industry segment can affect another. This requires industry analysis. Sometimes this research can be found in industry trade magazines. It is important to read and study these publications because they record and reveal what is happening in an industry.

Company. Monitoring and studying one's own company is essential to making decisions regarding every area of the company. The type of research conducted depends on what information is needed. For instance, a general study of the company can be done with a SWOT (Strengths, Weaknesses, Opportunities, Threats) analysis. Using a SWOT analysis, the company can attempt to critically and objectively determine its strengths and weaknesses, for example, and use this information for strategic planning.

Climate. The environmental considerations outlined and discussed in the previous chapter must be studied, both internally and externally. These include economic factors, the social and cultural climate, and corporate, political, legal, and ethical climates. For instance, it is important to know what is happening in the economy. The economy can affect everyone, and sport businesses are not excluded.

Sources of Information and How to Get Them

There are two categories of information sources: primary and secondary. As you learned before, *primary source information* is information created through one's own research—collected directly from the consumer via personal interview, phone surveys, or consumer questionnaires. *Secondary sources* are those sources from which you may obtain information that has been reported, published, or collected. There are also internal and external sources of information. *Internal sources* are those sources inside the sport company. *External sources* are those sources outside the sport company. There are primary internal and external sources, and there are secondary internal and external sources. A *primary internal source* is an interview conducted with one of the sport company's employees. A *primary external source* is an interview conducted with consumers. A *secondary internal source* is a report by one of the departments in the company. A *secondary external source* is a report issued by the United States Census Bureau.

Primary sources are those sources from which one collects the information directly. That is, when data is collected directly from the consumers, that is primary information. To do this, one must design a study for the collection of data. Designing a study is presented in the next section.

Finding existing information. Here are some ideas on where to find secondary information. A massive amount of information is contained on the Internet. Be careful of the sources of this information because there are websites that contain inaccurate information.

You can collect a wide array of information from local government offices and other nonprofit agencies. Some of these are the local chamber of commerce, department of health, city planning and zoning offices, city census offices, local colleges and universities, and local real estate or homebuilding offices.

Trade or industry-specific associations can also provide information, and nearly all of them have websites at which you can find a vast array of information. Table 4.7 includes research examples provided by the Sporting Goods Manufacturers Association. Tables 4.8 and 4.9 present examples of these associations. For almost every career, there is a professional association. Many of these associations track demographic and other data con-

Table 4.7. Examples of Research Available From the Sporting Goods Manufacturers Association
Sports & Fitness Participation Topline Report—
This report covers 117 sports and activities sampling over 40,000 Americans ages 6 and older. The report looks at activity levels and establishes participation trends in sports, fitness, and recreational activities in the U.S.
U.S. Trends in Teams Sports Report—
This report shows research about trends in team sports in the USA. Included is a report about what inspires young athletes to participate in sports and what motivates them to continue playing.
State of the Industry Report—
This is an annual overview of the state of the sporting goods industry in the USA, including research on the sporting goods and fitness market.
Tracking the Fitness Movement Report—
This research tracks several aspects of the fitness and exercise category from core participation to sales of equipment as well as health club membership.
Manufacturer's Sales by Category Report—
This research shows individual categories of sporting goods and fitness equipment sales, providing sales figures on over 30 categories. This research could help an individual/business determine where opportunities for entry or growth might be.

Table 4.8. Examples of Sport Business Industry Trade Publications

Bicycle Retailer and Industry News
Boating Insider Industry
Boat Show Exhibitor
PGA Magazine
Fitness News Magazine
Outdoor Retailer
The Park & Recreation Trades
Parks and Recreation Business
Outdoor USA Magazine
The Paddock Magazine (motor sports)
Sports Executive Weekly
SportsBusiness Journal

cerning their industry. The National Sporting Goods Association (NSGA), for example, tracks sporting goods sales and sports participation and publishes information such as the following:

Every year NSGA does its research study "The Sporting Goods Market" as a service to its members. The study, prepared by the independent research company of Irwin Broh & Associates, delineates the size and scope of the sporting goods market. At the same time, we gather brand share data on certain products. Each brand share report shows product sold by type of outlet, retail price range, major geographic regions and household income. It includes data on age and sex of major user. Reports include graphs showing year-to-year changes. The brand share data is based on a representative sample panel of 20,000 US households for equipment, 40,000 households for footwear. This panel is maintained by NFO, one of the most respected research companies in this field.

Table 4.9. Examples of Sport Business Industry Trade Websites

Surf Industry Manufacturers Association	www.sima.com
American Sportfishing Association	www.asafishing.org
National Sports Shooting Foundation	www.nssf.org
Fantasy Sports Trade Association	www.fsta.org
Sporting Goods Manufacturers Association	www.sgma.com
Sport Business Market Resource	www.sbrnet.com
The Horticulture Trades Association/Sports Turf Industry	www.the-hta.org
Dive Industry Association	www.diveindustry.us
UK Golf Trade Body	www.bgia.org.uk
Canadian Sporting Goods Association	www.csga.ca
Sporting Goods Intelligence Europe	www.abc-directory.com
Golf Course Industry	www.golfcourseindustry.com
Association of Fitness Industry Retailers and Manufacturers	www.afirmfitness.org
Sporting Goods Dealer	www.sportsonesource.com
Marine Industry Professionals	www.tradeonlytoday.com
Scuba Industries Trade Association	www.sita.org

Types of outlets covered in the report include: sporting goods stores, specialty sport shops, pro shops, discount stores, department stores, catalog showrooms, warehouse clubs, mail order, on-line/internet and other outlets. Brand data is reported specifically for K mart, Target and Wal-Mart in the discount store category and Sears in the department store category. "On-line/Internet" purchases, which are showing significant growth in both sports equipment and footwear, were added three years ago.

For footwear, specialty athletic footwear stores, family shoe stores and factory outlet stores replace catalog showrooms and warehouse clubs in types of outlets. For fitness equipment, TV shopping is reported.

Professional associations are another source of information. For example, the American College of Sports Medicine (ACSM) is a professional association for a variety of professionals and practitioners in areas such as sports medicine, athletic training, orthopedic medicine, and exercise physiology. The ACSM tracks and collects information about these areas. There are two outlets for the information: (a) annual conferences and meetings, and (b) newsletters and journals.

The NCAA is another example. The NCAA is primarily a governing association, but it also serves as a professional trade association, disseminating information to those working in college athletics to improve and enhance their management skills. The NCAA website and its publications, such as the NCAA News, serve as outlets for the dissemination of information. For more examples, reference Appendix B; it contains a list of several sport business trade associations.

Publications are another source of information and consist of magazines, newsletters, newspapers, reports, and journals, among others. Some of these sources are available on newsstands, some in bookstores, some by subscription, and others by membership in an organization. Consider, for example, the many sports magazines. To get an idea of how many there are, walk into any bookstore and look at the magazine section. On average, the section will contain over 50% sports and sport-related magazines. Each magazine holds information about that sport and its participants, equipment manufacturers, retailers, and other types of information. *Boating World* magazine publishes water sports participation data. *Golf World* magazine even publishes stock information. Appendix C contains a list of some sport business trade publications. Table 4.10 presents examples of trade sources of information for just one industry, the golf industry. As you can see, there is a lot of existing information that can come from a variety of sources. More examples are listed in Appendices B and C.

Step 3: Consider Hiring a Sport Marketing Research Company

If you cannot find existing information that answers your questions, and if you do not want to conduct the research in-company, consider hiring a research company that specializes in the type of research your company needs. There are numerous marketing research companies, so shop around for the one that you feel comfortable with, the one you believe will do the best job, and, of course, the one that you can afford. There are numerous marketing research companies with broad specialties, as well as those that fo-

Table 4.10. Examples of Trade Associations, Organizations, Exhibitions, Conferences, and Publications for the Golf Business Industry

Golf Industry Show	held annually
World Conference and Club Business Expo	held annually
GCSAA Education Conference	held annually
Women in the Golf Industry	www.wigi.info
PGA Magazine	www.pgamagazine.com
Golf Business Magazine	www.golfbusiness.com
Golf Course Superintendents Association of America	www.gcsanc.com
Golf Builder's Association of America (GCBAA)	www.gcbaa.org
Society of Golf Appraisers	www.golfappraisers.org
American Society of Golf Course Architects (ASGCA)	www.asgca.org
United States Golf Association (USGA)	
National Golf Foundation (NGF)	
International Golf Course Equipment Managers Association (IGCEMA)	
National Golf Course Owners Association (NGCOA)	ww.ngcoa.org
Club Managers Association of America (CMAA)	www.cmaa.org
CMAA Club Careers	www.clubcareers.org
The Environmental institute for Golf (EIFG)	www.eifg.org
Professional Golfers Association of America (PGA)	www.pga.com
Golf Business Development Magazine (GBD)	www.golfbusinessdevelopment.com
Golf Business Advisors	www.golfbusinesadvisors.com
Golf Course Industry Magazine	www.golfcourseindustry.com

cus on one or a few areas. A simple Google search using the words "sport marketing research companies" turns up several, such as Turnkey Sports & Entertainment, Performance Research, Leisure Trends Group, and IMF Sports Marketing Surveys. Another way to attain sport marketing research is with professors in sport marketing. Many universities offer programs in sport management in which their professors specialize in conducting research.

One example of a sport marketing research company is Collegiate Consulting (formerly NADCA Consulting) in Atlanta, Georgia. From the company's website, Collegiate Consulting states:

Collegiate Consulting is a comprehensive solutions-based consulting company focused exclusively on the collegiate marketplace. Featuring a team of experienced and proven individuals, Collegiate Consulting enables athletic departments and conferences to increase revenue, create efficiencies and maximize operations to succeed and prosper in a diverse climate. ("About Collegiate," n.d.)

The company began with a primary focus on college athletics and college sports conferences. It has since expanded to include consulting and research in a number of areas, such as ticket sales and employment (H. Ould, personal communication, February 16, 2012).

Another example is Joyce Julius & Associates. This company started by analyzing sport sponsorship and has expanded into several different marketing areas. On the company's website, Joyce Julius & Associates states:

> For more than 25 years, Joyce Julius & Associates has been measuring and evaluating corporate sponsorships from our headquarters in Ann Arbor, Michigan. In that time our methodologies have set the standard in sponsorship research. Our mission today, as it has been since the company's inception, is to provide industry-leading third party research, with an emphasis on accuracy, detail and accessibility. Joyce Julius & Associates measures and analyzes all forms of media, as well as on-site elements and promotions surrounding sponsorships. Through the utilization of powerful research tools, such as the digital tracking system **Image Identification Technology** (**IIT**) powered by Magellan, and **Recognition Grade**® methodology, which takes into consideration size, location, brand clutter and integration factors, Joyce Julius delivers accurate, timely and verifiable findings—every time. ("Welcome," n.d.)

Step 4: Determine the Research Design

If you cannot find existing information, or if the information collected doesn't answer your questions, then you will need to conduct the research. Perhaps you or someone in the company specializes in marketing research. Often a company has a research department whose job is to conduct all sorts of research for the business.

If you want to conduct the research yourself, or in-house, but are not sure about how to do it, consider consulting with methods on the Internet or in books about research methods. There are many books that will provide you with enough information to plan and conduct the research.

There are numerous research methods from which to choose. However, specific ones must be selected and matched to your research needs. This must be done to ensure you are conducting the right type of research in order to collect the right data. This is critical because if the method is not correct, then the information collected will be useless.

Determining the research design involves identifying the proper research method and determining the right sampling procedures. The following sections describe these procedures.

Step 4A: Sport Marketing Research Methods

A research method is a procedure, usually an established and tested one. That is, several research methodologies have been developed, tested, and perfected through the years. These methods have higher degrees of reliability and validity. *Reliability* is a measure of the level of consistency of the method and its results. *Validity* is a measure of the level of correctness of the method. That is, does the method actually test what it claims it will test? The higher the reliability and validity of a method, the more accurate the resulting data will be.

The research method selected by a sport business or organization depends on the purpose of the research. Research methodology is determined by the research question or need. In some instances, research is conducted to enhance understanding and knowledge; that type of research is called *basic* research. In other instances, research is done try to solve a practical problem; that is called *applied* research. Sport businesses typically conduct both basic and applied research, depending on need. Most businesses, however, more often conduct applied research because of their need to solve problems, answer questions, develop solutions, create products, test promotional strategies, increase sales, and address other practical needs. Examples of the more commonly used sport marketing research methods include the following:

- *Survey research.* The most popular technique used for gathering primary data is survey research. In this method, a researcher interacts with people to obtain information such as facts, attitudes, perceptions, and opinions. Some of the forms of survey research include personal interviews, mall-intercept interviews, telephone interviews, focus groups, mail surveys, and Web surveys. Sample surveys and questionnaires are given in Appendix F. The survey can be in a printed form, or it can be done in interview format. Either way, development of a list of interview questions or the survey questionnaire is essential to the research. All survey research requires that the questionnaires be consistent so that each person in the study will be asked the same series of questions.

  Questionnaires consist of three types of questions: closed ended, open ended, and scaled response. *Closed-ended questions* require the respondent to make a selection from a limited list of responses such as a multiple choice exam. *Open-ended questions* ask the respondent to give an answer in essay form. *Scaled-response questions* require the respondent to select from a range of usually intensive related answers such as most to least, higher to lower, strongly agree to strongly disagree. Closed-ended and scaled-response questionnaires are used most often. They are easier to analyze, but they are also more objective in nature. In contrast, open-ended responses are subject to the researcher's interpretation.

- *Focus group.* A focus group is a method in which a small group of individuals are brought together and guided through a discussion about a topic. The goal of a focus group is to bring out the ideas, opinions, and views of the individuals. The marketer then uses this information to guide decisions about the business or product for adjustments toward improvement.

  The use of focus groups has become popular in marketing research. In many cities, there are a number of companies that specialize in focus group research. You can be sure that as a marketing person in a sport business, you will most likely use focus group research at some point.

The goals of focus groups include generating ideas, revealing consumer needs and perceptions, and understanding consumer vocabulary. Generating ideas means that you will use this information to brainstorm ideas. Revealing consumer needs and perceptions means that you are seeking to adjust your current beliefs about the consumer or to be exposed to and learn about what they are thinking. Understanding consumer vocabulary means that you want to stay current about words and phrases that consumers are using.

- **Telephone Survey.** As you sit at home enjoying an evening of pizza and a movie, the phone rings. Your caller ID shows the words "Out of Area" or "Unknown." You know, however, that the caller is likely a telephone marketer. Still, the telephone is a viable method for conducting some marketing research. The method requires, however, that the sample be a true representative of your population.

  In recent years, cell phones, caller ID systems, voice mail, no-call lists, and general time constraints have worked against the successfulness of the telephone survey interview.

- **Mobile device survey.** Mobile devices, such as a smartphones or tablets (the iPad, for example), are growing tremendously in popularity as an additional way for businesses to directly reach consumers. As such, businesses are also using these devices as a way to collect information through mining for data, and sending surveys for the consumer to complete and return. Research about conducting research this way is in its infancy, so a business will want to be cautious about the quality of research and information collected in mobile device surveys. However, as these devices seem to be here to stay, businesses should utilize this outlet for research.

- **Social media survey.** Social media outlets, such as Facebook and Twitter, have blasted into the consumers' world and are used heavily. For instance, as of late 2011, Facebook was merely five years old and yet already had over 800 million users. Of course, businesses are heavily using these types of social media to advertise directly and indirectly to consumers, as well as using them for consumer research, primarily via surveys. As with research via mobile devices, the research about the effectiveness and quality of conducting research using social media is in its infancy in late 2011, businesses should still consider using them as a way to collect consumer information.

- **Mail survey.** "Snail mail," as it is called today, continues to be a good method for collecting information about your consumers. The mail survey can be a postcard insert or part of any other type of mailing to the customer.

- **Research via Internet.** Conducting research via the Internet is another method for collecting data about the consumer. Information can be obtained either through customer self-reporting survey, or through hidden measures. One research methodology problem associated with this method is that information is only attained from those individuals who have Internet access. That is, the negative aspect of Internet research is that Internet users do not currently reflect all segments of the population. Internet users are primarily the younger, more affluent, and better-educated segments of the population. However, as the percent of the population with Internet access increases, so will the projectability rates. As computer and Internet access prices continue to drop, more individuals in all segments of the population will begin to make these purchases and gain access to the Internet, thus making them accessible segments of the population for the marketer.

- **Observation research.** Observation research calls for observing people's behavior. This type of study is usually conducted when a company wants to determine buyer behavior. It is also used in studying consumers' reactions to products.

- **Purchase behavior research.** This is an area of research comprised of studying many factors of how consumers behave when purchasing and/or consuming. There are several methods. One method is consumer tracking when in a retail store. The system will track consumers' paths throughout the store in order to develop trends of movement. This information allows the marketer to strategically design the placement of everything inside the retail store.

  In fact, cell phone tracking software and GPS tracking software available through social media websites are being used willingly by consumers socially; however, some businesses and research companies are using these tracking systems for market research—tracking where someone goes and travels over time reveals patterns of behavior that can be used by companies for marketing, business, or advertising purposes.

  This system could also be used in sports stadia and arenas to track the movements of consumers as they move around inside and outside the facility. This information would help marketers make better decisions about arranging services and purchase points in and around the facility.

  Such systems are highly sophisticated and are raising ethical questions. For instance, there are companies that want to implant tracking device chips in personal clothing, shoes, and even under your skin. Some companies are claiming this is for "safety" reasons—that children can be located easily if ever taken or lost, that confused elderly adults can be located if they wander off, or that parents can know where children are at all times. While these might be considered ethical uses of such devices, there are unethical ways that the information can be used. For instance, it is already known that burglaries can take place because someone posts on a social media website that they are out at a restaurant, or posts pictures while on vacation in another state or country. Ill-minded individuals surf the Internet looking for these posts and, when found, move in to take advantage knowing that the homeowner is having margaritas in Mexico and won't be home for another week.

- **Test marketing.** Test marketing is the term used when conducting an experiment or test in a field setting. A company may use a group of individuals, a city, or a set of cities to test either the sales potential for a new product or to test differences in the marketing mix for a product. For example, a baseball bat manufacturer will select a number of college baseball teams to test a new bat. The test might last for a full baseball season. At the end of the season, the company will gather the opinions of the baseball players about the bat and use that information for the production of the bat. In a different example, a large sports facility, such as the Georgia

Dome in Atlanta, will test the offering of a new promotional item during sports events. The Dome marketing research staff can conduct interviews with people who bought the item to ask their reasons for purchasing the item. If it is determined that the item has potential for sustainable sales, then that information can be used in the decision for keeping that item.

• *Scientific research.* Research of a more formal and involved nature is typically labeled scientific research. It includes, for example, laboratory research for new product development such as the study and testing of new materials for sport apparel, research to design and increase the aerodynamics of a racing bike or a racing wheelchair, and physiological studies of elite athletes to improve a sport technique for enhancing performance.

There are numerous research methods, and not all are presented in this chapter. Full books are written about research methods (see Table 4.11), and all can be found with descriptions and instructions on the Internet. As a sport management professional, it is important to ensure that you have selected the appropriate research method for your purposes so that the information you collect will be of good quality and useful.

Step 4B: Sampling Procedures

A research sample is a representative group of people from a whole population. For instance, if there are two million people in a city in which you would like to collect data, you could try to collect the data from all two million or select a sample of the population from which to collect data. The size of the sample should be large enough and representative enough that the data can be a true representation of the whole population. The sample could be as small as 30. However, as the sample size increases and representation of the whole is increased, then the confidence level that the sample data is truly representative of the whole and can be inferred to the whole rises significantly.

Table 4.11. Examples of Research Methods Books
Research Methods in Sport Management
Authors: Ming Li, Brenda G. Pitts, & Jerome Quarterman Publisher: Fitness Information Technology Year: 2007
Research Methods in Sport Studies
Authors: Chris Gratten and Ian Jones Publisher: Routlege Year: 2010
Research Methods and Design in Sport Management
Authors: Damon Andrew, Paul Pedersen, and Chad McAvoy Publisher: Human Kinetics Year: 2011

To do this, the population must first be identified. This is the group from which the sample will be drawn. The researcher must also decide what kind of sample to select; that is, the researcher can choose a random sample or a convenience sample. A *random sample* is a way to select the members of a sample so that every member of the population has an equal chance of being selected. For example, if you want to survey a population of 20,000 season ticket holders but don't have the time or money to survey every one, you can use random sampling to get a smaller group. You can select the sample number to be 400. To reach 400, you can select every 50th person listed on an alphabetical list of all of the 20,000 season ticket holders. Thus, you obtain a random sample.

A *convenience sample* comes from using respondents who are convenient, or readily available/accessible to the researcher. For instance, if you elect to use a convenience sample of the season ticket holders, you select a sample because of its convenience for you. One way to do this is to assume that all people seated in luxury boxes are season ticket holders. They are easily available and convenient for you to access. You simply distribute surveys to all the people seated in the luxury boxes.

Most sampling procedures have weaknesses. It is important to know what these are and to analyze the data within those limitations. Refer to research design books in order to determine the best sampling method for your work.

Step 5: Conduct the Study

Careful and detailed planning is critical to the conducting of marketing research. The research design selected will usually call for specific procedures on conducting the study and collecting the data. The plans for conducting the study should include logistical procedures such as time frames, dates, times, places, materials, funds, and people involved. The plans should also include arrangements for collecting the data and storing it. For example, if the study is a study on sponsorship recall, this type of research methodology calls for the survey/interview technique. Usually, a mall-intercept approach is used. The researcher stays in one area and approaches people wandering by to participate in the study. Researchers must obtain permission to conduct surveys from the site's management personnel, decide how many surveys and researchers will be needed at the study site, determine what materials will be needed, and decide what to do with the completed surveys.

Step 6: Analyze the Data

The sixth step is to analyze the data. Since the study was designed based on a specific question, or to attempt to solve a problem, refer to the question or problem and determine if the data and its analyses answer the question, or provides enough information to help solve the problem. The purpose of data analysis is to interpret the information and draw some conclusions. Of course, the data analytical methods will have already been decided when the research method was chosen because the data must be collected in a specific way according to data-analysis methodologies.

Interpretation of the data can consist primarily of running the data through statistical and analysis procedures. If the data collected are numerical, some simple statistics applied to the data may help. Ask others in the company to study the information and tell you what they see. Compare the information to other studies and look for similarities and differences. Another idea is to take the information to a research expert, such as a sport marketing professor who conducts research, a sport marketing research company, or a general marketing research company, and ask for their analysis.

Practice by finding sets of data, studying them, and asking questions to interpret them. The more you practice, the better you will become at analysis.

Step 7: Use the New Knowledge

The final step is to determine how you can apply the new knowledge to the business in order to make decisions, develop strategies, and solve problems. The information may be used according to why you needed the information in the beginning. Why did you need the information? What was your research question? What was the problem you wanted to solve?

If you needed the information to understand why your indoor tennis club is losing consumers during June and July, the new information will help you decide what you need to do to retain consumers during these months. Let us say that the reason the club loses consumers in June and July is that they go to play tennis on outdoor courts so that they can be outside during the summer. What can you do? Your club has no outdoor courts. Can you afford to build outdoor courts? If not, is there another way to compete with the outdoor courts?

Here is a real example. When Dr. Pitts (one of the authors of this book) conducted a study of consumers at the Georgia Dome in Atlanta, Georgia, part of the survey revealed some angry fans. Further analysis showed that those sets of fans were sold seats behind obstacles that kept them from being able to see the event taking place. Pitts reported the findings to Carl Atkins, the general manager, and made a suggestion. The format of the event was changed and certain sets of seats were not sold for the event the following year. The study was repeated the following year and no angry consumers were found. This shows how research knowledge is used to make decisions that enhance consumer satisfaction for a product.

In the next chapter, there are several examples of consumer research and how the information from the research can be used.

CHAPTER SUMMARY

Research is critical for the sport business. Research is needed in the primary categories known as The 4 Cs—consumer, company, competitor, and climate. Every sport marketing person should know how to conduct research. The sport business needs information that is accurate, timely, interactive, and flexible in order to enhance success. Information and new knowledge come from research, and this information is used in formulating decisions and strategies in the sport marketing elements, the 4 P's—product, place, price, and promotion.

DISCUSSION QUESTIONS

1. What is sport marketing research? Why is it important?
2. What are the purposes of sport marketing research?
3. List and describe some research methods.

SUGGESTED EXERCISES

1. Interview people in a variety of sport businesses, organizations, or other enterprises in your city or community and ask them what kind of marketing research they conduct and why. Also ask them how they use the information to make decisions.
2. Identify at least 10 different places where you could obtain existing information in your city or community. Go to these places and research the types of information available there. Create a notebook of these resources and save this material for the future.
3. With a group of other students, and with the supervision of your instructor, develop a research study using surveys as a method. Conduct the study during a local sports event. Analyze the results and present your analysis to the class.

5

Segmentation, Target Marketing, and Positioning

INTRODUCTION

We live in a world that is growing in population, but shrinking in size (in relation to travel and contact). The population growth has escalated in recent years. At the turn of the 19th century, world population was at 1 billion. In just fifty years, the population exploded by 4 billion—an unprecedented period of time for population growth. It reached 6 billion in 1999 and a mere twelve years later reached 7 billion on October 31, 2011 (Population Reference Bureau, 2011). In other words, population growth has been increasing at a faster rate as the years go by.

Yet, although the number of people is incredible, the world is growing smaller in many respects. In relation to communications, travel, movement, news, and culture, for instance, the world's peoples meet, exchange ideas, influence each other, and are changed forever. You can read about the world population's many interesting, and concerning, facts at the Population Reference Bureau's website, www.prb.org.

There are advantages and disadvantages to merging peoples and cultures. For instance, as one measure of diversity, there are currently about 6,500 languages spoken around the world. Yet, as people and cultures merge, it is predicted that that number could drop to 3,000 by the year 2100. We live in an ever-growing multicultural society, and over time it continues to merge, mix, and change.

Just when marketing gurus thought they had the mass marketing theories and models completed and working well, the world started changing. Today, with ever-increasing numbers of populations and cultures in any given country, a marketing professional must constantly monitor the population, known in business language as *consumers*.

The United States is undergoing a transformation from a primarily mono-cultural society to a multicultural one. The total population of the United States is predicted to increase from 311 million in 2011 to 404 million in 2050 (Population Reference Bureau, 2011). Since the 1950s, the country has been shifting from a society dominated and controlled by whites to a society characterized by several groups, particularly Black, Asian, Hispanic, lesbian and gay, Jewish, disabled, and Native American. It is predicted that the white population will drop to 64% of the population by 2020—it is currently at 72% (223.6 million) according to the U.S. Census Bureau and the 2010 Census statistics. The Hispanic population is now the second largest population at 16% (50.5 million, or 1 in 6 individuals) whereas the African-American population is at 13%, and the Asian American population is at 5% ("2010 Census," 2011).

> **M-Marketing**
>
> is the attempt to reach a market through mobile devices, such as cell phones and tablet devices.

Businesses are using new marketing tactics such as relationship marketing, cause marketing, niche marketing, e-marketing, and the new M-marketing to communicate with these emerging markets. *Relationship marketing* is the attempt to develop a relationship with the consumer by trying to be more to the consumer than just a company from whom the consumer buys products. *Cause marketing* is the development of marketing tactics designed to recognize and support the cause of a group or organization. *Niche marketing* is targeting specific niches, or groups, that no other company targets. *E-marketing* is the attempt to reach a market through electronic media, specifically, the Internet. *M-marketing* is the attempt to reach a market through mobile devices, such as cell phones and tablet devices. As groups proliferate and cultures emerge, marketing professionals will need to stay knowledgeable about the changes and continue to develop marketing strategies to ensure success.

Marketing professionals in the sport business industry are in the same boat. It is not an industry existing in a vacuum as though untouched by the outside world. As noted in Chapter 1, the sport business industry is as multicultural as any population. Therefore, sport marketing professionals must continuously monitor growth and changes in consumers and develop sport marketing strategies to enhance success.

As the population and its many different groups proliferate, the importance of and need for segmentation, target marketing, and positioning increase. Segmentation is the marketer's tool to make sense of these numerous and various groups of people in order to make changes in product, price, distribution, or promotion strategies. Target marketing, positioning, and brand-awareness management are ways to determine a specific consumer segment to attract.

THE VAST AND VARIED SPORT BUSINESS INDUSTRY

Similar to human population growth, the sport business industry has experienced phenomenal growth during the past 50 years. It might make sense to you that as the number of humans increases, so does the number of sports and its businesses. But not all countries have populations of humans who participate in sports regularly, not all countries offer varied sports opportunities, and not all countries provide for a sports infrastructure that encourages sports participation. The United States is considered the top country in relation to the depth and breadth of its sport industry. As you learned in Chapter 1, the USA's sport business industry is massive.

It is this largess that requires organizing and categorizing in order to make sense of it all, and in order for sports executives and professionals to be able to navigate through it and enhance success within it. As with segmenting humans, a sport marketing professional must segment the industry. Part of this chapter focuses on industry segmentation and how it is used to enhance success.

SEGMENTATION

Segmentation is the division of a whole into parts. Putting things in order helps arrange them so that we can make sense of them. It helps make order out of chaos. For example, products in a sporting goods retail store are arranged by categories: Tennis goods are found in the tennis department; soccer goods are found in the soccer department; boating equipment is found in the aquatic sports department; and sports shoes are all found in the shoe department. The purposes for doing this are to make it easy for customers to find something, to make it easy for workers to stock the shelves, and to group similar items in a practical manner. This categorization is a method of segmentation—the division of a whole into relatively similar segments.

In sport business, the work of segmentation is done primarily in several areas: industry, product, and consumer. The industry is divided and grouped in a number of ways to make practical order of it. The product is divided into product markets (or segments) to understand the market for a specific product. The consumer market is divided and grouped in a number of ways to study consumers, to reach them, and to meet their needs, wants, and desires. The division of a consumer market into relatively homogeneous segments is *sport consumer market segmentation*. The division of the sport industry into relatively homogeneous segments is *sport industry segmentation*. The division of products into segments is *product market segmentation*.

Sport consumer market segmentation involves consumer analysis. Consumer analysis is the process of studying a total market or population and dividing the population into groups that have similar characteristics.

Sport companies want to know and understand the people who purchase their products, and companies also want to learn about the people who do not purchase their products. These data help the sport marketing professional make decisions concerning the company's product, price, distribution, and promotional strategies.

Sport industry segmentation involves industry analysis (also called competitive analysis). Industry segmentation is the process of studying an industry to divide it into industry segments that have similar characteristics. The sport marketing professional uses this information to analyze the segments, analyze which segment the company is in, and develop decisions and strategies for the sport company based on knowledge about the industry segments.

The Importance of Market Segmentation

Until the 1950s, few companies practiced market segmentation. Before that time, most of the U.S. consisted of a fairly homogeneous population that could be described easily—historical patriarchal family structure of white male, wife, three children, a dog and a cat; the man worked outside the home, the wife worked at home as a housewife. World War II had a significant impact on the country, changing the demographics.

Men were shipped off to war, and women were left to move into the jobs left vacant. Thus, a cultural shift took place that forever changed the previous social practices of males and females.

Today, the population is very different. It is distinctively different in relation to race, ethnicity, and national origin as evidenced by consumer groups of Hispanic Americans, Asian Americans, Latin Americans, Irish Americans, and African Americans. The population also comprises numerous different groups of people with different characteristics such as age, gender, race, ethnicity, religion, disability, national origin, sexual orientation, household status, lifestyle and relationship characteristics, cultural factors, social factors, class, income, education, and attitudes. For instance, today we hear about groups called the Baby Boomers, the Silver Fox market, the Pink Market, Generation Y, yuppies, guppies, Generation X, the Lost Generation, DINKS, and e-Gen. All of these became population segments with distinctive characteristics, posing challenges to marketing habits of businesses. Businesses were forced to conduct extensive research about the population of consumers in order to understand their characteristics so that product, price, and all other variables could be adjusted to what the consumer will actually purchase.

The same is true for the sport business industry. As was presented in Chapter 1, the sport business industry has realized phenomenal growth since the 1950s. Some of this growth is attributable to characteristics of people wanting to play sports and engage in fitness and recreation activities, and some is directly attributable to sport business professionals doing research to enhance success.

Segmentation is the first step toward understanding consumer groups, determining target markets, and informing marketing mix and positioning strategies. The determination of target markets is essential to the business. Target markets are those specific groups of consumers for whom the company produces its products and to whom the company tries to sell those products.

The Purpose of Segmentation

The primary purpose of market segmentation is specialization. The selection of target markets will come from segmentation, so it is a very important activity. Using consumer market analysis and segmentation, the sport company can select one or more consumer market segments on which to concentrate and specialize in meeting those segments' needs. Products, prices, services, advertising, and other promotional methods are developed for specific consumer market segments and with the competition in mind.

Take a look at the information in Table 5.1, and think about how just these few data are going to affect how we market a product in the United States today, in 10 years, or in 20 years. Businesses must monitor the many new, changing, or emerging population segments. More and more businesses are redesigning their products, prices, and promotional methods for these new markets. In pursuit of these markets, many companies are relying less on traditional forms of mass marketing and more on specialized media with a sharp target marketing focus. The shift toward target marketing is easier today due to the increase in target market media. For instance, as different markets have increased in

Table 5.1. United States Population Information	
The first billion in world population took from the dawn of humanity until 1830. The second billion took only 100 years—from 1830 to 1930. The population crossed 7 billion in 2011 and the United Nations predicts it will cross 8 billion in 2023, a rapid growth rate.[1]	In 2010, 30% of the world population is using the Internet on a regular basis but 78% of the people here in the United States are connected to the web. Additionally some 66% of those users have purchased something online.[4]
At the present growth rate of 1.1% per year, the United States' population will double to about 560 million in about the next 60 years, if current immigration and related trends continue. Each year over 3 million people are added to the U.S. population.[1]	After English and Spanish (8%), the next most common spoken language in American households is French yet studying of French in our schools has dropped by 25% in twenty years. The study of Chinese language has grown by nearly 35% in that same time.[6]
The average American spent just 8 hours reading educational books in 2009 but 121 hours playing video games according to the census bureau.[4]	Despite the rapid growth of the population in the U.S. the average American spends less time reading newspapers (158 hours in 2009) and more time watching television (1700+ hours in 2009).[7]
In 2010, 13% of the U.S. population is African American while 7.1% of privately owned businesses in the United States belong to African Americans.[2]	Inhabitants of American cities are exposed to an average of 5000 advertisements each day. This figure has nearly tripled in the last 30 years.[5]
Despite the recession, 75% of teens are receiving the same or more spending money from 2009 to 2010.[3]	The United States population increased by nearly 30 million from 2001 to 2010, a 9.7% growth rate.[2]

Sources: 1) CNN Wire Staff, 2011; 2) U.S. Census Bureau, 2012; 3) Seventeen Magazine, May 2009; 4) Internet worldstats.com; 5) New York Times.com; 6) Dobuzinskis, 2011; 7) Census.gov.

number, media outlets serving those markets have increased as well. Today, a sport marketing professional can utilize such media as cable-specific television, ethnic-centered magazines, market-topic magazines, Facebook, special websites, and other social media such as Twitter.

Companies in the sport business industry have also moved toward using target marketing. As pointed out in Chapter 1, there are sports, events, sporting goods, and other sport products and types of sport management and marketing companies specifically designed for and offering products to the many different markets. Targeting specific populations and increasing the use of special target market media is the future of marketing in sport business.

The sport industry has grown partially because most of the new segments of the population, which may be the fastest growing segments, are consumer driven. Take, for example, sporting goods and equipment. There are so many different segments of people participating in sports activities that equipment is becoming more customized. Golf clubs, for instance, has always come in a variety of sizes, weights, materials, colors, and lengths; but over the past 20 years, as the number and variety of people playing golf has increased, the golf equipment companies have created a large variety of equipment to

Target marketing allows for more focused and relevant advertising. Courtesy of
Stock.xchng

meet the demand. While there have always been stores that specialize in the sales of golf
equipment, stores have increased their inventory for variety. One such company, Golf-
smith, opened one of the first golf superstores in 1995 and then tripled their number of
stores between 2002 and 2007 in order to serve the varied demand from consumers.

In other equipment businesses, tennis rackets are also offered in a variety of sizes,
weights, and materials. Sports clothing comes in a variety of sizes, styles, and colors for
every age, gender, and sport. Sports shoes are offered in a variety of sizes, sport-specific
styles, and materials. Camping equipment is varied based on consumer preferences,
geography, and types of camping. There is a booming variety of aquatic-sports goods
and equipment: The air-jet engine is revolutionizing the boat industry. For powerboat
enthusiasts, there is a constant new variety of water toys such as the wakeboard; knee
board; the ski seat; the skurfer; single, double, and triple-person tubes; the ski board;
and barefoot skiing equipment. It is apparent that the new equipment is popular because any Saturday on any lake reveals that people using this new equipment outnum-
ber traditional water skiers by four to one.

Sports and other activities, sport organizations, and sport businesses developed and
designed by and for specific consumer segments are a fast-growing area of the sport industry. As pointed out in Chapter 1, many different populations in the United States
have been very busy developing their own sports organizations, businesses, clubs, leagues,
Olympics, and facilities specifically for their population.

Another growing area in the sport business industry includes those sport businesses
whose products are service and support. Some of those services include such products

as consulting, management, legal work, financial management, research, and marketing services. For instance, if you are a professional athlete and you desire legal and financial help, there are individuals and companies that provide this service. If your sport business needs research on why sales of its product are decreasing, there are companies that will do this work. If your business wants to know if it should put a newly designed hockey stick on the market, there are companies that will study this for you. If your company wants to find a sponsor for a beach volleyball event, there are companies that specialize in sport sponsorship management. They will not only find a sponsor, but they will also negotiate the contract and manage the entire process.

Other segmentation processes involve industry segmentation, product segmentation, and business consumer segmentation. As you learned in Chapter 1, the industry is massive and varied. Industry segmentation will provide important information toward understanding the industry as a whole, and the segments of the industry in which your company will do business. Product segmentation will provide categorization of products so that your company can study and understand a specific product market. This will provide vital information for making decisions about the product. And business consumer segmentation is for those businesses whose consumers are also businesses.

THE SEGMENTATION PROCESS

The segmentation process is a simple one, but each step must be carefully examined and analyzed so that it provides correct information for those who will be making decisions about market segments and then target markets. Figure 5.1 illustrates the steps in the segmentation process toward target markets. Remember that the primary purpose of segmentation is to understand and identify specific groups of consumers or an industry segment toward target marketing to inform marketing mix strategies.

Step 1. Select a market or industry

Step 2. Select one or more segmentation bases

Step 3. Select specific variables for segments

Step 4. Identify and define each segment

Step 5. Select one or more as target markets

Step 6. Develop marketing mix strategies

Figure 5.1. The Segmentation Process.

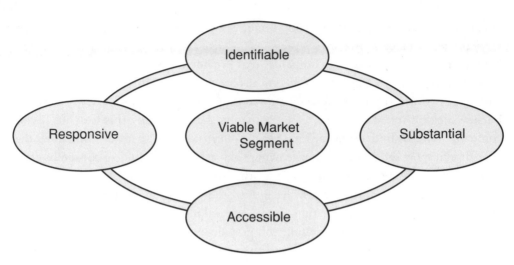

Figure 5.2. The Four Segmentation Criteria.

Step 1: Select a Population, Market or Industry

Determine which set of consumers or industry your company wants to consider for study. Use segmentation criteria to develop meaningful segments, as shown in Figure 5.2. Segmentation criteria are presented in the next section. For example, your company wants to consider the fastest growing population in the USA—the Hispanic population. Select this population to study and gather information for analysis. The information will guide decisions about whether or not to consider the Hispanic market as a target market and develop marketing mix strategies.

Step 2: Select Segmentation Bases (Variables)

Determine which bases and variables your company wants to use. Using specific segmentation bases and variables, as shown in Figure 5.3, determine specific markets based on the information. Segmentation bases and variables are presented in the next section. For instance, perhaps the data about the Hispanic population in Central City reveal it to be 50/50 male/female, ages 4 through 46, high school education, Catholic, play soccer, low-middle income, and 85% renters (as opposed to home-ownership), among other variables. Now your company can begin to determine if this segment is one that will be a potentially successful target market.

Step 3: Select Specific Variables

Within the bases, determine which variables your company wants to consider. Among the many variables, your company should narrow the focus to specific target markets within the whole Hispanic population. For instance, if your company is an indoor soccer arena, and your research shows within the segment that males aged 14 to 28 are the most avid soccer players, then your company might want to select these variables as a very specific market to target.

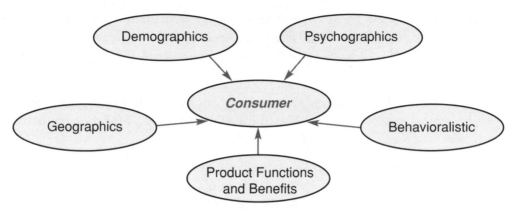

Figure 5.3. The Five Consumer Segmentation Bases.

Step 4: Analyze the Segment

Study, analyze, and determine conclusions about the segment(s) chosen. Which will be most beneficial to the company? Study all of the information collected about the segment, or many segments, looking for possible successful segments. Potentially successful segments are those that appear to be the ones that will be most likely to purchase your product.

Steps 5 and 6: Select Target Markets and Develop Marketing Mix Strategies

Determine which specific market(s) or industry segment(s) your company wants to target. Then develop marketing mix strategies based on your information about the target market(s) or industry segment. The marketing mix elements—product, price, place, and promotion—will be developed or modified and customized to each target market. This is where the common saying "give the consumer what they want" came from.

Target Market(s) Selection Strategies

From the segments, your company will select which one or more to make target markets. These groups are the ones for which the company will develop specific marketing mix strategies.

The target market will be the group or groups of consumers that the company will target for developing product, setting price, selecting distribution strategies, and creating promotional strategies. Every marketing mix element will be customized for each target market. The following are typical target market strategies.

Undifferentiated targeting strategy. This approach involves making no distinctions between any of the segments. Therefore, it is similar to mass marketing. This approach will work if the segments are so similar in characteristics that a distinct differentiation cannot be made. Marketing mix strategies will concentrate on the entire market. Some companies use this approach mixed with targeting individual differentiated target markets. For example, a company like Nike promotes its brand to the mass market. At the same time, Nike targets specific markets that are differentiated based on a number of segmentation variables, such as gender, age, and behavioral and other characteristics.

Single target market strategy. This approach involves selecting one target market. Whether this market is large or small, usually the strategy for using this approach is to "own" the market.

Niche target market strategy. This strategy is similar to single target marketing, but goes further in differentiating the market from others and is usually smaller in size. An example would be women over the age of 65 who exercise in a specific fitness center in a specific community. You can see how very restricted and small this target market would be. Typically, niche marketing will work if the company is the only one selling the product to its consumers. This strategy will be successful as long as the situation stays the same. However, once another company begins to offer the product, the targeting strategy will need to change.

Multi-segment target market strategy. This strategy involves the selection of two or more segments to target. Usually, this strategy can be the most successful in terms of efficiency and effectiveness. Even if there is very little difference between segments, people feel special when showered with attention. Larger companies with different products often use this strategy. Using Nike again as an example, this company manufactures numerous products, thus requiring numerous target markets.

In an example shown in Figure 5.4, a sporting goods retail store has identified its overall consumer segment as "sports participants." That segment can be massive if not further segmented. For this particular store in a central metro city area, the store's research helps further segment the "sports participants" into differentiated segments and target markets. The sport marketing team for the store has determined to use individual "sports" to divide and identify specific target markets. As an additional step, more target markets are identified using behavioral characteristics. The management team of the store will use this information to make decisions about what products to carry, how to price the products, when to carry the products, and how to use promotional techniques to increase potential sales.

As you can see through the use of the example, conducting research to delineate market segments, differentiating within those segments, and then selecting target markets provides key information needed in making decisions that guide the company.

THE FOUR CONSUMER MARKET SEGMENTATION CRITERIA

Sport marketing professionals use segmentation for several reasons. Segmentation helps identify groups of consumers with similar characteristics and purchase behaviors. Segmentation provides the sport marketing professional with valuable information that guides marketing mix decisions and strategies specifically customized for the consumer

Overall Market Segment	Specific Target Markets by Sport	Market Type by Behavioral Characteristics
• The Sports Participant: The individual who plays sports. However, in many cases, this individual is not the one making the decisions to purchase sporting equipment or clothing or shoe items; that individual can be a parent, an athletic director, or a coach. The segments include: individual participants, parents, league representatives, independent team coaches, school athletic directors, sports performance businesses.	• 1. Baseball—research shows 110,000 participants of baseball in the target city • 2. Softball—research shows 122,000 participants of softball in the city; aged 10 through 56; male and female • 3. Volleyball—research shows 32,500 participants of volleyball in the city; aged 14 through 54; mostly female • 4. Basketball—research shows 78,000 participants of basketball in the city; aged 7 through 55; equal male and female • 5. Football—research shows 14,000 participants of football in the city; aged 12 through 18; nearly all male • 6. Soccer—research shows 85,000 participants of soccer in the city; aged 5 through 55; equal male and female • 7. Golf—research shows 8,500 participants of golf in the city; aged 14 through 75; 60% male, 40% female • 8. Tennis—research shows 25,000 participants of tennis in the city; aged 10 through 65; male and female	• 1. Individual Sports Participants: These are the actual sports participants. Typically these are adult participants or older youths who have knowledge of equipment and income to purchase equipment and apparel of their own. • 2. Parents: parents buy on their own or are present at the purchase of over 90% of purchases for youth ages 5–18. This market is heavily influenced by their children in their relation to "hot" or best products to buy. They are also the market needing the most technical assistance from store sales staff. • 3. League Representatives: members of associations who are responsible for purchases for equipment and uniforms for leagues. Price and long-term relationships are important to this market. They have technical knowledge and want to deal with sales staff of same or higher technical knowledge level. • 4. Independent Coaches: Coaches are those teaching sports teams; they are responsible for the design and purchase of team uniforms and selection of specific equipment and shoes.

Figure 5.4. Market Segment and Target Markets for a Sporting Goods Retail Store.

group. Segments can be of any size and mix of characteristics. To be useful, however, segmentation methods should produce segments that meet certain criteria. The most useful criteria include identifiability, substantiality, accessibility, and responsiveness (see Figure 5.2).

Identifiable

Segments must be identifiable and measurable. Using the Hispanic population as an example, data about the population can be found from the U.S. Census Bureau and from most cities. This data both identifies and gives a measure of the population. In other examples, the Baby Boomers, Generation X, Generation Y, and the Millennials are each well-known market segments that have been identified primarily by birth years and measured.

Further, each market segment should be homogeneous within itself. That is, those within a segment should be as similar as possible. Segments should be heterogeneous between groups. That is, a segment should be distinguishably different from all others. These guidelines help the marketer determine similar and different characteristics within and between segments.

Substantial

Segments must be large enough to justify marketing mix customization and attention. Otherwise, the time and money spent on the marketing mix may never realize a return on investment or a profit. On the other hand, a population can be segmented using so many variables that each segment contains only one individual. The sport marketing professional must determine if and when the segment is large enough to justify customizing a marketing mix.

Accessible

Segments must be reachable with the customized marketing mix. This means that your company must be able to "reach" the market using means or media that the market uses or through which it can be accessed. Some segments are easy to reach, and others are hard to reach. For instance, hardcore baseball fans are easy to reach because they watch a lot of baseball. Therefore, we know where to find them and how to market to them. On the other hand, full-time RVers are hard to reach because they do not live at permanent addresses. An RVer is a person who has purchased an RV, or recreational vehicle, also known as a camper trailer. A full-time RVer is a person (or a couple) who has sold everything in order to live full time in the RV. RVers are constantly traveling, camping at RV parks, and enjoying life as RVers. There are a few magazines and websites targeting RVers that can be used as media through which to reach the RVers. And in a third example, the Hispanic population now has many ways to be reached: Hispanic TV stations, radio, magazines, newspapers, websites, and local organizations. The sport business can use any one or more of these media to reach, or advertise to, the Hispanic segments.

Responsive

Being *responsive* means that a consumer will respond to, or act upon, marketing activities. Segments must respond to a marketing mix customized to them. Otherwise, there is no point to having the customized marketing mix. If a segment does not respond to the customized product, price, distribution, or promotion efforts, maybe that segment need not be considered as a separate segment, or the marketing mix elements need to be modified. For example, if your sport business has decided to spend $10,000 for an advertisement on a website targeted to one of your target markets, you should measure whether or not consumers are responding to the ad. One measure commonly used is a coupon—a coupon can be tracked with specific identification tactics, such as a UPC code that gets swiped. A computer software system designed to track the coupon can give information about where the coupon came from, and how many have been used. If your company had predetermined that the 3,000 coupons used is a successful mark, and 2,895 coupons were used, then your company can conclude that the segment responded positively and successfully to your marketing mix.

BASES FOR CONSUMER SEGMENTATION

Sport marketing professionals use segmentation bases or variables (also called characteristics) to divide a total market into segments. These are characteristics that are divided into several categories. The choice of bases is crucial because an inappropriate group of bases will not be successful in relation to response to marketing mix. The key is to identify bases that produce a right mix of identifiability, measurability, substantiality, accessibility, and responsiveness in that segment.

Markets can be segmented using one or more bases and any number of variables within the bases. For example, a segment can be created using just gender as a variable. WNBA season-ticket holders can be segmented by gender. Markets can be segmented using multiple bases. For example, the WNBA ticket holders can be segmented into groups by gender, age, income, race, household status, zip code, favorite color, favorite movie, and so forth. The disadvantage of using multiple-base segmentation for this market is that it will create too many segments that are small in number and will probably not be of a substantial size to justify a customized marketing mix for each group. However, today's trend is toward the use of more bases rather than fewer because of the multicultural, multifaceted population; more segments want their differences recognized.

As mentioned earlier in this chapter, this trend has led to the development and increased use of relationship, cause, and niche marketing tactics. After all, these marketing strategies meet the most basic of marketing fundamentals—give the customers what they want.

In the sport business industry, companies commonly use one or more of the following five bases to segment markets: demographics, psychographics, geographics, behavior, and product functions and benefits sought (see Figure 5.3). Within each base are several individual characteristics or variables that must be considered. A more detailed description of these bases follows.

Demographics

Demographics are statistical data about a person or group. In the past, five demographics have typically been used: age, gender, income, race, and ethnicity (see Table 5.2). Today, additional demographics are used to deepen the segmentation of the population. The additional demographics include such characteristics as education level, sexual orientation, occupation, relationship status, religion, and social class. As you can see in Table 5.2, demographic information includes basic information about a person that can present a partial picture of the characteristics of that person.

Demographics are used commonly in segmentation in sport business. Using an example from sport marketing research, Table 5.3 shows the demographics of people who

Table 5.2. Some Demographics and Typical Breakdowns	
Demographic Variables	**Typical Breakdowns**
Age	Under 12; adolescent; teen; 18–24; 25–34; 35–44; 45–54; 55+ Baby Boomers 1945–1965; Generation X 1965–1985; Generation Y 1985–2005
Gender	Female; male
Relationship Status	Single; married; partner; divorced
Income	Under $10k; $10,000–19,999; $20,000–39,999; $40,000–59,999; $60,000–79,999 Under-$50,000; $50,000–99,999; $100,000–149,999; $150,000–199,999 Lower class; middle class; upper class; wealthy; super wealthy
Occupation	Clerical; sales; craftsman; technical; manager; professional; teacher
Education Completed	Middle school; high school; some college; college; graduate; doctoral or terminal
Race	White; Black; Asian; Hispanic; mixed; other
Nationality	American; French; German

attended a sports event and participated in that study. Note that the example shows some of the commonly used demographical data such as gender, age, ethnicity, sexual orientation, income, and education. By analyzing these data, the sport marketing professional can describe the consumers attending the event and use this information to help with decision making in marketing strategies. Several demographic characteristics are presented and described next.

Age

Age can indicate typical generational characteristics. For example, there are cultural differences between Baby Boomers, Generation Y, and Generation X populations. Two things are happening in the sport business industry in relation to age segmentation. First, current businesses in the sport industry are increasingly recognizing a greater variety of age segments as serious consumers of a variety of products in the industry.

Second, new companies and organizations have been started whose sole focus and product are age-specific segmentation. In the first instance, numerous existing sport businesses and organizations that offer sports activities and other sport-related products are recognizing more age groups as consumers and offering an increasing variety of products for those markets. The age groups range from the very young to the very old. Soccer organizations are offering leagues for age segments that range from the under-5-year-old division to the 50-plus division. In tennis, some tournaments offer age divisions such as the women's 60, 70, and 80 national clay court championships (United States Tennis Association, 2010). Swimming and track-and-field are two other sports in

Table 5.3. Example of Demographics from a Study at a Supercross Event. Atlanta, GA (2011)		
Variables	**Category**	**Percent of Study Participants**
Age	18–24	36%
	25–34	27%
	35–44	27%
	45–55	7%
	Over 55	4%
Gender	Male	67%
	Female	33%
Relationship Status	Single	49%
	Married	44%
	Partner	4%
	Divorced	3%
Ethnicity	African American	11%
	Caucasian	84%
	Asian/Pacific Islander	4%
	Hispanic	1%
Household Income In Dollars	Under 20K	14%
	20K to 39,999	24%
	40K to 59,999	19%
	60K to 79,999	11%
	80K to 99,999	6%
	100K to 119,999	15%
	120K +	11%
Occupation	Construction/Trade	10%
	Student	8%
	Service	8%
	Retail / Sales	7%
	Restaurant	6%
	Self-Employed	5%
	Medical	4%
	Office	4%
	Education	4%
Children?	Yes	52%
	No	48%

Source: Class Project on sport market research 2011; B. G. Pitts, B. Van Fleet, K. Olson, D. McDaniel, P. DeMatteo

which age, used as age-group divisions or leagues, are offered as age-related products. More recently, however, those age groups now include higher age brackets and are typically called the master's divisions. More sports organizations and businesses are doing the same.

Gender

Long ago, most spectator sports were limited to a few men's professional sports whose owners and marketers promoted to the male market. Today, however, with an incredi-

Table 5.4. Fan Facts About Women's Sports	
Danica Patrick's stockcar racing debut at the Lucas Oil Slick Mist 200 at Daytona International Speedway in 2010 is credited with a massive increase in viewership from the same event in 2009 with 2.4 million people tuning into the event, an 87% improvement. The event was televised on the SPEED network.[1]	When the wildly popular sisters Venus and Serena Williams played each other in the U.S. Open Women's final in 2001 more than 23 million Americans watched the match on TV. They are credited for overall growth of the sport as 2010 saw a 20% increase in overall viewership for the WTA.[4]
Superstars can have a huge impact on fan attendance. In 2005, attendance at LPGA Majors grew rapidly with the popularity of Annika Sorenstam. The combined attendance for the first three major championships of 2005 accounted for 288,798 guests, which was 14 percent higher than attendance figures for those same tournaments in 2004.[2]	Every game of the 2011 Women's World Cup was broadcast worldwide on the ESPN networks and WatchESPN.com. Additionally Twitter.com reported a new record for as 7,196 tweets were sent out, per second, during the end of the Women's World Cup final.[5]
The 2010 NCAA Women's Final Four games had a TV viewership of 3.5 million, and increase of 32% from 2011.[5]	The record-breaking attendance at the 2011 NCAA Women's Final Four Championship game was 17,473.[6]
Television viewership of the LPGA increased by 20% for events on cable, and 32% for events on the Golf Channel. LPGA.com saw an increase of 77% in daily visitors from 2010 to 2011; and overall traffic to the website increased by 52% during tournament weeks.[3]	Research shows that the number of U.S. high school girls playing sports rose from 8% of the number of boys in 1972 to over 70% in 2009. Between 1972 when Title IX was enacted, and 2010, the number of women's sports teams per college increased from 2 to 8.64.[7]
Sources: 1) Courchesne, 2010; 2) LPGA.com, 2005; 3) LPGA.com, 2011; 4) The Associated Press, 2010; 5) Messner, 2011; 6) The Associated Press, 2011; 7) ESPN W, 2011; 8) USCDornsife, n.d.	

ble number of hours of sports programming in a 24-hour period on dozens of sports television channels, and with more sports and other fitness and recreational activities televised or offered otherwise at an entertainment event, the sports spectator market has grown exponentially.

In addition, contrary to popular belief, sports spectators are not only males; and it's not only women who watch women's sports. In addition, it's not just a few men's sports that we see on television anymore. The number of women's sports and mixed-gender sports, some of which are setting records for spectatorship, is increasing. For instance, Table 5.4 provides several notes of numbers of spectatorship for women's sports.

In sports offered as a participant product, it is also a gender-bending period. Women's participation in sports, fitness and recreational activities is at an all-time high and shows no signs of slowing. Table 5.5 presents some facts about women's participation in sports.

The women's market is being felt across the sport industry in a number of ways. For example, Table 5.6 illustrates several instances. As girls and women have become serious participants, athletes, spectators, managers, owners, manufacturers, and consumers in a variety of ways in the sport industry, their consumerism and commercial value have risen dramatically.

Table 5.5. Participation Factors about Women's Sports	

• Over 3 million women women play sports each year.
• In 1971, 294,000 high school girls played interscholastic sports. Today 3.1 million play, much closer to the 4.4 million boys who play high school sports.
• According to the NCAA and U.S. Education Department. Between 1971 and 2005, female participation in collegiate sports increased 456 percent.
• A study published in 2007, for example, showed that playing on a high school sports team increased a young woman's chances of graduating from college by 41 percent.
• In 2007, the Olympic Charter was amended to include, for the first time in history, an explicit reference to women in sports.
    "The IOC encourages and supports the promotion of women in sports at all levels and in all structures, with a view to implementing the principle of equality of men and women."
      —Rule 2, paragraph 7, Olympic Charter
• During the 2004–05 season, 155,516 women participated in collegiate sports across all levels. This was an increase of over 6000 participants from 2001.
	• In 2011 15-year-old Rachel Hale becomes the first female in Vermont to win a state wrestling championship competing against male wrestlers; the third overall in the U.S.
	• A 2010 study by the Women's Sports and Fitness Foundation found that 53.7% of women in England surveyed wanted to participate in more sports than they do including over 70% of women age 16–34.
	• According to the U.S. Education Department. Between 1971 and 2005, female participation in high school sports increased 875%.
	• 42% of all athlete's at the Beijing Summer Olympics in 2008 were women, a growth from 38% at the 2004 Olympics in Athens.
	• In the 2010 Winter Olympics the U.S. team brought 93 female athletes; 43%.
	• The sports that saw the most female participants fro the U.S. at those 2010 Olympics were Ice Hockey, Speed Skating, and Alpine Skiing.
	• In 2011, on her third attempt since 2008, 60-year-old Pat Gallant-Charette from Westbrook, Maine swims across the English Channel in less than 16 hours. She is now the oldest American woman to swim the English Channel.

Sources:
1, 2, 3, 5, 6, 7, 8 —Women's Sports Foundation
4, 9 —Thomas, 2008.
10, 11—Olympic.org, n.d.
12 —2010 Olympic Report
13,14 —St. Lawrence County Branch, n.d.

Disability

Disability, or handicap, no longer restricts an individual's access to, or participation in, sports, fitness, recreation, or leisure activities or in sport business. The Paralympics, World Games for the Deaf, U.S. National Wheelchair Games, National Wheelchair Basketball Association Championships, and Special Olympics are some of the events that have been leaders in paving the way for the full participation in sport and sport business of people with disabilities. In addition, the Americans with Disabilities Act has helped open the door for many more opportunities in the sport industry for people with disabilities.

Disability sport is defined as "sport that has been designed for or specifically practiced by athletes with disabilities" (DePauw & Gavron, 1995, p. 6). These sports competitions are not as new as many of us think. For example, the First International Silent Games was held in 1924. The First U.S. National Wheelchair Games were held in

Table 5.6. Women's Consumerism and Commercial Value in the Sport Industry

- espnW launched in 2010 as a digital and content-driven business to better connect with female sports fans and athletes 18–34 with a web site, mobile applications and social media, with more planned for 2011.
- On October 22, 2001 ESPN secured an 11-year agreement to show the entire NCAA Women's Basketball Tournament. The deal also includes an agreement to air Division II basketball, women's soccer, softball, swimming, volleyball and indoor track.
- In 2010 the NCAA received $6.74 million dollars in ticket sales from the women's basketball tournament.
- Maria Sharapova is the highest paid female athlete in the world with earnings of $24.5 million dollars in 2009. She also signed a massive eight-year deal with Nike at the beginning of the year that could be worth as much as $70 million.

- 40% of the 6.6 million people attending Winston Cup races each year are women.
- Women purchase 46% of official NLF merchandise worldwide.
- Women account for 47.2% of major league soccer fans, 46.5% of MLB fans, 43.2% of NFL fans, 40.8% of fans at NHL games, 37% of NBA fans.
- Women make more than 80% of all consumer purchasing decisions
- As of 2011 six women have earned more than $10 million dollars during their LPGA careers including Annika Sorenstam at $22.5 million. Karrie Webb, Lorena Ochoa, Cristie Kerr, Juli Inkster and Se Ri Pak also qualify for this distinction.

Sources:
1, 2, 3—Eichelberger, 2011.
4—Badenhausen, 2010.
5, 6, 7, 8—Holland, n.d.
9—LPGA.com, 2012.

1957. The First International Games for Disabled were held in 1960. Many well-known marathons such as the Boston Marathon have wheelchair divisions, the first of which was established in the 1970s.

Many sports, fitness, recreational, and leisure activities today are modified in relation to rules and equipment for an individual or group according to disability. For example, for people with vision impairments to play softball, there is a softball with a chime inside so that the players can utilize their sense of hearing to compensate. In track, people with vision impairments use their hands to follow a string around the course or track. In water skiing, people with leg impairments have water skis modified so that the skier can sit on the skis. These are just a few of the numerous adjustments made to activities and equipment so that people with disabilities can participate.

Race and Ethnicity

Some groups in the United States have a single characteristic that places them in one market—race or ethnicity. People who are of Hispanic origin might all be categorized into the Hispanic market segment. People who are Asian might all be categorized into the Asian market segment. These segments, and a few others, are increasing as a proportion of the population in the United States while the proportion of whites is declining. The United States Census Bureau conducts a study of the population of the United States every ten years. The recent one done in 2010 revealed the percentages of the current population of the USA and these are shown in Table 5.7.

Table 5.7. U.S. Populations (2010)

Race	Number	Percentage of U.S. Population
Caucasian	223.6 million	72.4 %
African American	38.9 million	12.6 %
Other Single Race	19.1 million	6.2 %
Asian	14.7 million	4.8 %
Multiple Races	9.0 million	2.9 %
American Indian/ Alaska Native	2.9 million	0.9 %
Native Hawaiian/ Other Pacific Islander	0.5 million	0.2 %

Table 5.8. Strategies for Sport Marketers about the Black sports Consumer Market.

	Key Findings about Black Consumers		Strategies for Sport Marketers
1	The Black consumer market is a challenging segment with many cultural nuances that influence their thoughts and behaviors.	☞	Involve individuals with expertise in the Black consumer market in the designing of marketing strategies.
2	Black consumers have unique media consumption patterns.	☞	Use Black media outlets (particularly Black radio) to promote events.
3	Blacks respond more favorably to culturally based approaches of marketing communications.	☞	Advertisements and promotional messages should contain a theme and content that offer a reference point for Black audiences.
4	Blacks often seek a means of identifying with organizations as they decide whether or not to support their business.	☞	Engage in activities that allow Blacks to find a self-reference link to identify with the organization.
5	Black consumers often have an allegiance to patronize Black businesses.	☞	Conduct business with Black vendors to provide organizational needs, and involve them as corporate sponsors.
6	Black consumers often seek a cultural experience in their leisure activities.	☞	Amend the product/service with extensions that are culturally salient to Black consumers.
7	Black consumers are socially conscious individuals.	☞	Demonstrate a respect for the Black community through socially responsible/cause-related marketing.
8	Black consumers may have personal and structural difficulty accessing the existing channels of distribution.	☞	Distribute tickets through outlets that are easily accessible to Black consumers. Also, find creative ways of exposing the product to the Black communities.
9	Sport behaviors are often a result of socialization occurring during childhood.	☞	Invest in programs to include Black youth to nurture their involvement.
10	Just as any other community, the Black community also has opinion leaders.	☞	Form a support group of Black constituents from various realms of the community to serve as staff multipliers.

Source: Armstrong, 1998 .

	Table 5.9. Facts About the Hispanic Sports Consumer
1	A single year surge from 2009 to 2010 saw 24% more of the Hispanic population in the U.S. attending college. That marks an all-time high of 12.2 million Hispanics in college.
2	For the first time in decades, the growth of the Hispanic population in the United States is spurned more by domestic births than immigration. There were 7.2 million Hispanic Americans born between 2000–2010.
3	In 2010 31.8 million or 66% of the Hispanic population in the U.S. were of Mexican descent. In a distant second, there were 4.6 million Americans of Puerto Rican descent.
4	The number of Hispanic Americans participating in national elections has more than doubled from 2.9 million in 1986 to 6.6 million in 2010.
5	Hispanic Americans are less likely than both Blacks and Whites to access the Internet and use cell phones.
6	The average household wealth of Hispanic Americans fell by 66% from 2005 to 2009 as the population was hit hard by the great recession. However 2010 showed recovery with 3% more Hispanic Americans finding employment.
7	Marketing to the Hispanic culture should focus on the populations' tendency to place great emphasis on family values.
8	Hispanic Americans tend to locate in urban areas especially Southern California, Southern Florida, Southern Texas and Metropolitan Chicago.
9	Latino youths ages 16 to 25 are satisfied with their lives, optimistic about their futures and place a high value on education, hard work and career success.
10	English is spoken more commonly at work than at home by all generations. Hispanic immigrants report greater fluency in English if they are highly educated, arrived in the United States as children or have spent many years here.
	Source: The Pew Hispanic Center (PewHispanic.org)

These segments are also increasingly exercising their consumer and commercial value as sport businesses target them and as they create their own sport businesses and organizations to serve their sporting demands.

Articles appearing in the *Sport Marketing Quarterly* (*SMQ*) offer good advice concerning marketing to the African-American and Hispanic American sports markets. Tables 5.8 and 5.9 illustrate the points from those articles. Sport businesses wanting to target these segments would use this information to develop marketing mix strategies. With these segments, it would also be wise marketing to use cause-and-relationship marketing strategies.

Sexual Orientation: The Gay and Lesbian Sports Market

The lesbian and gay population comprise approximately 10% of the population, or 31 million. It is estimated that almost half, or 13 million, people who are gay or lesbian participate in sports, recreation, leisure, and fitness activities and that this market spends an estimated minimum average of $2,000 each per year, or a total estimated $22 billion in the sport industry.

	Table 5.10. Strategies to Reach The Gay and Lesbian Sports Market
1	Your company must identify as a "gay/lesbian friendly" to gain the necessary attention and trust of the gay and lesbian market.
2	The Gay and Lesbian Market has been enthusiastically labeled the "Dream Market" due to its overall buying power of $641 billion dollars.[2]
3	Research indicates that on average, gay consumers do not earn more than other Americans but have more disposable income because fewer are raising children.[1]
4	All men and women interpret imagery and data differently so research shows that the development of specific advertising strategies for gay males as well as distinctly different material for lesbian women will prove valuable.[1]
5	GLBT population does not fit into a single category of gender, race/ethnicity, age, nationality or socioeconomic status. It is a diverse group of people found in every gender and race worldwide.[2]
6	Form partnerships with lesbian/gay sports organizations and companies like Outsports.com or governing bodies like the Federation of Gay Games.[5]
7	Your Company must sponsor local and national gay sporting events like the Atlanta Gay Sports Alliance or the NYC Gay Hockey Association.[5]
8	Select appropriate media for advertising.[5]
9	Become a member of the IGTA (International Gay Travel Association) and be sure the IGTA logo is displayed on advertisements and websites.[4]
10	Keep in mind the Gay and Lesbian market is trending more and more towards technology with disposable income as 65% purchased a cell phone and 25% a new car in 2008.[3]
	Sources: 1. Witeck & Combs, 2006; 2. Oakenfull, 2007; 3. Baxter, 2010; 4. Community Marketing, Inc., n.d.; 5. Pitts, B. G., 1999b.

Similar to race or ethnic segments, the lesbian and gay sport market also have organized and started their own sport businesses. It is estimated that there are approximately between 3,000 and 15,000 sports events each year organized by, and targeted primarily to, the gay and lesbian market.

Like other groups, the lesbian and gay sport segment has its own Olympics—the Gay Games, held every four years. The Gay Games is an incredible success, having grown at a rate of 275% since the first games were held in 1982.

After identifying this market, the sport business should then develop marketing mix strategies customized for it. Further, it would be a good idea to develop relationship and cause marketing strategies similar to those suggested for race and ethnic segments. Table 5.10 presents a list of 10 strategies that a company might consider.

Income

Income is an important demographic for helping with decisions about several marketing elements, especially pricing strategies. Income is divided into two categories: disposable income and discretionary income. *Disposable* income is all money, after taxes, at your disposal. *Discretionary* income is all money, after necessities, to be used at your dis-

Table 5.11. Total Number of Snow Sports Participants Over 4 Years			
Season	Alpine	Snowboarding	Cross Country
2010	11,504,000	8,196,000	4,530,000
2009	10,919,000	7,421,000	4,157,000
2008	10,346,000	7,159,000	3,848,000
2007	10,362,000	6,841,000	3,530,000
Gender			
Male	60%	66%	55%
Female	40%	34%	45%
Source: www.snowsports.org			

cretion. Of course, it is discretionary income that sport marketing professionals study. The national average expenditure on recreational activity is about 8%. Therefore, if a person's discretionary income is $30,000, then the average amount of actual dollars spent for recreational and leisure activity is about $2,400. As the amount of income increases, so does the amount spent on recreational activity: An income of $50,000 yields about $4,000; an income of $75,000 yields about $6,000; and an income of $100,000 yields about $8,000. Anglers each spent an average of $1,046 for their sport.

Income has long been a demographic used readily in the sport industry. For instance, to which income segment do sports such as polo, sailing, yachting, scuba, snow skiing, and golf seem to be targeted? Although more income groups can afford golf today, there are still many golf clubs to which only the wealthy can belong. Table 5.11 illustrates the participation demographics of snowboarders and skiers. As you can see, the sport of

Table 5.12. Sales in the Snow Sports Industry				
Season	Apparel	Equipment	Accessories	Total
2010	$6.31 million 31.3%	$6.52 million 32.4%	$7.33 million 36.3%	$2 billion
2009	$5.82 million 32.8%	$5.61 million 31.6%	$6.32 million 35.6%	$1.77 billion
2008	$5.98 million 35.2%	$5.23 million 30.7%	$5.85 million 34.2%	$1.70 billion
2007	$6.64 million 35.8%	$5.63 million 30.4%	$6.24 million 33.7%	$1.85 billion
Source: www.snowsports.org				

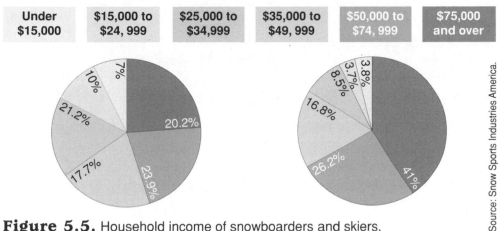

Under $15,000	$15,000 to $24,999	$25,000 to $34,999	$35,000 to $49,999	$50,000 to $74,999	$75,000 and over

Source: Snow Sports Industries America.

Figure 5.5. Household income of snowboarders and skiers.

snowboarding has grown over the years. In addition, you can see that snowboarding has been slightly dominated by males. As indicated in Figure 5.5, the largest segments are those whose household incomes are in the $50,000 to 74,000 and $75,000-and-over categories. Table 5.12 illustrates how much money is spent on snow ski equipment and apparel. As you can see, these are not inexpensive sports.

Table 5.13 illustrates how consumer market information is used to determine which sub-segments within a market primarily constitute the segment. In this example, we can see that the segment labeled "The Core" is the largest segment—56%—of all snow-boarders and that it accounts for $15.4 million in buying power whereas "Beginners" are close at 45%. A sport marketing professional working in the snow-sports industry segment would use this information to make decisions on product, pricing, and promotion and in establishing competitive strategies.

Relationship Status

Earlier in this chapter we mentioned different relationship segments identified in the U.S. population, such as the baby boomers. For each identifiable segment, there are specific demographic and psychographic information concerning life course variables

Table 5.13. The Snowboard Consumer Market Breakdown					
	Children (7–11)	The Core (Males 14–24)	The Employed (24 +)	Women (All ages)	Beginners (All ages)
Growth	17%	56%	30%	24%	45%
Buying Power	$8.73 million	$15.4 million	$11.3 million	Unknown	Unknown
Note: Overlap does not add up to 100%					
Source: www.snowsports.org					

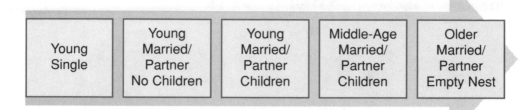

Figure 5.6. Relationship Life Cycle Possibilities.

such as household characteristics concerning marriage or domestic partnership, divorce, and children.

Other marketing information presents life-cycle information as actual cycles as though moving from point A to point B. For example, Figures 5.6 and 5.7 illustrate some of the possible relationship situations in one's life cycle.

Sport marketing professionals should monitor such demographics pertaining to their existing markets and potential markets. In today's world, it is a mistake to assume that everyone's relationship follows the old traditional route of young-single, married, married-with-children, and retired. For instance, in establishing membership categories, most fitness center and sports club businesses are moving away from the old traditional

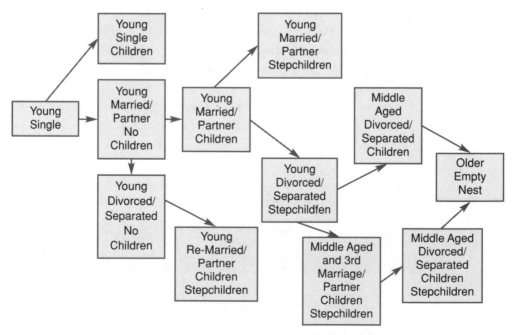

Figure 5.7. Modern Relationship Life Cycle Possibilities.

Source: Lu & Pitts, 2004

categories of "single" and "family" to more contemporary categories of "individual" and "household." In those businesses that might continue to use "family" designations, for instance, the definition is contemporary, and the member is given full control to define the family group. For example, the traditional definition of "family" was "married man, wife, and children." Today's definition includes several variations in order to be inclusive and more accurately reflect today's family groups.

Psychographics

Demographic information is a good start in describing and developing segmentation strategies, but demographics don't paint the full picture. Personality characteristics such as, favorite color, motivation factors, desires, attitude, and beliefs are some of the many other types of information that describe and define a person. These are called psychographics. Partially deriving from the word *psychological*, psychographic information is psychologically-related characteristics about a person. Table 5.14 presents a list of several psychographic variables. Note that many of these kinds of information are psychological and preference-based such as favorite color, favorite drink, prestige, happiness, and beliefs. Thus, they are subject to change as circumstances and situations in a person's life changes. For example, the way a people spend leisure time can change when they become a parent.

At the most basic level of psychographic information are basic human needs, wants, and desires. As Maslow's hierarchy of needs shows, in Table 5.15, people are driven by particular needs at certain times (Maslow, 1954). The most basic human needs are physiological—the needs for food, water, sleep, and shelter. These needs must be satisfied first because they are necessary for survival. Recent sports drink advertising, for example, attempts to appeal to the need to survive and thrive while participating in sports events.

Safety needs are second and include the need for security and protection and freedom from fear, pain, discomfort, ridicule, and harm. Sport marketing professionals often attempt to exploit the human's fear for safety and freedom from pain, for instance, by attempting to show, in ads, potential harming effects if certain actions are not taken.

Table 5.14. Some Psychological Factors Used in Segmentation	
Personality:	values, beliefs, habits
Physiological:	food, drink, sleep, shelter
Psychological:	affiliation, beauty, belonging, curiosity, esteem, independence, love, motive
Lifestyle:	household style, parent style, importance of life comfort, culture, financial resources, occupation and education, community
Desire for:	acceptance, achievement, comfort, fame happiness, identification, prestige
Freedom from:	anxiety, depression, discomfort, fear, harm, pain, sadness
Sources: Walthorn, 1979; Liebert & Spiegler, 1970; Kelly & Warnick, 1999	

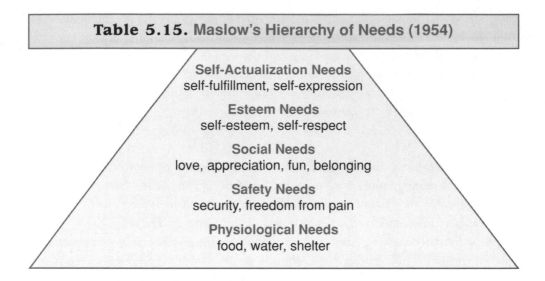

Table 5.15. Maslow's Hierarchy of Needs (1954)

Self-Actualization Needs
self-fulfillment, self-expression

Esteem Needs
self-esteem, self-respect

Social Needs
love, appreciation, fun, belonging

Safety Needs
security, freedom from pain

Physiological Needs
food, water, shelter

For example, an ad showing bones of extreme osteoporosis in someone who has not been active versus the healthy bones of someone who is active is an attempt to play on fear.

The human's social needs are commonly exploited in advertising. These include such needs and desires as love, acceptance, achievement, prestige, recognition, respect, satisfaction, appreciation, happiness, identification, sensual experiences, and status.

Many sport marketers use these in a variety of ways to reach consumers. These can be seen in, for example, such advertisements as promotions to encourage tailgating activities at sporting events such as football games, car races, and boat races. The ad for a softball bat that tells readers that the bat will make them the envy of the team and will give them more home runs is attempting to appeal to the need and desire for prestige and status, in the first instance, and achievement and satisfaction, in the second instance.

Esteem needs are those that include self-esteem and external esteem, or respect from one's group. These needs include self-respect and a sense of accomplishment, for instance.

The highest human need is self-actualization, which involves reaching a point in life at which the person believes he or she should be. This includes self-development, self fulfillment, self-expression, self-identification, and self-realization. To reach this need, the marketer attempts to speak directly to the individual about her or himself. Typically, in these ads you will find such phrases as "you've reached that point in life where you've accomplished everything you wanted" or "you've made it; now you can sit back and enjoy the good life." These tend to be directed more often at the mature markets.

Typically, psychographic information is categorized in three areas: personality, motives, and lifestyle. Personality characteristics are those traits, attitudes, and behaviors that make us "who we are." Many sport products are marketed on the basis of personality segments. In one area of the sport industry in which sporting events are marketed to spectators as consumers, this is most noticeable. The NFL markets primarily to certain male segments based on personality characteristics. Typically, those commercials show male groups with distinct personality characteristics such as the "serious couch potato fan," or "the crazy painted in-the-stands fan." The WNBA markets primarily to certain female personality segments. With slogans such as "We got next," the WNBA is attempting to reach those girls and women whose attitude toward male basketball players and fans is, "You've had your time. Move over, now. It's our turn."

Motives are those needs or desires that give humans a need for action, or motivation. Fitness center advertising usually always centers on motivation. In those ads are slogans and phrases such as "Summer's coming—can you fit into your bikini?" or "Body check—how do you look in the mirror naked?" These phrases are meant to motivate the human into wanting to get into great shape.

In a study looking at the motivations of sports participants and sports spectators, Milne and McDonald (1999) categorized motivation variables and Maslow's hierarchy of needs. Table 5.16 presents those motivational factors along with a brief description of each. In studying these, it is easy to see how a sport marketer could use them to segment consumers and to develop successful promotional campaigns in a number of sport industry businesses. For instance, people who exercise at a fitness center might be categorized in a "physical fitness" segment. This would be used as part of the message, slogans, or tag lines in advertising for fitness centers. In another example, those "achievement" segment. This need to achieve would then be used by the sport marketer in promotions to enter and participate in the event.

Lifestyle, life-cycle, and life-course factors are those characteristics concerning life situations. Although also used as a demographic, and described earlier in this chapter,

Table 5.16. Sport Participation Motivation Factors	
Physical Fitness	desire to be in good physical condition and improve health
Risk Taking	desire to participate in risky, thrilling, and extreme activities
Stress Reduction	desire to reduce anxiety, apprehension, fear, and tension
Aggression	desire to inflict aversive stimulus on another person, either in an attempt to reduce or increase aggressive levels
Affiliation	desire to be connected to or associated with something; confirms sense of identity
Social Facilitation	desire to be with others who enjoy the same activity
Self-Esteem	desire to enhance one's positive regard of self
Competition	desire to enter into a rivalry or contest with another, usually as a test of skill
Achievement	desire to accomplish a specific goal
Skill Mastery	desire to positively enhance performance
Aesthetics	desire to be near or part of the beauty, grace, artistry, and creative expression of sport
Value Development	desire to develop values such as loyalty and honest through sport
Self-Actualization	desire to fulfill potential
Source: Milne & McDonald, 1999	

Table 5.17. VALS 2 Psychographic Segments	
Actualizers	people who are successful, sophisticated, active, leader-oriented, and growth-oriented; seek to develop, explore, and express; and have high self-esteem, abundant resources, and a cultivated taste for the finer things in life
Fulfillers	people who are mature, satisfied, reflective, well-educated, well-informed, professionally employed, and comfortable; value order, knowledge, and responsibility; tend to be conservative; and are practical consumers concerned about value, quality, and durability
Believers	people who are conventional; traditional about family, church, community, and country; and conservative and predictable buyers
Achievers	people who are success-oriented in work and play; value control; live conventional lives; respect authority; are conservative; and favor established goods that demonstrate success
Strivers	people who are self-defined, easily bored, and impulsive; seek motivation and approval from the world around them; believe money means success; and emulate those who have more possessions
Experiencers	people who are young, vital, impulsive, and enthusiastic; seek excitement and variety; dislike authority and conformity; and are avid consumers, especially of clothing, fast food, movies, music, and videos
Makers	people who are practical, down-to-earth; value self-sufficiency; and are traditional in family, work, and play
Strugglers	people who are poor, ill educated, and lowly skilled; lack social bonds; live for the moment; desire immediate satisfaction and gratification; and are cautious consumers

lifestyle characteristics can be viewed as preferences and, as such, can be considered beliefs and attitudes.

Psychographic segmentation can include individual variables or can be combined with other variables in order to more accurately describe market segments. One such system, offered by Stanford Research International, is called VALS—Values and Lifestyles program (VALS 2, 1990). This system categorizes consumers by their values, beliefs, and lifestyles. Table 5.17 presents the segments as developed by VALS.

When this system is studied, it's easy to see how many different consumer groups in the sport industry can be segmented into these categories. For instance, those who participate in risky sports such as skydiving might be segmented into the "Experiencers" segment. Those who participate in polo might be categorized into the "Actualizers" segment. Then, using this kind of psychographic information, the sport marketer can develop promotional and advertising campaigns that have a higher chance of success.

Geographics

Geographic segmentation involves dividing or describing a population according to geographic regions or areas. Geodemographic segmentation involves using demographics, psychographics, and lifestyle information to segment a geographic location, area, or region.

The United States can be segmented according to purely geographic lines. The simplest division is North, South, East, and West. Beyond that, however, geographic segments with various factors or variables can be developed. For instance, there are segments with such labels as Westerner, Texan, New Yorker, Midwesterner, Yankee, Snowbird, and Southerner. Truthful or not, descriptions of people who live in these areas have been developed.

There are also segments divided by city population. These are called Metropolitan areas and Micropolitan areas—see Table 5.18. The US Census Bureau, as well as other government agencies and non-government organizations or businesses, tracks all kinds of population information. Go to the U.S. Census Bureau website and study the many ways population is tracked according to geography. This type of information is critical for businesses in making many different decisions for the company.

In sport business, there are sports that must take place in northern climates and sports that are better suited for southern climates. Snow skiing and water skiing are examples. This also means that a company whose products are either snow skis and equipment or water skis and equipment will want to distribute them primarily to those regions closest to where those sports take place—hence, geographic-segment marketing decisions.

Combining demographics and geography, most cities have areas that are segmented by income. There are neighborhoods and subdivisions in which the lower classes cluster and in which the upper classes cluster. This information could be used, for instance, in determining where to locate a private membership, high-priced golf and tennis country club.

Geographic segmentation is used to make distinctions between local, regional, national, and international markets or market segments. A sport company might be more successful at a local level than at a national level. On the other hand, a different sport business might be developed to compete specifically at the national or international level.

Table 5.18. Geographics: Metropolitan and Micropolitan Areas

Metropolitan and Micropolitan statistical areas (called metro and micro areas) are geographic entities defined by the U.S. Office of Management and Budget for use by federal statistical agencies in collecting, tabulating and publishing federal statistics.

  Metro and micro areas are collectively known as core based statistical areas (CBSAs). A metro area contains a core urban area population of 50,000 or more. A micro area contains a core urban area population of at least 10,000 (but less than 50,000). Each metro or micro area consists of one or more counties and includes the counties containing the core urban area, as well as any adjacent counties that have a high degree of social and economic integration (as measured by commuting to work) with the urban core. (U.S. Census Bureau, 2010).

Five Largest Changes in Metropolitan Areas Between 2000 and 2010 (all are increases in population)			
Houston, Texas	26.1%	Atlanta, Georgia	24.0%
Dallas-Fort Worth	23.4%	Washington, DC	16.4%
Miami, Florida	11.1%	Source: USCensus.gov.	

In many sports, sport marketers have developed levels of geographic-based competition toward which participants can strive. Within a sport, such as boat racing, a team must first complete or win local events, then regional competitions, in order to compete at the national race. In softball, as sponsored by ASA, for example, in order to be able to compete in the national championship, a team must first win at the local, state, and regional levels.

Behavioral

Consumers approach purchasing products based on a number of influencing factors. An obvious one is income; a wealthy person might have little regard for the price of a set of golf clubs, whereas a lower-middle-class person will probably seek to buy a set of golf clubs on the secondary market. Income will also affect where and when each consumer shops. The wealthy person is likely to purchase at the country club's pro shop or directly from the manufacturer, whereas the other person will seek clubs through secondary outlets such as yard sales, ads in bargain paper classifieds, or previously owned sports equipment sporting goods stores.

Many other influencing factors—of which most are demographics, psychographics, geography, location, and product use—affect a person's purchasing behaviors. These factors affect the consumer's decision-making process toward a purchase—a step-by-step process used when buying products. The typical process involves problem recognition, information search, evaluation of alternatives, purchase, and post-purchase behavior (see Table 5.19).

One area of study that helps the sport marketer understand consumers is the area of participant satisfaction; it is based on the question of why people participate in sports activities. Gaining an understanding of why people participate in a sports activity helps the sport marketer develop marketing strategies aimed at attracting new consumers and keeping current consumers.

A growing area of study within sport marketing concerning consumer behavior involves the study of spectators. Most of this research involves studying the factors that affect the spectator's decision to attend the event. In a study of why people attend NBA (National Basketball Association) games, researchers studied 14 factors categorized into four groups (Zhang, Pease, Hui, & Michaud, 1995). Table 5.19 presents the information from that study. You can see that the factors listed have to do with promotions, facts about the teams involved in the event, and the game schedule. These groups of factors are still used today in studying consumer behavior. Many other factors influence the purchase behavior of sports event spectators. Later in the chapter, Tables 5.20, 5.21,

Table 5.19. A Typical Consumer Decision-making Process	
All are affected and influenced by personal and social factors.	
Step 1	Problem recognition
Step 2	Information search
Step 3	Evaluation of alternatives
Step 4	Purchase
Step 5	Postpurchase behavior

Sociodemographic Factors	Economic Factors	Game Attractiveness Factors	Audience Preferences Factors
• Gender • Age • Relationship Status • Highest Educational Level • Number of Children (under 18) • Annual Household Income • Ethnicity • Occupation • Games Attend Per Year • Season Ticket Holder • Transportation Type • Distance To The Park Lu & Pitts, 2004	• Price of a ticket • Price of season ticket • Price of concessions • TV/Radio coverage of the home game in the local area • TV coverage of another sport event at time of the home game • Other sporting events in the area • Other activities taking place nearby • Other professional franchises in area	• Record (win-loss) of Home Team • Record (win-loss) of Visitor Team • Number of Star Players on Home Team • Number of Star Players on Visitor Team • Offensive Performance of Home Team • Defensive Performance of Home Team • Offensive Performance of Visitor Team • Defensive Performance of Visitor Team • Closeness of Competition • Games with Rival Teams • A Chance to see a Record-Breaking Performance by Team or Athlete • Special Promotion • Home Team's Place in the Division Standings • Home Team's Involvement in Race for a Playoff Spot • Advertising for Event	• Day games during the weekdays • Night games during the weekdays • Weekend day game • Weekend night game • Weather conditions • Cleanliness of the facility • Easy and/or multiple access to your facility • Availablity of parking at or near facility • Size of the facility (seating capacity) • The crowd behavior at the game • New stadium or arena • Number of years the team has been in the area • The variety of concessions available • Violence in the game • The design and color of the uniform • Going with family • Going with friends

Figure 5.8. Factors That Affect Attendance Model.

5.22, and 5.23 will present information from studies on factors that influence the purchase behavior of spectators for soccer, golf, and ice hockey events. Figure 5.8 presents a compilation of all of several factors from sport marketing studies (Lu, 2000). As you can see, there are many factors that play a part in the consumer's decision-making process concerning whether or not to attend an event. The sport marketing professional can use this type of purchase behavior information to develop or modify marketing mix strategies.

When compared to other types of products, sports events present a complex sport business problem for the sport management and marketing professional. This is perhaps unique in the universe of selling products. It is certainly different from factors that influence the purchase behavior and decision-making process of a consumer's decision to purchase such products as laundry detergent, a DVD movie, or property. Yet, selling sports events is similar to such products as a Broadway play, a circus, or a trip to Disney World. These are all entertainment products, and sports events fall into this category of product. Therefore, sport marketing professionals working for sport businesses that sell sports events can use research and information from studies in entertainment.

SOLVING A PROBLEM

The following sections detail the steps that sport marketers will follow in the problem-solution process.

Step 1: Problem Recognition

Do you feel thirsty after your soccer game? Did you break your softball bat? Does your sport company need research? These questions describe situations in which you might find yourself. In order to solve the problem, you first must recognize it. If you have learned that you will get thirsty at your soccer game, you will determine that you need a sports drink to take to the game. You need a new softball bat because you broke the one you have. Your sport business needs to know what consumers think about the new stadium, so you might need to hire a sport marketing consulting firm to do this research and solve the problem.

All of these are situations in which a problem has been recognized. The need for a solution develops.

Step 2: Information Search

The second step is seeking information to help develop the best solution. A person will consider such factors as money available, time available, and memory. These are internal factors that influence the knowledge or decision to purchase a particular product. Other variables that will influence this decision are external factors. External factors include information that a person receives from friends, family, advertising, and salespeople.

An information search can occur internally, externally, or both. The type of product needed or desired and its uses and functions will influence the extent to which the consumer uses internal, external, or both factors. Additionally, price can have a fairly significant influence. As presented in Chapter 9, the price of a product can affect consumers in a number of ways, such as influencing the consumer's willingness to spend, expectation of quality and performance, and post-purchase anxiety or comfort.

The type of product and its uses and functions will trigger an internal or external search, or both. For example, athletic tape needed to wrap a sprained ankle is a necessity. Most retail stores such as Walgreen's and Eckerd's carry only one or two brands, and they are practically identical to the general consumer, as most people are not trained in sports medicine. Therefore, there is very little, if any, information needed to make this purchase. However, if the consumer is considering purchasing a boat for skiing and other aquatic sports, the consumer is much more likely to employ a major external information search. The purchase of a boat requires some knowledge of the following: how the boat will be used (product uses and functions); how often the boat will be used; where the boat will be used; what size boat is needed or wanted; how many people the consumer expects to have on board on a typical outing; the activities planned while on the boat and using the boat; the kind of towing vehicle the consumer has; whether the boat will be towed (trailered) for each use; how far the boat will have to be trailered; the kind of terrain that will be covered in trailering the boat; the amenities needed or wanted in the boat such as stereo, toilet, water, built-in cooler, kitchen, built-in wet bar, and trolling motor; the kind of engine desired—outboard, inboard, stern drive, or jet drive; the kind of aquatic sports equipment needed or wanted—skis, kneeboard, skurfer, wakeboard, tubes, or barefoot skiing equipment; and the kind of safety equipment needed or wanted. As you can see, to purchase a boat, a consumer will need to collect much information that will help answer those questions and many more.

Consumers with prior knowledge or experience with a product are less needy of external information searches. They will rely primarily on the knowledge gained from the experience with the product from the previous purchase.

Steps 3 and 4: Evaluation of Alternatives and Purchase

After collecting information concerning the targeted product, the consumer will consider all alternatives, develop a set of criteria, weigh advantages and disadvantages, consider internal and external information again, and then begin to narrow the decision to finalist products. Again, as you can see in Tables 5.20, 5.21, 5.22, and 5.23, there can

Table 5.20. Promotion, Teams, and Schedule Factors that Affect the Consumer's Decision to Attend NBA Games.

Direction: Please rate the following variables that may have generally influenced you on making decision to attend the NBA games. Please circle only one answer (5 = very much, 4 = much, 3 = somewhat, 2 = a little, 1 = none).

Game Promotion (6 items)					
1. advertising	5	4	3	2	1
2. publicity	5	4	3	2	1
3. direct mail and notification	5	4	3	2	1
4. good seats	5	4	3	2	1
5. giveaway/prize	5	4	3	2	1
6. ticket discount	5	4	3	2	1
Home Team (4 items)					
7. win/loss records	5	4	3	2	1
8. league standing	5	4	3	2	1
9. superstars	5	4	3	2	1
10. overall team performance	5	4	3	2	1
Opposing Team (2 items)					
11. overall team performance	5	4	3	2	1
12. superstars	5	4	3	2	1
Schedule Convenience (2 items)					
13. game time (evening)	5	4	3	2	1
14. day of week (weekend)	5	4	3	2	1

Solution of Factor Analysis by Principal Component Extraction and Orthogonal Rotation ($N = 861$)

Source: Zhang, Pease, Hui, & Michaud, 1995

Table 5.21. Level of Involvement of Other Factors that Affect the Consumer's Decision to Attend Soccer Games.

	Total	Preboom	Boom	Postboom
Favorite team				
Don't have	11.5%	8.2%	6.7%	26.9%
Have	88.5%	91.8%	93.3%	73.1%**
Favorite player				
Don't have	34.7%	31.1%	31.0%	47.7%
Have	65.3%	68.9%	69.0%	52.3%**
Understanding rules				
Well	24.8%	45.6%	19.7%	13.1%
Enough	57.7%	49.8%	63.0%	53.7%
A little	15.5%	3.7%	16.5%	26.7%
Not at all	2.0%	0.9%	0.7%	6.6%**
Experience of soccer				
Don't have	64.2%	43.9%	70.0%	73.6%
Have	35.8%	56.1%	30.0%	26.4%**
When decide to go				
Day of game	5.2%	6.1%	3.8%	7.0%
Before day of game and after pregame	20.1%	17.3%	17.5%	29.4%
Before previous session	74.7%	76.6%	78.7%	63.7%
How to get information (M.A.)				
Newspaper	19.7%	24.0%	21.1%	11.3%**
TV/Radio	8.7%	8.7%	9.6%	6.4%
Soccer magazines	25.5%	31.5%	27.6%	14.0%**
General magazines	7.2%	6.7%	6.6%	9.5%
Friends/Acquaintances	23.4%	18.3%	19.2%	39.4%**
Posters	4.3%	3.8%	5.3%	2.4%*
Club newsletters	29.1%	31.0%	34.7%	13.5%
Others	19.3%	18.0%	19.3%	21.3%
How to get tickets				
Purchase tickets in advance	57.8%	56.3%	62.4%	48.3%
Purchase tickets at stadium	9.0%	11.0%	7.6%	10.0%
Purchase with package tour	1.8%	1.7%	2.0%	1.5%
Receive as a gift	21.1%	19.9%	17.9%	29.8%
Others	10.3%	11.1%	10.0%	10.3%**

Notes: $*p < .01$, $**p < .001$

Source: Nakazawa, Mahony, Funk & Hirakawa, 1999.

be many factors to consider. Some of those factors are alternative products. If the product is attending and watching a sports event, the example in Table 5.21 demonstrates that there are a number of alternative things to do that compete for the consumer's attention or purchase.

Step 5: Post-Purchase Behavior

The consumer may exhibit post-purchase behavior. This involves how the consumer feels, what the consumer thinks about the purchase, and whether or not the consumer is satisfied or dissatisfied in regard to the his/her expectations about how the product is performing. In other words, if the consumer went into the purchase with a certain set of expectations (product uses and benefits) and those expectations are being met, then

Table 5.21. (Continued).				
	Total	Preboom	Boom	Postboom
How to purchase tickets				
Through ticketing agency	37.1%	34.1%	35.6%	46.5%
Through supporter's clubs	39.2%	40.9%	43.0%	25.0%
At game	11.3%	14.0%	9.3%	13.3%
Others	12.3%	11.0%	12.0%	15.2%**
Transportation time (min.)				
Mean	75.0	73.9	74.3	78.1
Standard deviation	52.4	52.8	52.8	51.2
Size of party				
Go alone	13.0%	17.4%	11.8%	10.7%
Go in a pair	52.6%	50.0%	52.8%	55.4%
3 persons	12.8%	12.6%	13.5%	10.7%
4 persons	12.4%	8.9%	14.0%	12.8%
More	9.2%	11.1%	7.8%	10.4%**
Who to go with				
Friends	36.6%	39.9%	35.5%	36.6%
Work Friends	10.6%	10.5%	9.9%	12.8%
Social contract	4.8%	5.6%	4.0%	6.1%
Family/Relatives	42.8%	37.9%	46.6%	37.4%
Others	5.2%	6.1%	4.1%	7.1%**
Belonging to supporter clubs				
I am a member	45.0%	50.7%	50.1%	19.2%
I want to be	17.0%	14.6%	17.1%	20.7%
I do NOT want to be	37.9%	34.7%	32.7%	60.1%**
Frequency of attendance (games)				
Mean	4.4	6.0	5.1	1.7**
Standard deviation	5.3	6.0	5.2	3.3
Watching games on TV				
Often	67.0%	77.9%	71.2%	44.4%
Sometimes	25.7%	19.3%	23.3%	38.4%
Seldom	4.6%	2.0%	3.8%	9.4%
Almost never	2.7%	0.7%	1.7%	7.7%**
Watch other sports				
Don't	56.2%	36.9%	47.8%	41.4%
Do	43.8%	63.1%	52.2%	58.6%

Notes: *$p < .01$, **$p < .001$

Source: Nakazawa, Mahony, Funk & Hirakawa, 1999.

the consumer will probably be satisfied and feel comfortable with the purchase. If, however, the product does not perform to the consumer's expectations, then the consumer will probably be dissatisfied and feel uncomfortable about the purchase. For example, if a consumer buys tickets to a Super Bowl game and expects to have an enjoyable experience with a game that is exciting and close, yet the game turns out to be a large margin-of-victory game, then the consumer may be dissatisfied with the purchase. If, however, a consumer bought tickets to the final of the 2011 Women's World Cup, was a United States team fan, and expected to find a fair-sized crowd and an exciting game, that consumer was probably happily surprised to find that the U.S. team won the World Cup, crowd numbers were well above anyone's expectations, and the game was an exceptionally exciting one. This consumer will likely conclude that the purchase was above expectation and will be satisfied.

Sport business management and marketing professionals must take care not to promise too much in a product, lest that product not meet the claims made and thus adds to the consumer's dissatisfaction with the product. Too much post-purchase dissatisfaction can lead to the development of a negative image for the company. Consider, for example, the image problem facing several professional men's sports today in relation to some public opinion that the players are overpaid and get away with anything, that the league is a haven for criminals and encourages violence, and thus that the games are not worth watching and do not serve as a good role model for our youth. Sport marketing professionals are making attempts to counter some of these claims in order to maintain a supportive consumer base.

Product Functions and Benefits Segmentation

A consumer needs a product in order to satisfy a need or desire. Therefore, the product is a tool for the consumer to perform certain functions and realize certain benefits. A softball bat is a tool for the player to hit the ball, but a well-selected bat is what the player chooses in looking to improve hitting percentage, have more control, get more home runs, and enhance status among teammates and fans. A fitness center provides the potential for the consumer to get in shape, enhance health, lower blood pressure, meet people, grow stronger, lose those holiday-gained pounds, be a part of the cool crowd, fit into certain clothes, and/or get ready for the swimsuit season. As a matter of fact, the sport marketer uses these exact words to describe benefits when advertising for these products. Knowing how the consumer wants to use the product, the functions the consumer expects the product to perform, and the benefits the consumer expects to receive from the product is important for the sport marketing professional in developing marketing mix strategies that are well informed. This enhances the chances for success. Figure 5.10, presented later in the chapter, illustrates how the industry can be divided based on product functions. This model provides that the industry can be divided into three large categories based on similar product functions. This is important for the sport marketing professional to understand because it helps with describing the product, the business, and with positioning.

Product usage information can be utilized in a number of ways in the marketing mix. For example, there is a theory called the 80-20 rule. This means that 20% of all consumers generate 80% of consumption. This can be seen in fitness centers, for example, where a small group of consumers (about 20%) are responsible for the core (about 80%) of the consumption of the product. The rest of the consumers do not use the facility as much or as often. Sport marketing professionals have developed categories for these kinds of groups. Some of the categories include heavy users, medium users, light users, and non-users; high involvement and low involvement; hardcore fan and fan; and high loyalty, spurious loyalty, latent loyalty, and low loyalty. These kinds of segmentation categories can be used by the sport marketing professional to study consumers and develop appropriate marketing strategies.

Table 5.22. Entertainment Options that Affect the Consumer's Decision to Attend a Minor League Hockey Game.

Entertainment Option	1	2	3	4	5	Mean	SD
Professional and Amateur Sports							
Attend pro football games	44	26	16	6	7	2.7	2.5
Attend pro indoor soccer games	83	8	5	2	2	1.4	3.0
Attend pro basketball games	31	27	22	11	9	2.4	1.3
Attend pro baseball games	23	26	25	15	11	2.6	1.3
Attend intercollegiate games	40	21	18	10	11	2.3	1.4
Attend other sport shows	25	23	32	13	8	2.0	1.3
Recreational Participation							
Play recreational sports	16	15	24	18	27	3.3	1.6
Work out/Exercise	11	16	23	21	29	3.4	1.4
Travel	8	13	27	24	28	3.5	1.3
Arts							
Attend concerts	18	27	27	16	12	2.8	1.4
Attend movies	7	15	26	26	26	3.5	1.8
Television							
Watch sports on TV	7	11	17	25	41	3.9	1.6
Watch nonsports programs on TV	5	12	21	25	38	3.8	1.2
Dining and Night Clubs							
Attend bars/restaurants	8	7	20	28	37	3.8	1.3
Attend night clubs	35	23	18	12	12	2.5	2.5

*1 = Never; 2 = Occasionally; 3 = Sometimes; 4 = Often; 5 = Always

Source: Zhang, Smith, Pease & Jambor, 1997.

Tables 5.22 and 5.23 provide information from a study on sports participation and its influence on sports spectators. That is, the researchers were studying the relationship between a person's involvement as a participant in a sport and his or her involvement as

Table 5.23. Factors that Affect the Consumer's Decision to Attend a Golf Event as a Spectator.

Number of Professional Tournaments Attended (Past 5 years)	0	1	2–5	6–10	Over 10
	22.3%	8%	50.3%	12.6%	6.9%
	n = 39	n = 14	n = 88	n = 22	n = 12
Number of Professional Tournaments Viewed on Television (Past year)	0	1	2–5	6–10	Over 10
	1.7%	2.9%	14%	18.3%	62.3%
	n = 3	n = 5	n = 26	n = 32	n = 109
Years of Golf Played	Under 10	11–20	21–30	31–40	41–50	Unknown
	50%	21%	12%	9%	4%	4%
	n = 88	n = 37	n = 21	n = 15	n = 7	n = 7
Rounds of Golf Per Year	0	1–10	11–25	Over 25	Unknown
	13.7%	17.1%	18.3%	50.3%	.6%
	n = 24	n = 30	n = 32	n = 88	n = 1

Source: Lascu, Giese, Toolan, Guehring & Mercer, 1995.

a spectator of that sport. In general, the researchers found that high-involvement consumers—those who participate more frequently in the sport—are more likely to attend more of the sport's events in person, watch more on TV, pay more attention to activities offered at the live event, pay more attention to promotions associated with the event, and such consumers are more capable of correctly identifying the event sponsors.

BUSINESS CONSUMERS, B2B MARKETING, AND BUSINESS CONSUMER SEGMENTATION

If your business produces products for other businesses, then your consumers are business consumers. Business-to-business (B2B) marketing involves the marketing of products to individuals and organizations for purposes other than personal consumption (Lamb, Hair, & McDaniel, 1996). These consumers acquire products and services for purposes of manufacturing, production, resale, operations, enhancement of a company's position, or other business-related reasons. For example, if your company manufactures T-shirts to sell directly to a licensing and merchandising company for a sports event such as the national rodeo, then your consumers are business consumers. If your company conducts studies of sponsorship advertising and its effects for companies who are the sponsors or the companies who manage the event, then your consumers are business consumers.

Segmenting and targeting of business consumers is similar to segmenting and targeting of end consumers (those who purchase products for personal consumption). Business consumer segmentation involves categorizing businesses into groups with similar characteristics. Most sport business consumers can be categorized into the following groups: manufacturers, resellers, sports-governing bodies, institutions, and media sports enterprises. Manufacturers are those businesses that purchase products used to manufacture or produce other products, or that are used for the daily operations of the company. For example, the Hillerich & Bradsby Company (H&B) in Lousiville, Kentucky is a producer of baseball bats and ice-hockey equipment. To manufacture these products, H&B must purchase materials such as wood and plastics. Therefore, H&B is a business consumer. H&B also sells primarily to business consumers. Such companies as sporting goods retailers, distributors, and wholesalers who purchase H&B's products like their bats and golf clubs do so for resale purposes. Therefore, H&B must study, segment, and target business consumers.

Resellers include those businesses that purchase products for the purpose of reselling them for a profit. Sporting goods retail stores, for instance, are resellers: They purchase many products from many different companies in order to resell them for profit. Another example includes promotion and sponsorship management companies. For instance, a company that consults and manages sponsorship contracts must purchase signs for signage from a sign manufacturer. Therefore, they are a business consumer. Also, their products are targeted primarily to business consumers—those companies who want their sponsorship management products. In another example, a college licensing and merchandising company is a B2B company; it is both a business consumer and a company that targets business consumers. This type of company will purchase merchandise from manufacturers and producers, and sell it to their business customers.

Governing bodies include numerous organizations whose business is to govern various sports, recreational, and leisure activities; events; organizations; equipment; and facilities. The International Olympic Committee (IOC), for instance, governs everything involved in the Olympics enterprises. Its B2B product is primarily to stage, or produce (sell), a multi-sports event to end consumers, yet its transactions involve primarily selling the rights to broadcast the event to media sports enterprises such as TV and radio, rights to produce the event to a host organization, and sponsorship products to sponsorship companies. Thus, the IOC practically never directly sells the event to the end consumer.

Institutions are usually non-profit entities that include such organizations as schools, colleges and universities, faith-based sports clubs, city sports commissions, sports foundations, youth sports organizations, and city sports and recreation offices. They purchase such business products as facilities, office equipment and supplies, sporting goods, equipment, apparel, and promotional merchandise.

Media sports enterprises are those for-profit businesses that seek to broadcast sports events, sports-related shows, sports news, and sports-related material via media such as television, radio, magazines, video, DVD, and the Internet. Sports events broadcast on TV and radio are a common product. As pointed out earlier in this chapter, there are 235 hours of sports programming every 24 hours on 48 sports channels. Although many sports magazines, videos, DVDs, and Web products target end consumers, the companies that manufacture these products must transact with several businesses to purchase such products as the rights to the sports event for publications purposes, paper, videotapes, DVD disks, Internet website providers, and satellite distribution companies. Some of these companies also target businesses consumers with some of their products. For instance, trade publications are targeted to businesses.

Bases for Business Consumer Segmentation

Business consumer segmentation variables are a little different from end consumer variables. Whereas end consumer bases focus on human characteristics, business consumer bases must include business characteristics. Although it will be humans who make particular purchase decisions for the company, the company most likely has purchase criteria or policies that the buyer must follow. The following are brief descriptions of bases for business consumer segmentation, adapted from Lamb, Hair, and McDaniel (1996).

Geographic location. As presented earlier in this chapter, consumers can be segmented according to geographic location variables. Common variables using geographic locations include local, state, and regional. For instance, often various regions of the United States are known for certain sports: The West is associated with rodeo events; coastal regions are associated with ocean-related sports; the Rocky Mountain states are associated with winter sports and mountain-climbing sports; certain states such as Tennessee are known as basketball states, and certain states such as Texas are known as football states. Companies selling to industries that are concentrated geographically would benefit by locating close to those markets. For instance, surfboard companies will enhance efforts if they locate in coastal areas. In another example, sports agents might benefit if they locate in large city areas that can sustain several professional and semi-professional sports organizations.

Customer type. Segmenting by type of customer has benefits because the seller can concentrate marketing mix strategies. For instance, manufacturers of sports equipment can focus on retail stores, specialty stores, or distributors, developing marketing strategies specifically for one or more of these.

Customer size. Segmenting using this base is similar to segmenting end consumers based on levels of product usage such as heavy, medium, and light. This base involves volume. Your company might decide that its best strategy is to target those companies that purchase in large volume only.

Product use. Many products can be used in different ways, especially raw materials such as wood, plastics, and steel. How your customers will be using these products will determine how much they buy and other criteria. For instance, if a golf club manufacturer produces steel shafts, then the company will probably need to purchase a particular type of steel and a certain amount of steel. In another example, if a licensing company needs T-shirts for a very large sports event, such as the Kentucky Derby, then the company's use of the product for a once-a-year event will affect their purchase.

Purchase criteria. A company might purchase based on specific criteria such as price, quality, reputation, or delivery. If your company can deliver what the purchasing company needs when they need it, then this may be a reason to target this company.

INDUSTRY SEGMENTATION

Industry segmentation is the process of dividing or categorizing an industry into logical and/or similar parts, or industry segments. It involves industry analysis—the study of an industry. The sport marketing professional needs to know and understand the whole sport industry and, more specifically, its segments. This will help in determining where an individual sport business fits into a particular segment and into the whole industry. It helps in determining how events in the industry, or in a segment, will affect an individual sport business. This knowledge will help in marketing strategy.

Industry segmentation may be conducted in a manner similar to consumer segmentation, whereby one whole group is divided into categories of smaller groups based on homogeneous characteristics. The primary purpose for industry segmentation is competitive strategy formulation. Other reasons include identifying marketing opportunities and threats within a specific segment, to develop an appropriate marketing mix, and to inform resource allocation (Pitts, Fielding, & Miller, 1994).

Bases for Industry Segmentation

Segmenting of an industry is typically done primarily using two variables: products and buyers. An industry can comprise one product and one buyer. More typically, an industry segment comprises multiple similar products and buyers.

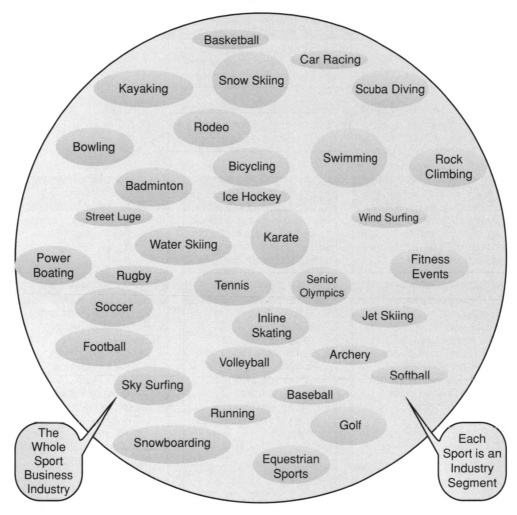

Figure 5.9. Sports as Segments of the Sport Business Industry.

The sport industry is divided into numerous segments by sports. The circle in Figure 5.9 illustrates all of the sports in the sport business industry. Inside are some of the numerous segments divided by sports. Often, the industry is mentioned according to "the basketball industry," "the softball industry," or "the running industry." Each segment is illustrative of everything that relates to a particular sport. For basketball, that would include basketball spectator sports, recreational sports, and equipment. If you work for a sport business that manufactures basketballs, you could consider your business as part of the basketball industry segment. Therefore, you would want to monitor every other manufacturer in this segment as well as basketball participation (consumer) rates. This information would help in strategizing.

Figure 5.10 is an illustration of the Sport Industry Model by Pitts, Fielding, and Miller (1994). This model categorizes the whole industry according to product function. Figure 5.11 shows the three segments identified by the model as a pie chart representing the whole industry as divided. If your company offers products whose function

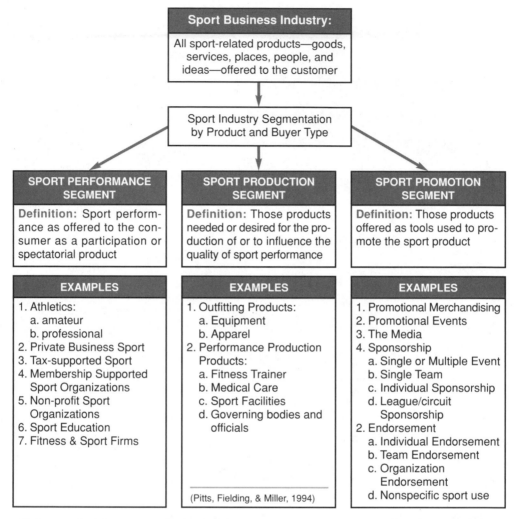

Figure 5.10. The Sport Business Industry Segment Model.

is promotion, then your company is categorized into the sport promotion segment. In this segment, you would want to monitor competitors and all consumers of these products. This knowledge will help with competitive strategy development.

Figure 5.12 divides the industry according to career fields (Parks & Zanger, 1990). Within each area might be different sports and different products, but each is similar in terms of area. For instance, there are numerous different professional sports. Those might be further subdivided by each sport, or by season into winter sports and summer sports. However, what makes them all similar is that they are all professional sports.

Figure 5.13 illustrates the sport industry as divided by financial size (Meek, 1997), with the largest segment at the top. As was presented in Chapter 1, the industry is large and varied; but all of the studies on the economic size of the industry showed that participant sports and sporting goods are the largest and second largest segments of the industry, respectively. Participant sports contains all those millions of average (nonprofes-

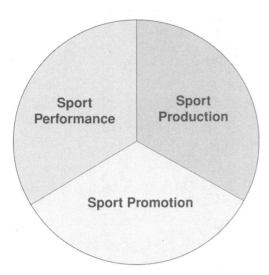

Figure 5.11. The Sport Industry and Its Segments as Divided by Product Function in the Pitts, Fielding & Miller Sport Industry Segmentation Model (1994).

sional) sports people participating in all those recreational sports on a daily basis, and all those people must have equipment and apparel in order to participate. So, their financial importance should come as no surprise.

Other methods include segmenting the industry by product. For example, baseball bat manufacturers study the "baseball bat industry;" athletic shoe manufacturers study the "athletic shoe industry;" golf course construction companies study the "golf course industry;" and a boat manufacturer studies the "boatbuilding industry." Each company needs to know what is going on in its specific area.

Industry Segmentation Information

Industry segment information is readily available. Appendices B and C offer information on sport business trade organizations and trade publications. *Trade* refers to a particular vocation, skill, knowledge area, profession, or business type. These businesses and publications offer information regarding industry information, research, and mar-

Source: Parks, Zanger, and Quarterman, 1998.

Figure 5.12. The Sport Business Industry as Divided by Career Fields.

Figure 5.13. The Sport Business Industry as Divided by Economic Size According to Meek (1996)

ket events. Segmentation information can also be found in numerous places on the Internet. Try doing a search through any Internet search engine, such as Google, and see what you can find.

Effective positioning tactics cause consumers to view a company's products more positively. Courtesy of Photos8.com

POSITIONING THE SPORT BUSINESS AND/OR PRODUCT

"Positioning" is how the business tells the consumer what to think about a product or business, often in comparison to other products. Positioning refers to the development of specific marketing mix elements to influence the consumer's perception of a product, brand, or company. For instance, a consumer might think that the golf clubs made by the Red Brand Company are better than those made by the Blue Brand Company because the Red Brand clubs are lighter, stronger, give more control, give more distance, and are higher quality clubs because they are more expensive. The Red Brand Company's product carries a particular place, or position, in the consumer's thinking.

The consumer could have developed this perception with no input. However, it might be more likely that the marketing tactics and strategies of the Red Brand Company influenced the consumer. For instance, the Red Brand Company could have used the phrase of "lighter, stronger, longer" so much in all of its advertising that the consumer was influenced by the words.

Positioning assumes that a consumer will compare products produced by different companies and could be influenced by the company's positioning tactics. Of course, if a product has been positioned to target a specific market, then that market will be more readily influenced because it already possesses the demographics and other segment variables for which the product was customized. For example, if a golf club company wants to target a wealthy segment and position the club to be the club for the wealthy, then the consumers in this segment are more likely to be influenced by the marketing mix strategies and are more likely to be attracted to that club.

Positioning is a critical element for the sport marketing professional. Most sport businesses have more than one market. Many products, therefore, have more than one market, and some products have more than one function (use). The sport business must develop the image of the product that it wants the consumer to hold. If there is more than one consumer market for a product, and if the product has more than one function, then the sport business must develop a position for each market and each function. Tables 5.24 and 5.25 present examples of positioning statements for different companies. Table 5.24 shows examples from companies with a single product focus, while Table 5.25 shows examples from companies with multiple products. Think about a company you would like to have and write a positioning statement for it.

There is a process to developing the positioning strategy for the product. Figure 5.14 illustrates that process and the steps are presented here:

Step 1: Identify the Target Market's Attribute Preferences

A market wants or needs a product for a specific function—the attributes of the product (refer to Chapter 8 for further study). Examine the market for those attributes. If the product and its consumer market are known, study the current market. If the product is new and the consumer market is not yet known, determine the potential consumer market.

Table 5.24. Level of Involvement Factors that Affect a Consumer's Decision to Attend a Golf Tournament.

| Variable | Involvement | | | |
	Low	High	t-Value	Prob.
Motivation for Attendance				
Proximity to golfers	3.99	4.39	140.94	.017
Live action	4.36	4.70	132.41	.007
Fitness motivation	3.07	3.44	138.73	.070
Personal love of golf	3.79	4.67	117.46	.000
Support for charity	3.47	3.93	139.98	.016
Golfing tips	3.07	3.86	135.44	.000
Excitement of the final round	3.78	4.33	140.00	.002
Promotions associated with event	2.49	3.10	133.65	.004
The company of friends	3.35	3.89	140.95	.005
Exposure to advertisements	2.45	2.95	136.31	.022
Ticket value	2.60	3.03	138.07	.055
Excitement of first two rounds	2.47	3.25	125.66	.001
Commitment to Golf				
Golf tournaments attended	2.45	3.07	142.41	.001
Golf tournaments watched	4.08	4.60	127.32	.001
Rounds of golf played	2.58	3.57	125.34	.000
Number years playing golf	11.75	17.92	138.65	.007
Golf Digest	.37	.56	142.74	.025
Use of golf for business	.19	.33	137.92	.053
Money spent last year	1.40	3.14	132.91	.003
Likelihood of attending similar event	4.04	4.72	101.22	.000
Ability to identify Cellular One as a sponsor	.14	.04	115.97	.045

Source: Lascu, Giese, Toolan, Guehring & Mercer, 1995

Step 2: Identify Current Positioning Strategy

How is the company currently positioning the product? How do competitors position their product? Typically, positioning can be found in the advertising for a product because advertising is how the company communicates to a market, so look there first.

Step 3: Analyze Current Position and the Market's Attribute Preferences

Study the current positioning strategy and the consumer market's preferred product attributes, and determine if they match. If the positioning strategy matches the consumer market's preferred product attributes, then the current positioning strategy is a match. If the current positioning strategy and the consumer market's preferred product attributes do not match, then it may be time to reposition the product.

Table 5.25. Examples of Positioning Statements.	
Road Atlanta	**360° Sports Academy, LLC**
Road Atlanta is recognized as one of the world's best road courses. Our multi-purpose motor sports facility is situated on 750 park-like acres in the rolling hills of Northeast Georgia. Road Atlanta is located 35 miles north of Atlanta and just minutes away from Chateau Elan, a 4-Star resort offering guests comfort and amenities such as three championship golf courses and a European-style spa. The facility is utilized for a wide variety of events, including professional and amateur sports car and motorcycle races, racing and driving schools, corporate programs and testing for motorsports teams.	360° Sports Academy is dedicated to developing student-athletes into leaders. We endeavor to empower student-athletes to be the best they can be. The overall takeaway from 360° Sports Academy is a holistic, life-building and applicable experience that will benefit all participants on many levels and empower the next generation of leaders. 360° Sports Academy offers a full spectrum of training programs for student-athletes and their parents. The topics, treated in-depth and addressed by subject matter experts, range from test-taking strategies, finance basics, health and wellness, and presentation/interview skills, to sports-specific athletic and game insights. techniques, and drills.

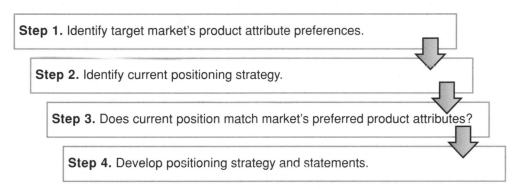

Step 1. Identify target market's product attribute preferences.

Step 2. Identify current positioning strategy.

Step 3. Does current position match market's preferred product attributes?

Step 4. Develop positioning strategy and statements.

Figure 5.14. The Positioning Development Process.

Step 4: Determine a Positioning Strategy

Using the research collected in the previous steps, determine a positioning strategy to meet the consumer market's preferred product attributes. Tables 5.24 and 5.25 present some examples for positioning statements for one product to target different consumer markets. Note how the statements for each different consumer market are specific to that market's preferred product functions. These are important for the company because some or all of the statements will be used in a number of ways, especially in promotional efforts.

CHAPTER SUMMARY

Because markets and industries are constantly changing, the sport marketing professional must constantly monitor and develop marketing mix strategies that will be beneficial for the company. Segmentation involves the study of markets and industries to divide a whole into parts in order to develop customized marketing mix strategies. In the sport industry, sport marketing professionals study primarily two broad categories: sport consumer markets, composed of end consumers and business consumers; and the sport industry, composed of a variety of industry segments.

Segmentation is the first step toward understanding consumer groups, determining target markets, and informing marketing mix and positioning strategies. Segmentation bases and variables are used to segment a consumer market or an industry. The choice of bases and variables is crucial because an inappropriate group of bases will not be successful in relation to responding to a marketing mix.

Target marketing involves the development of marketing mix strategies customized for one or more target markets or industry segments. These groups are the ones for which the company will develop specialized marketing-mix elements, strategies, and promotional campaigns.

Positioning involves communicating to the consumer what the company wants the consumer to think about the product. It is a critical element in marketing because it positions the product, or company, with a particular image about the product's functions in the consumer's mind.

DISCUSSION QUESTIONS

1. Describe how the population of your country has changed over the last 25 years and how it is going to change in the next 25 years. How will this affect the sport business industry?
2. What types of marketing strategies are sport businesses using more often for emerging markets? Describe each one and how it works.
3. What are bases for segmentation? Describe how they are used.
4. What is target marketing? Describe how to determine one or more target markets for a sport business.
5. What is positioning? Describe how to develop a positioning strategy for a product and a consumer market.

SUGGESTED EXERCISES

1. Using students in your class, conduct a study of demographics, psychographics, and other segmentation bases and variables using sporting goods as a basis. What did you learn about the class? How could this information be used if your company is a sporting goods retail company?
2. Write down a sports product that you purchased recently—one that is sold by more than one company. Create two columns. Label one column "My Buy" and the other column "Didn't Buy." In the "My Buy" column, create a list of all of the reasons you bought the product. In the "Didn't Buy" column, create a list of all of the reasons you did not buy the product from other companies. On another sheet, try to consider all the information you gathered to help you decide on your purchase and list them (family, friends, advertising). Write down all the things the people told you or that you remember from the advertising. Now compare all your notes and see if there is a relationship between any of them. Why do you

think you found a relationship between, for example, the reasons you bought the product from a specific company and the company's advertising for that product?

3. With a group, determine a way to segment the sport industry. First, determine a reason for segmenting the industry, such as pretending that your group is a television broadcasting company that focuses on extreme sports events. Develop bases for segmentation. Determine an appropriate marketing mix strategy for your company.

4. Your company is a team of the WNBA. You want to increase spectator attendance numbers for each game, but you also want to increase the number of games that many of your fans attend during a season. Develop a list of the factors that have an influence on attendance and design a study that will answer the questions you have for your fans.

5. Identify some different sport businesses such as a manufacturer and a sport facility. Identify different consumer markets for the products. Develop positioning statements for each consumer market.

6

Marketing Information Systems

INTRODUCTION

The amount of information that sport organizations generate daily is staggering. The major problem is that our thinking and skills have not developed quickly enough to accommodate this tremendous onslaught of data. It has been estimated that sport managers spend 80% of their time on information transactions (Horine & Stotlar, 2004). This phenomenon demands the development of systematic methods to process the abundance of information that is available and use it in marketing sports products and services.

Marketing information systems are used for information management. They have been referred to by many names—marketing information systems (MIS), computer information systems (CIS), and information asset management (IAM). Although no one title is singularly appropriate, the development and use of systems that can manage information for a sport organization or company is essential. Mullin (1985) said, "The MIS provides the link between the market and the marketer, and it is therefore the lifeline of marketing" (p. 210). Unfortunately, marketing information systems and database marketing in particular are not as well developed in the sport industry as they are in other business segments (Fielitz & Scott, 2003; Lefton, 2003).

Marketing information systems are generally characterized as a collection of data that is utilized by management in the operation and development of marketing programs and market-related decisions. In past decades, former coaches and athletes have managed many sport organizations. Marketing and management choices were often intuitive judgments rather than logical decisions based on data. Organizations can no longer remain competitive by using yesterday's decision-making styles. In today's environment, successful sport marketers must develop skills and abilities to interact with technology in making data-based decisions for marketing their products and services.

Hughes (2000) noted that each contact a company has with customers represents an opportunity to acquire customer information. Examples of these interactions include sales transactions, warranty cards, coupon redemption, and credit applications.

Advances in technology have enhanced corporate utilization of information. Typically, this information is used to develop a customer database. Hughes (2000) identified several benefits that this information can provide for marketers. First, the information allows marketers to access basic customer information such as name, address, and email—information that could facilitate direct marketing. More importantly, these data open communication channels through which marketers can establish and maintain a relationship with consumers. Through these relationships, marketers are able to increase consumer loyalty and thus encourage repeat purchases (Aaker, Kumar, & Day, 2000; Bonvissuto, 2005; Javalgi & Moberg, 1997). Most sport executives realize that repeat purchasers are essential for producing a higher lifetime value from each customer.

Sport organizations have access to a considerable amount of information about their customers. Some use it; some do not. Mullin, Hardy, and Sutton (2007) indicated that much of the information available to the sport marketer is either lost or not retrievable. Therefore, the purpose of this chapter is to assist sport marketers in the development and utilization of an effective marketing information system.

ID scanners at stadium gates can provide a valuable source of consumer information. Courtesy of Tempe Convention and Visitors Bureau

OBTAINING INFORMATION

The first step in building an effective marketing information system is to collect or generate useful data. But, you may ask, from where is the data obtained? Traditionally, sport organizations have not been as sophisticated as many other business operations in the collection and use of marketing data, so it is important to improve in this area of operations. Managers of sport organizations receive various kinds of information (i.e. sales reports, membership data) from within their organization and from other sources with which they must interact on an ongoing basis (Stotlar, 2009). These must be clearly identified and become main sources for marketing data.

Sources of MIS data are typically identified as being either primary or secondary (Mullin, 1985; Mullin et al., 2007; Stotlar, 2009). Primary research is research conducted with, or collected directly from, customers.

Sport organizations can, through technology, keep very accurate records of their clients and all people doing business with the organization. This includes both those who have purchased from the organization and those from whom the organization buys goods and services (Stotlar, 2009).

Health and fitness clubs have access to considerable amounts of information about their clients. All clients fill out application forms that include not only their name and address, but also typically their occupation and income. Many clubs also have an extended system that can track the programs and equipment used in the club by each member and can generate reports detailing individual and club usage. This information can be quite useful to the market manager in tracking renewals and future marketing campaigns.

In one study, Chen (2005) found that by examining data from a fitness center, managers could accurately predict which members where most likely to drop their membership. He analyzed the club's database across variables of gender, payment methods, residence, club visits, account status, and membership type. Chen was able to predict, with 82% accuracy, which members failed to renew their memberships. With national retention rates of only about 55%, club managers could certainly benefit from being able to forecast members who have a high potential to drop out.

The University of Northern Colorado Athletic Department implemented an MIS to better track the students attending athletic contests. Prior to implementation, students would just show their ID to access gate entrance; however, with the new system, the ID was scanned at the entry gate, providing the athletic department with current and reliable information on student attendance. This information was used successfully to push forward plans to locate a new stadium closer to the main student housing areas. The data could also be cross-referenced with basketball attendance to determine the ways in which basketball attendance differs from football attendance, and appropriate marketing efforts could then be initiated. As a side benefit, former students who had been accustomed to flashing their out-of-date IDs and proceeding through the gate were stopped and referred to the ticket window because the system could quickly verify their enrollment status.

Another innovative method for collecting marketing and consumer information was introduced at Colorado ski resorts. Several of the major ski resorts implemented computerized systems for validating and tracking skiers. The systems included scanners located at all lift locations across the resort. When skiers lined up for transport up the mountain, the lift operators scanned their lift tickets or season passes. Information collected through the process could then be analyzed and evaluated by resort managers. Specific information that would be valuable would be the types of terrain skied by the most skiers, the frequency and duration of runs, and the typical ski pattern for the majority of skiers on the mountain as well as the price and location of ticket purchase. The data could also be tabulated from week to week throughout the season, and individual reports could be generated for day-pass and season-pass holders. One interesting advantage of the system was discovered when two young season-pass skiers were reported lost at the end of a day skiing. Resort personnel were able to use the scanned data to locate the last ski lift accessed by the skiers, and a rescue was launched in the most likely areas where the boys would have skied. One boy was rescued, though the other unfortunately died. However, the rescue of the lone survivor would most likely not have been successful without MIS data.

The most popular methods for primary data collection for sport organizations are email surveys, blogs or chats incorporated into websites, and focus group interviews. Data generated through client questionnaires or surveys can be a valuable source of information about customers' attitudes toward products and services, as well as short-term demand trends (Stotlar, 2009). Primary data can enhance a sound quality-control system by eliciting feedback to be used in refining product and service offerings. Primary data collection can also take the form of pilot testing and product experiments. Those companies that manufacture sporting goods are continuously involved in this type of research, specifically in product development.

Unfortunately, some sport organizations discard valuable consumer information. Spoelstra (1997) found that when he joined the front office of the NBA New Jersey Nets, they were throwing away valuable data. When customers called the Nets to obtain a copy of the season schedule, the ticket office staff simply grabbed an envelope, wrote down the caller's name and address, and mailed the schedule. Because these people had expressed an interest in the Nets' product, Spoelstra felt that their names should be placed into an MIS for additional direct-mail marketing. Needless to say, Spoelstra changed the system. The development of this line of thinking could be seen through actions utilized by the Cleveland Cavaliers when they used data from Ticketmaster to place follow-up phone calls to recent ticket buyers in hopes that they would purchase tickets for future games (Bonvissuto, 2005).

Another technique often employed by fitness clubs is to capture data when guests of current members register at the front desk. The office staff is trained to enter the visitor's name into a "prospects" file that can be used in future marketing activities.

In the late 1990s, many sport organizations started to realize the value of collecting information and designed programs similar to the airline industry's frequent flyer programs. One of the first teams to initiate such a program was the San Diego Padres of MLB. In 1996, the Padres introduced the Compadres Club. In their first year of operations, they signed up 90,000 members. Forty-six percent of the club members increased their game attendance over that of the previous season. Other clubs (Anaheim Ducks, Los Angeles Angels of Anaheim, San Francisco Giants) quickly followed the model established by the Padres. Following their long-overdue World Series Championship in 2004, the Boston Red Sox worked with Relizon (a database marketing company working with many MLB teams) to implement the Red Sox Nation fan loyalty program. For $9.95, fans could become official citizens of the Red Sox Nation and receive preferential access to ticket sales and special edition commemorative souvenirs. In fact, the Red Sox sold all of their 2005 spring training tickets in six hours. They also increased sales of team hats by 200% and brought in $225,000 for the sales of commemorative World Series rings (Hiestand, 2005). Thus, for many MLB teams, database marketing is finally playing a part in their marketing strategies.

Professional sport teams are not the only sport entities to recognize the benefits of database marketing. NASCAR implemented its fan club in 2005 with a stated purpose of promoting a "direct connection between NASCAR, its drivers, teams, tracks, sponsors and its loyal fans" (Dyer, 2005). The three most common models of consumer loyalty programs are outlined below.

The first model is the points and prizes model. As you would expect, consumers earn points for purchases and eventually achieve point levels appropriate for prize redemption. A second, more structured model allows customers to continually accumulate points for awards. When specified point levels are attained, predetermined awards are distributed. This plateaus, perks, and prizes model has proven successful in numerous business segments. The third and least complicated loyalty program is the membership program. Customers are encouraged to join a corporate club that entitles them to special benefits and discounts. This model has been used as the basis of many sport fan clubs.

The Padres, and with some variation the other professional teams noted above, adopted the plateaus, perks, and prizes model. Padres fans were encouraged to join the Compadres Club by completing a club application. The types of data most commonly collected included personal data, demographic background, and purchase frequency/behavior. The personal information requested included name, address, email, phone and fax numbers, and date of birth. The demographic variables encompassed gender, age, marital status, ethnicity, number of children, education, household income, and occupation. In addition, some information was collected regarding the customers' lifestyle interests. Finally, application forms requested data relating to the applicants' purchase behavior. Factors such as where tickets were purchased, previous and future purchases, seating location, and media influences were also recorded. Collectively, these data would be of significant benefit to sport marketers if used properly.

Collecting email contact information opens the channels of communication between the company and its customers. However, email marketing has become so prevalent that many people have installed "spam blocking" software on their personal computers. The best way to avoid being blocked by consumers is to have the consumer request information from you (opt in), opening the lines of communication. Thus, the key to effective communication with your consumers is not by interrupting them, but rather by obtaining their permission to pursue a relationship. This is commonly called "permission marketing." Getting the customer to ask for information about products is much more effective than bombarding them with advertising asking for money.

Permission marketing starts with the contact. It provides the opportunity for the consumer to contact you for information. While this concept is not totally new, it has become more prominent with the growth of the Internet. Typically, the sport organization has a section of their website available for fans to sign up for club membership or for permission to receive special email notices. When sport organizations and corporations collect email addresses in their database, it is important to remember that the email address belongs to the customer. Developing trust with the consumers is critical if their email addresses are to be used for subsequent marketing activities. The best ethical position is to have a section of the email communication that would allow the consumer to "unsubscribe" with a click of the mouse if their trust is violated or if they decide to terminate the relationship.

McConnell and Huba (2004) note that sports teams should begin the development of a database by gathering as much feedback from their fans as possible. Teams like the Dallas Mavericks, Portland Trailblazers, and New Orleans Saints have established systems to gather input by creating "Fan Advisory Boards." The Miami Heat (NBA) developed a "buddy program" where members of the Heat staff were assigned to contact season ticket holders several times during the season. Many times the contact was initiated to notify the person of an upcoming event; sometimes it was just to ask if there was anything that the team could do for them. One Heat executive said, "there is nothing more important than our season ticket holders and it has brought our entire organization together to humanize this" (Migala, 2003).

Permission marketing was also implemented by English Premier League club Arsenal. Marketing firm CAKE Communications developed a downloadable program for the team's website that would provide team-related stories and information based on a customized profile supplied by the fan. This involved a "Skinker," a desktop icon (in this case an animated figure of the manager) that would pop up on the fan's computer screen with instant match results, video highlights, and news items. The results for Arsenal were impressive. In the first 12 weeks of the program, they had 50,210 downloads and 131,579 click-throughs to the team's website, an increase of 44.9% (Arsenal Case Study, 2005). The U.S. Olympic Committee uses a similar tactic when sending notices to their U.S. Olympic Fan Club members, including news stories and human interest pieces on select athletes and sports. Because club members have a special interest in Olympic sport, they welcome this information.

The practice of permission marketing is not confined to professional and Olympic-level organizations. Colleges and universities have also used the strategy. Sports information directors traditionally send press releases to media outlets from their database. The question arises, "Why not add season ticket holders and fan club members to the distribution list?" The Ultimate Fighting Championships, the University of Oregon, and other forward-planning sport organizations use their databases to allow select preferred customers to order event tickets before they go on sale to the general public (Migala, 2005). These practices can make the best customers feel special and increase their identification with the team.

Many sports retail companies ask customers to complete customer profiles when they order from the website. Then, when special promotions are available, the consumer gets an email notice based on the consumer's identified preferences or previous purchasing patterns. The key is to make sure that the offer is really special and not just an advertisement for regular merchandise.

Sport organizations are also consumers; therefore, every supplier to the organization should also be considered a potential consumer. A wide variety of products and services are purchased by your organization and represent another possible marketing opportunity. These companies could be contacted for ticket purchases, product donations, and sponsorship opportunities (Stotlar, 2009).

Secondary research is characterized by the fact that it is not conducted directly by the sport organization. Due to increases in technology usage, the information-vending business has become one of the fastest growing areas of the data business in sport marketing. The International Health, Racquet and Sportsclub Association (IHRSA) has been publishing quality data for the industry for over 25 years ("IHRSA Research," n.d.). IHRSA conducts an annual analysis of the fitness and exercise club industry with data from select health and fitness centers in the United States. Their data is exceptionally useful in establishing benchmarks for fitness club performance. For example, their 2011 data indicated that participating clubs had a median member retention of 71.1%. They also found that average revenues per club member were $653 per year and mean revenue per square foot of floor space was $47. Clubs in their sample also reported an increase in revenue per individual member from $732.10 in 2008 to $763.30 in 2009, an improvement of 4.3%. These are valuable benchmarks for those considering entering the health and fitness industry or simply evaluating their success in the market.

Several major companies are in the business of market research, including sport market research. A considerable amount of data can be obtained from these organizations, which collect and publish data about the sport industry.

Probably the most comprehensive information is available through Experian Simmons Market Research (formerly known as Simmons Market Research Bureau), which for over 60 years produced volumes of marketing research for all industries, including sports and fitness. Their data are presented in a variety of areas, and an entire volume is devoted to sports and leisure. Sport marketers will be most interested in the data on sports participation, attendance at sporting events and sports equipment sales. Experian Simmons details consumers by age, income, geographical location, occupation, education, marital status, and size of family. Access to Experian Simmons' research is available at most public libraries or on their website ("Experian Simmons," n.d.). Specifically related to sports is the collection of data available from the Sport Business Research Network's website (www.sbrnet.com). This company also works with the Sporting Goods Manufacturers Association and other trade groups to collect and disseminate industry data. For over 15 years, Turnkey Sports and Entertainment has been offering high quality data collection and analysis specific to professional sport and entertainment. They provide market-wide data and can create custom analyses for about any client. Although the customized data can be expensive, it is typically cheaper than conducting the analysis independently.

For example, the Sporting Goods Manufacturers Association, in association with American Sports Data, conducted a study of 10,000 children aged 10–18 regarding their participation, attitudes, and opinions surrounding sport. These data would be quite valuable in defining both market size and potential for sport retailers, and they would be essential when assessing operating efficiency of one's business. They would also be critical in making decisions regarding which business sector to enter (Wallenfels, 2005).

Manufacturers have become very ingenious regarding ways to build MIS data. For example, Nike placed a hand-tag on their Air Jordan youth apparel. This tag was an application form to join the Air Jordan Flight Club ("Nike.com," n.d.). Membership in the club included a poster, membership card, and special t-shirt, but most importantly, Nike obtained crucial contact information for young sports consumers. The Phoenix

Coyotes of the NHL held an online scavenger hunt for their young fans who had recently attended a Coyotes games. Through customer log-on, the Coyotes were able to
gather email and other pertinent data from their fans.

The sources for information are almost unlimited, but finding the information takes
a little time, imagination, and effort. For example, a national governing body such as
U.S. Swimming could easily access information from sporting goods retailers (or perhaps one of their sponsors like Speedo) detailing purchase information for recent customers. This information could in turn be entered into a database and included in future membership or marketing efforts.

As sport manufacturers and sport organizations collect market data, sport marketing
professionals need a marketing information system (MIS) to manage the data necessary
for making informed decisions. The accuracy and availability of marketing data are vital
for sport organizations because their fans, clients, participants, and consumers change
rapidly (Mullin et al., 2007). Therefore, the MIS must be designed to store, retrieve,
and assimilate the data in meaningful ways.

DESIGNING INFORMATION SYSTEMS

The MIS does not make decisions; it merely makes information available quickly, accurately, and in a form that marketers can interpret. In fact, sport icon Mark McCormack,
founder of IMG, noted "we can always find what we are looking for, despite all evidence to the contrary" (McCormack, 2000, p. 229). Refer to the model of marketing
information systems for sport organizations presented in Figure 7.1.

Marketing information systems must be integrated so that fragmented data can be
fused into composite pictures of individual consumers and specific sport markets. It is
imperative that when sport marketers are required to make decisions, they make informed decisions based on the best and most current information. All sport marketers
can make decisions, but the success of the marketing decision often depends on the
quality of the information on which it is based (Stotlar, 2009). It is the function of the
MIS to provide that information.

Mullin (1985) was one of the earliest sport marketers to recognize the value of a well-
managed MIS. He indicated that "the full value of an MIS is realized only when data
from various sources are integrated into a common database" (p. 207). Mullin described
the essential characteristics of an effective sport marketing database as follows:

1. A protocol must be established to collect data needed for the system.
2. The database must be linked to a central processing unit. An organization needs
   to have all of its data located in one centralized system.
3. Storage capacity must be planned into the system through a thorough analysis of
   anticipated data volume and characteristics.
4. The various databases (consumer files, accounting records, sales records, etc.) need
   to be fully integrated so that the data from one source can be contrasted and/or
   combined with data from another source.

5. The data must be retrievable in a form that the sport marketer can use for decision making.
6. Control mechanisms should be designed into the system to facilitate data security.

MAINTAINING DATA SECURITY

Two distinct types of security problems accompany the use of databases.

The first problem involves the software used to perform the various tasks. Because the information on the software program and the information that has been entered by the staff are stored on a home drive or flash drive, the characteristics of that site are important. Almost all computers use combinations of hard drives, flash drives and CD-ROMs. Larger computers may use removable hard drives and other storage systems. Although removable storage drives are relatively durable, they can be erased through exposure to any magnetic object. This totally destroys any information on the device, program, and/or files. These devices have also been known to "crash" on their own. Therefore, one of the most important aspects of data security is "backing up," which involves making a duplicate of all programs and information stored on disks. This may seem like much work, but the penalty for failing to back up work is that someone must reenter all of the information that was lost.

The second problem regarding security involves access to restricted information. Sport organizations consider their marketing information confidential. It is important that this information be reserved for viewing only by appropriate people. This restricted access is often accomplished through the password system (Westmacott & Obhi, 2001). The user must enter a predetermined password to gain access to MIS files. New developments in security are constantly evolving; systems that evaluate the user's eye geometry are currently being used in some corporations. These security measures are also quite important when any unauthorized access could cause severe problems for the organization.

GETTING THE SYSTEM TO WORK

Two mistakes are often made in the application of computer-based MIS systems in sport organizations. First, managers buy a computer with the idea that it is appropriate for the job at hand. Second, the people who will be using the system are often not involved in its testing and purchase. On many occasions, a well-intentioned administrator purchases a computerized data system to assist staff, only to discover that the systems and software will not perform the functions that the staff needs it to perform. The computer system and software should be purchased with specific requirements in mind, and the staff should be involved in the decision from the very beginning of the process.

Two basic types of programs are available—custom programs and commercial "off-the-shelf" business applications. Commercial software packages are readily available for the creation and management of marketing information, and they can handle the majority of information storage and retrieval needs of sport marketers. Each program has unique strengths and weaknesses, and many of them will allow the creation of custom forms for storing and retrieving marketing information. Another advantage is that many office workers will be familiar with the operation of the more well-known software programs.

In the event that an organization has special needs, a software program may be written especially for its applications. Although these programs will fit the organization's needs, they are generally expensive, and any future modification that is required will often mandate hiring the same person (or company) that designed the original program. It goes without saying that this situation would not leave the organization in the best market position.

A commercial database usually allows for individualized category ("field") names to be developed by the end user. The computer manages pieces of information using these "fields;" therefore, each piece of information by which the marketer may wish to sort, list, or search must have its own field, so it is important for the sport marketer to carefully review the ability of the program to handle files by fields. When considering either a custom-programmed package or a commercial one that allows for individualized fields for each file, the sport marketer must determine the exact information that will be needed.

Many commercial programs have companion software that will allow the sport marketer to create and move information from one application to another. Thus, a marketing director in a fitness center could write a memo on the word processor, have the MIS select the addresses of all members who had not been in for a workout in the past month, and merge the mailing list with the memo.

Considerable attention has thus far been devoted to various tasks and programs for the accomplishment of those tasks. One more type of program must be addressed: integrated database-graphics programs. These programs can also combine word processing, graphics, spreadsheets, database, and telecommunication. Use of this software facilitates sales reports, market projects, and communication with both clients and staff. This enables the user to purchase one piece of software that will do just about everything. Integrated software is more expensive, but the convenience of a "one-system" package is often worth the expense.

A well-designed database system can also perform many standard business tasks. Some MIS applications can perform accounts-receivable functions such as preparation of invoices, maintenance of customer accounts, and production of sales and other reports. In sport organizations, these functions are often applied to ticket sales or membership payments. The accounts-payable segment of the program would generally be widely applied throughout the organization, detailing all vendors with whom business is transacted. The features that often appear in this function are purchase-order control, invoice processing, check writing and control, cash-requirement forecasting, and vendor-information analysis. Programs may be designed for specific accounting and data management, but a truly integrated MIS can be adapted for a variety of uses in sport marketing activities.

In the sport setting, these features may surpass the needs and desires of the average sport marketer, but they should be fully compatible with the associated needs of the entire sport organization. The business computer industry has expanded so quickly in the past decade that it very likely that a commercially available package can be found to meet all of one's MIS needs.

WORKING WITH THE SYSTEM

It should also be pointed out that an MIS cannot be expected to solve problems efficiently as soon as the system comes out of the box. It takes about 20 hours for a person to become fully acquainted with the operation of any hardware system and about 40 hours to be become familiar with a specific software package. With the right system, access to the information is quick, and updating the material is much simpler than with conventional methods. Printouts of data should be available that include any combination of factors selected by the sport marketer. This will allow for effective sales and market planning.

PRODUCING RESULTS

The point of marketing research and data analysis is to better identify segments of the market that are most likely to purchase one's goods and services. The individual pieces of data in an MIS can reveal who bought what and when. However important that may be, what a sport marketer really wants to know is who will buy what and when. This is the aspect of sport marketing called *forecasting*. Forecasting is a distinct advantage provided by computerized MIS.

A marketing information system can assist in the interpretation of consumer data.
Courtesy of Arizona State University

Exactly what is forecasting and why is it necessary? Forecasting is the ability of the market manager to see how the future will be affected by anticipated or hypothetical decisions, the playing of "what if?" This is often referred to as "data mining." This can be very beneficial to sport marketers because hypothetical figures can be entered into the MIS for such items as sponsorship revenues, ticket prices, or membership fees. The program can then be manipulated to perform calculations detailing the financial and market consequences of those decisions.

Although MIS information is entered into the system in parts, sports marketers need to be able to look at that organization's data as a whole. There is a need for aggregate information to develop business and general marketing strategies, yet there is also a demand for synthesizing data to project individual consumer profiles. Sport marketers must clearly see the macro and micro perspectives of their consumer base. Therefore, both individual and aggregate information is needed for intelligent marketing mix decisions.

CHAPTER SUMMARY

All sport organizations deal with consumers, and consumer information is ideally suited to the storage and retrieval capabilities of the MIS. Having discovered the broad range of application for an MIS, it should be clear that marketing information systems will not immediately make a poor sport marketer competent or an inefficient salesperson good, but it is a tool that can be used by skilled employees and managers to assist in the performance of sport marketing tasks and decision making. Typical information contained in MIS files would include the consumer's name, address, email, age, occupation, and purchasing activity. It is precisely this type of information that is particularly suited to MIS and a well-managed database because of the need to continually update and change entries. Sport marketers can combine these data with other information in the corporation database to facilitate decisions on target markets and consumer profiles. Remember that the quality of one's decisions reflects upon the quality of the information upon which they were based.

DISCUSSION QUESTIONS

1. What are the essential characteristics of a well-designed marketing information system (MIS)?
2. What MIS sources would be available for an intercollegiate athletic program, and how would you go about setting up an MIS?

SUGGESTED EXERCISES

1. Select your favorite sport and consult www.SBRnet.com. See where you fit into the demographic segments presented.
2. Take a trip to your local fitness center or health club, and inquire about the types of information they have on their clients. Look at their application form if they are uncooperative with your first request.

Organizations and Professional Associations

Sporting Goods Manufacturers Association

200 Castlewood Drive
North Palm Beach, FL 33408
SBRnet
Richard A. Lipsey, President
PO Box 2378
Princeton, NJ 08543
Ph: (609) 896-1996
email: richard@sbrnet.com

SUGGESTED READINGS

Mitchell, S. (2003). The new age of direct marketing. *Journal of Database Marketing*, *10*(3), 219–229.

7

The Marketing Mix and the Sport Industry

INTRODUCTION

This chapter presents an overview of a significant portion of the sport marketing management model called the marketing mix, or "the 4 Ps." The marketing mix is crucial because its elements define the sport business. Therefore, much of the sport marketing professional's time is spent on the various functions within the marketing mix.

The marketing mix is comprised of four elements called the 4 Ps: product, price, place, and promotion. In this chapter we will define the marketing mix, present a description of its place in the sport marketing management model, provide a brief description of each of the elements of the marketing mix, and describe how the elements are combined to create the marketing mix for the sport company.

After this chapter, each of the following chapters are focused on the 4 Ps and their details, processes, and activities that are needed and performed for the success of each element.

THE MARKETING MIX

The *marketing mix* is the strategic combination of four elements, or functions: product, price, place, and promotion. At the heart of the decision-making process regarding the 4 Ps is the crucial information about the 4 Cs—consumer, competitor, company, and climate—that came from research and analysis of each (see Figure 7.1). This information is critical in informing every decision to be made concerning each of the 4 Ps.

> Creation of the marketing mix involves the process of discovering or developing the right combination of product, price, place, and promotion.

The development of the marketing mix involves determining the optimal combination of product, price, promotion, and place. Reaching the optimal combination depends on developing and manipulating each of the 4 Ps until each one is right for a particular consumer market and for the business. For the business, "optimal" means the combina-

> **Marketing Mix:**
>
> The strategic combination of product, price, place, and promotion decisions and strategies.

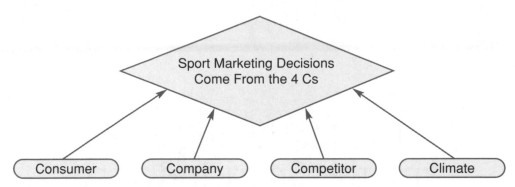

Figure 7.1. Information about the 4 Cs is necessary for making decisions and developing strategies about the Marketing Mix 4 Ps.

All decisions about the 4 Ps should be based on information gained from the research and analysis of the 4 Cs.

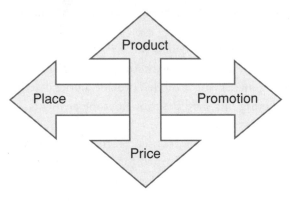

Figure 7.2. The Marketing Mix elements are interrelated.

tion that will sell, providing what the consumer wants and considers "optimal": the right product, at the right price, located where they want to shop, and perhaps involving some promotional incentives.

There are many variables of each of the 4 Ps that can be manipulated by the sport marketing professional. They are manipulated to meet the consumer's desires or needs or for competitive strategy, according to what the company can do within ethical, political, economical, and legal constraints and considerations. Remember, the 4 Cs constantly change and therefore require constant monitoring and research. When any one of the variables of any one of the 4 Cs changes, it can have an impact on one or all of the 4 Ps. A change has the potential to be positive or negative. It could be considered an opportunity or a threat to the company. The important thing is that the marketer knows about the change, studies it and its possible consequences—opportunities or threats—and makes decisions necessary to optimize or minimize those consequences.

Further, the 4 Ps are interrelated (see Figure 7.2). When a change is considered for one element, let's say "product," this will have an influence on the other elements. When a product is changed, promotions will need to be changed. Additionally, depend-

Creation of the marketing mix involves the process of developing the right combination of product, price, place, and promotion.

ing on the kind of change to the product, perhaps pricing and distribution will need to be changed. Therefore, it is important to think about all of the marketing mix elements when considering a change in one of them. The following sections explain each element of the 4 Ps.

Product

The product is what the sport company is offering to the consumer (see Figures 7.3, 7.4, and 7.5). The challenge is to produce the *right* product for the consumer. Products can be goods, services, people, places, and ideas. There are many products in the sport

Figure 7.3. The Marketing Mix: The 4 Ps.

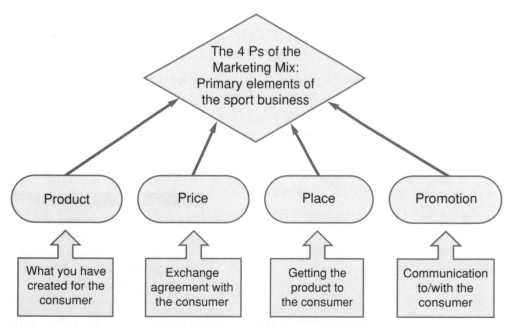

Figure 7.4. The Marketing Mix and Its Elements Known as the 4 Ps.

Product	Price	Place	Promotion
Functions	Objectives	Objectives	Objectives
Features	Flexibility	Channel Types	Promotion Mix
Accessories	Product Life Cycle	Market Exposure	Sales People
Utility	Terms	Distribution Goals	Advertising Methods
Use	Warranty	Transportation	Market Demand
Instructions	Sales	Location	Publicity
Installation	Special Order	Service	Public Relations
Service	Exclusivity	Intensity	Media Relations
Warranty	Psychology	Efficient	E-commerce
Product Lines	Perceived Value	Effective	M-commerce
Packaging	Discounts	Inventory Mgmt	Social Media Mix
Branding	Allowances	Warehousing	

Figure 7.5. The 4 Ps of the Marketing Mix.

industry. There are many consumers and competitors also. As you learned in Chapters 4 and 5, the sport marketer must determine exactly what consumers want, as well as analyze its competitors to learn what already exists in the market. As you will learn in Chapter 8, the process for developing the right product can be very involved.

The product can be manipulated, or differentiated as it is called in marketing. A tennis racket may be produced with a new shape or a new color. The sport center can offer new divisions in a volleyball league based on age, gender, or skill level. The same sport center could offer a new form of volleyball by simply changing some rules, court size, or number of players. As an example, beach volleyball can be played in a 2-player, 3-player, or 4-player format. All of the products offered by a company comprise the product mix. All products must be managed with specific functions and activities. The whole process is presented in Chapter 8.

Price

Price is the exchange value of a product. The challenge for the sport marketer is to determine the *right* price for the consumer. The price of a product can be manipulated in many ways. For example, promotional pricing can be used: 2-for-1 tickets to the game or 2-for-1 memberships to the fitness club, special sale prices on sports clothing during a holiday period, special sale prices on sporting goods equipment for seasonal sports, or price breaks as the quantity purchased increases. There are also long-term price-planning strategies that the sport marketer can use. Pricing strategies can involve numerous methods and planned for several different periods throughout the year. Chapter 9 provides detailed information on pricing.

> If the consumer believes that a product is overpriced or even underpriced, there is a good chance that the consumer will not purchase the product.

Place

Place is the process of getting the sport product to the consumer. It is also called distribution: distributing the sport product to the consumer. The sport marketer will analyze the types of distribution methods available and select those that will deliver the product to the right place. The right place means: where the consumer is, shops, or will travel. There are two types of distribution in the sport industry because of the types of products offered. First, *hard goods* are those products that must go from a manufacturing plant to a retail outlet and therefore must be distributed by actually moving product from one point to another. Second, there are products that cannot be moved physically in the sport industry. For example, a basketball game is not a product that can be moved to a retail outlet. The consumer must go to the place in which the game will be played (manufactured) in order to consume it.

The distribution (place) of a product can be changed. One can now purchase tickets to various sporting events through many different ticket outlets because they are distributed through many outlets. Sport facilities are becoming a one-stop shopping facility— many new arenas include hotels, shopping malls, and other attractions like fitness centers and amusement parks. Sport sold as a spectator product can change other factors in the way it is distributed to the consumer. For example, there are over 70 official Kentucky Derby Festival events prior to the actual Derby race, a sporting event that lasts about two minutes! Chapter 10 provides information about the detailed functions, activities, and strategies.

Promotion

Promotion is the element of marketing that many people in the general public think is marketing in its entirety. That's because promotion is the element that the general public sees and relates to as marketing. Promotion includes advertising and other promotional methods. These are designed to attract the consumer's attention. Therefore, the consumer believes that promotion covers the scope of the marketing effort.

Promotions can involve an appearance by well-known entities within a particular sport. Courtesy of Tom Campbell/Gold & Black Illustrated

> Though the public is often under the impression that promotion is strictly advertising, it is actually a process—the goal is to create enough interest in a product to convince a consumer to purchase it.

There are many promotional methods, strategies, tactics, and tricks available for the sport marketer to use, and there are some used in the sport industry that are rarely used in other industries. In one extreme example of trying to get the attention of the consumer and the media, when the first Super Bowl (at that time it was called the AFL-NFL World Championship Game) was played in 1966, organizers were so worried that the event would be ignored by the nation that they planned to create interest by staging a kidnapping of the silver trophy (Carucci, 1994).

Promotional methods include television commercials, print advertisements in magazines, direct-mail advertising, promotional pricing, "giveaways" at sports events, and press guides. Chapter 11 provides detailed information about promotion in the sport industry.

MANAGING AND MANIPULATING THE 4 Ps

All of the marketing mix elements are managed and manipulated by the sport marketer for two reasons: first, to stay in business and second, to be successful. The only way to do this is to offer products that will sell, at a price that will be paid, in a place where they will be bought, and using promotions that will attract the consumer.

The sport business professional uses the 4 Ps to develop the optimal combination for target markets and in response to changes in the market. It is the responsibility of the sport marketer to control and manage the marketing mix. Although each of the ele-

> Research is the foundation upon which all marketing decisions are made.

ments is developed through a specific planning process, they are not planned in a vacuum. The elements are interrelated (see Figure 7.2). As such, all decisions regarding one element must be done in conjunction with decisions regarding all other elements. In addition, decisions concerning the elements in the marketing mix must be made in relation to what is known about the 4 Cs—what the consumer wants; compared to what the competitor has; considered for its fit for the company; and considered within legal, ethical, social, cultural, and political climates.

THE INTERRELATIONSHIP OF THE ELEMENTS

As previously mentioned, the marketing mix elements are interrelated (see Figure 7.2). This means that each element affects each other element. The sport business professional must develop the optimal combination, basing decisions on information gained in the marketing research.

The consumer is looking for the right product, at just the right price, and that can be purchased at the right location. As you will learn in Chapter 8, the consumer does not arbitrarily buy products—the consumer is looking for something to satisfy a need or desire. From that perspective, the product and everything about the product take on characteristics beyond the intended function of the product.

> Consumer purchases are not arbitrary—the consumer is looking for a product that satisfies a need or desire.

This notion must be understood by the sport businessperson and used during the development of a marketing mix. For example, consider a consumer who wants a new pair of running shoes. The consumer's existing shoes are not quite worn out, but this consumer is becoming a "serious runner." A serious runner is a different person than a "recreational runner" and therefore has different product needs and beliefs about those needs. This runner believes that the shoes must be regarded in the running community as "serious runner" shoes. This is, in marketing terms, what can be described as a consumer who is image conscious, perhaps brand loyal, has high product knowledge, wants to fulfill a desire, and for whom price is not really a factor. The sport marketer, having studied the running market, understands the serious-runner consumer and recognizes what this particular consumer wants. Therefore, the sport marketer will produce a serious-runner shoe, and most likely, price will be no factor. The shoe will be advertised in serious-runner publications only, and the advertisements will carry the message and image that this shoe is only for the serious runner. In addition, the shoe will be sold only through serious-runner stores. This will add to the notion that the shoes are for serious runners only.

In this example, the sport marketer studied and understood this particular consumer. A product is produced specifically for this consumer; the price is set at what the consumer is willing to pay; the promotional methods imply the type of product for this particular type of consumer; and the product is offered for sale in specific places. This process and the decisions about the combination of the four elements are indicative of the interrelationship and impact of the elements. The primary strategy for the sport business in designing a marketing mix is to customize the marketing mix for a specific consumer market until the optimal mix is found. As the sport marketer identifies consumer market segments and selects target markets, the marketing mix elements are designed specifically for the consumer.

For example, if the sport marketer determines from research that the typical consumer of fitness center memberships is female; aged between 28 and 46; single; has one child; has an income range of $32,000 to $98,000; has an education level of at least a bachelor's degree; and has favorite sport and fitness activities that include weight training, working out on the stair climbing machine, aerobics, tennis, and volleyball; then the sport marketer can design the product—a fitness and sport center—for the consumer, price it for the consumer, develop promotional methods designed to attract the consumer, and place the facility in an area of the city in which a high percentage of those types of consumers live.

Also affecting the decision to open a fitness center is information concerning the industry and the competition. For example, if a fitness center already exists that offers exactly what the consumer wants, at the desired price, and in the right location, the sport marketer must determine if it will be feasible to open a fitness center. If reports of the fitness industry nationwide show that fitness center membership purchase is increasing, how does this compare to the local fitness industry?

In addition, the marketing mix should change as markets change. You have learned earlier in this chapter that the product, price, place, and promotional methods can be manipulated. Here is where constant research is needed. If it has been eight years since your company conducted any marketing research, the decisions and strategies are riskier as every year goes by. Most assuredly, the information of the 4 Cs has changed. It is very important that you constantly monitor the 4 Cs and make changes as needed on a consistent basis.

A good example of the kind of constant research a company should do is the research done on the Baby Boomer market. This is most likely a market you've heard about because they are mentioned in relation to practically everything in this country, from politics to retirement to toys to sports utility vehicles (SUVs). The Baby Boomer market has been given credit for making or breaking the success of many products, companies, and even whole industries, some of which are the fitness industry and the SUV industry.

Other examples of groups about which you may have heard are Generation X, Generation Y, the Millennials, the Techies, and the Dead Heads. Each of these is a market—a group of people (consumers) with some homogeneous characteristics or interests. They are studied and monitored constantly because their purchasing decisions and product needs and desires affect a company's marketing mix.

The information gained from research should be current. Therefore, research should be an ongoing process within the company. With a flow of current and accurate information, the sport marketer's decisions and strategies for the marketing mix can be much more successful.

CHAPTER SUMMARY

The marketing mix is the strategic combination of four elements commonly called the 4 Ps—product, price, place, and promotion. It is the component of the sport marketing management model on which the sport marketer will spend a great percentage of time. The marketing mix is designed based on information concerning the 4 Cs—consumer, competition, company, and climate.

8

The Product in the Sport Business Industry

INTRODUCTION

People seek to satisfy needs or desires, or to meet needed or wanted functions or benefits. To take care of a needed or wanted function or benefit, they seek goods, services, people, places, and/or ideas. Products perform as a satisfaction agent— the thing that will perform the desired function or provide a benefit (see Figure 8.1). Consider the following examples:

1. A softball player desires to improve hitting and enhance batting average. The player will search for the product that will fulfill those desires: the right bat.
2. Someone wants to lose weight and get into shape. This person decides that the product that will allow that individual to perform those functions is a fitness center. In order to get into the fitness center, the individual must purchase the opportunity to do so: a fitness center membership. The fitness center is offered as the opportunity for the person to fulfill those desires: the place to exercise.
3. A bicycle manufacturing company wants to increase sales and reach more markets. After much research, the company executive determines that the Internet

Figure 8.1. The Marketing Mix: The 4 Ps.

would be a good choice as an additional "store" for sales. The Internet is the product for this company that will perform the desired function; so the company will purchase an Internet domain and hire someone to design and manage a website. The bicycle company has sought services to meet needs.

4. While someone is playing tennis, the strings of the tennis racket snap. This person wants to continue playing tennis. In order to fulfill that desire, the racket's strings must be replaced. The service of stringing the racket provides the opportunity for the racket to be repaired so that the individual can fulfill the desire to once again play tennis.

These examples serve to partially explain why and how a person purchases a product: people are actually purchasing functions and benefits. The product is the satisfaction agent for those functions and benefits.

A definition of product should represent the breadth of the term. Therefore, *product* should be understood as a *concept* and as an umbrella term that includes goods, services, people, places, and ideas with tangible or intangible attributes. For instance, the softball player wants the softball bat for what it will *do* and the function it will fulfill, and not because it is simply a softball bat.

The sport marketing professional should strive to understand exactly what the consumer wants in order to offer just that. In the earlier examples, a fitness center is a "place" that provides the opportunity to fulfill desires for fitness, including weight loss, socializing, fun, relaxation and other benefits. In the example of replacing the broken tennis racket strings, the consumer receives both a good and a service: new strings and the job (service) of putting the strings on the racket. The bicycle company's need to increase sales and reach new markets is fulfilled by the creation of an Internet site.

PRODUCT DECISIONS AND STRATEGY
DEVELOPMENT USING THE 4 Cs

Developing decisions and strategies about every aspect of the product requires information about the 4 Cs—consumer, company, competitor, and climate (see Figure 8.2). Throughout the process of developing the product, information gathered about the

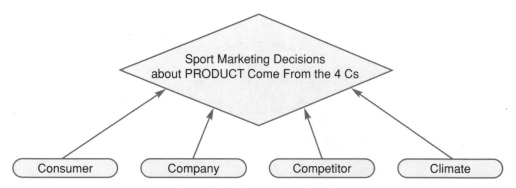

Figure 8.2. Information about the 4 Cs is necessary for making decisions and developing strategies about Product.

4 Cs will help the company determine many different variables about the product. The following sections present information about each of the 4 Cs and the factors that will influence decisions about the product.

Consumer

The consumer is the very reason for the product. Hence, a company must study and get to know everything possible about its consumers and what it is they seek in a product. As presented earlier, the consumer is looking to fulfill certain functions and/or benefits and thus is looking for a product that will satisfy those. For example, professional sports exist for the purpose of entertainment. Fans of professional sports love the entertainment they provide, including factors such as entertaining family, friends, or business associates. Thus, fans consume professionals sports for this and other purposes. Therefore, the sport marketing professional must be sure the product—professional sports—is providing entertainment. This can be accomplished through the actual game (or contest), or through peripheral products such as additional entertainment options during or surrounding the game, such as a fan interactive area, concessions, exhibits, and giveaways. This function will be identified and touted through the other marketing mix elements, such as place or promotion. In this example, place can be presented as the location of the arena in which the game is played. The city and its "family friendly atmosphere" can be used to promote the function of entertainment. Las Vegas, for instance, positions itself as "the city that never sleeps" targeting the consumer's desire to party and be entertained all night long.

Company

The company must provide products that are within its mission and purpose. It is one thing to try to fulfill the consumer's desires, but quite another to stay within and meet the company's mission and purpose. The mission and purpose of college sports, for example, was originally to provide extramural competitive sports opportunities for its students. Even though college sports has become big business, colleges and universities work hard to stay true to the original mission and purpose.

There are many factors about "the company" that will affect the decisions and strategies of this marketing mix element, the product. Figure 8.2 provides some of those factors, and the rest of this chapter focuses on presenting many of them.

Competitor

"Keeping up with the Joneses" is a cultural saying which means that one neighbor will do whatever it takes to try to do everything like their neighbor, the Joneses. However, is that what is best for them? In sport business, your company must make many decisions about itself in relation to its competitors—after all, if you are not studying your competitors, it can have a negative impact on your company. Therefore, it is strategically smart to know everything you can about your competitors. This information will give you the ability to make strategic decisions that will have a positive influence on your company. A good example to use here is sports. A coach wants his/her team to be competitive; a large part of that is to study the competition, get to know their players and plays, and learn their strategies. This knowledge will be used to make decisions, develop plays to counteract the competition, and develop plays and strategies that will enhance success. Figure 8.2 presents some of the factors about the competitor that influence product decisions and strategies. Many of these factors will be discussed in this chapter.

Climate

As one of the 4 Cs of sport marketing, climate has been a major factor in the current decade. The environment has been a major factor affecting nearly every company in a number of ways, and the economic recession has had a significant effect on how companies operate. In the past, slight recessions have only had a slightly negative effect on the sport business industry. However, when the recession of 2008 began and moved through the next couple of years, it became obvious that this particular recession was extraordinary in relation to its effects on the sport business industry. Sport companies slashed budgets, some sport companies went under, many sports companies scaled back on offerings, and sports events were cancelled because sponsoring companies either slashed their sponsorship support or completely terminated it.

It is very important that the sport business study all of the elements of the climate and fully understand the many possible effects that each one could have on the company. This way, specific and strategic planning can be done that will either minimize negative effects, avoid them completely, or have fully positive effects on the company.

UNDERSTANDING THE CONCEPT OF "PRODUCT"

Product has many elements and factors. Figure 8.3 illustrates some of those elements. It is not just a physical object that makes a product a product. It is the full sum of all the product's characteristics, either tangible or intangible. Therefore, it is critical to understand product as a concept. To develop an understanding of a *concept* of product, it is very helpful to consider definitions of product from a variety of marketing textbooks:

> A product is everything, both favorable and unfavorable, that one receives in an exchange. It is a complexity of tangible and intangible attributes, including functional, social, and psychological utilities or benefits. (Pride & Ferrell, 1991, p. 240)

> A product is a bundle of physical, service, and symbolic attributes designed to enhance consumer want satisfaction. (Boone & Kurtz, 1989, p. 271)

> A product is a set of tangible and intangible attributes, including packaging, color, price, quality, and brand, plus the services and reputation of the seller. A product may be a tangible good, service, place, person, or idea. (Stanton, Etzel, & Walker, 1991, pp. 168–169)

> A product is "the sum of the physical, psychological, and sociological satisfactions that the buyer derives from purchase, ownership, and consumption" and includes "accessories, packaging, and service." (Tarpey, Donnelly, & Peter, 1979, p. 178)

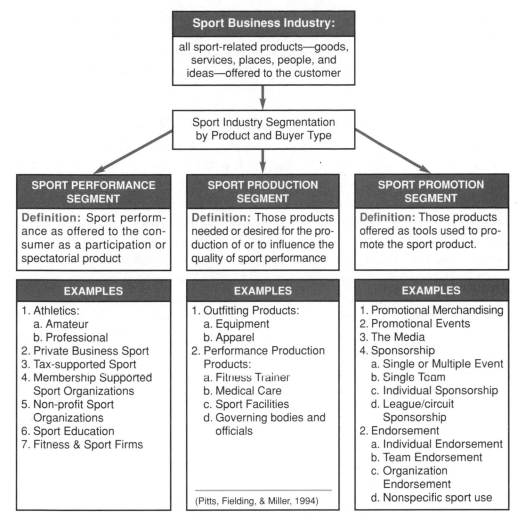

Sport Business Industry:

all sport-related products—goods, services, places, people, and ideas—offered to the customer

Sport Industry Segmentation by Product and Buyer Type

SPORT PERFORMANCE SEGMENT	SPORT PRODUCTION SEGMENT	SPORT PROMOTION SEGMENT
Definition: Sport performance as offered to the consumer as a participation or spectatorial product	**Definition:** Those products needed or desired for the production of or to influence the quality of sport performance	**Definition:** Those products offered as tools used to promote the sport product.
EXAMPLES	**EXAMPLES**	**EXAMPLES**

1. Athletics:
  a. Amateur
  b. Professional
2. Private Business Sport
3. Tax-supported Sport
4. Membership Supported Sport Organizations
5. Non-profit Sport Organizations
6. Sport Education
7. Fitness & Sport Firms
	1. Outfitting Products:
	  a. Equipment
	  b. Apparel
	2. Performance Production Products:
	  a. Fitness Trainer
	  b. Medical Care
	  c. Sport Facilities
	  d. Governing bodies and officials
	
	(Pitts, Fielding, & Miller, 1994)
		1. Promotional Merchandising
		2. Promotional Events
		3. The Media
		4. Sponsorship
		  a. Single or Multiple Event
		  b. Single Team
		  c. Individual Sponsorship
		  d. League/circuit Sponsorship
		2. Endorsement
		  a. Individual Endorsement
		  b. Team Endorsement
		  c. Organization Endorsement
		  d. Nonspecific sport use

Figure 8.3. The Sport Business Industry Segment Model.

Many of these definitions carry similar terms as descriptive characteristics of product, presented in the next sections.

TANGIBLE AND INTANGIBLE CHARACTERISTICS OF PRODUCT

A tangible product is something that is concrete, definite, discernible, and material. It is a physical object. A softball bat is a tangible product. It physically exists. An intangible product is something that is indefinite; it is not a physical object. When broken tennis racket strings need to be repaired, the task of replacing the strings is an intangible product, in this example, a service. Further, a tangible object is involved in this purchase. The consumer gets new strings, a tangible product, and the broken strings are replaced, an intangible product.

Professional sport events provide us with examples of intangible products. A professional men's basketball game is an intangible product. One can only watch the game.

Benefits realized include entertainment, socializing, fun, and a number of other personal satisfactions.

It is important that sport marketing decision makers understand the concepts of tangibility and intangibility. This knowledge guides decisions concerning product strategies and influences other marketing variables as well.

UTILITY AND BENEFITS OF PRODUCT

"Utility may be defined as the attribute in an item that makes it capable of satisfying human wants" (Stanton, Etzel, & Walker, 1991, p. 16). There are four types of utility: form, time, place, and ownership (possession). *Form utility* is the production of a product—using raw materials to create finished products. *Time utility* is getting a product to the consumer when the consumer wants it. *Place utility* is getting the product to the consumer where the consumer shops. *Ownership utility* is the ability to transfer ownership or possession of a product from seller to buyer (Boone & Kurtz, 1989).

Using the previous examples, let us consider utility. The consumer who wants a specific softball bat (form utility) to improve batting average wants the bat before the softball season begins (time utility) from a reputable sporting goods store close to where the consumer lives (ownership and place utilities). The sport marketer's job is to produce the bat from specific raw materials (form utility), get it on the market in advance of softball season (time utility), and distribute it to reputable sporting goods stores and other outlets (ownership and place utilities). It is only when the sport marketer completely understands the consumer's specific needs—what, when, how, why—that the marketer may make informed decisions concerning form, time, place and ownership utilities.

For the bicycle company that needs a website to increase sales and reach new markets, every utility is met. The company is getting a website through which to sell their products; it is getting the website when it is needed (immediately); it is getting the website from a well-known and respected company (an Internet service company); and it is getting the website close to where it is wanted—the Web designer they hired works in the main office suite.

The *benefits* of a product are everything the consumer derives from the product. In other words, benefits may include functions of the product and intangible benefits such as status, quality, durability, cost effectiveness, and others. For example, the consumer who wants to improve batting average expects that the selected bat will improve batting average. The sport marketer, based on an understanding of what the softball player wants, promotes the bat as a bat that will give the player a better batting average. Promotional messages such as "this bat has a bigger sweet spot," "the only bat for champions," or "the home-run hitter's dream bat" are strong suggestions to the consumer that this bat will give the consumer what he or she wants, a better batting average.

You should now have a good understanding of product. It is not simply a good or a service. It is something that functions in some capacity to fulfill a consumer's desire or need. The sport marketer must know what the consumer wants the product to do—its benefits—and guide the company toward meeting those demands—utility. The sport company produces a product *after* learning what the consumer wants.

SPORT PRODUCT

There is a vast array of products in the sport industry. Based on the definition presented in Chapter 1, we recognize the sport industry as broad and comprised of industry segments such as fitness management, recreational and professional sports; any product that fulfills the sport, fitness, or recreation-related needs or desires of a consumer is considered a sport product. This requires a broad concept definition of sport product. Drawing on the definition of sport and the sport industry in Chapter 1 and the general definitions of product in this chapter, the definition of sport product is "any good, service, person, place, or idea with tangible or intangible attributes that satisfies the consumer's need or desire for sport, fitness, or recreation-related products."

Return to Chapter 1 and reread the section on what exists in the sport industry. Using our definition of sport product, those are all sport products offered to fulfill consumer sport-related needs or desires. With so many sport products in this industry, it is necessary for the sport marketer to identify differing consumer needs and desires in order to create and offer products that will fulfill those needs and desires. The most common method is product classification.

SPORT PRODUCT MANAGEMENT

Product management presents a major challenge for the sport company. Products are what your company produces, if the company is a manufacturer, or what your company selects and buys, if your company is a wholesaler or retailer, in order to fulfill needs and desires of consumers. Effective management of the product is crucial to success. All of the factors and elements of what makes up a product should come from information about the 4 Cs, as illustrated in Figure 8.2. Every decision about the product should be informed by this information.

Product management involves deciding which products to offer, how to classify or define the product, knowing what product market and industry the product falls into, what type of product line to carry, when to keep or delete a product, as well as when to add new products. Additionally, proper management must include management of the product life cycle, product positioning strategies, new product development, product diversification, line extension, and product identification. This chapter presents many of the sport product management elements.

SPORT PRODUCT CLASSIFICATION

An initial step in developing products is to determine what type(s) of product(s) to offer. This task involves studying a particular product category, also known as a product market or an industry segment. The reasons for studying product categories or segments are similar to the reasons for studying and segmenting consumers. A thorough understanding of your product, its benefits and functions, and its utilities, along with understanding the same about your competitors' products, is critical to product management. Constant study of your product and all similar products will guide decisions concerning product development or diversification, pricing strategies, distribution tactics, and promotional strategies.

This information provides the basis for the sport company to define its product(s), make decisions concerning opportunities or threats, develop appropriate marketing plans, develop a successful product mix, and determine the right time for product differentiation and deletion.

One method of classifying products is based on the consumer. In this method, products are traditionally classified in two very broad categories: consumer products and business products. *Consumer products* are those products offered to the final consumer for personal or household use (Evans & Berman, 1987). *Business products* are those products offered to businesses or organizations for use in the production of other goods and services, to operate a business, or for resale to other consumers (Stanton et al., 1991).

The sport industry offers a wide diversity of products targeted to both business consumers and end consumers. In each category, products can be goods, services, people, places, or ideas. In relation to service products, they can be classified into one of three categories: rented-goods service, owned-goods service, or non-goods service.

A *rented-goods service* is the renting of a product for a period of time. Some examples in the sport industry include the following: a fitness center rents a fitness video to clients; a tennis center rents tennis rackets to members; a tennis center rents court time; a park near a lake rents jet skis on an hourly basis; a snow ski resort rents skis for a day or a week; a marina rents a houseboat for a weekend.

Owned-goods services include those services to repair or alter something that the consumer owns. Some examples of owned-goods services in the sport industry are: replacing broken strings on a tennis racket; getting golf clubs cleaned at the club; getting numbers, names, and logos put on a softball uniform; having a boat's engine repaired; and getting a wheelchair repaired in order to play a wheelchair basketball game.

Non-goods services do not involve a good at all. This category includes personal services offered by the seller. In the sport industry some examples are tennis lessons, golf lessons, or summer basketball camp; and a fitness center that offers childcare service on site. This category also includes those services offered by sport management or sport marketing companies that specialize in managing and/or marketing a sporting event for a consumer. For example, you hire a sport marketing company to market and manage every aspect of a large marathon in your city.

Business Products

Business products in the sport industry are those products offered to sport businesses for use in the manufacture of sport products, to operate a sport business, or for resale. Hillerich and Bradsby, manufacturers of the famous Louisville Slugger bats, purchase wood as a material used to make baseball bats (Pitts & Fielding, 1987). Consider the following variety of other types of business products offered to business consumers:

- A golf club manufacturer purchases graphite and other materials to produce golf clubs.
- A running shoe company purchases a variety of rubber, leather, and other materials to make running shoes.

- A bicycle manufacturer purchases aluminum to use in the manufacture of light-weight bicycles.
- A sport sponsorship management company purchases research services in order to help analyze sponsorship effectiveness.

If the sport marketer understands these types of classifications, the marketer will understand consumer type and what the consumer wants. Another method used in marketing to classify products is industry segmentation.

INDUSTRY SEGMENTATION

As previously discussed in Chapter 5, industry segmentation is another method used by marketers to classify products and buyers. *Industry segmentation* is defined as the division of an industry into subunits (industry segments) for purposes of developing competitive strategy. An *industry segment* is a combination of a product variety and a group of consumers who purchase it.

Some industries contain just one product. More typically, an industry contains a wide variety of products offered to a great variety of consumers—final and business. Trying to keep up with every product in the sport industry would be practically impossible. It becomes important and even necessary that the sport marketer focus on a section or segment of the total industry. This guides the sport marketer in the identification of marketing opportunities and threats within a specific product market and the development of an appropriate marketing mix (Day, Shocker, & Srivastava, 1979; McCarthy & Perreault, 1984; Porter, 1985).

The sport industry segmentation model (Pitts, Fielding, & Miller, 1994; presented in Figure 8.3 earlier) is a unique study of products in the sport industry. The authors used a portion of the Porter (1985) model for industry segmentation and used product function and buyer types in segmenting the sport industry. Three sport product industry segments were identified. These are the sport performance segment, sport production segment, and sport promotion segment. The information is important to the sport marketer in developing an understanding of the product segment within the sport industry in which the company's product(s) fits, identifying and monitoring the competition, and determining product management strategies (see Table 8.1).

Table 8.1. Three Reasons to Understand Sport Industry Segments	
1	To understand the company's product.
2	To identify and monitor competitors.
3	To determine product management strategies.

Sport Performance

The *sport performance industry segment* consists of sport performance as a product. Sport performance is offered to the consumer in two ways: as a participation product and as a spectatorial product. Each of these may even be considered separate segments as the marketing of participation and spectatorial products is different. However, they were placed in one category due to their similarities in function and benefit.

Functions and benefits include exercising, stress management, fun, activity, competition, and entertainment. Examples include basketball, hiking, boating, swimming, jogging, camping, Frisbee throwing, martial arts, and many, many more. These activities are offered in a variety of settings, to a variety of consumer markets, and in a variety of formats (a tournament, a league, a one-day event, a single event, a weekend event, lessons, clinics, seminars, and many more). Table 8.2 shows some examples of the variety of sport performance segment products.

Table 8.2. Products in the Sport Performance Industry Segment

SPORT PERFORMANCE INDUSTRY SEGMENT		
EXAMPLES OF SETTING	PARTICIPATION Collegiate athletics Pro sports Recreational leagues	SPECTATORIAL Collegiate athletics Pro sports Recreational leagues
FORMAT	League / Seminar Event / Camp Tournament / Lab Lessons / Olympics Clinic / Matches Rehabilitation	Games/matches/meets/contest
MARKETS	By age groups By gender and mixed By race By disability By sexual orientation By religion By skill level	By age groups By gender Special groups such as Girls or Boys clubs By race
FUNCTIONS AND BENEFITS	Fun Fitness gain Skill development Knowledge gain Weight loss Competition Stress management Entertainment Rehabilitative	Entertainment Fun Stress management Activity Support Source: Pitts, Fielding & Miller, 1994.

As a spectatorial product, sport performance is offered primarily in two ways: attendance at a sport event and spectating via television or video. Sport spectating has changed dramatically over the last few decades. The spectator is offered plush skyboxes, restaurants, and even a hotel in the sport facility; entertainment before, during, and after the event; and even spectator participation events during the sport event. These have become an integral part of the sport event spectator's package.

Sport Production

The *sport production industry segment* is defined as including those products necessary or desired to produce or to influence the quality of sport performance. Most sport participation requires specific equipment and apparel before it can be properly performed. The equipment and apparel afford the production of the sport performance. Further, in an effort to enhance performance, specific products or services may be desired. This creates a demand for a variety of products and product quality for the production of sport and to enhance the quality of performance.

For example, Venus Williams can probably play tennis with any tennis racket. However, she prefers custom-designed rackets in order to enhance performance. She also purchases a number of other products that influence her tennis performance, such as a personal fitness trainer, weight training equipment, a sports medicine practitioner, sports medicine equipment and supplies, and a professional tennis coach. Table 8.3 presents examples of products in the sport production industry segment.

Table 8.3. The Sport Production Industry Segment Examples	
1	Sport-specific equipment
2	Safety and protective equipment
3	Apparel: Clothing, shoes
4	Facility
5	Performance enhancing products: • personal fitness trainer • fitness equipment • sports medicine care • equipment and supplies • coaches • other staff
6	Governing organizations: • rules committees • officials: referees, umpires • governing associations • statisticians • scorekeepers, announcers, and other officials

Source: Pitts, Fielding & Miller, 1994.

Sport Promotion

The *sport promotion industry segment* is defined as those products used in the promotion of sport industry products. Refer to Table 8.4 for examples of products in the sport promotion industry segment. For example, college women's basketball can exist without promotion. However, it is enhanced, promoted, and in some situations partially funded by promotional tactics. The competitors in all segments of the industry use a variety of promotional products and techniques. This creates a demand for promotional products, events, methods, and people who specialize in promotion, marketing, public relations, and other related areas.

Table 8.4. The Sport Promotion Industry Segment Examples	
1	**Promotional Merchandise:** Merchandise with a logo, might include caps, cups, key chains, bumper stickers, decals, mugs, hats, t-shirts, dress shirts, ties, napkins, sweaters, jackets, clocks, shorts, sweatshirts and pants, blankets, stadium seats, pencil holders, stationary holders, pens and pencils, checks.
2	**Promotional Events:** Offering an event or activity along with a main sport event to bring attention to the product. Examples include holding a Beach Boys concert after a Major League Baseball game; offering a golf tournament to promote pre-game, half-time, and post-game events that surround the Super Bowl.
3	**The Media:** The media provide vast exposure for some segments of the sport industry. Sport marketers negotiate with television, radio, and print media for coverage of sporting events. The coverage promotes the sport event.
4	**Sponsorship:** Sponsorship is a two-way promotional tool. The sponsorship company provides funding for a sport event, which is a form of advertising for the company. Sport marketers use the funding to produce and manage the event. The company providing funding gains exposure and promotional benefits. Examples: Almost all college football bowl games have sponsors; many of the women's and men's professional golf tournaments have sponsors; the auto racing industry is practically driven by sponsors; the Olympics, Special Olympics, Gay Games, and Maccabiah Games all have sponsors.
5	**Endorsement:** Similar to sponsorship, endorsement is also a two-way promotional tool in the sport industry. Some examples: Mary Lou Retton's picture on Wheaties cereal boxes suggests her endorsement of that product; Michael Jordan's endorsement of Nike products.
Source: Pitts, Fielding & Miller, 1994.	

With a thorough understanding of the sport company's product, the sport marketer increases chances for successful sport product management strategies. However, sport products come and go. Sometimes, the product can be labeled a fad. In other cases, the product was simply not a good idea. If the sport marketer can identify the success level of a product, decisions can be determined that may save the life of the product or, at a minimum, save the company. This product analysis is called the *product life cycle*.

THE PRODUCT LIFE CYCLE

Just as people go through changes and stages throughout their lifetime, so do products. A person is born and then goes through childhood, adolescence, teenage years, young adulthood, adulthood, middle age, the senior citizen stage, and eventually death. A product begins life as an idea. It is then introduced onto the market, experiences a period of growth, a time of maturity, and will eventually decline in sales and then be taken off the market. One major difference between the person's stages and the product's stages is this: The person's stages may be measured using years of age. Death is certain. Although a product's stages may be measured using several factors, some of which are sales and profits, the amount of time in each stage can vary markedly. For example, a

The study of each product's life cycle will aid in the development of marketing strategies. Courtesy of Photos8.com

human's life span is estimated at approximately 74 years whereas a product's time on the market can range from just a few short days to hundreds of years.

The product life cycle is a concept popularized by Levitt in 1965 and is still applicable to and an important factor in today's market place (Levitt, 1965). It is a way to define and understand a product's sales, profits, consumer markets, product markets, and marketing strategies from its inception until it is removed from the market. Studying your company's products and understanding the product life cycle stage in which each product exists is imperative to planning marketing strategies. Through research, it is now known that (a) product lives are shorter now than in the past; (b) higher investment is presently required for new products; (c) the marketer may use the product life cycle to adjust marketing strategies; and (d) the marketer may strategically establish a more successful product mix in relation to the product life cycle concept, planning to establish products in each stage of the cycle so that, as one product declines, another product is introduced. As an example, let us look at fitness centers.

In the 1960s and early 1970s, fitness centers were known as health spas. The typical spa offered only a few products: a small weight room, a small pool, rolling machines, and locker rooms with a sauna and steam room. Typically, no exercise classes were offered, as the "instructors" were hired only to look good and sell memberships. With the "fitness boom" of the late 1970s, a new crop of fitness centers entered the market, and existing spas found themselves in the decline stage of the product life cycle. The new health-conscious consumer wanted more, and the new companies jumped into the fitness product market and offered much more in their facilities. Some of the existing spas changed, but some did not. Those that did not eventually lost out to the new multipurpose fitness centers.

Today's fitness centers offer a much greater product mix. In most, you will find a very large weight room, large pool, indoor running track, and a variety of exercise classes such as aerobics classes, swimming or pool exercise classes, fitness classes, and nutrition classes. There will usually be a few sports such as tennis, racquetball, wallyball, volleyball, and basketball. The locker rooms are large, clean, and airy with a full service of towels, shampoo, hair dryers, toothbrushes and toothpaste, and deodorants as well as plush carpeting, beautiful lockers, and big-screen television sets complete with a VCR for your convenience in viewing specific videotape programs also supplied by the center. In addition, you will probably find nice, large whirlpool baths, saunas, and steam rooms. There will be a number of other services such as a childcare service—sometimes a child-size fitness center itself, laundry service, full clothing services, sporting goods and apparel shops, restaurant and lounge, and a small business office area complete with phone, computer, fax, and copy machines so you can conduct business while at the center.

STAGES OF THE PRODUCT LIFE CYCLE

The stages of the product life cycle are introduction, growth, maturity, and decline. The product life cycle and its stages are illustrated in Figure 8.4. Sport management executives or marketers must be able to recognize in which stage of the product life cycle a product is at any given time. This determination will affect marketing strategy decisions.

Introduction Stage

The *introduction stage* occurs when a sport product is put on the market (offered to the consumer) for the first time. During this time, it is likely that no one knows the product exists. The sport marketer must promote aggressively to make distributors and consumers aware of the product. Typically, sales are practically zero and profits are negative.

At this stage, the sport company has invested in manufacturing and promoting the product but has not begun to receive profits from sales. The product that is offered is one that probably went through many stages of refinement such as idea generation, research and development, test marketing, and pilot trials. Investment during this period, for some products, may reach into the millions of dollars.

As Figure 8.4 indicates, sales are low and losses are common. There is also a high percentage of product failure during this stage. The sport company may have marketing research to show that there is a market for this product, but by the time the product finally hits the marketplace, many things could have happened. The market may be no longer interested, consumer needs or wants may have changed, or another company might have already entered the market and established share. The sport company must promote aggressively during this stage to create demand for the product.

Growth Stage

As demand for the sport product begins to develop and the product begins to sell, it enters the next stage in the product life cycle, the *growth stage*. As Figure 8.4 indicates, it is during this stage that sales and profits rapidly and steadily increase. Although sales and profits soar, the company may still be in danger. It is during this stage that competi-

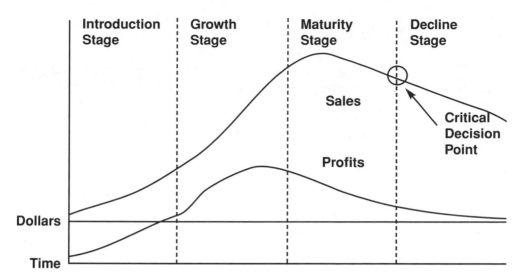

Figure 8.4. The Product Life Cycle Stages.

tors will enter the product market with identical or similar products. This competition will drive prices down, and profits will decline. Aggressive pricing promotions, adjustments in costs, legal action against imitators, and other marketing strategies will help to stabilize profits.

Maturity Stage

After the bumpy road, the sport product may finally reach the *maturity stage*. It may have found a steady place in the market. However, during this stage, there still are many competitors, and this keeps prices low, which keeps sales and profits down. It is also during this period that the product has been changed enough to finally meet the consumers' needs. Differences among competing products diminish. It is at this point, however, that companies will begin to promote any difference in their product that they believe will gain some market advantage. Usually, pricing wars begin and continue until one or more companies are driven out of the particular product market. Critical marketing decisions must be made at this point.

Decline Stage

During the *decline stage*, sales fall rapidly. There may be many reasons, some of which are new products on the market, a shift in trend, or new technology. Now the sport marketer is faced with the decision of terminating production of the sport product or making changes, sometimes drastic, to revive it. Of course, the sport marketer may also wait and see which companies drop out of the market. This can be a successful strategy because if a large number drop out, your company may become one of a few making the product and the cycle can be stopped. This tactic is risky as always when one plays a wait-and-see game.

It must be understood that the length of each stage can vary for any given product. The challenge to the sport marketer is to be able to recognize each product's life cycle

Table 8.5. Examples of Sport Products in the Product Life Cycle Stages			
	Participant Sport	**Sporting Goods**	**Spectator Products**
Introduction Stage	Slam Ball Ski Dancing Wakesurfing	Speed suits Wakesurfing	Slam Ball
Growth Stage	Snowboarding Wakeboarding	Snowboards Wakeboards	Snowboarding WNBA
Maturity Stage	Basketball Soccer	Golf Clubs PWC (Jet Ski)	PGA/LPGA NBA
Decline Stage	Field Hockey Croquet	Croquet Water skis	Ice Hockey

stage and make marketing decisions accordingly. For example, let's say that you are the manager/marketer for a multi-sport club. You are experiencing an unusual, sharp decline in participants in the adult tennis leagues. Upon investigation, you find that most of those clients are now playing tennis at a different club because it is offering childcare services all the hours that it is open. You are faced with a decision: Change what you offer or lose consumers to another company. Table 8.5 shows a variety of examples of sport products in various product life-cycle stages.

THE PRODUCT MIX

The product mix is a critical element of a sport company's business plan and marketing strategy. It is the sale of products and services that makes a company successful or may bring about failure. *Product mix* is the complete set of all products that the sport company offers to the consumer. It consists of all of the company's product lines and all related services. While there are some companies that offer only one product, there are many companies that offer two or more products. Making critical decisions and developing strategies about the product mix is important for the company's success.

Here are a few examples of product mix for different sport companies: a collegiate athletic program offers 12 women's and men's sports and promotional merchandise; a sporting goods manufacturer offers 10 different sport equipment products; and the local fitness center offers a variety of fitness and sport-related products, including a full range of exercise classes, tennis classes and leagues, volleyball leagues, swimming classes and open swim time, a clothing and sporting goods shop, childcare services, equipment repair, laundry service, towel service, a restaurant and lounge, and many others.

The product mix may be measured by its product lines and items. A *product line* is a set of closely related products. For example, as Table 8.6 shows, a fitness center offers fitness, sport, clothing, and equipment as four of its product lines. Within each product line, there are product items. A *product item* is a specific product within a product line. Aerobics classes are a product item in the fitness center's fitness product line. Ten-

	Table 8.6. Products in the Sport Performance Industry Segment		
SPORT COMPANY	**Product Assortment (Mix)**	**Product Line**	**Product Items Offered in the Product Line**

FITNESS CENTER	fitness
	weight loss
	restaurant and lounge
	aerobics
	weight training
	tanning
	massage
	testing-fitness; cholesterol
	sports leagues:
	  tennis
	  volleyball
	  swimming
	pro shop
		aerobics classes	low impact aerobics
			kid aerobics
			elderrobics
			advanced aerobics

		weight training	body building free weight training sport-specific strength events classes
		tennis	beginner's league intermediate league advanced leagues club tourney
COLLEGE ATHLETICS	women's sports men's sports	women's individual sports	track field swimming cross country tennis
		women's team sports	basketball volleyball soccer
SPORTING GOODS MANUFACTURERS	golf equipment tennis equipment	golf	golf clubs: 4 different sets golf balls golf umbrellas
		tennis	tennis rackets tennis string tennis balls tennis ball retriever

nis, volleyball, and swimming are product lines. Each of these may consist of a variety of classes, leagues and other product items. In another example, a sporting goods manufacturer offers three product lines: softball equipment, baseball equipment, and tennis equipment. The softball equipment line consists of a variety of product items: bats, gloves, batting gloves, softballs, and equipment bags. In a different example, a professional women's golf league offers two lines: watching professional golfers play, and souvenir merchandise.

The product mix of a sport company may be described by its width, depth, and consistency. The fitness center has a narrow width, for it offers product lines that are primarily of a fitness or sport nature. There are a wide variety of products offered within each product line, which means that the fitness center may be described as having depth. For example, the tennis line contains the following items: (a) classes for age groups of 5–7

	Table 8.7. The Center's Tennis Line	
1	**Classes Segmented By:**	Age Groups Skill Levels
2	**Instruction:**	Individual Lessons Lessons for Doubles Play
3	**Leagues Segmented By:**	Skill Levels: beginners to advanced Gender: women's, men's, mixed
4	**Clinics, Seminars:**	for coaching, for individuals, for play strategy, for rules knowledge
5	**Tournaments:**	—Intramural —Extramural

years old, 8–12, 13–15, 16–18, 19–21, 22–25, 26–30, and in five-year increments after 30; (b) classes for skill levels: beginner, intermediate, and advanced; (c) individual instruction; (d) leagues: skill groups ranging from beginner through advanced, and within each are categories for women, men, and coed singles, women, men, and coed doubles (see Table 8.7). There will most likely be other items such as special clinics or seminars, league tournaments, special tournaments, and competition with another center. The fitness center would be considered consistent, as its product mix is focused on products of a similar nature.

NEW PRODUCT DEVELOPMENT PLANNING

How does a sport company organize for new product development? The type of company and the products it offers will influence the eventual organization, planning, and process the company will use to develop new products. A fitness center that offers a variety of products must make a decision concerning the addition of new products such as new sports, fitness activities, or even a new line of tennis clothing in the pro shop. A tennis racket manufacturer will study the possibility and feasibility of manufacturing a new tennis racket. These are different types of companies: One is a manufacturer and the other a retailer. However, each must have and manage a new product development process. The process will involve hours, sometimes years, of analyzing information concerning factors such as consumer markets and product markets, cost of producing the product, cost to the consumer, capability of the company to produce the product, distribution possibilities and cost, as well as promotion possibilities and cost.

Consider another, very different example—the National Basketball Association (NBA). For the NBA, a new product might be an additional team in the league or a modification to the rules of the game of basketball. The addition of a new team to the league requires analysis of consumer markets and product markets, production (startup) costs, price (ticket prices) to the consumer, and many other decision factors. Modifying, adding, or deleting rules can change the game—the product—dramatically.

There have been many modifications to the game of basketball since it was invented. Some of those changes were instituted specifically to make the game more attractive to the consumer. For example, dunking was not allowed until the late 1970s primarily for safety reasons; rims and backboards were not made for dunking and would break. Another reason was that the dunk was not considered to be a skill. A stiff penalty was levied against a player who dunked either during the warm-up period before a game or during a game—the player was ejected from the game. Dunking became a tactic.

Coaches realized that a dunk motivated the team and excited the crowd. Specific players were instructed to dunk at key moments during the warm-up period before the game or during the game. It wasn't long before coaches, athletic directors, and others involved in selling the game realized that the crowds loved to see someone dunk the ball. Soon the rules were changed, and rims and backboards were modified to be safe for dunking. The dunk changed the game. Today there are even slam-dunking contests with large amounts of money, prizes, and titles involved.

New product development as a strategy is the addition of a new product to a company's product line. There are many reasons a company might consider developing a new product, including a need to stimulate sales, a desire to capture a new consumer need, a desire to improve the company's reputation, or a desire to expand.

New products are a constant event in the sport industry. In Chapter 1, we discussed many factors that have positively influenced the growth and development of the sport industry. Some of those factors are the consistent offering of new sports, new activities, new leagues, new sport organizations for all populations, and new sport equipment. There are, perhaps, more sport equipment and clothing products than sports when considering that most sport activities require a few pieces of equipment, special clothing, and footwear for each participant. In the sport industry, it can be quite confusing when trying to determine which comes first: the sport or the equipment. In some cases, ideas for a new sport develop first. James Naismith developed some rules for a new sport and used a soccer ball. That sport today is basketball and requires very different equipment than was first used.

Every year the Sporting Goods Manufacturers Association (SGMA) stages exhibitions of new sporting goods, apparel, shoes, and equipment. The SGMA has two exhibits: the SGMA Spring Market and the SGMA Fall Market. Thousands of sporting goods manufacturers and businesses are involved. They bring their most current products for display. People attending are buyers for retailers, wholesalers, distributors, and resellers.

Of course, not every new product introduced is successful. As a matter of fact, most new products fail. The failure rate is estimated to range between 33 and 90 percent. Companies spend tremendous amounts of money during the process of getting a new product to the market. There are many elements involved in new product development. Some ideas require years of research, which can involve scientists, technology, testing, manufacture of the new product, and promotion. However, even with all the money and time invested in producing the new product, there is no guarantee that the product will sell.

There are some common reasons that new product offerings fail. The primary reason is failure to match the product to the consumer's needs. If the product will not do what the consumer wants, the consumer will not buy it. Further, this may be the result of poor consumer research, the company's failure to stick to what it does best, and failure to provide a better product at a better value than the competition.

Good product management and planning can increase your chances of new product success. As was pointed out in Chapter 4 and earlier in this chapter, information and research are key in making decisions.

As pointed out earlier, there are many reasons that a company offers a new product. Sometimes, a new product isn't a totally new product. It is a product that has been modified as a means of offering a differentiated product or an improved product. For example, consider the variety of aerobics type classes offered today. Some examples are hard aerobics, soft aerobics, water aerobics, elderobics, jazzercise, and step aerobics. None of these are brand-new products. Rather, they are variations of the original aerobics product. In another example, arena football (football played in a small, indoor field with fewer players and a variety of rule modifications) might be considered a brand-new product because it is different from the original football sport. However, arena football is a variation of the original product. It is marketed as a different product—different from the regular 11-player game.

How many ways might one offer a new product? There are at least nine (Peter & Donnelly, 1991). Following are the nine ways with examples in the sport industry (see Table 8.8):

1. *A product that performs an entirely new function.* When the snowmobile was introduced, it performed a new function: motorized transportation across snow-covered areas in a small, personal vehicle.

2. *A product that offers improved performance of an existing function.* As an example, consider the introduction of new materials for wheelchairs. Aluminum and other composite materials offer the possibility for wheelchairs to be light and durable. This provides wheelchair athletes the capability to enhance performance in athletic feats.

3. *A product that offers a new application of an existing one.* Personal watercrafts (more commonly known as jet skis) were first introduced to be used as rec-

Table 8.8. Nine Ways to Offer a New Product	
1	A product that performs an entirely new function.
2	A product that offers improved performance of an existing function.
3	A product that offers a new application of an existing one.
4	A product that offers additional functions over an existing product.
5	When an existing product is offered to a new consumer market.
6	Offering a lower cost on a product can attract new buyers.
7	A product offered as "upgraded" or an existing product integrated into another product.
8	A downgraded product or the use of less expensive parts or components in the manufacturing process.
9	A restyled product.
Source: Peter & Donnelly, 1994.	

reational vehicles—new toys for play on the water. Today, personal watercrafts are used by police, emergency water rescue services, and Coast Guard operations for law enforcement, safety, and rescue functions.

4. *A product that offers additional functions over an existing product.* In one example, a fitness center may offer more sports and services than does another fitness center, thereby offering more functions to the consumer. In another example, weight-training equipment, one product is a single unit that allows the consumer to perform up to 12 exercises whereas another product is a single unit that offers only one exercise.

5. *An existing product that is offered to a new consumer market.* This may be done either by repositioning the product or offering the product in new markets (market development). In an example of the latter, the National Football League (NFL) is trying to gain market development by offering its product—football games—in European and Asian countries.

6. *A product that can attract new buyers with lower prices.* When a new material is used for golf clubs, the existing clubs may be offered at a lower cost. Softball bats are offered in a wide range of prices. A fitness center may offer specially priced memberships to first-time consumers for a limited period of time.

7. *A product that is offered as "upgraded" or an existing product that is integrated into another product.* In one example, fitness centers offer a variety of possibilities for "upgrading" a consumer's membership. The consumer may purchase one level of membership with the possibility of upgrading it to another level. In another example, computers have been integrated into a variety of sport equipment as a method of upgrading the equipment. Playing a round of golf indoors in a small room is possible with the use of a computerized golf course system. Through the use of video, screens, displays, sensors and other equipment, the consumer uses real golf clubs and golf balls to play a round of 9 or 18 holes of golf without leaving the room.

8. *A product that has been downgraded or that uses less expensive parts or components in its manufacture.* Many sporting goods and equipment manufacturers use plastics and other less expensive materials, parts, or components in their products. This changes the cost to produce the product and is sometimes promoted to the consumer as "new low price" or "we pass the savings on to the consumer" item.

9. *A restyled product.* Examples include the almost annual changes in sport clothing, running shoes, and other sporting equipment.

In another approach to offering new products, Ansoff (1957; 1965) developed *growth vectors*, which are used by most businesses today (see Figure 8.5). These are product strategies involving present or new consumer markets and present or new products, and they include market penetration, market development, new product development, and product diversification.

Market penetration is a strategy in which a company tries to sell more of its present products to its present consumer markets. *Market development* is a strategy in which a

Products → ↓ Markets	CURRENT PRODUCTS	NEW PRODUCTS
CURRENT CUSTOMERS	Market Penetration Strategy	New Product Development
NEW CONSUMERS	Market Development Strategy	Product Diversification

Market Penetration Strategy—push to sell more to improve position of present products

Market Development Strategy—find new customers for present products

New Product Development Strategy—develop new products for present consumers

Product Diversification Strategy—develop new products for new consumer segments

Figure 8.5. Product Market Growth Strategies.

company tries to sell its present products to new consumer markets. *New product development* is the creation of new products. *Product diversification* is a strategy in which new products are added in an attempt to meet the needs of new consumer markets.

NEW PRODUCT DEVELOPMENT PROCESS

There are some common stages in the new product development process within most companies. These are idea generation, screening and analysis, product research and development, test marketing, and commercialization (Boone & Kurtz, 1989; Peter & Donnelly, 1991; Stanton et al., 1991). Figure 8.6 represents the stages a sport company might utilize within a new product development process.

Stage 1: Idea Generation

Idea generation involves generating ideas for new products, product modification, or other types of product changes. Ideas may come from a multitude of sources. If the company has the resources, it may have a product research and development department, commonly known as a "R and D" department. It is the responsibility of the "R and D" people to generate product ideas, research them, and present feasible product ideas to company management. In other companies, product ideas must originate from employees. In either situation, the company management must create an atmosphere that supports idea generation.

Some companies offer incentives for those employees whose ideas eventually result in a successful product. Eventually, a decision will be made to take the next step and study the feasibility of a product.

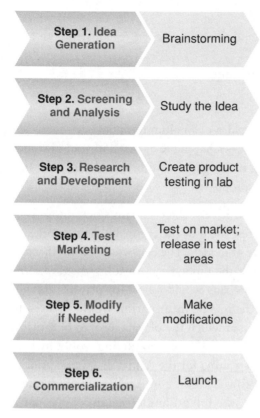

Figure 8.6.
The New Product Development Process.

Stage 2: Product Screening and Analysis

The next step is *product screening and analysis*. This involves determining the feasibility of a product. The process includes determining if the company can market a product profitably, if the product fits with the company's mission, if the company has all the necessary resources or technology, or if it might be beneficial to form partnerships with other companies. Based on the conclusions drawn from the research, a decision will be made, and the product could move into the next stage.

Stage 3: Product Research and Development

In the *product research and development* stage, product ideas with potential are converted. The type of product and its conceived functions determine the type of testing. If the product is a tangible item, a model can be produced. The model will undergo a number of tests in an effort to develop the best possible product.

Type of product requires further discussion here because there are many different types of products in the sport industry. Remember our definition of product earlier in the chapter. Product is a concept that includes goods, services, people, places and ideas. Also, remember that consumers are looking for a specific function—what the product will do. With this in mind, let us consider examples of each type of product and how it may be developed through testing.

Tangible Good

Softball bats provide a good example of a tangible good. The research and development department in a bat manufacturing company is considering the idea that aluminum might be a good material for bats. The purpose or function of a bat is to hit a softball. However, what the softball player wants is a bat that will hit a softball farther, consistently, and with control. The question the company should consider, then, is whether an aluminum bat will meet the needs of softball players. Other questions include:

- Can aluminum bats be made?
- What kind of aluminum can be used?

- How much will it cost the company?
- What kind of machinery and other equipment is needed to construct an aluminum bat?
- Where might the company get the aluminum?
- Will the aluminum bat function?
- How can it be tested?
- What will the consumer think about the idea of an aluminum bat?
- Will the consumer accept—and purchase—a bat made of metal instead of wood?
- Are any other companies considering making aluminum bats? If not, can this company possibly be the first with this product?

If most of these questions can be answered positively, the company's next move is to produce some bats made of aluminum and test them in the company's laboratories. A variety of aluminum would be used in a variety of models. The bats would be put through a battery of tests. The company could also test the models by providing them to some softball players, teams, and/or leagues. The company would follow the players throughout the league and receive feedback from them. The information would be used to make changes in the bat until reaching a point at which the players seem to be satisfied with the performance of one or more models. Further test marketing would include placing the bat on the market in a region and waiting for the results. If specific positive outcomes are reached, the company would consider going into full-scale production, getting the bats into more markets, and going into full promotion status.

Service Product

The testing of a service product could consist of the following process. A fitness instructor at a fitness center overhears customers discussing why the center does not offer childcare services. The customers say that they would come to the center more often if they did not have to spend the extra amount of time, effort, and money to find a sitter. The instructor thinks offering childcare might be a good idea and takes it to the center's manager. The manager also thinks it might be a good idea and organizes a committee, headed by the instructor, to study the idea. The committee, after studying the idea and surveying their members, concludes that the center has the space needed and could charge a small fee to cover the addition of an employee to manage the childcare center, and that the fitness center ought to offer the service for at least six months to test the idea.

Person

What might a company do if the company's products are people? As an example, consider a sport marketing and management company that specializes in managing and promoting professional athletes. The company's task is to try to find the best contracts and jobs for the athletes. The company uses the athletic and personal characteristics of the athlete as selling points. When the company considers the addition of a new product (adding another athlete) to its line of products (athletes already under contract), it will research many factors. Some of these factors are popularity of the individual, consumer markets (the variety and extent of demand for the athlete), cost to the company, and possible profitability. Further, the company might add the athlete for a one-year trial basis (test marketing).

Place

When the product is a place, research and development are contingent on factors such as the type of place (facility) and whether or not it exists. Let's look at an example of a facility that does not exist. The local state university has announced that it would like to have a new facility to house the women's and men's basketball and volleyball teams. The programs are very successful and have been nationally ranked in the top 25 for more than eight years. The existing facility was built in 1936. The process for determining the feasibility of this product can be very complicated. The university is a state-supported institution, which means that tax dollars are involved. The process might include the development of a committee to study the idea. The committee needs to gather information such as facility needs, the cost of such a facility, if resources exist or where the university might obtain the resources, if space (land) is available and obtainable, ticket price structure, who will use the facility, how many ways the facility might be used, expenses involved, consumer surveys, and other. This will involve working with contractors, architects, the state education department, state government, and many other agencies and individuals. The committee could perform all the research or hire a marketing company to do the work. In this type of situation, the university usually hires a marketing company to do the research. Be sure to hire a marketing company with experience in the sport industry and with specific experience in sport facilities and sport facility research.

When the testing is complete and the test results yield information, conclusions may be drawn about the product. The information from the research will guide decisions pertaining to moving to the next stage.

Stage 4: Test Marketing

The *test marketing stage* is the next step in the new product development process. Test marketing involves selecting a specific market area in which to offer the product. It is usually offered with a specialized marketing campaign. The primary reason for test marketing is to determine how the product performs in a real market. In selecting the test market area, some factors to consider are size, control of selected promotional media, cost, the consumer markets, and the product markets.

A sports wheelchair manufacturing company has developed a wheelchair for basketball. The company offers the wheelchairs in two large cities (test markets). The company's plan is to promote the wheelchairs in the two cities for a one-year period. If they sell well in the two test markets, the company will expand to additional large cities.

One may decide to skip this stage because it can be very expensive. The decision to skip test marketing should be based on the conclusion that the new product has a very high possibility of selling and being successful.

Stage 5: Product Modification

Modify the product if research and test marketing shows that changes are needed. This can be a critical stage because feedback from test consumers should be utilized to make modifications until the product is ready for more test marketing and modifications, and again until it is ready for the full commercialization and launch stage.

Stage 6: Commercialization

The final stage is *commercialization*. Full marketing strategies are planned, and the entire company prepares to make the necessary adjustments for the new product. Complete business and marketing plans are developed, implementation plans are identified, plans for production are developed, personnel considerations are established, and promotional efforts are determined. The product is finished and goes on the market.

Each sport company should organize its new product development process and attempt to manage the process for success. Management must remember, however, the high rate of unsuccessful new products and make a commitment to support the investment necessary for new product development.

DEVELOP THE PRODUCT POSITIONING STRATEGIES

Product positioning involves communicating a specific message about a product, or the business, to the consumer about exactly what the company wants the consumer to think about the product or the business. This is what is informally called "positioning the product." A product's position is the image or perception that the consumer holds about the product's attributes, quality, uses and other functions as these compare to other similar products. As was pointed out in the opening paragraphs of this chapter, a consumer does not simply purchase a product. The consumer is looking to satisfy needs or desires, or to be able to perform a certain function. The product is the tool that will satisfy that need or desire and/or perform the function.

Positioning was presented briefly in Chapter 5. In the remainder of this chapter, we will present how the product is communicated to the consumer based on the product's utilities and how the business wants to "position" the product in the marketplace. Figure 8.7 illustrates the step-by-step process that can be used when developing the positioning ideas and statements. Table 8.9 presents examples of positioning statements.

In the process (Figure 8.7), it is critical to point out that consumer research must be conducted in order to discover what the consumer wants in a product. What the consumer wants is what should be offered in the company's product. These wants can then be used in developing the positioning of the product. For example, the Red Rocket Jet Ski Company has identified two large consumer markets for its product—the recreational jet skier market and the industrial consumer market. The recreational jet skier consumer is looking for fun, whereas the industrial consumer is looking for a working tool. Each market has different desires and requires a product that will perform the function for which its consumers are looking. Therefore, these desires are incorporated into the positioning statements for those markets. This language will then be used

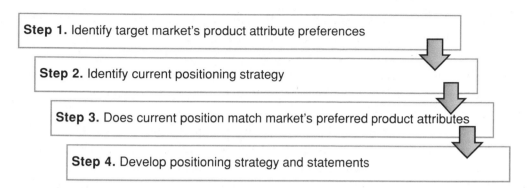

Step 1. Identify target market's product attribute preferences

Step 2. Identify current positioning strategy

Step 3. Does current position match market's preferred product attributes

Step 4. Develop positioning strategy and statements

Figure 8.7. The Positioning Development Process.

throughout all promotional materials and statements, as well as by salespeople when they present the product to potential consumers in the retail store.

For example, when a consumer walks into the jet ski store, a salesperson will approach and perhaps says something like this: "Hello! I see you are looking for some fun this summer, right? Well, we have several jet ski models that will make sure you have all the fun you can stand!" However, if the salesperson is the sales agent assigned to talk with the Coast Guard, the approach will be very different. The salesperson might state: "Hello, Ms. Johnson. How are you doing today? I understand you are looking to replace your fleet of rescue jet skis and that you are looking for something that you can

Table 8.9. Examples of Positioning Statements.	
Road Atlanta	**360° Sports Academy, LLC**
Road Atlanta is recognized as one of the world's best road courses. Our multi-purpose motor sports facility is situated on 750 park-like acres in the rolling hills of Northeast Georgia. Road Atlanta is located 35 miles north of Atlanta and just minutes away from Chateau Elan, a 4-Star resort offering guests comfort and amenities such as three championship golf courses and a European-style spa. The facility is utilized for a wide variety of events, including professional and amateur sports car and motorcycle races, racing and driving schools, corporate programs and testing for motorsports teams.	360° Sports Academy is dedicated to developing student-athletes into leaders. We endeavor to empower student-athletes to be the best they can be. The overall takeaway from 360° Sports Academy is a holistic, life-building and applicable experience that will benefit all participants on many levels and empower the next generation of leaders. 360° Sports Academy offers a full spectrum of training programs for student-athletes and their parents. The topics, treated in-depth and addressed by subject matter experts, range from test-taking strategies, finance basics, health and wellness, and presentation/interview skills, to sports-specific athletic and game insights. techniques, and drills.

customize with the Coast Guard logo. I also understand that you want the new fleet to last much longer than before, and to be more fuel-efficient. Well, we have a new line of working skis that I know meet all your needs." In the examples, you can see that even though the jet ski product is exactly the same product when it comes out of the manufacturing plant, there are two different functions that the product will perform based on what two different consumer markets desire.

Consumer perceptions can be measured through marketing research. The research will show what the consumer thinks about a product and how it compares to another company's product. This information is important in making changes to the product or to the image of the product. As is illustrated in Step 1 and Step 3 of the process in Figure 8.7, a marketer needs to know what the consumer wants, and the only way to that knowledge is through research.

PRODUCT IDENTIFICATION

Product identification involves establishing an identity for the product through the use of some identifying device. The primary purpose of product identification is to differentiate your product from other relatively homogeneous products. It may also be used as a strategy to increase the strength of the company or product image, to establish or to use an established reputation, and to facilitate market and product development strategies.

BRANDING

The most commonly used methods of product identification are branding and packaging. Branding is accomplished through the use of a brand, brand name, or trademark.

A *brand* is a name, symbol, term, and/or design intended for the identification of the products of a seller. It may consist of any combination of a name, word, letter, number, design, symbol, and color. A *brand name* is the word, letter, or number that can be vocalized. The symbol, design or coloring is the *brand mark*. It can be recognized by sight and not expressed vocally. For example, the brand mark of Nike includes the word "Nike" and a mark that looks like a well-rounded checkmark. Nike calls it a "swoosh." One would never know that the symbol actually has an identifying name, however, until looking into Nike's legal papers that describe the Nike brand name and mark. It is at this point that the brand name and mark may become what is commonly called a *trademark*.

Trademark is essentially a legal term. It is a brand that has legal protection; that is, it is protected from being used by other companies. Why would a company want to use another company's trademark instead of developing its own identity? The reason is to confuse and trick the consumer. The consumer purchases the product thinking that the product is from a well-known company. What the consumer actually purchased is a copy—an imitation of another company's product. These products have become known as "clones." For example, the consumer sees a mark that looks like the Nike swoosh on a pair of sneakers. The consumer purchases the product because the price is very low (compared to the price for the real Nike product) and believes it is a deal too good to pass up. In reality, the consumer purchased an imitation product.

Successful branding can make a product or company name instantly recognizable to consumers. Courtesy of Anna Cervova/Public-Domain-Images.com

Success in branding lies in selecting a good brand name and mark. The company should select something short, easy to pronounce, and easy to spell. A great brand suggests something about the product, and is unique. Other factors to be considered are ethics, market segments, and current events. A company can do harm to its image and its product if its brand name or mark is insensitive to cultures, populations, or specific current events. For example, in 1993, Converse intended to release a basketball shoe called the "Run 'N Gun" until community groups in Boston, where Converse is located, protested the implications of the name. The name is derived from a basketball term used to describe a specific type of play. The protesting groups, however, pointed out that in today's society the word "gun" means a weapon. Further, youths have actually been robbed and even murdered for their clothing and popular name brand shoes. Converse recognized its responsibility to young people, the impending bad press, and the possibility of a boycott and decided to change the name of the shoe. Its new name is "Run 'N Slam" (Moore, 1993).

THE 4 LEVELS OF BRAND BUILDING

There are four levels through which a consumer might progress in relation to branding. Any company will want consumers to insist on their brand and to purchase no other brand. It takes a lot of work and time to get the consumer to reach the top and fourth level, but it can be done. The sport company should engage in a number of marketing activities to build the brand. "Building" the brand means that the company is working toward the goal of having consumers recognize and perhaps prefer or insist on that brand. Figure 8.8 illustrates the levels of brand building.

Level 1: Brand Awareness

At the first level, *brand awareness*, a consumer is only aware of the existence of a particular brand. This is easily tested with a simple study—show consumers a logo mark with a multiple choice list of possible answers and ask them to choose the matching name and logo. Try this in class with several logos and see how many can be identified correctly.

Level 2: Brand Recognition

At the second level, *brand recognition*, the consumer is not just aware about a brand, but can recognize the brand and name it from memory. Using recognition research, if you show the consumer a logo, the individual can name the brand of the logo without any help or a list of multiple choices. This means that the company has done enough work putting the brand in front of the consumer that the consumer now has it stored in memory. For example, companies engage in sponsorship of sports events because it puts the company's brand in front of the eyes of the consumer. Testing this with simple sponsorship recognition surveys can measure whether the consumer is remembering the brand by sight.

Level 3: Brand Preference

At the third level, *brand preference*, the consumer has developed a preference for a specific brand and will often select it for purchase over other brands. Beyond the first step of making sure the consumer can identify a logo or other company mark is moving the consumer to the point where the company's product is well known by the consumer and is often preferred over other company's products. For instance, the "swoosh" mark of Nike is recognized worldwide, but how many consumers prefer the Nike brand over other brands? Certainly there are a good number because the Nike company holds a high-level market share. This means that Nike has done a good job with positioning their brand, following up with quality, making sure the products perform the functions wanted or needed by consumers, and creating demand for their brand.

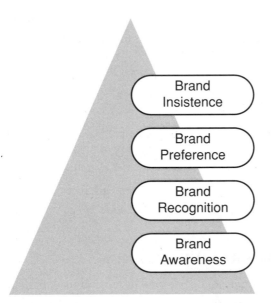

Figure 8.8. The Four Levels of Brand Building.

Level 4: Brand Insistence

At the fourth and top level, *brand insistence*, the consumer will purchase only a specified brand. It is, of course, the third level that is the goal of most companies. This level, however, is difficult to achieve due to the speed at which competitors can enter the market, and advertising can take place through direct media, such as mobile marketing. However, there are markets of consumers who insist on a particular brand for a given product. This can be measured through research.

PACKAGING AS A METHOD FOR BRANDING

Packaging is the activity of enclosing a product if it is a physical good. It involves designing and enclosing the product in some type of package or container in an attempt to differentiate the product from others. In addition, the package should protect the product, should be a convenient size, be easy to open and attractive so that it can be used as a promotional tool, and be honest. Although the sport marketer has many decisions to make concerning packaging, information guiding these decisions must also include consumer data. Because design and package costs are included in the final price of the product to the consumer, the marketer must know the price that a consumer is willing to pay for the product. Final decisions on packaging usually mean compromise when final cost becomes a major factor.

In the sport business industry, there are products for which packaging takes on a slightly different meaning. Sport marketers have developed a way to "package" sporting activity events in an attempt to make the event more attractive to a greater diversity of consumer segments. Packaging a sport event involves enveloping the event with an array of activities, benefits, and products. In one example, sport marketers trying to sell season tickets to collegiate women's basketball games create a variety of ticket packages. The lowest cost season-ticket package might contain just the tickets and nothing else. The most expensive ticket package might include VIP valet parking, a parking space, seats on or near the 50-yard line, admission to a pre-game and half-time reception, admission to a post-game party with the coach, and admission to the end-of-the-year banquet.

One of the shortest events in sport is surrounded by a month of activities. The event is a racing event over a distance of one mile and a quarter ("Derby Winners," 1993). The race lasts just a few seconds over two minutes. The event is the Kentucky Derby—a horse race. The Derby's first race was in 1875, and since that time, it has grown to a major money sport event with a record attendance of 165,307 in 2012 (Kentucky Derby sets attendance, 2012). There are "official" Kentucky Derby Festival events, and events and activities that are not registered as official Kentucky Derby Festival events. It started in 1956 with a parade and has grown to over 70 events and activities in 2012 (History, 2012), with countless unofficial events, parties, socials, and other activities. Furthermore, many of the events are sports activities, such as the following:

- Adidas Derby Festival Basketball Classic;
- BellSouth Derby Festival Volleyball Classic;

- Don Fightmaster Golf Outing for Exceptional Children;
- Fifth Third Bank Derby Festival $1 Million Hole-in-One Ladies Day;
- Fifth Third Bank Derby Festival $1 Million Hole-in-One Contest;
- King Southern Bank Derby Festival Foundation Pro-Am Golf Tournament;
- Meijer Derby Festival Marathon/miniMarathon; and
- U.S. Bank Derby Festival Great Balloon Race.

The Kentucky Derby race is held every year on the first Saturday in May. The official and unofficial events and activities that surround the Derby race provide a multitude of activities and entertainment for the consumer. Hence, the Kentucky Derby is a packaged sports event.

Sport event packaging goes beyond events and activities to include often-overlooked factors such as facility cleanliness, friendliness of workers and staff, and prompt attention to a variety of consumer needs while attending the event. Everything included in the package is designed to create an atmosphere in which the consumers believe that they are getting plenty more than just viewing the event.

The Super Bowl is another example of an event that is "packaged." There are several days filled with a variety of activities for the fans to engage in. Check the schedule for Super Bowl events and you will see dozens of activities listed. Some of the packaging involves additional benefits to go with ticket purchase. For instance, tickets to events can be "packaged" with additional items that give the tickets added value. For example, the top level ticket package might be called the Gold Medal package and include prime seats on the 50-yard line down close to the field, premium valet parking, access to super suites, free food and drink, access to pre-game activities, and access to post-game socials.

MAKING THE DECISION FOR PRODUCT DELETION

The time will arrive when some products no longer fulfill a consumer need or desire. A sport marketer must be able to identify that time and make the decision to eliminate the product. The decision should be based on an analysis of the product's situation: sales and sales trends, profits trends, cost analysis, and product life cycle stage. There are also indirect factors to be considered, such as the effect of eliminating a product on the company and employees, the effect on other companies, and the effect on the consumer.

If the sport company has decided to eliminate a product, there are some techniques that may be used in order to decrease the many effects that its elimination could have. For example, the product could be *phased out* over a period of time. This will allow everyone involved in its production and the consumer to begin to make the transition toward the day that the product is no longer offered.

CHAPTER SUMMARY

Products are the company. They provide benefits and perform functions that the consumer wants. In the sport industry there is a vast array of products. Product needs to be understood as a concept because a product involves tangible and intangible characteristics.

The wide variety of sport products available to the consumer in the sport industry requires some method of classification. Product classification typically involves an analysis of the consumer and, in particular, consumer needs and desires. The function of the product for the consumer is the reason for its existence.

The product life cycle is a concept that must be understood by the sport marketer. Product management strategies are influenced by the stages in which the company's products might be categorized in the product life cycle. Product mix and product development strategies are also influenced.

New product development is important to the sport marketer, as new products are a constant event in the sport industry. When the sport marketer understands the industry segment in which the company's products exist, informed decisions and strategies may guide the company to the successful addition of a new product.

The sport company must establish an identity for the product through product identification. This can include branding and packaging. Packaging is the activity of enclosing a product. There are some products in the sport industry that require a different kind of packaging—surrounding the product with an array of other products, activities, and events.

Product deletion is also a sport management and marketer's responsibility. A time may come when a product no longer fulfills the needs or desires of the consumer. At this critical point, a decision must be made concerning the elimination of the product.

DISCUSSION QUESTIONS

1. Define these terms: form utility, time utility, place utility, and ownership utility. Give an example of each.
2. What is product classification?
3. What is the product life cycle? What are the stages in the product life cycle?
4. What is the new product development planning process? What are the stages?
5. What is product identification? Why is it important? How is it used in the sport business industry?

9

Price and Pricing Strategies for the Sport Business Industry

INTRODUCTION

"What do I get for my money?"—This is a question asked by consumers everywhere. What consumers pay for something and what those individuals believe they get for their money varies from one consumer to another. What might be considered a "great deal" by one person may be considered a foolish deal by another. One person might think that paying a $1,000.00 for a ticket to see a college football bowl game is well worth it, while another person might see it as ridiculous and foolish.

Here is another example: Let us consider a conversation between two individuals about boats. Consumer A believes that Boat #1 is the better buy because the boat has more features and instruments than Boat #2. Consumer B believes that Boat #2 is a better buy because the engine has more horsepower. Consumer A points out that the price of Boat #1 is slightly lower than the price of Boat #2. Consumer B replies that the reason the price of Boat #2 is slightly higher is that it has a larger engine and engines are expensive. Consumer A argues that Boat #1 has more safety features such as a built-in automatic fire extinguisher in the engine compartment. Consumer B argues that Boat #2 has a good-looking color combination and that a more powerful engine is necessary to produce the speed and power needed when pulling water skiers. Consumer A states that water skiing isn't fun anymore and everyone's favorite toys are tubes, kneeboards, and wakeboards.

This discussion could go on for hours, days, or even weeks. Which consumer is right? Both are right insofar as each is willing to pay a particular price for what each believes is the best buy. Which one is truly the best buy? That depends on the consumer! The consumer defines "best buy" according to needs and desires. In addition, the definition will change from situation to situation and from product to product.

The price of a product in the sport business industry is the sport marketing mix element that is most difficult to determine. The sport marketing professional must consider that price is perhaps the most sensitive element of a product for the consumer.

The price, from the consumer's perspective, is the amount of money the consumer must sacrifice for a product. In addition, money is relative. Every consumer has a unique amount of money to spend and only a specific amount to spend for sport products. Many other factors affect the consumer's decision to buy.

In addition, there are factors that affect the determination of price, pricing objectives, pricing methods, and pricing strategies. The other broad factors are the other elements of the 4 Cs of sport marketing besides the consumer—company, competitor, and climate. This chapter presents the process of determining price and developing pricing strategies.

THE CONCEPT OF PRICE

Simply stated, price is "something exchanged for something," or what a consumer exchanges for a product (see Figure 9.1). A formal definition of price is the exchange value of something. *Value* is the quantitative measure of the worth of something. *Exchange* is the trading of something for something. The form of exchange may be money, services, or other forms of product exchange from the seller to the buyer. The first system of exchange was bartering, or trading. If you wanted corn, you might expect to trade wheat for it. If you wanted a little boat, you might have to trade a couple of cows for it. Eventually, something called money became the trading means of choice. Today, currency is the most common means in the process of exchange used by the consumer to obtain wanted or needed products.

Value is not an easy term to define. One definition states that value is a "quantitative measure of the worth of a product" (Stanton, Etzel, & Walker, 1991). Where do we begin to determine the quantitative worth of a product? Value can be determined by using any of a number of variables, and it can be determined by perceived value. *Perceived value* is what the consumer thinks is the value of something. There are no stated rules about determining price, but there are a number of factors and variables that affect the

Figure 9.1. The Marketing Mix: The 4 Ps.

determination of price. In the above example of trading two cows for a boat, the individuals involved would negotiate over the exchange. If the individual who wants the boat—the buyer—believes that two cows are too much to trade for the boat, that means that two cows are worth more than the boat. The individual with the boat—the seller—believes that the boat is worth two cows. The bartering, or negotiating, will continue until an agreement can be reached. If an agreement cannot be reached, we can conclude that the buyer believed that the value of the boat was not worth two cows. The buyer might decide to not make the trade, and the seller has lost a deal.

This is exactly what takes place in today's marketplace. Buyers and sellers negotiate over price. Negotiation takes place in more than one form—verbal and nonverbal. For example, negotiation over some products might be realized through nonverbal communication when the consumer decides not to purchase a particular product because of the price. This can force the seller to set a different price—or not make any sales. In the negotiation over some other products such as cars or boats, verbal negotiation takes place. The buyer and seller negotiate until an agreement can be reached. As a matter of fact, negotiation over price is expected for some products in the United States. In some other countries, negotiation over prices, sometimes called bargaining or haggling, is expected and part of the culture. For example, anyone who has been to certain cities in Mexico will agree that negotiation is commonplace among street vendors.

It is important to know the perceived value of a product when determining price. Courtesy of Bigfoto.com

If the buyer does not haggle over the price and pays the asking price, the buyer is considered foolish and an easy target by the seller. The seller will pass the word to other vendors. Some vendors consider the buyer rude if the buyer does not negotiate, and other vendors are insulted if the buyer does not negotiate.

There can be many factors involved in the determination of value, and it can have several meanings. This is because each individual involved in determining the value of a product has a unique perspective. Some of those variables include the following: attitudes, preferences, manufacturing costs, expected price, market value of the product, demand, time, beliefs, profit margin objectives, company needs, competitor's prices, laws, and economic values.

PRICE DECISIONS AND STRATEGY DEVELOPMENT USING THE 4 Cs

The sport marketing professional must consider many factors that affect price and pricing strategies. Information is critical to determining pricing strategies and methods.

Figure 9.2. Information about the 4 Cs is necessary for making decisions and developing strategies about Price and Pricing Strategies.

Product	Price	Place	Promotion
Functions	Objectives	Objectives	Objectives
Features	Flexibility	Channel Types	Promotion Mix
Accessories	Product Life Cycle	Market Exposure	Sales People
Utility	Terms	Distribution Goals	Advertising Methods
Use	Warranty	Transportation	Market Demand
Instructions	Sales	Location	Publicity
Installation	Special Order	Service	Public Relations
Service	Exclusivity	Intensity	Media Relations
Warranty	Psychology	Efficient	E-commerce
Product Lines	Perceived Value	Effective	M-commerce
Packaging	Discounts	Inventory Mgmt	Social Media Mix
Branding	Allowances	Warehousing	

Figure 9.3: The 4 Ps of the Marketing Mix.

This information comes from four categories called the 4 Cs of marketing (see Figure 9.2). However, most of these factors can be organized in order to consider them in a manageable manner. There are many elements of and factors about price that must be considered in the decision-making process, presented in Figure 9.3. Each of the 4 Cs is presented here with a brief description of how it relates to pricing.

Price can be a complex element of marketing for the sport marketing professional. Figure 9.4 shows a decision-making process based on collecting information about the 4 Cs that can be used as a model for developing pricing decisions and strategies. Each part of the model will be discussed in the following sections of the chapter.

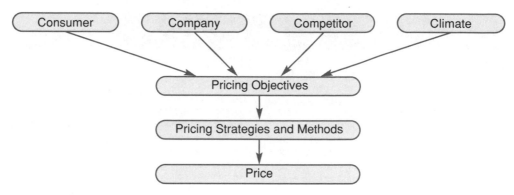

Figure 9.4. Process to Develop Effective Pricing.

Consumer

Although the price of something is a sensitive factor for the consumer, the consumer considers much more than the price in making a purchase decision. The consumer also considers factors such as product quality, warranty, company service agreement, refund policy, the consumer's image and reputation, and product bargain. Each factor is weighed in the consumer's analysis according to what the consumer will obtain for the price. For example, if the consumer is considering the purchase of a fitness center membership, he or she will consider services included in the membership package. Because this package costs more than another, how many services are included, and will the consumer use them?

· In addition to the factors mentioned, the consumer's buying decision is also affected by the decision-making pathway to a conclusion. Along the path, the consumer's decision process could be affected by the opinions of friends, family members, a significant other, and/or salespeople. The consumer could also be affected by age, income, education, geographic location, race, sexual orientation, and gender. Other factors include the consumer's personality, favorite activity, religion, and lifestyle. In addition, some consumers will research a product and its price to inform the decision to be made. There is information available through consumer product reports, product research labs, and government and private product testing organizations. The study of the consumer's consideration of price is an element of a specialized field of study called consumer behavior. We recommend that the sport marketing professional read extensively in this area.

If the product is professional or college sports, then the product is entertainment. Factors that affect attendance are critical to understanding *why* consumers buy tickets and attend games. Figure 9.5 shows the "Factors that Affect Attendance Model," in which many of the factors that affect the consumer's decision to attend a sports event. This model shows that such factors as simple as time and day of a sports game can affect the consumer's decision to purchase a ticket and go to a game. Therefore, what might be thought of as simple is actually a very important and critical element of scheduling sports games.

Sociodemographic Factors	Economic Factors	Game Attractiveness Factors	Audience Preferences Factors
• Gender • Age • Relationship Status • Highest Educational Level • Number of Children (−18) • Annual Household Income • Ethnicity • Occupation • Games Attend Per Year • Season Ticket Holder • Transportation Type • Distance To The Park	• Price of a ticket • Price of season ticket • Price of concessions • TV/Radio coverage of the home game in the local area • TV coverage of another sport event at time of the home game • Other sporting events in the area • Other activities taking place nearby • Other professional franchises in area	• Record (win-loss) of Home Team • Record (win-loss) of Visitor Team • Number of Star Players on Home Team • Number of Star Players on Visitor Team • Offensive Performance of Home Team • Defensive Performance of Home Team • Offensive Performance of Visitor Team • Defensive Performance of Visitor Team • Closeness of Competition • Games with Rival Teams • A Chance to see a Record-Breaking Performance by Team or Athlete • Special Promotion • Home Team's Place in the Division Standings • Home Team's Involvement in Race for a Playoff Spot • Advertising for Event	• Day games during the weekdays • Night games during the weekdays • Weekend day game • Weekend night game • Weather conditions • Cleanliness of the facility • Easy and/or multiple access to your facility • Availablity of parking at or near facility • Size of the facility (seating capacity) • The crowd behavior at the game • New stadium or arena • Number of years the team has been in the area • The variety of concessions available • Violence in the game • The design and color of the uniform • Going with family • Going with friends
Lu & Pitts, 2004			

Figure 9.5. Factors That Affect Attendance Model.

Company

Another important piece of the puzzle is one's company. What are the factors in the sport company that will affect setting the price of a product? Some of these are materials, equipment, rent or mortgage payment, payroll costs, maintenance, renovation, promotion, and dividends to stockholders. If the company is a manufacturer, it cannot put a price on a product that does not, at a minimum, cover the cost of producing the product. If it is a retailer or wholesaler, the price must at least cover the purchase of the product.

The type of sport company will also affect price determination. Generally, there are two types—nonprofit and for profit. Nonprofit sport companies include those that are supported by government funding, such as community recreation facilities, and nonprofit sport companies supported by membership fees, such as a YMCA. Usually, these are tax exempt. For-profit sport companies are the opposite—companies owned by individuals, groups, or large conglomerates that do not receive government funding support and are not tax exempt.

There is a difference in the costs associated with producing similar products in nonprofit and for-profit enterprises. For example, a nonprofit community fitness center receives a variety of tax breaks. Therefore, the total cost of producing the sport product is less than is the total cost for a for-profit fitness center. This allows the nonprofit sport company to set decidedly lower prices for the same products that the for-profit sport company offers. Hence, for-profit sport company owners complain that this is unfair competition.

Nonprofit sport enterprises gave special attention to raising prices, however, in the early 1990s. The reason was decreasing governmental and charitable funding. As state governments struggled to balance budgets during the early 1990s, the proportion of funding to recreation and sport facilities decreased. Nonprofit companies reported a decrease in charitable giving in the early 1990s due to the recession and the change in tax laws governing charitable giving—less of a given amount is deductible on a person's income tax calculations. As a result, some companies implemented higher fees. As government changes tax laws and these changes affect charitable giving, sport marketing professionals must become aware of these changes and how the changes will affect their businesses.

Raising fees will affect consumers and the companies. It will be up to the sport marketing professional to carefully analyze and estimate the effects of higher prices. As you will learn later in this chapter, the company might lose some consumers if prices are increased, but may make a greater profit.

Competitor

There is another factor the sport business cannot ignore: the competitor. More specifically, the sport marketing professional cannot ignore the competitor's prices and pricing strategies. When determining the price to place on a product, the marketer should give serious consideration to the price in the marketplace—prices being used by the competitors. For example, let's say that you are planning to build and manage an indoor soccer facility. Presently, there are three indoor soccer facilities in the same city. You decide, without investigating the competitor's prices, that you will establish the price, or league fee, for two of your products as follows:

1. Women's advanced league   —$400.00
2. Men's advanced league   —$400.00

When your facility opens, you get no entries in either league. Upon investigation, you discover that the consumers—soccer players—are buying the product (playing) at the other three facilities. You approach some of the players to ask why and find that they believe your prices are too high. You investigate the prices of the other facilities and find the following:

Facility A: Women's Advanced Fee   —$300.00
             Men's Advanced Fee   —$300.00

Facility B: Women's Advanced Fee   —$280.00
             Men's Advanced Fee   —$300.00

Facility C: Women's Advanced Fee   —$295.00
             Men's Advanced Fee   —$295.00

The amount that the consumers of indoor soccer are willing to pay has been established. The consumers have been paying a specific amount for soccer for quite a few years, and they are not willing to pay more. Finally, you decide that there is a simple solution. You will set the price below your competitors' prices. You set the fee at $100.00 for each of the leagues. This time, a couple of teams register and pay the $100.00, but there are not enough teams to fill the eight slots needed. Therefore, you have to cancel them and return the money to those who had registered.

Once again, you investigate by talking to the consumers. This time you discover that the consumers thought that the price you set was some kind of a hoax with plenty of other hidden charges that would eventually add up to the $400.00 you originally wanted to charge. In addition, some of them tell you that they were concerned with what they would get for only $100.00. In other words, they think that a price of $100.00 is too low to pay for soccer and that they will not get a quality product. This situation reflects two factors in price consideration: first, careful analysis of the competitor's prices; and second, the consumer's perception of the value for a product.

Climate

The climate includes those factors that are primarily external and that the sport marketing professional cannot directly control. These include factors such as laws pertaining to pricing, government regulations, the political climate, the economic situation, and local public attitude.

The economy can have perhaps the most direct effect on the sport company's pricing strategies. For example, since late 2008 the United States has been experiencing a recession involving high unemployment rates, which slows economic growth. Figure 9.6 illustrates the differences in spending in the U.S. between 2009 and 2010, reflecting the downturn in spending due to the recessionary economy. When consumers are not buying, the consumer price rate—known as inflation—usually falls. Therefore, if a company cannot raise prices to cover costs and company objectives, it is forced to change pricing strategies. For this recession this time, the sport business industry has been negatively affected in some areas, such as expensive clubs, pricey sports equipment, and sponsorship sales. Some sports events were canceled because the usual corporate sponsors either lowered or completely deleted their usual sponsorship spending.

The sport marketing professional cannot afford to develop something referred to as "tunnel vision." Tunnel vision means that the person has stopped paying attention to or studying all factors affecting a situation, and has become lazy or egotistical, paying attention to only one or a few factors. The sport marketing professional must constantly study all factors involved in order to make educated decisions.

PRICE ELASTICITY OF DEMAND

The sport marketing professional needs to understand a marketing concept called the elasticity of demand, defined as changes in the market (sales) when there is a change in price. *Elasticity* is a measure of consumer sensitivity (how consumers react) to changes in price. The following questions can help one understand this concept:

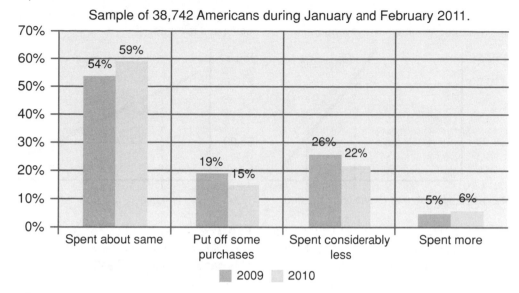

Figure 9.6. Effects of the Recessionary Economy During 2008–2010 on Spending for Sports, Fitness, and Recreation.

Source: The Physical Activity Council, 2011

1. What will happen if we raise the price of a sport product—if fewer consumers purchase the product, how many is "fewer?" How will that affect revenue, profit, and sales?
2. What will happen if we decrease prices—will more consumers purchase the products? How will this affect revenue, profit, and sales?
3. Is there any guarantee that a change in price will result in a change in consumer purchasing pattern?

The sport marketing professional can answer these questions only through estimation or experimentation; the marketer can attempt to estimate what will happen when a change is made to the price. The following example illustrates the concept of estimating elasticity of demand.

The cost of admission to the Wild Adventures Water Sports Park is $8.00 for a full-day pass. If the price is increased to $10.00, our first analysis is that there will probably be an immediate drop in attendance. This drop may level off, and the final effects will be minimal when we consider this situation over a long period, and if the increase in revenues from sales is equal to or greater than current revenue from sales.

If the attendance number decreases, we can conclude that the demand for this product is relatively inelastic. Refer to Figure 9.7, in which the graph illustrates the two-dollar increase and attendance figures. The graph shows that although the attendance number decreased from 320,000 to 300,000, total revenue increased from $2,560,000 to $3,000,000—an increase of $440,000, although there was a decrease of 20,000 buyers. This means that this situation is relatively inelastic because the change in price results in a parallel change in revenue.

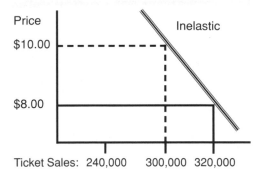

Change in Price created only slight decrease in sales, but an increase in revenue.

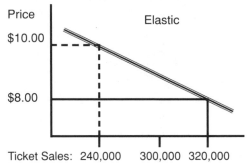

Change in Price created drastic decrease in sales and revenue.

Figure 9.7. Elasticity of Demand at the Wild Adventures Water Sports Park—This case is relatively Inelastic.

Figure 9.8. Elasticity of Demand at the Wild Adventures Water Sports Park—This case is relatively Elastic.

Figure 9.8 illustrates the estimate of what could happen if there were a drastic change in consumers. If the number of buyers drops from 320,000 to 240,000—a difference of 80,000 buyers—and this decrease results in decreased revenue, demand is relatively elastic: A change in price causes an opposite change in revenue—the higher price and fewer buyers resulted in a $160,000 decrease in revenue.

Determinants of Elasticity

What causes elasticity and inelasticity of demand? First, consider the situation at the beginning of the chapter: the consumers comparing two boats. Many factors affect their decision to buy. One factor is what they would "expect" to pay for a specific boat with a specific set of features. This "expected price" is what the consumer thinks the product is worth (McCarville, Crompton, & Sell, 1993). The expected price usually is one somewhere within a range of prices with relative minimum and maximum limits: a price most frequently charged, price for similar products, price of the brand usually purchased, or the price last paid (Winer, 1988). For example, the consumer might expect to pay between $100 and $300 for a one-year membership in a fitness center because that is the range of prices for that product in today's market. In another example, a consumer might believe that a fair price for a new pair of running shoes is "not over $80." If a consumer has "shopped around," this means that the consumer has compared prices of a product at two or more places. This is also precisely what the sport marketing professional should do. As one means of estimating setting a price, shop around—compare prices of the same or a comparable product. If the product seems to sell well within a specific range of prices, this is a fairly accurate estimate of "expected price," or what the consumer expects to pay and is paying. Some of the other factors that affect elasticity are presented in Table 9.1. They are discussed next.

Table 9.1. Factors That Affect Elasticity of Demand
• Product Necessity of Luxury
• Product Substitute Availability
• Frequency of Purchase
• Proportion of Income Available
• Economy
• Brand Loyalty
• Competition
• Quality of Product
• Product Specialization
• Time Frame of Demand

Necessity or Luxury Product

Price can be relatively inelastic if the product is a necessity and elastic if it is a luxury. For example, football pads are a necessity, and there are no substitutes. Therefore, the buyers must pay the set prices. On the other hand, going on a sports adventure trip is a luxury, and there are plenty of substitutes. Therefore, prices must be set specific to consumer markets because the consumer does not have to spend money for a trip.

Product Substitutability

Have you ever seen or heard these advertising words: "There is no substitute," "Accept no substitute," or "No other product compares?" The availability of substitutes for products can have a strong effect on elasticity. Those sport products or other products that can meet the consumer's needs, wants, or desires are direct competition for the consumer dollar. In research on recreation and leisure, *substitutability* has been defined as "an interchangeability among activities in satisfying participants' motives, needs and preferences" (Hendee & Burdge, 1974, p. 157). In the sports world, a definition offered in 1993 still holds true today: The term recreation substitutability refers to the interchangeability of recreation experiences such that acceptably equivalent outcomes can be achieved by varying one or more of the following: the timing of the experience, the means of gaining access, the setting, and the activity (Brunson & Shelby, 1993, p. 69).

Using this definition, the sport marketing professional must study two factors: what the consumer is looking for and the potential substitutes for their product. With this knowledge, the sport marketing professional can incorporate pricing and other marketing mix strategies to try to keep the consumer from selecting the substitute.

Frequency of Purchase

The frequency with which the consumer must purchase a product affects elasticity of demand. Frequency can be linked to necessity. For example, if a consumer has a consistent need for athletic tape to stock the sports medicine clinic, price can be set lower according to the frequency of purchase. In another example, if the sport product is such that there is a very low frequency of purchase, such as the need for a sport marketing study on building a new student recreation center for a university, price will likely be much higher.

Income

An individual's income limits the amount of money a consumer has available to spend on discretionary products after all the bills are paid. As income increases, the percentage of income a consumer has to use for food and bills decreases. This means that the percentage of income available for discretionary purposes increases. An individual with a lower income spends a larger percentage on food and bills and is therefore left with a smaller percentage for discretionary spending. For example, Consumer A's take-home income is $25,000 and Consumer B's take-home income is $50,000. Both use approximately 40% of their income for necessities such as mortgage, food, vehicles, insurance, utilities, phone, and cable/Internet. Consumer B has more discretionary income ($30,000) than Consumer A ($15,000) even though each uses the same percentage of income for necessities.

The Economy

The economy affects elasticity of demand. For example, how does recession impact consumer spending and price setting? The early 1990s were labeled the "Age of Disinflation" (Farrell & Schiller, 1993). Inflation is the rising price level measured in percentages over a period of time, usually annually. According to Farrell & Schiller, inflation in the United States reached double-digit proportions in the late 1970s and early 1980s; it reached 13.6% in 1980. Between 1990 and 1993, the inflation rate decreased from an annual 5.4% to a 1993 rate of 2.7% (Farrell & Schiller, 1993). Forcing this period of "disinflation" were recessionary factors such as high unemployment, slow economic growth, increased fierce global competition, and worldwide overcapacity. What this means to the sport marketing professional is that when the consumer has less money to

In economic slumps, sport marketers must reconsider current pricing strategies.
© Lucdenounce| Dreamstime.com

spend due to unemployment or is spending less money due to fear of losing employment, the company will begin to feel the effects. The sport marketing professional must either redesign pricing strategies or implement significantly radical ones.

On the other hand, sports activities seem to be sustained as compared to many other product markets during times of recession. It seems that Americans love their sports, recreation, and fitness activities, and they are more willing to forego the purchase of a washer and dryer in order to continue participating in their favorite activity. Moreover, these activities are thought to be therapeutic, stress-relief activities, adding to justification for not giving them up. However, the recent recession that began in late 2008 and has lasted several years is an unusually deep one, with unemployment higher than during other recessions. This recession has had a negative effect on the sport business industry.

Brand Loyalty

A consumer can become brand-loyal, meaning that the consumer will purchase only products of a certain brand. As an example, Consumer A believes the running shoes of the Smith Company are the best and the only shoe that fits everything the consumer is looking for in a running shoe; more important, the Smith Company is the only company in which the consumer believes. The consumer will buy shoes and probably other products from the Smith Company. Consumer B will buy running shoes from any company as long as they fit and the price is right. In this example, Consumer A is loyal to one brand. Most companies strive to create brand loyalty within their consumer bases. They will even use this as part of their advertising. Have you ever seen or heard the advertising slogans presented here?: "Our customers always come back" and "Once an Acme customer, always an Acme customer."

Brand loyalty applies to the sport industry in another unique way: something called the "hardcore fan." A hardcore fan is someone who picks and supports a particular team, or sport, and will stick with it through good times and bad. For example, a hardcore fan of a university basketball team whose college colors are gold and white may be heard to exclaim, "My blood runs gold!"

The Competition

The prices of the competition's products will affect elasticity of demand. Sometimes "price wars" evolve between two or more companies or between companies within an entire industry. For example, the fitness center industry experienced such phenomenal growth in the late 1970s and throughout the 1980s that the market became saturated with fitness centers. Almost all fitness centers offered the same set of products to the consumer. Therefore, the only difference between centers was the price. If the manager of a fitness center wanted to stay in business, prices had to be lowered—some prices were even below the cost of the product.

To be able to make educated decisions and to set marketing strategies that will compete best with the competition, the sport marketing professional must study the competition's prices and pricing strategies.

Product Quality

A sport product's quality will affect consumer purchasing and hence elasticity of demand. If the consumer knows, or even suspects, that a sport product is of poor quality, demand will be relatively elastic. Thus, if prices are increased, the consumer simply will not buy, believing that the product is not worth the increase in price.

Product Specialization

The specialization of a sport product will affect elasticity of demand. For example, a softball player must use a softball glove to participate in the sport. A softball glove is a specialized sport product. There are over 30,000,000 estimated softball participants over the age of six in the United States today. All of them must have this specialized piece of sport equipment to participate in softball. Therefore, the consumer (the softball participant) will purchase this product because it is the only product that performs the needed function. However, there are many softball glove manufacturers and retailers. The consumer has a wide range of choice. This keeps the price down.

Time Frame of Demand

Another factor affecting elasticity of demand is the time frame of demand: the amount of time a consumer has or is willing to take in the process of making a purchase. Following are three examples. If a soccer player needs athletic tape to wrap an ankle before a game and forgot to purchase the tape in plenty of time before the day and time of the game, the player will be under pressure and will pay almost any price for the tape. The player must stop at the closest store to purchase the tape and does not have time to shop around for the best price. In another example, consider the consumer who wants to buy a new softball bat. This individual currently owns a bat and is fairly satisfied with it. The new bat purchase is a consideration for the future. Therefore, this consumer is under no time pressure to purchase and can shop around for exactly the right product at the right price. In another example, a college athlete is pursued by several athlete-agents trying to persuade the athlete to retain their services if and when the athlete ever wants or needs an agent. The athlete can be under great time constraints as his/her senior year approaches.

DETERMINING PRICING OBJECTIVES
FOR THE SPORT BUSINESS

One of the most fundamental management skills necessary for positively affecting success is objective setting. Objectives give direction to determining the price and pricing strategies. Pricing objectives should derive from the marketing objectives that were established in line with the sport company's objectives and mission. A question the sport marketing professional must always ask first is "What results does the company expect to occur as a result of the price?" The objectives should be clear, forthright, quantitative, realistic, and achievable; and they should establish vision for the future.

Table 9.2 shows some examples of a variety of pricing objectives categorized by type based on the 4 Cs of marketing. Using the consumer as a basis for setting objectives, the

Table 9.2. Pricing Objectives Using the 4 Cs of Marketing			
Consumer	**Competitor**	**Company**	**Climate**
• Price sensitivity • Purchase decision • Fairness • Image • Need • Opportunity	• Meet competitors prices • Be a price leader • Stabilize the Market • Go for market share • Beat competitors prices • Discourage market entrants	• Meet the mission • Hit profit margin • Recover cost • Growth • Survival • Increase market share	• Economy • Laws on pricing • Manufacturing constraints • Environmental constraints • Political issues • Technological situation

company might determine that using image is important to setting price. For a consumer, image may be tied up in status quo. Keeping a level of prestige status quo will push the consumer to spend much more on a product than is necessary. Setting the price high sends a psychological signal that perhaps the product is of the highest quality and is a rare product only affordable by a few elite consumers. For example, even a softball bat can carry prestige. If the bat is given a prestigious name, given an unusually high price, and packaged with a leather carrying case with gold embossed initials, then the price is "justified" in the eyes of the consumer. Some consumers will happily spend upwards of the $400.00 price tag for the bat.

Using "company" of the 4 Cs for setting objectives, let's say the sport business wants to increase market share. Prices will perhaps be set lower, along with strong promotional incentives, in order to persuade consumers to purchase that company's product immediately instead of the competitor's. Sometimes, this might mean losses in profits for a period of time until the increase in market share is realized. After the share is gained, then the company can slowly begin to increase prices again.

Objectives are general aspirations toward which all marketing activities are directed. An objective is declared; then goals are formulated to meet the objectives. Objectives are open-ended statements. Goals are concrete and usually quantitative; goals have specific timelines. Further, company objectives and goals often involve more marketing elements, such as promotion and production, than pricing. For example, if a running-shoe manufacturer has an objective to become the largest market shareholder, then more than pricing strategies will be involved.

The sport marketing professional and management personnel of the sport company are responsible for establishing pricing objectives. Each objective has potential positive and negative consequences for the company and its consumers. The sport marketing professional and all management personnel must analyze the consequences, then make decisions based on this knowledge and on the direction in which they want the company to go. Once they have identified the objectives, the next step is to plan the methods and strategies that have the best potential in achieving the objectives.

PRICING METHODS AND STRATEGIES

After establishing pricing objectives, the next step in setting prices for sport products is deciding on specific methods and strategies. In this section we will present some common pricing methods and strategies that may be used in the sport industry, along with a brief description of each. A summary of these pricing methods can be found in Table 9.3.

Going-Rate Pricing Method

This method is also called status quo pricing, and it is applied when the company wants to keep prices at the going rate—the average price of competitors for same or equivalent products. For example, if the marketer was working with a fitness center, a check of all membership prices charged at fitness centers will be used to determine the going rate.

Demand-Oriented Pricing Method

Using this pricing method, the sport marketing professional ascertains the price that potential customers are willing to pay for a particular product. The price that potential customers are willing to pay can be determined through consumer surveys or studying the competition.

Price Discrimination Pricing Method

With this pricing method, different prices are charged for the same sport products (Berrett, Slack, & Whitson, 1993; Walsh, 1986). This method uses consumer demographics and other factors. For example, sport companies use variables such as the following:

- **Age**—senior citizen discounts; special rates for children
- **Income**—a sliding-scale pricing method according to income
- **Facility use**—peak prices for peak-use times
- **Corporate rate**—skyboxes sold to companies for luxury suites at the arena

Peak-Load Pricing Method

This is the method of charging different prices for the same products at different points in time. It is very similar to demand-oriented pricing. The peak-load method involves charging higher prices during times when product sales will be at their peak. For instance, the primary selling time for softball bats is in March, April, and May just prior to softball season. Prices for softball bats during this period will be a little higher than they will be during December and January.

Off-Peak Pricing Method

This pricing method involves setting prices lower during off-peak (lower-demand) times. Some fitness centers use this method. Because the high-use times are those times just before work (6:30–7:30 A.M.), during the lunch hour, and just after work (5:00–6:30 P.M.), fitness center management wants to encourage more use during the low-use times by offering price incentives. For example, the center can offer a member-

Table 9.3. Pricing Methods

- **Going-rate Pricing**—A method used when the company wants to keep prices at the going rate—the average price of competitors' prices. *Example:* All fitness center membership prices in the market are averaged to use to set your price.
- **Demand-Oriented Pricing**—Determining price based on demand for a product; can be found by setting price and watching sales, or by surveying consumers on what they are willing to pay. *Example:* Demand for a championship game is much higher than a regular season game and this can allow for prices to be set higher.
- **Price Discrimination Pricing**—Different prices are set for the same product using demographics, or using product differentiation factors. *Example:* Setting child's prices based on age; setting game ticket prices based on seating location.
- **Peak Load Pricing**—Method of setting different prices for the same product demanded at different point in time; higher prices are used during peak use times. *Example:* Peak use for snow ski activity is during winter months, so prices will be set higher.
- **Off-Peak Pricing**—Setting prices lower due to low use. *Example:* Prices for swimming are set lower during off-peak times, such as 9am to 11am.
- **Seasonal Pricing**—A pricing method used for sport products affected by the weather seasons. *Example:* Softball relies on warm summer weather; snow-skiing needs the snow of winter months.
- **Average Cost Pricing**—Using a formula to average price using costs and spread it across several markets. *Example:* Spreading the costs of all baseball leagues across all leagues to set one price for all.
- **Penetration Pricing**—Using price to gain market share. *Example:* A sporting goods manufacturer will set prices for their golf clubs lower than the competitor in order to gain consumers and increase market share.
- **Cost-Plus Pricing**—Setting price at a percent or desired profit above cost. *Example:* A soccer facility sets price at 30% above the cost as a predetermined profit margin.
- **Holiday Season Pricing**—Using a holiday of any kind to do holiday pricing specials. *Example:* An LPGA event organizer uses the tournament's special holiday weekend for special pricing.
- **Member Pricing**—Setting prices with special deals for members of an organization or entity. *Example:* Members of a sports club pay a lower price for a sports magazine subscription.
- **Break-even Pricing**—Most often used by non-profit organizations, prices are set according to costs only. *Example:* A local YMWCA sets prices for pool rental based only on the cost for the hour of use.
- **Single Price Pricing**—Use of one price for everything. *Example:* For 2 days, an NFL team offers all tickets for one price.
- **M-Pricing**—Setting special mobile device pricing, such as smart phones and tablet devices, is a way to encourage consumers to purchase your product through their m-devices. *Example:* A professional basketball team offers special ticket prices if a consumer uses their smart phone for the purchase.
- **Internet Pricing**—Similar to M-pricing, this method utilizes special pricing if the consumer uses the internet for purchases. *Example:* A sporting goods retailer offers a 5% discount and free shipping for any purchases made through their website.
- **Short-Term Pricing**—Using any excuse for a brief and short term pricing period. *Example:* The parks department offers a 3-day sale to purchase park passes for camping.
- **Product Line Pricing**—Using each product line as a price category differentiated by price only. *Example:* A tennis racket manufacturer offers tennis rackets by the price categories of "the $100 line," "the $200 line," and "the $300 line."
- **Secondary Market Pricing**—Determining price based on secondary market demand. *Example:* The used and/or consignment store "Play it Again, Sports" sets prices based on a value of used products and what the secondary market will most likely pay.
- **Rebate Pricing**—Using rebates as an incentive. *Example:* Sports Authority offers the "Biggest Rebate Ever!" sale for one week each year.

ship discount price to those who promise to only use the center in between those high-use times.

Seasonal Pricing Method

This pricing strategy is used when a sport product is affected by the seasons and usually relies on specific seasons. Snow ski resorts charge higher prices during winter when there is plenty of snow and skiers want to go skiing. Lower prices are charged during summer months. During the summer, houseboat rental fees are almost twice the amount charged during winter.

M-Pricing Method

M-pricing is based on M-marketing—the use of mobile devices (smart phones or tablet devices such as an iPhone or iPad) as a storefront, or an additional distribution avenue. Some sport companies will incentivize their products through special pricing offered only through a mobile device. For instance, every WNBA team offers tickets through several different ticket sales stores. Since shopping by mobile devices is new and is increasing in frequency at an incredible rate, the WNBA will offer special ticket sales if the tickets are ordered/bought through the mobile device. One reason for this is to promote consumer traffic toward the mobile device outlets. The WNBA knows that more and more fans are using their mobile devices for shopping. They use this research to target those fans for sales.

Internet Pricing Method

Similar to M-pricing, Internet pricing utilizes the Internet as an additional outlet/storefront to target those consumers who are increasingly using the Internet for shopping. This offers the company an additional way to increase sales. As an example, a fitness center will offer special Internet-only sales for new members. They might offer a coupon for 50% off membership prices if the consumer accesses, downloads, and uses the Internet-only coupon to purchase the membership.

Average-Cost Pricing Method

This method utilizes the following formula:

Average-Cost Price = Average Fixed Cost + Average Variable Cost

where

Average Fixed Cost = Total Fixed Costs / Number of Participants

and

Average Variable Cost = Total variable Costs / Number of Participants

The first step in average cost pricing is to determine which fixed costs and variable costs to use in the formula. Fixed costs are those expenses within the sport company that are constant, such as mortgage or rent, payroll, utilities, and phones. Variable costs are expenses such as short-term loan payments, temporary staff, short-term facility rental, and equipment purchases or rental. Once these have been determined, the formula can be used. Howard and Crompton (1980) give the following example:

IF Total Fixed Costs = $1,000

Total Variable Costs = $500

Projected Number of Participants = 100

THEN the Average Cost Price (ACP) = $1,000 / 100 + 500 / 100

THUS, ACP = $15

Penetration Pricing Method

This pricing strategy is used when the sport company wants to penetrate a market by using price as a primary marketing tactic. Prices are set relatively lower than other prices for the same products on the market. Penetration pricing is typically used as a first-time offering of a product. For example, a sport marketing company will soon be opening for business. The company's marketing professional determines that its pricing strategy will be penetration pricing. To try to secure consumers, prices for the company's services are set much lower than those of other companies. The company must use a promotion message that speaks to product quality. We have discussed the problem of setting prices too low; once the product achieves some market recognition, prices can be slowly increased over a period of time.

Cost-Plus Pricing Method

In this pricing method, the price of the sport product is based on the cost of the product plus a desired profit (Stanton et al., 1991). If the cost to produce one game of indoor soccer is $40, the price for a game will be $40 plus any amount of profit desired. Therefore, if the indoor soccer facility wants to make $60 of profit from each game, the price of one game will be $100. This will be multiplied by the number of games in a league round of play (usually 8–10 games). If there are 10 teams in the league and the schedule is a round-robin schedule, each team plays every other team once, a schedule that gives each team nine games. Apply the round-robin formula for determining how many games will be played (Byl, 1990):

$N (N - 1) / 2$ = Total Number of Games*

(*N is number of entries)

In this example we find that $10 (10 - 1)/2 = 45$ games. Hence, there will be 45 games in the league. If the price per game is established at $100, the total price for all 45 games is $4,500.

The next step is to determine what price to charge each team. The common method is to charge a league fee. Divide the $4,500 by the number of teams entering. Thus, $4,500 / 10 = $450. At this point in the formula, each team will pay a league fee of $450. Now add the "plus" amount to the $450. This amount can be any amount needed or desired, provided, of course, that the "plus" amount won't put the price out of reach for the consumer. The "plus" amount can be added according to goals and objectives for the company—for example, the company wants to start saving for the purchase of some equipment and wants to be able to purchase the equipment at the end of two years. Use the cost of the equipment divided over two years and divided among all teams in all leagues in all sports to determine the "plus" amount to add to each team's cost.

Break-Even Analysis Pricing Method

This method for pricing is determined through an analysis of costs and revenue, or more specifically, when the costs of producing the product equal the revenue taken from the sales of the product. If Central College sold $200,000 worth of tickets to its sports events and the events cost the college $200,000 to produce, the college broke even. In this example, however, Central College didn't make any profit. Break-even analysis will determine how many tickets need to be sold at what price to first break even; every ticket after that point is profit.

To use break-even pricing effectively, the sport marketing professional first determines the break-even point for a product using several different prices. This allows the sport marketer to determine total costs and revenue for each price being considered. Table 9.4 illustrates this method using different prices for tickets to Central College's events.

Short-Term Pricing Method

The many short-term pricing methods all involve selling a product at a discounted rate for a limited period of time. This type of method is used frequently in the sport business industry. Here are a few examples. A college athletics department will offer dis-

---

Table 9.4. Calculating the Breakeven Point Using Different Prices

Event Cost	Revenue Needed to Break even	Ticket Price Possibilities	Breakeven Point— tickets to sell
$200,000	$200,000	$2.00	100,000
$200,000	$200,000	$5.00	40,000
$200,000	$200,000	$7.00	26,666
$200,000	$200,000	$10.00	20,000
$200,000	$200,000	$15.00	13,333

If Central College sports events average 200 paying fans and there are 100 events, the total number of paying fans to all events is 20,000. If the events cost $200,000.00 and Central College wants to break even, they will need a price based on average fans attending all events. If Central sets the price of all tickets to all events at $10.00 and 20,000 fans pay, then Central will break even at $200,000.00. If Central were to lower the price to just $7.00, they would need to sell an additional 6,666 tickets to break even. If Central wants to make a profit, Central could raise the price slightly—any price over $10.00 would realize a profit. For example, raising the price to $15.00 would profit $100,000.00 and that is a 50% increase in revenue.

counted tickets to the women's volleyball games for a few days prior to the start of the season. An NBA team will offer a two-for-one, also called a BOGO (buy one get one), for a short period of time during a holiday. The LPGA will offer discounted tickets to a tournament for a brief time during the month before the tournament.

Product Line Pricing Method

This method involves setting specific price minimums and maximums for each product line. Acme Tennis Racket Company can carry three lines of rackets differentiated by price: the $500 line, the $300 line, and the $100 line. A sports facility will offer line sales based on seating arrangements and location of seats: the $10.00 ticket line, the $100.00 ticket line, and the $1,000.00 ticket line.

Single Price Method

This method involves setting just one price for everything the company offers. Most often, this method is seen in retail stores that specialize in a dollar store situation and is not used much in the sport business industry. However, one example is when a college sports department offers all tickets for one price no matter where the seat location is.

Secondary Market Pricing Method

This method involves determining the secondary market value of an item and establishing price. For example, the popularity and growth of the Play It Again Sports store is proof that there is a desire and a market for previously owned sports equipment. The store's management personnel establishes the value (price) of each item based on its condition and what it might sell for.

Holiday Pricing Method

This method is used for special pricing promotions during any holiday or holiday season. In the U.S., we are all familiar with the concept of "Black Friday." "Black Friday" is so labeled because it is the day during which sales are so high for so many sellers that their books go into the "black"—red ink is used when in the negative, and black is used when in the positive. Nearly every business in the U.S. uses holiday pricing. It offers a way to capitalize (monetize) nearly every holiday imaginable. For example, a sporting goods retail store will offer special sales during holidays such as July 4th, Labor Day, Thanksgiving, and Christmas. The sales will include special pricing promotions that might include discounts, coupons, and special pricing for certain hours.

PRICE IDENTIFICATION AS A PROMOTIONAL TOOL

Pricing can be used as identification, as a promotional tool, and as a way to "soften the blow." One reason to use pricing as an identification tool is to give the consumer a specific identification to the product through the price title. Using words that are softer to hear than the word *price* is done to attempt to have a calming effect on the consumer. Any trick that the sport business manager can use with the consumer should be used because it can positively affect sales.

The words used in place of price convey a definition of what the *price* is bringing, as well as what the consumer is getting. For instance, "licensing fee" determines that this involves receiving a "license" to do something and that there is a "fee." In other words, you must pay a price to obtain the legal right and permission of an owner to sell licensed merchandise. In another example, "admission" tells you that you are going to be admitted into something if you pay the fee for permission to gain entry. The alternative words give definition and identification to the product. This creative use of language is also part of the company's promotional efforts: Price is used as a promotional tool, illustrating the interrelatedness of marketing mix elements.

PRICE AND PRICING MIX MANAGEMENT

As Figure 9.4 (earlier in the chapter) illustrates, the sport business will determine price and pricing strategies using pricing methods, based on information gained from the 4 Cs as well as on pricing objectives set. Many factors of sports events as shown in Figure 9.5 must inform the sport marketing professional's decisions. Shown in Figure 9.5 (page 256) is the "Economic Factors" category. Several of these factors are related to price: price of a ticket, price of season ticket, and price of concessions. All of these must be considered when considering price and pricing strategies and methods.

Most companies will have several pricing strategies in place for any given period of time, and will have pricing strategies based on each target market. This is the pricing mix. As Figures 9.9 and 9.10 illustrate, a company's pricing mix can be quite involved. In these examples you see a small sample of pricing objectives, strategies, methods selected, and time frame set.

Pricing Mix		Smart Fit Fitness Center				Notes:	
Year 2013–2014		123 Main Street, Anywhere, USA					
Target Markets Identified		new consumers					

Objective	Strategy	Methods	Frame	Methods	Frame	Methods	Frame
Increase membership profit by 5%	Add 50 new memberships; Sales Promotions	1. 50% off coupon; local paper; website	Month of January	2. 2-for-1 coupon; local paper; website	Month of March	3. Holiday Pricing— 50% off coupon; Mobile push	July 1—4

Accounting Management—							
Method 1	# Sold	Method 2	# Sold	Method 3	# Sold	NOTES	Total
						Goal Set at 50; was goal met?	

Figure 9.9. Pricing Mix Management System for a Fitness Center.

Pricing Mix	Southeast University	Notes: (1) target student paper, online books store, and M-devices for students: (2) for alumni market, target the alumni newsletter and website
Year 2013–2014	123 Main Street, Anywhere, USA	
Target Markets Identified	(1) students; (2) alumni	

Objective	Strategy	Methods	Frame	Methods	Frame	Methods	Frame
Increase WBB ticket sales by 20%	Sales Promotions to 1–students; 2–alumni	1. BOGO 2. BOGO	Month of September	1. 50% off coupon M-device only; 2. 50% coupon website	1 and 2, for one week before 1st season game	3. Holiday Pricing— 50% off coupon; Mobile push	1. Black Friday; 2. M Monday

Accounting Management—							
Method 1	# Sold	Method 2	# Sold	Method 3	# Sold	NOTES	Total
Analysis						Were goals met?	

Figure 9.10. Pricing Mix Management System for a University Athletics Program.

In Figure 9.9, the Smart Fit Fitness Center is attempting to increase revenue by increasing membership sales. The example shows three methods selected, with time frames planned for each of the methods. At the bottom, an accounting is set up to take measurements of each of the methods and its outcomes. At the end of each pricing strategy, it can be analyzed for its effectiveness. If management thinks the strategy is working, then the strategy might be used on several other occasions and during other time frames.

In Figure 9.10, a university athletics department wants to increase ticket sales for the women's basketball program. This sample shows two target markets, students and alumni, and notes on what will be used to reach each market. The department's objective and goal is to increase sales by 20% through the methods that have been selected. With this chart, the sport marketing professional or someone charged with this responsibility can plan for each method and then chart each one's performance. After each one, an analysis can be made as to whether or not that method met the goal. The management staff can then determine if the methods used were successful and whether or not to use them again in the future.

In a study examining factors influencing fans' perceived value for NFL playoff games and buying through eBay, the researchers found that several factors were more influential in the fans' purchase (Drayer & Shapiro, 2010). Those factors included team performance, day of the game, face value of the ticket, population and income of the home city, and number of days before the event that the ticket was sold. These are like the information shown in Table 9.2 and Figure 9.5 (earlier in this chapter). Research, such as is presented in this chapter and throughout the book, collects factual information that the sport marketing professional must use in making decisions.

NASCAR runs its races at several different racetracks around the country (Sporting News Wire Service, 2010). Most of the speedways are locally owned and operated. To push ticket sales, local track owners have used several different pricing methods. Some of these have included the following. At the Michigan International Speedway, tickets were steeply discounted by 30% to attempt to fight the recession and the 18% decrease in tickets sold. They also used a "tiered pricing" method in which different prices were used for different events. Texas Motor Speedway used what they called a "backstretch busters" pricing method; a group of 3,000 seats in the "backstretch" portion of the speedway were sold at a deep discount. Owners of other tracks began to take notice because the methods were working, and they wanted to copy those methods—one form of studying competitors is to possibly copy what they do.

Sports Authority, a sporting goods retailer, uses rebate pricing occasionally. Once or twice a year, Sports Authority will announce and run its "Biggest Rebate of the Year!" offer. This catches the attention of those consumers who like using rebates and brings them into the store.

Determining the entire pricing mix and its management can be very involved. Every target market selected, as well as each pricing method, media method, and time frame for the methods is strategically planned and carried out. Each one will be analyzed as to its effectiveness and its ability to achieve the company's objectives. Whether management determines that the methods were successful or not, future plans can be modified toward a higher effectiveness and success rate.

Planning the pricing mix is, of course, based on information about the consumer and the company, and perhaps about the competitor and climate factors. Following a plan such as the one presented in Figure 9.4 (earlier in this chapter) gives the company a more effective and efficient process to determine pricing objectives, strategies, methods, and price.

CHAPTER SUMMARY

This chapter presented the marketing mix element "price." Price, as well as exchange and value, should be understood as broad concepts with many factors involved in their make-up. The 4 Cs of price determination were discussed, each in relation to its effect on price and the pricing strategy. The concept of price elasticity of demand and its effect on price was presented, along with the determinants of the elasticity of demand. Last, we looked at several pricing objectives, methods, and strategies that can be used by the sport marketing professional. The decision-making process for pricing is not an easy one for the sport marketing professional. Before establishing the price for a sport product, sport marketers must consider, study, and understand many factors. The sport marketing professional will be making educated decisions that will have increased positive potential when all factors have been analyzed and the pricing decisions are based on research.

DISCUSSION QUESTIONS

1. What are the factors to consider in determining price? Discuss each and give examples.
2. Discuss the concept of price elasticity of demand. Give some examples.
3. List some examples of pricing objectives for sport.
4. List and describe some pricing methods for the sport industry.
5. What is price identification? List examples of price identification found in the sport industry. Explain why these words are used.

SUGGESTED EXERCISES

1. Identify sport businesses, organizations, or other enterprises in your city or community that use these pricing methods and give the examples of each: going-rate pricing, demand-oriented pricing, price discrimination, seasonal pricing, short-term pricing, M-pricing, Internet pricing, and product line pricing.
2. Identify in your city or community some of the sport businesses, organizations, or other enterprises that use the price identification titles as presented in this chapter, such as licensing fee, admission, and purse. Develop a list of those businesses and the price identification titles. Describe each one and how it is used.
3. Select a sport business and interview someone there about the company's pricing strategies and methods. Give a presentation about this in class.

10

Place: Distribution Channels and Decisions in Sport Business

INTRODUCTION

A sport business has to get its product to the consumer, or, in some instances, get the consumer to the product (see Figure 10.1). Getting the product to the consumer involves those hard goods that are manufactured in a factory somewhere and need to be transported from there to retail stores. Getting the consumer to the product involves primarily sports activities in which the consumer will participate, or that the consumer will watch as a spectator. For example, when someone wants to consume (play) golf, that individual has to travel to a facility where he/she can play golf—a golf course. Or, when someone wants to watch a WNBA game, the person must travel to where the game will be played. These types of products are actually not manufactured until the game is played. At that point in time, the consumer is consuming the product at the same instant it is being manufactured. This is similar to someone going

Figure 10.1. The Marketing Mix: The 4 Ps.

to watch a theater play—the play is performed, which is the manufacturing of the product, while the consumer watches, which is the consuming of the product.

The process is called *distribution* (also called *place*). Different types of products require unique kinds of distribution strategies. There are many ways to distribute products. For example, there are tangible and intangible products, and each has to be delivered or transported in unique ways. There are many categories of consumers, such as the end consumer and the business consumer. Some distribution channels work best for different types of consumer, and there are different marketing channels with different costs involved. For example, the cost to ship one product in one package for next-day delivery for one consumer is much more expensive than the cost of shipping a large truckload of thousands of the product with a three-week delivery period to a retail store.

In this chapter you will learn about distribution in the sport business industry, the role of distribution in marketing strategy, the selection of a distribution network, and the types of distribution intermediaries available for moving and/or offering sport business industry products.

DISTRIBUTION DEFINED

The sport business must determine how to get its products from the manufacturer or producer to the consumer, or how to get the consumer to the producer. In the first instance, some sports products are hard goods, such as a tennis racket or a basketball, that need to be moved from the factory to the retail store. In the second instance, some sports products are participation or entertainment products. These products are sports activities or events, such as a professional basketball game, a soccer match, or a super cross race. With these types of products, the event (product) is staged at a facility where fans will gather to watch. The sport business will have made decisions regarding the facility in relation to location and other factors that will make the facility attractive to the consumer as a place in which to consume these types of products. As with all other marketing mix elements, information about the 4 Cs of sport marketing must be considered in order to make decisions about distribution that will be effective and efficient and work best for the company and the consumer (see Figure 10.2).

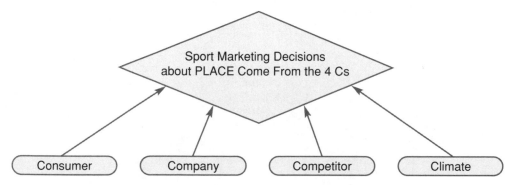

Figure 10.2. Information about the 4 Cs is necessary for making decisions and developing strategies about Place (distribution of the product).

Product	Price	Place	Promotion
Functions	Objectives	Objectives	Objectives
Features	Flexibility	Channel Types	Promotion Mix
Accessories	Product Life Cycle	Market Exposure	Sales People
Utility	Terms	Distribution Goals	Advertising Methods
Use	Warranty	Transportation	Market Demand
Instructions	Sales	Location	Publicity
Installation	Special Order	Service	Public Relations
Service	Exclusivity	Intensity	Media Relations
Warranty	Psychology	Efficient	E-commerce
Product Lines	Perceived Value	Effective	M-commerce
Packaging	Discounts	Inventory Mgmt	Social Media Mix
Branding	Allowances	Warehousing	

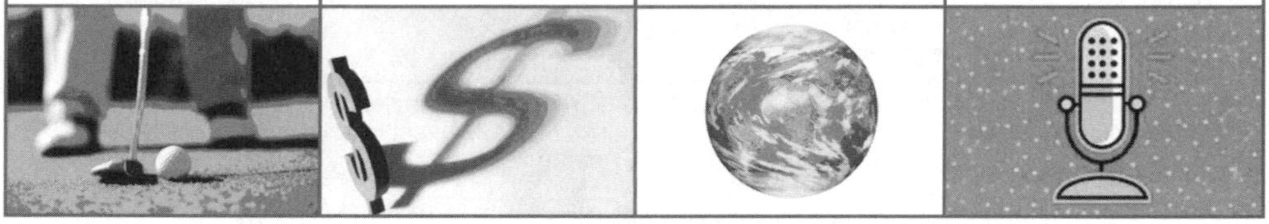

Figure 10.3: The 4 Ps of the Marketing Mix.

Distribution involves identifying distribution channels or intermediaries and determining the cost of distribution, the best distribution process for a specific product, and the distribution intensity. The distribution system is contingent on the type of product, the best interests of the sport company, the consumers, and other factors.

A *distribution system*, also called a *marketing channel*, includes the methods and channels used to deliver products from producer to consumer. An *intermediary* is an individual or organization through which products move from producer to consumer. Figure 10.3 illustrates some of the activities and elements of distribution as it relates to the marketing mix elements—the 4 Ps. Tasks in decision-making, such as determining channel types, transportation, and distribution intensity, are critical to developing successful distribution strategies and systems.

DISTRIBUTION DECISIONS

Distribution decisions in the sport industry depend on the type of product and consumer, among many other factors. In this section, you will learn about five different types of products in the sport industry and the kinds of distribution channels typically used for them. Those five product types are sports activities, sport goods, sport services, sports entertainment, and sport media. Table 10.1 provides several examples of different product types. It also provides information on distribution channel types that will be presented later in this chapter.

		Product	Distribution	Channel
Product Type	**Consumer Type**	**Examples**	**Type**	**Examples**
Sports Activities	End Consumers: Sports Participants	events & activities, such as leagues, tournaments, meets, races	Direct	Producer/Provider: Sports Complex or Organization
Sport Business Goods: 1. Sporting Goods 2. Business Goods 3. Promotional Goods	1. End Consumers, such as sports participants. 2. Business Consumers 3. End Consumers: fans, participants	1. Bowling ball, snow bike 2. Astroturf 3. Logo t-shirt; keychain	1. Complex 2. Direct 3. Complex	1. Sporting goods retailer 2. Direct sales: business-to-business 3. Retailers, vendors
Sports Business Services: 1. Sporting 2. Business	1. End Consumers: sports participants 2. Business Consumers: corporations	1. Racket stringing 2. Marketing research; sponsorship management	1. Direct 2. Direct	1. Producer—a person set up in a pro shop 2. Producer: business-to-business
Sports Entertainment: Spectator Sports	Two Types: 1. End Consumers: sports spectators 2. Business Consumers: corporations	WNBA, NASCAR, Olympics, X-Games, American Gladiators, PGA/LPGA, NFL	1. Complex 2. Direct	1. Ticket retailers and brokers 2. Direct sales
Media: 1. Sports Magazine 2. E-sports business 3. Industry Trade Magazine	1 and 2. End Consumers, readers of sports information 3. Business Consumers: retailers, producers, advertisers	1. Snow Boarding Magazine, Outdoors, Runner's World 2. CBS Sportsline 3. Sporting Goods Business, WinterSport Business, Sportstyle	1. Direct and Complex 2. Direct 3. Direct	1. Subscription; retail stores 2. Online 3. Subscription

Table 10.1. Examples of Distribution and Channel Types Based on Consumer and Product Types

TYPES OF PRODUCTS

There are two broad categories of products in the sport business industry: those products that must be manufactured and then moved from the factory to retail points for purchase by end consumers; and those that are produced in a place to which the consumer must travel and be present to consume. In the first category, products such as basketballs, tennis rackets, and motorcycles must be manufactured at a place of production, such as a factory, then moved from there to a location where the consumer will shop for that product, such as a retail store. In the second category are those products that must be staged or take place at a fixed facility or location. For example, the consumer will either watch a sports event at an arena, or participate in a sports activity such as hiking, skydiving, basketball, or working out. The following sections provide information about different types of products in the sport business industry.

Sports Activities: Participant Sport

Sports activities are participation products such as participation in basketball, bowling, scuba, hiking, sky diving, running, weight training, sailing, water skiing, golf, and snowboarding. The consumers of these products are people who want to participate in these activities for any number of reasons. Numerous sports, fitness, recreation, leisure, and sports tourism activities are offered to millions of different consumers today. Participant sport is one of the two largest segments of the sport business industry in the United States.

The activities are offered to the consumer in a number of ways, such as leagues, tournaments, championships, races, meets, regattas, outings, and adventure travel packages. All are offered at a fixed facility or a location. For instance, to participate in golf, the consumer has to travel to a golf course; to compete in a swim meet, the consumer must go to the swimming pool facility; and to go hiking in the Himalayas, the consumer has to travel to the mountain range. With these types of products, the facility or location is the "factory" for the product, and the consumer will manufacture the product at the same time as consuming it. This presents unique challenges for the sport business in relation to distribution. Distribution decisions must include such factors as geography, location, convenience, and quality of facility, among others.

Consumers of sports activities are end consumers, although there can be some business-to-business transactions surrounding the activity, such as sponsorship. The type of distribution for these products is direct: from producer to consumer. Examples of producers include city parks and recreation departments that offer basketball leagues; a privately owned sports complex that offers snow skiing; a sports organization that offers a roller hockey tournament; and a sports club that offers yachting tournaments, sailing races, or scuba outings.

Sporting Goods

Sporting goods are tangible goods such as sports equipment and apparel, artificial turf, facilities, and trophies. This type of product must be manufactured or produced in factories, shops, or plants and must be transported from the factory to a place where the consumer can purchase the good. Consumers include both end consumers and business consumers, depending on the product. As you can see in Table 10.1, some of these kinds of goods include sporting goods, business goods, and promotional goods.

The distribution system for these products will be either direct or complex, depending on the product type. Most sports equipment, for example, is manufactured in a factory and must be transported from that factory to where consumers can purchase the product. Snowboards are manufactured in a factory in Thailand. Snowboard consumers are in several countries, states and cities around the world. Therefore, the snowboards must be transported from Thailand to the many different places where the consumers can purchase them. Typically, snowboards are sold in sporting goods retail stores. The manufacturer must decide how to move the snowboards from the factory to the stores around the world. There are many marketing channel options available, such as transporting by truck, plane, or train. Usually, some combination is required. When more than one distribution channel is used, as with snowboards, the system will be complex rather than direct.

Sport Business Services

There are many different kinds of service products in the sport business industry. Some are offered to the end consumer and some are offered to the business consumer. They range from equipment repair, to golf cart cleaning, to pool maintenance, to sport marketing research, to athlete financial management. In fact, in a way, a sports facility offers service as a product—the facility is rented to different entities so that they can stage their events in the facility.

Many of those millions of sports participants are going to need their sports equipment cleaned, repaired, and/or maintained. This, of course, sustains a fairly large industry segment of services such as tennis racket stringing, golf club cleaning, pool maintenance, and equipment repair. For these products, which are primarily intangibles, the distribution is usually a direct exchange. For example, a tennis player with a racket in need of new strings and stringing takes the racket to a person who can perform this service.

Sports Entertainment

Professional sports exist as an entertainment product. Consumers watch professional sports events to be entertained in a number of ways. As has been presented in previous chapters, the "Factors that Affect Attendance" research shows several entertainment reasons people attend sports events (refer to Figure 9.5 in Chapter 9). Some sports events have been specifically created and produced as entertainment products for television. In the United States, the X-Games were created by ESPN.

Consumers of sports as an entertainment product include both end and business consumers. End consumers are those who are typically called "spectators." Spectators go to the event to watch the event and be entertained. Business consumers can be one of two types: those corporations that purchase the box seating (skyboxes or corporate luxury boxes) or those companies that purchase advertising, sponsorship, or other similar space at the event.

Sport Media

Some examples of sport media are sports television, sports magazines (print), Internet sports businesses, M-media (mobile devices), and industry trade magazines. The consumers of these media can be either end or business consumers. Consumers of sports magazines are end consumers—those who want to see and read about sports, fitness, and recreation activity.

Distribution of these products can be either complex or direct. Sports television is delivered directly through television channel providers, such as a cable or satellite TV provider. This is a direct transaction. Sports businesses on the Internet will carry out a direct transaction with the consumer via the Internet; however, delivery to the consumer involves a complex movement of the product.

THE DISTRIBUTION PROCESS

Figure 10.4 illustrates a simple process for developing the distribution system as based on information about the 4 Cs. Information will guide decisions and selection of each element of the distribution system. Management of the system is critical—each part of the distribution system should be monitored constantly to be sure it is effective and efficient. In fact, there are businesses that specialize in developing and analyzing distribution systems for companies. If the company is large enough, or in need of an analysis, management should seriously consider hiring a company that specializes in distribution systems to help. As shown in Figure 10.4, the first step is to determine what objectives the company wants to achieve with its distribution systems. This is important because distribution methods can then be selected that are best to help the company achieve its objectives.

Indirect distribution systems usually result in a higher final price for the consumer. Courtesy of Budgetstockphoto.com

DETERMINING THE TYPE OF DISTRIBUTION SYSTEM

A distribution system can range from direct (also called simple) to complex. A *direct distribution system* is one in which only the manufacturer and the consumer are involved directly, as depicted in Figures 10.5 and 10.6. In a direct system, the sport product moves from the manufacturer or producer directly to the consumer. There is no intermediary involved. A few examples include the following:

1. A sport sponsorship management company that sells services directly to a client.
2. A tennis pro who sells lessons directly to a student.
3. A sport facility construction company that sells directly to a college athletic department.
4. A city parks and recreation department that sells basketball leagues directly to teams.
5. A professional football championship game that sells directly to the spectator.

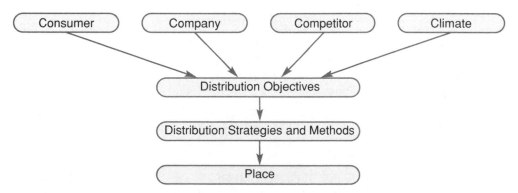

Figure 10.4. Process to Developing Effective Distribution.

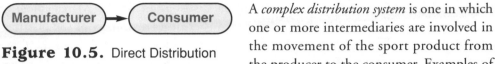

Figure 10.5. Direct Distribution System.

A *complex distribution system* is one in which one or more intermediaries are involved in the movement of the sport product from the producer to the consumer. Examples of routes of a complex system are illustrated in Figure 10.7. In one network, the product moves from the producer to an agent to a retailer and then to the consumer. In another network, the product moves from the producer to a distributor to a retailer and then to the consumer. In a third network, the product moves to a wholesaler and then to the consumer.

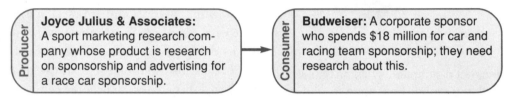

Figure 10.6. Example of a Direct Distribution System from Producer to Consumer.

In most instances in which intermediaries are involved, the final price of the product to the consumer is higher—hence, the popularity of a phenomenon called the "outlet store" or "factory-direct" store. No intermediaries are involved, which keeps the cost of moving the sport product very low. This results in a lower price for the final consumer and an increased profit margin for the manufacturer. When intermediaries are involved, the price of the product for the final consumer is driven up. For example, the manufacturer sells the sport product to a distributor who sells it to a retailer who sells it to the final consumer. Each entity involved must make a profit. Therefore, an aluminum softball bat that costs $3.75 to manufacture may be sold to the consumer for $39.95. Table 10.2 illustrates this process and what happens to the price of the product along the way to the consumer.

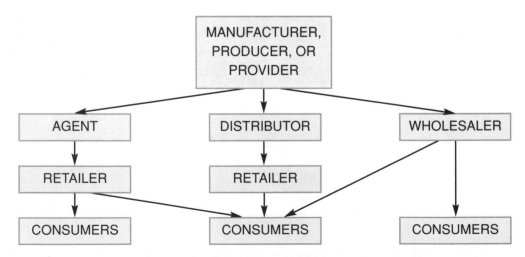

Figure 10.7. A Complex Distribution System in the Sport Industry.

Table 10.2. Example of a Sport Product's Increasing Cost as it Moves Through a Distribution System.	
Cost to Manufacture Bat	3.75
Packaging	1.25
Shipping Charges to Distributor	.50
Other Expenses Such as Advertising	3.50
Manufacturer's Total Cost	9.00
Manufacturer's Profit Margin	+3.50
Manufacturer's Price to Distributor	12.50
Shipping Charges to Retailer	.50
Other Expenses	.50
Distributor's Cost	13.50
Distributor's Profit Margin	+5.00
Distributor's Price to Retailer	18.50
Retailer's Expenses	2.00
Retailer's Profit Margin	+19.45
Retailer's Price to Consumer	$39.95

Although the costs of intermediaries drive up the final price of the product, many products would not be available to consumers if intermediaries did not exist. For example, it is not practical for a consumer who lives in Central City, Michigan, to travel to a running-shoe manufacturing plant in another country to purchase needed running shoes. Therefore, the manufacturer must move the product from the factory to Central City. To hold down cost, the manufacturer sells many products to retail stores in Central City. The running shoes are transported as part of a large shipment of goods to the stores in the city. To get the running shoes, the consumer simply shops at one of several sporting goods and shoes stores in the city.

THE DISTRIBUTION SYSTEM FOR HARD GOODS

The distribution system is comprised of distribution channels and intermediaries. A *distribution channel* is a route selected for a product to move from Point A to Point B. *Distribution intermediaries* are those individuals or organizations through which products are moved in the route from producer to consumer. The sport business management, as part of the overall marketing plan for a product, should have decided before a product is manufactured which intermediaries will be best for the company, the product, and the consumer. The determination of distribution intermediaries is a part of the development of a distribution plan.

Types of Distribution Intermediaries

There are a variety of distribution intermediaries available to the sport marketer. Some of these are listed and briefly described here:

Wholesaler. A wholesaler is a company that buys goods in large quantities specifically to resell to retailers or final consumers.

Retailer. A retailer is a company that buys goods to resell directly through their retail store to consumers.

E-tailer. An E-tailer is an Internet-based retail store.

Agent. An agent, usually a sales agent, is a person or a company who "moves" products (facilitates the sale) by taking orders from a buyer and placing the order with the producer.

Mail order company. This is a company that buys directly from a manufacturer or producer and offers the products through a catalog or electronic system.

Distributor. A distributor usually purchases products in order to sell them either to a wholesaler or a retailer.

Broker. A broker is an intermediary who serves as a go-between for the buyer and seller, usually working as an independent entity.

The distribution plan is called the *distribution system* (also sometimes called a distribution network, distribution channel, or marketing channel). The *distribution system* is the system developed for moving products from producer to consumer (Peter & Donnelly, 1993).

How does one construct a distribution system? There are many different systems because there are many types of companies, many types of products, and many different consumers with different needs. The distribution system selected must be one that is effective and efficient for the manufacturer or producer, the intermediaries, the product, the company, and the consumers. In addition, the company must give serious consideration to the environment. The management must not be fooled into thinking that the fastest or most economical method for moving products is also automatically environmentally friendly. A question a sport marketer or sport management executive will always face is one of ethics: If something is good for the company, is it okay for the environment, and is it ethical to proceed?

DEVELOPING THE DISTRIBUTION SYSTEM

At first glance, the task of selecting a distribution system might seem overwhelming because there are so many options. However, if the sport marketing professional first considers the factors that will affect the final selection, this will help guide the decision-making process.

An important element to remember is that the distribution system should be consumer driven. After all, it is the consumer who will purchase the product. Therefore, the product must be offered to the consumer when, where, and how the consumer wants it—time, place, and possession utility. One idea is to begin with the consumers of the product and trace the path from the consumer to the manufacturer.

Another important question to consider is which distribution options are available. Some sport marketers spend hours designing elaborate distribution systems only to discover that intermediaries do not exist or will not serve their needs.

Factors Affecting Selection

Some of the many factors that affect the development of a distribution system, or channel, are presented in Table 10.3. It is important that the sport marketing professional analyze each factor and understand how those factors are interrelated, and how the dis-

Table 10.3. Factors to Consider in the Selection of a Distribution System.	
The Consumer	Characteristics: number, geographical location Needs: purchase behavior, when needed, how needed, where needed Psychographic Characteristics: promotion
The Sport Company	Strengths: financial, location, availability of distribution options and weaknesses
The Sport Product	Type of Product: tangible, intangible, shelf life, packaging and shipping requirements
The Competitors	Characteristics: number, geographic location, distribution methods
The Climate	Legal: laws, regulations, policy Political: who is in office; what is "politically correct and incorrect" Economic: cost, inflation, and other economic factors Ethical: rights, issues, and other ethical considerations
Distribution Channels/ Intermediaries	Availability of Channels: what intermediaries exist and are available to you? Characteristics: types, location, cost, strengths and weaknesses, acceptance of product, ability to handle product
Distribution Intensity	Positioning the product
Adapted from Evans & Berman(1987), Boone & Kurtz (1992), Cravens & Woodruff (1986), and Peter & Donnelly (1993).	

tribution system considered fits with the overall marketing objectives. Within these factors are the components of the 4 Cs of marketing, and one of the 4 Ps. The factors are described in the following sections.

Consumer. Consumers want a product when, how, and where they need or desire it. This must be studied and understood by the sport company in order to know when, how, and where to distribute products.

Company. The position of the sport company will influence distribution. For example, the company might not be able to afford the higher-priced distribution channels or intermediaries and will have to select less expensive ones. The location of the company might be a barrier. If the company is in a city with no airport, distribution intermediaries will be limited to other forms of transportation.

Product. The type of product will influence how it is distributed. Shelf life, for example, is the amount of time a product can last before it loses quality. Of course, most of us know that fresh vegetables must be consumed before rotting, but what about sport products? What products have a long shelf life or a short shelf life? Here is an example of each. A Super Bowl game has a short shelf life; the game must be consumed at the moment it is produced. A basketball has a long shelf life; it can remain in a sporting goods store for a long time until consumed.

Products that are services require different distribution channels. A good is usually transported from producer to consumer through intermediaries. A service is usually sold directly to the consumer without the use of intermediaries.

Competition. Unless the sport company has the only product of its kind, the company has competitors. To stay in business, the company must take its competitors into consideration when making almost all business decisions. This information could help with ideas or could shed light on why the competitor always gets its product to the consumer first.

Climate. Laws, politics, the economy, ethical considerations, and environmental concerns will all have an influence on decisions about distribution. These should be constantly monitored so that the information gained can be used in determining distribution systems.

DISTRIBUTION BASED ON CATEGORIES OF PRODUCTS

Tangible products are physical objects. Most are manufactured in mass quantities at a factory and must be moved (distributed) to a place of purchase—retailer or wholesaler. For example, running shoes are manufactured in a factory and must be moved to a retailer to be sold.

Intangible products are not physical objects and include products such as services, places, and ideas. In addition, entertainment is included in this category. Most intangible products are not produced until ordered by the consumer. In a fitness center where laundry services are offered, the consumer must order the service, then simply leave dirty laundry in a bag in a certain spot. The center will perform the service and return the clean laundry to the locker area. Entertainment, however, is scheduled for a specific date, time, and place; the consumer must be available at that time and be able to go to the place where the event is offered. A basketball game, for example, can be offered as an entertainment product. The game will be scheduled at a specific date and time and in a sports facility. To consume the product, the consumer must travel to the facility and watch the game. In addition, the game is not produced, or manufactured, until the players play the game. Therefore, the consumer must be present when the game is played.

Another significant difference between the tangible running-shoe product and the intangible laundry service or basketball game is shelf life. The running-shoes and the laundry service have a long shelf life. The basketball game, however, has virtually no shelf life. The game cannot be manufactured and put on the shelf until a consumer purchases it. Instead, the game is simultaneously manufactured and

Tangible products have a longer shelf life, but the manufacturer must distribute them to accessible purchase locations, such as retailers. Courtesy of iStockphoto.com

consumed. If not immediately consumed, it perishes and that particular game will never be manufactured again. There is, however, a secondary product that the consumer may purchase to watch the game: videotapes/DVDs of that game.

Because of the perishable shelf life of spectator sports events, today's spectator sports marketers take great pains to increase what consumers receive for the amount of time and money spent at the game. Hence, most spectator sports events offer a variety of sideshows, concessions, services, souvenirs, and rewards in the form of door prizes or fourth-quarter drawings.

Regarding a different sport product, some providers of participation sports are offering the consumer more than participation for their money and time. To attract more runners, management personnel and marketers of many marathons and 10K runs offer much more than the race itself. Many offer the consumer T-shirts, concessions, pasta dinners, door prizes, rewards for every entrant and every person who crosses the finish line, childcare services, changing and shower services, medical care services, insurance, souvenirs, and photographs of the runner crossing the finish line. Some of these are included in the price of entry, and some are sold separately.

For some types of products in the sport industry, *how* and *when* the product is packaged and offered to the consumer are important parts of distribution. Almost all running events are held on Saturday mornings. Professional football games are held on Saturday, Sunday, or Monday evenings. Softball leagues are offered during the summer months and on weekday evenings. College women's and men's basketball games are played in evening slots. These are important elements of distribution called time, place, and possession utility. They are described in detail in the following section.

TIME, PLACE, AND POSSESSION UTILITY THROUGH DISTRIBUTION

Distribution offers time, place, and possession utility to the consumer. The product must be accessible to the consumer in the desired form, when it is needed. For example, a softball player needs to be able to purchase a softball bat before the season starts, usually in the summer; to buy the bat close to home; and to take possession of it when wanted.

Time utility is getting the product to the consumer when the consumer wants it. *Place utility* is getting the product to the consumer where the consumer wants it. *Possession utility* is creating possession of the product for the consumer. The distribution system is the channel through which the producer gets the product to the consumer when, where, and how the consumer wants it. For example, women's basketball fans want women's basketball at prime times (evenings, weekend evenings, prime-time slots such as seven or eight p.m.), in a great facility (in the same arena used by the men's team), and on a major broadcasting station (the major broadcasting networks, not the hard-to-find stations), and they want season tickets (giving them rights to specific seats for the entire season instead of "admission-at-the-door and no reserved seating"). Spectator sports marketers are listening, and more women's basketball is being offered in prime-time slots on major broadcasting stations, and pre-sold tickets and season tickets are being offered. This offers the product to the consumer when, where, and how the consumer wants it.

In another example, a manufacturer of sporting goods must distribute the goods to places where the consumer is most likely to purchase the goods. For example, Hillerich & Bradsby Co. (H & B), manufacturer of the famous Louisville Slugger baseball and softball bats, has a manufacturing plant in Louisville, Kentucky. Their bats, however, are sold around the world. Therefore, H & B must decide on the methods they will use to move the bats from the plant to places around the world where the consumer is most likely to purchase them. Those places are usually sporting goods retail stores and department stores with a sporting goods department. Some of the methods involved in moving the goods include moving them by truck, plane, ship, or train.

DISTRIBUTION INTENSITY

One of the elements of distribution on which the sport marketer must decide is the intensity of product distribution. *Distribution intensity* is the amount of distribution selected for a particular sport product. The degree of distribution intensity will affect sales of the product and is linked to positioning the product. Distribution intensity ranges from intensive to exclusive and is contingent on most of the same factors that affect the sport marketer's decisions on distribution channels. Table 10.4 illustrates the range of intensity.

The type of distribution intensity selected becomes part of the advertising message to the consumer primarily to let the consumer know where the product is available and to establish status quo for the product or company. An advertising message used to let the consumer know about the product's availability might be "widely available" or "available at all local sporting goods stores."

Table 10.4. Continuum of Distribution Intensity and Some Sport Product Examples.

	INTENSIVE	SELECTIVE	EXCLUSIVE
WHERE DISTRIBUTED:	everywhere possible	a few places	a few select places
EXAMPLES:			
Basketball Game	• TV and cable channels • radio taped for later broadcast • taped for sale - in-person	• in-person • only one TV channel • two radio stations	• in-person • only one TV channel
Softball Bats	• every sporting goods outlet possible • stores and department stores	• only half of all sporting goods stores	• only one select sporting goods store

Intensive Distribution. If the sport marketer chooses an intense distribution strategy, then the product will be offered in as many places as possible. In the examples given in Table 10.4, softball bats would be offered everywhere possible: all sporting goods stores, pro shops, department stores with sporting goods departments, and other outlets. A basketball game would be offered through as many outlets as possible: television channels, radio stations, in-person viewing, taped-for-later broadcast, and videotaped or captured digitally for later sale.

Selective Distribution. If the sport marketer chooses a selective distribution strategy, the product will be offered in a limited amount of places. The softball bats will be offered only in sporting goods stores. The basketball game will be offered through one local television station, one local radio station, and in-person viewing.

Exclusive Distribution. With exclusive distribution as a strategy, the sport marketer will offer the product in one or a small number of outlets. The softball bats will be offered in only one sporting goods store. The basketball game will be offered only through one television station or in-person viewing.

Another factor affecting the decision of distribution intensity is advertising dollars. In intensive distribution, much of the advertising effort is handled by the place of distribution. In exclusive distribution, much of the advertising effort lies with the producer, although the outlet selected can claim to be the exclusive outlet for the product.

Another factor to be considered is image. Exclusive distribution creates an image of prestige. The advertising message will sometimes include the words "available only at Samantha's Sporting Goods."

Exclusive distribution also allows for price increases. If your company is the only company with a product that has high demand, you can take advantage of the situation and assign higher prices than normal. For example, some television broadcasting companies pay for the rights to exclusively broadcast certain sports events. In this situation, the broadcasting company can increase the cost of advertising during the event. In some cases, the broadcast can go to a pay-per-view status in which consumers must pay specifically to view that particular event on television.

CHAPTER SUMMARY

A sport business must decide how to get its product to the consumer through a distribution system and strategies. The selection of a distribution system is affected by many factors, including the consumer, the company, the product, product positioning, the climate, and distribution systems available to the sport company. Distribution intensity will determine how extensively the product will be made available to the consumers. Different distribution channels work best for different types of products and different types of consumers. Each distribution channel has unique costs involved that should be given serious consideration in the selection process.

There are many different products in the sport business industry. Distribution decisions depend on the type of product, the consumer, the company, the climate, and the competitor, among other factors. The ultimate decision is to find the most appropriate way to get the product to the consumer, or the consumer to the product, when and how the consumer needs it, and in a way that meets the company's objectives.

DISCUSSION QUESTIONS

1. Describe the different kinds of distribution in the sport industry.
2. What are distribution intermediaries? Give some examples.
3. What are the factors that affect the selection of a distribution system?
4. What is distribution intensity? Why is it linked to promotion and positioning the product? Give some examples of each type.
5. What are some examples of different types of products found in the sport business industry? Develop what you think would be some appropriate distribution channels for these products.

SUGGESTED EXERCISES

1. List some sport products offered in your city or community. Create a distribution system for each. Research the real costs of the systems. Give a presentation in class.
2. For a tennis racket manufactured in Taiwan, develop a distribution system based on the fact that the tennis racket will be a high-priced, high-end product targeted to very serious amateur tennis players. Use as much real information as you can find to develop a full distribution plan.

11

Promotion in
the Sport Industry

INTRODUCTION

People will not buy a product if they do not know it exists. The purpose of promotion is to tell people about a product. From an academic standpoint, Irwin, Sutton, and McCarthy (2002) defined promotion as "the deployment of a fully integrated set of communication exchanges intended to persuade consumers toward a favorable belief or action as a tactical component of the overall marketing campaign" (p. 5).

Promotion is such an important marketing variable that companies have been formed for the sole purpose of selling promotional products. It is also critical for the service sector. According to Delpy (2000), "event organizers can no longer just open their gates and expect spectators to attend" (p. 8). Similarly, few clients will just drop by a sport business without prompting.

So many companies have been formed for the purpose of providing promotional support to sport organizations that "sport promotion" is considered an industry. There are marketing firms and sport marketing firms, advertising firms, agents who specialize in promoting sports people or teams, and companies that specialize in producing promotional products such as logo t-shirts, bags, cups, mugs, hats, towels, key chains, watches, jackets, flags, banners, trinkets, and drink coolers. Further, there is specialization within the promotion industry. One company, MultiAd Services (www.multiad.com) in Illinois specializes in the production of media guides, newsletters, scorecards, game programs, brochures/catalogs, and logo design.

If one needs inflatable displays, there are companies for that, too. For example, Inflatable Design Group (IDG) created a 25-foot inflated Spalding Basketball for a WNBA promotion (www.inflatabledesigngroup.com). Their other products have included customized inflatable entryways and many inflatable display structures with customized team logos that are used around the stadium for children. Another popular promotional product, especially for pro and college teams, is Fat Heads (www.fathead .com). These mural-sized graphics are used for commercial and in-home display.

There are companies that specialize in managing the logos, licensing, and merchandising for sport properties. For example, the Collegiate Licensing Company is a division of IMG Worldwide and represents a prestigious base of universities, bowls, and athletic conferences (www.clc.com). One of their services is to help their clients develop a base of licensees and retail outlets in order to successfully market licensed products. Their efforts are intended to target consumers of collegiate products and facilitate their purchase of licensed products. They also assist the marketing directors of their member institutions with establishing goals and a marketing strategy.

As in other industries, promotion is a very important communication tool in the sport industry. Again, people will not buy a product if they do not know it exists. In the sport industry, promotional communication is used to inform, educate, remind, and persuade.

PROMOTION AND SPORT PROMOTION DEFINED

The word *promotion* brings many concepts to mind—some good, some bad. Promotion is the function of informing, persuading, and influencing the consumer's purchase decision. Promotions include all corporate activities aimed at influencing consumers' purchasing attitudes and behaviors. (However, to some, promotions have come to mean some shady practice by which misrepresentation and inaccuracy are used to sway the public into unwanted or unnecessary purchases.) From a sport marketing perspective, promotion as applied to the sport industry is defined as the function of informing or influencing people about the sport company's products, community involvement, or image. In this definition, the many segments of people to whom the sport company promotes are a significant factor when developing promotion strategies. The sport company promotes to the end consumer, the business consumer, the general community, the business community, and the media.

According to Ries and Trout (1986), consumers screen and reject a considerable amount of the product and marketing information delivered via traditional communication sources. Thus, consumers may not be conscious of wants until their wants are stimulated by the sport marketer through an array of well-selected and designed promotional activities. Creating new concepts and ideas about consumer desires as well as products or services to fulfill them is difficult; therefore, sports marketers must be proficient in their promotional strategy to move the consumer to purchase.

One innovative idea was set in motion at the opening of the 57th St. Niketown store in New York City. The store utilized virtual reality, sport memorabilia, and computerization to showcase Nike technology. Shoe sizing was not performed with the standard Brannock device. Instead, customers just put a foot on the NGAGE digital sizing system, and the computer prepared a 3D image of the foot. Although the true benefit of this new system is unproven, it was an effective promotion and convinced many consumers that Nike was on the cutting edge of technology.

Promotions are an integral part of all communication efforts. Irwin et. al. (2002) noted that "communication is the foundation of all buying behavior" (p. 22). One of the objectives of promotion is the acquisition and retention of public acceptance of an idea, product, or service. This can be accomplished through effective communication with consumers.

The general literature on communication theory suggests that there are four essential ingredients in promotional communication: the sender, the message, the medium, and the receiver. For messages to convey clear and succinct meanings, the sender must accurately create the message and put it in an appropriate media form. When the receivers encounter a message, it must be decoded and interpreted. Interpretation of the message is influenced by the receiver's emotional status, perceptions of the sender, and cultural disposition, among other factors. The people to whom the sport company will communicate are existing and potential consumers. In addition, the sport company communicates to the general community, the business community, and the media. As a result, sport marketers use promotional communications to influence or change the attitudes, opinions, and behaviors of consumers in the sport industry.

For example, many sport companies want the general community to know that they care about the community. One way that this is accomplished is through the financial support of local children's recreation leagues. Companies often select a billboard in the community to disseminate the message. Companies may choose to have a message emblazoned on the billboard such as "We care. We are the proud supporter of the Central Children's Sports Leagues. Southland Sporting Goods—where your family shops for all your sporting needs." Companies may use more than one method to reach the audience. They may choose to post signs around the children's ballpark, send flyers through direct mail to everyone in the community, and hold a special sale in recognition of their involvement in the children's leagues. Each company must decide which methods will be most effective in gaining the attention of its audience and imparting the message.

RATIONALE FOR PROMOTION

There are other reasons for promotion because there are a variety of different messages a sport company wants to communicate to the people about its product or company. Effective promotions can facilitate a variety of marketing functions.

Promotion establishes an image. The sport marketer has a reason for being in business and a mission for the company. The company was designed based on a specific market segment. Therefore, the sport marketer wants to communicate a specific image to the consumer and the community. According to Ries and Trout (1986), a company's image is the sum of beliefs, ideas, and impressions held by consumers about the company and its products. The image may be luxury, prestige, convenience, cost savings, one-stop shopping, or creativity. The message of the promotion will communicate the company's image.

For example, if the company is a marina whose primary objective is to service and house large, expensive yachts, the promotional mix and message should communicate luxury and prestige. The marina's name might be "Class One Yacht Club." The communication through promotional methods such as advertising might be a slogan like "Your home is our home at Class One Yacht Club" or "Yachting is your luxury and your luxury is our business." Through the name of the company and the communication message in the slogan, the consumer is told that this marina is for the upper-class consumer who owns a yacht and that this company will take care of consumers in the fashion to which they are accustomed.

Promotion can reposition the image of a faltering product. For example, personal watercraft (PWCs), more commonly known as jet skis, began to develop a poor reputation because of the loud noise level of the engine, the recklessness of the drivers, the increase in accidents, and the increase in numbers invading previously quiet water areas without PWCs. The Personal Watercraft Industries Association (PWIA) and several PWC manufacturers have rallied to create a variety of promotional methods they hope will facilitate control of the reputation and turn it around. Their activities are directed at the end consumer, manufacturers, PWC rental businesses, and state and local water-governance organizations. Some of their activities include educational programs on safety (posters, videocassettes, brochures), research to decrease the noise produced by the PWC, rescue and education loan programs in which manufacturers lend PWCs to area Coast Guard offices or rescue units for their use and lend PWCs to lake and beach lifeguard stations for rescue operations. The cooperative promotional effort was successful in improving the reputation of the PWC and positively affected sales.

Promotion creates awareness for new products. As stated earlier, if people do not know your product exists, they will not buy it. If the sport company is planning to release a new product, no one will know unless the company implements an appropriate approach. Various sport companies orchestrate product launches using celebrity endorsers and press conferences. Many times, these promotional activities are coordinated through sport trade shows. An array of methods is integrated to publicize the offering.

Promotion alerts consumers to sales of which they would otherwise be unaware. The sport marketer must identify promotional methods and design a communication message that will tell consumers about the sale: dates, times, type of sale, purpose of sale, and any other information consumers might need. If the company is a sporting goods retail store and there will be a Thanksgiving sale, a promotion must be created to tell consumers about the sale. Another important factor is the decision about when and where to promote. For example, the Thanksgiving sale will be the Friday, Saturday, and Sunday after Thanksgiving. Perhaps the best promotion is an advertisement in the local newspaper, and the best time to run the ad is in the Sunday paper before Thanksgiving.

Promotion tells the consumer where a business is located, whether this is the physical site or the website.. Although this sounds like a simple message, it is very important. If the information is provided, the consumer does not have to spend extra time trying to find the business. This communication is usually handled within the promotion as a map depicting the location or as directions to the business. Sometimes a business will refer to a well-known landmark as a locater. For example, a well-known landmark in the city of Louisville, Kentucky, is the Water Tower—a historic city waterworks facility situated on the Ohio River. Businesses in the area use the Water Tower as a locater. A boat retailer's advertisements include the words "next to the Water Tower." A restaurant uses the same words. An indoor soccer facility uses the wording "located close to the Water Tower." The purpose of the message in the promotion is to establish the location of the business. For web-based companies, clearly presenting the Internet address serves the same purpose.

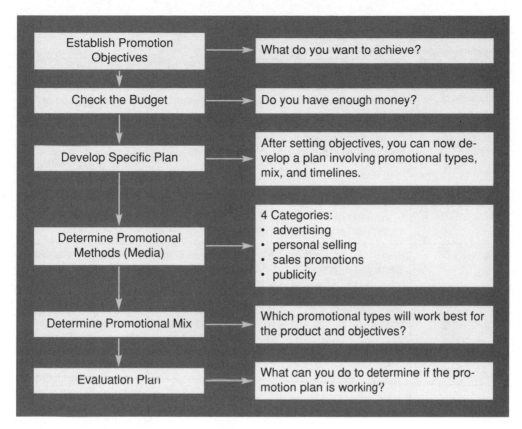

Figure 11.1. Promotional Planning Model.

PROMOTION PLANNING

Figure 11.1 illustrates the steps of promotion planning. Promotion planning is the process of developing all aspects of the company's communication effort. Many factors should be considered that will affect decisions concerning the promotion elements of the company's marketing mix. Some of these factors are the consumer, the competitor, money and other resources, product life cycle, and mission and objectives of the sport company. The following sections discuss the steps in the promotion planning process.

Set Promotion Objectives

In the promotion planning process, the first step is to establish promotion objectives. The establishment of promotion objectives is based on this question: What does your company want to achieve through promotion? The promotion objectives should emerge from the marketing objectives, which should emanate from the company objectives.

Promotion objectives are statements that specify exact results desired by the company. They are based on what the company wants to accomplish. The objectives are usually demand-oriented, education-oriented, or image-oriented; the overall objective is

Table 11.1. Sport Promotion Objective Types			
TYPES OF OBJECTIVES:	**DEMAND**	**EDUCATION**	**IMAGE**
PURPOSE	To affect behavior	To affect knowledge	To affect attitude or perception
OUTCOME DESIRED	Consumer purchases the company's product	To educate or inform the consumer about the company or its products	Consumer thinks of company in specific terms: good, positive, brilliant, creative, fun, serious, etc.
MESSAGE	• persuasive • demand oriented	• informative • reminder	• informative • persuasive
EXAMPLE	A sport shoe manufacturer uses a famous male basketball player to persuade the consumer to buy its shoes.	A new sport marketing firm is opening. It places an ad in a local business paper that tells story of company, what it does, its products and services, where it is located, and its hours of business.	A women's professional golf association uses TV and billboard ads to tell about its disadvantaged-youth golf-with-the-pros day held once a year. The association and the players pay for the youth to spend a day with the players golfing and participating in other events.

to affect behavior, knowledge, or attitude. Each promotional action selected must be based on the objectives of the promotion. Therefore, a sport company should select the specific type of promotion, or form of communication, based on carefully crafted objectives. Table 11.1 illustrates these objective types, purpose, outcome desired, message, and an example of each.

If the sport company wants to affect consumer behavior, demand-oriented objectives will be established. The behavior that the company wants to affect is purchase behavior. The company wants to persuade the consumer to purchase its products. With this as an objective, the company must design a promotional method and message that persuade the consumer to buy.

If the company wants to educate or inform the consumer about something, education-oriented objectives are developed. Usually, the company wants to educate the consumer about a characteristic of the company, its products, services, or other information. Typical information includes the location of the company, information on sales taking place and the company's offerings, or details about the company's products.

If the sport company wants to affect attitude or perception, it will develop image-oriented objectives. The company wants to assist consumers' formation of positive attitudes toward the company and its products. Marketers must strive to ensure a consistent image across all promotions.

Review the Budget and Other Resources

During the process of developing the objectives, it would be very wise for the sport marketer to know how much money is available for promotion and whether the company has other necessary resources available. This information will certainly have an impact on decisions made for promotional planning. Some promotional methods are expensive whereas others are inexpensive, and still others are free. Television advertising can be very expensive. On the other hand, staging an open house is relatively inexpensive. Realistically, the sport marketer must determine if there is enough money and other resources to pay for and follow through with the promotional methods selected. The sport marketer must also determine what promotional methods are available that are most effective for the objectives set within available resources.

The primary components of promotion in the sport industry include advertising, publicity and public relations, personal selling, and sales promotion. These components exist in conjunction with each other and can be used by the marketer separately or together to accomplish marketing and sales objectives.

After checking the budget and other resources needed for the promotional methods selected, the sport marketer must develop a detailed plan of action that involves selecting the most appropriate and effective promotional types, determining a promotional mix, and developing an evaluation plan.

Utilize Promotional Methods

As noted above, there are four general categories of promotional methods: advertising, publicity, personal selling, and sales promotions. Table 11.2 illustrates the four categories and specific promotional methods available for the sport marketer in each category. *Advertising.* Advertising can be defined as a message that informs and persuades consumers through paid media. We are all aware of effective and ineffective advertising. Think for a minute about ads that you have seen and enjoyed, but from which you

Table 11.2. Four Categories of Promotion Methods and Some Examples.

ADVERTISING	PERSONAL SELLING	SALES PROMOTIONS	PUBLICITY
• newspaper ad • magazine ad • television • radio ad • direct mail • billboard ad • ads on buses, grocery carts, walls, etc. • sponsorship • merchandising • the logo	• sales force • public speaking	• telemarketing • price • point of purchase display • newsletter • giveaways • target market specials • sponsorship • special events • open house day dinner, parties, etc. • exhibitions • merchandising	• press conference • press release • articles in local or other newspaper • coverage on TV or radio

cannot remember the product; in contrast, other ads immediately bring a specific product to mind. All advertising firms plan for success, but it is not always achieved. Consider the short-lived 1980s Reebok campaign "U.B.U." in contrast to Nike's long-running "Just Do It" advertising.

Advertising is a controlled medium. That is, the message delivered to the consumer is carefully crafted and controlled by the organization so that its content consists only of information that the organization wishes the consumer to receive. However, because the company controls advertising, its credibility with consumers may be low.

In sport, advertising can take many forms. There is advertising of sport products and services and advertising through sports events. The advertising of sports products and services is a multimillion-dollar industry. Advertising through sport is also a sizable segment of the industry. According to the International Events Group, as much as $18 billion of the total amount spent per year on all advertising is spent on sport-related advertising and sponsorship (Ukman, 2011).

A new form of sport advertising has developed around sport video games. If television advertising developed because people were spending hours watching TV, then consider that the average video game player spends 60 hours playing each game he/she purchases. Game developer EA Sports has been a leader in this integrated technology.

A primary motive for advertising in sport is that sports present a wholesome image and a wide demographic profile from which specific segments can be targeted. Advertising through sport events can also take the form of a sponsorship, as will be detailed in Chapter 13. Research on sponsorship through stadium advertising has shown that it is an effective media purchase, producing an effective return on investment (ROI; Ukman, 2004).

A popular advertising-related promotional activity conducted by many sport organizations is the trade-out, also known in the industry as VIK (value-in-kind). This process is seen most often when a sport organization gives something of value (complimentary seats, stadium advertising space, program ads) to the sponsor in exchange for products needed by the organization. With media sponsorships, the exchange is typically for advertising space or airtime that can be used by the sport organization for promotional activities.

Media trade-out programs within the university segment seek to do two things: increase the attendance at athletic events and increase overall support of the school's programs. Radio seems to be a viable choice as one of the media forms selected for trade-out campaigns. Many sport organizations trade out radio time for tickets at a cash-value ratio of about 4 to 1 favoring the organization (Spoelstra, 1997). Using coveted football or basketball tickets as barter, some universities have negotiated deals with major TV markets. Newspaper and billboard space can also be included in this strategy. This area presents a variety of issues. Many media sources always quote "full rate card" prices in the negotiations (this is similar to a "suggested retail price," which is rarely paid by consumers). On the other hand, the sport organizations occasionally inflate the prices printed on tickets that are included in trade-out and sponsor packages.

Some universities use TV and radio networks to blanket their region, as well as critical consumer areas in adjoining regions. During the summer and early fall, tapes can be made by players and coaches discussing their upcoming season. In this setting, all activities must be in compliance with collegiate rules. These plans have been particularly successful in encouraging advertisers who have rejected more traditional appeals for direct advertising. Additional coverage of this topic (specifically, dealing with leveraged media sponsorships) is in Chapter 14, Using Licenses and Logos in the Sport Industry.

Publicity. Publicity, although not identical to advertising, is often considered in discussion of the topic.

Irwin et. al. (2002) indicate that publicity differs from advertising in that, although it also informs and affects consumer attitudes, it is free. This includes the promotion or communication that comes from being mentioned in a magazine or being the subject of an article in the local newspaper. It has several benefits over advertising. First, because the information comes from a third party, it is seen as more credible and trustworthy. Second, it may also be consumed more readily by consumers who may avoid direct advertising. The disadvantage of publicity is that the company usually has no control over the content. This means that if the local paper wants to publish an article about a company, the reporter can write almost anything. Additional coverage of this topic is found in Chapter 12, Media Relations in Sport.

Sport marketers must realize that publicity alone will not sell tickets, raise funds, win supporters, retain members, or sell merchandise. Nevertheless, publicity can be helpful in conveying ideas to people so that these ends can be more easily achieved. Publicity efforts should be planned with these guidelines in mind:

1. Too much publicity can be poor public relations, because often at a certain point, people tend to react negatively to excessive publicity.
2. The amount of publicity absorbed is important, not the amount printed.
3. The amount of publicity disseminated does not necessarily equal the amount that appears in the media.
4. The nature of the publicity eventually tends to reveal the character of the institution or department it seeks to promote, for better or worse.
5. Some publicity received by an institution or department originates from outside sources.
6. Not all promotional activities result in publicity.

A successful publicity program depends on the development of an effective plan. This plan should incorporate the following elements:

1. identification of publicity needs;
2. recognition of appropriate media sources;
3. development of goals for each source;

4. creation of a specific methodology for targeted sources;

5. implementation through selected promotional materials; and

6. assessment of publicity outcomes.

Personal selling. Personal selling is defined as an oral presentation with potential customers for the express purpose of making a sale. Irwin et. al. (2002) expand the concept of personal selling with the term Person Contact to "convey the breath of promotionally oriented personal interaction that transpires within the sport industry" (p. 8).

Commitment to personal selling and personal interaction is key to effective promotions. There is an understanding among those in sales that communicating how a product or service can benefit the consumer is paramount. Central to this approach is the belief that without the salesperson, consumers would not be capable of realizing the benefits of consumption and that personal selling is therefore the most important aspect of the promotional mix. While not everyone in personal selling adheres to that philosophy, many do. The role of a salesperson is to provide the link between the organization and consumers, so that consumers' lives may be enhanced by the product or service to which they were introduced.

Personal selling is direct promotion between the seller and a potential consumer. The initial stage of personal selling has been termed the *approach phase*, "creating a favorable impression and building rapport with potential clients," and sets the stage for all subsequent interaction between the salesperson and the prospective customer (Pride & Ferrell, 2010, p. 444). Several authors (Miller, Shaad, Burch, & Turner, 1999; Pride & Ferrell, 2010) have noted the importance of establishing a relationship with the consumers before activating sales-related dialog. Personal selling includes selling face-to-face as well as via the telephone, videoconferences, and interactive computer links (Miller et. al., 1999).

In addition, considerable selling is done through television. Consider those television channels dedicated to bringing hundreds of thousands of products into consumers' homes. Professional salespeople host these, and a simple phone call to the company completes the purchase of any product offered on the show. Personal selling is a major element in the sport industry. There are salespeople in sporting goods stores, salespeople at sports apparel manufacturing companies who sell their products to retailers, promoters whose job is to sell a sport event to television and sponsors, telemarketers whose job is to sell tickets for the team, and salespeople whose job is to sell advertising space in the Super Bowl program. In the sport industry, an individual who is not trained as a salesperson can also act as one. For example, in men's college basketball, the players and coaches become salespeople for the program. They are scheduled to speak at local banquets and other activities. The coach usually has a local show aired once a week and the coach usually is hired by local businesses as a "pitch person" in advertisements for their products.

Success in personal selling depends heavily on locating potential consumers (Miller et al., 1999; Pride & Ferrell, 2010). In general, if salespeople can master one skill in selling, it should be the skill of prospecting. Two questions arise: "What exactly is a prospect?" and "What exactly is prospecting?" Irwin et. al. (2002) define a prospect as "a targeted individual or group with the potential (interest, need or want, and time/money resources) to purchase or utilize your products or services" (p. 108). Prospecting involves building a viable portfolio of potential clients and customers that positions the salesperson for work. Just as many executives go to the office, the person in sales consults the prospects' database. The question arises, just how does one go about creating a client base with potential customers? For the sport marketer, this often leads to the marketing information system discussed in Chapter 7, The Marketing Mix and the Sporting Industry. Also remember the traditional 80-20 business adage, according to which 80% of sales usually result from 20% of customers.

A substantial amount of interaction with consumers occurs through the Internet. For 2009, total Internet retail sales were estimated at $210 billion (Winters, Davie, & Weidenhamer, 2011). The Internet serves as an effective communication tool for interacting directly with consumers. Although a bit atypical from personal selling in that the consumers search for the company, rather than vice versa, the promotional methods most closely resemble personal selling. Yet, as with other advertising, the consumer must be able to find the company and products. One study indicated that 43% of customers came from search engine marketing ("Search Engine," 2011). In order to get the best results, most retailers actually pay the owners of the search engines (i.e. Google) on a performance basis to direct traffic to their company's website. Some have argued that websites are simply advertising offered through an alternative media; however, because customers can almost always engage immediately in purchasing products or services, this characterization does not fit.

Clearly, the Internet is a useful part of today's marketing and communication mix. For most sport retailers, the Internet provides excellent opportunities to promote services, sell merchandise, and communicate with existing members. In particular, the Internet is effective in publicizing up-to-date information, sales or special events. Sport organizations are also using websites for promotional activities. The Snow Industries Association, the Outdoor Recreation Coalition of America, and the Sporting Goods Manufacturers Association are among the organizations that use the Internet to gain name recognition and explain organizational services. Almost all of the professional sports teams use their websites to communicate with fan clubs (as discussed in Chapter 6, Marketing Information Systems). Through this medium, they typically offer special deals to club members and occasionally run trivia contests and other interactive activities. Fan clubs are particularly helpful in activating many of the promotions identified in this chapter.

Ski resorts also use the Internet extensively for promotional activities. This method seems to be particularly effective in this industry. Because snow conditions change quite literally overnight, resorts are quick to promote fresh snow and great skiing conditions via the Internet. In market research from Vail (Colorado), marketers found that 40% of their customers preferred the Internet as a source for gathering information about the resort (www.vail.com).

The Internet offers other promotional advantages over advertising. The mere fact that it is the consumer who seeks the information is powerful. Research has indicated that 60% of upscale, highly educated consumers (exactly those using the Internet) trust advertising a credible source for product information ("Search Engine," 2011). The objective is almost always to develop meaningful relationships with customers that increase overall company sales.

Sales promotion. The term "sales promotion" has been characterized as a general term to describe all communication instruments that do not fit into advertising, personal selling or publicity categories. Sales promotions are typically activities of short duration that are intended to move consumers to an immediate exchange. Sales promotions often consist of those promotional activities other than advertising, publicity, or personal selling; they are designed to affect consumer attitude or behavior. Some sales promotions include telemarketing, price promotions, point-of-purchase displays, newsletters, giveaways, sponsorships, merchandising, and special events. In the sport industry, several examples exist that can be categorized as sales promotions. Point-of-purchase displays are particularly effective. In retail sporting goods stores, displays of products are often used to tie the product with previous advertising. The phrase "as seen on TV" should be familiar to most sports consumers. Point-of-purchase displays can also initiate recall of sponsorship. A cardboard cutout of Olympic champion Lindsey Vonn in front of the ski section could stimulate the consumer's memory of her 2010 Gold medal and move the consumer to purchase the racket that sponsors her tournament play.

Many sales promotions in sport center on selling season tickets. Most professional sport teams develop DVDs for season ticket holders as part of the annual renewal campaign. In the past, they only sent a nicely worded letter and invoices to season ticket holders asking for renewal. The dynamic nature of sport and video is a great way to get the customer excited about the upcoming season.

Trade shows have also been effective sales promotions for sporting goods companies. The Sporting Goods Manufacturers Association has conducted a nationwide trade show for many years with the express intent of motivating large-scale retail chains to order merchandise "hot off the line." The International Health and Racquet Sportsclubs Association (IHRSA) has organized and run trade shows in the fitness industry for over 30 years with great success (www.ihrsa.org/trade-show). In 2010, the IHRSA trade shows hosted over 9,000 visitors and 700 industry suppliers. It enabled the suppliers to meet face-to-face with their customers in a relaxed and festive environment. Many club managers place orders directly at these shows because they are able to compare equipment from different companies firsthand and, based upon what they see, initiate the purchase. This type of activity is crucial to marketing success.

Discount coupons have been a popular promotion for many years. In 2008 the website Groupon (www.groupon.com) started localized intent-based couponing on an opt-in basis. This advertising support website sends daily deals to subscribers and has been very effective in driving both retail and Internet sales. Coupons are also available through corporate websites, providing an alternative to the traditional direct mail coupons. Coupon popularity has been attributed to four factors: a) the monetary (or discount) effect; b) the advertising effect—the coupons provide the consumer with product information; c) a reminding effect—they enhance awareness through repeated exposure to the coupon); and d) a utility effect—satisfaction is gained through the redemption process.

Sport organizations can also enhance the sales promotions of non-sport businesses through incentives. Situations in which purchasers receive free tickets to a sporting event with the purchase of a particular item may move them to purchase the item. Store appearances of a sport celebrity at point of purchase can also stimulate immediate sales.

Although sales promotions have been referred to as a "catch-all" category, they strike at the heart of marketing, prompting the exchange. Sales promotions must be incorporated with other elements in the promotional mix.

Determine the Promotional Mix

After establishing the promotion objectives, developing the budget, and considering promotional methods that will work best for the company, product, and consumer, the sport marketer must determine the promotional mix. The promotional mix is the combination of promotional methods that will help the sport company meet its objectives in the most effective way. It is rare that a sport company will use only one method—for example, a college athletic program uses only direct mail, a sport marketing company uses only journal advertising, a sporting goods retailer uses only newspaper advertising,

It is usually a good idea to diversify promotional methods in order to reach the widest audience. Courtesy of BigStockPhoto.com

or the Special Olympics uses only merchandising. It is more typical and much more effective for the company to use a mixture of these methods.

The decisions about which methods to use are contingent on many factors. Figure 11.2 illustrates many of the factors that affect the decision on promotional mix. Each of these is discussed briefly here.

Each promotional method serves a different function. Advertising on television can reach a large number of consumers, but it is expensive. Publicity can reach a large number of consumers but cannot be controlled by the company. Personal selling is effective if the salesperson is knowledgeable and influential, but it serves a very small number of consumers. Sales promotions are effective in different ways, depending on the type; each one attracts a different category and number of consumers.

The stage of product life cycle will affect decisions concerning the promotional mix (Stotlar, 2009). During the introductory stage, the company should aggressively promote the product. This means that the promotion budget will need to be extensive. During the growth stage, sales will increase. This means that revenue will increase. Promotional methods and aggressiveness will change, and money put into promotion will typically decrease. In the maturity stage, the pace of sales may slow and will eventually plateau. During this stage, however, the product is established and promotional objectives and methods change. If a product is approaching the decline stage, promotional objectives and methods must change to avoid disaster. If the product is allowed to continue in this direction, eventually all sales will cease. Typically, promotional objectives and methods become more aggressive and sometimes the product is repositioned and treated like a new product.

1	A different function for each method
2	The company
3	Stage of product life cycle
4	Access to promotional methods
5	Channels of distribution
6	Target markets
7	The competition
8	Geographic dispersement of the consumer market
9	The product
10	Push or pull strategy
11	Laws
12	Sport company resources

Figure 11.2. Factors Affecting Decision on Promotional Mix.

Channels of distribution will impact decisions on the promotional methods used (Irwin et. al., 2002). Managers of specific channels may have requirements that the sport company cannot or will not support. Based on their marketing experiences, many marketing managers often favor specific channels of distribution.

For example, stadium signage—a form of billboard advertising—has been found to be an effective promotional method for many companies (Stotlar, 2009). Although many of the companies using stadium signage are not sport companies, some are. Footwear companies who sponsor teams are very likely to include signage in their packages. Stadium signage's predecessor is the outdoor billboard. However, whereas a billboard has space and location limitations, and captures the attention of the consumer for only a few seconds as the consumer drives by, a sign in a stadium is in front of the consumer for as long as the event lasts, which can range from 1 to 5 hours. That amounts to a lot of impression time.

During an event such as the MLB All-Star Game, which lasts approximately 3 hours, signage and logos can make a significant impact on impression time. Spectators attending the event are surrounded by the signage, and consumers watching the event on television will also be impacted with the advertising. As the camera captures and focuses on players and the stadium, television viewers will see the advertising. In 2010, the familiar Nike "Swoosh" was the most-seen logo of the 18 apparel brands monitored during the Home Run Derby and MLB All-Star Game broadcasts, amassing nearly $2.3 million of comparable television exposure value when considering such factors as size and placement of the image on screen, as well as brand clutter and integration of the brand into the activity. Nike garnered a total of 13 minutes, 12 seconds (13:12) of on-screen time during the All-Star Game broadcast on Fox and 14 minutes, 4 seconds (14:04) during ESPN's coverage of the Home Run Derby (Joyce Julius, 2010).

The sport company's target markets will influence promotional methods. The promotional methods will need to be effective for each target market identified by the sport company. Target market factors to consider include geographic location and size as well as the associated demographic and psychographic characteristics. Some promotional method factors to consider are listed below in the form of questions:

1. Which method will catch the attention of the market? Only sport marketing consumer research can answer this question. A true understanding of the consumer will guide the sport marketer to decisions concerning the method to which the consumer will positively react.
2. What kind of message will attract the consumer, and will the consumer be able to understand it? Again, consumer research will guide the sport marketer to the answer. The sport marketer should develop the promotional message so that the consumer can relate to it and understand it. In other words, the sport marketer should consider writing the advertising message in the consumer's language.
3. Can the promotional method reach the intended target market? If a sport magazine is being considered as an advertising medium, does the target market subscribe to the magazine? For example, the Gay Games uses promotional methods that reach its specific target market: the lesbian and gay population around the world. Some of these methods are direct mail using postal mail and email lists of prior Gay Games participants and from lesbian and gay magazines and websites.

Competitors will affect the promotional method selected for the sport company. Although the promotional methods must be selected and designed for the consumer, equal attention must be given to competitors. Promotional methods selected can impact sport marketing strategies with increased market share and the outmaneuvering of a competitor in a specific area such as price, market penetration, and advertising message.

Geographic dispersal of the consumer market will affect the promotional methods selected. Personal selling may be best for localized markets. However, as the location of the sport company's consumers spreads geographically, the company will have to consider promotional methods that will reach the new consumers.

The product and its elements will also affect the promotional methods selected. The type of product and the characteristics and elements of the product will impact the method and message of promotion. Some of the characteristics include product type (good, service, person, place, idea), customized versus standardized, differentiation, quality, features, performance, design, and product life-cycle stage.

The decision to use a push or a pull promotion strategy will affect the promotional method used (Pride & Ferrell, 2010). The objective of both strategies is to get the product into the consumer's hands. A *push strategy* involves trying to move the product into the channels of distribution and encouraging sellers to increase sales volumes. The strategy usually involves offering a variety of awards and enticements to the channelers. Many sporting goods manufacturers use this strategy. A company will offer incentives or price breaks to a wholesaler or retailer that increases its sales volume. A *pull strategy* involves strong promotion directed toward the end consumer in order to affect the consumer's demand for the product. The consumer's demand for the product acts to "pull" the product through the channels. The sport company's promotional methods are designed to target the consumer and create demand. The consumer in turn asks for the product. For example, if a sporting goods retailer does not carry a specific product, a motivated consumer may ask that retailer to carry the product.

Local, state, and federal government agencies and consumer protection agencies have enacted laws, guidelines, and restrictions that will affect a sport company's promotional efforts. Some of these include the Federal Trade Commission, the Food and Drug Administration, the Securities and Exchange Commission, the United States Patent Office, and the Department of Justice. Other organizations and groups also work to control promotions. Some of these are the National Association of Broadcasters and the Better Business Bureau. Further, individual companies exercise ethical decision making in selecting and developing promotional methods.

Sport company resources will impact the promotional methods decision. There are two types of resources within a sport company—material and nonmaterial. Material resources include money, supplies, equipment, and the like. Nonmaterial resources include human resources. Does the sport company have the resources necessary to accomplish the promotional methods it is considering? The critical bottom line may be the ultimate factor affecting the company's decision concerning promotional methods.

As you can see, the sport marketer must consider and analyze many factors in the process of selecting the promotional methods and activities for the company.

Create Promotional Activities

Based on the marketing mix, business enterprises create special activities to promote their programs, products, or purposes. Stotlar (2009) indicated that promotions, as marketing tools, provide activities and incentives directly to consumers. One of the most notable names in sport promotion is Veeck. Bill Veeck Jr., one of baseball's most famous (and outrageous) promoters, is perhaps best known for sending a dwarf to bat

Well-executed promotional activities can spark interest in a product or franchise.
Courtesy of MediaFocus

in Major League Baseball. More noteworthy contributions included adding names to player uniforms and designing lighted, graphic scoreboards. His son, Mike Veeck, seems to have followed in the family tradition when he served as the marketing and promotions director for the MLB Tampa Bay Devil Rays (see graphic below for Veeck's promotional activities).

Perhaps Veeck's (Williams, 2000) most disastrous promotion was his 1979 Disco Demolition Night for the Chicago White Sox. The intent was to signal an end to the Disco era. Spectators were asked to bring old disco records to be piled up between the games of a doubleheader and blown up on the field. However, fans smuggled extra records into the stadium and began a "Frisbee" riot that resulted in the eventual forfeiture of the game.

Sample of Veeck's Notorious Promotions

- Twin Nights (buy one, get one free)
- Conversion Day (trade in an old Yankees hat for new Tampa Bay Devil Rays hat)
- Lawyer Appreciation Night (lawyers pay double)
- Free vasectomy giveaway on Father's Day
- Nobody Night (fans were locked out of the stadium and watched the game on a big-screen in the parking lot until official attendance[0] was recorded).

Intercollegiate athletics and interscholastic sports must likewise engage in promotional activities. The University of Texas started a promotion with their online magazine, giving Texas fans exclusive, behind-the-scenes content about the Texas football program. It included text, images, web links and full-screen, broadcast-quality video. Issues were automatically downloaded to a fan's computer and could be viewed an unlimited number of times at the fan's convenience. Fans from almost every state and many foreign countries downloaded the magazine. In addition, 53.2% of viewers clicked through to the Longhorns Store, generating incremental revenue. Incidentally, many subscribers were not season ticket holders or Longhorn Foundation members, which gave The University of Texas a whole new list of fans for their database (Plonsky, 2005).

Traditional promotions such as the "hat day," "bat day," and "poster day" events continue to be popular with both fans and sports organizations. The research on the effectiveness of such promotions varies. Boyd and Krehbeil (2003) found that about 40% of MLB teams used these types of promotional items. Interestingly, they found that if "giveaway" items were used for a game against an arch rival, attendance did not appreciably increase. On the other hand, when a giveaway item was used in a contest against a non-rival, attendance was positively affected. Overall, their research found that promotions in general increased attendance by about 20%. Liberman (2004) found that the most successful giveaway item, producing a 20.7% increase in attendance, was the jack-in-the-box toy (where a mascot or team player would pop out of a small box). A long-time favorite, the bobblehead toy produced increases of 15.3%. An interesting perspective was presented by Texas Rangers (MLB) Chief Operating Officer when he said that "the team doesn't view giveaways as inducements to buy tickets; they're rewards, and the team gives them out at high attendance games throughout the year" (Liberman, 2004, p. 21).

This also brings forward the aspect of protocol. Many teams have found that consumers "cherry pick" the games that have giveaway items. That is, they scan the teams schedule and choose to only purchase tickets to games at which there is a giveaway item. Many times, this defeats the purpose of the promotion (selling more tickets). In response, some teams have decided not to publicize the giveaway until closer to game day. Those who choose to use the giveaway as a reward also have some choices with protocol. The typical method involves giving the item to the first 1,000 fans into the stadium. However, many times season ticket holders, the most valued customers, are not among the first 1,000 into the stadium. Thus, the best customers do not get the reward that other fans receive. One method that solves this problem is to provide coupons for season ticket holders to use for item redemption at the stadium's customer service booth. An interesting side benefit is that oftentimes fans in the stadium may ask "Where did you get that?" and the response is "I am a season ticket holder." While there does not appear to be any research on this specific topic, it seems that this may be effective in both rewarding the best customers and increasing ticket sales.

Research studies into the effectiveness of these activities vary. In some cases, they produced large increases in overall attendance, whereas at other times they produced increases only for those specific events where people attended primarily to obtain the free novelty. Sport marketers should not jump to the conclusion that it is detrimental that a person attended an event for the express purpose of obtaining a free product. Sport can serve an effective (and profitable) role in linking consumers with products from sponsors.

The University of Tennessee launched some nontraditional promotions for their women's basketball contests. They had a face-painting night, balloon-making nights, and a petting-zoo night. At the petting-zoo promotion, animals were brought into the arena from local animal shelters for fans to pet and possibly adopt (Fechter, 1998). This type of promotion, which connects the university with a community-based organization, is often referred to as "cause-related." Cause-related promotions can be effective in drawing positive attention to sport programs.

The University of Arkansas women's athletic marketing staff created a program called "Read with the Lady 'Backs'" for children in grades K–6. The participants earned points, and prizes were awarded in various categories. The event produced significant public goodwill and helped form the image of the women's sport program as one concerned about the academic performance of children. NASCAR also had a "Race to Read Program" sponsored by Ford Racing. The promotion included a downloadable reading resources kit and participation incentives to encourage reading through the Race To Read program. Race To Read was designed to promote good and consistent reading habits through a promotional bookmark to track students' reading achievements and to reward participants.

Students visited the Ford Racing website to begin the program. The program suggested that each child read at least three books during the promotional period, fill out the Race To Read bookmark, and send it in to the specified address or email it from the association's website. Participating students received a free gift. The bookmarks submitted were tracked and the school with the most readers received a special recognition certificate and an appearance from Ford Racing NASCAR driver Jeff Burton.

Promotional activities that involve high school, collegiate, or amateur players require the exercise of considerable caution. Many sport-governing bodies have restrictive guidelines regulating the appearances of athletes in commercial activities. In some instances, if an athlete is associated with a specific product or company, he or she may be declared ineligible for amateur competition.

Some promotional activities seek to draw attention to the team/event/product by awarding prizes to those in attendance. Several sport teams have sponsored contests where spectators' ticket stubs were drawn at random for chances to win prizes by scoring goals (soccer, hockey), kicking field goals, or shooting baskets. These events are usually scheduled prior to the contest or between periods of play. The cost to the sport organization is minimal because the prizes can often be secured from sponsors as a trade-out for name recognition during the event or covered by relatively inexpensive insurance policies. These policies are offered through a myriad of companies that specialize in sport event promotions and contests. However, as with any business decision, one should investigate the company managing the promotion.

Several years ago, what seemed like a typical promotion went horribly wrong. During halftime of a Chicago Bulls NBA game, a 23-year-old office supply worker sank a

73-foot shot to win a million dollars. However, shortly after the event, it was discovered that the contestant had recently played college basketball, a violation of contest rules. With the payout in jeopardy, the Bulls held a press conference the following day and laid blame on the insurer. The insurer noted that the player had signed a waiver (which the Bulls administered *after* the shot) in which the stipulation was clear. Unfortunately, this promotion did not produce the intended result of positively impacting attendees (Cohen, 1993).

Just one year later, a similar controversy erupted in Miami, where the Florida Panthers (NHL) conducted a contest in which a fan could win a million dollars by shooting a puck the length of the ice toward a small opening in a template across the goal. The contestant shot the puck into the slot on the template, and an immediate celebration began. However, contest officials claimed that the puck had not passed "completely through" the opening as required. This promotion generated lengthy litigation rather than the intended promotional benefit. The oldest and largest company that handles promotions like these is the National Hole-In-One Association (www.hio.com). Based on a fee paid by the team, the company sets up the rules of the contest and guarantees the payout if the prize is won. Sport teams using this company include the Orlando Magic, Milwaukee Bucks and the Big East Conference.

Some of the many possible promotional activities associated with sport events that have proven successful are presented below:

1. Banquets to honor the participants of various sport teams through tributes to coaches, players, and support staff. These can be effective as award ceremonies where special acknowledgment and honors are accorded either employees or prominent citizens. To obtain the maximum promotional value, personal stories, pictures, and awards should be prepared.
2. Exhibitions of new products, protective sports gear, or the latest in sport and fitness fashion. These have also been proven to produce positive media coverage.
3. Team reunions in conjunction with a reception, dinner, and game.
4. Events, including guest days or nights for senior citizens, disadvantaged youth, Boy Scouts, Girl Scouts, and other groups who attend games. Often, these programs are enhanced by coordinating the event with a civic or service club where the members of the club provide transportation and supervision.
5. Sports clinics for various age groups in popular sports. These can expose and profile your staff for the media. Clinics can also be conducted on prevention and care of injuries, new fitness programs, or a myriad of other sport-related subjects.

One of the reasons that promotions are so popular is that they are relatively inexpensive and often do not cost the sport company at all. Other examples of successful promotional ideas include the following:

- Hosting a fun-run
- Hosting a celebrity tennis or golf tournament
- Holding a wellness fair

- Holding an open house at the sport organization
- Holding a live concert before or after a game
- Getting a famous athlete to make an appearance in the store to sign autographs
- Encouraging tailgating for events and contests
- Giving out "buy-one-get-one-free" coupons for a future contest
- Hosting a holiday tournament

One unique aspect of many sport programs is the desire of the public to associate with players, coaches, or employees. This can take many different forms—colleges and universities offer their coaches, fitness centers provide their instructors, and many corporations offer their leading salespeople for inspirational and informative talks. Many sport organizations circulate lists of speakers available to various organizations that may have the desire for guest speakers, whereas more aggressive organizations actively seek speaking engagements for their employees.

Develop Promotional Publications

Every sport organization will produce some type of promotional publication at one time or another. The purpose of organizational publications is usually to transmit knowledge or information to the public. A publication also communicates various aspects about the sport organization's style, approach, attitude, and image. For the publication to be effective, it must also be consistent. Herein lays the dilemma for managing promotional publications in many sport organizations. Should an organization create one single office that is responsible for all publications, or allow each department to produce its own publication to fit its individual needs?

Because publications are so crucial in the promotion and marketing of a company's goods and services, most sport organizations have one central unit that is responsible for the organization's publishing. Centralization of this promotional function reduces several publishing problems that have been encountered.

A major problem for many sport organizations is the dreaded desktop publisher. With the popularity of computer-based publishing programs for personal computers, everyone thinks they can be in the publishing business, and they can. Unfortunately, freedom of the press belongs to the person who has access to the internet. For an organization, this means that one can have untrained people creating and disseminating material to the public about one's products and services. The pitfalls here are tremendous. Poorly written, poorly designed, and inaccurate information may be presented to consumers without one's knowledge or control.

Three different methods of addressing this problem have been presented. The first suggestion is to have a centralized system, a franchise process, or an "official" publications policy. In the centralized system, one office handles all of the printing and publishing for the entire organization. This system affords the greatest amount of control and consistency and is very effective in protecting the organization from unprofessional or inaccurate publications. The limitations with this system are that it requires a relatively large staff and that the demands on one unit often fluctuate during different times of the year, which may create ineffective staffing patterns.

The franchising of publication operations can be effective because individual units are allowed to produce their own promotional materials. The franchise allows a representative from each unit to approve any publications from that unit. To qualify as a unit representative, a person has to undertake special training from a publication specialist. Not only do the units often have a better idea of exactly what they need, but they also often have a better idea of the unique benefits of the product or service in which the consumer may be interested. This option retains the advantages of having the centralized system in control, as well as decentralizing responsibility and workload.

The official publication method provides the least control of the three options. This policy limits the central publishing unit to the official publications of the organization (catalogs, brochures, advertising copy, etc.). All other units are free to produce their own (unofficial) newsletters or internal releases. This does eliminate the "publications police" that exist in the two previous systems; however, it also allows for the uncontrolled production of promotional literature. There is also a high probability that unofficial publications will find their way into the public eye, creating confusion and occasionally crises.

Regardless of the administrative structure, special brochures about a sport organization are effective in increasing exposure and publicity. Most commercial sport organizations use an annual report for communicating with both internal and external audiences. As a controlled medium, this document can be effective in creating favorable impressions about the organization in the minds of employees, clients, and prospective investors. In sport, these have been used by sporting goods companies, professional and collegiate teams, fitness centers, and commercial recreation enterprises.

Sport teams have, for many years, prepared and distributed game programs as promotional publications. Although sport teams have many advertising and promotional opportunities, game programs are still one of the most popular and reliable.

Game programs can be effective as a promotional tool by providing team history and contest information, and serving as a source of revenue. Industry data indicate that although attendance figures over the past few years at collegiate events declined, program sales increased significantly. The average sales data showed that about 1 in 10 football fans and 1 in 13 basketball spectators purchased a program (P. Kowalczyk, personal communication, 2011).

The philosophy surrounding the production and pricing of ads in the game program is of significant importance. If the sport organization is going to be competitive with other advertising media, then it is in the advertising business. If it cannot be competitive, it is really asking for philanthropy and contributions. This position/philosophy needs to be established early.

If the organization is in the philanthropy business, it must recover enough advertising revenue to offset printing costs. These advertisers must know that they will not receive the same exposure for their dollar as they would with other media. This does not, however, automatically mean that they will not purchase an ad. In many small towns, the advertisers are willing to support an organization through the purchase of an ad, irrespective of the cost-benefit ratio. Stotlar (2009) suggests that a sponsor should not be led to believe that he or she will receive the same advertising impact that other mediums offer. Rather, advertising in the game program should be explained as a way for the sponsor to support the athletic program with a donation and receive recognition in the form of an ad.

The way to determine if one's organization is truly in the advertising segment is to calculate a CPM (cost per thousand impressions). In doing so, the cost of advertising in the program is presented on the same basis as other media sources such as the local newspaper. Although ad costs are typically higher, very few people keep newspapers as souvenirs, whereas they often keep a program as a souvenir.

Irwin and Fleger (1992) presented several ways for sport marketers to manage game programs. The options they cite for producing profits and exposure provide valuable information.

Evaluate the Promotional Plan

The sport marketer must determine whether the promotional plan is effective or ineffective. He or she must therefore establish a method to determine whether or not the plan or parts of the plan are accomplishing the company objectives. The promotion objectives outlined what the company expected to achieve with the promotional plan. Did the plan accomplish these objectives? To answer that question, the sport marketer must assess the outcomes of the plan. Typically, this is performed through marketing research. Although Chapter 5 (Segmentation, Targeting, and Positioning in Sport Business) details marketing research, the following is a brief look at how it can be used for determining promotional effectiveness.

If the sport company wants to determine whether certain forms of advertising are effective, it can conduct a consumer survey. The survey will provide feedback for the sport marketer to analyze. In the analysis, the sport marketer must assess whether or not the advertising is accomplishing its goals. For example, the Blue Ridge Ski Resort wants to determine the effectiveness of direct mail advertising for its special two-for-one ski week. The sport marketer prepares a special skier check-in form that will be used for that week only. Questions on the form ask the skiers to identify where and how they found out about the special. If 50% state that they found out about the special in the direct mail they received, the sport marketer can make a subjective judgment about whether the promotional method was successful. If twelve people came for the special, 50% is six. Does an increase of six skiers who found out about the special through the direct mail mean that it was an effective method? Before we can answer that question, we must ask, "How many direct-mail pieces were sent to potential buyers?" If the answer is 1,000 pieces, 6 out of 1,000 could be determined unsuccessful. If the answer is 20 pieces, perhaps 6 out of 20, or 30%, may be considered to be a successful method.

Study Promotion Laws and Regulations

There are laws, guidelines, regulations, policies, and perceptions that affect promotion. The primary reason for regulation is consumer protection. The sport marketer must study and understand all of the regulations in order to produce a legal and ethical promotional plan. These areas are discussed in the following sections.

Laws. The sport marketer must know, understand, and apply the laws to the promotional plan. Federal regulation involves two primary laws: the Federal Trade Commission (FTC) Act and the Robinson-Patman Act. The FTC Act prohibits unfair methods of competition. One area of unfair competition is false, misleading, or deceptive advertising. The Robinson-Patman Act outlaws price discrimination and has two sections on promotional allowances. These sections state that promotional allowances must be fair and equal.

Regulation by other organizations. There are many organizations that affect promotional activities. For example, the Better Business Bureau is a nationwide company that works as a consumer advocate to control promotion practices.

Industry control. Many industries and individual companies work to affect promotional activities of their counterparts. These controlling mechanisms, although they are not law, are very effective in regulating ethical and tasteful promotional practices of companies.

Promotion and Ethical Issues. Every aspect and function of the sport business must follow ethical guidelines usually determined partially by the company and partially by the public. Ethical consideration should be given serious attention in areas including sociocultural issues and environmental issues. The sport marketer cannot afford to assume that the entire population of the United States or even other countries is of a similar culture and similar lifestyle. Serious attention to socioeconomic factors, cultural factors, and other such factors will exert a responsible leadership role for the business. In other words, it is critical that the sport marketer always work to "do the right thing" ethically and in socially responsible ways to position the company as people friendly and earth friendly.

Let us look at an example of how the entire process might work. Management of the Ship Shape Fitness Center has decided to target senior citizens. Their objective is to sell memberships to those senior citizens defined as 60-plus. Some products designed for and to be offered to this group are customized aerobics classes, one-on-one training, partner walking, water shaping, and a 60-plus tennis league. T-shirts will be specially designed to give as awards for milestones and league winners. The company develops the following message to be used as its primary promotion slogan: Fitness is good for you no matter how young you are! Management believes that this message is positive and keys on the 60-plus person thinking of her- or himself as young, not old. Promotional activities will include a one-week open house that will include activities designed to educate the 60-plus person about fitness. There will be exhibitions to show how fitness can be fun and an attainable goal. Management decides that the center will get 50, 60, or even 70-year-olds to perform the exhibitions. The objective for this is that the 60-plus person can see someone of his or her age exercising. The target group can relate to this much better than watching a very young and fit person exercising. The methods for communicating the message are selected based on the best method for reaching the audience.

From their marketing research, management learns that this market most likely does not work, that they are busy people and are not at home very much, and that they do not watch much television or listen to radio. Therefore, management concludes that the best way to reach the audience is through direct-mail advertising. The piece will be informative and simple, and will include information about the open house and the center. Other promotional methods will include coupons for two free days at the center, a special half-price membership fee for the first year, and special membership fee discounts for every year after that.

The sport marketer in this example has identified a target market, selected a positive message, and developed promotional methods specifically for the market. The products added were designed for the market, and the prices were identified based on the market's income. Communication is the tool used in getting the message to the consumer.

In conclusion, creating and managing promotion as a marketing element is difficult. Therefore, it is essential to unify all of the organization's executives on the role of promotions, the desired results, and the specific strategies to employ. Competition between specialists in various areas of the corporation can defeat the purpose of the promotional mix. For example, the advertising department may claim that it can do more to produce results than can the sales force. On the other hand, the public relations department may assert that its activities are more effective than advertising is. Therefore, a marketing manager must clearly understand the role of each component and be able to integrate promotional functions into the organization's overall business and marketing plan.

CHAPTER SUMMARY

Promotional systems are central to effective sport marketing because they relate directly to the consumer's decision to purchase. As the various promotional activities described in this chapter indicate, no single approach suits every situation. Promotions are limited only by one's imagination and more often than not, budget. Sport marketers must carefully analyze a particular setting, become knowledgeable about ideas tried by others, and create a promotional mix that best fits their specific organization and market conditions.

People will not buy a product if they do not know it exists, and promotion is the sport marketer's tool for communicating to the market about the company and its products. Sport promotion is the function of informing people about the sport company's products and influencing their purchase behavior. Promotion can shape a company image, reposition a product, create awareness for a new product, alert the consumer to sales, tell the consumer where the sport company is located, and inform the consumer about where a product can be purchased. The critical steps involved in promotion planning include establishing objectives, determining promotional methods deemed best for achieving those objectives, and developing a promotional mix. The sport marketer must know and understand the many factors that impact the development of the promotional mix. A master plan for all promotional activities should be developed, executed, and evaluated. Finally, the sport marketer must know the laws and the legal and ethical issues surrounding promotion in today's society.

The confidence of the manager is fundamental to the success of all promotional activities. Oftentimes, those who succeed are the ones who believe they will. Although it is highly unlikely that any sport organization can implement all the promotional methods outlined in the chapter, a complete study should be made of available opportunities. This chapter has provided some basic principles, guidelines, and practices that will improve sport marketers' confidence and chances for success.

DISCUSSION QUESTIONS

1. What is the process of communication?
2. What are promotional methods? Give some examples in the sport industry.
3. What are the factors that affect decisions about the promotional mix?
4. What are legal issues affecting promotion?
5. What are ethics, and what are some ethical issues the sport marketer should use in determining promotion strategies?

SUGGESTED EXERCISES

1. Conduct a study of three different sport businesses, organizations, or other enterprises in your city or community. Determine the promotional methods used by each.
2. Collect print advertising of a variety of sport products from numerous sources. Conduct a study of the ads and determine the target market(s) and the promotional message.
3. What are some populations recently objecting to the use of certain promotional messages and logos? In discussion groups, discuss the reasons and the ethical responsibility of the sport marketer.
4. Visit a local media outlet (radio, television station, or newspaper) and producer or editor to talk about their relationships with sports organizations. Prepare a contact sheet for that outlet complete with the names, position titles, and phone numbers of important people.
5. Investigate an advertising purchase for an athletic program or stadium scoreboard sign and determine if it is an equitable media buy compared to other advertising outlets.

PROFESSIONAL ASSOCIATIONS AND ORGANIZATIONS

National Association of Collegiate Marketing Administrators (NACMA)
24651 Detroit Road, Westlake, OH 44145

12

Media Relations in Sport

INTRODUCTION

Marketing communication cannot be limited to annual reports, advertising, and brochures. Interaction with the media is both a necessary and a valuable endeavor for any business. Historically, businesses interacted with the public mostly through face-to-face encounters. However, in our mass-mediated society, perceptions of your organization are delivered though multiple communication channels. Media and communication theorists have suggested that the expanded nature of communication in the global community and the speed with which information is transmitted mandate an understanding of media relations. Irwin, Sutton, and McCarthy (2002) note the importance of fulfilling the needs of the media. In fact, they say that the media should be treated like any other customer. The media need information and stories that are both interesting and newsworthy and fit the target market of the media's consumers. It is the sport marketer's job to create and distribute information for the media that meets those criteria. "For example, NASCAR significantly increased its coverage in USA Today by demonstrating that the race fan demographics characteristics matched those of the publisher's readers" (Irwin et. al., 2002, p. 174).

Media relationships will form a base from which all marketing and promotional strategies are launched. From the competency standpoint, the sport marketer must be knowledgeable about the specific formats, terminology, and personnel employed by the media. In the sports community, the title of the person who generally dealt with the media was "sports information director." However, due to the expanded role and the explosion of duties, many sport organizations are titling the person "director of communications."

Media is a broad term when used as a noun. It generally includes two categories: print and electronic. Within these categories, print media refers to newspaper and magazine professionals whereas electronic media typically includes television and radio. Although this classification system has worked well for many years, technology is rapidly blurring the lines of distinction. Many television stations are owned by publishers; publishers are producing vignettes for television and with electronic computer bulletin boards, some newspapers are never printed. Websites on the topic of sports are one of the most abundant. Thus, information about your programs, products and services is likely to appear in many places, many of which may even be unknown to you. Regardless of the labels placed on media outlets and media professionals, sport marketers must develop sophisticated skills and nurture productive relationships.

BUILDING MEDIA RELATIONSHIPS

The media must be considered as clients. Effective relations with media outlets will provide significant opportunities for communicating marketing concepts and product information with other clients and customers. Radio, television, and newspapers are the traditional media sources with which the sport marketer must become familiar. By providing a high-quality service to the media, all marketing functions can be enhanced.

One example of how *not* to build positive media relations occurred in 1999, immediately following Michael Jordan's retirement from basketball. Nike offered company chair Phil Knight to ESPN for an interview related to Jordan's announcement. However, Nike demanded that Bob Ley be replaced as the interviewer. Ley had served as the principal reporter on ESPN's documentary criticizing Nike's labor practices in Asian shoe factories. ESPN refused, and Nike received additional negative publicity rather than the positive exposure originally sought.

PRINCIPLES OF GOOD MEDIA RELATIONS

Sport marketers can develop confidence and respect by adhering to some basic principles or guidelines. According to Helitzer (2000), these include the following:

1. *Know the players.* A thorough understanding of the titles and responsibilities of media personnel will contribute greatly to your success. In the television environment, you will encounter executive producers, senior producers, talent (on-air hosts and reporters), and other production personnel. When dealing with print media, you will come in contact with editors, reporters, staff writers, and stringers (those who write for the publication on a part-time basis).

2. *Be accessible.* Everyone has a tight schedule and more work to do than time in which to do it. However, if you want media coverage, you will have to make yourself available on their terms. The only time when the media want you and are willing to wait for you is during a crisis in your organization.

3. *Be cooperative and non-combative at all times.* You will never win an argument with a reporter or writer. Even stupid questions deserve an answer. Remember, they do the editing and they will always have the last word.

4. *Appearance is critical.* Although you might think that this aspect of media relations applies only to television, this is not accurate. Your attire projects an image to all reporters. A person in formal business attire is almost always afforded more respect and credibility than a person in shorts and a golf shirt.

5. *Don't use jargon.* Instead, use words with which the public is familiar. In the sport industry, it is easy for us to use words and phrases that are unique to the field. Although we may believe that everyone should know the meaning of our words, this is not typically the case. Think before you speak, and rehearse the vocabulary that will be most effective with every audience.

6. *Use facts, not rumors, and be precise.* Gather as many pertinent facts as possible prior to talking to reporters. Although facts in some stories may initially be more detrimental than a rumor, specific examples confine a story whereas rumors tend to remove all boundaries. Good reporters will verify facts through alternate sources prior to airing or printing a report. Eventually, all of the facts will surface, and you do not wanted to be labeled a liar. Honesty and trust are critical to the survival and success of any organization.

7. *Don't stress or depend upon off-the-record accounts.* If you can see a camera, microphone, or reporter's notebook, assume that your words are being recorded. Remember, the job of the media is to get facts and report the story; asking a reporter to abide with off-the-record requests is unfair. Never say anything that you would not like to see in the media (i.e., there is no "off the record," and "the microphone is always on").

8. *Give as much service to the media as possible.* When news occurs, get the story out expeditiously. All reporters desire "hot" news, so you must be willing and able to supply the stories, pictures, and statistics they wish, in the form they need and on time.

9. *Treat stories as exclusive rights.* If a reporter uncovers a story, do not immediately give the same story to other reporters. Many reporters pride themselves on finding sensational news stories and believe that they should have the right to be the first to break the story.

10. *Recognize that timing is critical.* Breaking stories have a very limited shelf life, and if you want the publicity, you must provide all of the necessary information quickly and in a format that the media outlet needs. Remember that the media need news, not publicity.

PERSONNEL

Most college athletic departments employ a full-time person, typically called a sports information director (SID), to coordinate and manage the press and public relations activities for the college. The SID may have a staff ranging from one intern to a corps of employees, including an assistant SID, graduate assistants, secretaries, and several work-study students. It is the job of the sports information office to manage all of the public relations, media relations, and publicity activities for the athletic office. The sports information office develops the media guides, manages press day and the pressroom, develops the press packets, and makes up-to-the-minute statistics and general information available to the media. Although these activities are sales promotion activities, the target market includes the media and the activities are designed to influence consumers' attitude and perception.

In most sport corporations, media relations are managed by the communication directors or marketing managers. These companies also engage in media relations activities in an attempt to garner positive publicity through the media. In the college and university environment, communication directors are also responsible for posting news releases and game statistics on the organization's website as well as distributing them to the media outlets.

Specifically, retail sporting goods companies engage in similar strategies. For example, Reebok, adidas, Nike and others seek to maintain close trade relations with leading running-enthusiast magazines like *Runner's World*. Their objectives might include ensuring critical editorial coverage and proper running-product reviews. This does bring to question some ethical issues with regard to the relationship between publicity and advertising. It has been hypothesized that some magazine advertisers put a considerable amount of pressure on trade publications to provide favorable review or risk losing their advertising revenues. Since consumer-generated product review sites also exist, one should pay particular attention to these outlets. In some instances, companies have been known to pay bloggers to post positive comments across the Internet. Ethical standards suggest that any blogger compensated for comments should divulge that fact. Regardless of the type of sport organization, the personnel engaged in media relations must be highly trained and exhibit the highest of ethical standards.

TYPES OF MEDIA OUTLETS

Press Conferences

One essential aspect of providing service to media clients is identical to the basic concept of marketing: Provide what the client needs. Press conferences can provide that service, but should occur only when circumstances warrant their use. Too often, a media relations director will call press conferences to disseminate information that should have been in a news release. This causes the press to be wary of conferences. A press conference takes up a great deal of a reporter's day; therefore, if the press conference is to be a success, the information must warrant its occurrence.

Helitzer (2000) provides several considerations for planning a successful press conference. He recommends assessing the value of calling a press conference. Irwin et. al. (2002) and Helitzer (2000) discuss some of the more common reasons for calling a press conference:

1. A major change in personnel, including players, coaches, owners, or management
2. Scheduling of an important event, such as a title bout, championship game, or interstate rivalry
3. A change in facility location or name
4. Introduction of a new or revised product
5. Presentation or display of an award
6. Announcement of a new rule or policy
7. Announcement of a major sponsorship/partnership agreement
8. Crisis development

The timing of the press conference is also important. The key media people must be available at the scheduled time. Although it is not always possible to check everyone's schedule, the media do have some times that are better than others based on the media source (morning paper vs. afternoon paper; radio vs. television). The Internet, of course, is a live 24/7 operation.

Public perception of a company can be positively or negatively affected by how the company is represented in the press. © Tomispin | Dreamstime.com

If the decision has been made to conduct a press conference, the affected media must receive invitations. The invitation can be delivered to the media sources through the mail or in person. The former is the most efficient, though the latter is more effective. The key decision factors often revolve around the number of media invited and the amount of time that the organization has to issue the invitations. If the decision was made to send the invitation through the mail, it is also advisable to place a reminder call a few hours before the conference.

The preparation and selection of the conference site are also important considerations. Here, Helitzer (2000) has some specific criteria. There must be ample space for the anticipated number of attendees. Parking, seating, telephones, refreshments, and the amount of materials available must also be designed around the attendance factor. Attention should be given to the electrical facilities present at the press conference site. All communication media, including the public address system, the podium height and lighting, projectors, and multimedia equipment, must be checked before the conference. First impressions are critical in a press conference. The agenda or program for the press conference should be distributed along with any particular rules about the process of addressing the speakers.

Some sport companies work hard to influence the kind of publicity they receive through the media. For example, most university athletic departments stage a press day to which they invite reporters, journalists, and sports broadcasters. The media are encouraged to interview and photograph the athletes and coaches. Packets of material are offered to each individual. The packets contain information about the athletes and coaches, such as their records in high school, past seasons' records, highlights, hometown information, human-interest information, and expectations for the upcoming season. There is also plenty to eat and drink. The purpose of press day is to treat the press positively in the hope that the press will return the favor through their stories, reports, articles, and broadcasts. The treatment doesn't stop here. At every sport event during the season, there is a special room for the press. The pressroom will again contain packets of information, pictures, and current statistics about the season.

Although the primary objective of a media relations program is to draw attention to a person, organization, or event, sometimes attention is directed to the sport organization in negative situations. Accusations, accidents, and indiscretions can occur in any sport organization, and unfavorable publicity often results. One of the worst mistakes that a media relations practitioner can make is to give additional publicity to bad news by attempting to deny or explain the problem (Helitzer, 2000). In one-on-one communication, a dialogue can exist and a general conclusion as to the truth can be reached. However, mass media do not operate on a one-on-one basis.

It is certain that only part of the audience who saw or heard the original story will hear or see the rebuttal. Thus, the part of the audience who received only the rebuttal will begin to seek additional information and add impetus to the "crisis." Furthermore, those who received only the original story often remain unaffected by the rebuttal.

Too often, sport organizations attempt to use media for free advertising. To serve the media, provide what they need: news. A sport marketer's task is to make the available information look and sound interesting and newsworthy. This information could be that a new product is being introduced, announcements of new sales records, or even promotions and awards for company personnel. Traditionally, sport marketers provide much of their information to the media in the form of press releases.

Press Releases

Used by commercial, amateur, and collegiate sport organizations for many years, the press release has become a familiar tool for dealing with the media. It has become the most common form of communication in the sport industry. Several authors (Helitzer, 2000; Irwin et al., 2002) have presented criteria for successful press releases.

The press release must be written in a style that conforms to the style of the particular form of media even though releases are generally not used exactly as received. The journalist must present the information in a way that attracts audience attention. For electronic media, the information is crafted into a usable form by the media, and for newspapers it is redesigned to fit the specific space allotted. In both situations, the release should be written in a style commonly referred to as the "inverted pyramid" (Helitzer, 2000).

When scanning a newspaper, people want to see if a story is important to them prior to spending the time to read it. A headline is the first thing the reader will notice. There is some disagreement about whether a press release should have a headline attached. A recommendation would be to supply the headline and allow the reporter to make an editorial decision. In electronic media, people listen to the lead-in and make decisions about the relevance of the topic.

A standard element of all press releases is to identify the name of the organization, its phone number, and an appropriate contact person in the upper left-hand corner of the first page. The piece must include the essentials of who, what, when, why, where, and how. This should be accomplished in the first paragraph. The media can then decide if the story is worth attention. The first paragraph also may account for all the space the story is allotted in the paper. Thus, the news release must include the details of the story or event in descending order of importance.

Writing in this style (inverted pyramid) will more closely match the style of the reporter and will make it more likely that the information will appear in the media.

It is clear that simply grinding out releases is a costly waste of time and money. Helitzer (2000) and Irwin et al. (2002) report that only about 10% of the information received by daily publications through press releases is ever used. These data clearly indicate that most press releases never appear in print, and many are never even read, as the news media sort through daily stacks of releases in order to select those stories they believe to be of most interest or benefit to their clients.

The quality of presentation has a bearing upon whether or not a release is used, and competition is intense. One method of improving the chances that a release will be used is to meet the standards expected in preparing and delivering the story. Other useful tips for getting press releases into the media have been provided by both Helitzer (2000) and Irwin et al. (2002). When distributing press releases to the sports editor, the editor's name should also be included so that the person performing those functions will open it. Distribution times are very important because the print/broadcast deadline of the receiver can affect whether the release is available for use. If a news release is personally delivered, the person delivering it should try to avoid the front desk and present the release directly to the person who will make the decision on its use. Sport marketers must become familiar with the specific needs of different media outlets and their preferred method of receiving information. Due to advances in technology, most press releases are distributed electronically through email distribution lists. With one click of the mouse, a press release can be sent to hundreds of media outlets simultaneously. The following section examines the needs of the various media sources that may be used in the sport marketing field.

Newspapers, Magazines, and the Internet

Although newspapers were a mainstay of American culture, their popularity has declined significantly since 2005. Magazines (whether in print or electronic form) in sport, health, and fitness and other publications that carry featured sports stories continue to serve sports fans. Furthermore, specialized content websites and e-newsletters have experienced phenomenal growth. Data from 2010 indicated that Yahoo! Sports attracted 2.5 billion visitors (Miller, 2011). Almost all segments of the sport industry have specialized publications. Newsletters and magazines are not imposed upon readers; the reader purchases or accesses the content of their own volition. Thus, at the outset, there is some assurance of readiness to accept or expose oneself to the content. Generally, readers are interested in the content and the most influential citizens make it a practice of reading current newspapers and sport magazines (Irwin et al., 2002). Because these publications often are read at leisure, readers generally have time to digest the content of the items read and to formulate at least tentative opinions.

Maintaining a good relationship with the media can make it easier for a company to project a positive image. Courtesy of Stock.xchng

Sport marketing directors should make a point to get to know the outlets, publishers, the CEO, the editor, the editorial page editor, and finally the managing editor. This personal contact is critical to forming long-term relationships.

As a rule, magazines usually devote more space to stories than do newspapers. Internet postings are typically shorter than magazine articles and more closely resemble newspaper articles. Furthermore, magazines provide more specific material for the reader, so the impact of any story may be enhanced. Magazine articles also have a longer life than that of newspaper stories. Articles on the Internet have the longest usable life. Most people throw their newspapers away after reading them, whereas they tend to keep magazines longer and often pass them on to colleagues and friends, thus prolonging the impact.

A common complaint from newspaper and magazine editors is that the purpose of some sport organizations is to seek free advertising. Experienced media personnel are quick to recognize this tactic, which severely strains relationships. Another familiar complaint is that sport marketers often attempt to color or censor the material. Editorial personnel, on the other hand, rightly believe that it is their duty to the readers to remove any bias that may have been included. Finally, the sport marketer must never attempt to use influence or pressure tactics to get an item into or out of the paper. Although this has been attempted in instances where event sponsors have threatened to withdraw advertising from publications that did not give substantial media coverage to a sponsored event, the practice is considered unethical.

Many sport teams and events utilize the media to enhance their properties. In this process, sport managers often secure media outlets (newspapers and television stations/networks) as sponsors. This allows the sport organization to "leverage" the media for coverage. Because media coverage is vital to sport organizations, sponsorship benefits (i.e., on-site signage, tickets) are often provided to media outlets in exchange for advertising space in their paper or on their network. This exchange (often called "value-in-kind") benefits the sport organization because it offsets the cost of advertising, and it benefits the media outlet through preferential access to event or team coverage (Irwin et al., 2002). In some situations, the sport manager may also extend the advertising options to other sponsors (sometimes called a pass-through).

Many stories and releases are printed because they include an exciting photograph. Sports are action-packed activities, and high-quality photographs can catch the attention of editors and readers alike. A JPEG or other formatted photo with no more than two or three persons in the picture is preferred. You should identify photographs by including the information about the event and all people in the picture on a separate attachment. In addition, you should always credit the photographer, even if he or she is an organizational employee.

The major causes of rejection can be traced to common errors or omissions, including that the stories were poorly written and contained inconsistencies in tense, person and voice. If stories or press releases are continually rejected, arrange to have a conference with the editor, reporter, or others involved to determine any problems that may exist. The stated purpose of this meeting should be to improve one's service to the media, and it is hoped that the conference will result in a more positive relationship between the sport organization and the print media.

On some occasions, materials are obviously exaggerated or contain apparent inaccuracies. At other times, material cannot be distinguished from advertising and therefore conflicts with traditional editorial policies. Of course, newspapers and magazines are also valuable in calling attention to other forms of communication such as forthcoming speeches, event, radio, or television programs. It is through this avenue that many sport marketers encounter the electronic media. Because radio and television are instantaneous communication media, they present special needs to which the sport marketer must attend.

Radio

Sport marketers can use radio in a variety of ways. Probably the most common is for a team to broadcast its games over an official radio network. These distribution outlets are important in providing the game to fans who cannot attend in person or to those who enjoy the casual atmosphere of listening to sports events without visual cues or while traveling to the event site. Many organizations also broadcast their own audio over the web. Another example of sport radio is the ESPN Radio Network, which provides 24 hours of sport programming per week, 7 days per week through 5 designated studios, on the Internet and via satellite radio. In 2011, Sirius satellite radio had 9 all-sports channels.

Television

From the Olympic Games to a local coach's show, sport marketers will encounter television in many aspects of their work. Competition in the television industry increased markedly in the 1990s when over 150 new cable networks were established, and 400 new stations came into existence. From the addition of the Fox Sports Network as a competitor to ESPN, to ESPN's additional derivatives, the competition is fierce in the sport broadcast industry. In 2009, over 43,000 hours of live sporting events were broadcast over cable outlets. In addition, over 204 million video streams were viewed from sports sites. Sixty-six percent of Internet users had access to live video streaming in 2010, up from 9.5% in 2001. In 2010, more than 5 million viewers streamed the NCAA Final Four via CBS SportsLine (Miller, 2011).

Sports programming has increased 500% over the past 15 years, primarily due to the increase in the available program sources (Miller & Washington, 2010). The types of programming that are traditionally available include regularly scheduled contests (NFL, NHL, MLB, NBA, college games, motor sports, and horse racing), made-for-TV events (X Games, UFC, WWE, and celebrity sport events), and sport anthology or talk shows (NFL films, ESPN's *Outside the Lines*, etc.). Cable TV also offers a variety of sport-specific channels like the golf channel, the tennis channel, and GOL for soccer fans.

Regular network distribution is also changing. All of the major networks produce and telecast a variety of games on any given day. However, the local affiliates of the network select the contest that they feel will have the broadest appeal in the area. Yet because the other games are also available, the viewer can, for a fee, view other games via cable with a few flips of a switch. All of the professional leagues and many colleges and universities have pay-per-view options.

The International Management Group (IMG) formed a college division in 2007 when they acquired Host Communications and folded it into its college division along with the Collegiate Licensing Company (CLC). IMG College is the leader in collegiate marketing, licensing and media rights. Some of their top media contracts in collegiate sport include the University of Nebraska (13 years, $112.5 million), The Ohio State University (10 years, $110 million), and the University of Florida (10 years, $110 million) (IMG College, n.d.).

After 8 years of operation, the NFL Network reaches 85 million households. DirecTV added its "Super fan" platform to its existing Sunday Ticket in 2005, which allowed for interactive viewing of NFL games. The system allows viewers to watch up to 8 games simultaneously with switchable audio and provides real-time statistics. MLB.TV is a subscription service that allows users to watch live (and archived) *out-of-market games* on their computers via the Internet. Users can also port their MLB.TV subscriptions to watch through other devices like iPad, iPhone, Roku, and Android phones. The NHL televises games nationally on NBC and Versus (formerly OLN). In Canada, the NHL televises games nationally on CBC and TSN in the English language and on RDS in the French language. NHL Center Ice provides up to 40 games per week through a subscription similar to that of the NFL and MLB. The increase in this format has occurred because there are few, if any, additional costs to the producer, a limited hassle for the distributor, and consumers get the desired product at a reasonable price.

Pioneered in 2002 by the Yankees Entertainment and Sports (YES) Network, many sport teams have developed television programming (either wholly owned or leveraged with their media partners). The YES Network is a New York City-based, regional cable channel broadcasting a variety of sports events, with an emphasis on Yankees and New Jersey Nets basketball. Another example is Altitude Sports, started by Kroenke Sports and Entertainment and the owner of the NBA Denver Nuggets, NHL Colorado Avalanche and the MLS Colorado Rapids. The clear trend in the industry is for media outlets to "develop an equity position" in (in other words, to own) sporting events. ESPN controls all of the details of the X Games and therefore can shape the content to provide the best programming. Companies like the International Management Group own their own television production companies as well as the events so that they can protect the interests of their sponsors and athlete clients.

Pay-per-view has also grown substantially. HBO has traditionally led the way in pay-per-view sports with their boxing products followed by programming from WWE. From the mid-1990s with a Evander Holyfield v. Mike Tyson fight that had 1.4 million purchasers to the 2007 Oscar De La Hoya v. Floyd Mayweather bout with 2.5 million viewers generating $135 million dollars, HBO set the standard. More recently, the 2010 UFC bout "UFC 116: Brock Lesnar vs. Shane Carwin" generated 1.2 million purchases. Collectively the UFC now outsells both HBO and WWE in pay-per-view sales.

Securing Television Coverage

If one wants to have an event covered on television, the process is quite complicated. However, an overview may be helpful. To obtain coverage, content must be adapted to look like what the networks need. Television stations must pay for all programming; even reruns of *Friends* cost approximately $1 million per episode. A sport marketer must demonstrate to them that his/her event may be better and cheaper. Remember, the task is to prove it.

The first step is to contact the programming director, not the sports broadcaster. When the contact is made, a proposal must be presented for the coverage of the event. In general, lead time of approximately 6 to 8 months will be needed—12 if trying to obtain coverage on a network affiliate. As with most sport marketing areas, the sport marketer must be prepared. Some of the needed information includes data about television programming. For instance, one must know the difference between *ratings* and *share*.

The Nielsen ratings have long been the benchmark for measuring television-viewing patterns across the United States. The system is based on a selection of 4,000 households equipped with a "people meter." This device records the viewing patterns of the household. The resulting data are transformed into ratings and shares. *Ratings* represent the percentage of the total television households (approx. 95 million in the United States) that are tuned to a particular program. *Share*, on the other hand, is the percentage of those sets in use (at that specific time) which are tuned in to a given program. To be successful, one's event must be able to deliver competitive ratings and share for the station. The outline of the proposal should include the following points:

- Explanation of the event
- Benefits to the station—previous rating/share
- Level of involvement—production, wild footage, telecast only
- Facilities—camera hookups, knowledge of staff
- People and organizations in control—time/date, during event timing and running

Although the number of programming and outlet sources has increased, so has the competition across sport. However, with a lot of hard work, it is possible to present one's event on television.

MEDIA RELATIONS DURING A CRISIS

Sport marketers must know how to work with the media during a crisis—this section will briefly cover this topic. Sport organizations must manage the flow of information during a crisis to protect the reputation that the company has worked diligently to create. Managers must direct both the actual crisis and the public's perception of the crisis. The first step in this process entails the establishment of a crisis management team (Young, 1996). This team should have one designated director who will have the ultimate responsibility to control all information provided for the public and serve as the conduit for all information coming in to the organization. In some instances, this person is referred to as the "gatekeeper." Depending on the team director's public speaking skills and media savvy, this person may or may not be the spokesperson for the group. The crisis management team comprises the top management within the organization. For example, the USOC "Controversy" team for the Olympic Games included the USOC president, executive director, *chef de mission* (head of the U.S. delegation), director of public relations, and other staff as specified (United States Olympic Committee, 2008).

At the 2008 Beijing Olympic Games, a Chinese man wielding a knife stabbed Todd Bachman (father-in-law of Olympic Men's Indoor Volleyball Head Coach Hugh McCutcheon) and his wife. Bachman died and his wife was seriously injured. This incident was well handled by the USOC team, principally because they had a well-designed plan in place for crisis management.

Essentially, the role of the crisis management team is to plan, execute, and then evaluate. The crisis management plan should be more than a list of policies, procedures, and actions; it should reflect the full scope of organizational considerations regarding a potential crisis. Once the members of the team have been designated, the team director should select the spokesperson. Depending on the background and experience of this person, some additional training would most likely be appropriate. This training can assist the person in remaining calm, fielding questions from reporters, and crafting answers that will best serve the organization while simultaneously accommodating the media.

One of the responsibilities of the team director is to prepare and distribute the actual crisis plan. The plan should include the tasks for each member of the team and the sequence of actions required. Implementing the plan depends heavily on the equipment and facilities accessible. This "command center should be equipped with computers, modems, fax machines, copier, tape recorder, numerous telephones, pads of paper, pens, pencils, stationary, envelopes and a paper shredder" (p. 416). Other information that would be beneficial would be an organizational chart; a corporate contact sheet with names, addresses, and phone numbers of all key employees; and a copy of the updated database of media contacts. Consideration should also be given to creating a crisis kit that could be carried by key personnel who might be required to travel off-site to handle company problems. In this case, the computers should be portable with email and fax capabilities as well as a small printer.

Once the crisis has been defused, a thorough evaluation should be conducted immediately. It is critical that all elements of the plan area be analyzed to determine the effectiveness of each in resolving the situation. These actions have been found to be extremely constructive in preparing for and managing future crises.

CHAPTER SUMMARY

Media relationships are one of the most important factors in designing marketing communications. While the primary goal is the provision of accurate information for all media sources, the trend in the sport environment is for the media relations director to take a lead role in shaping the corporate image and brand. A decade ago, the NFL's communications director said that the role of the PR director in the league was to provide news stories, statistics and injury reports; but today's communication director takes a more proactive approach and helps shape the image of the franchise with the fans and the media (Supovitz, 2005). Unfortunately, they are not always successful (see side bar).

Productive media relationships require sophisticated skills and the highest of ethical standards. This mandates a high level of service, well-organized press conferences, professional-quality written material, and the development of personal relationships across all media outlets. Internet, radio and television programming are evolving in new directions, and top sport marketers will need to be current with technology and trends. As programming and outlet sources change, so will the competition across sport. Yet, with hard work, marketing functions can be enhanced through effective media relations.

The 2011 Super Bowl at Cowboys Stadium was plagued by two distinct crises. First, a falling-ice disaster after a freak snow storm was followed up with an even bigger crisis for fans, as the NFL announced that a number of temporary seats ticketed for Super Bowl XLV were not ready and some would not be available. The NFL stated that "Fans who are not accommodated with seats inside the stadium will each receive a refund of triple the cost of face value of their ticket. We regret the situation."

DISCUSSION QUESTIONS

1. What are the essential steps in obtaining electronic (television or radio) coverage of a sport event?
2. What are some of the differences between the impact of newspaper and magazine articles that would affect sport marketing?

SUGGESTED EXERCISES

1. Contact a sport organization and obtain permission to attend a press conference. Take notes and compare them with material in the text.
2. Working with a local high school and city newspaper, attend a sport event and write a press release after the event. Contact the local newspaper and deliver your release. Go over the content with a local college sports information director and discuss the quality of the release.

PROFESSIONAL ASSOCIATIONS AND ORGANIZATIONS

College Sports Information Directors of America/ CoSIDA
http://www.cosida.com/

13

Marketing Through Endorsements and Sponsorships

OVERVIEW

The purpose of this chapter is to describe how sport organizations can enhance their marketing efforts through athlete endorsements and sport sponsorships. Although non-sport companies have long used sport personalities and sports event to sell products, the contents of this chapter will be confined to sport organizations' use of endorsements and sponsorships. James (2002) noted that "people don't usually distinguish between sponsorships and endorsements and they are very different. Sometimes they can serve the same purpose, but a lot of times they don't. It all comes down to what your company's objectives are" (p. 15).

As explained in the sections of the text on marketing and promotional mix, the sport marketer must incorporate all available resources to satisfy the sport consumer. That process can be expedited through opinion leaders, individuals who have specialized knowledge of the sport product or service and who can influence others in the purchasing process. Poole (2005) found that 88% of consumers make product recommendations to their friends. Pride and Ferrell (2008) noted that opinion leaders are most effective when consumers in the target market share values and attitudes similar to those of the opinion leader. While one age group may find golfer Arnold Palmer trustworthy, a younger group may trust action sport athlete Shaun White (consecutive 4-time X-Games Super-pipe champion and multiple Olympic Gold medalist). The athlete must connect with and be readily recognizable to the audience.

This has been one of the main forces for the successful use of action sport athletes as endorsers. The growth of action sports across the globe has been tremendous, and many companies have followed the trend by signing niche athletes to promote their products. Sports such as snowboarding's half pipe, skateboarding, climbing, and even paintball have all seen double-digit increases in participation. The average snowboarder spends more than $400 per year on equipment and accessories ("Extreme Sports," 2005).

Sport marketers have used individual athletes through sport product endorsements with the hope that their endorsement will result in increased sales. For example, Olympic swimming star Michael Phelps helped push sales of Speedo swimming suits on a global basis after gold medal performances in both the 2004 and 2008 Games. This can be an effective component of sport marketing when matched to target markets and appropriately implemented with consumers.

The use of sponsorship marketing by sport corporations as a component of their corporate brand-management strategy is also prevalent in the sport industry. U.S. spending on sponsorship exceeds $16 billion per year with worldwide spending over $46 billion (Ukman, 2010b). Clearly, this represents an effective marketing element for sport and non-sport companies alike. This chapter will provide an overview of the use of both endorsements and sponsorship in accomplishing corporate marketing objectives.

OPINION LEADERS AND ENDORSEMENTS

Many sport companies use endorsers and opinion leaders because of their knowledge and power within certain groups. Brooks (1998) indicated that companies could use athletes as endorsers in four fundamental modes:

1. Explicit Mode—the athlete directly endorses the product
2. Implicit Mode—the athlete exhibits product use
3. Imperative Mode—the athlete recommends the product
4. Co-present Mode—the athlete simply allows his or her image to appear conjointly with the product

Research showed that sport celebrity endorsements positively affected Gen Y market word-of-mouth marketing and brand loyalty (Bush, Martin, & Bush, 2004). Snowboarder Shaun White brings in over $7.5 million in endorsements most significantly from his video game (for Wii, PS3 and PCs). White obtained his fame principally through the X-Games and benefitted significantly from the addition of snowboarding to the Olympics where he has won multiple gold medals. Other endorsers include Burton, Red Bull, Target, and Oakley (Mickle, 2010).

All of the major shoe companies use coaches as opinion leaders. Several college coaches are paid over $1,000,000 per year to outfit their team in specific shoes. The considerable economic value generated from the national television coverage of college football and basketball games provides the incentive. The exposure achieved through this endeavor comes not only in the arena but also through a company's support of the coach's summer sports camps where clothing for the coaching staffs, T-shirts, posters, and related merchandise can influence the impressionable youth market.

Youth programs represent the grass roots of the sport shoe market. If a sport marketer wants to move shoes, the youth market is the place to be (Medcalf, 2009). Establishing the purchasing patterns of customers early in their lives is a powerful tool in marketing. Both Nike and adidas employ this tactic and enter into agreements with amateur and high school basketball programs. Typically, programs receive about $2,500 in sport product for players and the coaches are outfitted in company apparel. The companies' strategy centers on the hope that not only will the players influence their peers, but they will also accessorize with additional company products.

It is not just the coaches and athletes of organized team sports that can be incorporated into endorsement as part of sport marketing plans. In the cheerleading and performance-dance industry, specialty companies often provide free shoes and apparel to the leading groups in the nation in an effort to influence the style selection and purchasing of other participants.

The manufacturers typically put the coaches under contract to guarantee specified actions and to protect the value of the endorsement. A typical contract calls for the following:

1. Give the company use of their name, nickname, initials, autograph, voice, video or film portrayals, facsimile signature, photograph, likeness and image.
2. Make the company shoes available to players and assistant coaches as well as cheerleaders, game personnel, and the team mascot.
3. Film a TV commercial and participate in two photo sessions, the results of which may be exploited by the company throughout the world in any manner determined by the company.
4. Make eight promotional appearances in the United States and one abroad, designated by the company.
5. Attend a company party and/or annual retreat.
6. Assist in the production of a promotional video on topics such as basketball fundamentals, physical conditioning, nutrition, academics, drug and alcohol education, and preparation for the real world.
7. Comment favorably upon the use of company products whenever possible.
8. Wear a sport jacket, sweater, or shirt bearing the company logo prominently displayed during all college basketball games and at other appropriate public activities.
9. Give the company four complimentary tickets to each game.
10. $5,000 will be deducted from the contract if team members do not achieve a 2.25 mean grade-point average each year.

Other tactics of using opinion leaders in sport have included product sampling and prototype testing as additional ways to receive input. Golf is one of the areas in which this is quite visible. One of the best reasons to sign an endorsement with a PGA player is to get feedback on product performance. A sport marketer must "get a player that can give you the right feedback in R&D and wants to be involved in R&D. The information you get from a pro is so different from what you get from a robot" (Seligman, 2005, p. 10). Product testing always generates a great deal of interest in the product and can be tracked to indicate the overall effect on sales. According to Seligman (2005) "Tour presence justifies a company's product in the eyes of the consumers" (p. 10). Often a product new to the market or even a prerelease prototype is distributed to key opinion leaders within an industry. In another example, Reebok often provides prerelease shoe models to top sales personnel in selected sporting goods stores to seed sales and generate product interest. This develops loyalty and can provide the company with reliable feedback on its products with minimal costs.

INDIVIDUAL ATHLETE ENDORSEMENTS

The use of individual athletes to endorse products has been a marketing practice in sport for decades. As early as the 1936 Berlin Olympics, adidas provided track star Jesse Owens with free shoes. Historically, the line between professional and amateur athletes was finely drawn. If an athlete was paid or received money from sport, he or she was a professional; if the athlete received nothing, he or she was an amateur. All of this has changed in Olympic sports, and although the Olympic Games offer no prize money, the athletes certainly collect from their endorsement deals. In 1981, the Olympic rules were modified. The International Olympic Committee (IOC) changed its regulations and allowed each international federation to establish its own standards on the receipt of monies and the effect on eligibility. At this time, the IOC no longer even refers to athletes as amateurs, but as eligible athletes. Many of the shoe and apparel companies provide cash incentives tied to medals won at the Olympic Games.

For many years, shoe companies engaged in bidding wars in an attempt to secure the next Michael Jordan. Tiger Woods was arguably the successor to Jordan, and signed a contract with Nike immediately following his final amateur match. The Nike contract (5 years, $40 million) was one of the highest in sport endorsement history. Tiger Woods renegotiated his Nike contract to 5 years, $100 million after the 2000 season, which featured wins in the PGA Championship, U.S. Open, British Open, and Canadian Open. His endorsement deals included: Nike—$25 million; General Motors—$7 million; Accenture—$8 million; EA Sports—$7.5 million; Upper Deck—$7 million; American Express—$7 million; Disney—$5 million; TLC Laser Eye Centers—$3 million; Warner books—$2.5 million; TAG-Heuer—$2 million; and appearance fees of $9 million, for a total of $89.4 million (Sirak, 2005). Golf's biggest star then spent 2010 weathering revelations about his adulterous sex life, a stint in sex rehab, a divorce and the loss of more than $35 million in endorsement revenue as well as his world No. 1 ranking (Miller & Washington, 2010).

Notwithstanding his troubles, Woods remained the American earnings leader in 2010 ($20 million in tournament earnings and $70 million in endorsements). Number 2 on the list was fellow golfer Phil Michelson earning about $10 million on the course and $52 million from sponsorships. LeBron James came in with a salary of $15 million and $30 million in endorsements including Nike's 10-year U.S. $90 million contract (Freedman, 2010b). Growth in the endorsement market allowed several athletes, particularly those in the NBA, to secure endorsements contracts into the tens-of-millions of dollars.

The late NASCAR driver Dale Earnhardt won seven Winston Cup Championships and in 1996 accumulated $2.5 million in winnings. However, by licensing his own name and likeness, he was able to generate an additional $8 million in endorsement earnings (Hagstrom, 1998). With his untimely death at the 2001 Daytona 500, Earnhardt merchandise became the sport's most coveted merchandise. His son, Dale Earnhardt, Jr., was the only NASCAR driver to break into Forbes Top 20 endorsers for 2010 with $4 million in salary and $22 million in endorsements.

Michael Jordan established the benchmark for endorsement earnings. Even after his retirement from basketball, Michael Jordan continues to derive profits from licensed merchandise and his signature Nike shoe and apparel lines.

The question remains: does the sponsorship of an individual athlete provide an adequate return on investment? Tiger's success on the tour helped push sales of Nike golf equipment from U.S. $100 million in 2000 to U.S. $350 million in 2005. When he switched to a Nike golf ball, their market share went from 1% to 3% in 3 months and to 10% the following year.

Trek's sponsorship of Lance Armstrong resulted in significant increases in sales of their $4000 tour model bike after Armstrong's 6th Tour de France win and, in fact, pushed the total market for the sale of road bikes to record levels ("Company Cases," 2005). Electronic Arts signed Woods for a video game bearing his name after his victory at the 1997 Masters and has had considerable success with the product for many years.

Internationally, Roger Federer replaced 2009 leader David Beckham as the 2010 top-earning foreign athlete, earning about $62 million. Beckham fell to third on the list with $40 million after Lionel Messi (FC Barcelona) at $44 million (Freedman, 2010a).

It has been more difficult for women to secure equivalent levels of individual endorsements. Serena Williams was the 2010 No. 1-ranked tennis player, but she was unable to match the earnings of Maria Sharapova. Sharapova's endorsements totaled $24.5 million from companies like Nike, Sony, Ericsson, and Tiffany. When combined with her $1 million in prize money, Maria Sharapova was the highest-earning female athlete. Other notables on the list were as follows. The Williams sisters came in at No. 2 and No. 3 on the earnings list; Serena made $20.2 million while Venus made $15.4 million. No. 4 on the list was racing's Danica Patrick, who pulled in $12 million. Patrick was the most popular driver in IndyCar in 2010. Her most notable sponsors are web designer GoDaddy.com, Peak Antifreeze, and Tisso watches. Figure skater Kim Yu-Na, who made $9.7 million, was ranked fifth. The 2010 Olympic gold medalist had an endorsement portfolio including Hyundai, Nike and Samsung Electronics (Badenhausen, 2010).

There is a continuing trend of companies seeking female athletes as product and service endorsers. According to many executives, female athletes are far less likely to generate negative publicity and are more accessible and personable with consumers. They will actually sign autographs and spend time with fans. In a 2003 study, Stone, Joseph, and Jones (2003) found that "endorsement opportunities for female athletes are growing and that elite female athletes may now be able to effectively compete with male athletes for some of the lucrative endorsement deals that have traditionally gone to men" (p. 101). Most corporations play down the "sex sells" controversy surrounding some women endorsers and instead portray their female endorsers as role models and athletically talented representatives of the company who can connect with consumers.

Unfortunately, some companies devalue women as athletes and focus on their physical attractiveness. According to Kaufman (1998), "How a woman looks still matters in endorsements and just about everything else. It's not right, but it's reality" (p. 48). Golfer Natalie Gulbis created a similar controversy with her 2005 calendar and layout in FHM magazine. Many considered the calendar to be too risqué, but the Ladies Professional Golf Association (LPGA) was also pushing the attractiveness of many of its top players. Former LPGA commissioner Ty Votaw said if Natalie was comfortable posing, they would support that decision. Research has shown that the more "feminine" and more attractive female endorsers received more endorsement opportunities than their less attractive colleagues (Fink, Cunningham, & Kensicki, 2004). However, recent studies have shown that highlighting female athletes' skills and level of expertise correlated positively with consumer attitudes and purchase intentions (Fink et al., 2004).

There is also a significant credibility problem with many athlete endorsers. Research indicated that over 79% of consumers thought athlete-endorsers added no value to the products they endorsed (Poole, 2005). Furthermore, other research indicated that most people believed the athletes were endorsing products just for the money and few people were able to match an athlete-endorser and the products that she or he endorsed (Fink et al., 2004). In general, basketball players were more often accurately recognized than were athletes in other sports, and male endorsers were more likely to be recognized than were female endorsers.

Endorsements with individual athletes do not exist without danger and controversy. One question that continues to cause controversy is "Who controls the rights?" Do team players have the right to select their own shoes, or do coaches have the power to demand that specific shoes be worn? Currently, the rights battle has been favoring the player, but it will remain an issue for some time to come.

Another issue relates to organizational control. This has been particularly evident in the Olympic Games. During the 1992 Barcelona games, the U.S. men's basketball team had uniforms sponsored by Champion, and individual players each had their own shoe contracts. However, the United States Olympic Committee had an agreement with Reebok for the medal presentation uniforms. Because the players had not signed the USOC agreement (requiring participants to wear the USOC-designated presentation apparel) and because wearing a Reebok logo conflicted with their shoe contracts, a serious problem arose. In the end, the players agreed to wear the Reebok uniforms, but unfolded the collar or otherwise covered the manufacturer's logo.

This controversy continues. At the U.S. Olympic Swimming Trials, swimmer Michael Phelps wore the compulsory U.S. Swimming Speedo-logoed cap. However, at the conclusion of the race, he slid off the approved cap to reveal his VISA sponsored cap underneath.

Similarly, control issues can be observed in Formula 1 racing, where car owners have the rights to signage on the car and driver's suit, yet the drivers own the rights to their helmets. Several of the Formula 1 drivers make as much as U.S. $500,000 from their helmet sponsorships. Thus, conflicts can arise if drivers pursue sponsors that may conflict with the car's primary sponsor. At the Tour de France, the rules control the riders, but not their equipment cars; as a result, sponsors literally cover the cars with logos and advertising.

Almost all sport organizations (NCAA, the NFL, the NBA, Major League Baseball, and the IOC) have so-called "billboard rules." These rules limit the size and number of logos that can appear on uniforms and equipment. Even with the tight rules, many sport marketers find loopholes.

CHOOSING AN ATHLETE ENDORSER

As noted earlier, the principle rationale for selecting an athlete endorser is that person's status as an opinion leader. The principle issue for the marketer is to pick an athlete spokesperson with the right set of characteristics that will be able to produce the most favorable response from consumers. Research (McDonald, 1998) has shown that the best endorsement value is generated from situations in which a high level of congruity exists between the image of the athlete and the image of the product. Moreover, for some products, certain sports would be more effective in producing positive consumer response than would others. This determination can only be made through extensive market research.

Martin (1996) suggested several steps needed for marketers to determine the right athlete for a product endorsement:

Choosing an athlete to endorse one's product involves research to discover which athlete can most effectively match the product's image. Courtesy of Mark Turney/ U.S. Marine Corps

1. The image of the product must be assessed through market research with customers.
2. Marketers should then measure the image factors associated with a variety of sport activities.
3. Once the images of the product and the sport have been assessed, the marketer should select an athlete(s) from the sport that most closely matches the images of the product.
4. The final step is to evaluate the athlete's ability to enhance the consumers' perception of the product.

According to Martin's (1996) research, "careful consideration of the perceived degree of fit between images of the product and images of the sport can significantly increase the positive evaluation of the endorsement by an athlete from the chosen sport" (p. 37).

ENDORSEMENT TRENDS

Although sport marketers can still benefit from individual athlete endorsements, the risk is high (e.g., Tiger Woods, Kobe Bryant, Latrell Sprewell, Mike Tyson). As noted earlier, Veltri (1996) indicated that the power of athletes in endorsing products has varied. As a safeguard, many endorsement contracts have special clauses to cover instances in which a player or coach is involved in some horrid scandal. Contracts often have a special termination clause allowing for termination of the agreement at any time if the person wears another manufacturer's product, commits any act that "tends to shock, insult or offend" the community, violates any league rule, or becomes "disabled/incapacitated and unable to perform." Players can recover from negative incidents, however. In 2004, NBA player Kobe Bryant was accused of sexually assaulting a woman, resulting in some of his endorsements being cancelled or simply not renewed. Once the case was settled, his major sponsors once again began using Kobe in the advertising, and he has regained prominence on the court and with his endorsements (#7 in 2010 earnings). As a result of the problems and risks associated with individual athlete endorsements, many sport sponsors are more inclined to sponsor events.

EVENT SPONSORSHIPS

The initial question that must be addressed is whether a company should use sponsorship in lieu of traditional advertising. Sponsorship offers a number of distinct advantages over more conventional advertising techniques. Sponsorship spending has grown at a rate three times that of advertising. While advertising delivers a straightforward commercial message, sponsorships connect with people through a different source. Within the sport industry, marketers must understand the role of sponsorship as a marketing tool. Sponsorship involves a company being prepared to make a commitment and support an activity; it says the company is going to be more people oriented than advertising suggests. In several ways, sponsorship is longer lasting in the terms of its commitment (Stotlar, 2009).

Sponsorship has been defined as "a cash and/or in-kind fee paid to a property (typically sports, arts, entertainment, or causes) in return for access to the exploitable commercial potential associated with that property" (Ukman, 2004, p. 154). Essentially, the primary goal of sponsorship is to augment marketing communication (Ferrand & Pagés, 1996). The sponsorship of sports activities ranges from local beach volleyball tournaments and fun runs to the Olympic Games. Deals range in scope from a $2,500 sponsorship of youth sport to the $85–130 million sponsorship of the 2012 Olympic Games. Collectively, these events can provide sport marketers with an array of opportunities to market their products and services. As outlined at the beginning of this chapter, this discussion of sponsorships will be limited to their use as marketing tools for sport organizations.

Worldwide, corporate spending on sport sponsorship increased dramatically during the 1980s and 1990s. 2005 U.S. spending on sponsorship totaled $12.09 billion. In 2010, U.S. sponsorship spending reached $16 billion per year with worldwide spending over $46 billion. European corporations contributed $12.9 billion, followed by Pacific Rim countries with $10.6 billion, and Central/South America spent an additional $3.8 billion. (Ukman, 2010a).

Numerous companies engage in sport sponsorship activities in almost every sport organization from local fitness centers and high schools to the Olympics and professional sport leagues. As the number of sport organizations desiring an affiliation with sponsors has grown, the leverage in the industry has changed. This has created a situation in which the sponsor can weigh the offers from competing organizations seeking sponsors and keep prices down. As a result, during the early part of the 2000–2010 decade, the momentum shifted from the sport organizations to the sponsoring corporations. In today's environment, it is increasingly important for sport managers to be skilled in the methodologies and techniques of sponsorship as a marketing component. A successful sponsorship arrangement can serve as a positive marketing vehicle for any sport organization.

As with the fit between image and individual endorsers, perceptual fit between the image of a sport and that of a sponsoring company is critically important. Research on examined consumer reaction to terms such as sophisticated, rugged, exciting, and wholesome in relation to both companies and the sports being considered for sponsorship. This research concluded that creating a good perceptual fit between the sport and a sponsor could contribute to brand equity for the sponsor. Thus, the prevailing research (Martin, 1996; McDonald, 1998) confirms that both sponsorships and endorsements are more effective if there is a high level of congruence between the image of the sport/athlete and the image of the corporation.

Stotlar (2004) provided a model that would serve sport marketers in the evaluation and implementation of sponsorship programs (see Figure 13.1). The author recommends that the sponsorship be considered as part of the comprehensive assessment of corporate objectives. All too often, the question that marketers ask is "What can sponsorship do for us?" A better question is "What do we need to do, and can a sponsorship accomplish that objective?" As such, sponsorships should be selected with attention to specific criteria.

RATIONALE FOR PURSUING EVENT SPONSORSHIPS

Sport organizations can buy into event sponsorship for a variety of marketing reasons. In the past, many organizations were attracted to sport properties to cultivate the social benefits. Sport executives could associate with star players, play in celebrity golf tournaments (the current price tag for a top PGA player to appear in a pro-am event is $150,000), and host parties for their friends in conjunction with the event. Although these reasons may still exist, their prominence has clearly decreased. In today's business environment, shareholders and boards of directors demand measured return on investment from sponsorship activities.

Thus, decisions to sponsor sport-related properties must be linked to business-related objectives of the company. One must "look at an event to help meet a marketing objective, then make sure it meets sales promotion, PR, and internal employee morale needs" (Ukman, 2004, p. 6). There must be a match between the organization's target market and the property's audience (or participation base). An obvious example of this can be seen in adidas' sponsorship of the Boston Athletic Association that owns and operates the Boston Marathon. In their deal ($400,000 per year through 2023), adidas supplies 12,000 jackets and shoes for staff and volunteers; they also have the right to put flyers in all participant race packets, display on-course signage, distribute logo blankets for the

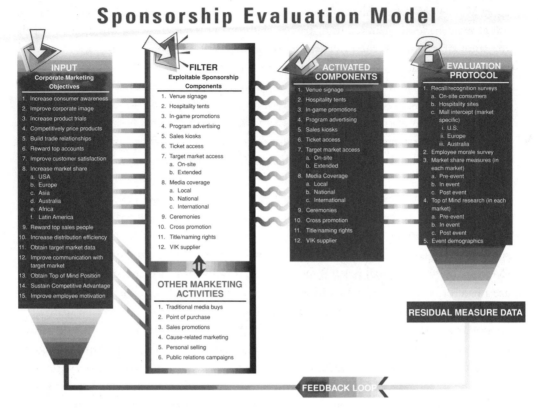

Figure 13.1. Sponsorship Evaluation Model

from Stotlar, D. K. (2004) Sponsorship evaluation: Moving from theory to practice. *Sport Marketing Quarterly*, *13*, 1, March 2004.

top finishers, and have exclusive sales of logoed apparel. Because of its historical ties with soccer, adidas signed a sponsorship agreement with FIFA and the World Cup through 2014 for an estimated $351 million (Woodward, 2005). Adidas executives estimated that their sales of World Cup-related products for 2010 was $1.8 billion.

The participants and fans of those events clearly represent the core customers for adidas' many products. Sport companies must also look for direct product sales at sponsored events. Thus, adidas would be more inclined to sponsor a road race if it could access the participants through on-site sales points or obtain the event's database for future marketing initiatives. For the 2010 World Cup, adidas secured the rights as sole supplier of official merchandise.

Sponsorships have also been effective in promoting the image of the sponsor. Thus, adidas/Reebok, through its sponsorship of the NFL, NBA, and NHL could generate consumer impressions and further position the brand through "authentic" association with the leagues. Ferrand and Pagés (1996) proposed that sponsorship can be effectively used in image management. Companies can use sport sponsorship to establish an image in the consumer's mind, solidify an existing image, or modify the consumer's image of the company. Companies must rationally select the appropriate event or group to sponsor in order to maximize the communication potential. Then, "the sponsor must consider the image of the event, the sponsor's present image, and the desired future image of the sponsor or its brand" (Ferrand & Pagés, 1996, p. 279). This was clearly evident when Tom Wade, the chief marketing officer of the PGA tour was asked about their sponsorships. Wade noted that "companies are judged by the company they keep"—a slogan also used with the International Olympic Committee's TOP Programme some years ago (Ukman, 2004, p. 4). Wade went on to discuss the importance of a partnership between the organization and its sponsors, stating that "Corporate relations are our life and blood" (p. 4). This is reflected in the fact that the PGA tour staff assigned 75% in sponsor service and 25% in sponsorships sales. Wade said that with "more than 100 major companies as sponsors, we can't afford a lot of turnover because there aren't another 100 companies to replace them" (p. 4). The PGA also established a dedicated website (www.pgamarketingcenter.com) to service their sponsors and attract new sponsor business. Along with Wade, many other industry experts support the aspect of relationship building in sponsorships. The Baltimore Ravens put a similar emphasis on sponsorship service at about 80% of their duties (Rocklitz, 2005).

However, changes in corporate expectations have mandated more utility from sponsorship associations. One company's director of sponsorships stated this point clearly when he said, "We are no longer satisfied with enhanced image; give us opportunities for on-site sales, well-developed hospitality packages and dealer tie-ins and we'll listen" (qtd. in International Events Group, 1992d, p. 5).

The key trend in today's sponsorship environment is activation. A sport marketer at a corporation seeking sponsorship opportunities must look beyond signage to strategies that connect with the consumer in meaningful ways. Activation has taken on many forms over the years, but it essentially means that the sponsorship connects the product directly with the consumer. Gatorade has been seen prominently on the sidelines for sports activities for over 40 years. Their sponsorship of professional and college teams has provided them with an authenticity that would be impossible to replicate through traditional advertising.

Sport-related businesses, like most corporations, desire to be seen as community citizens with a responsibility to contribute to the wellbeing of the communities where they do business. In support of this concept is the message delivered by a special events manager: "Customers want companies that care about them, that give back to the community" (qtd. in International Events Group, 1992d, p. 5). As an example, a local bicycle shop could sponsor a triathlon to influence competitive riders and also could sponsor a child's bike safety class. These strategies are often labeled as "cause-related marketing." While there are many examples of sport companies supporting worthy causes, one of the most successful was Nike's support for the Lance Armstrong Foundation (cancer research). Many cause-related efforts fail because the company is really trying to use the cause for its own self-interest. Consumers can typically see through this rather easily. In Nike's case, the yellow bracelets (sold for $1 each) did not include the Nike swoosh or other marketing logos. Rather, Nike subtly showed their support by selling more than 50 million bracelets in the first year. Since its inception, the program has raised more than $400 million to support cancer research and related causes (Burleigh, n.d.).

A close examination of the reasons that a business should become involved in sport sponsorships is essential. Understanding how sponsorship activities can help accomplish business goals is one of the key elements in selecting successful sponsorship opportunities. These must be specific to each event that the sport marketer intends to approach.

DEVELOPING A WINNING STRATEGY

The sponsorship relationship between a sport entity and event owners must include advantages to both parties, whereby the product's market value and profits are increased and the event benefits as well. A key component for success is the measurement of return on investment (ROI). Sport managers must be fully cognizant of the data that demonstrates the accomplishment of specified corporate objectives. For example, data indicate that 73% of NASCAR fans choose to purchase products of NASCAR sponsors over others (Ukman, 2004).

These data should be provided by the event owner, but are occasionally collected by the sponsor. Sport organizations that use sponsorship as a marketing tool must be prepared to evaluate sponsorship in the same manner as other marketing efforts. "The general measurement mentality has been to simply transfer advertising metrics [the criteria against which objectives are measured] and proceed to sponsorship without considering either the differences that the sponsorship environment requires" (Ukman, 2004, p. vii). Her four-step approach includes: 1) setting objectives and baseline measures, 2) creating the measurement plan, 3) implementing the plan, and 4) calculating the return on the sponsorship.

Sport marketers can also employ professional market research firms to collect the data. One such company is Joyce Julius and Associates, which conducts research in sponsor exposure and publishes the results in a publication titled *The Sponsor's Report* that measures logo time on televised sports broadcasts. The data showed that Tiger Woods' victory in the classic 2005 Masters, when the Nike ball teetered on the lip of the cup, garnered more than $10 million of television exposure for Nike during CBS' telecast (Joyce Julius, 2005). According to their research, logos for Nike, Nike One Ball, and Nike's Tiger Woods Collection were clearly seen on screen for a total of 30 minutes and four seconds. When compared to the estimated cost of a 30-second commercial during the CBS broadcast, Nike was credited with $10,824,000 of in-broadcast exposure value.

One of the aspects of sponsorship that has attracted sport-related companies has been its ability to reach consumers by breaking through the clutter in advertising. Marketing managers have used sponsorship as an avenue to present their message to consumers in a more relaxed atmosphere and to support their other marketing efforts. Sport events are also attractive because they can provide a cross-sectional exposure when compared to other marketing avenues available to the sport marketer (Stotlar, 2009).

Media attention is another important factor in selecting an event to sponsor. Good events have the potential to generate considerable media coverage. This type of message can be particularly effective because consumers typically see this in a different light than they see traditional advertising. Another related facet of media coverage and sponsorship is that if an event has a media sponsor, discounted or free coverage can often be obtained by tagging their promotional messages. Such a situation exists with the annual Bolder Boulder road race in Boulder, Colorado. The local NBC affiliate and Saucony shoes sponsor the event. Not only is Saucony granted sponsorship of the race, but it also receives logo presentation on all TV spots promoting the race. Similarly, Saucony can benefit from the televised coverage of the race, which will have several prominent sponsor banners strategically located for the cameras. Media coverage also provides a reliable and measurable method to calculate return on investment.

Although the number of times the sponsor's name was mentioned by the announcers, the column inches of print devoted to the event, and the number of times the corporation's banner was seen on national television are important, the raw data do not always reflect the whole picture. Consider, for example, an announcer who, in the middle of a race, says, "Her Saucony shoes have fallen apart, and she'll have to finish this race barefooted." What is the economic value of that? Other sport marketing research firms criticize value reports because some of the calculations are based on rate-card advertising costs. Most major corporations purchase advertising at a substantial discount. Thus, some of the reported value assessments may be inflated.

Before undertaking a sponsorship, criteria should be developed for evaluating possible opportunities. This process has been discussed extensively (Irwin & Assimakopoulos, 1992; Mullin, Hardy, & Sutton, 1993; Stotlar, 1993). Irwin, Assimakopoulos, and Sutton (1994) provided an inventory detailing the typical factors to be considered as companies deliberate engaging in sponsorship activities:

- Budget—affordability, cost effectiveness, tax benefits
- Event management—past history, organizing committee
- Image—match to products and services offered
- Target market—demographics, geographical reach
- Communications—media exposure, audience size, and demographics
- Sponsor mix—match with other sponsor's products and image
- Level of involvement—title sponsor, in-kind supplier, exclusivity
- Other opportunities—wholesaler tie-ins, on-site displays, signage, product sampling, merchandising.

It is critical that all of the components of the sponsorship agreement be detailed in a written contract. Many of the terms and elements provided in a sponsorship lack industry-wide standards, and any confusion must be minimized. Reed (1990) developed an excellent checklist for companies to use when working with an event (see Figure 13.2). If an event owner offers a sponsorship that can meet your criteria, is ethically grounded, and gives you service and data with which to justify continuation, sport sponsorships can be a successful marketing tool for sport organizations.

SPONSORSHIP RIGHTS

1. Sponsor's Official Status
- ❏ As only sponsor?
- ❏ As only sponsor in a category?
- ❏ Right to veto other sponsors for reasons of incompatibility? Any conflicts with official suppliers?
- ❏ What about sponsorships at other sites or related events?

2. Signs at the Event
- ❏ How many?
- ❏ What is the size and placement of sponsor's name relative to others? Who pays?
- ❏ Distance from others' signs? Sign on curtain?
- ❏ Billing on marquees?
- ❏ Signs on vehicles (sound trucks, courtesy cars, etc.)?
- ❏ Any conflicts with permanent signage or arena suppliers?

3. Advertising Credits
- ❏ On stationery?
- ❏ In name of event? On program cover?
- ❏ In program advertisement?
- ❏ In all advertising?
- ❏ In all print advertising only? In television billboards?
- ❏ On souvenirs (T-shirts, bumper stickers, etc.)?
- ❏ In Press releases?

4. Sponsorship Fee
- ❏ How paid? When paid?
- ❏ Secured by letter of credit or escrow?
- ❏ Refundable if television ratings are poor?

5. Merchandising Rights
- ❏ Can the sponsor sell T-shirts, mugs and similar souvenirs?
- ❏ Can the sponsor manufacture its own souvenirs or buy from the promoter at cost? Who gets the profit on merchandising efforts?

6. Ownership of Television Rights
- ❏ Who owns and controls?
- ❏ If the promoter owns, does the sponsor have right of first refusal on available spots? Is there an estimated rating and/or a rebate for low ratings?
- ❏ Does the sponsor get opening/closing credits or billboards?
- ❏ Does the sponsor have rights to use footage of the event for current and/or future advertising?
- ❏ Will the Promoter get all rights necessary from participants to allow use of clips in commercials without further compensation?

7. Public Relations and Personal Appearances
- ❏ Can the promoter commit key personnel or talent to personal appearances on behalf of the sponsor?
- ❏ Can the promoter commit its spokespersons to mention the sponsor's name whenever possible?
- ❏ Does the sponsor have the right to erect a courtesy tent?
- ❏ Can the promoter commit the key personnel participating in an event to attending post-event parties in their honor?
- ❏ Does the sponsor get free tickets (for key customers, tie-in contests. etc.)?

8. Future Options
- ❏ Does the sponsor have the right to renew its sponsorship on the same terms and conditions (plus a fixed increase in the price)?
- ❏ Does the sponsor have the right of first refusal for subsequent years?

TRADEMARKS
1. Sponsor's quality control
2. Promoter's quality control
3. Ownership of special logos

LIABLITIES
1. To observers
2. To participants
3. To the site
4. To innocent bystanders
5. For infringement of trademarks
6. For contractual commitments in the event of rain, broadcast interruption, force majeure events

Adapted from—Reed, M. H. (1990). *Legal aspects of promoting and sponsoring events.* Chicago, IL: International Events Group.

Figure 13.2. Sponsorship Contract Checklist.

THE OLYMPIC GAMES AND SPONSORSHIP

Marketing is a basic function and central dimension of the Olympic enterprise, and as with other sport organizations, it requires specific planning and the performing of distinct activities. Leading up to the 2012 London Games, the International Olympic Committee officially surpassed the $1 billion sponsorship mark in 2011. Olympic and amateur sport organizations have, over the past several years, become very dependent upon sponsorship income. Olympic organizations are essentially resource-conversion machines. These organizations obtain resources from sponsors and convert them into specific products and services that are provided to the public. To accomplish this, Olympic organizations must create an exchange with the sponsor (Stotlar, 2009). Typically, these exchanges have been in the form of signage, logo presentation, hospitality opportunities, and identification with high-level teams and athletes. There are plenty of opportunities for sale in the Olympics: television, commercials, product licensing, product exclusivity at the Games, team sponsorships, Olympic Movement sponsorships, awards presentations, training center support, product endorsements, and almost anything a marketer could devise (Rosner & Shropshire, 2011; Stotlar, 2009).

Sport sponsorships between Olympic organizations and corporations have existed for many years. In 1896, Kodak had an ad in the official program of the first modern Olympics, and by 1928, Coca-Cola had begun its long-standing relationship with the Olympic movement. Sponsorship and the Olympics have a prolonged relationship and one that has increased significantly in complexity.

In 1985, the IOC hired ISL Marketing to create a program to facilitate corporations interested in sponsoring the Olympic Games (Rosner & Shropshire, 2011). The Olympic Partner (TOP) Programme was the creation. The TOP Programme brings together the rights of the IOC as owner of the Olympic Games, the two Games Organizing Committees, and the National Olympic Committees throughout the world as partners

The Olympics provide an excellent (if expensive) way for brands to reach a global market. Courtesy of Stock.xchng

in one four-year sponsorship program (Rosner & Shropshire, 2011). This process also accomplished another major goal of any sport marketer: to make it easier for consumers to buy one's product. Another factor in this formula was the IOC's restructuring of the games so that an Olympic Games (Summer or Winter) would occur every two years instead of both Games occurring in one year with a four-year cycle. This would allow sponsors to gain more long-term benefits and would spread the payments over an extended period.

The system was designed to allow a limited number of sponsors to receive special treatment and benefits on a worldwide basis and achieve exclusivity and protection in their Olympic sponsorship activities. Specifically, TOP sponsors would receive the following benefits (Rosner & Shropshire, 2011; Stotlar, 2009):

1. Product exclusivity—Only one sponsor would be allowed for any product category. This meant that if Coca-Cola and Visa were members of the TOP, then Pepsi and American Express would not be allowed to become involved with Olympic sponsorship on any level, including internationally, nationally, or with the organizing committee.

2. Use of marks and designations—Each participant was granted the right to use the solitary Olympic rings and to use them in combination with all National Olympic Committee (NOC) designations. This gave them worldwide and local impact. Companies could also use the "Official Sponsor" and "Official Product" designations. All Organizing Committee logos were also available to sponsors.

3. Public relations and promotional opportunities—Sponsors were given special tie-ins and media events to increase their exposure.

4. Access to Olympic archives—The IOC made articles from its archives in Switzerland available to sponsors for special exhibits and displays. Film and video archives were also available.

5. Olympic merchandise and premiums—Clothing and apparel bearing the Olympic logos could be used for sales incentives and marketing activities. Visa had to reorder company shirts five times in 1996.

6. Tickets and hospitality—Sponsors received priority access to seating at both the Winter and Summer Games.

7. Advertising options—Each participant in TOP was given first chance at souvenir program ads and the option (where possible) of television commercial purchases.

8. On-site participation—Point-of-purchase and product display were included in the package. Companies would also have certain rights to concession areas and space for product sampling. For example, Kodak provides each athlete in the Games with a disposable camera and supplies the 900 photojournalists with 175,000 complimentary rolls of film.

9. Research—Each sponsor would receive a full research report on the public's reception of their participation and an assessment of the valued-added benefits. Research after the 1998 Games showed significant improvements in product image for TOP participants.

10. First right of negotiation for the next quadrennial—Those who were satisfied with TOP would have the option to continue in their product category. (Rosner & Shropshire, 2011; Stotlar, 2009)

For the 2008 Summer Olympic Games in Beijing, 9 TOP sponsors were secured, with each paying about $100 million for TOP Partner status ("2010 Marketing Fact File," 2010). Since the 1985 development of TOP, sponsorship has become an integral part of the Olympic movement. Over the last two decades, TOP served two major goals of the IOC: It made the IOC less dependent on television revenues, and it assisted all countries in the world with sport development through a shared-revenue system.

TRENDS AND GRASSROOTS SPONSORSHIP

One of the most important issues that sport marketers should look into is how their corporation can benefit from sponsoring at the grassroots level. Many sport-related companies are realizing that speaking to consumers in a local environment may be more persuasive than nationwide involvement. However, some caution should be exercised when working with grassroots events. Event personnel are often largely composed of volunteers with unproven success. When sponsoring their event or property, one's corporate reputation is in their hands.

The movement to event sponsorship and away from individual endorsement should continue, as consumer data show that the credibility of individual endorsers is low. Events can be successful for the sponsor regardless of who wins, and they are less likely to become entangled in controversy (i.e., Tiger Woods, Mike Tyson theory). However, the scandal surrounding the Salt Lake City 2002 Olympic bid showed that events are not immune to controversy that could adversely affect sponsors. The very nature of the event can also cause trouble for sponsors. For instance, animal rights activists have threatened to boycott products from the sponsors associated with the Iditarod dogsled race because of alleged cruelty to animals. The Professional Rodeo Cowboys Association moved to diminish the possibility of controversy through the publication of a brochure detailing the methods employed to safeguard animals used in rodeo events.

Another interesting sponsorship trend appeared when sport computer game manufacturer Electronic Arts began selling sponsorship on outfield walls and other signage in its video games. These sponsorships proved to be very effective in targeting youth markets.

Sport marketers can certainly look toward including the arts and social issues in their marketing campaigns. Consider these three noteworthy examples. The Denver Nuggets of the NBA had a very successful program exchanging game tickets for handguns. For many years, the United States Sports Academy used various sponsors to support a sport art museum housed on its campus. In relation to social issues, an event was started in 1993 to honor the late college basketball coach Jim Valvano and raise money for cancer research. The college basketball tournament entitled "Coaches vs. Cancer" and the Jimmy V Foundation raise over $1,000,000 annually.

The power of the Internet has also made it possible to expand one's dominion for securing candidates for endorsements and events for sponsor partnering. Many sport organizations post a Request for Proposals (RFP) on their websites in order to facilitate a wide range of companies looking to partner through sponsorship. Shoe manufacturer Airwalk also used its website to attract potential endorsees through an online application form. Airwalk's Internet strategy seemed particularly appropriate given the lifestyles of its primary clientele.

In the dynamic worlds of sport and finance, new trends will certainly emerge. The challenge for sport marketers is to keep abreast of the industry and creatively seek opportunities to use sponsorships and endorsements to market products and services.

CHAPTER SUMMARY

The purpose of this chapter was to describe how sport organizations could enhance their marketing efforts through athlete endorsements and sport sponsorships. Because of their knowledge and power within certain groups, sport companies can effectively use opinion leaders to increase product sales. Opinion leaders can also be used in product sampling and prototype testing. Endorsement of products by individual athletes has been a marketing practice in sport for decades, yet its popularity has wavered. A credibility problem with individual endorsements exists because many consumers believe that sports celebrities endorse products only for the money. The scope of all marketing strategies and tactics must also include attention to the organization's social responsibility and ethical business practices.

A trend that appears to be successful is cross-promotion, whereby several companies band together around an athlete or event to gain additional exposure. The objectives for sponsorship center on market communication. Event sponsorship can provide companies an opportunity to interact with clients and customers on a large scale, whereas choosing an individual athlete as a spokesperson can enhance brand awareness and consumer loyalty. The company can use sport sponsorship to communicate to the market that it is a successful and socially responsible firm that produces and sells quality products (Ferrand & Pagés, 1996). The concerns for the future are whether the sport sponsorship and endorsement fields are saturated and whether sponsors will switch to other areas like the arts and regional festivals to accomplish their objectives.

DISCUSSION QUESTIONS

1. Describe the advantages and disadvantages of having an individual athlete as a product endorser.
2. Compare and contrast the sponsorship rights available through each level of Olympic sports: IOC, NOCs, NGBs, IFs.

SUGGESTED EXERCISES

1. Attend a local sport event where sponsors have signage displayed in the venue. After exiting the event, ask patrons which, if any, of the sponsors they can remember.

PROFESSIONAL ASSOCIATIONS AND ORGANIZATIONS

IEG Sponsorship Report
International Events Group
640 North LaSalle, Suite 600
Chicago, IL 60610-3777
www.sponsorship.com
1-800-834-4850

Sports Market Place
Franklin-Covey
7250 N. 16th Street
Phoenix, AZ 85020
www.sportscareers.com

SUGGESTED READINGS

Stotlar, D. K. (2001). *Developing successful sport sponsorship plans.* Morgantown, WV: Fitness Information Technology.

14

Using Licensing and Logos in the Sport Industry

OVERVIEW

Licensing is the act of granting to another party the right to use a protected logo, design, or trademark. Although trademark licensing may be traced back hundreds of years, dramatic growth occurred in the 1980s and 1990s. Comic book heroes, cartoons, schools, professional teams, clubs, causes, characters, and many other subjects became featured designs on clothing. In 2010, the worldwide licensing industry was worth approximately $170 billion at retail, with the U.S.A. generating approximately $110 billion and Europe generating $34 billion. In North America, the sport leagues (NBA, NFL, NHL, etc.) own the license properties of the clubs. The market of sport licensing in Europe is more complex, as one must negotiate with each club to use the license of a team. Sport typically accounts for about 17% of the licensing industry's global revenues.

Sales of sport-related merchandise subsided in the late 1990s due in part to changes in fashion trends. The market showed steady growth from 2000–2008 with a slight drop-off in 2009 (Miller,

Trademark licensing allows franchises to increase brand visibility through merchandise sales. Courtesy of U.S. Navy

2011). Regardless of fluctuations in market conditions, licensing can be an effective component in branding strategies for many sport entities.

Historically, sport organizations have found it desirable to initiate efforts to protect the investment in their name and marks through trademark licensing. Through such programs, sport organizations could receive name recognition and substantial revenue. In 1963, the National Football League established its licensing program to bring the protection of team names and insignia under central control. On the collegiate scene, the University of California at Los Angeles (UCLA) began its licensing program in 1973 (Irwin & Stotlar, 1993). Other sport organizations quickly began to establish licensing programs.

On the revenue side, about $17.9 billion is attributable to the U.S. professional leagues plus NASCAR (Miller, 2011). In 2010, each NFL team received over $10 million from the league's licensed product sales of over $30 billion. The other professional leagues reported significant revenues as well. The National Basketball Association realized $1.8 billion in sales, followed by Major League Baseball at $3 billion and the National Hockey League at more than $730 million (Miller, 2011).

The industry has not been devoid of turmoil. The significant declines in the late 1990s pushed three of the biggest companies producing licensed sportswear into bankruptcy. Pro-Player and Starter went bankrupt in 1999, and in 2000, Logo Athletic filed for bankruptcy. Sales of licensed professional sport apparel declined 30–40% in 2000, yet the succeeding 10 years saw modest growth until the economic downturn of 2009. This situation has led many of the professional leagues to re-examine their licensing programs. The move has been to reduce the number of licensees and work on partnership between the league and the licensee.

The profits generated from licensing are not limited to professional teams completing in league play. NASCAR was able to generate over $1.1 billion annually in licensed product sales (Miller, 2011). Individual events have also been capable of deriving significant revenues from licensed products. The 2010 World Cup (soccer) revenues from licensing were estimated at $3 billion in worldwide sales. World Cup managers set up 200 official World Cup shops in South Africa and a total of 3,000 outlets for licensed merchandise. Adidas alone sold more than $1.8 billion in licensed goods.

Sport organizations such as the United States Olympic Committee receive significant licensing revenues that account for approximately 25% of their budget ("2010 Media Guide," 2010).

Olympic organizations develop programs to create Olympic Games-related products, merchandise and souvenirs for consumers through licensing agreements that grant the use of Olympic marks, imagery or themes to third-party companies that market and manufacture the products. Olympic Games licensing programs are managed by the Olympic Games Organizing Committees under the direction of the International Olympic Committee (IOC). Licensing revenues from Beijing were $163 million from 68 licensees, and Vancouver 2010 came in at $51 million from 48 licensees (International Olympic Committee, 2011).

Collegiate sport entities also profit measurably from the sale of licensed products. Collegiate licensing is a $4 billion a year industry, about 80% of which is handled by the Collegiate Licensing Company (CLC). CLC serves as the exclusive licensing agency for over 200 collegiate properties located in 44 states across the U.S. Current clients include the Bowl Championship Series (BCS), the Rose Bowl, the Heisman Trophy and the NCAA (including the Men's and Women's Final Four, the College World Series, and all NCAA Championships), as well as many of the most recognized colleges and universities across the U.S., including Texas, Notre Dame, Florida, Michigan, Georgia, North Carolina, Alabama, Penn State and Arizona ("About CLC," n.d.). The CLC originated in the 1980s to assist colleges and universities across the U.S. in strengthening the market for licensed apparel through leveraging retailers. Through their assistance, universities are better able to secure shelf space in the market and establish a defined protocol for dealing with organizational licensing and merchandising. Furthermore, their clients can work to set more uniform royalty fees and payment schedules. Typically, royalty rates for colleges and universities run about 8% of the price at wholesale. The CLC was acquired by IMG as part of their IMG College service in 2006.

Michigan's longstanding deal with Nike was replaced by adidas in 2008. The deal reportedly pays the university $7.5 million per year (Vosgerchian, 2007). Adidas also has deals with UCLA, Nebraska and Tennessee. Nike still has sponsorship and licensing rights at the University of Texas at Austin and the University of North Carolina, among others. Many universities have licensing and sponsorship deals generating over $1 million in annual licensing revenues.

In a new licensing twist, the CLC has also contracted with EA Sports, the nation's leading producer of sports video games to offer games linked to the most popular college teams in the country (Ryan, 2005). However, in 2010, former UCLA basketball player Ed O'Bannon filed a class action lawsuit against the NCAA and CLC in federal District Court in San Francisco on behalf of himself and other former student-athletes.

O'Bannon was angry after seeing his highlight clips from 1995 being used to promote NCAA broadcasts. O'Bannon's legal argument is that requiring student athletes to sign away their rights of publicity in perpetuity is a violation of Section 1 of the Sherman Antitrust Act. The NCAA believes that prohibiting college athletes from receiving payments for their athletic skills preserves the amateur nature of the college game, and therefore promotes, not restrains, competition in the market for college sports and sports products. Thus, the NCAA can, without compensation to the athletes, license their names and images for apparel, video games, broadcasts, and highlight DVDs, long after they have graduated from college.

The current trend in collegiate licensing is to broaden distribution channels and to maximize brand exposure across multiple markets (Freifeld, 2005). Several large companies (like the CLC) entered the business to assist sport organizations in the management of their licensing programs. In these organizations, the licensing agent helps in the protection of an organization's logo or marks. The CLC developed seven basic goals with short-term and long-term strategies (Battle, Bailey, & Siegal, 1991; Bhonslay,

1999a; Conklin, 1999; Freifeld, 2005). The consortium not only affects its members (over 200 in 2011), but it also directly and indirectly affects nonmember schools. Their goals include the following:

1. To attract, maintain, and strengthen a prestigious base of universities, bowls, and athletic conferences.
2. To attract and maintain a base of licensees sufficiently large to cover all potential market segments and distribute all marketable products.
3. To identify retailers that are current or potential carriers of collegiate merchandise and show them the requirements and opportunities of collegiate licensing.
4. To identify consumers of collegiate products and encourage them to buy licensed products.
5. To improve the effectiveness of current methods of enforcement and to develop new methods.
6. To establish marketing programs that can expand the market for "Officially Licensed Collegiate Products" and take advantage of synergistic marketing, advertising, and promotional programs.
7. To provide unparalleled services to member institutions and licensees and to develop a database and reports to give management the information needed to analyze, evaluate, and manage progress toward the goals previously listed.

Four factors led to the development of organized sport licensing (Irwin, 1990). One of those factors was the increased popularity of sport and the resulting media coverage. Successful athletic teams, especially in football and basketball, have been a rallying point for the public for many years. Increased popularity led to greater attendance at games, which led to increased media coverage. This, in turn, led to increased popularity, higher attendance figures, and even more media coverage. Stadiums and arenas were enlarged, front pages of major newspapers carried the outcomes of major sports contests, and television magnified sports and multiplied their popularity. Today, sporting events receive headline coverage virtually year round.

Another development during the 1970s was the technology involved with screen printing or silk-screening, which greatly expanded the licensing industry. Blank garments were easily acquired from a number of mills and could be printed to meet any demands. Printed T-shirts became a communications medium during the 1970s. Adults, as well as children, were part of a market that grew dramatically throughout the 1980s.

In sport, the demand for imprinted goods was advanced through fan pride, loyalty, and desire to support the team by wearing team colors and designs. Anyone who has attended major events knows the emotions that fans generate in support of their teams or favorite player. People found themselves extremely attracted to their favorite school, team, or player and desired a means through which they could express their feelings. As the market for imprinted products expanded, fans sought licensed goods as a method of expressing their support.

During the 1980s, the costs of running competitive sport programs increased dramatically. As a result, the sale of imprinted sport merchandise was activated to help build revenues. Parallel with the increases in sales, problems began to occur with logo abuse and counterfeit merchandise.

During the 2000 Major League Baseball "Subway Series," 24 federal marshals confiscated items from 80 bootleggers. After the final World Series Game, the NYPD raided one factory and retrieved $1 million in counterfeit goods and an official MLB logo-disk containing all of the League's protected marks. With these levels of abuse, sport managers quickly decided that they needed greater control over the use of their marks to prevent the obnoxious designs, poor-quality merchandise, and product liability risks that they were beginning to face.

In a sport licensing program, the marketer typically grants a manufacturer the right to use the organization's logo (or indicia) in the production and sale of merchandise. The licensee is required to sign a contract, pay royalties, and adhere to strict licensing regulations. Royalties for licensed goods typically run about 8–15% of the price for which an item is sold.

As a marketing vehicle, licensing enables sport organizations to generate consumer awareness and interest through logoed products, all with minimal capital outlay. The established protocol for licensing revenues in most professional sport leagues is to engage in profit sharing. All of the major professional leagues collect royalty payments through league subsidiaries normally called "Properties" (e.g., NBA Properties, NFL Properties). These entities collect all licensing revenues and then distribute them equally across all teams in the league.

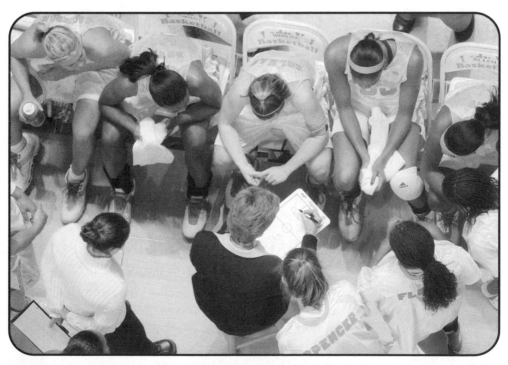

Profit sharing benefits both sport organizations and manufacturers. Courtesy of UT Lady Vols Media Relations

Although teams and events have profited from licensing, sport leagues have also entered the market. The NBA, PGA Tour and NASCAR began to open retail outlets to sell not only team and player/driver items but also organizational apparel. These sport organizations believed that they could build strong brands around their own logos (NBA, PGA Tour, NASCAR). The USOC also initiated similar brand-building activities in the late 1990s. The market for sport-logoed items is no longer limited to the team's home city, campus, or a local market, but extends around the globe.

To ensure standardization and quality, many souvenirs such as clothing, mugs, or novelties bearing sport logos are put through rigorous marketing and approval processes. Each item is checked for both quality and design. Products of inferior quality can be rejected, and strict labeling requirements can be enforced so that consumers can identify the merchandise as authentic. In addition, the product manufacturers can be required to carry product liability insurance, which protects the organization if legal action is filed because of an incident involving a licensed product.

Because of the popularity of sport licensing and trademarks on manufactured items and the potential revenue, commercial, professional, intercollegiate, and amateur sports organization marketers must develop a significant knowledge base in this area. There has also been an increasing amount of litigation in this field, and the guidelines governing the use of sports trademarks are still being established in the courts (Wong, 2002). As the national and international markets for merchandise bearing sport logos, names, and indicia develop, sport administrators will be required to seek legal avenues to protect their market, products, and marks. However, most sport organizations know little about how to protect their marks or how to license legally protectable properties to second parties for commercial use (Irwin, 1990).

Another aspect of licensing involves licensing a business name to other businesses. This is similar to a concept with which you may be familiar, franchising. Under licensing agreements, sport organizations such as fitness clubs (e.g., Gold's Gym) purchase the right to use an established name, and operate the business independently. However, in a franchise arrangement, the proprietor must purchase the franchise rights and typically agree to relinquish some operational control. Included with the purchase are restrictions on business practices often relating to facility size, mandated equipment, and audits/inspections by corporate officers. Although many of the benefits associated with franchise and licensing are best suited for start-up businesses, a recent trend has been for existing businesses to switch over to a recognized industry name through this process.

THE LEGALITIES OF TRADEMARK LICENSING IN SPORT

The case law governing sport licensing is sparse but has developed rapidly based on traditional trademark law. Sport organizations therefore must develop a firm legal basis for requiring that users of their trademarks obtain permission to use the trademarks and for requiring that the users pay royalties for the privilege. In order to more fully understand trademark licensing, one must be familiar with the following principles, terms, and definitions surrounding trademark law ("A Weighty Matter," 2004).

Trademark Principles

The Federal Trademark Act of 1946, Lanham Act 45, 15 U. S. C. 1051-1127 (1946), commonly known as the Lanham Act, governs the law of trademarks, the registration of trademarks, and remedies for the infringement of registered trademarks (Griffith, 2003; Wong, 2002). The Trademarks Law Revision Act, which went into effect in 1989, was Congress's first overall revision of the Lanham Act since 1946. The revised Lanham Act created major changes in federal trademark law that are highly relevant to sport trademark registration and licensing. *Sports Edge* magazine suggests that manufacturers that encounter problems with trademark infringement email the U.S. Commerce Department for help. The fundamental aspects in the use of trademarks are (Irwin, 1990):

1. Trademark: "Any word, name, symbol, or device, or any combination thereof used to identify and distinguish the goods of one person from those manufactured or sold by others."
2. Service mark "Any word, name, symbol, or device, or any combination thereof used to identify and distinguish the services of one person from the service of others."
3. Collective mark: "A trademark or service mark used by members of a cooperative, association, or other collective group or organization."
4. Mark: "A shorthand reference to any type of mark, including trademarks, service mark, and collective marks."
5. Registered mark: "A mark registered in the United States Patent and Trademark Office, as provided under the Act." (United States Department of Commerce, 1993, p. 1)

Infringement of a Trademark

The Lanham Act defines trademark infringement as the reproduction, counterfeiting, copying, or imitation, in commerce, of a registered mark "in connection with the sale, offering for sale, distribution, or advertising of any goods or services on or in connection with which such use is likely to cause confusion, or to cause mistake or to deceive without consent of the registrant" (United States Department of Commerce, 1993, p. 7).

Secondary meaning. Secondary meaning is a mental recognition in the buyer's mind that associates symbols, words, colors, and designs with goods from a single source. It tests the connection in the buyer's mind between the product bearing the mark and its source (Wong, 2002). Certain terms that are selected or invented for the express purpose of functioning as trademarks may be classified as inherently distinctive. Such marks are protectable and can be registered immediately on use. One such example would be the swoosh created by Nike. However, some potential marks describe products or services, geographic designations, or personal surnames. To qualify for protection as a mark, the courts require evidence that such a term has acquired secondary meaning; that is, consumers associate the products or services under the term with one particular source (Wong, 2002). The example here is that one shoe company produced a football shoe called Montana. They claimed that it was a generic reference to a geographical region. Football player Joe Montana, his agent, and eventually the courts disagreed.

Laches. Laches may arise when a party fails to assert a right or claim within a reasonable time, and the other party relies on this inaction to claim use of the other party's mark (Wong, 2002). An example of just this case arose when the University of Pittsburgh tried to stop Champion from producing sweatshirts with the Pitt logo. The court in this case said that because Pitt had previously allowed Champion to use its logo, it could not now prevent its use by Champion.

Each of the types of marks described earlier is protected equally under the Lanham Act. Sport organization names, team names, and logos may be described as trademarks, service marks, or collective marks (Wong, 2002). Any of these marks used on items such as clothing and novelties as well as services is entitled to protection. Registered marks are not always confined to team names and indicia. In the not-too-distant past, sports facilities registered their names, including the 1988 Olympic Oval in Calgary, Wrigley Field in Chicago, and Fenway Park in Boston.

Because of the complexity of managing a sport-licensing program (integrating financial, promotional, and legal responsibilities), there have been organized efforts to control the use of sport organizations' logos, trademarks, and copyrights. As a result, organizations have been faced with a serious dilemma: internal versus external management (Irwin & Stotlar, 1993). Irwin's (1990) research and subsequent publications shed considerable light on this decision.

Another twist of the licensing setting occurred in 2000 when Nike signed an arrangement with British football (soccer) club Manchester United for $432.3 million (10 years beginning in 2002) to manage its licensing program. Not only did Nike obtain exclusive worldwide sales of merchandise,

Operational Protocol Factors in Sport Licensing

- Program Governance and Leadership
- Designated internal licensing authority
- Principal licensing assignment full-time
- Direct report to central administrator
- Licensing policy committee assembled
- Professional licensing agency assistance
- Program Protection and Enforcement
- Legal specialist consultation
- Majority of logos registered as trademarks
- Licensee application and screening process
- License issuance and renewal procedures
- Basic agreement nonexclusive
- Execution of joint-use agreements
- Execution of international licenses
- Product sample required for quality control
- "Licensed product" identification required
- Counterfeit logo detection procedures
- Counterfeit logo reduction procedures
- Program Promotions and Public Relations
- Proactive recruitment of licensees
- Proactive recruitment of retailers
- Licensee/retailer public relations program
- Advertising used to promote products/program
- Publicity used to promote products/program
- Licensing program information published
- Revenue Management
- Advance payment required
- Uniform royalty charged on all products
- Written royalty exemption policy
- Royalty verifications routinely conducted
- Royalty verifications conducted by specialist
- Written royalty distribution policy

but they were also authorized to run the worldwide merchandising program for the team. Previously, Manchester United had established stores in China, Singapore, Kuala Lumpur, Dubai, Kuwait, Dublin, and Cape Town. Manchester United and Nike formed Manchester United Merchandising Limited (MUML), a joint-venture business controlled by Nike (Kaplan, 2003).

Research by Irwin (1990) examined the pros and cons of internal versus external management and found that most organizations are better off handling their own programs. Specific factors in program design were established against which sport organizations could judge their programs. A review of these operational factors seems appropriate (Irwin 1990; Irwin & Stotlar, 1993).

The advantages and disadvantages assignable to internally and externally managed licensing programs must be reviewed within the context of the organization's resources. Internally managed programs are generally more expensive to run, but they yield higher profits. External or agency-managed programs usually offer easier access to wholesale and retail networks and may have better nationwide success.

Many sport organizations utilize agencies to initiate a licensing program. The agencies typically have a higher level of expertise, more manufacturing contacts, and an understanding of all of the management factors that must be addressed. Once the licensing program is operating efficiently, the sport organization can bring the program in-house and obtain greater control. Furthermore, profits can be maximized by avoiding the 30% commissions normally charged by agencies.

Sport licensing is a journey, not a single destination. All factors affecting the program must be considered. Irwin's (1990) conclusions prescribed a licensing paradigm. The major components of a licensing system should include:

1. An examination of the feasibility of assigning a full-time licensing administrator.
2. An evaluation of the cost-effectiveness of internal versus external management of the program based on internal resources and potential markets and profits.
3. Identification of a single administrative authority for licensing agreements.
4. The development of policy for the issuance of exclusive and nonexclusive license agreements.
5. The design of specific royalty and exemption policies.
6. Application procedures for issuance/renewal of licenses.
7. A process whereby licensees must disclose financial stability, distribution intent, and licensing references.
8. A request for advance payments from licensees as earnest money to be applied to future royalties.
9. The establishment of a uniform royalty rate calculated on the net cost of the licensed item sold.
10. The requirement to furnish finished samples of the licensed merchandise.
11. The requirement to furnish certificates of insurance pertaining to licensed merchandise sold.
12. The federal registration of at least one of the organization's marks.

13. The required use of licensee identification on all merchandise distributed (hang tag, label, etc.).

14. A plan for the allocation of royalties received by the organization.

15. An enforcement policy including the responsibility to police merchandisers and issue cease and desist orders.

16. Consultation with trademark law specialists as needed.

17. The performance of compliance review with licensees.

18. The recruitment and recognition of licensees on a sustained basis.

19. The development of licensing brochures or guidelines for distribution to prospective licensees.

20. The reporting structure for the licensing administrator within the organization (p. 151).

Many of the professional baseball teams (Chicago Cubs, Atlanta Braves, San Francisco Giants, and New York Yankees, among others) have developed methods that borrow strengths from both systems. Although MLB administers the licensing program for all baseball clubs, these clubs aggressively began to sell their own merchandise through specialty catalogs, corporate-owned retail stores, and online sales. Not content with collecting only the 10% royalty provided by MLB, these organizations began selling the merchandise directly to their fans to bring retail profit margins to the team. These profit margins averaged 50% after expenses were taken from the typical 350% markup from wholesale cost. Almost all major professional sport teams operate retail stores in addition to their website merchandising. Regardless of the system employed, the major objectives of any sport licensing program are threefold: (a) Protection—to protect the trademarks of the organization, (b) Public Relations—to create a favorable image and positive exposure for the organization, and (c) Profit—to maximize revenues (Irwin, 1990).

Trademark Licensing Agreements

Program enforcement procedures include all methods of securing and exercising protection of the sport organization's property rights in its name, logo, seals, and symbols. As sport licensing programs are constructed and policy parameters are established, licensing administrators typically develop contractual relationships with licensees as a part of the program enforcement protocol (Irwin, 1990). The primary legal base for this contractual relationship has been the licensing agreement. This agreement should provide for controls, checks, and balances regarding the exclusivity of mark, usage, royalty management, and quality control (Irwin, 1990). Previous empirical data have indicated that the authority to grant and execute licensing agreements on behalf of the organization came primarily from upper-level administration.

According to experts in the industry, the elements that should be examined in a licensing agreement include, first and foremost, the parties entering into the agreement. The pertinent definitions encompassed in the agreement should be defined and all service marks and trademarks covered by the agreement must be delineated. The contract should also describe the specific products to be licensed, the duration of the agreement, and terms under which the agreement can be terminated or modified. It is also imperative that the royalty and payment structure be addressed, complete with details providing for audits. Specifically, the contract should define the royalty on net sales without deduction for shipping, advertising, or even returns or uncollectible accounts. The agreement should prescribe the reporting procedures and the payment methods and schedule. Other areas traditionally covered would include the types of products to be licensed, the rights for approval, ownership of artwork and designs, insurance and indemnification, and the territory governed by the agreement. Finally, it is crucial for the organization to restrict the ability of the licensee to assign the license to subcontractors.

Although licensing contracts are intended to control the use of registered marks, the situation may be spinning out of control. Battles are continually fought over who has the right to control. This issue has surfaced most frequently in professional sports. The NFL instituted a program to capture what seemed to be lost revenues. Although the league obtained royalties from the sale of team-logoed items, the players were attracting sponsorship dollars from corporations for displaying corporate logos on shoes, gloves, and sideline hats. In a move to profit from these images during the game, the NFL established the Pro Line program. This program required companies who wished to have their logo visible during an NFL game to pay a fee to the league. In some instances, depending on the scope of the license, the fees surpassed $50 million per year.

To many, this action seemed like extortion. The league was restricting the rights of player to wear shoes and other items that were not specified as "uniforms" under the collective bargaining agreement. Therefore, if a player wanted to wear a shoe from a company that had not paid the fee to the league, he would have to tape over (spat) the logo. The league even went so far as to hire former players to police the sidelines looking for unauthorized logos.

All of the professional leagues have reduced the number of licensees in a strategy to assist their licensing partners by allowing "strategic exclusivity" in particular segments of the market in order to maximize the value of the brand. In this sense, a lesser number of licensees is better, more manageable, and more profitable.

CHAPTER SUMMARY

As evidenced by the financial data presented earlier, sport licensing has (since its inception) achieved substantial commercial success. The development of this industry has obviously had a considerable impact on manufacturers, retailers, and consumers. The future of sport licensing seems very bright and appears to be on solid legal ground; a good foundation has been laid, and the present multi-billion-dollar market should easily expand. However, styles and trends can change as quickly as they evolve, and there seems to be some disparity over the strategy in the market place. The trend in collegiate licensing to broaden their distribution channels and sign as many as 380 separate licensees is in stark contrast to the trend in professional sports to minimize licensees and maximize each licensee's exclusivity and profitability. In the author's opinion, the professional sports team approach seems to represent a better partnership which will, in the long term, serve both organization and licensee better. With a clear focus on all three elements of a sound licensing program (protection, profit and public relations) sport organizations can continue to manage successful licensing programs.

DISCUSSION QUESTIONS

1. What are the laws that affect licensing and trademarks?
2. What factors led to the development of organized sport licensing?

SUGGESTED EXERCISES

1. Investigate the origins of NFL Properties, Inc. Who was their first licensing director?
2. Develop a sport logo and determine the procedures and costs for registering that mark in your state.
3. Contact a sport organization with a registered mark(s) and request a copy of its graphic standards manual.

15

Social Media in Sport Marketing

by Doris Lu-Anderson, California State University Long Beach;
and Natasha T. Brison, Georgia State University

INTRODUCTION

Electronic technology is having a tremendous impact on sports and the sport business industry. Chapter 1 (see Table 1.17) explained that mobile devices and Internet technology are creating new methods of promoting sports and sport businesses, and are being used as new distribution channels. The growth of social media venues and marketing use for exposure and distribution has been increasing. Many sports fans, for instance, not only check their favorite teams and athletes on the Internet but also download apps to their mobile devices to follow scores and updated news. Some hardcore fans watch games on their mobile devices and discuss games with other fans on Facebook and Twitter when they are not at the game, and while at the game.

Social media has had a tremendous impact on consumers' shopping behaviors and businesses' marketing approaches. This chapter presents the social media concept and its influence on sport consumers and sport businesses.

WORLD WIDE WEB (WWW) AND INTERNET TECHNOLOGY

The explosive development of the World Wide Web (WWW) and Internet technology has greatly impacted sport marketing. Sport organizations and related entities have been exploring this new media to identify the most effective strategies to reach the target group and marketing objectives. Sport businesses are utilizing various new media platforms to market their products to consumers and business clients, from selecting and developing domain names, official websites, blogs, and online marketing advertising to utilizing YouTube and social media sites.

The improvement of Internet technology leads to a lower cost of computer storage, broadband, and accessories. Also, individuals find it is easier and faster to contact each other via various applications and electronic devices. For example, people can use email and Skype to contact friends, family, and business associates who live on the other side of the world within seconds and at low cost. Fans can follow their teams' scores and news on the Internet or electronic devices. Moreover, because more public information is available in cyberspace, corporations no longer monopolize information in the marketplace (Huang, 2009a, 2009b). The stakeholders of the sport franchises (e.g., owners, staff, community residents, fans, vendors) can easily retrieve information about the franchise's business development and team performance on the Internet.

WEB 1.0 AND WEB 2.0

Web 1.0 is referred to as the static websites resulting in a one-way flow of communication (Belch & Belch, 2011). Fans can retrieve team schedule and ticket info from an official Web 1.0-based website. Later, the term "Web 2.0" was introduced by Darcy Di-Nucci, a consultant of electronic information design, in January of 1999 (Cervinschi & Butucea 2010). In 2004, the term was defined further by Tim O'Reilly at the O'Reilly Media Web 2.0 Conference. He termed it as "a collection of open-source, interactive and user-controlled online applications expanding the experiences, knowledge, and market power of the users as participants in businesses and social processes" (William & Chinn, 2010, p. 426).

Web 2.0 denotes a new era of web application. Under the concept of Web 2.0, the World Wide Web is a decentralized platform where users participate, collaborate, interact, and share. With this concept, several pioneers have innovated various websites and social media networks, including Wikipedia, YouTube, Flickr, Facebook, Twitter, Linkedin, Digg, MySpace, SlidesShare, Yelp, Groupon, Google+, etc. Some of the Web 2.0 websites focus on publication, some focus on networking, online games (e.g., Zynga), or sharing. The websites with emphasis on interacting with the end users usually generate tremendous interest from marketers.

SOCIAL MEDIA

Social media has brought a new concept to the sport industry and helped create a booming growth in sport marketing communication. Clavio and Kian (2010) indicated that it is a trendy "new" media marketing tool with an unknown potential and possible growth. Web 2.0 allows users to use web applications to interact with other end users with user-friendly clicks. Social media applies the idea of Web 2.0 and expands to numerous operation systems. Users can easily create an account and start to build their network via friends' email or common background and interests. The more friends that the users include in their connection circle, the

Social media provides a low-cost, nearly instantaneous way to communicate with fans and consumers. © Nalaka174 | Dreamstime.com

more "'information threads" can be shared. A simple icon such as "like," "comment," or "share" permits users to engage with the topic. Also, the "User Generated Content (UGC)" feature lets users be the topic initiator, receiver, or participant.

The social media outlets facilitate people to engage with others who have similar interests, background, and experiences (Fullerton, 2010; Williams & Chinn, 2010). Therefore, after logging in a social media account on a computer, smartphone, or other electronic device (such as the iPad), people can connect with their friends, family, interest groups, business clients, favorite teams, favorite athletes, or favorite stores with just one click. The increased popularity of social networks has fueled a new opportunity for marketers (Fullerton, 2010). Included in this evolving communication is consumer-generated media (Petersen, Miloch, & Laucella, 2007), which then complements traditional internet information sources.

Because the computer infrastructure and electronic devices (e.g, smartphones, iPads) are widely used in the global market, people often use social media to search for and share information. Sport entities have found social media to be an easy and inexpensive way to communicate with fans. Therefore, many sport organizations and athletes have added social media links to their official websites in an effort to push news directly to the fans' accounts and provide a venue for feedback. Professional sport teams, college athletic departments, and conferences have Facebook fan pages and Twitter accounts to disseminate news. Professional athletes such as Yani Tseng of LPGA, LeBron James of the NBA, Tony Hawk of pro skateboarding, and Georges St-Pierre, professional mixed martial arts fighter, all have a Facebook fan page and/or Twitter account so they can easily share updates with fans and the press. Indeed, social media offers athletes a different news distribution channel to keep fans informed of their current status and career decisions, and similarly, these same features have driven fans or followers to athletes' social media sites (Sanderson, 2011). Sport organizations such as the International Olympic Committee (IOC), USA Volleyball Association, Rock 'n' Roll Marathon, Nike, action sport apparel companies, and retail fitness and sport clubs have all adopted social media outlets (or social networks) such as Facebook, Twitter, and YouTube channels as additional promotional mix elements and message distribution channels.

Facebook was invented in a dorm at Harvard University in 2004 by a student, Mark Zuckerberg, and now is one of the largest social forums used by people around the world. As of September 2011, one of the most recognized social media websites, Facebook, has passed 800 million users (Olivarez-Giles, 2011). In February 2012, Facebook filed for an Initial Public Offering (IPO), which is the first sale of stock by a company to the public. Twitter was established in 2006 as a social media tool by Biz Stone, Evan Williams, and Jack Dorsey as another venue to connect people with other people (Johnson, 2009; Schultz, Caskey, & Esherick, 2010). Each Twitter post allows up to 140 characters to send messages (tweets) with photos and location. Twitter has close to 360 million users as of April 2011 (McMillan, 2011).

A professional networking website, Linkedin, was started out in the living room of co-founder Reid Hoffman in 2002 and launched in May 2003 (Linkedin, n.d.). Linkedin allows members to manage and share their professional identities online and engage with their professional networks, access shared knowledge, and search business opportunities. Linkedin became a public held company in May 2011 and has more than 135 million members worldwide as of November 3, 2011 (Linkedin, n.d.).

Another popular social media site, YouTube, was created by Chad Hurley, Steve Chen, and Jawed Karim in February 2005 and officially launched in December 2005 (YouTube.com, n.d.). YouTube was bought by Google in November 2006 for US $1.65 billion. As of May 2011, YouTube has about 3 billion daily views (Wauters, 2011). YouTube allows users to upload, view, share, and comment on videos. Many people, young and old, use YouTube to share videos with family and friends. In the sport industry, companies also use YouTube to distribute images. Based in San Diego, Sector 9 is a popular skateboard brand. With a limited marketing budget and knowledge of skaters' preference to watch footage, Sector 9 has its own YouTube channel to share skateboarding and surfing (long board) videos of their endorsed athletes. Skateboarders and surfers can share footage with a click. A big name in the industry, ESPN, uses YouTube to provide past videos on its YouTube channel as well. For marketers, YouTube offers a great and convenient vehicle to disseminate images and share with other potential customers. The continuous sharing of video clips can generate buzz and news.

Even though marketers have been utilizing social media outlets, they are still not really sure how to formulate effective tactics (Ang, 2011). Ideas and strategies have been presented in print media and cyber space. Before going further, reviewing the fundamental marketing communication concept will be helpful to lead us to identify the best strategy to integrate the organization's marketing and communication resources.

THE NEW WAY OF COMMUNICATION

In the traditional communication process, communication transmits from the source provider (e.g., newspapers and magazines) to the message receiver (e.g., audience and end users) unilaterally or bilaterally. On many occasions, the information is disseminated through various layers or messengers to reach the public. However, the individual consumers have limited opportunities to communicate with other users. This process requires much time for the sport organizations to learn the end user's reaction. Figure 15.1 shows the evolution of communication.

Via social media, sport businesses or organizations can send messages directly to business clients and individual consumers. They use in-house marketing teams or outsourced units to operate social media communication. In addition to the traditional promotional mix, the marketing teams can use blogs, social networks, wikis, and video sharing sites to send the information. In the meantime, the end users can share their opinions directly with other end users and with the sport organizations (see Figure 15.1). The community that the end-users form offers direct reactions and possible sales opportunities for the sport organizations.

For example, Lauren Cochran, the senior manager of marketing for the Philadelphia Flyers (NHL), stated that their franchise uses social media to enhance fans' visits to the official website. Social media also creates two-way communication for the sport franchise and fans, allowing them to communicate and engage in the Flyers' community

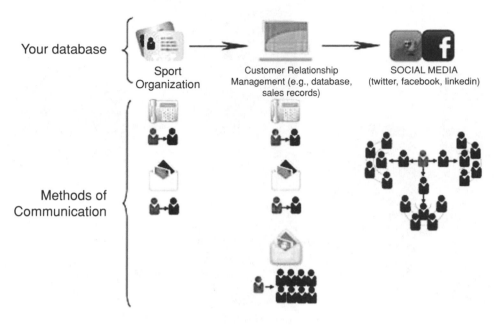

Figure 15.1. Evolution of Communication.

Adapted from Goodlife, 2009

more easily. For the sport team, social media is the new vehicle to drive traffic, create leads, increase sales, and conduct data collection about the customers (Paciolan, 2011).

In Figure 15.2, the sport organization or athletes use an in-house marketing team or outsource to a marketing agent to communicate with business clientele and consumers. In addition, to use traditional promotional mixes such as advertising, personal selling, sponsorship, sales promotion, and public relations, they also integrate social media into their dissemination of information. By using social media outlets, the organization can engage with consumers and receive direct feedback. The organization no longer needs to wait for a long time to receive feedback from the end-users. Likewise, fans and followers do not have to wait too long to obtain direct information from the organization.

Furthermore, the communication procedure has changed. In early days when a sport organization needed to make an announcement it would send a

Consumers access social media from many on-the-go devices, including smartphones, laptops, and tablets. © Geotrac | Dreamstime.com

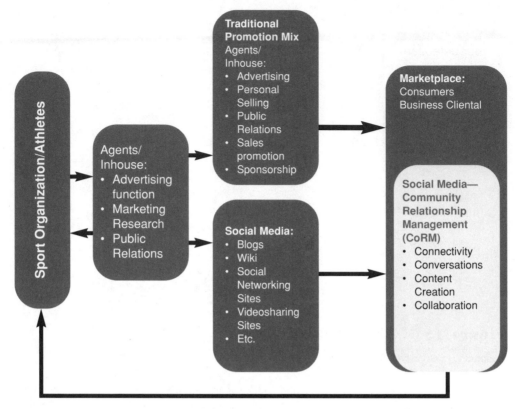

Figure 15.2. Social Media Communication Paradigm in Sport Industry.

Revised from the New Media Communications Paradigm by W.G. Mangold & D. J. Faulds (2009), Social Customer Relationship Management Model by M. Wu (2010), and the Community Relationship Management (CoRM) Model by L. Ang (2011).

press release to the media. With social media, sport franchises can break their own news first, post it to websites, send emails to journalists and directly to subscribed fans. Media outlets can pick up the news on the wire (Paciolan, 2011). Pro athletes also perceive the messages they post to social media sites as small individual press conferences (Sullivan, 2011). Instead of interviewing athletes directly for their opinions about specific news, journalists use quotes from athletes' posts.

Sport organizations integrate traditional and new communication mediums to reach the target market and objectives. It is the same for colleges. For example, many college alumni associations hope to strengthen the relationship with alumni through sport. The Florida State University Alumni Association posts game-day information on its official website and sends the information via email. In the message, the local alumni chapter and game viewing location options are listed. The local alumni chapter is responsible for forming a regional alumni club and delivering game viewing activity information. In the past, the local chapters used print newsletters or emails to update the members, but it is time consuming and expensive to use hard copy publishing and mail distribution. Due to the low cost and interactive features, more local alumni chapters now use social

Figure 15.3. An Example of University Alumni Association Using Social Media to Strengthen Alumni Community Relationship.

media to distribute information and react to each other's discussion threads in real time. For the alumni, it is a fun way to connect with each other and show their support for the university. For the university, it is a way to reinforce the alumni relationship, strengthen the university brand, and generate ticket sales and fundraising opportunities (see Figure 15.3).

SOCIAL COMMUNITY CUSTOMER RELATIONSHIP MANAGEMENT

Customer relationship management (CRM) has been widely used in industry and business to coordinate an organization's interactions with clients and potential customers. The goal is to find and attract new clients, cultivate customer relationships, and develop customers (Fullerton, 2010; Kotler & Keller, 2009). Professional sport teams use their customer database to determine the preferences of fans and their lifestyles. In this way, they can better serve the needs of fans and develop improved loyalty.

Following a similar concept, social media can be applied to bond with customers. In the marketplace, social media emphasizes cultivation of a community and strengthening of customer engagement. Therefore, researchers have developed a model of social community relationship management (CoRM) (Ang, 2010; Kane, Fichman, Gallaugher, & Glaser, 2009).

Ang developed a 4Cs model of social CoRM to display the concept—connectivity, conversations, content creation, and collaboration. The model is merged in the Social Media Communication Paradigm in Sport Industry (see Figure 15.2). The components of the 4Cs, with application examples, are as follows:

1. **Connectivity:** A large community of users needs to be developed to strengthen network communication. Various sport entities and athletes have created Facebook fan pages to encourage the fan community online. Fans connect with other fans who share similar interests.

   a) **Individual Athlete:** Many individual professional sport athletes have a Facebook fan page and/or a Twitter account. For example, professional beach volleyball player Misty May-Treanor's fan page has more than 625,000 fans. She updates her tournament results and clinic and charity activities regularly. The fans can easily receive her information and other fans' responses. Also, the fan page will show if there are other fans of Misty May-Treanor in this fan's network. Furthermore, Facebook will suggest that current users invite individuals who have similar interests but are not yet in their network. Thus the user's social network will expand.

b) **Local Chambers of Commerce:** They can develop fan pages to connect with businesses, residents, and visitors. For example, Key Largo, Florida is famous for its rich marine life and water sport activities. The Key Largo Chamber of Commerce uses a fan page to inform visitors of local weather, water sport events, and business activities to connect with followers all year round.

c) **B2B (Business-to-Business):** B2B businesses use social media to connect with their clientele as well. People are familiar with Linkedin as a professional networking tool. However, companies also use it strategically to create business leads for the organization. A social media and inbound marketing consultant, Peter Rastello, suggests that business owners can create a Linkedin group which relates to their business and start to collect members with a common interest (e.g., linking a scuba diving business and scuba divers). Members of the group can share news, business opportunities, and opinions. Also, the sport entity should link the official business website, blog, and social media applications on the Linkedin company home page (Rastello, 2010).

d) **Retail Sport Business:** Social media is an easy, inexpensive and effective marketing communication tool for small business owners because they can post outreaching messages anytime and anywhere. More importantly, successful brands on social media do not do hard-sell nor preach to their fans; instead, they engage with them (Vahl, 2011). An owner of a retail gym franchise, LA Boxing Carlsbad, echoes this idea. He states that his social media strategy is to create a sense of community and share the experience at the gym. He stated: "People who are fans on the Facebook are already our members. Therefore, there is no need to do more sales pitch on the fan page (R. Motano, personal communication, July 5, 2011). He uses pictures, videos, short description, humorous messages, and nutrition information to engage customers. At LA Boxing, the franchise headquarters has a main Facebook fan page to establish corporate brand image and attract business clients. At the local level, many franchisees have their own Facebook fan page and/or Youtube channel to bond with local customers. Franchisees can use local consumer behavior and lifestyle to customize the social media marketing initiatives because even the nearby neighborhood may have different customer preferences on using social media (R. Motano, personal communication).

e) **Sport Teams:** Social media platforms are fast and effective vehicles for teams to gather fans and interact with them. It is a two-way communication system which also collects fans' contact information and their consumption behavior data. For example, the Philadelphia Flyers push messages out to fans to offer exclusive content and promotions, and they create polls and questions to seek fans' feedback. Lauren Cochran, the senior manager of new media for the Philadelphia Flyers, shared that their fans cheer together for the team (Paciolan, 2011). Their social media contest during playoffs was very successful; it collected over 10,000 names after only 2 days of social media contests. The team uses the leads to nurture customer relationships and to develop sales opportunities.

The New Jersey Devils use social media extensively. The team founded its Mission Control program in February 2011 to serve as its social media hub for both the team and the arena, allowing fans to utilize the space and monitor messaging (New Jersey Devils, 2011). Will Carafello, the director of marketing for the Devils, said that to implement this Mission Control program, the team selected and trained 25 enthusiastic and tech-savvy fans to provide social media coverage, live chat, intermission tweet-ups, and more. They have been receiving positive feedback from fans and team. Currently the Devils have 250,000+ fans on their Facebook fan page. To be social media environment-friendly, the franchise even offers iPad rental in the arena (Paciolan, 2011).

f) **Independent sport coach and fitness instructor:** Coaches and fitness instructors who teach at various facilities can use social media to stay in touch with the members and clients after class. Messages can be about their teaching schedule, teaching philosophy, and activity pictures.

2. **Conversations:** A website's news feed offers the latest information about an individual or a sport organization. The users can easily click "like," "share," or "comment" to offer feedback. In the world of social media, having conversations with other users is fast and low cost. Through this type of "viral marketing" on social networks, information is spread out in real time to create buzz and distribute news. For example, the U.S. Olympic Team receives limited media coverage. Fans of Team USA do not have a direct platform to communicate with the team and other fans. The U.S. Olympic Team updated the current competition schedule of Team USA at the regional and national level on its Facebook fan page. Fans who "like" the U.S. Olympic Team on Facebook will automatically receive news updates and are able to create conservations with other fans that follow the team.

Another example of integrating traditional advertising with social media is a regional fast-food chain based in San Diego, California: Jack in the Box. For Jack in the Box, it is a challenge to retain frequent fast food users in a competitive market. The chain's marketing team decided to initiate a major marketing campaign that included a Super Bowl commercial, official company website, YouTube channel, Facebook page, and Twitter account. According to Terry Graham (2011), the chief marketing officer of the company, the storyline of the campaign started from the world without Jack. The first 30 seconds of the commercial was aired during the 2009 Super Bowl; in the commercial, the chain's mascot, Jack, was hit by a bus. For many years, Jack had been built to make customers feel they bonded with him (and through him, the brand). After the Super Bowl commercial, fans chatted with each other on the company's blog, Facebook page, Twitter account, and YouTube channel. The commercial was viewed repeatedly on YouTube. More than 80,000 "get well" messages were shared; 84,000 fans signed up for regular updates on Jack's condition; more than 2.3 million visitors flocked to hanginthere jack.com; and 900,000 fans visited coupon pages. Jack in the Box was the only regional player in the Top 10 list of 2009 Super Bowl ads on Yahoo Video, which received 763,000 views. Also, 500 PR placements and more than 90 million impressions were circulated. Overall, it is considered that consumers highly reengaged with the brand. (Graham,2011; "How to Make," 2010).

Teams also use social media to ask fans for advice. The Red Sox posted questions about a game time change. The post received more than 4,300 Facebook likes and 650 Twitter responses from fans. Thus, the conversation over social media has become as part of a Red Sox's media toolbox (Fisher, 2011).

Exercise apparel brands utilize social media to interact with customers frequently. For example, lululemon athletica is a Vancouver-based yoga and running apparel company. Growing from a clothing design and yoga studio, lululemon has become a multimillion dollar apparel business. The revenue of lululemon has grown from $148 million in 2007 to $711 million in 2011. Although the company has developed to become an international corporation, executives want it to stay organic and be truthful with *Yogis* and runners. Lululemon uses Facebook, Twitter, YouTube, Flickr, and a company blog to bond with customers. Messages include updates about new products, activity pictures, spiritual words, activities, questions. These are effective in generating feedback and conversing directly with customers. Also, the regional stores have their own social media pages to include more local activities with customers.

3. **Content Creation:** Successful media offers user-generated content (Ang, 2011). Sport organizations offer the news or conversation topics, and users are invited to share their feedback, pictures, or other visual materials. For example, the Mammoth Mountain Ski Resort in California releases news year round on social media. Followers are informed of the snow conditions and activities. Also, fans share their pictures, videos, and comments, which can create news buzz. For instance, the University of Southern California's skiing/snowboarding team posts their skiing and snowboarding footage on the Mammoth Mountain fan page via YouTube, which generates more buzz for the ski resort and the team. GoPro, the company behind the versatile GoPro action camera, encourages users to share their films on its fan page, which allows other Go Pro users to watch and post feedback.

4. **Collaboration:** One of the most well-known Web 2.0 methods, wiki, offers a platform for people to contribute on certain topics or projects. The most popular wiki, Wikipedia, includes numerous pages devoted to various sport teams' history,

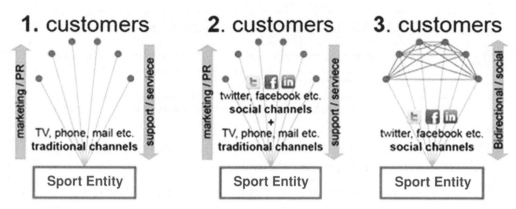

Figure 15.4. Social Customer Relationship Management Evolution.

Adapted from Wu, 2010,

player information, stats and more. Fans are able to contribute directly to the building and updating of these pages, keeping other fans informed about their favorite sport teams and organizations.

Michael Wu (2010) presented the evolution of social customer relationship management (see Figure 15.4). In this transforming process, marketing and PR from the sport entity has shifted from one-way support and service for customers to bidirectional feedback and social activity. Customers now have more opportunities to interact with other customers and also read the communication record between the sport entity and other customers, including customer reviews. The conversation becomes more transparent. Therefore, organizations need to listen and work with their fans to co-create value with them. Wu said, "You may have 10,000 employees watching the social stream, but the whole world is watching yours" (Wu, 2010, "My Perspective" para. 4)

CUSTOMERS LIKE SOCIAL MEDIA NETWORKING

Many spectators and customers receive event information from social media. Two marketing studies from Georgia Dome Research indicated that fans received game-related information from social media. For example, Pitts and DeMatteo (2011) noted that 32% of fans heard the Atlanta Football Classic (AFC) via social networking .The other study which surveyed fans at Southeastern Conference (SEC) Men's Basketball Tournament found that 12% of participants learned the game information from social media (Pitts, Boreland, Haynes, Rodgers, Shuyler, Staten et al., 2011).

Student customers spend hours on the Internet and mobile devices every week. Thus, they also like to receive campus activity messages via social media pages. For example, a study on campus recreation centers found that 32.9% of participants heard about the program on its Facebook fan page, and 54.5% from the official website. Furthermore, 45.2% of participants would like to be notified about upcoming activities via the Facebook fan page, and 59.5% prefer updates via the official website (Lathrop, 2012).

Table 15.1. Tips for Successful Social Media	
1	Post regularly and provide feedback. Consider consumers' viewing frequency.
2	Focus on customer engagement.
3	Offer links to your website, blog, Facebook, Twitter, YouTube channel, and Flickr stream, etc.
4	Create the proper balance of team information and promotions (particularly sales messages) and remember—no hard sales pitch!
5	Understand the customer and customize the social media style and tone.
6	There is no fast track. Put in the time and effort to build the community.
7	Be open and honest. Social media is about being authentic and personal, so be sure to follow this principle.
8	Tell the organization's story.
9	Have special offers for fans only.
10	Show outside links to the product or brand to maximize the buzz.
11	Ask fans to invite their friends.
12	Add a poll to the fan page to that the sport organization can discover fans' needs and wants.
13	Make it fun.

Summarized from: Vahl, 2011; Rastello, 2010; Warner, 2011.

Another study on intramural sport noted that 71.1% of participants want to receive activity messages from Facebook, 34.2% prefer Twitter, and 55.3% like intramural websites (Gross, 2012). These studies indicate that fans and customers do like to be informed through more traditional media such as official websites, newspapers, flyers, and word-of-mouth; but they also like to receive messages from social media. Therefore, sport organizations and campus recreation program should integrate traditional promotional tools with social media networks to keep customers informed and engaged. Table 15.1 contains tips for utilizing social media to successfully promote an organization.

THE LEGALITIES OF SOCIAL MEDIA IN SPORT MARKETING

The use of social media in marketing provides both benefits and opportunities for companies to promote brands. Companies have been able to not only use advertising and marketing dollars for additional campaigns but also reduce their budgets by utilizing Facebook and Twitter. Although these campaigns appear to help promote a company's brand, implementing a Facebook or Twitter marketing campaign is not without legal issues. The purpose of this discussion is to educate marketers about potential legalities that may arise when using social media in sport marketing.

There are two primary organizations that monitor and/or regulate advertising and marketing practices in the United States. The first is the Better Business Bureau (BBB); the second is the Federal Trade Commission (FTC). Serving communities in both the United States and Canada, the BBB was founded in 1912 with a vision to encourage "an ethical marketplace where buyers and sellers can trust each other" and a mission "to be the leader in advancing marketplace trust" (Council of Better Business Bureaus, 2012c, para. 1; para. 2). The BBB works to further its mission by creating a network of businesses that consumers can trust and alerting consumers when a business fails to adhere to certain marketplace standards. The organization provides services for both consumers and businesses. Consumers are able to conduct research on businesses and charities through the BBB's database of reviews. Searches may be conducted by business name, type, website URLs, phone numbers, or email addresses. If a consumer has a dispute or disagreement with a business, the BBB acts as a mediator for resolving the dispute. In 2010, the BBB received over 874,000 complaints in the U.S. and Canada, of which 75.5% were settled (Council of Better Business Bureaus, 2012f). For businesses, the BBB has a Resource Library, Specialized Programs and Services, and Advertising Review Services. Under the Advertising Review Services, businesses will find the National Advertising Review Council (NARC), the National Advertising Review Board (NARB), and the National Advertising Division (NAD) (Council of Better Business Bureaus, 2012d). The NARC was created to provide "guidance and set standards for truth and accuracy for national advertisers;" it also sets the policies for the NAD and the NARB (Council of Better Business Bureaus, 2012e, para. 1). The NAD's mission is to "foster public confidence in the credibility of advertising" (Council of Better Business Bureaus, 2012b, para. 1); this is achieved by providing a "low-cost alternative to litigation" for advertisers and regulators, and decisions are provided within 60 business days (Council of Better Business Bureaus, 2012a, para. 1). The NARB handles appeals of decisions by the NAD. Although most advertisers voluntarily adhere to the NAD decisions, it is important to note that the NAD cannot enforce its decisions, but it can refer matters to the Federal Trade Commission.

Created in 1914 under the Federal Trade Commission Act (FTCA), the Federal Trade Commission (FTC) is the regulatory agency that prevents false advertising and unfair competition among businesses. Section 5 and Section 12 are the primary sections for enforcement and regulation. Section 5 prohibits persons, companies, or organizations from engaging in unfair or deceptive acts in interstate commerce; Section 12 prohibits false advertisements that are likely to induce the purchase of consumer goods. For sport marketers, the most applicable FTC guideline which may be enforced through either Section 5 or Section 12 relates to the advertisements or marketing campaigns that will include athletes, celebrities, or general product consumers as endorsers. The first FTC guidelines regarding endorsements and testimonials were established in 1975 and finalized on January 18, 1980. The guidelines were drafted to assist companies with determining proper advertising conduct when utilizing endorsements. The FTC defines endorsements as "any advertising message (including verbal statements, demonstrations, or depictions of the name, signature, likeness or other identifying personal characteristics of an individual or the name or seal of an organization) that consumers are likely to believe reflects the opinions, beliefs, findings, or experiences of a party other than the sponsoring advertiser, even if the views expressed by that party are identical to those of the sponsoring advertiser" (16 CFR §255.0[b]). If an endorser is hired to promote a brand or product, FTC Guideline 16 C.F.R. §255.5 requires that he or she must fully disclose any "connection . . . that might materially affect the weight or credibility of the endorsement (i.e., the connection is not reasonably expected by the audience)."

PRACTICAL IMPLICATIONS

"Social media appears to be a force to be reckoned with when it comes to marketing, sponsorship opportunities, and connecting with a fan base" (Kishner & Crescenti, 2010, p. 25). Unfortunately, when choosing to conduct marketing activities through social media outlets such as Facebook or Twitter, sport organizations should be cautious about the marketing methods used to promote their brand and influence consumer purchase intentions. A few sponsors and advertisers, such as 1-800 Flowers and Coastal Contacts, Inc., have associated consumer perceptions of brand image and their intent to purchase on the company's number of Twitter followers, Facebook "likes," and Klout score, and as a result, marketing campaigns have focused on increasing consumer fans on these sites. Coined "like-gating" or "fan gating," the practice is defined as companies' encouraging consumers to "like" them on Facebook, or perform some other social media network function, in exchange for "something." This something may include freebies or entrance for contests, promotions, or sweepstakes, and access to offers is limited until the consumer clicks the "like" button or agrees to "follow" the brand.

In 2011, the BBB saw an escalation in consumer complaints regarding companies looking to boost their social media image by increasing the number of friends on Facebook or followers on Twitter. The decision by the NAD was the result of a complaint by 1-800 Contacts, Inc., a competitor of Coastal Contacts, Inc., an online supplier of contact lenses and eyeglasses. Coastal Contacts was offering a promotion through its Facebook page which expressed the claim: "Like this page! So you too can get your free pair of glasses!" There were additional terms and conditions that applied to the promotion that were not available until after the consumer "liked" the advertiser's Facebook page. For example, the company had a limit on the number of glasses available, and certain brands were not included in the promotion. Coastal also boasted through comments on its page about how many consumer "likes" it had obtained. The NAD determined in its investigation that the Coastal Facebook page "likes" reflected a "general social endorsement," and although accurate in this case, there was concern that the display of "likes" on a company's Facebook page would give the impression that consumers actually liked the brand, when in fact they chose to "like" the company to get a free gift or to enter a promotional contest. The NAD recommended that Coastal make several modifications to its page which included identifying that the supply is limited, including the cost of shipping and handling, and enhancing the "conditions apply" notice (NADNews, 2011). The BBB stated "that marketers must be careful what they promise in exchange for a 'like' on Facebook and that they are not using misleading or artificial means to inflate the number of Facebook likes"(Delo, 2011). Furthermore, if marketers choose to engage in practices that may potentially mislead consumers, their companies could become the subject of false advertising claims with the Federal Trade Commission.

For example, in 2011, Hyundai Motor America was under investigation with the FTC regarding whether the company violated Section 5 of the FTCA in connection with a blogging campaign designed to build interest in ads that were to premiere during the broadcast of Super Bowl XLV (Engle, 2011). Hyundai hired an outside marketing agency to conduct its marketing efforts, and unbeknownst to Hyundai, the agency created a campaign which gave bloggers gift certificates for including links to videos of Hyundai upcoming Super Bowl ads in their social media posts. The inquiry focused on whether these bloggers had been informed about the FTC guidelines regarding discloser for such incentives. The FTC ultimately decided not to recommend enforcement action based on several factors: 1) Hyundai did not know about the use of these incentives; 2) a small number of bloggers actually received the certificates; 3) some did disclose that they were receiving incentives for posting the information; 4) the actions were not those of Hyundai employees but of an individual at a marketing firm; 5) the actions were contrary to the published social media policies of both Hyundai and the marketing firm; and 6) upon learning of the misconduct, the marketing firm promptly addressed it (Engle, 2011). The result is not to say that there was no violation, but that the FTC chose not to pursue enforcement. Marketers should view this matter as a suggestion for proper conduct in not only how campaigns should be conducted but also in how misconduct should be handled.

Another legal issue pertaining to utilizing social media relates to social media squatters and the need for companies to protect their trademarks. The Federal Trademark Act of 1945, or the Lanham Act as it is often called, defines trademark infringement as the reproduction, counterfeiting, or copying in commerce of a registered mark in connection with the sale or advertising of any goods which may cause consumer confusion as to the origin of the mark (15 USC 1114). If a sports organization chooses to use social media, the company should beware of individuals and competitors that may choose to register usernames containing another company's trademark with the intent to either sell the username to the mark holder or to market its own products under the username.

It is imperative for companies to protect their marks, even if it takes years to clean up the "squatting." For example, both Coca Cola and Nike have been victims of Twitter squatting. Coca Cola complained directly to Twitter and succeeded in getting the Coca Cola identity returned. In 2009, if you put Nike in the Twitter search box, approximately 175 results returned with none of them being identified as the brand's official account (Lee, 2009). Fortunately for Nike, today this is not the case, and this highlights the fact that marketers and companies alike need to recognize that social media is a powerful outlet to reach its consumer base and an attractive target for infringement.

When considering potential legal concerns, attention should be focused on not only knowing basic rules of conduct but the importance of controlling what consumers see about the brand in the social media marketplace. It should also be noted that the information provided is only to bring to light a few of the potential legal issues associated with using social media. Marketers should be aware that the legal issues are not limited to those discussed here, and it is ultimately the responsibility of marketers, businesses, and marketing agencies to understand the legal environment that relates to the practice of marketing and social media.

CHAPTER SUMMARY

Social media has brought a new set of communication tools to the sport industry and prompted booming growth in sport marketing communication. It is a trendy "new" media marketing tool with an unknown potential and possible growth. Sport entities have found social media to be an easy and inexpensive way to communicate with fans. Therefore, many sport organizations and athletes have added social media links to their official websites to push the news directly to the fans' accounts and receive feedback. Further, the entire communication process has been changed by social media. Sport franchises and athletes sometimes break the news on their own social media page first.

Sport organizations and fans can interact directly with the new communication process. Fans and customers can exchange feedback and share their stories via social media. The concept of social community relationship management (social CoRM) is the idea of engaging customers through connectivity, conversations, content creation, and collaboration. Fans and customers like to receive ticket and activity information sent by the sport organizations.

Because the communication becomes transparent, sport organizations need to be sincere in listening and working with their fans and influencers to co-create the value of the organization and create a bond with consumers. With careful planning when integrating traditional marketing with social media, the sport organization and athletes should be able to maximize the marketing performance and reach the objectives.

DISCUSSION QUESTIONS

1. The growth of social media forms has made a major impact on the way advertisers and sport entities reach their customers. Explain how social media has changed the marketing environment and practice.
2. What are the essential elements in effective social media marketing?
3. Identify one sport organization or event which engages with customers on their social media outlets effectively. Describe the successful tactics that are used by the organization.

SUGGESTED EXERCISES

1. Analyze a sport organization's official webpage to see how they utilize social media to make themselves. Discuss the results with your team and provide suggestions and comments to the organization.

2. Working with a local sport organization or a sporting event on campus (e.g., 5K run with softball team to raise money for charity) and identifying their social media strategy and who is in charge of social media content approval and implementation.

3. Review the social media policies at various sport organizations, such as college athletics, professional sport leagues, and International Olympic Committees. Find out if the organizations have regulations on athletes and staff using social media before the game and during competition. If so, what are those regulations?

SUGGESTED READINGS

Belch, G. E., & Belch, M. A. (2011). *Advertising and promotion: An integrated marketing communications perspective* (9th ed.). New York, NY: McGraw-Hill Irwin.

Sanderson, J. (2011). *It's a whole new ballgame: How social media is changing sports.* New York, NY: Hampton Press, Inc.

Appendix A

Sport Business Organizations
Contact Information

CONTENTS

Age-Related Organizations and Businesses

Amateur Athletic Union
AAU National Headquarters
PO Box 22409
Lake Buena Vista, FL 32830-1000
407-934-7200
407-934-7242 (Fax)
http://www.aausports.org

American Youth Soccer Organization
12501 S. Isis Avenue
Hawthorne, CA 90250
800-872-2976
http://www.soccer.org

AUSSI Masters Swimming
148A Ferguson Street,
Williamstown VIC 3016
Australia
Telephone: 03 9399 8861
Fax: 03 9399 8863
http://www.aussimasters.com

Boys & Girls Clubs of America
1230 W. Peachtree Street, NW
Atlanta, GA 30309
404-487-5700
http://www.bcga.org

Charlie Tarricone's American Basketball Consulting Services
1305 Campus Drive
Vestal, NY 13850
607-724-8155

Moreno Valley
14177 Fredrick Street
Moewno Valley, CA 92552
909-413-3000
909-413-3750 (Fax)

National Adult Baseball Association
NABA
3609 S. Wadsworth Blvd., Suite 135
Lakewood, CO 80235
800-621-6479
303-639-6605(Fax)
http://www.dugout.org

National Alliance for Youth Sports
2050 Vista Pkwy
West Palm Beach, FL 33411
561-684-1141
561-712-0119 (Fax)

National Senior Games Association
PO Box 82059
Baton Rouge, LA 70884-2059
225-766-6800
225-766-9115 (Fax)
http://www.nsga.com

PrepUSA
PO Box 97427
Tacoma, WA 98497
253-581-5324
253-756-2900 (Fax)

U.S. Budokai Karate Association
100 Everett Road
Albany, NY 12205
518-458-2018

Young American Bowling Alliance (YABA)
800-514-2965 ext. 3158
414-421-4420 (Fax)
http://www.bowl.com

Youth Basketball of America, Inc.
10325 Orangewood Blvd
Orlando, FL 32821
407-363-YBOA
407-363-0599 (Fax)
http://www.yboa.org

Auto Sports Racing Organizations and Businesses

American Rally Sport Group, Inc.
3650 South Pointe Circle, Suite 205
Laughlin, NV 89028
702-298-8171
951-737-5519 (Fax)
http://www.rallyusa.com

Boston Performance Group
18 Fordham Road
Allston, MA 02134
617-787-8035
617-787-6492 (Fax)

Cotter Group
SFX/Cotter Group
6525 Hudspeth
Harrisburg, NC 28075
704-455-3500

Kelley Racing
9350 Castlegate Drive
Indianapolis, IN 46256

NASCAR/National Association
for Stock Car Auto Racing
(public relations)
PO Box 2875
Daytona Beach, FL 32120
386-253-0611

PacWest Racing Group
4001 Methanol Lane
Indianapolis, IN 46268
317-297-2500
317-297-2100 (Fax)

Pep Boys Indy Racing League
4565 W. 16th Street
Indianapolis, IN 46222
317-484-6526
317-484-6525 (Fax)

Rally School Ireland
Gola Scotstown
Co. Monaghan
047 89098
047 89223 (Fax)

Disability Sport Organizations and Businesses

American Blind Bowling
Association
411 Sheriff Street
Mercer, PA 16137
742-745-5986

Canadian Blind Sports
Association
7 Mill Street, Lower Level, Box 1574
Almonte, Ontario, K0A 1A0
Canada
613-256-7792
613-256-8759 (Fax)

Disabled Sports USA
451 Hungerford DR, STE 100
Rockville, MD 20850
301-217-0960
301-217-0968(Fax)
http://www.dsusa.org

International Blind Sports
Association
http://www.ibsa.es/eng

International Paralympic
Committee
Adenauerallee 212-214
D-53113 Bonn
Germany
Tel: +49-228-2097 200
Fax: +49-228-2097 209

National Foundation of
Wheelchair Tennis
940 Calle Amanecer, Ste B
San Clemente, CA 92672
714-361-3663

National Sports Center
for the Disabled
PO Box 1290
Winter Park, CO 80482
970-726-1540
303-316-1540
970-726-4112 (Fax)
http://www.nscd.org

National Wheelchair Basketball
Association
6165 Lehman Drive Suite 101
Colorado Springs, CO 80918
719-266-4082
http://www.nwba.org

Skating Association for the Blind
and Handicapped
1200 East and West Road
West Seneca, NY 14224
716-675-7222
http://www.sabahinc.org

USA Deaf Sports Federation
102 North Krohn Place
Sioux Falls, SD 57103-1800
605-367-5760
605-367-4979 (Fax)
http://www.usdeafsports.org

U.S. Association of Blind Athletes
33 N. Institute Street
Colorado Springs, CO 80903
719-630-0422
719-630-0616
http://www.usaba.org

U.S. Cerebral Palsy Athletic
Association
200 Harrison Avenue
Newport, RI 02840
401-848-2460
401-848-5280 (Fax)

Wheelchair Sports, USA
1668 320th Way
Earlham, IA 50072
515-833-2450
http://www.wsusa.org

Fitness Organizations and Businesses

American Council on Exercise
4851 Paramount Drive
San Diego, CA 92121
800-825-3636
858-279-7227
858-279-8064 (Fax)
http://www.acefitness.org

American Fitness Professionals
and Associates
PO Box 214
Ship Bottom, NJ 08008
609-978-7583
http://www.afpafitness.com

Association of Women's Fitness
and Health
273 South Centerville Road
Ashburn, VA 20147
http://www.association-of-womens-fitness
   .org

National Gym Association
PO Box 970579
Coconut Creek, FL 33097-0579
954-344-8410
954-344-8412 (Fax)
http://www.nationalgym.com

Nebula Fitness
PO Box 54
1142 North Center Street
Versailles OH 45380
800-763-2852
937-526-9411 (Fax)
http://www.nebula-fitness.com

Professional Fitness Instructor
Training
PO Box 130258
Houston, TX 77219-0258
800-899-7348
713-868-8086
713-868-2683
http://www.pfit.org

The Fitness Zone
800-875-9145

International Sports Organizations and Businesses

British Athletics
http://www.british-athletics.co.uk

Canadian Association for the Advancement of Women and Sport and Physical Activity
N202-801 King Edward Avenue
Ottawa, ON, Canada K1N 6N5
613-562-5667
613-562-5668 (Fax)
http://www.caaws.ca

Fédération Internationale de Football Association (FIFA)
PO Box 85
8030 Zurich, Switzerland
+41-43/222 7777
http://www.fifa.com

General Association of International Sports Federations
Villa Le Mas 4, boulevard du Jardin Exotique, MC 98000, Monaco
+377 +97 97 65 10
+377 +93 25 28 73 (Fax)
http://www.agfisonline.com

International Amateur Athletic Federation
Stade Louis II—Avenue Prince Heredi-taire Albert
MC 98000 Monaco
377 92 05 70 68
377 92 05 70 69 (Fax)
http://www.iaaf.org

International Olympic Committee
Chateau de Vidy
Case Postale 356
1007 Lausanne, Switzerland
41.21 621.61.11
41.21 621.62.16
http://www.olympic.org

North American Sports Federation
PO Box K
Drifton, PA 18221
570-454-1952
http://www.nasf.net

Media Organizations and Businesses

CBS SportsLine
http://www.sportsline.com

CNN/SI
http://www.sportsillustrated.cnn.com

ESPN
http://www.espn.go.com

Fox Sports
http://www.msn.foxsports.com

The Sporting News
http://www.sportingnews.com
USA Today
http://www.usatoday.com

Minority Sports Organizations and Businesses

African American Sports

African American Golf Association (AAGA)
309-682-1482
http://www.aagagolf.com

Black Coaches Association
Pan American Plaza
201 S. Capitol Ave. Suite 495
Indianapolis, IN 46225
317-829-5600
317-829-5601 (Fax)
http://www.bcasports.org

Black Entertainment and Sports Lawyers Association
PO Box 441485
For Washington, MD 20749-1485
301-248-1818
301-248-0700 (Fax)
http://www.besla.org

Gay and Lesbian Sports

Atlanta Lesbian Health Initiative
http://www.thehealthinitiative.org/about.php
Chicago Metropolitan Sports Association
http://www.chicagomsa.org/cmsa_new/

The Chiltern Mountain Club
http://www.chiltern.org

Federation of Gay Games
584 Castro Street Suite 343
San Francisco, CA 94114
415-695-0222
http://www.gaygames.com

Georgia Gay Rodeo Association
PO Box 7881
Atlanta, GA 30357-0881
770-662-9510
http://www.georgiagayrodeo.com

Hotlanta Volleyball Association
PO Box 8144
Highland Station
Atlanta, GA 31106
770-621-5062
http://hotlantavolleyball.org

International Gay and Lesbian Aquatics
http://www.igla.org

Interanational Gay and Lesbian Football Association
http://www.iglfa.org

International Gay Rodeo Association (IGRA)
http://igra.com

International Gay Bowling Association (IGBO)
http://igbo.org

Native American Sports

Iroquois Nationals Lacrosse
http://www.iroquoisnationals.com

National Sports Organizations and Businesses

National Association of Intercollegiate Athletics (NAIA)
23500 W. 105th Street
PO Box 1325
Olathe, KS 66051
913-791-0044
http://www.naia.org

National Auto Sport Association
PO Box 21555
Richmond, CA 94820-1555
510-232-NASA
510-412-0549 (Fax)
http://www.nasaproracing.com

National Bicycle League
3958 Brown Park Drive, Ste D
Hillard, OH 43026
800-886-BMX1
614-777-1625
614-777-1680 (Fax)
http://www.nbl.org

National Collegiate Athletic
Association
PO Box 6222
Indianapolis, IN 46206-6222
317-917-6222
http://www.ncaa.org

National Golf Foundation
1150 South US Highway One, Ste 401
Jupiter, FL 33477
561-744-6006
http://www.ngf.org

National Junior Colleges
Athletic Association
1755 Telstar Drive, Suite 103
Colorado Springs, CO 80920
719-590-9788
719-590-7324 (Fax)
http://www.njcaa.org

National Softball Association
PO Box 7
Nicholasville, KY 40340
859-887-4114
859-887-4874 (Fax)
http://www.playnsa.com

USA Basketball
5465 Mark Dabling Blvd.
Colorado Springs, CO 80918-3842
719-590-4800
http://www.usabasketball.com

U.S. Specialty Sports Association
215 Celebration Place, Suite 180
Celebration, FL 34747
(321) 939-7640
(321) 939-7647 (Fax)
http://www.usssa.com

Professional Sport Organizations and Businesses

American Bowling Congress
5301 S. 76th Street
Greendale, WI 53129
1-800-514-bowl
http://www.bowl.com

American League of Professional
Baseball Clubs
350 Park Avenue
New York, NY 10022
212-339-7600
212-593-7138 (Fax)

Association of Surfing
Professionals (North America)
PO Box 309
Huntington Beach, CA 92648
714-848-8851
714-848-8861 (Fax)
http://www.aspworldtour.com

Association of Tennis
Professionals
201 ATP Tour Boulevard
Ponte Vedra Beach, FL 32082
904-285-8000
904-285-5966 (Fax)
http://www.atptennis.com

Association of Volleyball
Professionals (AVP)
6100 Center Drive, 9th Floor
Los Angeles, CA 90045
310-426-8000
310-426-8010 (Fax)
http://www.AVP.com

American Basketball Association
9421 Holiday Drive
Indianapolis, IN 46260
(317) 844-7502
(317) 844-7501 (Fax)
http://www.abalive.com

Continental Basketball
Association
1412 W. Idaho St. Suite 235
Boise, ID 83702
208-429-0101
208-429-0303 (Fax)
http://www.cbahoopsonline.com

International Korfball Federation
PO Box 85394
3508 AJ Utrecht
The Netherlands
http://www.ikf.org

International Shooting Sport
Federation
ISSF Headquarters
Bavariaring 21, D-80336
Mynchen, Germany
+49-89-5443550
+49-89-5443554 (Fax)
http://www.issf-shooting.org

Major League Baseball (MLB)
350 Park Avenue
New York, NY 10022
212-339-7800
212-355-0007 (Fax)
http://www.mlb.com

Major League Soccer (MLS)
110 E. 42nd Street, 10 Floor
New York, NY 10017
212-450-1200
212-450-1300 (Fax)
http://www.mlsnet.com

National Basketball Association
(NBA)
645 Fifth Avenue
New York, NY 10022
212-407-8000
212-832-3861 (Fax)
http://www.nba.com

National Football League (NFL)
280 Park Avenue
New York, NY 10017
212-450-2000
212-681-7599 (Fax)
http://www.nfl.com

National Hockey League (NHL)
1251 Avenue of the Americas
47th Floor
New York, NY 10020-1198
212-789-2000
212-789-2020 (Fax)
http://www.nhl.com

National League of Professional
Baseball Clubs
350 Park Avenue
New York, NY 10022
212-339-7700
212-935-5069 (Fax)

National Bicycle League
3958 Brown park Drive, Suite D.
HIlliard, OH 43026
614-777-1625
614-777-1680 (fax)

Religion and Faith-Based Sports Organizations and Businesses

Athletes in Action
651 Taylor Drive
Xenia, OH 45385
937-352-1000
http://www.athletesinaction.org/

Fellowship of Christian Athletes
8701 Leeds Road
Kansas City, MO 64129
816-921-0909
http://www.fca.org

Maccabi USA
Maccabi USA/Sports for Israel
1926 Arch Street 4R
Philadelphia, PA 19103
215-561-6900
http://www.maccabiusa.com

National Christian College Athletic
Association
NCCAA National Office
302 West Washington Street
Greenville, SC 29601
864-250-1199
864-250-1141 (Fax)
http://www.thenccaa.org

OC International
PO Box 36900
Colorado Springs, CO 80936-6900
719-592-9292

Sport Market Research Organizations and Businesses

Joyce Julius & Associates, Inc.
1050 Highland Drive, Ste E
Ann Arbor, MI 48108
734-971-1900
734-791-2059 (Fax)
http://www.joycejulius.com

Simmons Market Research
Bureau
230 Park Avenue South, 3rd Floor
New York, NY 10003-1566
212-598-5400
212-598-5401 (Fax)
http://www.smrb.com

Society for American Baseball
Research
812 Huron Road, Ste 719
Cleveland, OH 44115
216-575-0500
216-575-0502 (Fax)
http://www.sabr.org

Sport Business Research Network
PO Box 1417
Princeton, NJ 08542
609-896-1996
609-896-1903 (Fax)
http://www.sbrnet.com

Sport Marketing Agencies

International Management Group
(IMG)
IMG Center, Suite 100
1360 E. 9th Street
Cleveland, OH 44114
216-522-1200
216-436-3187 (Fax)
http://www.IMGworld.com

Proserv, Inc.
1401 North Street, Suite 203
Escanaba, MI 49829
906-786-1699
888-598-5208
http://www.proserv-inc.com

R.L.R. Associates, Ltd.
7 W. 51st Street
New York, NY 10019
212-541-8641
212-262-7084 (Fax)
http://www.rlrassociates.net

Sporting Goods and Apparel Manufacturers and Retailers

Sporting Goods Manufacturers Association
200 Castlewood Drive
North Palm Beach, FL 33408
561-842-4100
561-863-8984 (Fax)
http://www.sgma.com

Action & Leisure
45 E. 30th Street
New York, NY 10016
212-684-4470
212-532-6194 (Fax)

Adams USA, Inc.
610 S. Jefferson Avenue
Cookville, TN 38501
800-251-6857
http://www.adamsusa.com

Adidas–Salomon AG
Social and Environmental Affairs
World of Sports
Adi-Dassler-Strabe 1-2
91074 Herzogenaurach Germany
+49 (0) 9132/84-0
+49 (0) 9132/84-3242 (Fax)
http://www.adidas-salomon.com

Airwalk Footwear
http://www.airwalk.com
Bike Athletic Company
3330 Cumberland Blvd.
Atlanta, GA 30339
678-742-TALK
http://www.bikeathletic.com

Bolle America
9500 W. 49th Avenue
Wheat Ridge, CO 80033
800-554-6686
303-327-2200
303-327-2300 (Fax)
http://www.bolle.com

Discus Athletic
PO Box 5186
Martinsville, VA 24115
540-632-6459

Hillerich & Bradsby Company, Inc.
800 W. Main Street
Louisville, KY 40202
800-282-2287
502-585-5226
502-585-1179 (Fax)
http://www.slugger.com

Nike, Inc.
PO Box 4027
Beaverton, OR 97005
800-344-6453
http://www.nike.com

Reebok International, Inc.
PO Box 1060
Ronks, PA 17573
800-934-3566
http://www.reebok.com

Scott USA
PO Box 2030
Sun Valley, ID 83353
208-622-1000
208-622-1005 (Fax)
http://www.scottusa.com

Sims Sports, Inc.
888-360-SIMS
http://www.simsnow.com

Skis Dynastar Inc.
PO Box 25
Hercules Drive
Colchester, VT 05446-0025
802-655-2400
802-655-4329 (Fax)
http://www.dynastar.com

Spalding Sports Worldwide
150 Brookdale Drive
Springfield, MA 01104
1-800-SPALDING
http://www.spalding.com

Tecnica USA Corporation
19 Technology Drive
W. Lebanon, NH 03784
800-258-3897
603-298-8032
603-298-5790 (Fax)
http://www.tecnicausa.com

Wilson Sporting Goods Company
8700 W. Bryn Mawr Avenue
Chicago, IL 60631
773-714-6400
773-714-4550 (Fax)
http://www.wilson.com

Sports Logo and Licensed Merchandise Organizations and Businesses

Art's Pro Sports Apparel & Things
http://www.citivu.com

B&J Collectibles, Inc.
801 Corporate Circle
Toms River, NJ 08755
732-905-5000

BestSportsGifts.com
Summit Bldg.
13575 58th Street N
Clearwater, FL 34620
727-593-8692

eCompanyStore
5945 Cabot Parkway Bldg 200, Ste 150
Alpharetta, GA 30005
800-975-6467
877-588-8932
678-942-3101 (Fax)
http://www.ecompanystore.com

InstantPromo.com
Executive Graffiti Inc.
361 S. Camino Del Rio
Suite 202
Durango, CO 81303
970-247-8344
970-247-8345 (Fax)
800-255-1334

LogoProducts.cc
The Backyard Store
3419 Northeast Parkway
San Antonino, TX 78214
888-814-7531

Nikco Sports
516 Trade Center Blvd.
Chesterfield, MO 63005
800-345-2868
636-777-4070
636-777-4071 (Fax)

Racing USA, Inc.
228 Commerce Parkway
Pelham, AL 35124
205-985-5280 (fax)
http://www.racingusa.com

Rugby Imports
855 Warren Avenue
East Providence, RI 02914
800-431-4514
401-438-2727
401-438-8260 (Fax)
http://www.rugbyimports.com

Selinda's
PO Box 1732
Suwanee, GA 30024-0973
678-482-8239 (phone and fax)
http://www.selindas.com

Twenty-Four Seven Incentives, Inc.
5435 S. Gibralter Street
Aurora, CO 80015-3767
303-699-5012
303-699-2931 (Fax)
http://www.247incentives.com

Wendy Havins Promotions, Inc.
4060 Palm Street, Suite 604
Fullerton, CA 92835
888-556-9010
714-525-3330
714-525-3495 (Fax)
http://www.whpromotions.com

Sport Sponsorship Management Organizations and Businesses

ACC Properties
412 E. Boulevard
Charlotte, NC 28203
704-378-4400
704-378-4465 (Fax)

AJ Sports Inc.
9229 Sunset Blvd, Ste 608
Los Angeles, CA 90069
310-550-5922
310-274-3280 (Fax)

API Sponsorship
1775 Broadway, Room 608
New York, NY 10019
212-841-1580
212-841-1598 (Fax)

Barnes Dyer Marketing, Inc.
15510 Rockfield Blvd, Ste C
Irvine, CA 92618
714-768-2942
714-768-0630 (Fax)

Genesco Sports Enterprises, Inc.
214-237-6945
http://www.genescosports.com

Marketing Event Partners, Inc.
6075 Barfield Road, Suite 200
Atlanta, GA 30328
404-256-3366

Miramar Sports & Special Events
PO Box 27
El Granada, CA 94018
650-726-3491
650-726-5181 (Fax)
http://www.miramarevents.com

Premier Management Group
919-363-5105
919-363-5106 (fax)
http://www.pmgsports.com

Vantage Sports Management
222 W. Comstock Avenue, Ste 208
Winter Park, FL 32789
407-628-3131
407-628-3121 (Fax)
http://www.vantagesportsmanagement.com

State Sports Groups

Florida Sports Foundation
2930 Kerry Forest Parkway
Tallahassee, FL 32309
850-488-8347
850-922-0482 (Fax)
http://www.flasports.com

Water Sports Organizations and Businesses

American Water Ski Association
1251 Holy Cow Road
Polk City, FL 33868
863-324-4341
863-325-8259 (Fax)
http://www.usawaterski.org

American Windsurfing Industries Association
1099 Snowden Road
White Salmon, WA 98672
800-963-7873
509-493-9463
509-493-9464 (Fax)
http://www.awia.org

International Jet Sports Boating
Association
3303 Harbor Blvd. Suite E-3
Costa Mesa, CA 92626
714-751-8695
714-751-8609 (Fax)
http://www.ijsba.com

Irish Surfing Association
Easkey Surf and Information Centre
Easkey, Co. Sligo, Ireland
+353 (0) 96 49428
+353 (0) 96 49020

Sail America
850 Aquidneck Avenue, B-4
Middletown, RI 02842-7201
800-817-SAIL
401-847-2044 (Fax)
http://www.sailamerica.com

Super Boat International
Productions, Inc.
1323 20th Terrace
Key West, FL 33040
305-296-6166
305-296-9770 (Fax)
http://www.superboat.com

Unlimited Light Hydroplane
Racing Association
12065 44th Place
South Tukwila, WA 98178
206-315-1716
206-767-2157 (Fax)
http://www.ulrs.org

U.S. Lifesaving Association
http://www.usla.org
U.S. Windsurfing Association
5009 South Lake Drive P.O. Box 99
Chelsea, MI 48118-009
877-386-8708
http://www.uswindsurfing.com

Water Polo Canada
Unit 12-1010 Polytek
Gloucester, ON K1J-9H9
Canada
613-748-5682
613-748-5777 (Fax)

Water-Skiing Federation,
International
PO Box 564
6314 Unteraegeri
Switzerland
+41 41 7520099
+41 41 7520095 (Fax)
http://www.iwsf.com

Women's Sports Organizations and Businesses

Canadian Association for the
Advancement of Women and
Sport and Physical Activity
N202-801 King Edward Avenue
Ottawa, ON, Canada, K1N 6N5
613-562-5667
613-562-5668 (Fax)
http://www.caaws.ca

U.S. Women's Curlng Association
c/o Kettle Morain Curling Club
PO Box 244
Hartland, WI 53029
http://www.uswca.org

Women's Basketball Coaches
Association (WBCA)
4646 B Lawrenceville Hwy
Lilburn, GA 30047-3620
770-279-8027
770-279-8473 (Fax)
http://www.wbca.org

Women's Basketball Hall of Fame
700 Hall of Fame Drive
Knoxville, TN 37915
865-633-9000
http://www.wbhof.com

Women's International Bowling
Congress, Inc. (WIBC)
5301 S. 76th Street
Greendale, WI 53129
414-421-9000
414-421-4420 (Fax)
http://www.bowl.com

Women's National Basketball
Association (WNBA)
645 Fifth Avenue
New York, NY 10022
212-688-9622
212-750-9622 (Fax)
http://www.wnba.com

Women's Ocean Racing Sailing
Association
PO Box 2403
Newport Beach, CA 92663
714-840-1869
714-846-1481 (Fax)
http://www.worsa.org

Women's Pro Fastpitch (WPF)
4610 S. Ulster Drive, Suite 150
Denver, CO 80237
303-290-7494
303-415-2078 (Fax)
http://www.profastpitch.com

Women's Sports Foundation
Eisenhower Park
East Meadow, NY 11554.
800-227-3988
516-542-4700
516-542-4716 (fax)
http://www.womensportsfoundation.org

Appendix B

Sport Business Trade Organizations

Adventure Cycling Association

Adventure Cycling Association's nonprofit mission is to inspire people of all ages to travel by bicycle for fitness, fun, and self-discovery. Established in 1973 as Bikecentennial, Adventure Cycling is the premier bicycle travel organization in North America with 44,700 members nationwide.

> 150 East Pine Street
> P.O. Box 8308
> Missoula, MT 59807
> 406-721-1776
> http://www.adventurecycling.com

American Association for Leisure and Recreation

Promotes school, community, and national programs of leisure services and recreation education.

> 1900 Association Dr.
> Reston, VA 20191-1598
> 703-476-3400
> http://www.aapherd.org

American Sportfishing Association

Ensures a healthy and sustainable resource (more fish), increases participation in sportfishing through promotion and education (more anglers), and helps member sportfishing companies increase their business (more profits).

- Offers trade shows (ICAST), annual meeting, management conference, Future Fisherman Foundation, Fish America Foundation, American Sportfishing newsletter

> 225 Reinekers Lane, Suite 420
> Alexandria, VA 22314
> 703-519-9691
> 703-519-1872 (Fax)
> http://www.asafishing.org

American Sportscasters Association, Inc.

Promotes professionalism and enhances the image of professional sport broadcasters.

- Sponsors Hall of Fame, Sportscaster of the Year, Sports Personality of the Year

> 212-227-8080
> http://www.americansportscasters.com

Athletic Footwear Association
Serves to promote the athletic footwear industry.
- Offers generic marketing programs, market research programs, and annual meetings
  407-840-1161

Club Managers Association of America
Promotes and advances friendly relations between and among persons connected with management of clubs and other associations of similar nature. Assists club officers and members through their managers to secure the utmost in successful operations.
- Offers annual Assistant Club Managers conference, managerial openings list, club management forums, premier club services, international staff exchange program, publications

  1733 King Street
  Alexandria, VA 22314
  703-739-9500
  703-739-0124 (Fax)
  http://www.cmaa.org
  cmaa@cmaa.org

European Fishing Tackle Trade Association (EFTTEX)
Organizes annual trade show available to anyone involved in the fishing tackle trade.
- Offers newsline, members website page, annual international business reception (EFTTEX Show Report)

  71 St. John Street
  London EC1M 4NJ
  England
  +44 20 7253 0777
  +44 20 7253 7779
  http://www.eftta.com
  info@eftta.com

Golf Course Superintendents Association of America
A professional membership organization for golf course superintendents in the United States., Canada, and throughout the world. Advances the art and science of golf management, collects and disseminates practical knowledge of the problems of golf course management and a view toward more economical management of golf courses.
- Offers job listings, seminars, continuing education, certification, *Golf Course Management* magazine, GCSAA News Weekly

  1421 Research Park Drive
  Lawrence, KS 66049-3859
  800-472-7878
  785-841-2240
  http://www.gcsaa.org
  infobox@gcsaa.org

Ice Skating Institute

Provides leadership, education, and services to the ice skating industry.

- Offers annual World Championship competition, ISI EDGE (bimonthly professional journal), *Recreational Ice Skating* (quarterly magazine), education foundation, annual conference, and trade show

> 17120 N. Dallas Pkwy., Suite 140
> Dallas, TX 75248-1187
> 972-735-8800
> 972-735-8815 (Fax)
> http://www.skateisi.com
> ISI@SkateISI.com

International Health, Racquet, & Sports Club Association

Exists to enhance the quality of profitability of its member clubs through education, information, networking, and marketing opportunities, group purchasing, legislative support, and public relations.

- Offers *Club Business International* (CBI) magazine, IHRSA/Boys and Girls Clubs of America Program, passport program, annual trade show, annual conference, annual international convention

> 263 Summer Street
> Boston, MA 02210
> 800-228-4772
> 617-951-0055
> 617-951-0056 (Fax)
> http://www.ihrsa.org
> info@ihrsa.org

National Association of Charterboat Operators (NACO)

Unifying force for the charterboat industry with more than 3,300 members, realizing major successes in combating and challenging government regulation.

- Offers The NACO Report (bimonthly newsletter), Group Rate Liability Insurance Program, drug testing compliance program, government regulation and lobbying, annual conferences and meetings

> PO Box 2990
> Orange Beach, AL 36561
> 251-981-5136
> 866-981-5136
> 251-981-8191 (Fax)
> http://www.Nacocharters.org

National Association of Sports Commissions

Fosters cooperation and sharing of information and professionalism among local and regional sports commissions and authorities.

> 9916 Carver Road, Suite 100
> Cincinnati, OH 45242
> 513-281-3888
> 513-281-1765 (fax)
> http://www.sportscommissions.org

National Bicycle Dealers Association (NBDA)

Exists to aid the growth of cycling in America through research, education, and advocacy.
- Offers Bicycle Retail Education Conference (BREC), inter-bike bicycle trade expos, articles, books, and resources

> 777 W. 19th Street, Suite O
> Costa Mesa, CA 92627
> 949-722-6909
> http://www.nbda.com
> info@nbda.com

National Scholastic Surfing Association (NSSA)

Promotes the sport of amateur surfing, provides top quality, structured events and encourages the merits of academic achievement for the benefit of its members.
- Offers eight competitive conferences, National Scholarship Program, rulebook, annual National Championships, current news, and news archives

> Janice Aragon
> PO Box 495
> Huntington Beach, CA 92648
> 714-536-0445
> 714-960-4380
> http://www.nssa.org
> jaragon@nssa.org

National Skating Suppliers Association

Provides information, merchandise, and resources to skating manufacturers and distributors.

> 130 Chestnut Street
> PO Box 831
> North Attleboro, MA 02760
> 800-325-1917
> http://www.skatingsupplierassoc.org

National Ski and Snowboard Retailers Association (NSSRA)

Develops, improves, and promotes the business of ski retailers, ski shops, ski areas, and other members of the ski industry; improves communication with the ski industry.

> 1601 Feehanville Drive, Suite 300
> Mt. Prospect, IL 60056-6035
> 847-391-9825
> 847-391-9827 (Fax)
> http://www.nssra.com

National Sporting Goods Association (NSGA)

Consists of retailers, dealers, wholesalers, suppliers and sales agents in the sporting goods industry. Committed to providing members with up-to-date information.

- Offers annual management conference, NSGA newsletter, retail focus articles, industry research and statistics, TeeTeam Dealer Summit

> 1601 Feehanville Drive, Suite 300
> Mt. Prospect, IL 60056-6035
> 847-296-6742
> 847-391-9827 (Fax)
> http://www.nsga.org
> info@nsga.org

Ontario Association of Sport and Exercise Sciences (OASES)

Provides fitness appraisal certification, training, and national CSEP certification for fitness consultants by offering workshops, support to member through certification, and training for personal trainers who promote safe, effective physical activity.

- Offers Fitness Certification Appraisal, courses and conferences, job opening postings, Vanguard newsletter, workshops

> http://www.oases.on.ca
> info@oases.on.ca

Roller Skating Association International

Promotes roller skating and established good business practices for skating rinks. Represents skating center owners and operators, teachers, coaches, and judges of roller skating and manufacturers and suppliers of roller skating equipment.

- Offers *Roller Skating Business* magazine, annual convention and trade show, insurance services, advertising, and vendor information

> 6905 Corporate Drive
> Indianapolis, IN 46278
> 317-347-2626
> 317-347-2636 (Fax)
> http://www.rollerskating.org

Sporting Goods Manufacturers Association

Represents manufacturers of sporting goods equipment, athletic footwear, and sports apparel in the areas of legislation, marketing information, market protection and growth, consumer safety, international trade, product liability, and program funding.

- Offers research reports and related studies, annual events, The Super Show, annual conference, advanced management education program, Coalition of Americans to Protect Sports (CAPS), exhibitor manual

  200 Castlewood Drive
  North Palm Beach, FL 33408
  561-842-4100
  561-863-8984 (Fax)
  http://www.sgma.com
  info@sgma.com

Women's Basketball Coaches Association (WBCA)

Promotes women's basketball by unifying coaches at all levels to develop a reputable identity for the sport of women's basketball and to foster and promote the development of the game in all of its aspects as an amateur sport for women and girls.

- Offers annual national convention, WBCA Coaches Poll, and publications including *Women's Basketball Journal, Coaching Women's Basketball, Fastbreak Alert*, and *At the Buzzer*

  4646 Lawrenceville Highway
  Lilburn, GA 30047
  770-279-8027
  770-279-8473 (Fax)
  http://www.wbca.org
  wbca@wbca.org

Women's Sports Foundation

Promotes participation and provides information in the area of sport and fitness to women and young girls.

- Offers job listings, newsletter, resource center, biennial summit

  Eisenhower Park
  East Meadow, NY 11554
  800-227-3988
  516-542-4700
  516-542-4716 (Fax)
  http://www.womenssportsfoundation.org

Appendix C

Sport Business Industry Trade Publications

Aquatics International
Focuses on design, management, and programming of public and semi-public swimming pools, waterparks, beaches, and other water-oriented facilities.
  Frequency: 11 times per year
  Circulation: 30,000
  888-269-8410

Archery Business
Archery related trade publication.
  Frequency: 7 times per year
  Circulation: 11,000
  800-848-6247

Athletic Business
For owners and operators of athletic, recreation, and fitness facilities.
  Frequency: 12 times per year
  Circulation: 42,000
  505-988-5099

Bicycle Retailer and Industry News
Offers news and features about the bicycle industry for retailers, manufacturers, and distributors of equipment, bike wear, and accessories. Covers in-depth market news and analyzes one of the fastest-growing segments of the golf market.
  Frequency: 18 times a year
  Circulation: 6,500
  949-206-1677
  http://www.bicycleretailer.com

Black Belt Magazine
Martial arts trade publication.
  24900 Anza Drive, Unit E
  Valencia, CA 91355
  Frequency: 12 times a year
  661-257-4066, x. 10
  http://www.blackbeltmag.com

Boxing Monthly
Provides worldwide information and current news on the sport of boxing.
  Frequency: 12 times per year
  Topwave Ltd.
  40 Morpeth Road
  London E9 7LD
  United Kingdom
  +44 0 181 986 4141
  +44 0 181 896 4145 (Fax)
  http://www.boxing-monthly.co.uk
  bmsubs@mmcltd.co.uk

Coaching Women's Basketball Magazine
The official coaching trade magazine for women's basketball.
  http://www.wbca.org/education/wbca-publications

Club Industry
Business magazine for health club owners and operators.
  Frequency: 12 times per year
  Circulation: 30,000
  215-643-8100

Fitness Management

For owners and managers of athletic and health facilities.

Frequency: 12 times per year
Circulation: 25,000
323-964-4800

Fly Fishing and Fly Tying

Provides practical and technical information in the area of fly fishing and fly tying.

Frequency: 11 times per year
Rolling River Publications Ltd.
Aberfeldy Road, Kenmore Perthshire
Scotland PH15 2HF
+44 0 1887 830526
+44 0 1887 830526 (Fax)
http://www.flyfishing-and-
   flytying.co.uk

Fly Fishing Retailer

Focuses on the health, development, and success of the fly fishing industry. Covers issues, detailed information, and brings them into focus for retailers, manufacturers, and raw-goods suppliers for this marketplace.

Frequency: 5 times per year
Circulation: 4,900
949-376-6260
http://www.flyfishingretailer.com

Full Court Press: The Women's Basketball Journal

An online magazine and news website for professionals and fans of women's basketball.

http://www.fullcourt.com

Golf Operator Magazine

A golf course management and marketing magazine.

http://www.cunninglyclevergolfoperator
   .com

Inside Lacrosse Magazine

For coaches and fans of lacrosse.
http://insidelacrosse.com

NCAA News

Primary means of communication for NCAA with its more than 1,100 member institutions, organizations, and conferences, as well as the news media and other persons interested in staying abreast of developments in college athletics.

Frequency: 52 times per year
Circulation: 25,000
317-917-6222
http://www.ncaa.org

Outdoor Retailer

Focuses on specialty sports retailers of backpacking, mountaineering, camping, hiking, climbing, cross-country skiing, padding, mountain biking, adventure travel, snowboarding, snowshoeing, and related clothing.

Frequency: 2 trade shows per year with
   publications
Circulation: 18,000
http://www.outdoorbiz.com

Poundbury Publishing Ltd.

Magazine publishing company which currently publishes six magazines, four of which are sport related.

Prospect House
Peverell Avenue East, Poundbury
Dorchester, Dorset DT1 3WE
United Kingdom
+44 0 1305 266360
+44 0 1305 262760 (Fax)
http://www.poundbury.co.uk

Procycling

Worldwide voice of international professional road racing, distributed in every country where there are English-speaking fans of cycling.

Frequency: 12 times per year
+44 (0)207 6086300
http://www.procycling.com
feedback@procycling.com

Ski Area Management

Trade publication for the skiing industry conveys event, product, and company information.

45 Main Street North
PO Box 644
Woodbury, CT 06798
203-263-0888
203-266-0462 (Fax)

Sport Business.com

Provides daily on-line information and news concerning sport business.

Frequency: Daily
6th Floor
Elizabeth House
39 York Road
London
SE1 7NQ, UK
+44 (0)20 7934 9000
+44 (0)20 7934 9200 (fax)
http://www.sportbusiness.com

Sport Business Research Network

Provides a fee-based service, focusing on the sporting goods and sports marketing industry including: sports equipment sales, participation, broadcasting, sponsorship, and marketing. Providing sporting goods industry with current news and information concerning the market.

Frequency: 12 times per year
PO Box 2378
Princeton, NJ 08543
609-896-1996
609-896-1903 (Fax)
http://www.sbrnet.com
richard@sbrnet.com

Sporting Goods Business

Over 30 years old, *SBG* covers and analyzes the sporting goods business.

Frequency: 18 times per year
Circulation: 24,700
646-654-4997
http://www.Sportinggoodsbusiness.com

Street & Smith's Sports Business Journal

Authority on sports. Business journal devoted to news of the industry.

Frequency: 49 times per year
Circulation: 17,000
120 West Morehead Street, Suite 310
Charlotte, NC 28202
704-973-1410

Women's Basketball Online

"Where women's basketball meets the Internet."

http://wnba.womensbasketballonline.com

Appendix D

Sport Business Academic Journals
and Associations Directory

CONTENTS

Sport Management Academic Curriculum Standards

1993–2008: In May 1993 the first NASPE-NASSM Sport Management Curriculum Standards Manual was published through a joint task force of membership involving scholars and practitioners in sport management representing the National Association for Sport and Physical Education (NASPE) and the North American Society for Sport Management (NASSM). The manual and the review council are listed here. More information can be found through the NASSM or NASPE websites (www.nassm.org, www.aahperd.org/naspe/template.cfm)

The Manual:

NASPE-NASSM Sport Management Curriculum Standards and Program Review
Published by NASPE, can be purchased through NASPE or NASSM.

The Curriculum Standards Review Council:

NASPE-NASSM Sport Management Program Review Council
Made up of six council members, one director and several reviewers; can be contacted through NASPE or NASSM organizations.

2008–present: Commission on Sport Management Accreditation

In 2008, a new committee started and took over the task of curriculum standards review and approval—the Commission on Sport Management Accreditation (COSMA). A new system of review and accreditation resulted. The new information can be found at the following websites.

The COSMA Manuals: http://www.cosmaweb.org/manuals
COSMA Home Website: http://www.cosmaweb.org/

Sport Business Management Journals

—journals developed specifically for the field of Sport Management

Asian Sport Management Review
　Sports Management Association of Taiwan
　Yumen Street, Taipei, Taiwan
　Website: http://e-jasm.jp/docs/aasm/asmr01.pdf

Asian Journal of Sport Management
　Contact: Asian Association for Sport Management

Choregia: Sport Management International Journal
　An online journal.
　Website: www.choregia.org/index.html

Entertainment and Sports Lawyer
　Forum on the Entertainment and Sports IndustriesAmerican Bar AssociationWebsite:
　　http://www.americanbar.org/groups/entertainment_sports/contact_us.html

European Sport Management Quarterly
　European Association for Sport Management—publishers
　Website: www.easm.net

International Journal of Sport Communication
　Human Kinetics Publishers
　Website: http://www.humankinetics.com

International Journal of Sport Finance
　Publishers: Fitness Information Technologya division of ICPE/WVU-CPASS
　West Virginia UniversityWebsite: http://www.fitinfotech.com/IJSF/IJSFWVU.tpl

International Journal of Sport Management
　American Press PublishersWebsite: http://www.americanpresspublishers.com/IJSM.html

International Journal of Sport Management and Marketing
　Website: www.inderscience.com

International Journal of Sports Marketing and Sponsorship
　IMR Publishers
　Website: http://www.imrpublications.com/journal-landing.aspx?volno=L&no=L

International Journal of Sport Management, Recreation & Tourism
　Website: www.ijsmart.eu/

Journal for the Study of Sports and Athletes in Education
　Left Coast Press Publishers
　Website: http://www.lcoastpress.com

Japanese Journal of Management for Physical Education and Sports
Japan Society of Physical Education, Health and Sport Sciences
Japan Society of Physical Education, Health and Sport Sciences, Kishi Kinen Taiiku
Kaikan, 1-1-1 Jinnan, Shibuya-ku, Tokyo 150-8050
Website: http://taiiku-gakkai.or.jp/

Journal of Intercollegiate Sport
Human Kinetics PublishersWebsite: http://journals.humankinetics.com/jis

Journal of Issues in Intercollegiate Athletics
An online journal of the College Sport Research Institute
Website: http://csri-jiia.org/index.html

Journal of Japan Society of Sports Industry
Nogakushorin Bldg., 6F, 3–6, Kandajinbo-cho, Chiyoda-ku, Tokyo 101-0051 Japan
Website: http://www.jstage.jst.go.jp/browse/sposun

Journal of Korean Society of Sport Management
Editor, Cho, Han-beom
Kookmin University
Department of Sport Management
chohb@kookmin.ac.kr

Journal of Sport Administration and Supervision
Middle Tennessee Sport Management—Publishers
Website: http://www.jsasonline.com

Journal of Sport Management
Official Journal of the North American Society for Sport Management
Human Kinetics Publishers
Website: www.humankinetics.com/jsm

Journal of Sports Economics
Sage Publications
Website: www.jse.sagepub.com

Journal of Sports Engineering
Official journal of the International Sports Engineering Association
http://www.springer.com/materials/mechanics/journal/12283

Journal of Venue and Event Management
Online journal of the Department of Sport and Entertainment Management
University of South Carolina
Website: http://www.hrsm.sc.edu/JVEM/index.shtml

Korean Journal of Sport Management
Korean Society for Sport Management
Cho, Han-beom—Editor in Chief
Kukmin University
Seoul, Korea

Marquette Sport Law Review
  Marquette University Law School—publishers
  414-288-7090

Seton Hall Journal of Sports and Entertainment Law
  Seton Hall University School of Law
  Wolfgang Robinson, Editor in Chief
  One Newark Center
  Newark, New Jersey | 07102 |
  973-642-8500

Sport, Business and Management: An International Journal
  Emerald Publishers
  Website: www.emeraldinsight.com/products/journals/journals.htm?id=SBM

Sport Management and Other Related Topics Journal
  The SMART Journal
  Dr. Jason W. Lee, University of North Florida, Editor
  University of North Florida
  Website: www.thesmartjournal.com

Sport Management Education Journal
  A journal of the North American Society for Sport Management
  Human Kinetics Publishers
  Website: www.nassm.com/InfoAbout/SMEJ

Sport Marketing Quarterly
  Fitness Information Technology—publishers
  West Virginia UniversityWebsite: www.fitinfotech.com

Sport Management Review
  Journal of the Sport Management Association of Australia and New Zealand
    (SMAANZ)
  Website: http://www.smaanz.org/index.html

The Sports Lawyers Journal
  Published by the Sports Lawyers Association
  Edited by the students of Tulane University School of Law.
  Tulane University Law School
  Website: http://www.law.tulane.edu/tlsjournals/slj/index.aspx

Villanova Sports and Entertainment Law Journal
  Villanova University School of Law
  Website: http://www.law.villanova.edu/Academics/Journals/Villanova%20Sports
    %20and%20Entertainment%20Law%20Journal.aspx

Sport Business Industry Related Journals

This is a sample of the many journals in which you will find sport, recreation, leisure, fitness and sport tourism related research and material. Additionally, refer to the many journals in the areas of business, such as the *Journal of Marketing*, and law for research and material in foundational and related content areas.

Australian Leisure Management
Australian Leisure Management—Publishers
Website: www.ausleisure.com.au

Current Issues in Tourism
Taylor and Francis Publishing Group
Website: http://www.tandfonline.com/toc/rcit20/current

Electronic Journals of Martial Arts and Sciences
EJMAS
Website: Ejms.com

International Journal of Hospitality Management

Elsevier Publishing Company—Journals
Website: www.journals.elsevier.com/international-journal-of-hospitality-management/

International Review for the Sociology of Sport
Sage Publications
Website: http://irs.sagepub.com/

Journal of Aging and Physical Activity
Human Kinetics PublishersWebsite: journals.humankinetics.com/japa

Journal of Hospitality Marketing & Management
Taylor and Francis Publishing Group
Website: www.tandfonline.com/loi/whmm19

Journal of Leisure Research
National Recreation and Park Association
Sagamore Publishing LLC
Website: http://js.sagamorepub.com/jlr

Journal of Park and Recreation Administration
National Recreation and Park Association
Sagamore Publishing LLC
Website: http://js.sagamorepub.com/jpra

Journal of Philosophy of Sport
International Association for the Philosophy of Sport—PublishersWebsite: http://iaps.net

Journal of Sport and Social Issues
SAGE PublicationsWebsite: www.jss.sagepub.com

Journal of Sport Behavior
University of South Alabama—publisher
http://www.usouthal.edu/psychology/journal.html

Journal of Sport History
North American Society of Sports History (NASSH)
Website: www.nassh.org/NASSH_CMS/index.php

Journal of Sport & Tourism
Taylor and Francis Publishing
England
Website: www.tandf.co.uk/journals/rjto

Journal of Sustainable Tourism
Taylor and Francis Publishing
England
Website: www.tandf.co.uk/journals/rsus

Journal of Vacation Marketing
SAGE Publications, Inc.
Website: http://jvm.sagepub.com/

Leisure Sciences
Taylor and Francis Publishing
Website: www.tandf.co.uk/journals/titles/01490400.asp

NASSM News
Newsletter of the NASSM
Nassm.com

NCAA News
Newsletter of the NCAA
Website: www.ncaa.com

NIRSA Journal
Official Publication of the National Intramural-Recreational Sports Association
Website: www.nirsa.org

Quest
Human Kinetics Publishing Inc.
Website: journals.humankinetics.com/quest

Sociology of Sport
The Official Publication for the American Society of Sociology of SportHuman Kinetics Publishers
Website: http://journals.humankinetics.com/ssj

Women in Sport and Physical Activity Journal
Official Publication of the National Association of Girls and Women in Sport
aahperd—Publishers
Website: www.aahperd.org/nagws/publications/wspaj/

YouthFirst: The Journal of Youth Sports
YouthFirst Organization—Publishers
Website: http://youthfirst.info/publications/journals/

Sport Business Management Professional Academic and Scholarly Associations

ALGEDE—Latin American Sport Management Association
Asociación Latinoamericana de Gerencia Deportiva (ALGEDE) (Latin American
Sport Management Association)
President: Dr. Rosa Lopez de Amico, Pedagogic Experimental University Liberator in
Maracay, Venezuela, South America
Conference—The ALGEDE conference is biannual. The first two were held in 2009
and 2011; the third will be in 2013 in Columbia.
Website: www. algede.afpr.br and www.algede.com

Asian Association for Sport Management (AASM)
Publication: Asian Journal for Sport Management
Conference: Annually

College Sport Research Institute
Publication: Journal of Issues in Intercollegiate Athletics
Conference: Annually usually in April at the University of North Carolina at Chapel
Hill campus
Website: http://exss.unc.edu/research-and-laboratories/college-sport-research-insti
tute/overview/

European Association for Sport Management (EASM)
Publication: European Sport Management Quarterly
Conference: Annually in September
Sports Institute of FinlandKaskelantie
10–19120 Vierumäki
+358/40/586.74.93
Website: http://www.easm.net

*International Association for Sports and Leisure Infrastructure
Management*
website: www.iaslim.org

Japan Society of Sports Industry
Website: http://www.jstage.jst.go.jp/browse/sposun

North American Society for Sport Management
   Publications: Journal of Sport Management; NASSM News
   Conference: Annually in June
   Website: www.NASSM.org

National Association for Sport and Physical Education
   1900 Association DriveReston, VA 20191
   703-476-3410
   Publications: Journal of Coaching Education, Journal of PE and Dance

National Collegiate Athletic Association
   Publications: The NCAA News, Champion Magazine
   Conference: Annual
   700 W. Washington Street
   P.O. Box 6222
   Indianapolis, Indiana 46206-6222
   317-917-6222
   ncaa.org

Sport Management Association of Australia and New Zealand (SMAANZ)
   Publication: Sport Management Review
   Conference: Annually in November
   Website: www.smaanz.org

Sport Marketing Association
   Publications: Sport Marketing Quarterly (partner)
   Conference: Annually in October
   Website: www.sportmarketingassociation.com

World Association for Sport Management
   This association is new and as of the publication date of this book does not yet have a
      journal or conference. Therefore, continue to search for information about this
      association to follow its development.

Sport Management Conferences, Congresses, Conventions, and Exhibitions

ALGEDE—Latin American Sport Management Association
   Conference every two years (last one held in 2011)

European Association for Sport Management (EASM)
   Holds annual conference for Professors, Instructors, Students, and Industry Practitioners
   Website: www.Easm.net

Florida State University Conference of Sport Administration
  Sport Management
  College of Education
  Florida State University
  1002 Tully Gym, Tallahassee, FL 32306-4280
  Phone: (850) 644-4813

National Golf Course Owners Association
  NGCOA Annual Conference and Trade Show
  Website: www.ngcoa.org

North American Society for Sport Management
  Holds annual conference for Professors, Instructors, Students, and Industry Practitioners
  Website: www.nassm.org

Sport Management Association of Australia and New Zealand
  Holds annual conference for Professors, Instructors, Students, and Industry Practitioners
  Website: www.smaanz.org

Sport Marketing Association
  Holds annual conference for Professors, Instructors, Students, and Industry Practitioners
  Website: www.sportmarketingassociation.com

Appendix E

Sport Marketing Research Briefs

For Love or Money: Developing and Validating a Motivational Scale for Fantasy Football Participation

Brendan Dwyer—Center for Sport Leadership
Yongjae Kim—Kutztown University of Pennsylvania

The past two decades has seen an explosion of research attempting to understand why people attend sporting events. Understanding the motivations of sports consumers can help organizations and businesses alike in tailoring their business plans and marketing strategies to their audience. Specifically, the demand for sport has been the primary focus of the majority of this research, for understanding consumer motivation provides vital information for sport marketers (Sloan, 1989). An important component of this understanding is the development of ways to measure customer demand for sport (Trail, Anderson, & Fink, 2000; Trail & James, 2001; Wann, 1995). This knowledge is incredibly important for sport managers as they look to provide services and products that are in line with the demands of sport consumers.

Fans through a variety of means including television, event attendance, print publications like magazines and newspapers, the Internet and even radio broadcasts can consume the sports medium with ease. Therefore, the best way to understand the motivations behind the consumption of sports is to investigate all these different methods as well as the frequency to which they are used.

Despite all the research that has already been done on these sport consumers, one significant group has been largely overlooked to this point and that is the media dominant fan. These individuals tend to consume sport through methods other than attending games. While these fans of the sport represent professional sports' largest fan base, a comprehensive psychographic assessment of this group of consumers is lacking (Pritchard & Funk, 2006). Within this impressive group of sport fans are those who participate in fantasy sports.

This activity is also called Rôtisserie or Fanalytics. Fantasy sports are games, generally found online, in which participants act as mock general managers or owners of a sport franchise. These mock teams are completely customizable, interactive, and involve nearly every major professional sport from professional football to bass fishing and golf. Fantasy sports are primarily online services but can often include a in-person component where fans have the opportunity to socialize and interact while also actively following their favorite sports and teams. These fans have an opportunity to interact with friends, family and even complete strangers that share in their passion for sport. The competition is based on real statistics and can be updated on a play-by-play basis while games take place.

This study looked at fantasy football participation due to its massive popularity (> 20 million participants) and its status as the gateway activity for other fantasy sport games (Fantasy Sports Trade Association [FSTA], 2008).

Players typically join leagues during the summer and participate in drafts sometime before the beginning the actually National Football League (NFL) season in order to be prepared for the games. Individual NFL players are selected to fantasy teams based on perceived potential to perform at a high level and amass strong statistical seasons. These statistics are typically measured on the total output in the form of touchdowns, yards from scrimmage, receptions, points allowed by defense, etc. The schedule of competition in fantasy leagues usually falls in line with the NFL's weekly slate of games where players participate in head to head matchups. These scoring schedules can also be modified for daily participation where players can be more actively involved in roster changes and manipulation of their teams' starting lineups. Players require access to current information about players and teams in order to perform at a high level in the fantasy sports environment. That need generates a higher consumption of sports by these participants in fantasy sports.

Specifically, fantasy sport websites, such as Yahoo.com, ESPN.com, and CBSsports.com, have become the primary vehicle through which fantasy owners draft players, check scores, conduct research, and perform daily and weekly functions associated with the activity. Simultaneously, as the Internet has grown into a primary means of communication and entertainment for consumers, fantasy football have become one of the most popular activities among NFL fans. The use many online sites is a must to stay up to date on the quickly changing landscape of professional sports.

The popularity of fantasy sports, in general, is evidenced by the fact that nearly 30 million Americans and Canadians currently participate in some kind of fantasy sport league (FSTA, 2008). Most fantasy sports participants are active in multiple leagues throughout the season. This high level of commitment has recently transformed the fantasy sports world into a highly lucrative business. The FSTA has estimated the total market impact of fantasy sports to be $4.48 billion, each year, with $800 million spent directly on fantasy sport products and services like league fees and magazines. Another important factor to consider is just who these consumers are as fantasy sports include arguably the most sought after demographic in American business (Caucasian, male, 18–45, bachelor's degree and $78,000 annual income). As a result, fantasy sport has emerged as an easy, cost-effective means of reaching an engaged and lucrative group of consumers (Leporini, 2006).

Even with the constantly growing popularity of this activity and the incredible marketability of the participants, there is still very little research on the motivational factors that drive them. Given this fact, the current study was exploratory in nature with a twofold purpose. First, the intent was to examine what motivations lead to participation in fantasy football and second to develop a comprehensive motivational scale. Specifically, this study examined fantasy football from a Uses and Gratifications (U&G) perspective to understand how fantasy football participants use this media to fulfill their unique needs and wants.

The study helped to understand what psychological needs are fulfilled by participation in fantasy football. The most intriguing component of the results centers on the relationship between gambling and participation in fantasy sports as gambling is a proven avenue to encourage the consumption of sports. However, a lack of criterion-related validity with regards to this factor resulted in settling on three more consistent factors. These factors are consistent with previous research and include social interaction, entertainment/escape and competition motives.

Dwyer, B., & Yongjae, K. (2011). For love or money: Developing and validating a motivational scale for fantasy football participation. *Journal of Sport Management, 25*(1), 70–83.

The Jordan's Furniture "Monster Deal": A Legal Gamble?

Eli C. Bortman—Babson College

In the Spring of 2007, Jordan's, a Massachusetts area furniture dealer, attracted the attention of local fans, media, and sport marketers with an innovative promotion entitled "Jordan's Monster Deal." The retailer used television commercials with the energetic president of Jordan's Furniture enthusiastically announcing, "EVERY Sofa, EVERY Sectional, EVERY Dining Table, EVERY Bed, EVERY Mattress . . . can be YOURS FREE if the Red Sox win the World Championship in 2007."

Jordan's furniture had the right to designate itself as the "Official Furniture Store of the Boston Red Sox" because it was a sponsor of the organization. The title of this promotion played off the famed left field wall at Fenway Park typically referred to as "The Green Monster."

The Jordan's brand is very well known in the Boston area and has three stores in suburbs of the city and one in Southern New Hampshire. The retailer also has a history of engaging and entertaining television advertising techniques and promotions (Knapp, 1988). Even though the promotion seemed innocent at first look, the filing of a law suit against the retailer brought up an interesting question: Did Jordan's "Monster Deal" constitute illegal gambling?

Initially, the suggestion that this promotion could be considered an illegal gambling transaction drew skepticism but the Commonwealth of Massachusetts has two state statutes, one civil and one criminal, which may or may not have applied to this case.

In fact, a few Massachusetts Supreme Judicial Courts had already addressed similar activities. This article investigates the gambling issues that surround these types of insured sport promotions under Massachusetts law, and discuss implications of this ruling for sport managers both in Massachusetts and the numerous other states with similar legal restrictions.

Jordan's furniture was not the first retailer to offer a money-back promotion based on the outcome of a sport team's season. In fact this type of promotion has become increasingly popular in recent years. Similar promotions have been seen in the Chicago area based on the outcome of Chicago Bears game as well as the Los Angeles area based on a college football contest between USC and UCLA. Another Boston retailer, Alpha Omega jewelry, even offered partial refunds on engagement rings tied to the Red Sox performance the day the ring was purchased.

These cases have most likely answered the questions of illegal gambling practices in these promotions in favor of the retailers but it has become vitally important for sports managers to investigate the laws in their perspective states before engaging in a similar promotion.

Bortman, E. C. (2009). The Jordan's Furniture "monster deal": A legal gamble? *Sport Marketing Quarterly, 18*(4), 218–221.

Marketing Murderball: The Influence of Spectator Motivation Factors on Sports Consumption Behaviours of Wheelchair Rugby Spectators

Kevin K. Byon—University of Georgia

Michael Cottingham II—Southern New Hampshire University

Michael S. Carroll—Troy University

It has been found that Spectator motivation is one of the most important variables affecting the consumption behaviors in sport (e.g. Funk, Mahony & Ridinger, 2002; Trail, Fink & Anderson, 2003). This phenomenon has been studied in various contexts, including women's professional basketball (Funk, Ridinger & Moorman 2003), professional baseball (Trail & James, 2001) and men's professional basketball (Pease & Zhang, 2001) as well as new domains such as mixed martial arts (Andrew, Kim, O'Neal, Greenwell & James, 2009; Kim, Andrew & Greenwell, 2009) and soccer and ski-jumping (Mehus, 2005). However, so far, this research has focused mostly on non-adaptive sports, which shows a need to investigate the motivations of spectators of adaptive sports in order to better understand that group.

This study was designed to investigate the link between spectator motivation and consumption among sports fans including continued patronage intentions and online media consumption within wheelchair rugby events. Respondents to this survey were attendees of five matches involving registered United States Quad Rugby Association (USQRA) teams held in the Midwestern United States. A random cluster sampling technique was used in data collection. 105 questionnaires were found to be usable for the purpose of data analysis. The modified version of the Motivation Scale for Sport Consumption (MSSC; Trail & James, 2001) was used to measure spectator motivation. A total of seven factors were included in the MSSC: (a) achievement, (b) knowledge, (c) aesthetics, (d) drama, (e) escape, (f) physical skill and (g) social interaction. To better understand how spectator motivation could explain sports consumption behaviors, two behavioral loyalty constructs were measured, including continued patronage intentions (Söderlund, 2006) and online media consumption, which was adapted from Fink, Trail and Anderson (2002).

A Confirmatory Factor Analysis (CFA) was used to examine the psychometric properties of the MSSC. In addition, two multiple regression analyses were used to examine the relationships between spectator motivation factors and sports consumption behavior factors. The CFA results indicated that the MSSC demonstrated sound psychometric properties in the wheelchair rugby setting. The results of the multiple regression analyses indicated that the most statistically significant predictors of continued attendance at these events were physical skill and knowledge.

The results of this study have the potential to benefit the wheelchair rugby teams and league, which often operate with limited marketing budgets. Suggestions for practitioners to increase continued patronage intentions are as follows. With respect to the physical skill motivation factor, wheelchair rugby organizers should recruit teams to compete based more on their skill level than geographical convenience. With respect to the knowledge motivation factor, event organizers should consider providing an information booklet that includes a short explanation of the rules of the sport, an explanation of the disability classification system and an introduction to the athletes on the home team. In addition, event organizers should consider providing "fan days" in which fans can try the wheelchairs and play the sport, to increase their tactile knowledge of the game.

Finally, with respect to online media consumption, developing short educational vignettes, strategically placed on websites to educate prospective fans, can increase knowledge. With respect to the vicarious achievement factor, more wheelchair rugby teams should develop team websites and consider using social networking sites to develop various groups to provide information and foster fan identification with the team.

Byon, K. K., Michael Cottingham, I., & Michael S., C. (2010). Marketing murderball: The influence of spectator motivation factors on sports consumption behaviours of wheelchair rugby spectators. *International Journal of Sports Marketing & Sponsorship, 12*(1), 76–94.

The Relationship Between Spectator Motivations and Media and Merchandise Consumption at a Professional Mixed Martial Arts Event

Damon P. S. Andrew—Troy University

Seungmo Kim—Hong Kong Baptist University

Nick O'Neal—King of the Cage

T. Christopher Greenwell

Jeffrey D. James

This study's purpose is to explore the nine selected motives impact the consumption of media and merchandise among consumers of Mixed Martial Arts (MMA). This study builds off previous research by investigating the relationship of motivations and consumption at a large MMA event. A one-way MANOVA was computed to test for gender differences in relation to attendance motivations in this study. After a variety of differences among spectator motives were identified, two separate backward deletion linear regression analyses revealed notable relationships between spectator motivations and consumption of media and merchandise for both males and females. This suggests the need to implement a varying marketing strategy for males and females in order to best take advantage media and merchandise consumption among MMA spectators.

The popularity of the sport of MMA has grown significantly in recent years. Not only has the largest North American promoter of the sport, the Ultimate Fighting Championship (UFC), grown by leaps and bounds, but other professional organizations tied to MMA such as Bellatar Fighting Championship, King of Cage and Strikeforce have appeared on the scene. Many amateur MMA organizations and events have also started promoting fights at a local level. MMA has also competed well with other popular sports in television ratings. According to Spike TV, UFC 75, held in the United Kingdom on September 6, 2007, recorded a 3.1 overall rating, surpassing the ratings for college football games, NASCAR, and the U.S. Open tennis tournament televised on the same Saturday night. The sport has had had great success in drawing the attention of men in the 18–49 years old demographic (Pishna, September 2007). Spike TV reported:

> UFC 75 scored 2,503,000 [men in the 18–49 years old demographic] compared to 2.3 million for Oregon vs. Michigan [college football] on ABC; 2.1 million for NASCAR on ABC; 1.3 million for Virginia Tech vs. LSU [college football] on ESPN;

> 1.3 million for Notre Dame vs. Penn State [college football] on ESPN, and 546,000 for the U.S. Open Women's Tennis Final on CBS. (Pishna, September 2007)

UFC's reach as a leading promoter of MMA in the world has even grown beyond the United States. In fact events are now televised UFC events are televised in over 100 countries and in 17 different languages (Show, 2009). This rapid increase in popularity of MMA provides sport managers an opportunity to study a sport in its formative years of growth and better understand what attracts customers and fans. While some sports such as soccer have struggled to gain traction with American consumers, MMA has shown impressive growth as evidenced by the large number of organizations promoting events and the high attendance of live events in conjunction with rapidly increasing television ratings.

So far there has been little empirical research done to understand the motives for watching and participating in MMA but prior studies have suggested that different motives exist for watching individual sports as opposed to team sports (Kim, Greenwell, Andrew, Lee, & Mahony, 2008). Studies have also shown that the motives of sports consumers may be different in other countries (Kim, Andrew, & Greenwell, 2009). However there is still need to understand the motivations of MMA consumers. This study will add to the knowledge of MMA consumers by examining motives for attending live events, buying merchandise, and watching events on television.

The findings from this research will help sport managers understand the MMA consumer and what attracts them to the sport with regards to media and merchandise. The importance of consumer knowledge also adds considerable insight into the growth of the sport. Whereas consumers in many countries have grown up with various martial arts ingrained within their culture, those in the United States are less likely to know about the rules, strategies, and techniques associated with the sport. The results from this study suggest many people attend to increase their knowledge of the sport and fulfill their desire to learn.

With regard to media consumption behavior, aesthetics, knowledge, and drama were common motives that predicted media consumption behavior for both male and female consumers, while violence only predicted male consumers' media consumption behavior. Interestingly, the influence of drama on media consumption behavior was very different compared to past research concerning an amateur MMA event (Kim, et al., 2008).

Andrew, D. S., Seungmo, K., O'Neal, N., Greenwell, T., & James, J. D. (2009). The relationship between spectator motivations and media and merchandise consumption at a professional mixed martial arts event. *Sport Marketing Quarterly, 18*(4), 199–209.

The Role of Involvement in Sports and Sport Spectatorship in Sponsor's Brand Use: The Case of Mountain Dew and Action Sports Sponsorship

Gregg Bennett

Mauricio Ferreira

Jaedeock Lee

Fritz Polite

The ability of a company to create a recognizable and well-liked brand is an essential component to measuring success in business approach and marketing strategy (Allenby, et al., 2002), and researchers are constantly looking for empirical evidence explaining that the use of brand names is a major stream in marketing literature (Fennell, Allenby, Yang, & Edwards, 2003). In the last one hundred years or so, studies have examined the relationships between several variables (e.g., psychographics, age, gender, and other demographics) in an effort to develop better understanding of consumption rates and brand use (Shaw, 1912; Smith, 1956) so strategies can be created and implemented to increase brand use.

Firms often sponsor sporting events to communicate with targeted consumers via demographic and psychographic variables (Bennett, 1999; Cliffe & Motion, 2005; Fennell & Allenby, 2004; Nicholls, Roslow, & Dublish, 1999; Roy & Cornwell, 2004), in hopes of creating more recognizable brands. The sponsorship of certain sporting events, venues or teams can provide brand exposure to areas or people that are more difficult to reach through traditional media outlets (IEC, 2004). The Mountain Dew brand's decision to sponsor action sport events is one prime example of this strategy at work. This sponsorship provides access to a coveted target market, consisted of primarily young males (Bennett, Henson, & Zhang, 2003). In fact, Browne (2004, p. 174) connects the "reinvigoration" of the Mountain Dew brand and increases in brand use (sales) to this long standing decision to sponsor action sporting events. The growing popularity of action sports and the impressive amount of investment the athletes and events have attracted from various brands is noteworthy (Bennett, Henson, & Zhang, 2002; Browne,;2004).

While the easy access to target markets is an obvious advantage of sponsorship, many brands will choose to activate the sponsorship through television and event attendance. For that reason, live spectatorship of sporting events can be crucial in the use of sponsorship. However, sponsors must often be prepared to sign contractual agreements for inaugural events without historical evidence of attendance or viewership for the event. That creates some uncertainty about the expected success of these new sponsorships. Research has shown that highly involved consumers of sport will likely consume the sport through live event attendance more than those who are not as involved (Stone, 1984), sponsors must rely on the expectation that those who are deeply committed to a sport will eventually watch and attend its events. This topic leads to the primary focus of this study, "which has not yet been addressed in the sponsorship literature: a) how is involvement, sport spectatorship, and target markets related to sponsor's brand use?

As such, the purpose of this study was to examine the relationship between involvement, demographic characteristics, action sport consumption, and use of an event sponsors brand. We sought to examine the degree to which involvement with action sports (enduring and behavioral), demographics (age and gender) and action sports consumption (spectatorship, participation, and video gaming) actually predict Mountain Dew use among those attending an action sports event."

This study will contribute to previous research by detailing how sport consumption, and brand use are related while considering sports sponsorships. The proposed model will examine how sport spectatorship affects the relationship between involvement in action sports and brand use.

The study found that age, gender and event spectatorship did have a direct impact on brand use (purchase). Also that event attendance mediated the relationship between commitment to the sport, participation, video gaming, and brand use.

Bennett, G., Ferreira, M., Lee, J., & Polite, F. (2009). The role of involvement in sports and sport spectatorship in sponsor's brand use: The case of Mountain Dew and action sports sponsorship. *Sport Marketing Quarterly, 18*(1), 14–24.

An Examination of Sports Sponsorship From a Small Business Perspective

J. Terence Zinger

Norman J. Reilly

This paper responds to the need for more investigation into the "conceptual underpinnings of sponsorships" (Gardner & Shuman, 1988, p.44) by investigating the spectrum of opportunities that are available to small firms—whether as sports donors or as bona fide sponsors—through the prism of small business Stages of Development theory. A multiple case study approach is employed to explore the nature of sponsorship activities being undertaken by small enterprises and to contribute to the advancement of the authors' 'philanthropy-sponsorship' continuum.

This research makes two contributions. First, it presents the classifications of 'patronage' versus 'semi-strong sponsorship' versus 'fully functioning sponsorship' relationships, based on the nature of the expected benefits. Second, it evaluates the small business/sports property interface from the perspective of small business phases of development and proposes a framework for linking the small firm to sports sponsorship outcomes.

Within a reasonably short time frame, sport has emerged as an effective vehicle for building brand awareness, reaching target audiences and burnishing the corporate image (Seguin & O'Reilly, 2008).

Whereas substantial research has been directed towards the obligations of the sport organisation (as sponsee) in cultivating sponsorship partnerships, this exploratory study examines the implications of the ever-increasing growth in sponsorships for small enterprises (as sponsors) and considers what type of sponsorship activity is feasible for a given small business.

While resources are limited for many small enterprises, there may well be untapped sponsorship opportunities, as they seek cost-effective marketing and public relations vehicles, while sport properties (particularly at amateur level) search for relief from persistent funding shortages.

This research focused on six case studies from small firm sponsors. The sample was drawn from a larger study of 80 companies, where support was found for several sponsorship 'best practices', including the value that sponsors ascribe to exclusivity, as well as the importance of tangible, identifiable benefits for both sponsor and sponsee. However, the small enterprises featured in this paper showed a tendency to treat their sponsorship endeavours as a natural adjunct to their extensive charitable activities, with three of the six being highly influenced by a sense of community. While these small firms appeared to be successful in negotiating suitable packages of rights and benefits and in one case was able to secure a certain level of exclusivity, there was little effort directed towards researching and differentiating between sponsorship opportunities.

The Stages of Development theory provides a workable approach to breaking down the population of small firms into useful subgroups. To facilitate further analysis, the six cases were also classified by their perceived level of organisational complexity. For instance, employee relations was found to be an important factor in two of the higher level firms. In addition, there was evidence that even beyond the early phases of small business development, the attitudes and personal interests of the entrepreneurs seem to have an influence on sponsorship activity, at times dominating commercial considerations.

The discussion emphasises the need for the small business owner to be fully aware of the nature of the organisational commitment that may be necessary to derive the full benefit available through sponsorship arrangements. Once the business enterprise starts to envision an involvement that will extend beyond pure patronage, it must address the sundry challenges that accompany the development of an effective sponsorship programme. The need for continual measurement of the effectiveness of the sponsorship, as well as the importance of developing activation programmes, can place burdensome demands on the sponsor's organization.

This paper's contributions include the development of a philanthropy-sponsorship continuum, some new insights into the nature of sponsorship at the small enterprise level and a proposed framework that might be helpful in relating the array of patronage and sponsorship opportunities to the different categories of small business.

Zinger, J., & O'Reilly, N. J. (2010). An examination of sports sponsorship from a small business perspective. *International Journal of Sports Marketing & Sponsorship, 11*(4), 283–301.

The Use of Sport Celebrities in Advertising: A Replication and Extension

Brody J. Ruihley

Rodney C. Runyan

Karen E. Lear

The use of sport celebrities to bolster advertising is an important factor reaching a target market of sports consumers. It has been questioned whether the use of this strategy has decreased as more and more sports celebrities are involved in negative off-field issues. This study will further the investigation of the use of these sport celebrities in advertising. Using a content analysis, the study replicates the work of Stone, Joseph, and Jones (2003). By replicating the Stone et al. content analysis, we provide validation for the earlier work, as generally called for by many leading researchers. Extending the study into the most recent decade enlarges the current literature, as it enables the identification of change in the way marketers use celebrity athletes in print advertising. By investigating the issue of race in such ads, we extend the current literature to explore advertisers' use of African-American endorsers to promote specific products. We find this research to generally support the earlier study; however, not all trends predicted by Stone et al. have materialized. Other results show that there is a significant discrepancy in the endorsement activity of African-American athletes compared to Caucasians, with Caucasians receiving a disproportionate amount of the opportunities in endorsements compared to their participation rates in sport.

According to Stone et al. (2003), celebrity athlete endorsements in print advertising declined from the 1980s to the 1990s. They posited that this decline was due (in part) to the concern advertisers might have regarding possible negative consequences of ill-behaved athletes. Since the 1990s, there has been tremendous growth of advertising in media other than print (television, Internet, etc.). Thus, holding advertising volume constant, there should be fewer ads appearing in print periodicals in the new millennium, leading to the proposition of four thoughts. First, there will be considerably fewer ads featuring celebrity athletes. Second, there will be significantly more female athletes used as endorsers in ads. Next, that the number of ads featuring a Caucasian athlete will be significantly more than those featuring an African American athlete. And lastly, the use of African American athletes as endorsers will significantly increase from the 1980s period to the 2000s period.

This study replicated previous findings that there would be fewer *Sports Illustrated* ads featuring athletes, as endorsers during the 1990s period than were featured during the previous decade and also that there would be growth in the use of non-celebrity models as endorsers. The only disparity involved the hypothesis stating that the number of ads featuring female athletes as endorsers would increase significantly between the two periods. These results indicate six ads featuring female athletes in the 1980s period and seven ads featuring female athletes in the 1990s period, thus we cannot confirm the Stone et al. finding of a significant increase in the use of female endorsers.

Our three main topics of discussion focus on trends in the use of celebrity athletes in advertising, the use of female athletes in advertising, and race of athlete endorsers in advertising. We conclude with a discussion of the limitations of the current research and recommendations for future research.

The research through content analysis of advertisements in *Sports Illustrated* shows several noteworthy trends. This study confirms previous findings that there was a decrease of the use of celebrity athletes in advertisements from the 1980s to the 1990s but also that these types of endorsements bounced back the following decade. In the 2000s, the research showed that the use of celebrity athletes as endorsers increased from the previous two decades. These results contradict the previous predictions that marketers would be scared away by the rising controversies surrounding celebrity athletes. Even though behavioral issues are present among celebrity athletes, brand owners have continued to use them to endorse products.

The content analysis also found that a significant increase in the use of female athletes as celebrity endorsers occurred between the two periods. It appears that marketers use female athletes at a much higher rate than twenty years ago.

The research also shows that while there was a great increase in the use of African American athletes as celebrity endorsers, there was a greater increase in the use of Caucasian athletes. This shows that there is at best stagnation in the use of the African American Athletes as endorsers.

The scandal facing Tiger Woods during late 2009 may or may not have a negative effect upon other African-American athletes in terms of endorsement opportunities. The ubiquity of Woods' endorsements, and the depth of his relationships with those marketers were well known. Nike has long marketed a separate line of Tiger Woods golf equipment, and as of this article's completion, Nike planned to continue that relationship (Vranica, 2009a). But other marketers may be more cautious in the future. When such a presumably bankable athlete such as Woods is seemingly not beyond scandal, other athletes appear to be even riskier in terms of endorsement.

Ruihley, B. J., Runyan, R. C., & Lear, K. E. (2010). The Use of Sport Celebrities in Advertising: A Replication and Extension. *Sport Marketing Quarterly, 19*(3), 132–142.

Not Just a Party in the Parking Lot: An Exploratory Investigation of the Motives Underlying the Ritual Commitment of Football Tailgaters

Jenna Drenten

Gara Okleshen Peters

Thomas Leigh

Candice R. Hollenbeck

The purpose of this study is to investigate the motives behind the ritual of football tailgating and how those motives influence ritual commitment. By using an ethnographic approach with methods including observation of ritual tailgaters, informal conversations, and formal interviews. The research shows that four basic motivations exist within this population. These motivations among tailgaters include involvement in the event, social interaction with other participants, inter-temporal sentiment (retrospection and prospection), and the feeling of an identity within the community of tailgaters. It can be inferred from the data collected that the commitment of consumers to the ritual of tailgating motivates participants to continue tailgating over time. Theoretical and sport marketing implications are discussed.

The origin of tailgating can be traced to New Brunswick, New Jersey in 1869 where the first intercollegiate football game occurred in America between Rutgers and Princeton. Before the game, a group of fans had gathered to eat, drink and generally socialize in what is widely considered the first tailgating party. This activity has clearly become a fixture of college football spectatorship.

Studies have already focused on identifying factors that motivate consumers to attend sporting events (Garo & Garcia, 2007; James & Ross, 2004; Koo & Hardin, 2008; McDonald, Milne, & Hong, 2002; Swanson, Gwinner, Larson, & Janda, 2003; Wann, Grieve, Zapalac, & Pease, 2008); however, only one study before this current study specifically examined the motives behind social pre-game rituals surrounding sporting events. In a two-stage study at the University of Illinois, James, Breezeel, & Ross (2001) identified two primary motives that individuals continue tailgating: 1) to escape their normal routines and 2) to enjoy social interaction. Although important, the work of James et al. (2001) is limited because it focuses more on the act of tailgating as a leisure activity and less on the how meaningful the ritual itself can be. The present study takes a different approach by examining tailgating in a way that details the emotional connection to such a consumption ritual.

There has been a steady influx of research on rituals within the study of marketing but the concept of investigating a long-term commitment to rituals like tailgating is limited. There is a need for research on what motivates this behavior. Drawing from theory on ritual commitment and reversal synergy, the research shows that motives with a dual nature and the negotiation processes that accompany these factors influence a tailgater's commitment to the ritual over time.

The findings of this study identify a wide variety of factors at work with respect to the perpetuation of the tailgating ritual over time. For instance, tailgating is not driven simply by an interest in being social. Instead, there is an underlying negotiation of competition and connection among consumers of the event that leads to that long-term commitment to the tailgating ritual.

The most important contribution of this study is arguably the identification of taking a more holistic view of the overall tailgating experience. The separate themes identified by this research, such as camaraderie and nostalgia do not necessarily detail the consumer's commitment to the ritual in the long-term. "Rather, the constant negotiation due to the dual nature of the motives is essential to ritual commitment. The findings of this study show that it is the overall experience itself that is important, not an individual act or individual motivating factor. The process by which the dual themes interact and are negotiated creates meaning and motivates the consumer to perpetuate and commit to the ritual over time."

The findings from this research are important for a variety of sports venues including universities, sports leagues (e.g., NASCAR, NFL), and businesses interested in using sponsorship marketing with teams and leagues. These venues would like to capitalize on the commitment of consumers to the ritual of tailgating before events.

"By focusing marketing efforts on reflecting the underlying dualities of sport-related rituals, rather than only promoting the ritual itself, marketers can use these latent motives to foster ritual commitment."

Drenten, J., Peters, C., Leigh, T., & Hollenbeck, C. R. (2009). Not just a party in the parking lot: An exploratory investigation of the motives underlying the ritual commitment of football tailgaters. *Sport Marketing Quarterly, 18*(2), 92–106.

Communicating With Consumers Through Video Games: An Analysis of Brand Development Within the Video Gaming Segment of the Sports Industry

Galen Clavio

Patrick Kraft

Paul Pederson

The increasing popularity of the sports video game genre has provided advertisers with new avenues for marketing and product placement. Video games, once seen as kids' games and strictly recreational tools, have transformed into vivid, life-like representations of a wide variety of situations. Sports video games in particular have been embraced in the marketplace, with the genre holding 40% of the console gaming marketplace. Chief among the demographic groups that purchase sports video games is Generation Y; a highly desirable target market for advertisers that comprise consumers aged 18–34. As video games have advanced technologically, advertisers appear to have taken notice, with industry-wide expenditure on in-game product placement rising sharply—from $50 million in 2004 to a projected $120 million in 2006.

The purpose of this study was to examine whether companies are using the sports video game genre for the purposes of branding and product placement, and if so, to what extent this utilisation is taking place. The study examined the highly popular PGA Tour/Tiger Woods golf game for the Playstation and Playstation 2 consoles from 1997–2006, utilising the content analysis method to measure the amount of product and brand placement present in the various menu options for each year of the series. The study used the brand image, name or logo as the unit of measurement.

The results of the study reveal that advertisers are indeed using sports video games for the purposes of branding and product placement, and that this utilisation is a relatively new phenomenon. For the first seven years of the series, there was only one incidence of branding. However, in the final three years of the series, from 2004–2006, there were 2,099 unique occurrences of branding and product placement. Furthermore, the number of incidences of branding in each game more than doubled from 2004 to 2006, while the number of brands represented in the game nearly doubled over that same time span. Certain brands had a much larger presence than others, with adidas, the Nike family and Oakley accounting for more than two-thirds of the total branding impressions recorded. In all, 24 distinct brands were identified over the life of the series, including such niche companies as Cobra, Precept and Under Armour.

These results indicate that sports video games are increasingly seen as viable marketing avenues by companies and by advertisers. The growing number of visible company brands, coupled with the increasing number of available products, indicates a desire by these companies to have their brands seen and utilised by users of this game series.

Clavio, G., Kraft, P. M., & Pedersen, P. M. (2009). Communicating with consumers through video games: An analysis of brand development within the video gaming segment of the sports industry. *International Journal of Sports Marketing & Sponsorship, 10*(2), 143–156.

Virtual Advertising in Sports Events: Does it Really Work?

Matthias Sander

Claudia Fantapié Altobelli

This is an investigation of the effects of virtual advertising in the setting of a sports broadcast. An analysis of virtual advertising will allow the results to be linked to variables like brand awareness and repeated exposure. The research will also examine the attitudes of advertising as a whole and its impact on impact on attitudes of virtual advertising. The results show that most participants can identify virtual advertising and that a positive opinion of advertising in general is linked to a positive attitude towards virtual advertising.

Virtual advertising can be defined as a technology that allowed superimposed digital images to appear in the backgrounds of a television broadcast (Cianfrone et al, 2006; Pyun & Kim, 2004). This paper will provide some early feedback on the effects of this growing tool in advertising and will serve as an exploratory study to provide further insight into its effectiveness.

It was expected that participants would recognize virtual advertising as such but the study attempts to discover what factors influence the effectiveness of this marketing revolution. It can be assumed that factors such as brand awareness and frequency of exposure would influence the effectiveness of virtual advertising. (Tellis, 1997; Longman, 1997; Pieters & Bijmolt, 1997; Turley & Shannon, 2000; Sander, 2004). For the sake of comparison, the influence of the same factors were measured for traditional advertising.

142 participants were shown an 18-minute video clip from a televised soccer match as the case study for this research. These participants were students at a German university.

The research shows that most of the participants did in fact recognize virtual advertising and the model gives an excellent explanation for the effect of the variables (brand awareness, duration of exposure and frequency of exposure).

How often a viewer is exposed to the advertised material is clearly shown to be a significant factor in how effective the ads will be. The research also showed a positive correlation between participants attitudes about all forms of advertising and their opinions on virtual advertising.

"In conclusion, this investigation provides fundamental data for further research on consumer responses to virtual advertising in sports broadcasts. However, there is only a little conclusive evidence regarding the effectiveness of different kinds of virtual advertising (e.g. 3D animation, animated virtual advertising) so far. More effort has to be made in this direction."

Sander, M., & Altobelli, C. (2011). Virtual advertising in sports events: Does it really work? *International Journal of Sports Marketing & Sponsorship, 12*(3), 225–239.

Understanding Women's Collegiate Volleyball Spectators From the Perspectives of Sociodemographics, Market Demand and Consumption Level

Ryan Zapalac

James J. Zhang

Dale G. Pearse

U.S. intercollegiate athletic departments typically see women's volleyball as a sport with little opportunity to generate revenue and that poses a problem for many schools. The challenge of managing the disparity between budget and revenue is coming to the forefront and athletic programs are constantly fighting debt. One option for these programs to examine may be tackling new or lesser-used marketing opportunities within various sports like women's volleyball. There has been minimal research into the market demand of spectators of women's volleyball and so this study will study the spectators of the sport from the perspectives of socio-demographics, market demand and consumption.

265 spectators from seven women's college volleyball games at three NCAA Division-I schools participated in a survey for this research. Spectators were presented the survey at random as they entered the facility.

The questionnaire included sections on the three focal points of this study mentioned earlier. A factor analysis showed four common themes within market demand including promotion, affiliation, attractiveness and affordability. The factors that influence game consumption among participants were attendance, frequency, the purchase of merchandise, the purchase of tickets and season ticket ownership.

"A canonical correlation analysis also showed that the market demand factors were positively predictive of the game consumption factors." The study of these results signifies that market demand factors must be emphasized in the marketing plans of women's college volleyball. The implementation of these factors could help increase revenues from the sport and thereby increase profitability for the athletic departments.

The findings implied the need to emphasize market demand factors when marketing intercollegiate women's volleyball games. Placing an emphasis on these factors could result in increased revenues from this sport, leading to increased profitability for collegiate athletic departments.

"Collegiate sport marketers may want to emphasize an increased volume of promotional efforts that focus on affiliation with a university to foster increased attendance at women's volleyball games."

However, the analysis did not show any noteworthy relation between market demand factors and the purchase of merchandise. This suggests there may be some other factors not studied in this research that effect game day sales.

Zapalac, R. K., Zhang, J. J., & Pease, D. G. (2010). Understanding women's collegiate volleyball spectators from the perspectives of sociodemographics, market demand and consumption level. *International Journal of Sports Marketing & Sponsorship, 11*(4), 320–343.

Appendix F

Examples of Surveys and Questionnaires for Research

Overview: The purpose of Appendix F is to provide examples of research instruments commonly used in sport marketing. The examples are survey instruments. A brief overview of each instrument is provided offering the topic of study, its purpose, the type of instrument, methodology, and some uses of the information. The survey instruments included are real surveys from actual research in sport marketing.

Activity: Actual studies may be conducted using any of these instruments with appropriate guidance and supervision of the sport marketing course instructor and/or the authors from whom these instruments derived. (Use of these instruments without the supervision of the instructor is NOT recommended and should not be attempted.)

Survey 1: Sponsorship Recognition

Topic of Study: Sponsorship and Sports Events

Purpose in Sport Marketing: Sponsors spend money as a method of advertising to increase brand awareness. Sponsors of sports events would like to know if this category of advertising is reaping results, such as brand awareness and increased sales of the company's products. With positive results, sponsor company decision makers will most likely continue to use sponsorship as an advertising form.

Sports event managers desire sponsorship to gain business relationships and as a form of funding the event. Managers would like spectators to support the sponsors as a reward and a show of support for the sponsor's support. This would help in the triangle relationship between the event manager, the sponsor, and the spectator.

Purpose of this study: To measure sponsorship recognition.

Instrument: Survey

Directions: Please circle your answer or place an X in the spaces provided. All replies are strictly confidential. Thank you in advance for your assistance!

1. Have you noticed sponsor signs or booths at the stadium
   or surrounding area for the season? ❑ Yes ❑ No

Below, answer Yes or No if you think there is a company as a sponsor. If you answer Yes, identify the *one or more companies* you can remember.

Is there a soft drink sponsor?
a. Pepsi   b. Coca-Cola   c. RC Cola   d. Mountain Dew   ❏ Yes   ❏ No

Is there a bank sponsor?
a. Capitol City Bank   b. Barnett Bank   c. Sun Trust
   d. Government Employees Credit Union   ❏ Yes   ❏ No

Is there an American automobile manufacturer sponsor?
a. Chevrolet   b. GMC   c. Ford   d. Dodge   ❏ Yes   ❏ No

Is there a hotel sponsor?
a. Winn Dixie   b. Bruno's   c. Albertson's   d. Publix   ❏ Yes   ❏ No

Is there a video rental company sponsor?
a. Blockbuster   b. Greg's Video   c. Video 21
   d. Movie Gallery   ❏ Yes   ❏ No

Is there a sports magazine sponsor?
a. Sports Illustrated   b. ESPN—The Magazine
   c. Women's Sport & Fitness   d. College Football Weekly   ❏ Yes   ❏ No

Is there a medical/health facility sponsor?
   a. Tallahassee Memorial HealthCare
   b. Tallahassee Wellness Center
   c. Orlando Orthopedic Clinic
   d. Tallahassee Regional Medical Center   ❏ Yes   ❏ No

Is there an ice cream company sponsor?
a. Ben & Jerry's   b. Baskin Robbins   c. Edy's
   d. Haagan-Daas   ❏ Yes   ❏ No

Is there an internet company sponsor?
a. monstor.com   b. travelocity.com   c. Yahoo! Sports
   d. careerbuilders.com   ❏ Yes   ❏ No

Is there a sports retail sponsor?
a. Jumbo Sports   b. Play It Again Sports
   c. Champ's   d. Finish Line   ❏ Yes   ❏ No

Is there a local television station sponsor (individual)?
a. WTWC-NBC   b. WCTV-CBS   c. WTXL-ABC
d. WTLH-FOX   ❏ Yes   ❏ No

2. Are you more likely to buy the products of sponsor companies
   of this season because they are sponsors of the (event)? ❏ Yes   ❏ No

3. How long have you been a (event) season ticket holder (in years)? _____

4. Are you a member of the (club) Boosters also?   ❏ Yes   ❏ No

Please offer some information about yourself (all information is kept confidential).

5. What is your gender? ❏ Female ❏ Male

6. What is your age? _____

7. What city and state do you live in? _____

8. Which category below best describes your total, annual household income?
   ❏ 0–$10,000   ❏ $10,000–29,999   ❏ $30,000–49,999
   ❏ 50,000–69,999   ❏ $70,000–89,999   ❏ $90,000–109,999
   ❏ $110,000–129,999   ❏ $130,000–149,999   ❏ $150,000–over

9. What is your highest level of education attained? _____
   ❏ grade school   ❏ some high school   ❏ high school graduate
   ❏ vocational/technical school ❏ some college   ❏ college degree
   ❏ some post graduate work   ❏ master's degree   ❏ doctoral degree

When you have completed the survey, please enclose it in the postage-paid, addressed return envelope provided, and drop it in the nearest postal box.

Thank you for participating.

Methodology: As you can see in the example, sponsorship recognition asks the study participant to "recognize" the sponsor company (or brand) in a particular product category. The typical protocol is multiple choice. (For more specific directions, refer to research methods books and sport marketing literature.)

Surveying takes place during the event away from areas where sponsors' signs would be visible—usually, just outside the arena. The researcher approaches people who attended the event and asks if they would participate in marketing research and complete a survey.

A second surveying technique is to mail the survey to the attendees and ask them to complete it and send it back. This requires gathering a mailing list with names and addresses of people who attended the event. Sometimes, mailing lists are available that contain season ticket-holders, for example.

Sources: (1) Slattery, J., & Pitts, B. G. (2001). Paper presented at the annual conference of the North American Society for Sport Management, Virginia Beach, Virginia, May 29–June 3, 2001. Available from the authors, Florida State University. (2) Cuneen, J., & Hannan, M. (1993). Intermediate measures and recognition testing of sponsorship advertising at an LPGA tournament. *Sport Marketing Quarterly, 2*(1), 47–56.

Survey 2: Purchase Intention

Topic of Study: Purchase intent; Support of sponsors of sports event

Purpose in Sport Marketing: The purpose of this research is to determine if sports event attendees (spectators) intend to support the sponsors of the event by purchasing the product of that company. Some research is showing that consumers of sports events are more influenced to purchase certain products (of sponsoring companies) and less influenced to purchase others. For example, certain food product companies, such as pizza and sub sandwiches, seem to enjoy more support from attendees than others. The reasons need further investigation. However, if the owner of a more formal restaurant that offers more formal cuisine determines through research that the market (spectators) at certain sports events are less likely to purchase their product, then that owner might decide that advertising (through sponsorship) at this sports event is not producing successful results. This type of research can help answer those questions.

Instrument: Survey

Directions: Please circle your answer or place an X in the spaces provided. All replies are strictly confidential. Thank you in advance for your assistance!

Please rate how likely you are to purchase the products of the following sponsors of this event due to their sponsorship of this organization.

1 = definitely will not buy
2 = probably will not buy
3 = might or might not buy
4 = probably will buy
5 = definitely will buy

	1	2	3	4	5
1. Piccadilly Restaurant	1	2	3	4	5
2. Subway	1	2	3	4	5
3. Papa John's	1	2	3	4	5
4. US Airways	1	2	3	4	5
5. U.S. Cellular	1	2	3	4	5
6. Furrin Auto	1	2	3	4	5
7. Comp-U-Wiz	1	2	3	4	5
8. Snookers Billiards Room	1	2	3	4	5
9. Blockbuster	1	2	3	4	5
10. Budweiser	1	2	3	4	5
11. All State Insurance	1	2	3	4	5

Also, please rate your attitude towards these companies as a result of their sponsorship of (event).

1 = more favorable attitude due to sponsorship
2 = somewhat more favorable attitude
3 = doesn't make a difference in opinion about the company
4 = somewhat less favorable attitude
5 = less favorable attitude due to sponsorship

	1	2	3	4	5
12. Piccadilly Restaurant	1	2	3	4	5
13. Subway	1	2	3	4	5
14. Papa John's	1	2	3	4	5
15. Airways	1	2	3	4	5
16. Cellular	1	2	3	4	5
17. Furrin Auto	1	2	3	4	5
18. Comp-U-Wiz	1	2	3	4	5
19. Snookers Billiards Room	1	2	3	4	5
20. Blockbuster	1	2	3	4	5
21. Budweiser	1	2	3	4	5
22. All State Insurance	1	2	3	4	5

23. Does the type of signage a person has at an event influence your likelihood to purchase something from that company?   ❏ Yes   ❏ No

24. Have you ever purchased the products of any (event) sponsors in the past?

                                                                              ❏ Yes   ❏ No

If yes, which companies? And why? _____

25. Estimate the number of games you attended last season (1999-2000):
    ❏ 0-10   ❏ 11-20   ❏ 21-over

Estimate the number of games you will attend this season (2000-2001):
    ❏ 0-10   ❏ 11-20   ❏ 21-over

Please offer some information about yourself (all information is kept confidential).

26. What is your gender?
    ❏ Male   ❏ Female

27. What is your age? _____

28. What city and state do you live in? _____

29. Which category listed below best describes your total, annual HOUSEHOLD income?
    ❏ 0-$10,000   ❏ $10,001-29,999   ❏ $30,000-49,999
    ❏ $50,000-69,999   ❏ $70,000-89,999   ❏ $90,000-109,999
    ❏ $110,000-129,999   ❏ $130,000-149,999   ❏ $150,000-over

What is your highest level of education attained?
    ❏ grade school   ❏ some high school   ❏ high school graduate
    ❏ vocational/technical school ❏ some college   ❏ college degree
    ❏ some post-graduate work ❏ master's degree   ❏ doctoral degree
    ❏ law degree

THANK YOU FOR PARTICIPATING!

Methodology: This instrument attempts to determine the level of purchase intention. As you can see in the example survey, the attendee is asked to rank their level of intention as listed from "definitely will not buy" to "definitely will buy." Surveying takes place during the event. The researcher approaches people attending the event and asks if they would participate in marketing research and complete a survey.

A second surveying technique is to mail the survey to the attendees and ask them to complete it and send it back. This requires gathering a mailing list with names and addresses of people who attended the event. Sometimes, mailing lists are available that contain season ticket-holders, for example.

Sources: (1) Slattery, J., & Pitts, B. G. (2000). Purchase intent of attendees of minor league hockey. Unpublished study. Available from the authors. Florida State University. (2) Shannon, J. R., Turley, L. W. (1997). The influence of in-arena promotions on purchase behavior and purchase intentions. *Sport Marketing Quarterly, 6*(4), 53–59.

Survey 3: Market Competitor's Influence

Topic of Study: Market competitors

Purpose in Sport Marketing: The purpose of this research is to determine the level of influence of the competition in the marketplace for your sport business. This information will be used in determining product differentiation and positioning in promotional efforts.

Instrument: Survey

Marketing Survey Form

Purpose: This survey is for the purpose of providing better service to the Xxxx (professional team name) audience. The collected information will be solely used for research, and your name will not be identified. Your sincere and honest response is greatly appreciated.

Entertainment Options: Please rate how much you participate in the following activities (5-Always; 4-Often; 3-Sometimes; 2-Occasionally; 1-Never).

1. Attend professional indoor soccer game	5	4	3	2	1
2. Attend a concert	5	4	3	2	1
3. Attend intercollegiate games	5	4	3	2	1
4. Attend professional basketball games	5	4	3	2	1
5. Attend a night club	5	4	3	2	1
6. Attend professional baseball games	5	4	3	2	1
7. Watch sports on TV	5	4	3	2	1
8. Play recreational sports	5	4	3	2	1
9. Attend a movie	5	4	3	2	1
10. Watch non-sport programs on TV	5	4	3	2	1
11. Work out/Exercise	5	4	3	2	1
12. Travel	5	4	3	2	1
13. Attend professional football games	5	4	3	2	1
14. Go to bar/restaurant	5	4	3	2	1
15. Attend other sport shows	5	4	3	2	1

ATTENDANCE INFORMATION. Please fill in the blanks.

How may Xxxxx home games have you attended this season? _____

How many total Xxxxx home games do you plan to attend this season? _____

How many Xxxxx games will you attend next season? _____

DEMOGRAPHIC INFORMATION. Please provide the following information.

Age: _____

Gender: _____

Ethnicity (circle one):   a. Caucasian   b. Black   c. Hispanic   d. Asian   e. Other

THANK YOU FOR YOUR COOPERATION AND ASSISTANCE!

Methodology: This instrument attempts to determine which competitors in the area are supported by consumers. The attendee (spectator) is asked to rate their involvement in the competitor's products. The attendee is also asked to provide information about their level of involvement in your product (event). This information can be analyzed and the influence of your competitors can be evaluated. Surveying takes place during the event. The researcher approaches people attending the event and asks if they would participate in marketing research and complete a survey.

A second surveying technique is to mail the survey to the attendees and ask them to complete it and send it back. This requires gathering a mailing list with names and addresses of people who attended the event. Sometimes, mailing lists are available that contain season ticket-holders, for example.

Source: Zhang, J. J., Smith, D. W., Pease, D. G., & Jambor, E. A. (1997). Negative influence of market competitors on the attendance of professional sport games: The case of a minor league hockey team. *Sport Marketing Quarterly, 6*(3), 31–39.

Survey 4: Economic Impact, Sports Event

Topic of Study: Economic impact, sports event

Purpose in Sport Marketing: The purpose of this research is to determine the financial (economic) impact of a sports event (or business). This information is useful in several ways. It can help the organizers of the event determine how much money the event is responsible for bringing into an area and how much of that money is spent on different areas, such as lodging, food, entertainment, transportation, event admissions (the sports event and other connected events), retail shopping, and event souvenirs. These types of information can help the organizers and local businesses involved (called stakeholders) in decision-making for the future of the event. The information can also be used to garner further support for the event from local government offices, current stakeholders, and potential stakeholders. The information is also used to ascertain the commercial value of the event which is sometimes used to inform prices for advertising and sponsorship fees, broadcasting fees, and other aspects of the event.

Instrument: Survey

Event Economic Impact Survey

Directions: Simply write your answers or an X in the spaces provided. Thank you in advance!

1. Why are you attending the event?
   - ❑ athlete/participant   ❑ cultural/participant   ❑ exhibitor/sales
   - ❑ spectator   ❑ event worker/staff
   - ❑ media with magazine (which one?) _____
   - ❑ media with film crew (which one?) _____
   - ❑ media with TV (which one?) _____
   - ❑ media with newspaper (which one?) _____
   - ❑ media other (which one?) _____

2. With whom did you come to the event?
   ❏ family only   ❏ partner only   ❏ friends only
   ❏ alone   ❏ both friends and family/partner
   ❏ organization (please fill in): _____

3. How many are in your party (including yourself)?

4. Would you have come to city either now or in the next 3 months if the event were not held?
   ❏ Yes   ❏ No

5. If yes above, how many days longer was your stay (if any) than it would have been if the event had not been taking place? _____

6. How many nights did you spend in city? _____
   In other cities? _____

7. Where (other cities) did you stay? _____

8. If you stayed overnight, where did you stay in city?
   ❏ hotel/motel   ❏ with friends/relative   ❏ RV   ❏ camping
   ❏ hosted housing   ❏ hostel   ❏ apartment ❏ other

9. Have you attended the event previously?   ❏ Yes   ❏ No
   ❏ 1982   ❏ 1986   ❏ 1990   ❏ 1994

10. Do you plan on attending the event again in (Year)?   ❏ Yes   ❏ No

11. Where do you live?
    Country _____   City _____   State _____   Postal Code _____

12. What is your source of information about the event?
    ❏ radio   ❏ newspaper   ❏ TV   ❏ friends
    ❏ website   ❏ direct mail from the event
    ❏ local (city) sports organization   ❏ other

13. How many event SPORTS events did you attne/participate in? _____

14. How many event CULTURAL/ARTS events did you attend? _____

15. Please estimate (in even US dollars) how much you spent on each of the following items during your entire stay for the event in city. Your responses are very important to the study. if you can not covert to US dollars, note what currency you are listing:

    food & beverages (restaurants, concessions, grocery stores, etc.) $ _____
    fees (to participate in the event) $ _____
    admission fees (sports events and other shows) $ _____
    night clubs, lounges, & bars (coverage charges, drinks, etc.) $ _____
    retail shopping (clothing, gifts, etc.) $ _____
    event souvenirs $ _____
    loding expenses (hotel, motel, etc.)   _____
    private auto expenses (gas, oil, repairs, parking fees, etc.) $ _____
    commercial transportation (airlines, bus, train, rental car, etc.) $ _____
    any other expenses (please identify) $ _____

16. What is your age? _____

17. What is your gender?
    ❏ female   ❏ male   ❏ other

18. What is your sexual orientation?
    ❏ lesbian   ❏ gay   ❏ bisexual   ❏ heterosexual

19. Please describe your household, "I live . . ." (check one and fill in the blanks):

    I am the only adult in my household. I have _____ children.
    I live with my spouse/partner/lover of years. We have _____ children.
    I live with a friend/roommate. I have _____ children.
    Other: Please describe: _____

20. Which category listed below describes your total, annual HOUSEHOLD income in US dollars? (or specify currency)
    ❏ 0–$10,000   ❏ $10,001–29,999   ❏ $30,000–49,999
    ❏ $50,000–69,999   ❏ $70,000–89,999   ❏ $90,000–109,999
    ❏ $110,000–129,999   ❏ $130,000–149,999   ❏ $150,000–plus

21. What is your highest level of education?
    ❏ grade school   ❏ some high school
    ❏ high school graduate   ❏ vocational/technical school
    ❏ some college   ❏ college degree
    ❏ post-graduate work   ❏ doctoral degree

22. What is your occupation? (If retired, please check "retired" and list former occupation.)
    ❏ professional/tehnical   ❏ clerical/office worker   ❏ homemaker
    ❏ craftsperson   ❏ retired
    ❏ salesperson/buyer/agent   ❏ service worker   ❏ other:

Methodology: This instrument attempts to determine several aspects of economic impact of the event, such as how much money the attendee spends on transportation, lodging, food, and other items by simply asking the attendees to report on the amount of money they spent. Further, the instrument gathers information concerning length of stay, future plans to attend, how many people in the group, how they learned about the event (tells the event marketer which advertising media were effective), in what other activities the attendees participated while in the area, and what other cities were visited by the attendees. Surveying takes place during the event. The researcher approaches people attending the event and asks if they would participate in marketing research and complete a survey.

A second surveying technique is to mail the survey to the attendees and ask them to complete it and send it back. This requires gathering a mailing list with names and addresses of people who attended the event.

Source: (1) Pitts, B. G., & Ayers, K. (2001). An analysis of visitor spending and economic scale on Amsterdam from the Gay Games V, 1998. *International Journal of Sport Management, 2*(2), 134–151. (2) Turco, D. M. (1997). Measuring the economic and fiscal impacts of state high school sport championships. *Sport Marketing Quarterly, 6*(3), 49–53.

Survey 5: Consumer Behavior, Level of Involvement

Topic of Study: Consumer behavior; level of involvement

Purpose in Sport Marketing: The purpose of this research is to study the consumer. The area of research in this study focuses on the influence of an individual's level of involvement with a product as a determinant of level of consumerism. More specifically, how does the consumer's type and frequency of involvement with a particular sport affect their consumption? In this particular study, the authors focused on the spectators at a golf event and attempted to determine if their commitment to play golf, watch golf on TV, attend golf events, money spent on golf, and even use of golf for various activities (such as business and networking) affected their level of involvement as a golf spectator. This type of research can help determine if high level or low level of involvement consumers are more or less likely to attend more similar events. (Typically, research shows that high level involvement consumers of a sport are more likely to attend events.) This information is useful in studying markets, which is then used in making decisions on a number of sport marketing elements concerning the company and product.

Instrument: Survey

Personal Involvement Inventory

important	—	—	—	—	—	—	—	unimportant*
of no concern	—	—	—	—	—	—	—	of concern to me
irrelevant	—	—	—	—	—	—	—	relevant
means a lot to me	—	—	—	—	—	—	—	means nothing to me*
useless	—	—	—	—	—	—	—	useful
valuable	—	—	—	—	—	—	—	worthless*
trivial	—	—	—	—	—	—	—	fundamental
beneficial	—	—	—	—	—	—	—	not beneficial*
matters to me	—	—	—	—	—	—	—	doesn't matter*
uninterested	—	—	—	—	—	—	—	interested
significant	—	—	—	—	—	—	—	insignificant*
vital	—	—	—	—	—	—	—	superfluous*
boring	—	—	—	—	—	—	—	interesting
unexciting	—	—	—	—	—	—	—	exciting
appealing	—	—	—	—	—	—	—	unappealing**
mundane	—	—	—	—	—	—	—	fascinating
essential	—	—	—	—	—	—	—	nonessential*
undesirable	—	—	—	—	—	—	—	desirable
wanted	—	—	—	—	—	—	—	unwanted*
not needed	—	—	—	—	—	—	—	needed

*Indicates item is reversed scored. Items on the left are scored (1) low involvement to (7) high involvement on the right. Totaling the 20 items gives a score from a low of 20 to a high of 140.

Methodology: Surveying takes place during the event. The researcher approaches people attending the event and asks if they would participate in marketing research and complete a survey.

A second surveying technique is to mail the survey to the attendees and ask them to complete it and send it back. This requires gathering a mailing list with names and addresses of people who attended the event.

Source: Lascu, D. N., Giese, T. D., Toolan, C., Guehring, B., Mercer, J. (1995). Sport involvement: A relevant individual difference factor in spectator sports. *Sport Marketing Quarterly*, *4*(4), 41–46.

Survey 6: Consumer Behavior, Purchase Intent, The Internet

Topic of Study: Consumer behavior, purchase intention, the Internet

Purpose in Sport Marketing: The purpose of this research is to study consumer behavior. More specifically, the purpose of this study was to examine consumer confidence about Internet purchases and purchase intention of sport product on the Internet. The sport company might use this information to design and use the Internet as a distribution channel.

Instrument: Survey

Survey Instrument

1. In the next 12 months, do you think you are likely to buy XXXXXX over the Web?

Definitely will buy   1   2   3   4   5   Definitely will not buy

2. Overall, the thought of buying XXXXXXX over the Web causes me to be concerned with experiencing some kind of loss if I went ahead with the purchase.

Strongly Disagree   1   2   3   4   5   Strongly Agree

3. All things considered, I think I would be making a mistake if I bought XXXXXXX over the Web.

Strongly Disagree   1   2   3   4   5   Strongly Agree

4. When all is said and done, I really feel that the purchase of XXXXXXX over the Web poses problems for me that I just don't need.

Strongly Disagree   1   2   3   4   5   Strongly Agree

5. The thought of buying XXXXXXX over the Web causes me concern because some friends would think I was just being showy.

Strongly Disagree   1   2   3   4   5   Strongly Agree

6. Purchasing XXXXXXX over the Web would cause me to be thought of as foolish by some people whose opinion I value.

Strongly Disagree   1   2   3   4   5   Strongly Agree

7. Purchasing XXXXXXX over the Web will adversely affect others' opinion of me.

Strongly Disagree   1   2   3   4   5   Strongly Agree

8. The demands on my schedule are such that purchasing XXXXXXX over the Web would create even more time pressures on me that I don't need.

Strongly Disagree   1   2   3   4   5   Strongly Agree

9. Purchasing XXXXXXX over the Web could lead to an inefficient use of my time.

Strongly Disagree   1   2   3   4   5   Strongly Agree

10. Purchasing XXXXXXX over the Web will take too much time or be a waste of time.

Strongly Disagree   1   2   3   4   5   Strongly Agree

11. Purchasing XXXXXXX over the Web would be a bad way to spend my money.

Strongly Disagree   1   2   3   4   5   Strongly Agree

12. If I bought XXXXXXX over the Web, I would be concerned that the financial investment I would make would not be wise.

Strongly Disagree   1   2   3   4   5   Strongly Agree

13. If I bought XXXXXXX over the Web, I would be concerned that I really would not get my money's worth from the tickets.

Strongly Disagree   1   2   3   4   5   Strongly Agree

14. Purchasing XXXXXXX over the Web would not provide value for the money I spent.

Strongly Disagree   1   2   3   4   5   Strongly Agree

15. As I consider the purchase of XXXXXXX over the Web, I worry about whether they will perform as well as they are supposed to.

Strongly Disagree   1   2   3   4   5   Strongly Agree

16. If I were to purchase XXXXXXX over the Web, I would be concerned that they would not provide the level of benefits that I would be expecting.

Strongly Disagree   1   2   3   4   5   Strongly Agree

17. One concern I have about purchasing XXXXXXX over the Web is that eyestrain could result due from looking at the computer.

Strongly Disagree   1   2   3   4   5   Strongly Agree

18. I am concerned that using the Web may lead to uncomfortable physical side effects such as bad sleeping, backaches, and the like.

Strongly Disagree   1   2   3   4   5   Strongly Agree

19. I am concerned about the potential physical risks associated with purchasing XXXXXXX over the Web.

Strongly Disagree   1   2   3   4   5   Strongly Agree

20. Considering the possible problems associated with an online XXXXXXX vendor's performance, a lot of risk would be involved with purchasing them over the Web.

Strongly Disagree   1   2   3   4   5   Strongly Agree

21. I am confident about the ability of an online XXXXXXX vendor to perform as expected.

Strongly Disagree   1   2   3   4   5   Strongly Agree

22. If you purchase XXXXXXX over the Web, your credit card details are likely to be stolen.

Strongly Disagree   1   2   3   4   5   Strongly Agree

23. I am concerned that if I purchase XXXXXXX over the Web, the vendor will not keep my personal information private.

Strongly Disagree   1   2   3   4   5   Strongly Agree

24. The thought of purchasing XXXXXXX over the Web makes me feel psychologically uncomfortable.

Strongly Disagree   1   2   3   4   5   Strongly Agree

25. The thought of purchasing XXXXXXX over the Web gives me a feeling of unwanted anxiety.

Strongly Disagree   1   2   3   4   5   Strongly Agree

26. The thought of purchasing XXXXXXX over the Web causes me to experience unnecessary tension.

Strongly Disagree   1   2   3   4   5   Strongly Agree

27. To me, the World Wide Web is:

important	1	2	3	4	5	unimportant
of no concern to me	1	2	3	4	5	of concern to me
means a lot to me	1	2	3	4	5	means nothing
matters to me	1	2	3	4	5	doesn't matter
boring	1	2	3	4	5	interesting
unexciting	1	2	3	4	5	exciting
appealing	1	2	3	4	5	unappealing
fun	1	2	3	4	5	not fun
says nothing about me	1	2	3	4	5	says something about me
tells me about a person	1	2	3	4	5	shows nothing about a person

28. In general, I would be one of the last people to buy something over the Web.

Strongly Disagree   1   2   3   4   5   Strongly Agree

29. If I heard that a product I wanted to buy was available over the Web, I would be interested enough to buy it in this manner.

Strongly Disagree   1   2   3   4   5   Strongly Agree

30. Compared to most people, I purchase few, if any, items over the Web.

Strongly Disagree   1   2   3   4   5   Strongly Agree

31. In general, I would be among the last in my circle of friends to buy something over the Web.

Strongly Disagree   1   2   3   4   5   Strongly Agree

32. I would buy something over the Web even if I had not heard of the online vendor before.

Strongly Disagree   1   2   3   4   5   Strongly Agree

33. I like to buy things over the Web before other people do.

Strongly Disagree   1   2   3   4   5   Strongly Agree

34. In selecting from the many XXXXXXX vendors operating on via the Web, would you say that:

I would not care at all   1   2   3   4   5   I would care a great deal
as to which one I use   as to which one I use

35. Do you think that the various XXXXXXX vendors operating on via the Web are all very alike or very different?

They are all alike   1   2   3   4   5   They are all different

36. How important would it be to you to make the right choice of Web-based XXXX XXX vendor?

Not at all important   1   2   3   4   5   Extremely important

37. In making your choice of Web-based XXXXXXX vendor, how concerned would you be about the outcome of your choice?

Not at all concerned   1   2   3   4   5   Very much concerned

38. What is your age? _____

39. What is your gender? ❑ Male? ❑ Female

Methodology: Surveying takes place during the event. The researcher approaches people attending the event and asks if they would participate in marketing research and complete a survey.

A second surveying technique is to mail the survey to the attendees and ask them to complete it and send it back. This requires gathering a mailing list with names and addresses of people who attended the event.

Source: Pope, N., Brown, M., & Forrest, E. (1999). Risk, innovativeness, gender, and involvement factors affecting the intention to purchase sprot product online. *Sport Marketing Quarterly, 8*(2), 25–34.

Survey 7: Fan Attendance Survey

Topic of Study: Consumer behavior, factors influencing attendance

Purpose in Sport Marketing: The purpose of this research is to study consumer behavior. More specifically, the purpose of this is to examine the many factors that influence the consumer's decision to attend a sports event. This information is useful in making decisions concerning several aspects surrounding the event over which the marketer has control, such as, parking fees, ticket prices, seating assignments, cleanliness of the facility, and friendliness of the staff. There are other factors that the marketer has limited or no control, such as, parking, weather, competing events or entertainment, and quality or outcome of the event.

Instrument: Survey

Part I—Demographics

Directions: The following information is being requested for statistical purposes only. Please answer the following questions by placing a mark or circle on the appropriate box.

1. What is your gender? ❑ Male? ❑ Female

2. What is your age?
   ❑ 13–18   ❑ 19–24   ❑ 25–29   ❑ 30–34   ❑ 35–39   ❑ 40–44
   ❑ 45–49   ❑ 50–54   ❑ 55–59   ❑60–64   ❑65–69   ❑70+

3. What is your marital/household status?
   ❑ Single   ❑ Married/Partner   ❑ Divorced   ❑ Widowed   ❑ Others

4. What is your highest education level?
   ❑ Elementary   ❑ Junior High   ❑ High School
   ❑ Undergraduate   ❑ Graduate

5. How many children are in your household? (18 yr. old and under)

6. What is your annual household income?
   ❑ Less than $19,999   ❑ $20,000–$29,999   ❑ $30,000–$39,999
   ❑ $40,000–$49,999   ❑ $50,000–$59,999   ❑ $60,000–$69,999
   ❑ $70,000–$79,999   ❑ $80,000–$89,999   ❑ $90,000–$99,999
   ❑ $100,000–$109,000   ❑ $110,000–$119,000 ❑ $120,000+

7. What is your ethnicity?
   ❑ African American   ❑ Caucasian   ❑ Asian
   ❑ Hispanic   ❑ Others:

8. What is your occupation category?
   ❑ Blue collar   ❑ Clerk   ❑ Education
   ❑ Housewife/husband   ❑ Management   ❑ Military
   ❑ Professional   ❑ Sales   ❑ Student
   ❑ Technical   ❑ Others: ❑ Your title:

9. How many games do you attend each year? _____ games

10. Are you a season ticket holder? ❑ Yes ❑ No

11. What kind of transportation do you use when you come to the stadium?
    ❑ Driving a car   ❑ Bus   ❑ Taxi
    ❑ Motorcycle   ❑ Subway   ❑ Walk
    ❑ Others:

12. How many miles did you travel to get to the game?
    ❏ 0–10   ❏ 11–24   ❏ 25–49   ❏ 50–74   ❏ 75–100   ❏ 110+

Part II: Factors

Directions: Please circle the number that best reflects your perspective opinion.
    ❏ Factor   ❏ Influence Rating

How do the following factors influence your attendance at home games?

1 = Not at all
2 = Very little
3 = Somewhat
4 = Very much
5 = Extremely

1. The price of a ticket. 1   2   3   4   5
2. The price of season ticket 1   2   3   4   5
3. The price of concessions 1   2   3   4   5
4. TV/Radio coverage of the home game in local area 1   2   3   4   5
5. TV coverage of another sport event at time 1   2   3   4   5
   of your home game
6. Other sporting events in the area. 1   2   3   4   5
7. Other activities taking place nearby 1   2   3   4   5
8. Other professional franchises in your area 1   2   3   4   5
9. Record (won-loss) of home team 1   2   3   4   5
10. Record (won-loss) of visitor team. 1   2   3   4   5
11. Number of star players on home team 1   2   3   4   5
12. Number of star players on visitor team 1   2   3   4   5
13. Offensive performance of the home team 1   2   3   4   5
14. Defensive performance of the home team 1   2   3   4   5
15. Offensive performance of the visitor team 1   2   3   4   5
16. Defensive performance of the visitor team 1   2   3   4   5
17. Closeness of competition. 1   2   3   4   5
18. Games with rival teams 1   2   3   4   5
19. A chance to see a record-breaking performance 1   2   3   4   5
    by a team or athlete
20. Special promotion (hat day, poster day, etc.) 1   2   3   4   5
21. Home team's place in the division standings 1   2   3   4   5
22. Home team's place in the league standings. 1   2   3   4   5
23. Home team's involvement in race for a playoff spot 1   2   3   4   5
24. Media advertising 1   2   3   4   5
    (TV, radio, newspaper, Internet, etc.)
25. Day games during the weekdays 1   2   3   4   5
26. Night games during the weekdays 1   2   3   4   5
27. Weekend day games. 1   2   3   4   5

28. Weekend night games 1   2   3   4   5
29. Weather conditions 1   2   3   4   5
30. Cleanliness of the facility 1   2   3   4   5
31. Easy and/or multiple access to your facility 1   2   3   4   5
    (via subway, highway, transit, etc.)
32. Availability of parking at or near facility 1   2   3   4   5
33. Size of the facility (seating capacity) 1   2   3   4   5
34. Crowd behavior at the game 1   2   3   4   5
35. New stadium or arena 1   2   3   4   5
36. Number of years the team has been in the area 1   2   3   4   5
37. The variety of concessions available 1   2   3   4   5
38. Violence in the game 1   2   3   4   5
39. The design and color of uniform 1   2   3   4   5

Methodology: The people to be studied include any group of potential consumers. The sport business might determine to target any group of consumers in order to assess general attitudes toward purchasing their product via the Internet.

Sources: (1) Lu, D. (2000). Factors affecting attendance in professional baseball: A comparison of Taiwan and USA. Paper presented at the Florida Association for Health, Physical Education, Recreation, and Dance annual conference, October, 2000. Paper available from the author, Florida State University. (2) Zhang, J. J., Pease, D. G., Hui, S. C., & Michaud, T. J. (1995). Variables affecting spectator decision to attend NBA games. *Sport Marketing Quarterly*, 4(4), 29–39.

Appendix G

Example of Survey Formatting—A Real Survey Conducted at the 2011 Atlanta Football Classic at the Georgia Dome in Atlanta, Georgia

The following page shows a real survey used to collect consumer information at a sports event, the Atlanta Football Classic held at the Georgia Dome in Atlanta, Georgia. This replication shows how special formatting is used to get questions and responses into a format easily used by the study participant. This survey was created using Microsoft Word.

Activity: With the supervision of your course professor, create your own survey with formatting using a software program of your choice.

Complete This Survey And Receive A Free Refreshment At One Of Our Concessions! (while quantities last)

Please help with some important research that will be used confidentially by the Georgia Dome. Thank you!!

I. Factors that Influence Your Attendance and Event Experience

Which of the following factors influenced your attendance and game-day experience? Please circle the number that best reflects your opinion on a scale of 1 (No Influence) to 5 (Strong Influence) or NA (Not Applicable).

1. Price to attend the event	1 2 3 4 5 NA
2. Media advertising/promotion of the game	1 2 3 4 5 NA
3. The long-time rivalry between the two teams	1 2 3 4 5 NA
4. Your favorite team's win-loss record	1 2 3 4 5 NA
5. The opponent	1 2 3 4 5 NA
6. Entertain a client(s)	1 2 3 4 5 NA
7. Entertain the family	1 2 3 4 5 NA
8. A chance to enjoy historically Black college football	1 2 3 4 5 NA
9. Half-time entertainment	1 2 3 4 5 NA
10. Crowd behavior at the game	1 2 3 4 5 NA
11. The overall atmosphere of the game	1 2 3 4 5 NA
12. Entertainment opportunities with the game	1 2 3 4 5 NA
13. The 100 Black Men organization and its mission	1 2 3 4 5 NA
14. Events such as job fair, college fair, parade	1 2 3 4 5 NA
15. Atlanta as a premier destination for African-American culture and history	1 2 3 4 5 NA
16. The Georgia Dome as a venue for hosting this event	1 2 3 4 5 NA

II. The Georgia Dome

1. Have you ever attended an event at the Georgia Dome? ❑ Yes ❑ No
2. What other types of events do you attend at the Georgia Dome? _____

3. Please rate the following facility services and amenities at the Georgia Dome on a scale of 1 (Poor) to 5 (Excellent). NA = (Not Applicable).

• Facility location	1 2 3 4 5 NA
• Directional signage	1 2 3 4 5 NA
• Professionalism/courtesy of staff	1 2 3 4 5 NA
• Food quality	1 2 3 4 5 NA
• Food variety	1 2 3 4 5 NA
• Seating comfort	1 2 3 4 5 NA
• Sound	1 2 3 4 5 NA
• Content and clarity of video/ message display boards	1 2 3 4 5 NA
• Stadium temperature	1 2 3 4 5 NA
• Cleanliness of the facility	1 2 3 4 5 NA
• Facility security	1 2 3 4 5 NA
• Access/traffic flow	1 2 3 4 5 NA
• Parking	1 2 3 4 5 NA
• Overall rating of your experience at the Dome	1 2 3 4 5 NA

4. What specific improvements would you suggest be made to the Georgia Dome to enhance your game-day experience? _____

5. What form of transportation did you use to get to the Georgia Dome—circle one: car—MARTA—taxi—other: _____

III. Atlanta

1. How do you rate the following city services? From 1=Poor → 5 = Excellent

• Airport	1 2 3 4 5 NA
• MARTA	1 2 3 4 5 NA
• Hotel(s)	1 2 3 4 5 NA
• Taxi	1 2 3 4 5 NA
• Entertainment opportunities	1 2 3 4 5 NA
• Security downtown	1 2 3 4 5 NA
• Restaurant selection	1 2 3 4 5 NA
• Overall Rating for Atlanta	1 2 3 4 5 NA

2. What more can be done to improve Atlanta city services/features/amenities? _____

IV. Economic Factors

1. What is your motivation for attending this event? Please check below . . .
❑ Alumni ❑ Parent ❑ Student ❑ College Fan
❑ Basketball Fan ❑ Family ❑ Friend ❑ Other: _____

2. With whom did you attend this event? Please check below . . .
❑ Family only ❑ Partner only ❑ Alone ❑ Friends only
❑ Family, friends, and partner ❑ School Club/Organization
❑ Business associate: Name of organization
❑ Other (please specify) _____

3. How many are in your party (including yourself)? _____

4. Did you come to Atlanta specifically for this event? ❑ Yes ❑ No

5. If your answer to #4 is NO, how many days did you add in order to attend this event? _____

6. How many nights total did you stay in Atlanta? _____

7. If you stayed overnight, where did you stay? Please check below . . .
❑ Hotel ❑ Friends/Relatives ❑ Camping/RV
❑ Other: _____

8. Have you attended this event previously? ❑ Yes ❑ No

9. If your answer to #8 is yes, how many times? _____

10. Do you plan to attend this event again? ❑ Yes ❑ No

11. Where did you get information about the event—check ALL you used:
❑ TV ❑ College Newspaper ❑ Friends ❑ Family
❑ NCAA Website ❑ Local Newspaper ❑ Facebook
❑ Twitter ❑ College Website
❑ ESPN Website ❑ Radio
❑ Dome Website ❑ Other: _____

12. Where did you purchase your ticket(s)? _____

13. Please estimate (in even U.S. dollars) how much you spent on each of the following items during your entire stay for this event.
• Food and beverages (restaurants, concessions, grocery stores)
$ _____
• Admission fees (this event and other related events)
$ _____
• Nightclubs, lounges, bars (cover charges, drinks, etc.)
$ _____
• Retail shopping (clothing, gifts, etc.)
$ _____
• Event souvenirs
$ _____
• Lodging expenses (hotel, motel, etc.)
$ _____
• Private auto expenses in the city (gas, parking fees, etc.)
$ _____
• Commercial transportation (public transit, taxi, car rental)
$ _____
• Other expenses (please specify) _____
$ _____

V. Demographics—Please tell us about yourself!

1. What is your gender? ❑ Male ❑ Female

2. What is your age? _____

3. Where do you live? City _____ State _____ Zip Code _____

4. What is your personal/committed relationship status—check one below.
❑ Single ❑ Married ❑ Partner ❑ Divorced

5. What is the highest level of education you have completed—check one below
❑ Some High School ❑ 1st College degree ❑ In Doctoral Program
❑ Finished High School ❑ In graduate school ❑ Have Doc. Degree
❑ Some College ❑ Master's Degree ❑ Other: _____

6. How many children (18 and under) are in your household? _____

7. What is your income: _____ OR check one below:
❑ Under $20,000 ❑ $20,000–$39,999 ❑ $40,000–$59,999
❑ $60,000–$79,999 ❑ $80,000–$99,999 ❑ $100,000–$119,999
❑ $120,000–$139,999 ❑ $140,000–$159,999 ❑ $160,000 or more

8. What is your ethnicity?
❑ African American ❑ Caucasian/White
❑ Asian/Pacific Islander ❑ Hispanic/Latino
❑ Other (please specify) _____

9. What is your occupation? _____

10. Any additional comments? _____

THANK YOU FOR YOUR PARTICPATION AND ENJOY THE 2011 BANK OF AMERICA ATLANTA FOOTBALL CLASSIC!

Index

About the Authors

Brenda G. Pitts, EdD

Dr. Pitts is currently a professor in sport marketing in the graduate sport administration program at Georgia State University in Atlanta, Georgia, after having spent 6 years at Florida State University and 12 years at the University of Louisville. Dr. Pitts is author/coauthor of several sport marketing textbooks and numerous publications and presentations, primarily in sport marketing and published in several scholarly journals such as the *Journal of Sport Management*, *Sport Marketing Quarterly*, *Journal of Vacation Marketing*, *Sport Management and Other Related Topics Journal*, and the *International Journal of Sport Management*. She has consulted in sport marketing for several sport businesses, has reviewed materials in sport management, and spoken at numerous conferences. Her international stops have included such countries as Japan, Sweden, South Africa, Hong Kong, Singapore, Malaysia, France, Australia, Germany, Hungary, England, The Netherlands, Scotland, Cyprus, Belgium, and France. In recognition of her scholarly achievements, Dr. Pitts was the recipient of the Dr. Garth Paton Distinguished Service Award in 2004 and the Dr. Earle F. Zeigler Scholar Award in 2000; one of the first Research Fellows of the North American Society for Sport Management in 2001; and a nominee for the Sport Management Council's 2007 award. Some of Dr. Pitts' service accomplishments have included: member of the committee that wrote the Sport Management Curriculum Standards (first published in 1993), served on the first Sport Management Program Review Council; program chair of two NASSM conferences (1990 and 2004), and was a council member, President-Elect, President, and Past-President of NASSM, 1990–1995. Dr. Pitts is a founding member of the Sport Marketing Association and was the Vice-President for Academic Affairs for the first three years of the new Sport Marketing Association, managing the conference program and editing the three conference papers books. In addition, she was an Editorial Board Member (1991–1998) and later co-editor-in-chief of The Sport Management Library (1998–2000), a project that has produced more than 20 textbooks in sport management.

David K. Stotlar, EdD

Dr. David K. Stotlar teaches on the University of Northern Colorado faculty in the areas of sport marketing, sponsorship, and event management. He also serves as Director of the School of Kinesiology & Physical Education at the same institution. Dr. Stotlar has had more than 60 articles published in professional journals and has written several textbooks and book chapters in sport management and marketing. He has made numerous presentations at international and national professional conferences. On several occasions, he has served as a consultant in sport management to various sport professionals; and in the area of sport marketing and sponsorship, to multinational corporations and international sport managers. Dr. Stotlar was selected by the United States Olympic Committee as a delegate to the International Olympic Academy in Greece and the World University Games Forum in Italy and served as a venue media center supervisor for the 2002 Olympic Games. He has conducted international seminars in sport management and marketing for the Hong Kong Olympic Committee, the National Sports Council of Malaysia, Mauritius National Sports Council, the National Sports Council of Zimbabwe, the Singapore Sports Council, the Chinese Taipei University Sport Federation, the Bahrain Sport Institute, the government of Saudi Arabia, the South African National Sports Congress, and the Association of Sport Sciences in South Africa. Dr. Stotlar's contribution to the profession includes an appointment as Coordinator of the Sport Management Program Review Council (NASPE/NASSM) from 1999–2001. He previously served as Chair of the Council on Facilities and Equipment of the American Alliance for Health, Physical Education, Recreation and Dance, and as a board member and later as President of the North American Society for Sport Management. Dr. Stotlar was a member of the initial group of professionals inducted as NASSM Research Fellows. He is also a founding member of the Sport Marketing Association.